A HISTORY OF
CHRISTIAN THOUGHT

A HISTORY OF
CHRISTIAN THOUGHT

By

DR. J. L. NEVE

Professor Emeritus, Hamma Divinity School
Wittenberg College, Springfield, Ohio

Volume Two

HISTORY OF PROTESTANT THEOLOGY

By

O. W. HEICK, PH.D.

With Contributions by

DR. J. L. NEVE

on

The Post-Reformation Developments
and
First Fundamental Steps into the Modern Age

THE MUHLENBERG PRESS
PHILADELPHIA : PENNSYLVANIA

Printed in United States of America
UB173

FOREWORD

The following pages constitute the second volume of Dr. J. L. Neve's HISTORY OF CHRISTIAN THOUGHT. As the interested reader will remember, Professor Neve was called to his eternal reward on August 12, 1943, a few days previous to the completion of Volume One. I therefore wish to express here my deeply felt gratitude to my esteemed teacher with whom I had been associated since 1936 in the preparation of this work. Professor Neve was an inspiring teacher and sympathetic friend. As a scholar he was possessed of a keen mind. Though firmly grounded in the Confessions of his Church, he wrote, as a historian, "with malice toward none," being always mindful of the dictum of Ph. Marheineke that the "peace of history" must rest over the mind and work of the investigating theologian. His was a long and useful life. In the Lutheran Church of America he will always be remembered for his persistent endeavors to lead his brethren in the old General Synod, prior to the merger of 1918, to a more genuine understanding and deeper appreciation of the historic Confessions of the Church.
Requiescat in pace et lux aeterna ei luceat!

While in the first volume the authors have discussed the development up to and including the seventeenth century, the present volume deals with the modern age after 1700. To this volume Professor Neve has contributed eight chapters on developments in the eighteenth century, in Germany, Holland, France, and England; and four chapters for the nineteenth century on Kant, the religion of German Idealism, Schleiermacher, Hegel and the Hegelian theologians. My special field of study has been modern thought on the Continent, beginning with the Confessional revival about 1840, Great Britain in the nineteenth and twentieth centuries, and Amercian theology since Jonathan Edwards.

I wish to express my appreciation to Professor P. Nyholm, Blair, Nebraska; Professor A. T. Kantonen, Springfield, Ohio, and President C. Bergendoff, Rock Island, Illinois, for information afforded on the history of Scandinavian theology both in America and in the home lands. I also had the privilege to study, in typewritten form, Professor C. G. Carlfelt's lectures on Recent Swedish Theology, delivered at the Luther Academy of Dubuque, Iowa, in July, 1942. To Professor F. E. Mayer, St. Louis, Missouri, I am indebted for his careful reading of the manuscript and many important suggestions. Professor F. K. Krueger, Springfield, Ohio, and the Rev. H. Gieschen, Omaha, Nebraska, have rendered me a like service for some parts of these chapters. I am likewise grateful for facilities afforded by the libraries of Wittenberg College, Springfield, Ohio; Nebraska University, Lincoln, Nebraska; Oberlin College, Oberlin, Ohio; Princeton Theological Seminary, Princeton, New Jersey; Augustana Seminary, Rock Island, Illinois; and Fort Hays Kansas State College, Hays, Kansas.

Since acknowledgement for quoting from copyrighted material has been made, in most cases, at every particular instance, I desire here to express my gratitude to *The Christian Century* for permission to quote from the remarkable series of contributions, "How My Mind Has Changed" (1939), and to Professor V. Ferm for permission to quote from his composite volumes *Contemporary American Theology,* published by the Round Table Press.

Due to the exigencies of the war, the publication of this Volume has been delayed a considerable length of time. I should therefore refer its readers to some important books which have appeared since the completion of the manuscript:

Reinhold Niebuhr, *The Nature and Destiny of Man* (New York, 1941-43); D. C. Macintosh, *Personal Religion* (New York, 1942); C. E. Raven, *Science, Religion and the Future* (New York, 1944); A. C. Garnett, *A Realistic Philosophy of Religion* (New York, 1942); F. G. Bratton, *The Legacy of the Liberal Spirit* (New York, 1943); D. E. Roberts and H. P. Van Dusen (eds.), *Liberal Theology* (New York, 1942); S. J. Case, *The Christian Philosophy of History* (Chicago, 1943); Wilhelm Jaeger, *Humanism and Theology* (Milwaukee, 1943); E. S. Brightman (ed.), *Personalism in Religion, a symposium of twelve essays in honor of A. C. Knudson* (Boston, 1943); A. C. Knudson, *The Principles of Christian Ethics* (New York, 1943); W. K. Anderson (ed.), *Protestantism, a Symposium* (Nashville, 1944); A. C. Zabriskie, *Anglican Evangelism* (Philadelphia, 1943); Nicholas Berdyaev, *Slavery and Freedom* (New York, 1944); *The Thomist, nineteen essays in honor of Maritain* (New York, 1943); Jacques Maritain, *Christianity and Democracy* (New York, 1944); R. E. Brennan, *Essays in Thomism by J. Maritain and others* (New York, 1942).

Among biographical and historical studies we may mention A. I. Abell, *The Urban Impact on American Protestantism* (Cambridge, 1943); A Koch, *The Philosophy of Thomas Jefferson* (New York, 1943); Edward Gill, *A. T. Robertson: A Biography* (New York, 1943); C. R. Sanders, *Coleridge and the Broad Church Movement* (Durham, 1942); Charles Williams (ed.), *The Letters of Evelyn Underhill* (London, 1943).

Students of the New Testament will be interested in F. C. Grant, *The Earliest Gospel* (New York, 1943); E. P. Booth (ed.), *New Testament Studies* (New York, 1943); T. S. Kepler (ed.), *Contemporary Thinking about Jesus* (New York, 1944); C. J. Cadoux, *The Historic Mission of Jesus* (New York, 1944).

For studies in Lutheran Theology we refer to C. H. Little, *Lutheran Confessional Theology* (St. Louis, 1943); Theodore Graebner and P. E. Kretzmann, *Toward Lutheran Unity* (St. Louis, 1943); P. W. Spaude, *The Lutheran Church under American Influence* (Burlington, 1943).

Brunner's *The Divine-Human Encounter* has recently been translated into English (Philadelphia, 1943).

In addition to treatises on Christianity and the war by Karl Barth (see p. 178), the reader should refer to his later booklet, *The Church and the War* (New York, 1944). Among other publications on the Christian interpretation of the war, we note C. C. Morrison, *The Christian and the War* (New York, 1942); Paul Hutchinson, *From Victory to Peace* (New York, 1943); E. M. Poteat, *The Four Freedoms and God* (New York, 1943); H. A. Freeman (ed.), *Peace is the Victory* (New York, 1943); and William Temple, *The Hope of a New World* (New York, 1941). All these are outstanding. This discussion, in books and articles, of the Christian interpretation of war is, very likely, the greatest contribution of the past triennium to the history of Christian thought.

Among the prominent scholars referred to in this volume, we mention the following who have recently passed from the scene of their earthly labors: M. Reu (d. October 14, 1943); W. A. Brown (d. December 15, 1943); James Moffatt (d. June 27, 1944), and Archbishop William Temple (d. October 26, 1944).

OTTO W. HEICK.

A HISTORY OF CHRISTIAN THOUGHT

Volume Two: History of Protestant Theology

TABLE OF CONTENTS

Book Four

Developments in Post-Reformation Theology

CHAPTER FOUR

THE THEOLOGY OF THE "INNER LIGHT"

CHAPTER FIVE

THE ENGLISH DEISTS: FIRST STEPS IN RADICAL LIBERALISM

CHAPTER SIX

THE FRENCH NATURALISTS OF THE SEVENTEENTH AND
EIGHTEENTH CENTURIES

CHAPTER SEVEN

GERMAN RATIONALISM

CHAPTER EIGHT

THE OLD SOCINIANS OR UNITARIANS

BOOK FIVE

New Attitudes to Religion and Christianity

SECTION ONE

Continental Theological Thought with Special Emphasis on German Theology after 1800

CHAPTER ONE

IMMANUEL KANT: HIS IDEAS ON RELIGION

CHAPTER TWO

GERMAN IDEALISM AND ITS RELATION TO CHRISTIANITY

CHAPTER THREE

SCHLEIERMACHER

CHAPTER NINE

THEOLOGICAL THOUGHT BETWEEN THE TWO GREAT WARS

Appendix

SECTION TWO

Theological Thought in Great Britain

CHAPTER ONE

INTRODUCTORY REMARKS

Presbyterians, Methodists, and Baptists. 15 Religious Idealism as opposed to conservative Christianity: Quakers, Mormons, Christian Science, and various Theosophical societies.

BOOK FOUR
Developments in Post-Reformation Theology

The developments here to be discussed comprise two groups. The one is comparatively conservative, the other is radical. The conservative movements were these: (1) Syncretism in Germany; (2) Arminianism in Holland; (3) Arminianism, issuing into "Latitudinarianism" in England; (4) The Theology of the "Inner Light" as productive of Independentism and Spiritualism and leading into positions of Liberalism.

The radical developments show us the following movements: (1) English Deism; (2) French Naturalism; (3) German Rationalism at its first appearance; (4) Unitarianism in England and in America.

Chapter One

GEORGE CALIXTUS AND THE PRINCIPLES OF SYNCRETISM

Literature: W. GASS, *Georg Calixt und der Synkretismus,* 1846. T. HENKE, *G. Calixtus und seine Zeit,* 2 vols., 1853-56. Much use has been made in this chapter of H. SCHMID, *Geschichte der synkretistischen Streitigkeiten,* 1846; it is a work of the most helpful kind. See also the very good articles in the *Protestantische Realenzyklopaedie (PRE)* on *Georg Calixt* (III, 644 ff.), on *Synkretismus* (XIX, 239 ff.), on *Synkretistische Streitigkeiten* (XIX, 243 ff.), on *Abr. Calovius* (III, 648 ff.), on *Joh. Musaeus* (XIII, 572 ff.). Cf. J. H. KURTZ, *Church History* (Eng. ed, 1888 ff.), p. 159, see also A. THOLUCK, *Geist der luth. Theologen Wittenbergs,* 1852. With all its value, this last mentioned work is very misleading in judgments which have been fittingly corrected in the latest (third) edition of the *PRE* as referred to above. See the corresponding articles in the *New Schaff-Herzog Encyclopedia;* also in the *Lutheran Encyclopedia* (pp. 464 ff.) and *Religion in Geschichte und Gegenwart (RGG).* To this literature the writer may add his own book *Lutherans in the Movements for Church Union,* 1921, pp. 81-109. The most valuable and thoroughgoing Vol. IV (1927) of OTTO RITSCHL, *Dogmengeschichte des Protestantismus,* devotes eleven chapters (pp. 231-473) to this whole subject. It is the best treatment extant.

I. FACTORS IN THE DEVELOPMENT OF CALIXTUS

In order to estimate the principles in the movement here to be studied we must understand the training and development of this theologian of irenics. He was a student in the University of Helmstedt for six years, and then was professor in that same school for forty-two years from 1614 to 1656.

Helmstedt was different from the other universities of seventeenth century Lutheranism. This institution was opposed to the Formula of Concord, and served as a place of refuge for those Melanchthonians who were uprooted by the Crypto-Calvinistic controversies in electoral Saxony. Among the professors in this school, especially the professors of philosophy, there were ardent advocates of humanism (among them the learned John Casselius and the brilliant Cornelius Martini of Antwerp). History, the ancient classics and philosophy were much studied, not to support Biblical doctrine, but for their own sakes. These Helmstedt professors were not hostile to theology. Reason was not exalted to a position of opposition to theology. They did oppose the "barbarism of polemics" as practiced between the churches, and they held that education in the classics, ancient philosophy and history would make theology more palatable. H. Schmid, author of the well-known standard work on Lutheran Dogmatics, fittingly remarks: "The staleness and immoderateness of polemics, yea, the coarseness that characterized the controversies of the time find their explanation largely in the neglect of the *humaniora;* for in classical antiquity there lies a spirit of moderation and fine culture, which, to their great detriment, the Lutheran theologians had been losing more and more."

We mentioned that Helmstedt was Melanchthonian in character. The father of Calixtus, who opposed Flacius and afterwards the Formula of Concord, had been a pupil of Melanchthon in Wittenberg after Luther's death. In the Melanchthonian-humanistic atmosphere of Helmstedt, young Calixtus received a broad education, spending four of

the six years in a study of the humanities. He was a brilliant student and upon graduation was soon selected as a candidate for professorship. His chief interest was the
history of the ancient Church, an interest clearly manifested in his later writings.[1]
Humanism, when dissatisfied with the present, flees into antiquity, there to discover
correctives for the misdevelopment of the centuries.

Following his graduation and before undertaking his professorship, Calixtus traveled
extensively. He visited many German universities, also traveled in Belgium, Holland,
England and France, making a close study of the churches, particularly their creeds.

II. THE THEORIES OF CALIXTUS AND THE REPLY OF LUTHERANISM

1. Calixtus on fundamentals and non-fundamentals. Calixtus appealed for mutual
recognition and co-operation between the churches on the basis of existing agreement in
the fundamentals of Christianity. As to organic union, however, he was open-minded
enough to see that there ought to be agreement also on some non-fundamentals. On
this subject there had been definite expression by the Lutheran Nik. Hunnius and
others.[2] In our next two chapters on Arminianism in Holland and in Great Britain we
shall see that tolerance and mutual recognition on the basis of a distinction between
fundamentals and non-fundamentals were widely advocated.[3] It was a sentiment that had
developed as a reaction against the confessional polemics in the seventeenth century.

Calixtus conceived of a fundamental doctrine as follows: It is a doctrine that is
necessary to be believed for salvation; a doctrine which no one, be he layman or theologian, can ignore without endangering his salvation. He included as fundamental such
doctrines as belief in eternal life, resurrection of the body and soul, that eternal life
will be a life with God, that salvation comes only through Christ, through the work of
the Holy Spirit in the holy Christian Church.[4] Following Bonaventura, he classified the
Church's teaching into three divisions: (1) *Antecedentia:* religious matters, which man,
without the aid of revelation, can know by his own reasoning—*e.g.,* the facts of providence, the immortality of the soul, knowledge of the Scriptures. (2) *Constituentia:*
real matters of faith, the objects of revelation for the salvation of man, his sinfulness
and God's grace in the acts of redemption. These were to Calixtus the real fundamentals.
(3) *Consequentia:* more or less theological doctrines derived from fundamentals and
incorporated into the creeds—*e.g.,* predestination, personal union of the two natures in
Christ, the doctrine of the Supper.[5]

2. Appeal to tradition and to the Apostles' Creed.

a. As to confessional standards for the fundamentals necessary to be believed for
salvation, Calixtus appealed to *the doctrinal tradition of the early Church* of about the
first five centuries, to the *consensus quinquesaecularis.* Though Calixtus held the Scriptures to be the sole source of salvation (*unum, primum et summum principium; Haupt-
prinzip*) yet he insisted that the teaching of the early Church constituted a real criterion

---

[1] Cf. his *Apparatus Theologicus,* 1628, his *Orationes Sellectae,* 1659, and various books on history of
ancient dogmas.

[2] See the thorough review of this situation by O. Ritschl, *op. cit.*

[3] Our reference is to Jacob Acontius and the *Confession* of the Arminians by Episcopius in Holland, and to
Edward Stillingfleet in England and John Dury in Scotland.

[4] Schmid, referring to Calixtus, *Ad Moguntinos,* theses 30-40.

[5] *Ad Moguntinos,* 66, 71, 44; cf. Schmid, *op. cit.,* pp. 156 ff., 187 ff., 267 ff., 270 ff.

of fundamental truth (an *alterum principium secundarium* or *subordinatum*).[6] Abraham Calovius (1612-86), of the Wittenberg University was the outstanding opponent of Calixtus, and he had many supporters among the Lutheran theologians. He attacked Calixtus on his theory of tradition as a secondary standard of truth and insisted that the Scriptures are the only infallible norm of true doctrine.[7]

b. Later, Calixtus spoke less of tradition, having settled upon the *Apostles' Creed* as representing what was fundamental in the teaching of the early Church. He argued that the ancient Church in its earliest form was certainly in possession of all the truth needed for salvation. But on this point again Calixtus found Calovius to be his ready opponent. The latter rejected the claim that the Apostles' Creed represents a complete doctrinal norm of truth for all time and contains the fundamentals of the Scriptures in such a way that nothing needs to be added, amplified or defined.

We must remember that Calixtus appealed to antiquity mainly to support his claim of a virtual union (*communio interna*) between the churches.

Before proceeding further, we will interpose a few critical remarks on the present problem. While the Apostles' Creed represents an admirable expression of the rudiments of Christian truth, yet it is only a general outline upon which were to be erected the individual parts of the Christian faith, the *fides quae creditur*. This growth was to take place through the process of progressive doctrinal experience, chiefly in conflict with error. The Apostles' Creed, as it developed out of the Baptismal Formula, thus represents the formulation of the first doctrinal experience of the Church. Later developments could be expected naturally. To demand of the Church after the Reformation that it should limit its public confession to the statements of the Apostles' Creed would be equal to compelling the full-grown man to return again to the stage of development of the boy.

3. The Apostles' Creed and later creeds. Religion in contrast to theology.

a. The position of Calixtus. Baur, the founder of the Tuebingen School, once said that Calixtus undertook to lead the Church back from theology to religion. And indeed, his attempt to put the Apostles' Creed into contrast with the other creeds of Christendom was an endeavor to establish religion and theology as opposites. That this cannot be done in entire harmony with the genius of Lutheranism will be shown in Chap. III, pp. 33 ff.

As has been pointed out, Calixtus had established himself upon a distinction between fundamentals and non-fundamentals. Fundamental, he said, is what is necessary to be known and to be believed for salvation. To the plain statements of the Apostles' Creed nothing of a fundamental nature can be added. The later more elaborate creeds contain fundamentals only where the substance of that creed is repeated in a practically identical form; wherever the later creeds offer interpretation and qualification of the Apostles' Creed, there they no longer express fundamentals. Such interpretive and supplementary matter which was necessitated by the activity of the heretics has no significance for the ordinary Christian; it is material for teachers only, by which these should be guided in their work.[8]

---

[6] Schmid, *op cit.,* p. 148 f.

[7] Calovius, *Syncretismus Calixtinus,* pp. 10, 143. For a more exclusive review of the controversy see Neve, *op. cit.,* p. 86.

[8] Cf. Schmid, pp. 148 f., 151 ff., 160. Our references must largely be to the lucid discussions of this book; H. Schmid writes of the difficulty for any mind of today to work through the writings of Calixtus.

Many of the Church's teachers, however, Calixtus continued, have made the mistake of delving too much into mysteries, such as the Trinity, the two natures of Christ, original sin, the relation of God's grace to man's will in conversion and other matters. They should have contented themselves with simply teaching what is clearly revealed and needs to be known for salvation. So Calixtus, as an irenic, argued in his zeal for bridging the chasms between the churches and tried to make the differences appear to be of minor consideration. He lamented that the terms of the school had been permitted to coin the expressions of pure religion; such statements, for instance, as this, that he who repents and believes in Christ and accepts His merit has forgiveness of sins and shall have eternal life (p. 162). He did not deny that occasions might arise when a teacher is compelled to go beyond the clearly revealed statements of Scripture (p. 152). But this, he said, should be done only in theological discussion, with much reticence and with a consciousness that man will always be denied a full insight into the mysteries of the Christian faith (p. 154). He always repeated that such doctrinal differences are not fundamental for salvation and, therefore, do not affect the virtual union (*communio virtualis*) between the churches.

Regarding the later more theological creeds, Calixtus made a distinction between the creeds of the first five centuries and the creeds of the Reformation age. He looked upon the former as confessional testimonies of the fundamental period of the Church's life, but they are theological in character and for that reason their acceptance is not necessary for salvation. As to the confessions of the Reformation, he would again say: Either they repeat the plain statements of the Apostles' Creed, and in such parts they are fundamental for salvation; or they interpret that creed and deduce additional doctrines from it (*per consequentiam*), in which cases they constitute no articles of faith, but are intended to serve only the teachers of the Church. He even went so far as to call the doctrinal differences between the churches "*quaestiones annatae*" (pp. 200, 209).

b. Reply from the Lutherans. The opponents of Calixtus (Calovius, Huelsemann, Dannhauer and also the mild Musaeus) had a different appreciation of the more theological creeds of Christendom, and it cannot be denied that in the main they were more correct in their positions. To them, as was stated, the Apostles' Creed was merely a general outline of the Church's faith, a first attempt to state the essentials of truth. The statements of this creed, they would say, expressed the Christian faith seminally, with the need of development and further unfolding.

The leading objections of Calovius were as follows: The Apostles' Creed was not formulated for the purpose of giving to the believers of all ages a really complete summary of the Christian faith. And the later creeds of the ancient Church do not make it their object to interpret or to supplement the Apostles' Creed; they were simply written to meet the errorists of the age, such as Arius, who denied the full divinity of Christ, the Macedonians who denied the personality and the divinity of the Spirit, the Nestorians and Monophysites who held fundamental errors regarding persons and natures of Christ. In meeting these teachers, the Church found itself called upon to state other features of revealed truth, which were essential and fundamental, but had so far not been generally recognized. Calovius took the position that all revealed truth is fundamental for salvation in one or another way, and that in the later creeds of the first five centuries, as also in those by the Reformation, we have new and needed statements of Scripture truths. And those, he insisted, have their significance not merely for the teacher of the Church, but for every soul. It is for this reason that the confessions of Lutheranism contain articles of faith, that must also be *counted among the fundamentals.*

Calovius pointed to the undeniable fact that the various errors, which had been the occasion for the development of the creeds, constituted temptations and dangers for the life of the Church; that the rejection of these errors in the creeds had much to do with the faith of the Church; and for this reason the creeds offer important messages for the common Christian, even if it is the special duty of the teacher to interpret those messages.[9]

4. The inner union claimed by Calixtus. On the basis of his theory of fundamentals and non-fundamentals in connection with his distinction between Apostles' Creed and later creeds, Calixtus declared that there is a virtual union (*communio interna*) between Lutherans and Reformed, and even Rome, that needed only to be recognized. He admitted that an outward union (*communio actualis et externa per sacramentum*) was not possible as long as these churches were wrongfully charging each other with fundamental errors. He admitted that the doctrine of the Lord's Supper was a serious obstacle to an external union between Lutherans and Reformed,[10] but not because of the doctrinal difference in itself—for it is not a fundamental doctrine—but because of the place of this sacrament in the cultus of the Church and because of the tenacity with which the churches hold to their differing opinions.[11]

The Lutherans admitted that they had much in common with the Reformed. Notwithstanding hard words that fell in the controversy, they did not seriously regard the Reformed like Jews and heathen, not even as sects like the Anabaptists and Socinians. They accorded them the name of a church.[12] But they denied the existence of a real union in the faith. And the differences, to them, were differences in the faith. Calixtus insisted upon distinguishing in every doctrine between the what (*quid*) and the how (*quomodo*), that is between the substance and the manner of teaching it. But the Lutherans answered: It is not enough to know that Christ is the Saviour, but it is also necessary to know how He saves; the teachings on the way of salvation, on the means of grace and on man's attitude are by no means non-fundamental matters. It is in the conflicts on these very important doctrines, they insisted, that the differences as to commonly accepted doctrines appear. Dannhauer declared: The churches accept the words of the creed, but they disagree in the meaning of them, which shows that the assumption of an existing union is after all a deception.[13]

The Lutherans refused to distinguish between fundamentals and non-fundamentals after the theory of Calixtus. Their arguments were as follows: The Scriptures speak of no such distinction and draw no line. Truth is an organism. In this organism there are parts of seemingly minor importance, but even these cannot be removed without

---

[9] Calovius, *Syncretismus Calixtinus,* pp. 143, 150, 153, and many other places; also *Digressio de Nova Theologia,* p. 910. Cf. Schmid, *op. cit.,* pp. 147 ff., 200 ff., 247-53, 291 ff., 409 ff.

[10] Schmid, pp. 172, 187 ff., 191 ff., 232 ff.

[11] *Ibid.,* pp. 172, 175-77, 187 ff., 191 ff., 232.

[12] *Ibid.,* pp. 211, 306.

[13] His *Mysterium Syncretismi,* p. 45; cf. Schmid, p. 290 ff.

injuring the whole. Dannhauer declared it to be a mistake to call only those doctrines articles of faith which must be believed for salvation; many doctrines of Scripture, which are not fundamental in that sense, are nevertheless articles of faith because of the help and comfort they give to the seeking sinner and to the Christian. As such he mentions the doctrine of the real presence of Christ's Body and Blood in the Supper.[14]

Calixtus took the position that no church could call itself the true Church, because all churches, Rome included, have the fundamentals of the Apostles' Creed. He regarded the Lutheran Church as the purest in theology, but in matters necessary for salvation he could see no difference. The greater or lesser purity, he said, was touching not the religion but merely the theology of the churches.[15]

It was in connection with the problem of an existing virtual union between the churches that the question was asked: Who is a heretic and what is a heresy? Here Calixtus had to express himself. In consistency with his leading views he said: We must distinguish between error and heresy. Departure from the statements of the Apostles' Creed constitutes a heresy, and a heretic, in this sense, is not in the union of faith with other Christians. But departure from the teaching of the later creeds and from the doctrinal matters derived from the Apostles' Creed *per consequentiam* constitutes an error which does not affect the union of faith.[16] A heretic, then, in the proper sense of that term, is he only who rejects an article of faith as it is plainly expressed in the Apostles' Creed.[17] Furthermore, it is one who rejects that article of faith consciously and who intentionally makes himself the cause of a schism, not one who by providence finds himself in a schismatic communion.[18] As has been said, the Lutherans objected to the distinction between Apostles' Creed and later creeds in this discussion. Calovius declared that such a definition of heresy was certainly opposed to the practice of the Church which demanded subscription to the later creeds as proof of orthodoxy.[19] He further reminded Calixtus that if adoption of the Apostles' Creed only is sufficient as evidence of orthodoxy then even the Arians, Socinians, Arminians and Anabaptists could not have been charged with heresy.[20]

As we have seen, Calixtus did not demand an organic union of the churches as long as serious theological difficulties stood in the way, but he pleaded for the recognition of an existing union (*communio virtualis*) on the fundamentals of the Apostles' Creed. On this basis he demanded an attitude of mutual recognition of one another as true churches, all being orthodox in the fundamentals of the faith. The Lutherans declared that if there were a real inner union in the matters pertaining to salvation then the obstacle for an external union would be removed and the full union should be consummated, but they denied the existence of such an inner union, and therefore declared that a recognition, such as Calixtus was advocating, would be infidelity to truth.

Even the milder University of Jena with John Musaeus took this position. Rejecting the theory of Calixtus regarding the fundamentals, these Jena theologians declared that the Church is steward not merely over a certain number of doctrines that seem to be particularly important, but over all revealed truth that is helpful in leading souls in the way of salvation. They argued that if the Lutheran Church is serious in her particular confession and is appealing to the Scriptures with good conscience she cannot recognize the opposing churches as orthodox and evangelical, but is in duty bound to testify against their errors; otherwise she would be espousing the principle that one conception

---

[14] Schmid, *op. cit.*, pp. 217, 293.
[15] *Ibid.*, pp. 172, 221, 225.
[16] *Ibid.*, pp. 172 ff., 260 ff. Cf. Calixtus, *Desiderium et Stud.*, etc., Sect. 6 *De Tolerantia*, thesis 4.
[17] *Ad Moguntinos*, th. 86.
[18] Calixtus, *Epicrisis Theol.*, th. 44.
[19] Schmid, p. 262. Calovius *Syncretismus Calixtinus*, pp. 164. 167.
[20] Schmid, p. 263. Calovius, *Digressio*, p. 923.

of religion is as good as another.[21] They recognized with the Formula of Concord that in other churches there are many true Christians who are erring innocently. These, they said, can be regarded as brethren. But, it was added, there is not always a way of knowing their inner attitude and, therefore, the rule will have to be that individuals must be judged after their public confession in the church in which they are members. As to recognizing other churches as true churches the position was taken that this could not be done consistently when these had confessionally established themselves upon positions subversive of the creed of the church from which recognition is expected.

III. AN ESTIMATE OF THE PRINCIPLES OF CALIXTUS AND OF THE LUTHERANS OF HIS AGE

1. *Distinction between Church and individual.* The distinction between fundamentals and non-fundamentals, when applied to the question of mutual recognition, in the hope of union, cannot be made by asking: What is indispensable for the individual to know and to believe in order to be saved? Calixtus failed to distinguish between Church and individual.

Regarding the individual, salvation depends upon an attitude of the soul to Christ, not upon the knowledge and acceptance of a fixed number of doctrines. But it is also true that having faith in Christ the intellect is not altogether passive. The Gospel which is accepted calls for a doctrinal expression even in the mind of the ordinary believer. But no hard and comprehensive rule can be made as to the details of such doctrinal expression. For an individual with little religious training, when it comes to the last struggle, it may be only one thought centering about Christ as the Saviour from sin, consequently much less than is contained in the Apostles' Creed. In another individual again, who grew up in a Christian environment under careful instruction in Scripture truth, a much larger insight into divine truth would be natural, so that elements of even the later creeds would be embraced in his confession. And then again, it is one thing not to know or not to have a clear conception of fundamental truth, and quite another to reject such truth with purpose and against conviction. It should also not be denied that a larger religious knowledge is helpful to the soul in finding the way of salvation.

But through the whole discussion it was left out of consideration that the question is an altogether different one when the object in view is the mutual recognition of the churches and when the aim is to prepare the way for church union. Here the Lutherans were right when they took the position that all Scripture truth is fundamental which aids the Church in its work of winning souls for Christ and of leading the congregation of believers in all truth.[22]

Calixtus demanded that churches of different creeds should recognize each other as "true" churches. To support his demand he asked his Lutheran opponents: Can the members of other churches not be saved? God Himself adopts His children, and we must recognize them as brethren in the faith.[23]

Such argument sounded well and was bound to make the position of Calixtus popular. But his argument was forcing the question by cutting the knot of a problem which he was unable to solve theologically. He was too persistent in ignoring the

---

[21] Report of the Jena faculty, published in Calovius' *Historia Syncretismi*, pp. 999 ff.
[22] See the fine discussion of Stahl, *Lutherische Kirche und Union*, pp. 339 ff.
[23] Schmid, *op. cit.*, p. 173.

difference of Church and individual in the discussion of this question. His argumentation was too much upon the presupposition that one church is as good as the other, and here he failed to see that church membership is or ought to be a matter of conviction and of conscience. The Lutherans expected the other churches also, as most of them were actually doing, to refuse to them full recognition and actual union so long as there was no agreement in matters of faith.[24]

We must admit, however, that the Lutherans of the age of Calixtus inclined to the mistake of making Christianity and the salvation of the individual too much dependent upon orthodoxy of faith. Many of them overlooked the fact that a sincere Christian can live in doctrinal errors and may even defend them. They said: When he has been sufficiently instructed then the responsibility is upon him. But considering the tenacity of prejudices, the natural fidelity to the church into which an individual was born and the influence of environment, the seventeenth century Lutherans were not right when they took the position that "sufficient instruction" is bound to convert the lover of truth. They were defective in their psychology. But in this they were right: that in the relation of church to church, recognition of an existing internal union and public fellowship in the faith must be regulated by the public profession.

2. The teaching of Calixtus as a reaction against the orthodoxism of his age. From the standpoint of conservative Lutheranism the positions of Calixtus, as they have been viewed, cannot be accepted. This has been the practically unanimous verdict of the Lutherans of his own age (the more liberal Jena School included), of the great Lutheran theologians who wrote in the second third of the nineteenth century, and of Lutheranism in America.[25] F. Kattenbusch in his article on Symbolics[26] offers the following severe judgment which weighs heavily if we consider his decidedly liberal theological position: "The Syncretism of the seventeenth century deserves no sympathy. He who really knows George Calixtus cannot judge him with any special appreciation (*ehrend*); neither as man nor theologian does he stand upon a higher level than his much-scolded opponent Abraham Calovius." Phil. Schaff, in his *Creeds,* on this subject, was too uncritical in following Tholuck, whose judgments in the works quoted in our Literature have been proven to be very unreliable. Prof. J. Kunze, in his article on Calovius, says: "Tholuck's judgment betrays the narrow position of the pietistic-unionistic school."[27]

It cannot be denied that in the age of Calixtus Lutheranism was in need of correctives. Orthodoxy had degenerated into orthodoxism.[28] The continuous controversies between Lutheranism and Calvinism had led to an intellectualism and to a preaching of pure theology in the pulpits, which yielded little bread to Gospel-hungry souls. The Ubiquity was a favored subject for discussion in the sermons. The appeal to the congregation was of such a nature that the layman was hardly regarded a full Christian unless he was a theologian. And with it all went a polemics that in most cases was out of place in the pulpits.

---

[24] For a complete discussion of the problems here involved the writer must refer to his interpretation of Article VII of the Augsburg Confession in his book, *The Augsburg Confession* (1914), pp. 92 ff., and in *Introduction to the Symbolical Books of the Lutheran Church,* 2nd edition (1927), pp. 181 91.

[25] We refer to the article "Georg Calixt" in Meusel, *Kirchl. Handlexikon* I, 632 ff.

[26] In the *PRE,* XIX, 204, 35 ff.

[27] *Ibid.,* III, 653, 24.

[28] Cf. Kurtz, *Op. cit.,* Sec. 159.

The Lutherans of the seventeenth century went too far in identifying religious truth with the theological and dialectical formulation of the same. In the practical life of the Church there are situations where, in the application, a distinction between religion and theology must be observed. In denominational problems it has not alway" been easy to distinguish properly between the *fides qua* and the *fides quae creditur*, tha' is, the subjective and the objective faith. In the distinction of Calixtus between the simple facts of the Apostles' Creed and the later creeds of a more theological nature, we have the reaction against the intellectualism of the seventeenth century Lutheranism. But the theory of Calixtus was not acceptable. His distinction between religion and theology was too mechanical. It must never be left out of view that to a certain degree theology, true Scriptural theology, will always have to be the form of the objective faith, without which a healthy subjective faith cannot be cultivated in the Church.

3. *The "Internal Union."* Calixtus' assertion of a practically existing internal union (*communio interna, virtualis*) could be made only by an almost entire abstraction from the objective faith. Common recognition of the Apostles' Creed did not mean much, because the differences appeared in the interpretation of that creed.[29] That internal union, then, had a certain degree of reality only when regard was had to the *fides qua creditur*, that is to the relation and attitude of the heart to God and His Son as Saviour from sin.

The Pietists, especially the newly converted among them, are always unionists when it comes to denominational problems. The profound impression from their religious experience leads them to regard all as brethren in the faith who have had a like experience. But, if the spiritual development and growth of such a newly converted individual is normal, then the time is bound to come when he feels the need of linking his religious experience with the doctrinal experiences of the historic Church. The Church's doctrinal experience is crystallized in the creeds. So, then, purely pietistic Christians develop into confessional Christians with denominational interests.

4. *Calixtus' failure to appreciate the Reformation.* We mean the Reformation as a creative epoch in the doctrinal development of the Church. Prof Tschackert, an advocate of irenics as to the relation between the Lutherans and the Reformed and strongly opposed to the seventeenth century Lutheranism and sympathetic with Calixtus, writes on Georg Calixt in the *Realencyklopaedie* (III, 647 ff.): "As regards his irenics, we shall acknowledge and highly appreciate his good intention. But in taking the position that the Apostles' Creed and the *consensus quinquesaecularis* are the best representation of Christianity he proved that he did not have the proper appreciation of the religious content of the Reformation. Upon the standpoint of Calixtus the historic reformation of Luther loses its specific value. The natural consequence was indifferentism towards the confessions of the Church, which, in a number of cases, evidenced itself in the conversion of Lutheran princes and princesses to Roman Catholicism." Calixtus was Lutheran in name, but he ignored the historic foundation of his church. Dannhauer remarked correctly that in following Calixtus, the Lutheran Church would have to cease praising Luther and his Reformation and apologize for the schism that had been caused in Protestantism. Even Baur (*History of the Christian Church*) felt constrained to remark that from the standpoint of Calixtus and in consistency with his theories the Reformation needed not to have taken place. Characteristic of his position was the

---

[29] Cf. Dannhauer, *Mysterium Syncretismi*, p. 45.

answer he gave to Prince Anton Ulrich of Brunswick, who had asked him whether a Protestant princess could marry with good conscience a Roman Catholic king and embrace his faith. He answered: (1) The Roman Catholic Church does not err in the foundation of faith and the matter of salvation. (2) Consequently the changing of one's church relationship from Protestantism to Roman Catholicism is permissible.[30]

5. *Humanism.* The humanistic trait in Calixtus had much to do with his liberal views in dealing with denominational problems. Baur remarked that Calixtus favored a development from the purely Christian to the generally human. (*"Er lenkte von der Religion zu dem allgemein Menschlichen."*) Here, perhaps, was the real root of his conflict with Lutheranism. In the Introduction to this chapter we have acknowledged that humanism could have had a beneficial influence upon the seventeenth century Lutherans. We had reference, however, only to form, method, temper. Humanism makes the theologian freer, more scientific, and helps him to draw lessons from history and psychology. But it also inclines to a criticism of the foundations. The hand of God in history is ignored. The Reformation is looked upon as a misdevelopment.

IV. SYNCRETISM AS A MOVEMENT

1. *The charge of syncretism.* The term "syncretism" came into frequent use as a charge against Calixtus and his followers. The term stigmatizes the endeavor of combining in one Church opposing confessions of faith. The term is derived from the Greek *synkerannymi* (συγκεράννυμι), to mix together. But it is perhaps more correct to think of the *"Syncretismon"* by which the old Cretans, being in disagreement with one another, meant (according to Plutarch) that they should always be united against a common foe. In this sense it had been suggested also by Zwingli, Bucer, Melanchthon that they should form a *Syncretismon,* meaning by that a united front against Rome, even if a full doctrinal union could not be realized.[31]

2. *Jena versus Wittenberg: striking the balance in the controversy.* It has been emphasized again and again that Lutheranism cannot agree to a clear-cut separation between religion and theology, especially not after the suggestions of Calixtus. But it has also been indicated that the seventeenth century Lutherans had lost themselves in an intellectualism which ignored entirely the necessary distinction between confessional substance and matters that are purely theologumena. Here the later Wittenberg had been leading.

The real defect in the position of the Wittenberg University came into light in an abortive confession, composed and proposed by Abr. Calovius. It was his *Consensus Repetitus,* etc., of 1664.[32]

This new symbol against syncretism went far beyond the Formula of Concord in rendering decisions on theological problems. Following the order of the Augsburg Confession, we have in eighty-eight sections always first the true doctrine, introduced by a *profitemur;* then follows with a *rejicimus,* the rejected error; finally there is a proof quotation from the writings of the Helmstedters (Calixtus, Hornejus, Latermann,

---

[30] Meusel, *Kirchl, Handlexikon* I, 634-f. Cf. Schmid, *op. cit.,* pp. 200, 209.

[31] Zwingli, *Opp.* ed. Schueler, VII, 390; VIII, 577. *CR* I, 917; C. Schmidt, *Melanchthon,* p. 655; Hering, *Unionsversuche* I, 64 ff., 283 ff. *PRE,* XIX, 239 ff.

[32] As to full title and related matters see: Schmid, *op. cit.,* p. 367; Meusel, II, 20. *PRE.* XIX, 248, 53 ff.; 254, 51 ff.; Schaff, *Creeds* I, 351.

Dreier). Among the things rejected as downright heresies are the following: that the article of the Trinity is not clearly revealed in the Old Testament, and that the believers of the Old Testament should not have known this doctrine; that the Angel of Jehovah is not Christ; that the Old Testament believers did not know and believe the doctrine of Christ's person and office; that even outside of the sacrament Christ is not bodily present with all believers; that Creationism is not a heresy; that the existence of God needs not be proved by theology; that newly born children have no real faith; that John in Chapter 6 speaks of the Lord's Supper; that Romanists and Calvinists can belong to the true Church; that they can have a hope of salvation and are not to be condemned to eternal death. Consent to these matters was required for church fellowship. It was the intention to place the Helmstedters outside of the Lutheran Church. Calovius published one work after the other to prepare the Church for an adoption of his symbol.

But Wittenberg no longer truly represented the Lutheran Church. John Musaeus with the faculty of the Jena University stepped in as a regulating factor and did a valuable service to Lutheranism. He criticised the Wittenberg theologians that in their controversy against Calixtus they had not sufficiently distinguished between necessary articles of faith and matters in which *salve fide et caritate* there may be disagreement. He demanded the recognition of "open questions."

A characteristic passage from the Jena circle may here be quoted: "In the detailed and thorough discussion of necessary articles of faith, in the interpretation of difficult passages of Scripture, in the dealing with philosophical questions relative to their bearing upon necessary articles of faith, in the method of polemics and in like matters, even orthodox and doctrinally pure theologians cannot always be expected to agree. This is especially true of the men at high schools, for they have not been called to lecture before their audiences without further thought of what they have learned of their teachers or read of other theologians; but they are to consider carefully special difficulties and should aim as much as possible to elucidate and to interpret. If this be done, then it cannot be otherwise but that sometimes there will be dissensions in the manner of teaching, in formulating and defending the doctrines of faith," etc. Estimating the theological situation, attention was called to the fact that in matters of knowledge convictions mature gradually and that frequently many have to render their contributions before the full truth is seen. For such ventilation of thought, it was said, there must be toleration in the Church. Progress should not be barred by too much insistence upon conformity to detail.

The Jena theologians were far from agreeing with Calixtus in his manner of distinguishing between fundamentals and non-fundamentals. Here they were in entire harmony with Wittenberg. To the honor even of the seventeenth century Lutherans it can be reported that the *Consensus Repetitus* was never adopted. The large work of Calovius, his *Historia Syncretistica*, was also practically confiscated by the government of Lutheran Saxony.[33]

Our special point of interest in this chapter has been in the critical review of positions taken by George Calixtus, in which the theology of the Reformation is for the first time toned down to a level of mild interdenominationalism and to positions later

---

[33] *PRE,* XIX, 261, 5 ff. For literature on the whole subject see Schmid, *op. cit.,* 377 ff.; Gass, *Georg Calixtus,* p. 112; Tschackert in *PRE,* XIX, 248, 46 ff.; *Der Jenaschen Theologen ausfuehrliche Erklaerung,* 1677, printed in Calovius, *Historia Syncretistica,* 1685, pp. 1009 ff.; Kunze on *Musaeus* in *PRE,* XII, 376 ff.

occupied by the union movements. In the form of a reaction against the seventeenth century theology in the spheres of Lutheranism it contained in itself seeds of liberalism that were not yet noticed. The syncretistic movement, at that time, was crushed. But the union movements of succeeding ages revived Calixtinian tendencies of irenics in the Moravian movement and in the Prussian Church Union. The "Syncretism" of Calixtus addressed itself to the Lutheran part of Protestantism. We shall see, in the following two chapters, how the same tendencies asserted themselves in domains of the Reformed churches, in Holland and in England.

Chapter Two

ARMINIANISM IN HOLLAND

Literature: The writings of Arminius: Latin, J. ARMINII, *Opera Theologica*, Lugd. Bat., 1629; in new ed. at Frankfort, 1631 and 1635. Translated from the Latin into English by J. NICHOLS, London, 1825-28 (2 vols.); Buffalo, 1853 (3 vols.). J. NICHOLS, *The Life of Arminius*, London, 1843. Also the articles on Arminius and Arminianism in MEUSEL. *Kirchl. Handlexikon*, in *Protestantische Realencyklopaedie*, (*PRE*) and the corresponding article in the *New Schaff-Herzog*, also in the *Encycl. Britannica*, and in L. STEPHEN'S *Dictionary of World Biography*. Compare also the historically orientating article by E. G. A. BOECKEL given as an introduction to the Canons of Dort in his *Bekenntnisschriften der evangelisch reformierten Kirchen* (1847) pp. 508-13. As to an easily obtainable well balanced review, we refer to PH. SCHAFF, *Creeds of Christendom* I, 509-15. Compare CHARLES HODGE, *Systematic Theology* (1874) II, 316 ff., 327 ff. We have a detailed investigation of the whole situation by O. RITSCHL, *Dogmengeschichte des Protestantismus* III (1926), 314-339; also by R. SEEBERG, *Lehrb. d. DG*, IV, 3d ed. (1920), 676-700. (Cf. LOOFS, *DG* and FISHER, *History of Doctrine*.) A critical review is given by G. F. OEHLER, *Lehrbuch der Symbolik*, 2d ed., 191-196. Among English church histories we mention one by W. WALKER. Cf. also J. TULLOCH, *Rational Theology*, 2 vols., 1872. Also G. B. WINER, *Comparative View of Doctrines* (in Clark's Foreign Theological Library, 1873). Also G. L. CURTISS. *Arminianism in History*, 1890. Also J. L. GIRARDEAU, *Calvinism and Evangelical Arminianism Compared*, 1890.

From the Church of Luther we shall now, for the next two chapters, step over to territories of Calvinism (Holland and Great Britain). In our study of the syncretism of George Calixtus we found ourselves still on Lutheran ground, although it should not be overlooked that similar synergistic tendencies were moving in Holland (the distinction between fundamentals and non-fundamentals) and also in England (cf. the influences of an irenic theology, as with Stillingfleet and others). But in both Holland and England the background was Calvinism, or Arminianism as its counterpart.

At another place, in Volume One, at the close of the chapter on John Calvin, we gave an enumeration of the standards of Calvinism, chief among which we mentioned Calvin's *Institutes* (1559), the *Heidelberg Catechism* (1563), the *Second Helvetic Confession* (1566), the *Canons of the Synod at Dort* (1619), and, most important, the *Westminster Confession* in Great Britain (1647), with two *Catechisms*. For an extensive review of the history of the Westminster Assembly and its work read Philip Schaff, *Creeds of Christendom*, I, pp. 727-829, and for a brief review of outstanding Reformed and Presbyterian Confessions of faith and their significance, see our *Churches and Sects of Christendom* (1940). pp. 313-321.

We shall not give here an analysis of the *Westminster Confession*, but shall refer the student to our *Churches and Sects*, particularly to our discussion of the historical points of emphasis concerning doctrine and practice of the Reformed Churches in their differences from Lutheranism (pp. 321-352).

The Arminian movement began with a controversy on predestination, but this was only the starting point of the conflict. In the discussion we shall speak first of this starting point and then, second, of the further development of Arminianism.*

---

* Originally published 1931 as an article of the author in the *Princeton Theological Review*, and here revised and republished by courtesy of the publishers.

I. Arminianism as It Started

1. The immediate cause of the conflict was on the one side the emphasis on Calvin's double predestination in the form of supralapsarianism as contrasted with infralapsarianism, and on the other side the opposition to this teaching. In the thought of the Reformed theologians after the death of Calvin, these two terms refer to the logical order of the decrees in discussing the subject. Charles Hodge wrote on the meaning of supralapsarianism as follows: "According to this view, God, in order to manifest His grace and justice, selected from creatable men (from men to be created) a certain number to be vessels of mercy, and certain others to be vessels of wrath. In the order of thought, election and reprobation precede the purpose to create and to permit the fall. Creation is in order to redemption." [1] Then Hodge speaks of infralapsarianism: "God, with the design to reveal his own glory, that is, the perfections of his own nature, determined to create the world; secondly to permit the fall of man; thirdly, to elect from the mass of fallen men a multitude whom no man can number as vessels of mercy, etc." [2]

Calvin did not express himself clearly or consistently on this matter. "As it was not in his day a special matter of discussion, certain passages may be quoted from his writings which favor the supralapsarian and other passages which favor infralapsarian view." [3]

In the writings of Beza also there are expressions not irreconcilable with in infralapsarianism.[4] But, as is pointed out by O. Ritschl[5] to whom we are indebted for these references, the burden of his teaching throughout was the supralapsarian conception of predestination.[6]

D. V. Koornheert, a scholarly layman, of whom we shall hear more a little later, wrote against this teaching. He gathered a following, and the demand was for a revision of the Belgic Confession. Jacob Arminius, known for dialectical skill and for loyalty to Calvinism, was asked to reply to him. But on closer study of this problem he turned against Beza and all the strict predestinarians. As professor at the University of Leyden (1603) he soon was in conflict with his colleague, Francis Gomarus, a rigid Calvinist.[7]

It is in the emphasis upon this conception by strict adherents to Calvinistic principles and in the determination of a more or less rationalistically inclined anti-Calvinist group of men who wanted to get rid of every vestige of the Biblical doctrine of predestination that we must see the historical cause of the conflict here to be described.

2. The conflict soon resulted in a schism affecting the whole of the Reformed Church in Holland. Arminius died in 1609. The scholarly and able Simon Episcopius became his successor in the university and the spokesman for his followers. It was he especially who systematized and developed the "Arminian" views. The Arminians, in 1610, expressed their position in five articles (*Articuli Arminiani sive Remonstrantiae*) which gave to them the name *"Remonstrants."* [8] The adherents of the official church

---

[1] *Systematic Theology* II, 316. [2] *Ibid.* [3] *Ibid.*

[4] Cf. *Tractationes Theologicae*, ed. II, Genevae, 1582, III, 406 b; see also his argumentation at the Montbeliard Colloquy in the *Acta Colloquii Montis Belligartensis*, Tübingen, 1587, pp. 523 ff.

[5] *DG*, III, 295 f.

[6] See his *Tractationes*, I pp. 81 (10), 173 (2), 179 (5), 196 (5), 683, 684, 687; III, 403 a.

[7] Fisher, *op. cit.*, p. 338; Seeberg, *op. cit.*, IV, 671 ff.; Ritschl, III, 319 f.; Tulloch, *op. cit.*, I, 11 ff.

[8] These articles are published by Schaff in *Creeds*, IIII, 545 ff., in Dutch, Latin and English (from which we shall quote below). The Preface, the five negative articles and the conclusion are here omitted. E. G. A. Boeckel, in his above mentioned *Bekenntnisschriften der evangelisch-reformierten Kirche* (Leipzig, 1847) gives a German translation of the whole (pp. 544-53).

issued a *Counter-Remonstrance.* All endeavors to reach an agreement were of no avail. So the question came before the famous Synod of Dort, convened on November 13, 1618, and lasting till May 9, 1619, during which time there were held 154 formal sessions and a large number of conferences.[9] The whole Dutch delegation, consisting of 84 clerical and 18 secular commissioners, was orthodox. There were 28 foreign delegates of Reformed churches: from England, Scotland, the Palatinate, Hesse, Nassau, East Friesland, and Bremen. King James had instructed the English delegates to "mitigate the heat of both sides." Some of the German delegates were urging the same thing. But such voices were ignored. The representatives of Arminianism, thirteen in all, were treated as persons under indictment and were excluded from participation in the proceedings. The result was the condemnation of the five articles of the Remonstrance and the drafting of five decidedly Calvinistic "Canons." The Belgic Confession and the Heidelberg Catechism were formally adopted.[10]

3. *The doctrine of predestination in the discussion of the Synod.*

a. The *general situation* is characterized by Schaff with the following remark: "The Arminian controversy is the most important which took place within the Reformed Church. It corresponds to the Pelagian and the Jansenist controversies in the Catholic Church. It involves the problem of the ages, which again and again has baffled the ken of theologians and philosophers, and will do so to the end of time: the relation of divine sovereignty and human responsibility."

b. The *"Five Articles" of the Remonstrants* together with the "explanatory theses" which they were required to lay before the Synod [11] may guide us in stating what was their teaching on predestination:

Point 1: God had simply decreed to save all who would believe in Christ and persevere in this faith to their end; and to condemn all who continue to refuse Him. In this act there is no reference to individuals. Thus predestination is reduced to the mere foreknowledge of God.

Point 2: Christ died for all men and for every man, obtaining "for them all . . . redemption and the forgiveness of sins"; only that "no one actually enjoys this forgiveness of sins except the believer." They protest against distinguishing between the general fact of Christ dying for all and His actually dying for the elect only (theses 2, 4).

Points 3 and 4[12]: "Man has not saving grace of himself, nor of the energy of his free will, inasmuch as he, in the state of apostasy and sin, can of and by himself neither think, will, nor do anything that is truly good (such as saving faith eminently is); but it is needful that he be born again—and renewed in understanding, inclination, or will, and all his powers." Art. 4, speaking of the absolute need of divine grace, adds: "But as respects the mode of the operation of this grace, it is not irresistible, inasmuch as it is written concerning many, that they have resisted the Holy Ghost." In the background of these two articles, supplemented by the theses, are the thoughts expressed and unexpressed: The sinner, while not free in the doing of the good, is still expected to prepare

---

[9] On the composition and history of this synod which was representative of the whole of Reformed Protestantism, see Schaff, *Creeds,* I, 512-15.

[10] Schaff, in his *Creeds of Christendom,* III, gives these *Canones Synodi Dordrechtanae* in Latin (pp. 550-80), then the English abridgment, as adopted by the Reformed (Dutch) Church in America (581-97). The Latin text is found also in Niemeyer's *Collectio* and the German in the collections of Boeckel.

[11] Given by Müller, *Bekenntnisschriften der reformierten Kirche,* pp. lix ff.

[12] After English translation by Schaff, *Creeds,* III, 546 f.

himself and to take the decisive steps. The divine call is always seriously meant, the distinction between an external and an internal call being rejected. There is no calling of the reprobates just for the purpose of hardening them, for removing their excuse and for punishing them more severely. There is no secretly predestinating divine will. The given grace is sufficient for the salvation of all. (These are statements contained in the theses.)

Point 5: Perseverance, resistance in temptation are through the assistance of the Holy Spirit and by the help of Christ; they are not, however, the result of an absolute decree. Believers, therefore, can fall into grievous sins and persevere in these. *They can only hope that they may persevere and be confident that divine grace will always be at hand and be sufficient* (see besides Art. 5 the theses upon this subject). The basis for all these statements is, after all, the belief in a certain freedom of the will in spiritual things and the denial of a real predestination.[13]

c. The *Canons of Dort*[14] are the reply of the Synod to the "five points" of the Remonstrants. Points 3 and 4 are taken together. Under each of these heads, "articles," or statements of positive doctrine, are first given. These are then followed by "rejectory articles" directed against the opponents. The articles show that the leaders at Dort were not deceived as to tendencies and principles of the Remonstrants, that were not expressed in the articles which they had submitted.[15] The question of supralapsarianism versus infralapsarianism was evaded at the Synod. But the infralapsarians were decidedly in the majority there, especially among the delegates from England and from Germany. There are in the Canons no really supralapsarian statements. In their entirety they represent the orthodox Reformed system as pivoting around the doctrine of predestination.[16]

In the following we shall try to give the essentials of these "Five Points of Calvinism."

Point 1: *Of Divine Predestination.* All men have sinned in Adam, are under God's curse and deserve eternal death. Christ was sent for the salvation of all believers. The wrath of God is upon those who believe not this Gospel, because the cause of this unbelief is "in man himself." [17]

But on the other hand, the messengers of God go only "to whom He will and at what time He pleaseth" (Art. 3).[18] Faith "is the free gift of God," and "that some receive the gift of faith from God and others do not receive it, proceeds from God's eternal decree . . . according to which decree He graciously softens the hearts of the elect, however obstinate, and inclines them to believe while, in His just judgment, He leaves the non-elect to their own wickedness and obduracy" (Art. 6).

There is emphasis upon the fact that the predestination for salvation pertains to "a certain number of persons," to an "elect number" that cannot be "diminished" (Arts. 7, 10, 11, 15).

As to the non-elect or reprobate there is the statement that "others are passed by in the eternal decree" (Art. 15).

---

[13] Cf. Seeberg, *op. cit.*, IV, 678-82; see also Schaff, *Creeds*, I, 516-19.

[14] In reviewing the *Canons of Dort* we have before us the Latin text and the English abridged text, both given by Schaff, *op. cit.*, vol. III, also the German text by Boeckel (see above), and the careful review by Seeberg, IV, 683 ff.

[15] See II below, also the footnote in Seeberg, IV, 690.

[16] Cf. Seeberg, IV, 685.

[17] Schaff, *Creeds*, III, Art. 5, see pp. 581 ff.

[18] There is a similar statement in the Augsburg Confession (Art. V): *Ubi et quando visum est Deo.*

What is God's motive in this double "eternal decree"? The election for salvation is "out of mere grace," "to the sovereign good pleasure of His own will," "for the praise of the riches of His glorious grace" (Art. 7). The *reprobate* has fallen into his state "out of His sovereign, most just, irreprehensible and unchangeable good pleasure," "for the declaration of His justice" (Art. 15).

To meet the troubling thoughts of imperfect Christians the following article (Art. 16) is added: "Those who do not yet experience a lively faith in Christ . . . and do nevertheless persist in the use of the means which God has appointed for working these graces in us, ought not to be alarmed at the mention of reprobation, nor to rank themselves among the reprobate, but diligently to persevere . . . and with ardent desires devoutly and humbly to wait for a season of richer grace. Much less are they to be terrified . . . who cannot yet reach that measure of holiness and faith to which they aspire . . ."

To these articles on Point One the synod attached a *"rejection of errors"* in nine paragraphs.[19] Among these was this, that the whole of predestination is simply the general truth that God will save all who believe and persevere (Art. 1); also that this predestination is conditioned upon the right use of the "light of nature" (which would be Pelagian), and upon the foreseen attitude of man in repentance, faith, and perseverance (Arts. 4, 5); also that the elect may be lost, which would be in conflict with the immutability of God (Arts. 6, 7); that God cannot have decreed to condemn anybody (8); finally that the evangelization of some peoples is to be explained by merits that these had before others (9).

Point 2: *The Death of Christ and the Redemption of Men thereby.* The justice of God demands also the eternal punishment of the sinner unless satisfaction be made. He cannot do this in His own Person (Arts. 1, 2). Thus God gave His Son who became a curse for us and rendered the satisfaction. His sacrifice and satisfaction were of infinite value and, therefore, sufficient to expiate the sins of the whole world. They were sufficient for the reason that Christ was not only "really man and perfectly holy," but also the only begotten Son of God. This gospel is to be preached to all. Those, thus called, who do not believe, perish because of their own desert (Art. 6); those who believe and are saved "are indebted for this benefit solely to the Grace of God given them in Christ from everlasting. . . . For this was the sovereign counsel and most gracious will and purpose of God the Father that the quickening and saving efficacy of the most precious death of His Son should extend to all the elect, for bestowing upon them alone the gift of justifying faith, thereby to bring them infallibly to salvation: that is, it was the will of God, that Christ by the blood of the cross . . . should effectually redeem out of every people . . . all those, and those only, who were from eternity chosen to salvation" (8).

The *rejectory paragraphs* are directed against the teaching that Christ had suffered without regard to special persons (Art. 1); that Christ, by His satisfaction, had merely opened the way for the Father to offer salvation under new conditions to be met by man in the use of his free will (Art. 3); that a federation of grace had been established in which God had declared Himself satisfied with faith and with an obedience which, while it is imperfect, is yet worthy of eternal life (Art. 4); that all men must be

---

[19] Latin by Schaff, *Creeds*, III, 556 ff., German by Boeckel, *op. cit.*, 520 ff.; cf. Seeberg, *op. cit.*, IV, 690 ff.

regarded as having been adopted into that federation of grace so that nobody is under condemnation because of original sin (Art. 5); that in reality the death of Christ was not necessary for those who loved God and were His elect (Art. 7).

Points 3 and 4: *Of Man's Corruption, his Conversion, and the Manner of this Process.* Man, through a false use of his freedom, and under temptation by the devil, sank into the state of the Fall: "entailing on himself blindness of mind, horrible darkness, vanity and perverseness of judgment." He "became wicked, rebellious, and obdurate in heart and will, and impure in his affections" (Art. 1). His children and "all the posterity of Adam, Christ only excepted, have derived corruption by their original parent, not by imitation, as the Pelagians of old asserted, but by the propagation of a vicious nature in consequence of a just judgment of God" (Art. 2). Man, therefore, is under God's wrath, "incapable of any saving good, prone to evil, dead in sin, and in bondage thereto; and, without the regenerating grace of the Holy Spirit men are neither able nor willing to return to God, to reform the depravity of their nature, nor to dispose themselves to reformation" (Art. 3). However, there is "in man, since the Fall, the glimmerings of a natural light whereby he retains some knowledge of God, of natural things, and of the difference between good and evil, and discovers some regard for virtue, good order in society, and for maintaining an orderly external deportment. But so far is this light of nature from being sufficient to bring him to a saving knowledge of God, and to true conversion, that he is incapable of using it aright even in things natural and civil" (Art. 4). Not even "the law of the decalogue" can bring salvation. "For though it discovers the greatness of sin, and more and more convinces man thereof, yet as it neither points out a remedy, nor imparts strength to extricate him from misery, and thus being weak through the flesh, leaves the transgressor under the curse, man cannot by this law obtain saving grace" (Art. 5).

"What, therefore, neither the light of nature nor the law could do, that God performs by the operation of His Holy Spirit through the Word or ministry of reconciliation" (Art. 6). This call is not feigned, but serious (Art. 8).

If there are those that do not accept the call nor persevere then "the fault lies in themselves" as also in those who "though they receive it, suffer it not to make a lasting impression on their heart. Therefore, their joy, arising only from a temporary faith, soon vanishes and they fall away . . ." (Art. 9). The accepting of the call by others is not to be ascribed to the proper exercise of a free will, but to God's eternal election; it is this election that makes the call efficient (Arts. 10, 11).

Thus the regeneration does not come about through teaching, moral persuasion (which would lead into Pelagian conceptions), but through a supernatural work of God. After this divine work has taken place and man is renewed, then the will itself becomes active (Art. 12). Thus faith is to be considered "the gift of God" (Art. 14). But in all this, the *"grace of regeneration does not treat men as senseless stocks and blocks, nor take away their will and its properties, neither does violence thereto;* but spiritually quickens, heals, corrects . . . that where carnal rebellion and resistance formerly prevailed a ready and sincere spiritual obedience begins to reign" (Art. 16). The last article emphasizes the need of the means of grace: "the sacred precepts of the gospel, in the exercise of the Word, the sacraments *and discipline*" (Art. 17). The Lutherans never included "discipline" among the means of grace.

To these articles a number of very interesting *rejectory paragraphs* were attached.

In reading them we must keep in mind the Socinian influences which we shall have occasion to point out below as having contributed to the historical background of developing Arminianism. The Synod rejected the teaching that original sin in itself was not sufficient to merit temporal and eternal punishments for the whole race (Art. 1); that spiritual gifts and virtues, such as goodness, holiness and justness in the will, cannot have been present in the first man and that for this reason he cannot have fallen from them (Art. 2); that in man's spiritual death the spiritual gifts cannot be separated from his will, because this will was never depraved, but was merely hindered through the darkness of mind and irregularity of passions (*per tenebras mentis et affectuum inordinationem* [20]), so that after the removal of these hindrances (*impedimenta*) man again is free and can choose in his own free powers as he wills (Art. 3); that the unregenerate is not entirely dead in his sins, but can hunger and thirst after righteousness (Art. 4); that man in his depraved and natural condition is able to use the general grace which he has in the natural light . . . so correctly that in this way he can gradually attain to a larger evangelical saving grace (Art. 5).

Regarding the communication of grace the following sentences are rejected: that in a true conversion God *cannot infuse into the will* new qualities, ways (*habitus*) or gifts, and that, therefore, the faith of conversion is no divinely infused quality or gift, but an act of man . . . (Art. 6); that the grace of conversion is nothing but a persuading (*lenis suasio, Anraten*) which produces the consent of the will (Art. 7); that *man can resist grace* and that it is in his power to become regenerated or not (Art. 8); that the cause of conversion must be seen in the *co-operation* (the Lutherans spoke of "synergism") between grace and free-will, and that grace does nothing until man's will first has moved and made the decision (Art. 9).

Point 5: *Of the Perseverance of the Saints.* God has liberated the regenerated from the dominion and service of sin though not yet altogether from the body of sin and from the infirmities of the flesh. Daily sins of infirmity are a constant cause for humiliation before God, for flying for refuge to Christ, for mortifying the flesh and for pressing forward to perfection. If left to their own strength the converted could not persevere in grace. They are not always so influenced and actuated by the Spirit of God that they be not led into temptation and do not fall into grave sins—"sometimes by the righteous permission of God." "By such enormous sins, however, they very highly offend God, incur a deadly guilt, grieve the Holy Spirit, interrupt the exercise of faith, very grievously wound their consciences, and sometimes lose the sense of God's favor, for a time, until on their returning into the right way by serious repentance, the light of God's fatherly countenance again shines upon them" (Arts. 1-5).

But God, . . . according to His unchangeable purpose of election, does not wholly withdraw the Holy Spirit from His own people; . . . nor suffer them to proceed so far as to lose the grace of adoption and to forfeit the state of justification, or to commit the sin unto death. But He preserves in the elect "the incorruptible seed of regeneration" from perishing and by His Word and Spirit effectually renews them to repentance so that they may again experience the favor of a reconciled God" (Arts. 6, 7).

The cause for this is to be seen in *"God's free mercy,"* not *"in their own merits and strength." "With respect to God, it is utterly impossible . . . that they should totally fall*

---

from faith and grace ... and perish in their backslidings ... since His counsel cannot be changed, nor His promise fail, neither can the call according to His purpose be revoked, nor the merit, intercession and preservation of Christ be rendered ineffectual, nor the sealing of the Holy Spirit be frustrated or obliterated" (Art. 8). The assurance for this preservation of the elect the true believers find "according to the measure of their faith" in the "Word of God," in the "testimony of the Holy Spirit" and in a serious and holy desire to preserve a good conscience, and to perform good works" (Arts. 9-11). "This certainty of perseverance" will not excite in believers a "spirit of pride" nor make them "carnally secure"; it is, on the contrary, "a real source of humility." "Neither does renewed confidence of persevering produce licentiousness ... , but it renders them much more careful ... lest by abusing His fatherly kindness, God should turn away" (Arts. 12-13).

On this fifth point the Synod added the following *rejections of opposed errors:* that the perseverance of believers is not the effect of election, but a necessary condition for man to comply with in his own free will (Art. 1); that while God furnishes the needed strength for perseverance it is dependent upon man's will whether he wants to persevere or not (Art. 2); that believers and elect can definitely fall from grace and commit the sin against the Holy Spirit (Arts. 3-4).

Regarding the assurance of salvation the following sentences are rejected: that a special revelation alone could give such an assurance (Art. 5); that the teaching of such a guarantee of salvation would furnish a comfort for the flesh and be detrimental to the religious and ethical life (Art. 6); that the difference between those who believe only for a time (*fides temporariorum*) and those of permanent, justifying and saving faith consists merely in the element of duration (Art. 7).

II. The Genius of Arminianism in the Light of Its Further Development

1. The Remonstrants in their "Five Articles" of 1610 *had moved in very guarded statements.* In the minds of their subscribers there was much more than was there expressed. If this was not yet completely developed, it was in process of development on the basis of principles that were discernible. This was clear to the Synod of Dort in 1618 as may be seen from the many rejectory statements attached to its "Canons." [21] We learn it especially also from the Confession which was prepared, 1622, by Episcopius for the Remonstrants after their condemnation at Dort. [22]

2. The theological liberalism of later Arminianism had already been foreshadowed by certain pioneer influences in Holland. [23] We can observe in the Netherlands a certain confluence of humanistic and practical-mystical tendencies. Settled doctrines and strict church forms were not in favor. The call was for tolerance, for the simple devotional teachings of the Bible and for a universal religion fit to promote morality. The Bible alone was to be authority, and binding Confessions were to be declined. Seeberg whose

---

[21] These rejectory parts are omitted by Schaff in his abridged English text, *op. cit.,* III, pp. 581 ff., but they are given in his Latin text, III, pp. 545 ff. We have them also in German by Boeckel, *op. cit.,* pp. 516 ff.

[22] This document of a considerable length appeared in Holland in Dutch (1621) and in Latin (1622): *Confessio sive declaratio sententiae pastorum, qui in foederato Belgio Remonstrantes vocantur.* It was also printed in the Latin works of Episcopius (2nd ed. in London, 1678, cf. Part II, 75-94). In German this most interesting document is given by Boeckel and covers 86 pages (pp. 554-640). We miss it in Schaff, *Creeds,* III, where we should have had an English translation of it.

[23] Our references are especially to Seeberg, *op. cit.,* IV, 667-75, and to Ritschl, *op. cit.,* III, 314-19. See also the introductory remarks of Walker in his chapter on Arminianism, *op. cit.,* p. 453 f.

observations we are here following illustrates this whole peculiar situation by an exhibition of the teachings of two men: Jacob Acontius and D. Koornheert. Acontius represents the mild humanistic views of Erasmus. His book *Stratagemata Satanae* (1565) went through twelve editions and was much read in Holland and England. Obligatory Christian teaching was to be reduced to certain essentials. He demanded tolerance and the abrogation of execution for heresy. Koornheert was less conservative than Acontius. He delighted in criticism of the Church. Still he took the Scriptures as standard in matters of faith. But the traces of Socinian rationalization are observable. He suggested modifications of doctrine in a number of respects: Scripture, he declared, knows nothing of original sin, the imputation idea in connection with the doctrine of justification is to be rejected, the redemption of Christ consists in making man righteous, the teaching of predestination in the sense of Calvin is a fundamental error because it makes God the author of sin.[24] We shall fail to understand Arminianism if we do not consider this whole historical background of the controversy.

3. The Theological leaders of the movement after the death of Arminius (1609) *all contributed considerably to develop the real genius of it.* The following names must be mentioned: Uytenbogaert (d. 1644), Vorstius (d. 1622), Episcopius (d. 1643), Grotius (d. 1645), Curcellaeus (d. 1659), van Limborch (d. 1712). As to the theological positions that were taken the following should be mentioned:

In JACOB ARMINIUS already can be seen the traits of the movement as a whole. In his first pastorate he won distinction as a preacher and pastor of an irenic spirit. The change of conviction regarding predestination, which drove him into a study of the Scriptures, developed into differences on other matters. More than once was he accused of a defection from Reformed orthodoxy.

UYTENBOGAERT, the special friend of Arminius, who functioned as leader in 1610, when the Articles of Remonstrance were drafted, was opposed to making the Church a school of theologians. With Arminius he emphasized the devotional import of religion. The Bible as such was to be authority, confessions and catechism were not to have binding force.[25]

VORSTIUS, having cultivated a relationship with the Socinians, had fundamental antipathies against the theology of the Reformed Church, especially against the traditional conception of the atonement, and this position, naturally, affected his attitude on other doctrines, especially predestination and justification. He protested against a dogma in conflict with reason.[26]

GROTIUS contributed the much discussed "governmental" theory of the atonement. Starting from the idea that God in His relation to the sinner should not be thought of as an offended individual demanding satisfaction, he taught that God was to be regarded as "a great moral ruler." The death of Christ, therefore, "was not a payment for man's sin—which is freely forgiven—but a tribute to the sanctity of the divine government, showing that while God remits the penalty, He vindicates the majesty of His divine government." Thus Grotius aimed to meet the objection of the Socinians against the Anselmic theory. This "theatrical" explanation of the atonement, however, was not

---

[24] The literary sources for these statements are given by Seeberg, *op. cit.*, IV, 672 ff.

[25] See the article on this man in the *PRE*, XXI, 510-18 and the same in the *New Schaff-Herzog*.

[26] See the special references to his writings by O. Ritschl, *op. cit.*, III, 339-43. Cf. article in *PRE*, XX, 762 ff., and in *New Schaff-Herzog*.

followed by the Arminians, but men like Episcopius, Curcellaeus and Limborch rather followed their teacher Arminius and developed conceptions leading in the direction of Socinianism or into lines of thought which formerly had been dwelt upon by the Franciscans against the Dominicans (*acceptilatio*).[27]

EPISCOPIUS, as special spokesman, covered in a well balanced way all the characteristic tenets of Arminianism.[28]

CURCELLAEUS was a relentless critic of traditional dogmas. In a positive way he contributed to the teaching of the Arminians, especially their subordinationism in the conception of the Trinity.[29]

LIMBORCH, finally, the only one of the Arminian theologians to leave us a complete system of dogmatics including ethics,[30] again called attention to the distinction between fundamentals and non-fundamentals. His theology was later called "rational supernaturalism." With Vorstius he insisted that nothing must be found in Scripture that is not agreeable with reason.[31] As to particulars he was a subordinationist, taught the freedom of the will, spoke of faith as an act of obedience, favored a moralistic Christianity and aimed to avoid the traditional terminology of dogmatics.[32] In him we see a flexibility of theology that is characteristic of Arminianism.

4. *The doctrinal tenets of later Arminianism* are summarized and itemized in the view of a conservative writer as follows: "According to its whole genius (*Geistesrichtung*) it gradually made dogma second to ethics; it saw in Christ pre-eminently a new lawgiver, not the redeemer. In the dogma of the Trinity it inclined to the subordination of the Son and the Holy Spirit to the Father. Original sin was taken as an inborn weakness. The image of God in man was not seen in a righteousness and holiness given him at the creation, but was taken to consist merely in the dominion over the creatures, as with the Socinians. In the receiving of divine grace (in conversion) there was taken to be a co-operation of man by virtue of an inborn moral freedom. The substitutional atonement of Christ and His fulfilment of the law was denied to have been sufficient in itself, but was merely a free act of love which was accepted as sufficient. For this reason there can be no justification of the sinner as an imputation of Christ's merit in the sense of a forensic justification. The sacraments have only a ceremonial significance. Baptism was the ceremony of an admission of believers into the Church. Infant baptism had little favor, because children cannot believe. The Lord's Supper offers only a moral strengthening of faith and love." [33]

5. *Standards of Faith.* In the special Confession already mentioned, which was prepared by Episcopius, and published by the Remonstrants after their excommunication and banishment, they took occasion to express themselves on standards of faith.

Authority of Confessions. Their leaders had been writing against confessions. Now the Remonstrants published one themselves. This forced them to a long and very interesting discussion of creeds and confessions in the introduction to their document.[34]

---

[27] On Grotius, cf. Ritschl, *op. cit.*, III, 343-56 and the church histories and the encyclopedias.

[28] Cf. Ritschl, *op. cit.*, III, 356-61.

[29] Cf. the above-mentioned literature.

[30] *Theologia Christiana;* five editions appeared in the years 1686-1730.

[31] Cf. Oehler, *Symbolik*, p. 197.

[32] Ritschl, III, 364-69.

[33] Meusel, *Op. cit.*, on Arminianism.

[34] The text of it is given in the *Opera Episcopii*, II, pp. 71 ff.; in German translation by Boeckel, *op. cit.*, pp. 554-72.

They say that conditions can arise in the Church that will make confessional statements a matter of necessity. They are a means of defending truth against error, of pointing out fundamentals in distinction from non-fundamentals. Still they must not become decrees of what is to be believed; not norms and rules of faith, by which truth and error are to be judged. But their purpose is merely to indicate what the writers of these confessions believed regarding religion. And by such indications they may aid the less informed and the careless as beacon lights. They must not be put on a level with the Scriptures. They are not tests of truth, not even in the sense of being entitled to render the decision where the meaning of Scripture is doubtful. Nobody is tied to the view of the confession if he becomes convinced in his conscience that it does not agree with Scripture.[35] With all the truth in these statements, the document of the Arminians left out of consideration that in critical and decisive moments the confession of the Church must serve as a bond of union. There are moments in the Church's life when believers will need to know who is fellow-believer and who is not. Episcopius also overlooked the fact that the confessions can claim to represent stages of religious experience in the life of the Church and on that account are bound to have at least a derived authority that cannot, as a rule, be attributed to other religious literature.[36]

The Scriptures. In reading the Confession of Episcopius one cannot fail to be impressed with his energy in stressing the authority of the Scriptures.[37] He held that this authority does not rest upon decrees of the Church, ancient or modern; the Word has its authenticity in itself, is established upon God's veracity and is in need of no official interpreter because it addresses itself to the individual Christian. But while admitting the authority of Scripture they had already spoken of it in their *Confessio Remonstrantia* (I, 10) as merely "directive." They had a milder conception of the inspiration of the Scriptures, especially regarding the historical books of the Bible.[38]

6. *Estimates:* John Tulloch, an Englishman and a representative of an opposing theology (Presbyterian), writes: "Arminianism was a great deal more than a dogmatic theory. It was also, or at least it rapidly became, a method of religious inquiry. . . . The method alone has given to it enduring significance in the history of Christian thought. It revived the suppressed rational side of the original Protestant movement, and, for the first time, organized it into a definite power and assigned to it its due place both in theology and the Church." [39]

Schaff writes: "Calvinism represented the consistent, logical conservative orthodoxy; Arminianism an elastic, progressive, changing liberalism." [40] He continues: "Their literary and religious influence has gone far beyond their organization. Their eminent scholars . . . have enriched exegetical and critical learning and liberalized theological opinions, especially on religious toleration and the salvation of unbaptized infants. Arminianism in some of its advocates had a leaning towards Socinianism, and prepared the way for Rationalism. Many Arminians adhered to the original position of a moderated semi-Pelagianism." [41]

---

[35] Cf. Boeckel, *op cit.,* especially pp. 560 f.

[36] The writer has written on this matter more in detail in his *Introduction to the Symbolical Books,* 2d ed., pp. 31-39; also in *Lutherans in the Movements for Church Union,* pp. 153-62.

[37] Boeckel, *op. cit.,* pp. 572-78.

[38] Cf. Oehler, *op. cit.,* p. 197; also Tulloch, *op. cit.,* I, 28.

[39] *Ibid.,* I, p. 19.

[40] *Op. cit.,* I, p. 509.

[41] *Ibid.,* I, p. 516

Oehler, referring to their principle of "natural supernaturalism," which they applied to exegesis, remarks that with all their influence upon theology and with all their scholarship they contributed their part to putting the stamp of Latitudinarianism (*Verflachung*) upon the Biblical branches of theology.[42] Limborch laid down the principle that exegesis must never find anything in the Scriptures that is not in agreement with reason.[43] Historic Latitudinarianism developed chiefly in England.

In giving these estimates from the various sources we feel that the following from E. Troeltsch deserves to be mentioned as food for much thought. He remarks that the Arminians, in opposition to the confessionally governed churches "widened the sphere of the natural." [44] It was here that the idea of Hugo Grotius of a natural law (*lex naturae*), of a state emancipated from the civilization of the Church, of an ethics independent of the motives derived from the Christian religion, first found a place. The conservative Protestant Church of today recognizes of course an independent philosophy, and with this an ethics such as also the Reformation had spoken of under the term *justitia civilis*.[45] But the danger for religion came when under the sway of Deism and its successors the Church itself came into the temptation of turning away from "theological ethics," and when psychological analysis alone was to furnish and exhibit the motives for the doing of the good. In the last analysis it was this new emphasis on ethics that stimulated the "Arminian" attitude to predestination and synergism in England. The impulses for this movement came from the new philosophy (Montaigne, Charron, Spinoza, Hobbes). The English empiricists took up the problem in their development of an analytical psychology. It is in the light of these philosophical undercurrents that we must study the further development of Arminianism, especially in its influence upon England.

---

[42] *Symbolik*, p. 197.
[43] Cf. *Theologia Christiana* I, 12.
[44] See his article on the "English Moralists" in the *PRE*, XIII, 441 (line 20).
[45] Cf. the Augsburg Confession, Art. XVIII.

Chapter Three

ARMINIANISM IN ENGLAND

As *literature* on Arminianism in England we mention: W. WALKER, *History of the Christian Church*, pp. 457 ff. G. P. FISHER, *History of Christian Doctrine*, 1906, pp. 353 ff. The articles pertinent to the topics treated here in the *Protestantische Realencyklopaedie* (*PRE*) and the *New Schaff-Herzog;* also the *Encyclopedia Britannica* (11th Ed.), and the *Dictionary of National Biography*, 1885. The work of special value for us here is JOHN HUNT, *Religious Thought in England*, 3 vols., 1870 ff.; also JOHN TULLOCH, *Rational Theology and Christian Philosophy in England in the Seventeenth Century*, 2 vols., 1872. R. SEEBERG, *DG*, IV, 634 ff., on "Anglo-Saxon Rationalism and Conservatism," etc., cf. 694 ff., on "Old and New Calvinism." This chapter appeared as an article in the *Bibliotheca Sacra*, 1931, and is here reproduced with some minor alterations, by courtesy of the publishers.

There are two things that must be kept in view if we want to speak of the influence of Arminianism upon England: (1) *The liberalistic trend of that movement brought Rationalism;* and (2) *the emphasis upon the more practical aspects of religion produced a church life which viewed Christianity primarily as a force for moral transformation.*

Beginning with the first of these two influences of Arminianism, we must think of that wide sphere of theological interests which we have described in the preceding chapter. The conflict at Dort was not merely on predestination. It was not really a faith but as Tulloch put it, "a method of religious inquiry," which "revived the suppressed rational side of the original Protestant movement," or, as Schaff said: "It liberalized theological opinions." We should guard ourselves, however, against insisting that in Arminianism there is a necessity of being driven on into Rationalism; we are not justified in saying more than Schaff when he added: "In some of its advocates it had a leaning toward Socinism, and prepared the way for Rationalism." [1] But with the coming of Arminianism to England we soon see in that country a gradual rationalizing of its Calvinistic theology in evergrowing circles. It progressed to such an extent that "Latitudinarianism" as a general condition of England's theology was the result. Together with other influences, especially from philosophy, it created an atmosphere for the propagation of the radical rationalism that appeared in the English Deists and in the Unitarians of England and America.

The second influence of Arminianism in England and America, to which we must refer, is the communication of a certain practical type of Christianity, such as appeared in Methodism and later became a controlling religious influence in America. We take the term "Methodism" in its generic sense as covering the type of religion in many of the English denominations outside of the Methodist Church. When we speak of Arminianism in connection with the Methodist Church and related churches we do not think especially of the liberalizing trait in Arminianism, which we analyzed in our observation of developments in Holland and shall study further in this chapter. But we mean here the strongly synergistic trait of Methodism in its evangelistic practice. We see this trait in the fundamental aversion to consideration of the doctrine of pre-

---

[1] *Creeds of Christendom*, I, 515.

destination; in materially modifying conceptions in that strong emphasis upon the unimpaired spiritual powers of man before his conversion, in which he is urged to lay hold on saving grace; and in the stress that is put upon man's action in general.[2]

We shall now see how Arminianism gradually began to find favor in England. Here it was to have even a greater influence than in Holland.

I. CALVIN'S INFLUENCE IN ENGLAND

The voices of Calvinism in the stricter conception of predestination had been heard in England. Here we do not think of the Puritan movement in its ecclesiastical features, but we must note especially the doctrinal type of Calvinism in Scotland and England after James I (1603-25). After the temporary abolition of the Prayer Book and the over-throw of Archbishop Laud the Westminster Assembly was convened (1643-47) which created the famous *Westminster Confession* with "larger" and "shorter" Catechisms.[3] King James I had sent commissioners to the Synod of Dort (1618) to help condemn the doctrines of Arminius. He had, however, instructed them to "mitigate the heat on both sides," and to advise the Dutch ministers "not to deliver in the pulpit to the people those things for ordinary doctrines, which are the highest points of schools and not fit for vulgar capacity, but disputable on both sides." [4] But the emphasis was upon Calvin's double predestination, including reprobation. The *Lambeth Articles*[5] were strongly Calvinistic. James I, while refusing to incorporate them with the authorized standards, was a high Calvinist during the first part of his reign, and public expression in this direction was not lacking. WILLIAM PRYNNE wrote his book, *Anti-Arminianism,* and urged the bishops to extirpate the "Arminian thieves and robbers." Bishop DAVENANT denied the universality of divine love. Replying to an Arminian treatise under the title of *God's Love to Mankind,* he showed the danger of magnifying this common love, lest it might obscure that special love which God had for His chosen.

Puritan dogmatism in the seventeenth century had certain features in common with the Lutheran theology of the day. John Tulloch, himself a Scottish Presbyterian, has tried to give a characterization of it. We give part of it, to be compared with our observations in another connection:

"Dogmas are rigorously carried out to their consequences. The letter of Scripture is itself turned into logic, and the divine idea, living and shapely in its original form, is drawn out into hard and unyielding propositions. Nothing is more singular, nor in a sense more impressive, than the daring alliance thus forced between logic and Scripture. The thought and the letter, the argument and the fact, are inwrought. This identification of Scripture with its own forms of thinking was the very essence of Puritanism and gives it something of its marvelous success in an age when argument was strong and criticism weak. To do justice to Puritanism, it must be admitted that it did not only bring its ideas to Scripture, but supposed that it found them there. . . . Calvinism was only Chris-tianity reduced to a system. . . . Calvinistic speculation has always this true element of sublimity in it. It soars directly to the throne of God, and seeks to chain all its deduc-tions to that supreme height. But it fails to realize how far men's best thoughts are

---

[2] Read in this connection critically Seeberg, *op. cit.,* IV, 634 ff.
[3] Schaff, *Creeds,* III, 598-673.
[4] *Ibid.,* I. 513.
[5] *Ibid.,* III, 523.

below this height and how much human weakness and error must mingle in the loftiest efforts to compass and set forth divine truth. . . . It barely recognizes even now in the sphere of theology that truth is not all on one side. It still looks with jealousy on that more tolerant spirit, both of faith and of criticism, which labors to distinguish the essential from the accidental, and so to penetrate and sift all systems as to lay bare the multiplied influences of time, place, and character, which have mingled in their production, and stamped and colored them with their own impress and hue." [6]

Also among the leaders of the Independents, later, there were the representatives of the strictest kind of Calvinism. Cromwell complained in Parliament that Bishop Neile of Winchester gave countenance to divines who preached Arminianism.[7] John Owen, a strong Congregationalist, defended Calvinism in most radical terms: God had settled the fate of the reprobates from all eternity, without regard either to their unbelief or their impenitence. To say that Christ died for all, means in reality that He died for none. An atonement as a price for all, and yet effectively applied to none, is a price not paid. As one of the worst heresies of Arminianism, Owen pointed to the belief that even pagans who had never heard the Gospel might be saved. He admitted that pagans who had made endeavors after an upright life, had their reward here in outward prosperity or peace of mind. They may also have a reward hereafter in a diminution of the degrees of their torments. But they cannot be out of torments (entirely), for by nature they were corrupt and (therefore) from all eternity (they were) children of wrath.[8]

II. First Steps in the Direction of Arminianism

James I (1603-25), in the latter part of his reign, grew indifferent to the specific points of emphasis in strict Calvinism. The Calvinistic insistence upon the point that the temporal ruler cannot be the head of the Church made the kings of England suspicious of high Calvinism. It was this political opposition to Calvinism that first opened the gate for the entrance of Arminianism into England, although the expression of this opposition was at first only sporadic. Richard Montague defended Arminianism in connection with the publication of two books which he wrote against those who believed that faith, once possessed, can never be lost.[9] It was strongly opposed especially by Carleton, a delegate to Dort, who would not admit that the denial of Peter had been a real fall: "A Christian cannot fall totally and finally." The appeal was to Augustine who was declared to have made a great difference between those who are regenerated and justified only sacramentally, and those who have had this experience according to God's election.[10]

Arminianism was soon on the increase. The story is told that Bishop Morley, who survived the Restoration, once was asked "what the Arminians held" (as to tenets and opinions), and he answered that "they held all the best bishoprics and deaneries in England." [11]

Even a high churchman, such as Archbishop Laud, combined with his theories

---

[6] *Op. cit.*, I, 66 ff.
[7] Hunt, *op cit.*, I, 149.
[8] *Display of Arminianism*, pp. 156-260.
[9] *A Gagg for the New Gospel* and *Apello Caesarem*. Cf. Hunt, *op. cit.*, I, 151.
[10] Read the details of this discussion by Hunt, I, 154.
[11] Tulloch, *op. cit.*, I, 124.

of the episcopacy the doctrines of Arminius.[12] It may seem strange that Laud, as head of the Anglican Church, should have created a gateway through which Arminianism came in and was strengthened in England. The immediate cause for it was, as has already been suggested, his and the crown's opposition to the orthodox Presbyterians. It was this turn in the political development of England that gave to the theology of the Episcopal Church in that early day a liberal tendency. Doctrinally there is no real inconsistency in this, when we remember that Rome also is semi-Pelagian and has been opposed to predestination in any form. Laud promoted his cause by favoring those who were anti-Calvinistic, and by passing injunctions forbidding the clergy to preach on subjects connected with predestination. On the surface this seemed to be only a political measure. But Laud was a consistent Arminian. On the Bible, for instance, he offered this thought, which had been defended so strongly by the followers of Arminius in Holland: "We must distinguish between the Word of God and the Scriptures. Before Scripture was written—that is before it was Scripture—it was God's Word." [13]

In the controversy with some of the Independents over the article on baptism, to be incorporated in the Westminster Confession, the Arminians did not hesitate to express themselves in favor of baptizing infants. They took the position that all are redeemed, and that, therefore, children also should receive the seal of the covenant of redemption. If they did not keep the conditions of the covenant the blame rested with them. This was in harmony with what the Arminians in Holland had been emphasizing.

JOHN GOODWIN (d. 1665), an Independent, renounced decidedly the specific dogmas of Calvin. The problem of Scripture interpretation was much upon his mind. He wanted to stand upon the Scriptures, but insisted that in many of the Calvinistic points of emphasis these were misinterpreted: for instance, when the Presbyterians found their form of government taught in the Bible; or when the ministers quoted the Scriptures as commanding that heretics, blasphemers and idolators were to be put to death; or when the doctrine of the Trinity was spoken of as expressly taught in Scripture or by the Word of God without further qualification of that term. Hunt quotes him as follows (I, 263): "The true and proper foundation is not ink and paper, not any book or books, not writing or writings, whatsoever, whether translations or originals, but that substance of matter, those glorious counsels of God concerning the salvation of the world by Jesus Christ which are indeed represented and declared both in the translations and the originals, but are distinct from both. . . . The Word of God had a beginning and was extant in the world, nay, in the hearts and consciences of men before there was any copy of the Word extant in writing, either in the one language or the other." "Moses," he continued, "was the first penman of the Scriptures, but the Word was from the beginning. . . . Matthew, the first penman of the New Testament, did not write till eight years after the ascension, but the foundations of the Christian Religion were long before that." In a writing Sion College Visited, he said, "that Jesus Christ and not the Scriptures, was the foundation of the Christian Religion." The question as to whether pagans may be saved was much discussed in that day. On this, Goodwin expressed himself in a paper, the Pagan's Debt and Dowry, in these words: "The Scriptures intimate that there is a capacity in all men, by the light of nature to know that some atonement

---

[12] Read in this connection critically the brilliant review of "Anglicanism" by Tulloch, op. cit., I, 37-64. Schaff remarks: "The distinctive Arminian doctrines of sin and grace, free-will and predestination have been extensively adopted in the Episcopal Church since the reign of Charles I." Creeds, I, p. 516. Cf. Tulloch, n. 64.

[13] Cf. Hunt, op. cit., I, 169, 170; cf. II, 141. Cf. the next chapter on "The Theology of the Inner Light."

has been made for sin. St. Paul declares that they have heard the Gospel who have heard that sound which goes out day and night from the heavens unto the end of the world. In all ages there have been grains of seeds of piety in men's hearts. What men have actually known in the light of nature is considerable, but not to be measured by what they might know." Expressions like these are interesting, because they show that a mildly liberalized theology had entered the Protestant Church of England. They also illustrate the fact to which we have referred, that Arminianism was not just a dogmatic theory on the doctrine of predestination, but that it was a state of mind and a "method of religious inquiry." Many Arminians have been known for fostering Biblical criticism and an unbiased exegesis.

In the study of the rise of Arminianism in England the name and theology of RICHARD BAXTER (1615-1691) ought not be passed by although he was not really an Arminian. However, in Baxter's independency of theological inquiry there was the unconscious tendency toward the Arminian attitude. We know him as a theologian of fervent piety, especially as the author of *The Saints' Everlasting Rest* (1649) and of a large devotional literature. His biographer, Wm. Orme, who enumerates his publications under 168 titles, published in 1830 his practical works in twenty-three volumes, republished by H. Rogers in four volumes in 1868. His political, historical, ethical and philosophical works have never been printed. Richard Baxter was a man of much learning and ingenuity. He had developed a mediating system of theology, which came to be known as "Baxterianism." It was a theology which—much like Pietism in Germany —furnished foundations for his type of ardent piety, but which after him, through the independency of inquiry and the whole attitude of mind, contributed to breaking down the forms of doctrine and polity in which conservative theology in England had been aiming to preserve the positive contents of Christian teaching. The following observation guides us—a statement of A. H. Newman in his long and comprehensive article on "English Theology in the Nineteenth Century" (in *PRE*, XXIII, 401): "Under the influence of Socinianism and Deism, the Presbyterian congregations of England during the Eighteenth Century, that had come from under the influence of Baxter, landed almost all in anti-trinitarian tracks of thought and, after 1800, even began to call themselves Unitarian." This is a most interesting observation. It reminds of a similar development in the Lutheran Church. German Pietism was much like Baxterianism. It was a needed reaction to the intellectualism of the seventeenth century and a corrective to the orthodoxism of its day. But in its theology it paved the way for the Rationalism that was coming. It is told that John Salomo Semler, the rationalist, was a pietist who conducted family devotions with much fervor. Why is it that movements which are necessary and good in themselves offer the impulses for developments to be deplored? In the case of Pietism, the history of doctrine has given the reason. The degeneration of Baxterianism into Unitarianism (Arianism) also has its explanation.

There was nothing in the theology of Baxter that would not do honor to his piety and that was not consistent with the ardor of his truly religious interest. His motto was that familiar and attractive remark of Rupert Meldenius, a pupil of John Arnd: "In essentials unity, in non-essentials liberty, in everything charity." [14]

---

[14] *In necessariis unitas, in non necessariis libertas, in omnibus caritas.* This statement sounds so well that most people will dislike any endeavor at criticism. But there are two questions that must here be asked: (1) Is it not possible to confound "non-essentials" with matters in the periphery of a vital problem, that have, after all, a determining influence upon the essentials? And (2) while we will insist, of course, that the needed criticism

Among the essentials in which there should be unity in the church, Baxter counted the recognition of the supernatural. In his writing on the evidences for the truth of Christianity he points to the testimony of Scripture that miracles were wrought and to the fulfilment of prophecy. At the same time he emphasized that man should not rely alone upon the illumination of the Spirit, but accept reason also as the gift of God even if reason has to be rectified, purified, illuminated. This is true, of course. He eliminated from his concept of faith the idea of implicit trust without proper evidence. The truth of Christianity, in the end, must rest upon an "objective cause" which we have in the evidence itself as contained in the Scriptures. To see properly, however, the Spirit's illumination is needed. A great part of our sanctification consists in the rectifying of our reason. The grace which we have received may be measured by the degree of sanctified reason which we possess. This is all correct, and we know how this was meant by Baxter. But this proving of Christianity by its evidences, in which his age did so much, is a two-edged weapon. It may prove the point to some minds, but it may also pave the way for a Rationalism which Baxter would have refused to follow. He speaks of Christians as being the most rational of men.[15]

It was only natural that a prolific writer such as Baxter should have dealt also with the Calvinistic doctrine of predestination. Here also he mediated. He reconciled himself to the decrees of the Synod of Dort because of the statements incorporated therein that Christ had died for all men. He thought that this statement relieved him from preaching a divine reprobation. At the same time he and the Baxterians claimed certain fruits of the death of Christ for the elect exclusively; the grace of a true faith, repentance and the higher Christian life, the peace of conscience, inner affiliation with the Church as the congregation of believers, the hope and assurance of eternal life, justification on the day of judgment, and glorification of soul and body in the resurrection. Baxter and his followers believed that the beneficiaries of these fruits of the death of Christ were few. As to the rest of mankind they would speak of a divine reprobation only because of the unbelief and impenitence foreseen. This position, if it meant anything at all, was a subversion of the first principles of Calvinism. (See *The Denominational Reason Why*, etc., Hunt I, 265; *PRE*, II, 488 ff.; cf. the *NSH*).

III. THE RATIONALIZING TRAIT OF ARMINIANISM

Bishop JEREMY TAYLOR (d. 1667) was an outspoken Arminian.[16] Hunt: "There are but few doctrines on which Taylor's views would not exclude him from the common pale of the orthodox in the judgment of the majority of Christians, of whatever sect or party" (p. 334). Still he was, strictly speaking, not a member of the "Rational Theology group" (see below). He lived before their time.

In his *Liberty of Prophesying* (1647) he advocated tolerance. He was opposed to

of error be conducted in the spirit of charity, has it not often been the case that this Christian "charity" degenerated into the absence of a positiveness in the testimony for a truth that cannot be sacrificed? It is to be admitted, of course, that many very ardent advocates of truth have overdone it in insisting upon unity in matters that in reality have little or nothing to do with fundamentals of the faith. Reconciliation of the contending factors in the Church was the aim of Baxter's theological writings. Among special works of this group were his *Methodus Theologiae* and *Catholic Theology*. G. P. Fisher has given an elaborate exhibition of Baxter's teaching in two articles of the *Bibliotheca Sacra* IX, 135 ff., and 300 ff.

15 The reference here is to certain chapters in *The Saints' Everlasting Rest*, to *The End of the Doctrinal Controversy*, *The Unreasonableness of Infidelity*, *More Reasons for the Christian Religion*, *The Scripture Gospel Defended*, Cf. Hunt, I, 271-277.

16 See the complete sketch of his life and work by Tulloch, *op. cit.*, I, 344-410. Cf. Hunt *op. cit.*, I, 334-360, also Fisher, *op. cit.*, p. 364 f.

the sharp theological definitions in the Nicene and the Athanasian Creeds, especially to the damnatory phrases of the latter.[17] He insisted that errors of understanding are not heresy. Heresy is a matter of the will and not of the intellect (386 ff.). He speaks of the "Catholics" as a party, who took it upon themselves to determine what was heresy and what was not. It was the general councils that created heretics, he said, but councils are not infallible; they have contradicted one another (401 ff.). The uncertainty of the meaning of the Scriptures should make men tolerant. Here he, with many others, voiced a growing feeling of his age in reacting against the persecuting methods of the state under influence of the ruling church parties. The history of England in the seventeenth century is marked by a very general discussion of the liberty of conscience.[18]

It was especially in his expression on such subjects as Original Sin, Regeneration, Grace and Good Works, that he labelled himself as an advocate of Arminian opinions. On these subjects he was out of harmony with the Thirty-nine Articles of the Church of England. He was an outspoken opponent of Augustine as well as of Calvin. Although a bishop of the Anglican Church, he did not hesitate to say that we can rely neither upon apostolic nor later traditions to be infallible. The moralistic trait is conspicuous in his writings. "He sets a higher value on a good life than on an orthodox creed. He estimates every doctrine by its capacity to do men good. Religion was meant to make us more just and more merciful, and it is a sufficient reason for the rejection of any doctrine if it does not serve that object. We may then conclude that it is not sound." [19] The trouble with words like these is that a historic system of sane doctrine is estimated with the bias of the rationalist who fails to account for the regenerating and sanctifying forces in the credal statements of a religion to which he is opposed, and, in addition, fails to explain the temporary shortcomings of such a religion by the individual representatives as men of their own peculiar temper, time and civilization.

JOHN MILTON (d. 1674), the friend of Hugo Grotius, and many of the original thinkers of that day, had naturally the Arminian attitude of mind. In the *Apology* he defended the Remonstrants against *Smectymnus*.[20] His independence of mind had already appeared when he was a student in Cambridge about 1625. In a tract on education, 1644, he denounced the traditionary scholastic methods as "an asinine feast of sow-thistles and brambles." There was reason for such language when we learn that themes such as the following were discussed: "The music of the spheres," "whether day or night is more excellent," "whether there are not partial forms of an animal in addition to the whole," "how many angels can find place on the point of a needle." He was a relentless opponent of force in matters of religion. On subjects such as the Trinity, the relation of Christ to the Father, personality of the Holy Spirit, predestination, he favored the Arminian ways of expression and often even spoke as if in harmony with Unitarians and Arians. But he held to Bible revelation as the source of religious knowledge.[21]

IV. THE "CALIXTIAN" TRAIT IN ARMINIANISM

A study of the later development of Arminianism in Holland shows the general

---

[17] Tulloch, *op. cit.*, I, 372 ff.

[18] See the tables of contents in Hunt, *op. cit.*

[19] *Ibid.*, I, 341.

[20] This peculiar title for a book was a word formed from the initial letters of the names of the authors: Stephen Marshall, Edmund Calamy, Thomas Young, Matthew Newcommer, and William Spurtstow.

[21] *PRE*, XIII, 78; cf. *NSH;* also Tulloch, *op. cit.*, II, 16 f.

interest of the seventeenth century in the distinction between fundamental and non-fundamental articles of Christian belief. The so-called "syncretistic controversies" in Germany, which we have studied in Chapter One, revolved about that distinction.

A man of Arminian tendencies who produced a work in England on that same subject was EDWARD STILLINGFLEET (later Bishop of Worcester, d. 1699). We may condense the long title of his writing into the words of his biographer, J. Tulloch,[22] and call it *The Irenicum of a Comprehensive Church*. The book which appeared on the eve of the Restoration (1659) and was reprinted three years later (1662), the year in which the Act of Uniformity was passed, was an appeal for confessional peace. He explains Christianity "as a religion of peace and tolerance." The design of Christ was "to ease men of their former burdens and not to lay on more." "What possible reason can be assigned or given why such things should not be sufficient for communion with a church, which are sufficient for eternal salvation?" "What ground can there be why Christians should not stand upon the same terms now which they did in the time of Christ and His apostles? Was not religion sufficiently guarded and fenced in by Him? The grand commission the apostles were sent out with, was only to teach what Christ had commanded them—not the least intimation of any power given them to impose or to require any thing beyond what He himself had spoken to them or they were directed to by the immediate guidance of the Spirit of God."

In these utterances of Stillingfleet we must distinguish between the differences touching doctrine and those regarding church polity. Both are not of the same significance in a history of doctrine. On the church polity question the whole situation in England (conflict between Episcopalians, Presbyterians and Independents; Conformists and Non-Conformists) added a difficulty that has not existed upon the Continent. Stillingfleet refers to this when he remarks on "an unhappy controversy to us in England, if ever there were any in the world." [23]

As far as matters of doctrine are concerned it must be remarked that, indeed, much in this *Irenicum* of Stillingfleet reminds us of the positions of Calixtus in his distinction between fundamentals and non-fundamentals. It must be admitted, of course, that the awful intolerance of that age, coupled with persecution without end, as had been the case in England up to the Toleration Act of 1689, justified the plea for an *"Irenicum."* But as to the correctness of Stillingfleet's argumentation for church union on the basis of recognizing the fundamentals and ignoring non-fundamentals, much is to be considered that does not lie on the surface of his proposition. Is it always possible to force a mutual recognition of doctrinally differing churches or tendencies in the church by dismissing the matters of disagreement as non-fundamental and non-essential? While lying in the periphery they may have a determining and qualifying effect on the things in the center. Stillingfleet asks: "What ground can there be why Christians should not

---

[22] *Op. cit.*, I, 411-63; cf. Hunt, *op. cit.*, I, 135 ff.

[23] It is here that we observe an interesting difference between the Lutheran and the Reformed church families. The Lutherans mention only two things as constituting the special work of the Church: the teaching of the gospel and the administration of the sacraments. The government of the Church (*regimen ecclesiae*), although a needed interest, is not a co-ordinated *tertium quid* (cf. *Augsburg Confession* V and XXVIII). The churches under the influence of Calvin have laid more stress upon church government as *de jure divino* appointment. (Cf. the *Belgic Confession*, XXX; the *Westminster Confessions*, XXI.) In England the church government question became an especially aggravated problem because over against the watchword of the Anglican Church, "no bishop, no king," the Puritans and Independents established themselves upon the principle that the Church of Christ can recognize only an ecclesiastical, or rather a spiritual rulership. There has been a large literature in England on the subject. For an exhaustive study of the problem see Henry A. Clark, *History of English Noncon-formity*, 2 vols., 1911-13.

stand upon the same terms now which they did in the time of Christ and His apostles?" But has the Church not learned very essential things since the days of Christ and His Apostles? Calixtus wanted to unite all churches upon the Apostles' Creed. Schaff remarked: "It must be admitted that the very simplicity and brevity of this creed, which so admirably adapts it for all classes of Christians and for public worship, make it insufficient as a regulator of public doctrine for a more advanced stage of theological knowledge." [24] Surely, the Church has grown in the understanding of the Scriptures. A creed, to be sufficient today, must contain statements on matters on which the phrases of the Apostles' Creed have received different interpretations by the various denominations of Christendom. To make the Apostles' Creed the basis on which to unite the denominations would be equal to compelling grown and matured men again to return to the state of development of the child.

NOTE: In this connection we should also make mention of the life-work of JOHN DURY (DURAEUS), a Scotchman (d. 1680), who spent fully fifty years of untiring activity in England, and chiefly on the Continent (Germany), in the futile task of reconciling in the manner of Calixtus the difference of opinion between the "Syncretists" and the confessional Lutherans. The writer has a brief review on this remarkable man in his book *The Lutherans in the Movements for Church Union* (pp. 70 ff.). (As to further literature on John Dury see *PRE*, V, 92 ff., and the same article in the *NSH;* also the *Dictionary of World Biography* (XVI, 261 ff.). Here is an account of all his writings on "Irenics," about fifty in number. Cf. Ritschl, *op. cit.,* IV, 264, 266 ff., 333, 349, 450.)

V. RATIONAL THEOLOGY

This is a name that was given to the common endeavors of a group of men who, about the time of the civil war, stressed the importance of reason in matters of religion. Usually three men are mentioned, who were closely related to each other as friends: Lord FALKLAND, JOHN HALES and WM. CHILLINGWORTH.[25]

Lord FALKLAND, who stood in the center, may be characterized by an expression such as this: To those "who follow their reason in the interpretation of the Scriptures God will either give grace for assistance to find the truth, or His pardon if they miss it." [26]

JOHN HALES had been at the Synod of Dort and been greatly impressed by the address of Episcopius and offended over the treatment accorded the Remonstrants. Still it cannot be proven that he, at that time, actually turned against Calvinism.[27] However, he argued vigorously for the claims of reason in the interpretation of Scripture and the criticism of dogma.[28] He insisted on the distinction between dogmatic and religious differences. This took him into the argumentation of fundamentals and into deliveries on "heresy" and "schisms" in which he expressed himself like Calixtus, the Arminians in Holland and like Stillingfleet.[29]

WILLIAM CHILLINGWORTH, the most prominent theologian in this group, was "a churchman of the moderate and liberal class. The basis of belief is affirmed by him to be Scripture, the truth of which is established by just reasoning, with the full right of private judgment. Charity must be used with regard to those who differ." [30] These

---

[24] *Creeds of Christendom,* I, 16.
[25] Tulloch, *op. cit.,* has the biographies of these men. Cf. also Hunt, *op. cit.*
[26] Tulloch, I, 76 ff.
[27] The remark "I did bid John Calvin goodnight," quoted by Fisher, *op. cit.,* p. 363, is not sufficiently established. See Tulloch, I, 190.
[28] Hunt, I, 370.
[29] Tulloch, I, 228, 232; Hunt, I, 369, 373, 374, 466.
[30] Tulloch, I, 323-36; II, 2-5; Hunt, I, 212, 359, 374, 377 f.

men and others were opposed to party strife, to Anglican narrowness with regard to usages and to Puritan dogmatism. All may be called Arminians. They marked a revival in the freedom of inquiry which had characterized early Protestantism. They favored comprehensiveness and inclusiveness and stressed the inner, spiritual side of Christianity as contrasted with conformity to outward institutions. They were liberal, but not radical. Many of these men did their part in trimming the wings of the overbearing Deists and Freethinkers."

VI. LOCKE AND THE REASONABLENESS OF CHRISTIANITY

This was the age of JOHN LOCKE (1632-1704) with his insistence upon the supremacy of human reason, with the concepts expressed in his *Letters on Toleration* and with his demand for a comprehensive Church. Locke aimed to show in his famous *Essay Concerning Human Understanding* and in other writings that religious conviction as well as any other knowledge is subject to criticism. Religion must be reasonable, at least it cannot contain anything that is against reason.[31] But men are bound to differ as to whether certain religious views are reasonable. He refused to recognize religion as based upon "innate ideas" which, because given by God, can claim to be incontestable. The mind of man is a blank, and convictions, also religious convictions, arise from impressions received by sensation and combined by the mind into ideas. The religious views, convictions, and creeds of individuals and churches, are therefore of a diverse nature, and on that account, subject to criticism. The Church, therefore, should be inclusive, comprehensive and tolerant of all religious views. It was with these thoughts that John Locke aided and encouraged both the men of Rational Theology and the men of Confessional Irenics.

VII. LATITUDINARIANS

The Latitudinarians, partly identical with the men of Rational Theology and supported also by theologians of the "Cambridge School," should here be mentioned. The term "men of latitude" was fastened upon all of a broad and mediating type who were opposed to the church polity of the Laudian School and the doctrinal strictness of the Puritans.

Even the Socinians (Unitarians), Deists and Atheists were frequently called by that term. But the Latitudinarians with their liberal views of varying degree were not radicals as a rule. They were Arminians. Against the strict Calvinism they preached the freedom of the will and the universality of redemption through Christ. They were rationalists in that they were convinced that in theology nothing can be true that is false in philosophy; that the results of science must be recognized; that theology must co-operate with philosophy; that the masses must be held to the Church by accommodation policies.

The Latitudinarians of all types had a practical way of preaching. Such was the comment on them by Bishop BURNET, himself a Latitudinarian: "This set of men contributed more than can well be imagined to reforming the way of preaching, which among the divines of England before them was overrun with pedantry, a great mixture of quotations from the Fathers and ancient writers . . . full of many sayings of different

---

[31] The reference is to his *Reasonableness of Christianity*, 1695.

languages." Of the new preachers, he says: "Their style was clear, plain, and short. They gave a paraphrase of their text, unless where great difficulties required a more copious enlargement: but even then they cut off unnecessary shows of learning and applied themselves to the matter in which they opened the nature and reasons of things so fully, and with that simplicity that their hearers felt an instruction of another sort than had commonly been observed before, so that they became very much followed. . . . " [32]

As prominent representatives, names such as the following are mentioned: BURNET, TILLOTSON, WHISTON, SPENCER; also NORRIS, GALE, CUMBERLAND. Archbishop JOHN TILLOTSON (d. 1694), who was prominent as a preacher, may be taken as a general type of the English Latitudinarians. They represented a remarkable blending of conservatism with rationalism.[33] Some lost themselves in radicalism, as, for instance, BURY, who declared that all Christian doctrines outside of repentance and faith are non-essentials.[34]

The aim of the Latitudinarians, especially during the years between 1689 and 1699, had been to mediate between and to unite the Episcopalians and the Presbyterians who stood face to face in hopeless discord. But they failed and were crushed between the two extremes.[35] Tulloch, altogether too ardent in his advocacy of rationalism and liberalism in religion, celebrates the men of this type as "the true authors of our modern religious liberty." Considering the intolerance on the part of both their ecclesiastical opponents in that day, there may be truth in this judgment. But to the historian there will always be the weighty fact that Latitudinarianism, as like movements on the Continent, soon lost itself in indifferentism and thus became unproductive in theology. In a general way, however, it may be said that the whole movement, including all the liberal tendencies that we have been studying in this chapter, together with the Cambridge School, must be looked upon as precursory to the Broad Church of the middle of the nineteenth century, which was represented by such men as S. T. Coleridge, T. Arnold, Hare, Maurice, Kingsley, the authors of the *Essays and Reviews,* Conybeare, and Colenso. This development we shall note later.

---

[32] Quoted by Fisher, *op. cit.,* p. 367.

[33] See quotations from Tillotson's sermons by McGiffert, *Protestant Thought before Kant,* pp. 194 ff.

[34] Cf. his *Naked Gospel,* 1690; followed by his *Latitudinarius Orthodoxus,* 1697.

[35] Cf. Tulloch, *op. cit.,* II, 1-5.

Chapter Four

THE THEOLOGY OF THE "INNER LIGHT": FACTORS CONTRIBUTING TO THE CONFESSIONAL DISINTEGRATION

Literature: R. H. GRUETZMACHER, *Wort und Geist*, 1902. This is the best discussion of the principles of Spiritualism. We have a very good historical account of all the persons and factors of the movement on the Continent in the work of P. TSCHACKERT, *Die Entstehung der lutherischen und der reformierten Kirchenlehre samt ihren innerprotestantischen Gegensaetzen*, 1910, pp. 121-157. R. SEEBERG, in his *Dogmengeschichte*, Vol. IV^a gives a valuable description of the whole spiritualistic movement with its background in the outgoing Middle Ages. See LOOFS, *Dogmengeschichte*.[4] We mention also the article by UHLHORN on the Anabaptists in the *PRE*, I, 481 ff. Compare ERBKAM, *Geschichte der protestantischen Sekten in der Reformationszeit*, 1848. L. KELLER wrote in a way decidedly favoring the Anabaptists under the title: *Die Reformation und die aelteren Reformparteien*, 1882. Against him there appeared H. LUEDEMANN, *Reformation und Taeufertum in ihrem Verhaeltniss zum christlichen Prinzip*. Of the spiritualistic movement we have the account by SEBASTIAN FRANCK in his *Geschichtsbibel*, 1531; among *recent* works, HENRY S. BURRAGE, *A History of the Anabaptists in Switzerland*. See especially the *Religious Bodies* II on the Baptists and Quakers in America (U. S. Government, 1926).

E. TROELTSCH has written much on the whole development of thought through this movement, more especially pertaining to its social aspects. See his *Sociallehren der christlichen Kirchen und Gruppen* (translated into English from the 3rd edition). E. H. CORRELL, *Das schweizerische Taeufermennonitentum*, 1925. Furthermore we should mention the books of RUFUS M. JONES, *Spiritual Reformers of the 16th and 17th Centuries* (1914), and *Studies in Mystical Religion* (1909); also A. P. EVANS, *An Episode in the Struggle for Religious Freedom* (the Sectaries of Nuremberg), 1924. One who wants to view the situation from all sides and especially the doctrinal interests must study Luther's reaction to the Spiritualists of his day. His anti-Spiritualistic thoughts are presented in fine historical review by T. TSCHACKERT in the above-mentioned work, pp. 162-196. Cf. also our book on *Churches and Sects of Christendom* (Baptists and Quakers).

In the preceding listing of literature we have aimed to mention only the works of a more general type. There are many monographs on Spiritualism in various localities. We refer to the following: The publications by J. LOSERTH, covering Tyrol, Lower Austria and Bohemia. See also P. WAPPLER, *Thomas Muenzer und die Zwickauer Propheten*, 1908. A. NICOLADONI, *Joh. Buendelin von Lintz und die oberoesterreicher Taeufergemeinden*, 1893. E. MUELLER, *Geschichte der Bernischen Taeufer*, 1895. P. BURCKHARDT, *Die Baseler Taeufer*, 1898. NITSCHE, *Zur Geschichte der Wiedertaeufer in der Schweiz*, 1885. K. REMBERT, *Die Wiedertaeufer in Herzogtum Juelich*, 1899. F. ROTH, *"Zur Geschichte der Wiedertaeufer im Oberschwaben,"* *Zeitschrift des historischen Vereins fuer Schwaben u. Neuberg*, 1902.

There are also books that deal with the individual leaders of the movement; to these we shall refer in footnotes in the ensuing discussion.

I. THE MOVEMENT ON THE CONTINENT

The question will be asked: What have the spiritualistic teachings of the men, here to be reviewed, to do with the tendencies toward confessional disintegration? Most of them belong to the age of the Reformation. Why should they be spoken of in a chapter to be inserted between Arminianism and Deism? In order to interpret the situation correctly we need to remember that with the following chapters on English Deism, French Naturalism and German Rationalism we are approaching the period when the source and criterion of truth shift decidedly from the objective to the subjective.

In the Reformation we studied a movement that accepted a religion of objective facts. Luther and Zwingli, Melanchthon and Oecolampadius, Calvin and Beza, Cranmer and Knox, were all conservative, or what many today would call "evangelical." They did not question the revelation of God through the Scriptures. The Word, as speaking to us from the pages of the Bible, was to them the voice of God. While there was not agreement between the Lutherans and the Reformed on the conception of the sacraments, both sides settled upon definitions that were to secure in one sense or another Baptism and the Lord's Supper as means of grace. And all accepted the theology of the so-called ecumenical creeds, received from the ancient Church.

But there was already another fundamentally different type of theology at work. We call it the theology of the "Inner Light," the theology of "Spiritualism." It refused to accept the Scriptures as such, that is, the "letter," as the Word of God. The Bible was nothing but an empty letter. The Spirit was to be the teacher. The Bible would only become the Word, if man would read it with a certain preparation of a spiritual nature. In other words, the Word was thought to be in man. Hence, the frequent confusion between the Spirit of God in man and man's own spirit. As a rule, there was opposition to fixed doctrines. Luther's doctrine of justification was spoken of with much contempt; it was said to have opened the door for all kinds of sins. There was objection to the teaching of original sin, which was looked upon as weakening man in his own efforts. The emphasis was upon personal experience. Christ had not suffered for our redemption, but to give us an example. His suffering helps us only if we act in suffering as did Christ.

The sacraments were looked upon as empty ceremonies; at best as symbolizing a baptism by the Spirit or, in the case of the Supper, as suggesting an inner communion of the soul with Christ. They were regarded as belonging to the childhood of the Church; now we have to do with more weighty matters: with faith and repentance. The baptism of infants was seen as an initiation into the pope's church, as a magic of no avail. The cry was: "Away with the outward church, with forms of worship, with the office of the ministry; the true church is a matter of the Spirit." But not only the Church but also society was to be reformed. Here we touch upon the ideals of Thomas Muenzer and upon movements connected with eschatological expectations. Christ Himself was to appear. Then there would be no need for government and law. He would then put the sword into the hands of his followers so that the godless could be annihilated and the millennium realized.[1]

Before we can give a classification and a description of the representatives of this Spiritualism we may show in general how some leading historians have been writing on the origin of this movement.[2] The views of recent historians concerning the relation of the Spiritualists to the Reformation varied greatly among themselves.

Some, e.g., *Rothe, Dilthey, Troeltsch,* consider them as the first really consistent representatives of the Reformation principle, as the men who for the first time actually

---

[1] See Seeberg, *op. cit.,* IV³, 27 ff.

[2] We are indebted to Prof. R. Gruetzmacher for a special communication on the development as far as Germany is concerned. In connection with other literature we shall make free use of this orientating sketch.

broke away from Roman Catholicism, and cast out of the Church the essentially Roman elements. Troeltsch declares: "As a whole, the movement may be judged to be an off-shoot of Protestantism. Here it actually started. And it was the ideas of the Reformation from the subjective side, which it developed with consistency." [3] But Troeltsch feels immediately that he should add the following: "In making this statement we must not overlook, however, that Anabaptism, on the one hand, harked back to before the Reformation, and, on the other hand, went far beyond it." Thus we see that this scholar who has championed this movement so much acknowledges the close relation that existed between this Spiritualism and the mysticism of the Middle Ages. A. Ritschl, in his *History of Pietism* (see the introduction to Vol. I) had viewed the movement almost exclusively as an after-effect of medieval mysticism. Seeberg follows this conception in the main and, therefore, deals with the Spiritualists before he comes to the Reformation itself, viewing them as "a pre-Reformation system reappearing in the age of the Reformation." [4]

R. GRUETZMACHER, in the above-mentioned communication, expresses his attitude to these conceptions as follows: "The spiritualistic views of these men are neither an original product of the Reformation period, nor are they entirely out of relation to the Reformation as a movement. Their origin may be traced to the very beginnings of Christian theology, and even beyond that early time to Platonism, to the Jewish philosophy of a Philo with its speculative tendency, and to Neo-Platonism. Origen, Pseudo-Dionysius and Scotus Erigena are a few of the significant representatives of this school of thought among the earlier Christian theologians." In the mysticism of the Middle Ages the movement broadened, and both tendencies, the more naturalistic and pantheistic type and the type inspired by and modified through historical Christianity, have their followers. Thus the views that came to life again among the Spiritualists in the Reformation age are in the last analysis pre-Reformation in character; they embrace Middle Age ideas. And yet an appreciable number of the exponents of this movement were influenced more or less by the Reformation. They started with the same questions that were raised by the Reformers, and the conclusions reached by the Reformation did not leave them unaffected. At the same time their position with regard to the confessional principles of the Reformation is nearer to Zwingli, Capito, and Oecolampadius than to Luther and Melanchthon. We must distinguish between various types. There were the men who stood closer to the Reformation, and there were those who were entirely removed from its influences. Again, there are a few men, such as Muenzer and Karlstadt and the Anabaptists in general who were essentially practical reformers and not theologians. To these we cannot give much space in a history of Christian doctrine. Our main interest will be in the men of creative ideas, who contributed to later religious thought.

1. The first leaders in the movement: Muenzer, Karlstadt and Schwenkfeld. These three men, contemporaries of Luther, were among the first exponents of spiritualistic views. They were alike in that they started from Luther and his principle of the Word, but they all energetically insisted upon an immediate revelation still to be experienced. To these three men, however, the assumption of a direct or immediate

---

[3] *Protestantisches Christentum und Kirche in der Gegenwart.* Cf. I, section 4, 1906.
[4] *Op. cit., DG* IV³, 19 ff.

evelation by the Spirit was merely for the purpose of securing a theoretical basis for
he solution of some special concrete and practical problems.

THOMAS MUENZER (d. 1534) spoke of a divine "something" that slumbers in the
ecesses of the soul. But this must be set free through a special supernatural intervention
f God. Such conceptions were in entire accord with the mysticism of the Middle Ages
cf. Nic. Suso). As the chief content of this divine revelation we have that expectation
f the nearness of the end, the demand for a rigorous ethics (so different from that of
uther) and the establishment of a community of saints upon an ethical-social basis.
All this looks like a revival of Montanism.[5]

A. B. KARLSTADT used this new revelation to bolster up his peculiar view of the
ord's Supper and his ideals for the reform of worship. He did not yet know of any
nnate, indwelling Word. But he conceived of God working in the soul through special
llumination. The external Scriptures go parallel with that illumination, but in such a
nanner that through the divine illumination alone they attain true value and a proper
neaning. The sacraments can contain and bestow a heavenly gift no more than the
xternal Word.[6]

K. SCHWENKFELD (d. 1561), also a contemporary of Luther, is of far more impor-
ance in the History of Doctrine than the two men just mentioned. Luther wrote in
ard words against him. But R. Seeberg (DG, IV, 32) calls him *"einen bedeutenden
und ernsten Mann."* [7] Even today there are organizations that are propagating his views.
The scholars on history of doctrine are interested in the publication of his writings.
(See below.)

Schwenkfeld was the originator and typical exponent of a mediating spiritualistic
heology. He was always willing to admit that it was through Luther that he had found
he Gospel. But he opposed Luther and perseveringly maintained against him a concep-
ion of the means of grace in which the importance of the external Word and its preach-
ng was minimized. To Schwenkfeld the Bible is only an imperfect human image of
vhat God wrought directly within the hearts of the prophets and apostles. Thus the
criptures have no decisive meaning for the inception of the religious life in man; they
nly show forth that life and bear witness of it. It is not the Word which brings the
pirit, but the man who is filled with the Spirit brings that Spirit with him to the Word.
The divine light must be brought to the Scriptures, the Spirit to the letter, the truth
o the image, and the master to his work." [8]

As distinguished from a more Socinian type of the Spiritualists, of which we shall
oon speak, he believed in the supernatural character of the work of the Spirit. He
leclined the naturalistic conception of the Word as an innate rational-ethical possession
f every man. Not everybody possesses by nature this "internal living Word." There
nust be a spiritual renewal. But this comes without the Scriptures through the Spirit
vhich he identifies, peculiarly, with the historical incarnate Jesus.

His estimate of the sacraments was the natural result of his separation of the

---

[5] For literature see the articles in the PRE the New Schaff-Herzog, the RGG, the Hastings *Encyclopedia*.
[6] Cf. his writing *Concerning Priesthood and the Sacrifice of Christ,* 1523.
[7] For objective estimates see Erbkam, *Geschichte der protestantischen Seckten,* 1848, pp. 358 ff.; R. Gruetz-
nacher *Wort und Geist,* pp. 158 ff.; cf. also his article in the PRE XVIII, 72-81. Cf. the New Schaff-Herzog;
lso P. Tschackert, *Entstehung,* etc., pp. 157 ff.; K. Ecke, *Schwenkfeld, Luther und der Gedanke einer evange-
ischen Reformation,* 1911. See the *Religious Bodies,* Vol. II, on the Baptists and Quakers. U. S. Government,
926.
[8] *Concerning the Holy Scriptures,* VI, 5.

heavenly and the human in the Word when conceived as the means of grace. They were to him no real means for an impartation of grace. Baptism, be it of the infant or of the adult, is not necessary. He accepts as religiously valuable only the spiritual baptism by Christ Himself. Such baptism has nothing to do with the external rite. There can be nothing more in the performance of the rite than a symbolical pointing to the baptism with the Spirit of Christ. His doctrine of the Lord's Supper was in harmony with his general view of the means of grace. He denied any connection between bread and wine and the body and blood of Christ. Over against Luther's realism, he set forth a spiritual influence through the symbolical significance.

Contrary to this persistent separation between the earthly and the heavenly in the means of grace, he so closely joined the humanity of Christ to His divinity that the human nature was almost entirely displaced by the divine and deified after the manner of monophysitism in the Ancient Church: Christ's body, in its flesh and blood, was not from Mary, but from God. He brought it with Him from heaven. It was not our nature which He adopted. And through the work of His redemption this humanity became absorbed by His divinity. The distinct natures in Christ are thus denied.

He differed from Luther also on other matters, especially in his minimizing of justification. Here we have an emphasis upon the moral element at the expense of the religious. "God does not count anyone righteous in whom there is nothing of his essential righteousness." [9]

In his "immediacy of the Spirit," Schwenkfeld was a Spiritualist, and in his whole development he was a natural result of the great German spiritualistic and mystical movement among the laymen in the later Middle Ages.

He had no appreciation of the institutional side of the Church and was therefore opposed to forming organizations. His whole interest was in the experience of the individual, and for that reason he was absolutely unable to establish a Church devoid of the characteristics of the sect.

His followers emigrated largely to the United States of America. In 1734 about 200 of them landed in Philadelphia and settled in Montgomery, Bucks, Berks and Lehigh counties in Pennsylvania. Here they were forced to organize to maintain their identity. In connection with Hartford Seminary in Connecticut, they are publishing at Leipzig (1907 ff.) the *Corpus Schwenkfeldianorum*. As to the unpublished documents that were awaiting publication, see above-mentioned article by R. Gruetzmacher in the *PRE.*

Note: Here would be the place to speak of the Anabaptists proper: HUBMAIER, DENCK, HAETZER and others. But while identified with the spiritualistic movement the Anabaptists represented essentially a practical and moral rather than a doctrinal movement. They, as also the Mennonites, must be discussed in Church history and more especially in Christian Symbolics or in a description of the denominations of Christendom.

We should, however, take note of the fact that the spiritualistic trait in the Anabaptist family of churches has given much stimulation to theological thought, although they have been an outstanding factor in the process of confessional disintegration. The Baptists of England and America were fundamentally congregational and knew of no binding creeds beyond the principles of the local congregation. Doctrinally, most of them followed a Calvinism modified by features of Arminianism, with borrowings from Socinianism as an after-effect. The theology of the "Inner Light" easily leads to theological liberalism. Side by side with this tendency, however, a strict conservatism either of the Calvinistic or of the Arminian type (Fundamentalism) maintains itself with much tenacity.

---

[9] *Epistulae* I, p. 812.

2. Spiritualists of a naturalistic and rationalistic type. We have had occasion to remark that the men reviewed so far (Muenzer, Karlstadt, Schwenkfeld) were mystics of the supernaturalistic type. The Baptists and Mennonites also established themselves upon supernatural grounds. But there was also a group of Spiritualists who represented a sometimes veiled and sometimes boldly and clearly expressed religious naturalism and rationalism.

a. The most important of this group was SEBASTIAN FRANCK (d. 1542).[10] He treated with sharp criticism the Scripture principle of the Reformation. The Bible to him is full of self-contradictions. Its interpretation is varying and unreliable. It does not have the power really to bring about a new, moral life. The Scriptures are in the last analysis the human letter as contrasted with the divine Spirit. God cannot reveal Himself through the letter but only through the Spirit. This Spirit he calls the "Word of God," "Spirit of God," "Mind of Christ," "Understanding of the Scripture." These terms are, however, used only by way of accommodation to traditional expressions. For the Spirit according to this idea is not a supernatural gift of God, but a natural possession of man. "The light is already kindled in the lantern of our hearts, and the treasure is even now hid in the field, secreted in the precious soil of the soul. Whosoever would but allow this flame to burn, rather than to prefer the lamp of the flesh (Bible), whosoever would but look within himself and seek this treasure, would not find it on the other side of the sea, nor be forced to look for it in heaven, for the Word is in us." [11]

The careful student will observe that the human and the divine in Franck's teachings are identified with one another in a pantheistic way. With him, the Holy Spirit of revelation becomes the spirit of man as a divine element. To be sure, this divine element is at first only potentially present, and hindered in its development by that which is sensual and sinful, but man is fully capable of himself to bring the divine within him into full consciousness and power, and to conquer sin by his own strength. This is not done primarily through a moral and ethical activity, but through quiet and patient waiting. One is here reminded of that quietism which was in part promulgated by the mysticism of the Middle Ages and by the later Spanish mystics.

Man becomes a believer by calling into life the Word that dwells within him, and by yielding himself to the dominion of the indwelling Spirit of God. It is purely a psychological procedure; it does not depend upon any contact of man with the transcendent God through historically transpiring events.

Regarding the person of Christ it may be said: "The whole gospel of Franck can be fully presented without the necessity of even naming Christ." [12] Franck uses the name of Christ often, but He is to him just another expression for the *anima naturaliter christiana* of Tertullian, and not at all the historical Jesus. He also lacks a vital consciousness of sin. Christ is pictured as freeing us from error, but in the last analysis this Christ can at all times be identified with the universal presence of God in the human reason. In conclusion it may be said: Franck sacrifices the peculiar character of Christianity as a religion of redemption and with it the basic position of Christianity in order to pro-

---

[10] See Article in *PRE*, VI, 142 ff., R. Gruetzmacher, *Wort und Geist.* P. Tschackert, *Entstehungsgeschichte,* p. 154 ff. Seeberg, *DG*, IV³, 22 ff. The first to call special attention to Franck was F. Latendorf, *Franck's erste Sprichwoertersammlung,* 1876. H. Ziegler, *Seb. Franck's Bedeutung fuer die Entwicklung des Protestantismus;* also *Seb. Franck, kurze Darstellung seines theologischen Standpunktes.*

[11] Quoted by Hegler from *Spirit and Scripture* by S. Franck, 1882, p. 91 ff.

[12] Hegler, p. 150.

mulgate in its stead a rationalistic-pantheistic religiousness. He prepared the way, both positively and negatively, for modern religious liberalism. Troeltsch therefore is right when he asserts (approvingly) with regard to Franck: "The doctrine of the Spiritualist concerning the 'inner light' contains the germs of modern religious subjectivism, of a psychological theology of experience which finds in the religious concepts of history merely symbols and suggestions and in all dogmas only the fruits of the original and fundamental element which is the religious consciousness, and therefore holds all religions alone to the authority that comes from the subjectivity of personal conviction allowing them free reign to take the most varying forms in expression. The divine Spirit, thought of in psychological concepts, has gradually and quietly transformed itself into the natural reasoning faculty of man's spirit." [13]

b. THEOBALD THAMER (d. 1569) follows the premises of the naturalistic-ethical conception to their logical conclusions.[14] For him the original revelation of God lies in conscience and nature. The Bible is the truth only where it agrees with both of these "Conscience is the true and living mercy seat where we approach God. Outside of the conscience there is no grace. God does not speak to us except through conscience, so that it is unvarnished truth, that although a person may hear the external Scripture for a thousand years, and does not have the living Word, the divinity of Christ or the conscience within his soul, it will do him no good." [15] Thamer unmistakably represent the conception of an ethical self-determination which he puts in place of the Christian revelation. Socrates supported the same position before him, Kant after him. Conscience takes over all the functions of Christianity. This received much stress later by the rationalistic leaders of England (cf. Shaftesbury), France, and Germany.

c. At this place we shall insert a brief reference to VALENTINE WEIGEL (d. 1588) He was one of the few who contributed in an original way to the further development of Spiritualism in Germany. We cannot give space for a review of his system, which may be studied in the encyclopedias, in the histories of philosophy, in Gruetzmacher' *Wort und Geist,* and through his own writings. We shall simply call attention to the fact that although he touched upon religion he stressed that "God, Spirit, and Word are within us," and that therefore "the spiritual understanding flows forth from within." [16] He arrives at an outspoken pantheism: God and the universe coincide and become one. God finds himself and arrives at personality and activity only in and with the universe. The variation in the divine immanence is to be explained on the basis of the presence of good and evil in the world. Evil is but a necessary concomitant of all that is created. From the beginning God has imparted the necessary power to the soul of man to overcome it. Redemption is the gradual process by which the divine principle in man achieves mastery over the anti-divine principle inhering in his created nature. As the best means for bringing about man's subjective deification Weigel recommends patient waiting and yielding to the divine through a repression of the individual will. This reminds us of Franck and of the mysticism of the Middle Ages. Weigel complicated and confused his otherwise inherently consistent pantheistic and psychological system by joining it to the central thoughts of Christianity. And, on the other

---

[13] *"Protestantismus und Kirche"* in *Die Kultur der Gegenwart,* p. 514.
[14] See R. Gruetzmacher, *Wort und Geist.* Cf. *PRE,* XIX, 580 ff.
[15] Quoted by A. Neander *Th. Thamer,* 1842, p. 28.
[16] *Gueldener Griff,* chap. 12.

and, he stripped Christianity of its historical and supernatural content. He had but few points of contact with the Reformation, and these lay in the mutual connection with mysticism.

There continued to spring forth from the fertile soil of Spiritualism in Germany a long line of agnosticizing thinkers, mystically and pantheistically inclined. They offered no new and really constructive principles of which a history of Protestant theology needs to take note. Weigel was out of the ordinary among these. His contribution lay in his ideas for developing and recasting that peculiar mode of thought into the monistic and idealistic pantheism favored by so many in the present day.

II. SPIRITUALISTIC RELIGION AND THEOLOGY IN ENGLAND: THE QUAKERS

Literature: There is the thoroughly objective and sympathetically written article under the title *Quaker* by R. BUDDENSIEG in the *PRE*, XVI, 356-380 (English in the *NSH*). Next in importance in this class of literature comes J. HUNT, *Religious Thought in England*, 1871, I, 239; II, 286-304. On the relation to Deism there are fine observations in G. V. LECHLER, *Geschichte des Englischen Deismus*, 1841, pp. 61-66. In the many writings of RUFUS M. JONES we have the special authority on the Quakers in general and particularly in America. On branches in America we refer to the Government's publication on the *Religious Bodies*, Vol. II, 1926, 608-32. As sources we mention especially the *Journal* of GEORGE FOX, and ROBERT BARCLAY, *An Apology for the True Christian Divinity* (both stereotyped editions).

1. Background and atmosphere.

a. The study here to be followed takes us into the *time of the English civil war,* which took place in 1640-1649. This movement was religio-political in character, but in such fashion that the religious interests predominated. Under the despotic reign of Charles I, in which he was aided by Archbishop Laud, the Independents feared the reintroduction of Roman Catholicism. In 1643 Anglicanism was overthrown, and the Puritans (Presbyterians) assumed the reins. But the republican form of church government which they introduced represented such a forced union of power and of faith that the reaction of a more radical Independency was the result. The demand was: Freedom for all religious parties! This triumphed in the succession of Oliver Cromwell (1649-1660). But *individualism,* now in the saddle, insisted upon running its course to the limit. The Erastians and Levellers demanded the absolute independency of the individual religiously and politically. The Baptists brought this demand to a formal expression by practicing the baptism of adults only: The individual believer must determine for himself. The religious atmosphere out of which Quakerism grew is indicated by a sect such as the "Seekers" who questioned the right of the existing dogma and, therefore, professed to be merely seekers of the truth.[17]

b. A sect of special interest in this respect was the *"Familists,"* or *"Family of Love."* [18] It was a sect of Anabaptists that had come from Holland. Henry Nicholas of Amsterdam was its originator. The interest was in special revelation by dreams and mystical experiences. Nicholas felt himself called to introduce a new era in the Church and for this purpose formed a society. The Spirit of love within the heart was making the "inner righteousness" real. There was opposition to external ordinances such as the sacraments, all interest was in the baptism of the Spirit and in the communion through the Holy Ghost. The "letter" was of no value to them compared with the Spirit. The

---

[17] G. V. Lechler, *op. cit.,* p. 61. Cf. the article by Kattenbusch in *PRE*, XVIII, 126 f.; see the *NSH*.
[18] See the article by Loofs, in *PRE*, V, 750 ff.; but especially Hunt, *op. cit.,* I, 234-8.

literal statements contained in the New Testament were spiritualized: Christ's cruci
fixion meant the crucifying of the natural man; the resurrection meant our rising t
newness of life; Christ's return for judgment meant that the natural man was to b
governed with righteousness; angels and devils were taken to be good and bad men wit
their virtues and vices; the seven devils which possessed Mary Magdalene were th
seven deadly sins, and so on.

c. We have a striking example of the enthusiasm and fanaticism among the Quaker
around 1654 in a man like JACOB NAYLOR, a friend of George Fox, who claimed to b
the "Son of God" and the "King of Israel" and as such held a triumphant entrance a
Bristol. He was punished at the whipping post and the mark B (blasphemy) was burne
upon his forehead. Fox protested to the Parliament against this punishment and sough
to defend Naylor[19] who himself later publicly repented, 1660.[20]

2. In the Quakers we have a decided reaction against church forms. George Fox an
his followers took offense when John Smyth, pioneer in the Baptist movement, felt tha
he had to baptize himself, thus stressing the importance of an outward form.

The Quakers protested also against "the idolatry of the Bible," against "worshippin
the records instead of the Spirit which gave the records." We see, it was the same posi
tion that we met among the Spiritualists in Germany. John Hunt (I, 238) quotes
minister who had said in his church: "We have a sure Word of prophecy. It is th
Scriptures by which all doctrines, religion and opinions are to be tried." George Fo
who was present could not restrain the Spirit within him, and he cried out: "It was no
the Scriptures, but the Holy Spirit by which holy men of God gave forth the Scripture
whereby opinions, religion and judgments are to be tried." Hunt observes correctl
(II, 298): "This was simply transferring to the Spirit what Protestants generally ha
ascribed to the Scriptures."

The Quakers would not limit inspiration to the age when the Scriptures wer
written, and they would not admit that the spirits of men after that age could have n
inspiration. In terms of church history this was Montanism, and Montanism is the out
standing trait in the Spiritualism here under discussion. But we know well enough tha
Rome always expressed something of this same belief in its conception of tradition
The high Anglicans have similarly held that in a sense the Church is inspired (c
Thirty-Nine Articles). Barclay in his standard work for the Quakers quoted Calvin
"He only whom the Holy Ghost has persuaded can repose himself on the Scripture wit
a true certainty." The French, the Dutch, and the Westminster Confessions have simila
expressions. Melanchthon appealed to "pious men" for a correct interpretation of Scrip
ture, and Luther demanded that the true theologian must be a regenerated person (*hom
renatus*). It should not be overlooked, as Hunt remarks, that the early Quakers had th
same reverence for the Scriptures as had other Christians. They received the Bible a
a rule of faith that could not be contradicted by new revelations. We may say that th
conflict which the Spiritualists on the Continent and the Quakers of England introduce
concerning the distinction between the "Word" and the "Scriptures," touched upon
point which comparative Symbolics has always regarded as a real crux of theology.

3. Critical survey of the situation. How are we to judge regarding that radica
distinction between the Holy Scriptures, or the written Word, or the objectively preache

---

[19] *Letters*, 46.
[20] See in the *PRE*, XVI, 361, lines 20-50; cf. *NSH* on "Quakers."

Word, on the one hand, and the Word of God, the real Word, on the other hand? Ought these two forms of the Word to be contrasted with the emphasis which such contrast received in the Anabaptist and Quaker movements?

Many points of special emphasis in the camps of reacting or protesting denominations point to errors in the official Church. In Rome there was functioning the *ex opere operato* principle: Scripture, sacraments, rites and ceremonies bring spiritual benefits without the response of the believer's heart.[21] Against this doctrine the Anabaptists and the Quakers, like the forerunners of the Reformation, reacted and protested: It is not the form that works, but the Spirit of God. And with Zwingli they would say: salvation from God directly, without the mediation of church acts. The form also in Scripture and sacrament can be nothing more than a symbol and is nothing more than psychologically didactical. It was on this subject that the public conflict between Zwingli and Luther arose.[22] Calvin dealt with practically the same problem when he distinguished between an external call through the Word in the case of the reprobates where the Spirit is not present to make it effective in their hearts, on the one hand, and the really serious call of the predestinated where the Spirit is actually working through the Word.[23] Luther wrote much against the above-mentioned *ex opere operato* principle of Romanism. He stressed that the minister of the Gospel must be a regenerated person, and that faith is the receptive means for the spiritual influence from the Word as well as from the sacrament. But he insisted upon the inseparable organic relation of the earthly and the heavenly elements in the means of grace. For him, the Word, written as well as preached, was thus a real means of grace. With this the principle of the immediacy of the Spirit cannot co-exist. Most of the members of the Reformed churches today are in practical agreement with the Lutherans on this subject; as well as many in the churches of spiritualistic origin. But it was the historical mission of Luther and his associates to be witnesses in this matter.

The Church cannot bear this spiritualistic distinction between the outer and the inner Word, simply because it destroys the universality of grace and makes salvation through Christ uncertain. If such a distinction is to be admitted, then the efficient promise of the Gospel is not a real foundation of spiritual comfort for the individual Christian; then he is established upon the uncertain foundation of a secret election, or, if he has given up Calvinism for Arminianism, upon his own individual experiences (emotional or rationalistic). This was the religious interest of Luther in his opposition, though he was sometimes too impetuous and too violent against the Spiritualists in their distinction between the outer and the inner Word.

There is a point with regard to the Word of Scripture which Luther himself saw, but which was left unnoticed by his contemporaries in general as well as by the Lutheran theologians of the seventeenth century. It is the thought of *the relation between the human and the divine in the inspiration of Scripture*. The Word of God, far from being merely a collection of writings, a collection of reports on history, faith, and morals, is, in its deepest meaning, the revelation in the person of Christ, in whom "the Word became flesh and dwelt among us." In the Bible we have an organism of the divine and the human, as may be observed in the mysterious relation between the two natures in Christ. It is in this sense that K. Girgensohn in his *Grundriss der Dogmatik*

---

[21] This is rejected in the closing paragraph of Art. XIII of the Augsburg Confession.

[22] For the sources on both sides see the extensive literature referred to by Seeberg, *op. cit.*, IV³, 376 ff., and compare our review in Book Three (Vol. I, pp. 289 f.).

[23] See the *Canons of Dort*, Chap. I, Art VIII; *Westminster Conf.*, Chap. X, on the basis of the *Consensus Genevensis* on "External Election." Cf. C. Hodge, *Syst. Theology* III, 483.

(p. 134), points to that mysterious relation and warns against the separation of the divine an
the human in the conception of the inspiration of Scripture. If we keep in mind this dynami
relation between the divine and the human factors in the Scriptures then we will have littl
trouble regarding the problem of their inspiration.[24]

4. In closing let us *review briefly the particular tenets of Quakerism*. Among th
Quakers of the second generation were WILLIAM PENN (d. 1670) and ROBERT BAR
CLAY (d. 1690). We shall see in their doctrinal formulations that Spiritualism incline
to and actually develops into the leading principles of Socinianism. This was pointe
out with relentless persistency by Charles Leslie[25] and also by George Keith, an apostat
from Quakerism.[26] The spiritualistic interpretation of Word and Sacrament as the mean
of grace is apt to produce one of two things: either an increased spirituality or a pro
nounced rationalism. Rationalism, frequently, is the successor of Pietism. Pietistic Halle
among the German universities, was the first to yield to Rationalism.

The theology of Penn included a rejection of the doctrine of the Trinity as expresse
in the Nicene and Athanasian Creeds.[27] In Christology the emphasis was not upon th
historic Christ, but upon the "Christ within us" who was declared to be in all men. Thi
reminds us of the Logos doctrine of the early Apologists. This idea is similar to tha
expressed by Zwingli when he spoke of the noble men of paganism as being within th
reach of salvation irrespective of any knowledge of the Gospel. So Penn pointed t
Plato, Plotinus, Seneca, Epictetus, and Antoninus as men who had been obedient to th
light of the "Christ within us." Hunt remarks: "It is shown by Penn in his treatise *Th
Christian Quaker,* in the fashion of Lord Herbert, that the heathen knew all the grea
principles, or doctrines of religion. The sublimest passages of Scripture concerning th
one God are paralleled by passages from pagan authors. Pythagoras and Plato, Socrate
and Cleanthes, believed in conscience as the light of God in the soul of man. It is furthe
shown by many quotations that the pagan philosophers were virtuous men, that the
believed in the immortality of the soul and the recompenses of the life to come. Pen
does not stop with allowing the heathen merely a knowledge of what is called natura
religion. He maintains that they had a knowledge of Christ's coming, and anticipate
His teaching." (II, 292.)

It was statements such as these that laid the Quakers open to the charge of bein
established upon the principles of Deism.

Barclay, the real dogmatician of the Quakers (in his *Apology for the True Christia
Divinity,* the standard work for Quaker doctrine), was much interested in proving th
objective character of the Spirit's immediate revelation. He based it upon passage
such as these: "The Spirit shall teach you all things," and: "I will put my laws in
their minds, and write them in their hearts." Penn supported Barclay by saying: "
was the Spirit which taught Moses the history of creation and the fall of man, two thou
sand years after the events . . . . the facts of Christ's life were revealed to the prophe
centuries before they happened." [28]

The Quakers also used the language of Socinianism in their refusal to take th

---

[24] Compare the article on "Inspiration of Scripture" in Meusel, *Kirchliches Handlexikon.*
[25] Cf. Hunt, *op cit.,* II, 303 f.
[26] *Ibid.,* II, 300 f.
[27] *Works* I, p. 30.
[28] Cf. *Ibid.,* II, 294.

death of Christ as a satisfaction for sin and in their rejection of an imputed righteousness.[29]

The particular details concerning the Quakers as an organization cannot be discussed in a history of doctrine: they must be dealt with in studies on the denominations of Christendom.[30]

---

[29] Penn's *Works* I, 61.
[30] Cf. in our *Churches and Sects of Christendom*, the chapter on the Quakers.

Chapter Five

THE ENGLISH DEISTS: FIRST STEPS IN

RADICAL LIBERALISM

Literature: W. WALKER, *History of the Christian Church*, 1918, pp. 487 ff. A. C. McGIFFERT, *Protestant Thought Before Kant*, 1911. A. V. G. ALLEN, *The Continuity of Christian Thought*, 1894, pp. 347-69. One of the best books that is highly praised also by English writers is G. V. LECHLER'S *Geschichte des englischen Deismus*, 1841. Cf. article "Deismus" by E. TROELTSCH in the *Protestantische Realencyklopaedie* (*PRE*) Vol. IV, and the corresponding article in the *New Schaff-Herzog Encyclopedia* (*NSH*) Vol. III. J. LELAND, *Deistical Writers*, 5th (best) edition, 1837. J. TULLOCH, *Rational Theology and Christian Philosophy*, 1897, Vol. I. J. HUNT. *Religious Thought in England*, 3 vols. ABBEY AND OVERTON, *The English Church of the 18th Century*, 1878. A. S. FARRAR, *A Critical History of Free Thought* (Bampton Lectures, 1862). LESLIE STEPHEN, *History of English Thought* (Quarterly Review, 1877). M. PATTISON, "Tendencies of Religious Thought in England," 1688-1750, in *Essays and Reviews* (American Edition, Boston, 1861). On the "Relation of John Locke to English Deism" we refer to the able and thorough dissertation under the title by S. G. HEFELBOWER (University of Chicago Press, 1918). For convenient references to the philosophical background we refer to N. E. CUSHMAN, *A Beginner's History of Philosophy*, 1911, 2 vols., and to F. TILLY, *History of Philosophy*, 1927; also T. SIMON, *Grundriss der Geschichte der neueren Philosophie* (1920). As to the editions of the deistic writings and the contemporary controversy in connection with them the *Dictionary of National Biography* (1885-1900) will be of much service.

Thus far in this volume we have followed the first unintentional influences leading to confessional disintegration by describing the unionistic efforts of George Calixtus; also by characterizing the genius of Arminianism in Holland and its influence upon England as issuing in Latitudinarianism. Subsequently we have studied the liberalizing influences inherent in the theology of the "Inner Light." Now we shall present in the following three chapters the first steps in radical liberalism: the English Deists, the French Naturalists, and the German Rationalists. These three connected movements aimed at the complete overthrow of the faith of the Reformation. Upon this follows a review of the Unitarian movements.

We have today become accustomed to the statement that the German universities have been the fountain of theological liberalism. But Tulloch is correct when he says that "the home of rational thought was certainly not in Germany in the earlier times of Protestantism." [1] Holland was in a special sense the starting point for the radical liberalism in the seventeenth century. Thither came Descartes, and there he laid the foundations of modern philosophical rationalism; there Spinoza constructed the greatest of all rational systems; there Bayle published his famous *Dictionary*. From Holland the new influences spread first to her neighbors to the south and to the west. France had the first of her "Naturalists" and England her "Deists" before Germany had her age of

---

[1] *Rational Theology*, I, p. 8. Cf. Allen, *op. cit.*, p. 357.

Rationalism. In England the freedom of the press had been declared in 1693, and the establishment of this principle invited the liberalists of that early time to publish their views. The philosophy of John Locke, which made reasonableness the criterion of truth, dominated the age. Alexander Pope, "the prince of rhyme and the grand poet of reason," wrote his *Essay on Man* (1732-34) in which he declared:

> "For modes of faith let graceless zealots fight.
> His can't be wrong, whose life is in the right.
> On faith and hope the world will disagree,
> But all mankind's concern is charity."

The books of the "free-thinkers" in England were widely read in Germany. Baumgarten reviewed them in his *Nachrichten von merkwuerdigen Buechern* (Halle, 1752-58). Thorschmidt published a *Versuch einer vollstaendigen engellaendischen Freidenker-Bibliothek* (Halle, 1765-67). Thus we see that the beginnings of theological liberalism were in England.[2]

The tardiness of the Germans in responding to the liberalizing tendencies of the age was due to the very conservative principles of the Lutheran Reformation with its strong emphasis upon the objective side of religion, and particularly to the definiteness with which Luther rejected humanism, certain spiritualistic positions of Zwingli, and the ideas of the "Spiritualists" (Anabaptists). A further reason may be seen in the rich religious content that characterized the Lutheran theology of the seventeenth century.[3]

Note: If Germany is regarded as holding the leadership in problems connected with theological liberalism the reference must not be, as Tulloch remarked (above), to "the earlier times of Protestantism." But it is true that in the age of "reconstruction" (during the first third of the 19th century) it was the philosophical and religious thought of German thinkers that inspired S. T. Coleridge, the "Schleiermacher of England," to his philosophy of idealism, and to his views on religion and theological subjects. It was under the influence of his impressions from German philosophy and theology that foundations were laid not only for the Broad Church movement in England, but also for the forms in which Modernism is appearing in England and America today.

1. The Deistic movement was an expression of aversion to the positive and the historical forms of religion. It was the result of the tendency of the age to divorce theology from philosophy, or religion from philosophical rationalism. Descartes had simply wanted to reconstruct theology without breaking with established dogma. But the drift of the development was toward a complete divorce. The individual in his insistence upon absolute freedom of thought emancipated himself from all external authority. In the term of A. Collins, he wanted to be a "free-thinker."

There were many causes for the resentful attitude of thoughtful observers to the established forms of religion. We refer to the manner in which the confessional controversies were fought in that day, to the unhistorical use of Scripture on the dogmatical points of difference between churches and individuals, to the excessive claims of the churchmen backed by political power, to the tyrannical abuse of royal prerogatives so completely in contrast to the ever growing spirit of political and religious liberty. All

---

[2] Besides Tulloch, as quoted above, see Troeltsch, Article on "Aufklaerung" in *PRE* II, 234, 17; also M. Pattison, *op. cit.*

[3] Present-day critics who decry this theology as being barren of religious value surely fail to account for the rich devotional material which kept proceeding from this source in the form of catechisms, prayer-books and especially in the great hymns of that age (the chorales).

these things contributed to making the official forms of religion objectionable. In their protest against these the Deists were unable to be conservative reformers; in history they will always be known as the group which took first steps to inaugurate radicalism into Christian theology.

a. The aim of the Deists was to find a religion that all would want to recognize—a "natural religion" that might serve as a common ground for the critical examination of supernaturalism of any form. But it was felt in that day of strong emphasis upon dogmatics in theology that this natural religion had to present itself in the form of a system. The theory of knowledge to be employed was empiristic-sensualistic, and the system to be constructed was to be of the mechanistic sort. The practical interest was in the moral elements of religion. This theology was in reality nothing but a theory of morality. The natural law of the old Stoics (*lex naturae*) was much studied. The movement was a criticism of supernaturalism. And since this criticism had to be conducted with constant reference to statements of the dogmaticians of supernaturalism it became a religious philosophy. The aim in it all was at a religion in harmony with scientific thought, a religion liberated from the supernatural and from a special interest in a beyond, a religion, at the same time, in which the confessional differences would be looked upon as the natural variations of an historical situation. We shall have occasion to say more on this below in connection with the discussion of Lord Herbert of Cherbury.

b. The name "Deist," which was applied to these men, is in need of qualification. The term "Deism," as employed by present-day theology, refers to the thought of a transcendent God who created the world, but who, by withholding His immanence, left the world to take care of itself. This was unconsciously among the free-thinkers in England the conception of the universe built upon the basis of the Newtonian observations. As yet it was not the developed system which it was later when philosophy and theology came to distinguish between deism, pantheism and theism. The English Deists had nothing to do with a deism as opposed to theism. They called themselves "Deists" because they were opposed to atheism. But, naturally, the content of their belief in God, in which Christ as redeemer and mediator had no place, did not go beyond a personal "first cause" that had established a realm of law in which the world was moving in an unchangeable mechanical order. The more fitting name, therefore, was the one claimed by A. Collins (1713): "Free-thinkers" (see below).[4]

c. Orientation as to time and phases in the history of Deism. English Deism was a product of the reasoning spirit which was stimulated by political events, and it ran a course parallel to the gradual emancipation of the individual from the all-embracing power of absolute government in the state. It was a movement that covered a century and a half (from Herbert of Cherbury to David Hume, 1624-1776), and was in essential harmony with Naturalism in France, while it anticipated practically all the positions of German Rationalism. It had a period of youth (Herbert, Hobbes, Blount), a period of maturity (Toland, Collins, Tindal, Morgan, Annet, Middleton), and a time of old age (Shaftesbury, Mandeville, Dodwell, Bolingbroke, Hume). Arising during the reign of Charles I, it flourished in the period extending from the revolution of 1688, and it decayed toward the close of and in the times following the reign of George II.[5]

---

[4] For further study we refer to Troeltsch, *PRE*, IV, 24-39; cf. *NSH*. See W. Walker, p. 481. T. Simon, *op. cit.*, p. 39.

[5] A. S. Farrar, *op. cit.*, pp. 15-164, cf. M. Pattison, *op. cit.*, p. 293.

2. Philosophical background. In a study of the English Deists we need to review carefully the general philosophy of that age, because their theology was nothing but a system of philosophy as all natural theology must be. The significance of the English Deists lies in the fact that they became the founders of our modern philosophy of religion.

In the following paragraphs we shall present short accounts of the philosophical views of Bacon, Spinoza, Hobbes, and Lord Herbert of Cherbury (called the "father of English Deism"). We must also have a few orientating remarks on the relation of John Locke to the Deists, and finally we must study the significance of Hume for the dissolution of Deism.

Note: We might have included in these reviews a paragraph on *Descartes.* Of this philosopher one might be reminded when reading the remark of McGiffert: "The rationalism of the period was of all sorts and degrees, *but in every phase of it there was the tendency to reject or modify the medieval estimate of man.*" But the conservatives of today will not admit that a truly historical conception of the Reformation is irreconcilable with a properly modern estimate of man. This is our reason for not including the philosophy of Descartes in the following reviews.[6]

a. FRANCIS BACON (1561-1626) aimed at certainty in his suggestions for a method of arriving at knowledge. His special interest lay in the tangible matters of the natural sciences, that is in the things observable by sense-experience. Bacon was an empiricist. Descartes also aimed at certainty, with this difference, however, that he sought it in the intellectual utterance of consciousness. Here we have the early indication of the development of two differing types of theology: the theology following the philosophy of English empiricism with Francis Bacon, Thomas Hobbes and John Locke as first guides, and the continental (German) theology of idealism following Leibnitz and his successors.

What are the special points of interest in the philosophy of Bacon when we keep in mind that here it is our object to trace the influences contributory to the religion of the English Deists? The answer must be about as follows: (1) Bacon rejected the syllogistic-demonstrative method of scholasticism, upon which theology had been relying. In his inquiry after a reliable method for finding truth he declared against deduction from a general principle except when this principle or hypothesis is already identical with an actual experience. Bacon insisted that all thinking must be established upon experience arrived at by induction. (2) Among the misleading conceptions or prejudices ("idols") of which we must rid our mind in the pursuit of this method he names also the "idols of the tribe," concepts peculiar to man's constitution, among which Bacon counted the teleological view of things, a mistaken notion because it ignores the mechanistic character of causality. (3) As a child of the age when philosophy and science were passing out of the hands of the theologian, he drew a sharp line between the work of science and that of theology. Philosophy was to be secularized. His optimism as expressed in the *New Atlantis* was for the future of science, the mastery of nature ("knowledge is power"). He had no intention to discredit religion, or to deny to theology its legitimate sphere. But he warned against an unreasonable confounding of the divine with the human. Mediating causes, if they are not known, must not be traced to the working of God, because this would result in a conviction not resting on

---

[6] As to editions of the works of the philosophers we must refer the reader to the newest encyclopedias and to the histories of philosophy. Among the latter we mention the careful footnotes in A. Weber (Eng. translation), in W. Turner and Windelband (Eng. translation). B. Rand, *Modern Classical Philosophers,* 2d ed., offers a convenient selection.

truth. The findings of science are not to be feared because, properly considered, they will support faith and discredit superstition. The source of theology must be seen in the divine revelation through the word of God, not in the natural light nor in the dictates of reason. This must be done even where the testimony of God runs counter to reason. Still, the "natural light" in man, if this is taken as the remnant of an original purity and insight in the human race, should be looked upon as sufficient to yield some reliable information on matters of the moral law, even though it is not perfect. "Natural theology," as a part of philosophy, furnishes proof against atheism, but it is not sufficient to establish religion on a positive basis. The boundaries between sacred theology and the natural theology of philosophy should not be confused.

The Deists, as we shall see, went beyond these last mentioned suggestions of Bacon. To them the "natural light" in man was sufficient to establish the real, the true religion, the "natural religion." It is interesting to follow in the English literature of that day the evolution of Bacon's term "natural theology" to that of "natural religion"; which was first used by A. Bury.[7]

b. The Influence of SPINOZA (1632-1677). Spinoza's influence on the English Deists was much greater than that of Bacon. This is especially seen, when one examines the writings of the time after Lord Herbert of Cherbury and Thomas Hobbes, and of the time when the English Deists were at the height of their activity. There was something in Spinoza's pantheistic system as a whole that commended itself to free-thinkers everywhere, even if they were not really pantheists. The pantheism of Spinoza, as expressed in his *Tractatus de Deo et homine,* was not understood nor discussed in his day; later on it was taken up by German philosophy. Goethe was a follower of Spinoza, while Hegel's pantheism was of a different type. The best and most lucid description of the difference between Spinoza's and Hegel's pantheism, in our estimation, is that by Luthardt in his popular Dogmatics *Christiliche Glaubenlehre* (1906), p. 130 ff. It is the supernatural features of Christianity which are bound to disappear in a system like that of Spinoza. Farrar remarks: "Its influence on the question of revealed religion will be obvious. It admits that the phenomena which we attribute to miracle in the process of revelation are facts, but it denies their miraculous character. They are the mere manifestation of some previously unknown law, turning up accidentally at the particular moment; some previously unknown mode in which the all-embracing substance manifests itself. In this view all religions become various expressions of the great moral and spiritual truths which they embody, and true piety consists in rising beyond them to the vision of the higher truths which they typify, and the practice of the principles which they enjoin as rules." [8]

It was especially in his *Tractatus Theologico-Politicus* that Spinoza expressed himself on revealed religion. His aim was to defend liberty of thought as a requisite for the safety of both state and religion. In his critical investigation, in which he surveyed the Jewish and Christian religions, he came to the conclusion that certainty on the subject of revealed religion is impossible and that the fundamentals of faith are all contained in natural religion which he identified with his philosophy of pantheism. The Deists (with John Locke) never tired of writing on the "natural law" (*lex naturae or lex*

---

[7] See the article on "Latitudinarianism" in the PRE and NSH. Cf. F. Kattenbusch, *Die deutsche Theologie seit Schleiermacher* (1927), p. 14 f.

[8] *Op. cit.,* p. 153 f.

rationis). They also wrote a great deal on miracles, prophecy, the Canon, the principles of interpretation; and all these were subjects on which Spinoza had expressed himself in his *Tractatus*. It is of interest to note that Spinoza had already concluded (Chap. 8) "from supposed marks of editorship that the Pentateuch and the historical books were all composed by one historian who was, he thought, probably Ezra, Deuteronomy being the first composed." Spinoza took the first steps in emphasizing the need to interpret the Scriptures historically. It is to be admitted, of course, that here was a lesson to be learned. But the Deists, in following this hint, were too radical simply because they were radical in all their aims.

Spinoza, like Hobbes, Herbert of Cherbury, and others, had the idea that philosophy and religion do not have the same interest in actual truth. He emphasized with Hobbes that religion is an interest of the state for the purpose of safeguarding good morals, but that philosophy, as the only means of discovering truth, must be independent and enjoy absolute freedom of thought. In this connection he proposed the idea, later emphasized by Kant and now very familiar in the circles of Modernism, that for religion it is a matter of indifference whether the stories of Scripture are true or not. Such a position overlooks the fact that religion ceases to be a real motive for piety if its historicity is called into question.

c. THOMAS HOBBES (1588-1679). In his *Leviathan* Hobbes agreed with Spinoza in giving the state absolute control over the functioning of religion in society. But he developed an elaborate theory of this position, which was directed against the unlimited license, urged especially by the Dissenters, in matters of religion. According to Hobbes the state has the right to determine the type of religion best adapted for creating social well-being, and is justified in interfering with the freedom of conscience. But this part of his philosophy, although involving the matter of religious toleration, is of no special interest for our present purpose. Here we must limit ourselves to his psychology.

The philosophy of Hobbes marked the turning away from the traditional treatment of ethics, the discrediting of theological ethics and the introduction of a new psychology as the basis for ethics.[9]

We know the language of Scripture along this line. It speaks of the eternal value of the soul, its God-likeness in the original state; it traces the observable influences upon the soul for good back to supernatural influences from God and His Spirit, as well as the influences for evil to the devil. We know also what the Church taught. It taught upon the basis of Scripture the natural depravity of man as dating from the Fall and the influence of saving grace as a divine and supernatural creative act. This teaching involved a psychology, of course. We have something of that in the writings of Augustine and in Melanchthon's *De Anima* (also in Luther's *De Servo Arbitrio*). But it is readily seen that in the ages before Descartes and before the appearance of the natural sciences there could be only the rudiments of an analytical psychology. And it must be admitted, of course, that the interest of the conservatives in the Church before, during and after the Reformation was in the metaphysical and supernatural matters concerning the order of salvation.

Hobbes, in his *Leviathan*, turned against these positions of the Church. He took psychology out of the hands of the theologian. Interest shifted from theological ethics

---

[9] Our special reference here is to the very profound article by E. Troeltsch in the *PRE*, XIII, on the "English Moralists." Cf. the *NSH*.

to civil or social ethics. Here Hobbes had had his predecessors: Even a good Christian like Hugo Grotius had laid down the principle of the independence of the state from the Church. The Arminians had labored to widen the sphere of the purely natural.

Hobbes received his stimulus from the conditions in England after the revolution (1642-49) which had brought about the dissolution of existing society. Cromwell at the head of the army of the Independents had established a commonwealth in which an unsettling spiritualism and puritanism was holding society in a state of restlessness. He had been forced to establish a dictatorship, which he had to maintain with an iron hand against the threatening influence of the fanatic extremists and restless spiritualists. It was during this time that Hobbes published his *Leviathan* (1651). He felt the necessity of establishing a modern theory of absolute monarchy in contrast to the democratic revolutionists as well as to the completely antiquated divine right theorists like Filmer in his *Patriarcha*. This monarchial government was to rest upon the basis of purely secular or human ethics, derived from man's natural conceptions of right and wrong. Starting with the Aristotelian conception of an original state in which there was a war of all against all (ἄνθρωπος ἀνθρώπῳ λύκος) Hobbes attributes to man's reason and sense of self-preservation the desire to end this anarchic and chaotic state of affairs by establishing an organized society through the transfer of supreme authority from this society to a governor. This is done in the form of a contract. Organized society through its spokesman, the king, adopts an official religion, and has the absolute right to do so, for the purpose of securing the happiness of all.

The question then arises: What is the most natural and beneficial system of ethics to be adopted by the state? It was this question that created a special interest in an analytical psychology, and on this Hobbes set the English thinkers of the 17th and 18th centuries at work. This new psychology was empirical in character. It ignored the metaphysical teachings of Bible and Church concerning the nature of the soul, the influence of divine grace upon the natural faculties of man and the impulses bound to be received from a divinely revealed destiny. It sought the laws for ethical action merely in the natural functions of the mind and in an immanent psychological analysis of these. While the decisive step in this direction was taken by Hobbes, he had his predecessors, the French Naturalists, such as Montaigne and Charron, who, following the old Stoics, had already been endeavoring to record the psychological laws underlying the motions of feeling and will.

It is especially the mechanistic character of the psychology of Hobbes to which we must call attention. In his struggle for a new theory of knowledge he arrived at the two statements: "All that exists is body," and "All that occurs is motion." All knowledge and all willing are traced to impressions upon the brain received through the nerve senses from external objects.[10]

The fundamental principle of Hobbes' philosophy was the mechanical conception of the physical world. This was an assumption of his age under the influence of Kepler, Galileo and the French scientists. But Hobbes extended its application to the mental sphere, and the psychology which we have described was the result. Upon the basis of his mechanistic psychology he theorized that the idea of deities was originally produced by the fear of hostile beings thought of, though mistakenly, as having an incorporeal

---

10 *Leviathan*, I and VI.

existence. Man investigates as to the causes of interference with his welfare and discovers something which he conceives of, mistakenly, as spirit. A like faith of many individuals leads to organized religion and to a worship of the deity.

If we remember that the outstanding trait in the English Deists was the naturalization of religion, then it is clear what influence upon them the philosophy of Hobbes must have had.

We see more of a real pioneer of English Deism in a philosopher who died about thirty years after Hobbes:

d. LORD HERBERT OF CHERBURY (1582-1648). This man of attractive personality was in a special sense the real pioneer of English Deism. He is beautifully described by J. Hunt, I, 441-61, and there are many references to him in Vol. II of the same work. He had been stimulated to thought on the problems of religion by visits to France and by direct or indirect contact with the liberalists of the age. Toward the close of his life he published the following writings: (1) *De Veritate*, to which he appended two shorter treatises—*De Causis Errorum*, and *De Religione Laici*—; and (2) *De Religione Gentilium*. The first of these offers a theory of the laws of knowledge; the second is built upon the first and presents a critique of faith or religion.

We cannot here go into the details of his argumentation but must content ourselves with presenting only a few leading thoughts of his writings as a whole. The test of true religion, he said, lies in its universality. There are the common religious conce*r*tions (*notitiae communes*) among all men of every race. In these we have the essentia*i*s of religion. True religion has its foundations in the natural instincts, in the truths which are intuitively perceived. He enumerates five such truths that are common to all religions: (1) The being of God; (2) the duty to worship him; (3) the practical-moral character of divine worship; (4) the duty to repent of sins and to forsake them; (5) divine retribution, partly here and partly hereafter. These have frequently been styled the "five points of Deism," and their author has been called the "father of Deism." The position is taken that this "religion of nature or reason" is innate in man. There are no atheists; atheism is an abnormality. The priests of the various religions added to these innate religious ideas a multiplicity of deities to be worshiped through ceremonies, oracles which they alone could interpret, and means of expiation which they alone could dispense. Christianity returned to an emphasis of the above mentioned essentials of religion. But in the process of doctrinal development the true religion was soon overlaid with the divisiveness and sectarianism of religious conceptions which characterized the age of the writer.

Supernatural revelation is not spoken of as impossible, but its probability in individual cases is tied to conditions which make it practically superfluous. Reason is the real authority in matters of truth and error; revelation is uncertain, although it may be admitted that there can be things beyond reason. In the heathen religions, as in Christianity with its Bible, we must try to find the real truth, the real word of God. And this will be found to be covered generally by the above mentioned "five points."

The significance of Lord Herbert in the history of theological liberalism lies in his predication of subjective reason (*sana ratio*) as the principle of religious truth. In this respect he was on common ground with Descartes, Spinoza and many of the advanced thinkers of the age. In England the points of conflict between Churchmen and Puritans had ceased to attract attention, and the appeal was to the powers and prerogatives of reason. It was the age of reason in all countries, an age in which freedom of political and religious thought was demanded. In religion and ethics the thinkers went back of the Scriptures to the standards of philosophical thought. We shall withhold our criticism of the situation until we have reviewed the other English Deists who are also regarded as having contributed to the ideas of theological liberalism.

e. *The Relation of* JOHN LOCKE (1632-1704) *to the Deists and to the Church.* What is the criterion or norm with regard to the claims of revelation? What is the relation of revelation to natural religion? On these problems in which the Deistic movement was vitally interested Locke expressed himself first in his *Essay on Human Understanding* (1689). The claims of revelation, by pagans, sectarians and dogmatists, must stand the test of reason applied to the external situation and an inner believability. The truths of divine revelation, which, according to Locke, we cannot have by innate ideas, must commend themselves to reasonable metaphysics and ethics, to a knowledge arrived at by perception in the way of experience.[11] If in such a way the reliability of the truth of revelation has been established then we may allow a posteriori a favorable prejudice with regard to some mysterious details. If we ignore this criterion of reasonableness in the foundations of Christianity[12] then the most absurd matters might be introduced as revelation. The central teachings of Christianity, however, should be derived exclusively from the Gospels and the Acts, which stress the moral demands for participation in the Messianic kingdom and are identical with the laws of natural religion. The Christian religion, different from all pagan religions and philosophies, presents the natural religion in its purity, perfection and with authority. With this fundamental position Locke combined a certain belief in miracles and inspiration of Scripture.

These supernatural features made his teaching on the relation between the religion of nature and that of revelation somewhat acceptable to many of the moderate Conservatives. This class of clergymen, mostly of a Latitudinarian type, would have expressed the situation with the following words of M. Pattison (p. 297): "Christianity is a résumé of the knowledge of God already attained by reason, and a disclosure of further truths. These further truths could not have been comprehended by reason. When divinely communicated, however, they approve themselves to the same reason which has already put us in possession of so much." [13]

The Deists were encouraged by Locke in emphasizing the practical identity between natural and revealed religion, making natural religion the norm and criterion of the revealed. Thus the question has arisen whether Locke was the "father of Deism" or not. Considering the fact that the Deists as "free-thinkers" took a fundamentally different attitude towards religion than was the case with the seriously minded and religiously inclined Locke, it would not be correct to put him with the Deists.[14]

3. *A first echo of the new teaching.*

a. CHARLES BLOUNT, in his first writing (*Anima Mundi*, 1679), emphasized the relative perfection of natural religion among the non-Christians. In the translation of Philostratus' *Life of Apollonius of Tyana* he evidently desired to discredit the super-

---

[11] On the difference between Lord Herbert and Locke regarding the "innate ideas" read John Hunt, *op. cit.,* (I, 452) who is of the opinion that "both seem to mean much the same thing."

[12] Cf. his writing *The Reasonableness of Christianity*, 1695.

[13] For further illustration, see the discussion of Archbishop Tillotson by McGiffert, *op. cit.,* pp. 194-200.

[14] See E. Troeltsch *PRE*, IV, cf. *NSH*, also J. Hunt, *op. cit.,* I, 459, II, 183, 249.

natural character of Christ by paralleling His miracles with those attributed to non-Christians.

b. His friend CHARLES GILDON, who later retracted, published the *Oracles of Reason* which contained articles by himself, Blount and others.[15] It was suppressed by the authorities as the "worst calumny of Christianity."

4. *The autonomy of ethics.* The EARL OF SHAFTESBURY (d. 1713), left as his chief work three volumes on *Characters of Men, Manners, Opinions, Times* (2d ed., 1714). His significance lies in his tracing the ethical to the conscience, which is autonomous; it must not be sought in an external authority (cf. Hobbes on the State). The sense for the ethical as an instinct is born into us, the same as the sense for beauty. The selfish and the social instincts are in our nature. It is the pleasure in the beholding of the harmony of these that constitutes virtue, which produces happiness. While pedagogically helpful and needed because of human depravity, it is wrong in principle to promote virtue by praise or punishment and by promise of rewards, as preachers do on the basis of the Bible; love is the driving motive of Christianity.

While reason should not be taken as an outward authority (cf. Locke) true revelation will be in agreement with reason; else it is deceptive, even if it should be attested by miracles.

The excrescences of religion can best be met by ridicule and irony. The constant practice of Shaftesbury in this kind of writing provoked books of protest from the camp of the Conservatives (see below).[16]

5. *The warfare against the supernatural.*

a. In the general attack upon the supernatural J. TOLAND (d. 1722) published a book entitled *Christianity Not Mysterious, or a Treatise showing that there is nothing in the Gospel contrary to Reason nor above it, and that no Christian doctrine can be properly called a Mystery* (1696). This book had several editions. Pressing the question of authority in matters of religion, he rejects tradition and the authority of the Church and Scripture as it was usually interpreted. Reason is proclaimed as the only principle of authority. Even the divine source of Scripture can be established only by reason. He admits that the use of reason can suffer perversion; it should then be restored to its original power. The criterion of unimpaired reason must be sought in the force of evidence. There may be revelation as a means of information, but the teachings of revelation must satisfy man's reason. From this standpoint he draws the conclusion that in Christianity there can be nothing mysterious. There cannot be even the appearance of a conflict between reason and the Gospel. In this statement Toland goes beyond the position of Spinoza, Herbert, and Hobbes, who admitted, as we have seen, that in Christianity and Scripture there may be something beyond the faculty of reason. The statement of Toland was made in order to prove that the essence of the Christian religion is found in that "natural religion" which all peoples and races are alleged to have in common. Christianity is something "sectarian," to use the present-day term, a special branch of the real religion.[17]

---

[15] The contents are described by Farrar, *op. cit.*, 174 f.

[16] Cf. Hunt, *op. cit.*, II, 343 f. Simon, 44.

[17] It is not difficult to understand that it was in the atmosphere of this distinction between natural religion and the estimate of historic Christianity as a sectarian form of the natural or universal religion that Masonry was organized. This was in 1717.

In his denial of the mysterious element in Christianity Toland asks whether the very conception of faith does not demand a supernatural object. He denies this by pointing to the reasons for faith in Scripture: We must satisfy ourselves that the Biblical writings are genuine as to authority, and we must be convinced that the contents of the writings are worthy of God. Our reaction is that this is right so far as it goes, but Toland overlooks the fact that the believer finds something in the Scriptures which lies beyond the intellectually demonstrable, something that is seen and felt only by the intuitive vision of the spiritually-minded reader.[18]

b. ANTHONY COLLINS and THOMAS WOOLSTON *on prophecy and miracle.* Among the attacks on the supernatural there was a publication by Collins (d. 1729) on the conception of the Old Testament prophecies, their bearing on the New Testament reports, and the results derived from this consideration for the proper estimate of Christianity. This work bears the title *A Discourse of the Grounds and Reasons of the Christian Religion* (1724). The Christian religion is viewed as an allegorized Judaism, a "mystical Judaism," a religion of reason, developed and perfected by the allegorization of the Jewish religion of reason.[19]

The conflict was continued by Th. Woolston (d. 1731) as spokesman for Collins in his *Discourse on the Miracles of Our Saviour* (eight treatises, 1727-30). In overbearing and very offensive language, he ridiculed the literary conception of the Biblical records. A severe controversy resulted from the publication of this book. In the battle between the natural religion of the Deists and the supernatural religion of Christianity the Church was cut to the quick. This gave a strong stimulus to the development of Christian apologetics, and many scholars came forward to defend the Bible. Lechler, in writing on this conflict, speaks of some sixty publications which appeared in connection with it.[20]

c. Later on, PETER ANNET (d. 1768), in his desire to reply to the defenders of miracles who had been pointing to the Biblical eye-witnesses, undertook to tear down this part of the bulwark. He wrote *The Resurrection of Jesus Considered in Answer to the Trial of Witnesses* (1744), suggesting that Christ may not have been really dead after his burial. He spoke of Paul as the founder of a new religion and questioned the genuineness of his writings. All supernaturalism was rejected.

d. CONYERS MIDDLETON (d. 1750), with like radicalism, fought the inspiration of the Bible, the possibility of miracles, etc., and aimed to wipe out all difference between sacred and profane history. Middleton, however, was in England the first to point out that we must take into consideration the historical conditions of a movement before we can understand its significance.[21]

6. *On the general conception of religion.* Several of the Deists devoted themselves to a constructive statement of the tenets of Deism. As examples of such attempts we offer a brief review of Tindal's and Chubb's ideas.[22]

---

[18] Hunt, *op. cit.,* II, 236-51.

[19] We cannot go into the details of the whole debate. Lechler gives a very complete and lucid repor:, *op. cit.,* pp. 266-288. Troeltsch offers a brief review in the *PRE.* See also Hunt, *op. cit.,* II, 369-99.

[20] *Op. cit.,* pp. 298-323. Hunt, *op. cit.,* II, 400-431.

[21] See Troeltsch, in *PRE,* IV, p. 546, 15-40.

[22] Bolingbroke might have claim to a review at this place if we consider his general aims. But he was more brilliant than solid and therefore we shall prefer to let the untutored T. Chubb, a man of much moral earnestness take his place. As to the views of Lord Bolingbroke see J. Hunt, *op. cit.,* Vol. III, 148 ff.

a. MATTHEW TINDAL (d. 1733) published the book *Christianity as Old as the Creation, or the Gospel a Republication of the Religion of Nature* (1730). The leading ideas are as follows. Reasonable living, which leads to happiness in life, is religion and constitutes the morally good. A follower of John Locke, Tindal admits no innate ideas in men, but to this rule he makes an exception—the desire for happiness. This he calls the only innate principle of the mind. Religion is essentially a reasonable way of living. Fundamental to all religions is the recognition of the law of nature which is always perfect, plain, simple, and universal. The divisions in religions have been dealing with the non-fundamentals, with matters not truly religious. The criterion of the true religion is the universality of the natural religion. From the identity of the Christian religion with natural religion Tindal argues that Christianity can have no articles of faith that are not in agreement with reason. Those who object to this, he says, aim after all to explain religion with the aid of reason. Many things in the Bible must be rationalized in order to make them acceptable. Tindal overlooks the fact that there is a difference between using reason in the interpretation of Scripture and the laying down of a rule that there can be nothing mysterious and miraculous in revelation. The misleading thought of Tindal is seen in the demand that was under-lying the title of his writing: Christianity must be identical with natural religion, other-wise it cannot be true. If Christianity teaches more than is contained in natural religion, then such additions belong to the realm of superstition or to the corruption of true religion. And this was the real position of the Deists. The views of Tindal, together with those of Chubb, are representative of the views of Deism on religion as a whole.

b. THOMAS CHUBB (d. 1747) was a common workman who by a remarkable interest in theological controversies had trained himself to a clear presentation of thought in writing. In his book *The True Gospel of Jesus Christ* (1738) and in a defense of that book *The True Gospel of Jesus Christ Vindicated* (1739) he aimed to show that Christ had wanted to teach simply the moral law, the "law of reason," the "law of nature." Christianity is simply the religion of obeying the moral law or the dictates of the con-science. If this law has been violated, then there must be repentance and reform, which will be followed by divine forgiveness. This is the whole doctrine of salvation. There can be no inclusion of doctrines and opinions in this Gospel of Christ. Such matters as His divinity have nothing to do with man's salvation. Christ was not really the Son of God; He was man, and as such He is our example. The doctrine of an imputation of Christ's righteousness is harmful because it deprives men of the incentive to rely entirely on the moral law for their salvation. We see that Chubb anticipated in an especially clear and simple way the *rationalismus vulgaris* which was soon to flourish particularly in Germany.

7. Estimate of the Deists. In addition to the few critical remarks of a general nature which were expressed under *3 a-c* of this chapter, we further offer a few state-ments regarding the significance of the English Deists. (1) While it is true that the French Deists (Naturalists) were more radical than some of the English writers (Tindal, Toland, Chubb), yet most of the latter were men who took the first step in really radical liberalism. They remind us of that type of criticism which in the history of Christian thought was further cultivated by Voltaire, Frederick the Great, Emperor Joseph II, Benjamin Franklin, Thomas Jefferson, Thomas Paine, and later by Robert Ingersoll.[23]

---

[23] See the remark by Walker, *op. cit.,* p. 492.

(2) Not counting such philosophers as Herbert and Hume, who strictly speaking did not belong to this group, they were throughout small men in the field of literature. Troeltsch characterizes them as second- and third-rate men who had the real *intelligentia* of England against them.[24] (3) Most of them bear the marks of laymen who undertake the discussion of philosophy and religion without having the requisite training for such a task. This was one reason why their work was purely negative and non-constructive. (4) In making human reason the criterion of revelation in the sense of religious philosophy, they failed to appreciate the appeal which the Holy Scriptures have always had to the soul of man; and therefore they did not feel the need of crediting to the Bible any special significance for the life of the Church. This applies more to the French than to the English Deists. In discussing the relation between natural religion and revelation, the chief interest of the English Deists was in such subjects as the probability or improbability of the prophecies and miracles. It did not occur to them—nor, for that matter, to their conservative opponents—that the much-discussed special revelation might be viewed as a history of redemption. (5) The Deists had no interest in the so-called Arian or Unitarian controversy concerning the Person of Christ which was going on in England at that time. Allen remarks: "As there had been no special message, there was no necessity for a supernatural messenger" (p. 364). (6) It cannot be denied that the assaults of the Deists upon the Faith of the Church served the purpose of calling attention to matters in theology which needed to be rectified. (7) Finally, we must note the fact that the whole deistic inquiry, taken together with the philosophical influences surrounding the movement, created the "philosophy of religion" which serves today as an auxiliary branch of systematic theology.[25]

8. *Replies from the camp of the conservatives.* It is impossible within the space at our disposal in this chapter to present, to classify, and to give a critical review of all the writings which proceeded from the conservative quarters of the Church against the Deists. They were very many. All we can do is to mention the outstanding replies and characterize the methods in refuting their foe. The student will want to read what the historians of the 17th and 18th centuries wrote on that great controversy.[26]

a. *Names for Orientation.* Against Lord HERBERT came a reply from THOMAS HALYBURTON: *Natural Reason Insufficient;* from RICHARD BAXTER a writing under the title *More Reasons for the Christian Religion and No Reason Against It.* Against C. BLOUNT we have CHARLES LESLIE in his *Short and Easy Method with the Deists* which converted C. GILDON who had been writing on the side of BLOUNT, and who wrote the *Deist's Manual.* LESLIE added the following writings: *The Growth of Deism, The Five Crowns of the Church, The Growth of Error.* JOHN TOLAND'S book, *Christianity Not Mysterious,* drew forth many replies: STEPHEN NYE, *Historical Account of the New Testament;* JOHN RICHARDSON, *The Canon of the New Testament Vindicated;* J. JONES, *A New and Full Method of Settling the Canonical Authority of the New Testament;* T. MANGEY, replying to TOLAND'S *Nazarenus;* T. BRETT, on the same subject; JAMES PATERSON, *Anti Nazarenus.* Against the Earl of SHAFTESBURY we see writings by J. BROWN who criticized his derisive methods in the *Essay on the Characteristics;* by JOHN BALGUY in *A Letter to a Deist;* by Bishop BERKELEY in *Minute Philosopher* and

---

[24] *PRE*, IV, 534, 59.
[25] See the remark of Troeltsch, *Ibid.*, 533, 7.
[26] We refer especially to J. Leland, 5th ed., to J. Hunt's 3 volumes; to Farrar, *op. cit.*, pp. 221 ff., to L. Stephen; to Abbey and Overton; to R. Buddensieg's excellent article on "J. Butler" in *PRE*, III, 594-602.

A Vindication of the Theory of Vision; by Bishop WARBURTON on SHAFTESBURY'S method of ridicule. J. BUTLER, in his book on the *Analogies* which will be reviewed below, has frequent references to SHAFTESBURY, especially regarding the conscience. The writings of A. COLLINS (*Discourse of Free-Thinking* and *Grounds and Reason for the Christian Religion*) "engaged the whole Church Militant in controversy" (Hunt, II, 379). Among his opponents were: WM. CARROLL, objecting to a place for reason in theology; R. BENTLEY in *Eleutherius Lipsiensis;* F. HARE in *A Clergyman's Thanks for Eleutherius Lipsiensis;* D. WILLIAMS in *A Letter to the Author of Free-thinking;* J. ADDI-COMBE; Bishop CHANDLER on Old Testament prophecy; S. CLARKE in *A Discourse Concerning the Connection of the Prophecies of the Old Testament and Their Application to Christ.* Against THOMAS WOOLSTON there were N. LARDNER, S. BROWN, and Bishop SMALBROKE on the miracles. Against MATTHEW TINDAL (*Christianity as Old as Creation*) we have: S. CLARKE, *Truth and Certainty of the Christian Religion,* in his Boyle Lectures; H. STEBBING, the Abraham Calovius of England[27] wrote against TINDAL by praising CLARKE'S book; J. CONYBEARE wrote a *Defense of Revealed Religion;* J. LELAND published *An Answer* to Tindal; J. JACKSON replied in his *Remarks on Christianity as Old as Creation;* Bishop GIBSON wrote against him in one of his *Pastoral Letters.* Against CHUBB'S *The True Gospel of Jesus Christ* there came a reply from J. HALLET, and another from G. BENSON. Against LORD BOLINGBROKE there were writings by LELAND and WARBURTON. This mere index may serve as a guide for the student who desires to follow special studies along this line.[28]

b. The Conservatives admitted a natural religion in addition to the revealed. They denied, however, that the two are identical, or that the latter came as the culmination of the former. They protested especially against the endeavor of the Deists to make natural religion the norm and criterion of the revealed. Whereas the Deists sought to naturalize religion, the Conservatives strove to supernaturalize it. They emphasized a special revelation. Against the "five points" of Lord Herbert, Thomas Halyburton advanced the following objections: (1) Those five points cannot be regarded as being generally acknowledged; (2) The element of truth in the Gentile religions is not a matter of independent discovery, but is a remnant of the original divine revelation; (3) Purely natural religion is insufficient for salvation because of the weakened condition of sinful man.[29] It was upon these statements that many of the replies to the later Deists were based. They reiterated that religion in its depths cannot be comprehended by the reasoning mind; that even natural religion presents points of difficulty to pure reason; that the noblest of heathen philosophers had altogether mistaken notions about God and immortality. It goes without saying that in many respects the conservatives of that day used methods and emphasized points which sound unnatural in the ears of the conservative theologian of today. We have learned to view revelation as a history of redemption, and this has given us apologetic weapons which were entirely unknown to men in that day.

c. Among the above mentioned writers against the Deists there was one whose book was so extraordinary that we must devote a special paragraph to it. It was the

---

[27] Buddensieg, *PRE*, III. 597. 35.
[28] Use Hunt, *op. cit.*, and be guided by his topical index in Vol. III. Cf. *Dictionary of National Biography.*
[29] Cf. Lechler. *op. cit.*, p. 54.

Analogy of Religion by JOSEPH BUTLER, bishop of Durham (d. 1752).[30] This work was in those days the completest and best answer to be given to the Deists' objections to a revealed religion; and it was destined to hold, for a long time, a distinct place in English literature. Published in 1736, it was remarkable in this respect that no opponent felt safe in risking a reply. It exercised an influence upon men of widely differing types of religion: for instance, upon J. H. Newman who became a Roman Catholic cardinal, and upon James Mill, the radical philosopher. Butler disconcerted the Deists by admitting that an absolute proof for the facts of revealed religion cannot always be given. But from man's experience regarding the present world-order he drew conclusions for the reasonableness and probability of a higher order. "The difficulties of revelation, admitted to be embarrassing in themselves, cannot be counted as destructive to religious belief, inasmuch as difficulties of a similar nature beset the recognition of nature as a coherent and systematic whole" (*NSH*). So Butler took the Deists on their own ground. Here lay the significance of Butler as an apologist. It was in the nature of his aim, however, that his proof was more negative than positive. As a philosopher he was in no wise comparable with a man like R. Cudworth of the Cambridge School (see below), and thus he was unable to establish Christianity upon a new speculative foundation. Such, indeed, was not his aim. But he did succeed in proving what he set out to prove.

9. *The men of the Cambridge school* (BENJ. WHICHCOTE, J. SMITH, R. CUD-WORTH, H. MOORE). This school flourished in the second half of the 17th century. Although adherents of it were Arminian and Latitudinarian in their advocacy of the freedom of inquiry, in their aversion to confessional controversies, in their defense of toleration, and in their emphasis upon religious life as opposed to form, they represented nevertheless a theology which contributed to the overthrow of Deism. We refer to the philosopher of that school—RALPH CUDWORTH (d. 1688). In his great work, *The True Intelligent System of the Universe* (1678), he endeavored particularly to refute Deism. To him the God of the Deists was a God of fatalism; such a conception was bound to be of serious consequence with regard to the clear distinction between good and evil as well as with regard to man's freedom. To the above-mentioned work of Cudworth, Bishop Chandler added a posthumous treatise under the title: *A Treatise Concerning Eternal and Immutable Morality* (1731). A century later another admirer of Cudworth published from his manuscripts a *Discourse on Moral Good and Evil* (1838). This rational type of theology, which argued from the foundations of Neo-Platonism, had a speculative depth which stood as a formidable witness against the shallowness of the Deistic writings. McGiffert gives a fitting characterization of the men of this school, when he speaks of "their emphasis upon reason as a faculty by which we may enjoy a direct vision of spiritual realities hidden from the senses and inaccessible by the ordinary processes of discursive reason" (p. 192).[31]

10. HUME'S *philosophy of skepticism and its consequences for Deism.* DAVID HUME'S philosophy of skepticism (1711) was a logical development of the philosophy of the English empiricists. All of these had spoken of experience as the foundation of

---

[30] See *Dictionary of National Biography,* and compare Hunt, Farrar, Abbey-Overton, L. Stephen, Buddensieg, Allen.

[31] See Fisher, *op. cit.,* 368 f. Allen, 340 ff. Tulloch in his *Rational Theology* has devoted the entire Vol. II to this school. On Cudworth see *PRE,* IV, 346 ff.; cf. *NSH.* The German church-historian Mosheim translated in 1733 Cudworth's *Intellectual System* into Latin (2nd ed., 1773). This was for the purpose of introducing Cudworth to the scholars of Europe. Birch, in an English edition of Cudworth's works (1845), translated the Latin biographical notes of Mosheim.

knowledge. Bacon sought to arrive at facts by observation and experiment. Hobbes traced all knowledge to sense-perceptions. Locke explained the acquired ideas in man by pointing to experience, either external or by sensation or reflection. Then came Hume who said: If nothing can be reality but that which is traceable to real experience, then there are two things which must be entirely eliminated, namely substance and causality. *Substance,* as existing back of qualities, conditions and actions, has never been really observed. Its reality for man is not in its materiality but in the sensations. It is just an idea, an imagination, a fiction. All matter, as far as we know it, is only a mental condition, a mental habit. It is not a conception based upon real experience, but consists only of isolated impressions and ideas. In this he agreed with Berkeley. *Causality* also is ruled out. Upon the basis of "laws," outside of strict mathematics, it cannot really be proved that one thing necessarily follows another in the relation of cause and effect. We cannot trust deductions which are not mathematically verified. And since all deductions under consideration here are neither mathematical nor experimental, we know nothing of realities outside of ourselves. Berkeley (1684-1753), before Hume, had denied the reality of matter ("things"). Hume agreed that we have no certainty with regard to the existence of matter. But he went beyond Berkeley by carrying his skepticism to the question of the certainty of the mind. We shall express his reasoning in the popular language of W. Durant in his *Story of Philosophy* (p. 281): "We know the mind, said Hume, only as we know matter; by perception, though it be in this case internal. Never do we perceive such entity as the 'mind'; we perceive merely separate ideas, memories, feelings, etc. The mind is not a substance, an organ that has ideas; it is only an abstract name for the series of ideas; the perceptions, memories and feelings *are* the mind; there is no observable 'soul' behind the processes of thought." This was skepticism carried to such an extent that all grounds for certainty in matters of religion seemed to disappear.[32]

We must now consider what effects this skeptical philosophy had upon the tenets of Deism.

a. The Deists, following Locke, had made reason the criterion in matters of religion. Now *Hume denied reason the right to create and derive truth from itself,* because this would mean speaking of things of which there can be no real experience. So the Deists, with the conservatives, lost the foundation upon which they had been building.

b. Furthermore, with the ruling out of cause and effect, *the customary deistic arguments for the existence of God were lost.* Hume argued that on the basis of real experience we know nothing of God as the Creator of the world. The teleological proof falls, because we cannot draw any analogy between a human intelligence which creates small things and a divine intelligence which created the universe. By doing this we should overlook the fact that the world is finite and that creation is beset with many imperfections. The cosmological proof falls with the admission that there is no necessity in causality. In addition to this the following question would be in order: Why may not the world, like God, have its cause in itself? Neither can there be anything in the moral proof which claims that the presence of evil in the world necessarily calls for a just and omnipotent God who will right the wrongs which we behold. We might just as well

---

[32] The writings of Hume were: *A Treatise on Human Nature, Enquiry Concerning Human Understanding* (in Rand), *Dialogues Concerning Natural Religion, Natural History of Religion.* On editions see Weber and Turner.

conclude that there is a God who is evil or unjust or powerless or who exists as a blind force.

c. Another dogma of the Deists was the *immortality of the soul.* They argued that the soul is an immaterial and therefore an indestructible substance. But Hume said: We know of no such substance. The Deists taught that the injustices of this life demand an equalization by a just God in a future life. But, said Hume, we do not know that there is a God; and if there should be one, how do we know that there will be an equalization? Eternal punishments for temporal transgressions are in themselves a gross injustice. And, according to experience, the soul is more likely to be mortal than immortal, when we consider how all things in this world fade and pass away, and especially when we observe how the soul is affected by the weaknesses and aging of the body.

d. Regarding *miracles* Hume was more on common ground with the Deists, at least in his aversion to admitting the reality of supernatural happenings. He simply insisted that experience is the source of all knowledge, and thus denied the probability of the individual miracles. But by his strict adherence to 'his principle he succeeded in throwing overboard all deistic endeavors of such men as Woolston, Annet and Middleton to allegorize and rationalize the miracles of the Bible.

e. Finally, Hume contributed not a little to the dissolution of Deism by overthrowing its fundamental presupposition: namely, that *the "religion of reason" had been monotheistic in origin and that only gradually it had been adulterated by priests into polytheism, until it was finally restored to its pristine purity by Christianity* (cf. our review of Lord Herbert). Beginning with the crudest factors of experience, Hume insisted that religion did not originate in reason, but in the feelings of primitive man, and that therefore polytheism was the primary form of religion. Assuming that there has been a gradual evolution from the lower to the higher, he traced the development of religious systems, ethics and philosophy in an ascending scale throughout the ages, and claimed that under the influence of powerful natural events it came to pass that monotheism superseded polytheism.

With regard to his personal attitude toward religion the books of Hume offer conflicting reports. In his *Natural History of Religion* he even declares himself on the side of theism and professes to arrive at it by reasoning. But then, again, he finds "ignorance the mother of devotion," declares all to be an inexplicable mystery, and loses himself in skepticism.

We have now studied the philosophical criticism by which Hume uprooted Deism. However, the effects of it were not seen immediately, for his writings were comprehended only gradually.[33] For the moment his ideas—so far as their general influence was concerned—were considered in line with the ideas of Voltaire in France. It is evident that the English people had grown tired of the "free-thinkers." Pattison makes the remark: "The decay of interest in the topic is sufficiently marked by the fact that the opinions of Hume failed to stimulate curiosity or antagonism. His *Treatise on Human Nature* (1739) fell dead-born from the press." However, it is of the greatest importance to keep in mind that the fundamental philosophical ideas of Hume had a profound influence upon Kant and through him upon the final development of German Rationalism.

---

[33] See Pattison, *op. cit.,* p. 293; cf. *PRE*, IV, 549, 20 ff.

Chapter Six

THE FRENCH NATURALISTS OF THE SEVENTEENTH AND EIGHTEENTH CENTURIES

INTRODUCTORY OBSERVATIONS

Literature: E. TROELTSCH, from a theological standpoint which will not be shared by even the most moderate among the conservatives, has written a very comprehensive and informing article on *"Aufklaerung"* in *Protestantische Realencyklopaedie* (*PRE*), II, 225-41, which must not be passed by in a study of this whole subject. In abbreviated form this article has been transposed into English by the *New Schaff-Herzog Encyclopedia* (*NSH*), IV, 141-47. See the large literature on this subject as quoted *ibidem* (p. 147). It must be remembered that Troeltsch has written much on this subject after the date of that article. We should also refer to his article on "Deism" in the *PRE* (IV, pp. 532-59) and *NSH* (III, 391-97). The second part of this very informing article reviews the French Naturalists. As to further literature on the subject the reader is referred to the *Dictionary of National Biography*. Much information will also be found in the Histories of Philosophy, such as WEBER, WINDELBAND, TURNER, CUSHMAN, TILLY. To W. DURANT, in his *Story of Philosophy* (1926), this sketch is indebted for a few significant quotations. Compare also the ably written book by T. SIMON, *Grundriss der Geschichte der neueren Philosophie in ihren Beziehungen zur Religion* (1920). The French literature on the subject, which is considerable, is given by Troeltsch in the *PRE* (IV, 532 f.) and in the *NSH* (III, 397).

The Naturalism of France here to be reviewed is a section out of the movement usually described by the term "Enlightenment" (*Aufklaerung*). It covers the beginnings of the new philosophy (Descartes, Spinoza, Leibnitz, Hobbes, Herbert of Cherbury, Locke, *et al.*) and the particular movements known as English Deism, French Naturalism and German Rationalism.

All the above named movements represent the first concerted steps into radical liberalism. The faith of the Reformation is rejected in all its fundamentals.

It will be correct to speak of a "Naturalism" in France, in distinction from the Deistic movement in England. The two are in many ways the same. Both had their interest in the religion of reason, in a natural religion. But while the more prominent among the English Deists, men like Toland and Tindal, labored to relate this natural religion to revealed religion, this endeavor was absent in France. French Naturalism was not theological in character. This is easily explained. The France of Louis XIV was not Protestant as was England, and in France it was the policy to use the official Roman Catholic Church to hold the individual in the bondage of political absolutism. This naturally produced a reaction among the French liberalists against the Church. In England where the press had been free (since 1693) and religious freedom was recognized in ever increasing degrees this antipathy to traditional religion was not against the Church as such. In France the development drifted from the deism of Voltaire into the atheism and mechanical materialism of Lamettrie, Diderot, and von Holbach, until with the idealism of Rousseau a certain new element became engrafted upon the movement. The whole development issued into the French Revolution.

1. Precursors. Several men are to be mentioned as precursors of the movement.

One was the skeptic MICHEL DE MONTAIGNE (1533-92), who liked to express the fundamental note of his thinking in these two questions: "What do I know?" and "What matters it?" He had observed the abuse of religion in politics, and in his pessimism he charged religion itself with inciting controversies, the turmoil of wars, intolerance, and vices.

P. CHARRON (d. 1602) also sounded the note of skepticism. In opposition to the policies of Louis XIV this attitude of mind became more and more the atmosphere of the cultured in France. At first this skepticism was negative. But through Voltaire some positive content was received from the English Deists and from the natural philosophy in England.

P. BAYLE (1647-1706), author of the *Critical Dictionary,* pointed to the impossibility of a religion established upon reason. This was directed against John Locke who had insisted upon the harmony between religion and reason. The objection of Bayle led the skeptics of his age to abandon revelation and to hold to reason. Voltaire thanked Bayle for having taught him the art of doubt. Bayle also raised the question: How can there be a good God and so much evil in the world? Rejecting the customary explanations as unsatisfactory, he suggested that the simplest solution would be in the Manichaean admission of a good and an evil God. If there is only one God, then, he said, we must drop either His goodness or His omnipotence. Leibnitz wrote against Bayle in his *Theodizee.* He also insisted upon the absolute independency of morality from religion: Religion would adulterate the morality of the state. On this basis he demanded a separation of the state from the church, with absolute tolerance which should include also the atheists.

2. VOLTAIRE'S *real name was Francois Marie Arouet* (1694-1788). "In Voltaire eighteenth century France had its keenest wit. No philosopher, vain, self-seeking, but with genuine hatred of tyranny, especially of religious persecution, no one ever attacked religion with a more unsparing ridicule" (Walker). This does not mean that he was an atheist. In a letter to Diderot he insists upon recognizing "a great Intelligence," a "Workman infinitely able," who "has made everything that exists." [1] Against the materialistic Holbach he spoke of "a divine organizing intelligence." [2]

On a visit to England (1726-29) he became a Deist. He believed in the existence of God and of primitive natural religion, consisting of a simple morality. But he rejected all religion that was based on the authority of the Bible or of the Church. While in entire agreement with Locke in the insistence on toleration he, like Bayle, differed from Locke in his views on the harmony between revelation and reason. Still as we saw, he could admire the wisdom of God who had constructed this universe. He believed in the so-called teleological proof of God's existence, and combined with it also the cosmological. Everything in this world has its cause in something else. This concatenation of causes must lead us back to a final cause, which is God.

He had his doubts on immortality, but later he included this with the existence of God as necessary to be believed for the upholding of order in society. "If God did not exist, it would be necessary to invent him." [3] At Ferney, just inside the Swiss border, near France, where he had found his home (1758) he erected his own church with the inscrip-

---

[1] Tallentyre, *Voltaire in His Letters,* 1919, p. 81.
[2] See the article "Providence" in his *Philosophic Dictionary.*
[3] Pellissier, *Voltaire Philosophe,* 1908, p. 172.

tion: *"Deo erexit Voltaire."* His final faith is quoted by Durant, p. 265. Outstanding among his many writings was the *Essay on the Spirit and Morals of the Nations* (1754-58) (*Essai sur les moeurs et l'esprit des nations*), and his *Dictionary of Philosophy* in ten volumes (1746), reprinted in English by E. R. DuMont (1901). To these we may add as characteristic of his method in attacking religion the *Examen important de M. Bolingbroke* (1767).

His visit in England had converted him to the natural philosophy resulting from the work of Newton and Clarke. From Locke he accepted the theory of knowledge. The main principles of his ethics were those of Shaftesbury. The English Deists in general gave him the critical method and his conception of a natural religion. He praised the moral life, and taught that on virtues and vices the voice of reason is absolutely reliable. He rejoiced over the coming of the "Age of Reason." To him, however, it was only for the *honetes gens;* the common people (the "canaille"), the shoemakers and the servants were to have no part in the glories of this condition. This is a frequently recurring remark in his voluminous writings. It was here that Rousseau differed fundamentally from Voltaire (see below).

In following the English Deists he stripped their views of their religious and theological interests, reducing religion to simple morality and rational metaphysics. In his investigations he employed historical and ethnological material to a greater degree than the English Deists had done. In this way he contributed effectively to the creation of a "philosophy of history" and a "philosophy of religion." The rise of the positive religions was to be studied in children and savages. Ignorance and fear in the presence of the laws of nature explain the rise of religious ideas. This is applied to Biblical history. It was in these investigations and criticisms that Voltaire made many frivolous statements which among those not fully informed in the Church have earned him the reputation of having been an atheist. Voltaire was frivolous, but not an atheist. But with his frivolity he taught his age to mock at essential things in religion.

His special points of emphasis may be summed up as follows: (1) The relativity and analogies between the various religions; (2) The natural-pragmatistic explanations of the Jewish-Christian religion with the interest of putting Christianity in a co-ordinate relation to the pagan religions and stripping the history of Christianity of its sacred character; (3) The inclination of people in olden times to believe in miracles and the absence of miracles in the ages historical in character; (4) The extension of paganism as compared with the smallness of Judaism and Christianity; (5) The antiquity of the human race as compared with the newness of Christianity, etc. Here, as in this whole sketch, we cannot go into criticism but can only report.

By thus engaging in these investigations Voltaire created a systematized theory of the history of religions: In the tribal God he saw the beginning of polytheism. Monotheistic Judaism produced the Christian and Mohammedan religions. Moses was a shrewd politician. The prophets were enthusiasts like the dervishes, or else epileptics. Jesus, to him, was a good man, but vain and enthusiastic, a visionary like George Fox. He deceived his age by miracles. His disciples were deceived deceivers, falsifiers, and tricksters. The Christian religion received life only through its union with Platonism. The doctrinal controversies of the Church then produced the barbarism of the Middle Ages with all the shedding of blood in consequence of the conflicts that marked the

Reformation and post-Reformation ages. Now the age of reason is opening the gates for a common morality which will bring peace and harmony to all.[4]

In his younger years Voltaire was an optimist, although he took exception to the teaching of Leibnitz that this is the "best of worlds." The earthquake at Lisbon (1755) settled him in a bitter pessimism.[5]

3. *The Development toward Materialism.* ETIENNE DE CONDILLAC (1715-80) was the philosopher of sensualism.[6] Locke had distinguished between outward and inner perceptions (sensations, reflections). Condillac wanted to deduce all activity of the mind from outward perception. All life of the individual, even revelation, is deduced from sensation. He was not a materialist, but the drift is toward materialism.

CLAUDE HELVETIUS (d. 1771) applied sensualism to the sphere of the ethical: We are trained by our environment. Egotism is the motive of all our action. The proper ambition is to be cultivated. Religion besides this idea is superfluous. True religion is identical with morality and knows of no mysteries. The Church is criticized because it deals with private vices and ignores the interests of society.[7]

4. *The Materialists.* JULIEN DE LAMETTRIE (1709-51).[8] Descartes in his *Treatise on the Passions of the Soul* said that the limbs can be moved by the objects of the senses, and by the spirits *without the aid of the soul* (I, 16). Lamettrie extends this term to man. The mind is a function of the physical organism, a mere secretion of the brain. The only difference between the brain of man and the brain of an animal is development. There can be no immortality because the spirit (mind) perishes with the brain. Neither can we speak of a divine mind governing the universe, because the principle of life, movement and sensation is in matter. But matter is animated, the universe is full of souls. At this point he admits that souls are more than machines.

Upon the foundation of this materialism Lamettrie erects a corresponding ethics. The purpose of life is happiness. Of course he admits that there is a happiness of a higher and lower value, a happiness of a more lasting and a passing sort. But nothing must interfere with that happiness. Repentance and pangs of conscience are to be rejected because they make man unhappy. Atheism is necessary for the realization of this happiness. It must be held in mind, of course, that this radicalism was the reaction against a persecuting church. The writings of Lamettrie, however, have become a store-house for all his successors in materialistic thought.

DENIS DIDEROT (1713-84) was editor of the famous *Encyclopédie* or *Dictionnaire Raisonné* (1751-66). He had D'ALEMBERT as his chief assistant. They were assisted by men such as Voltaire, Rousseau, von Holbach *et al.* (the "Encyclopedists"). The special writings of Diderot do not give us a unified philosophy because he passed through a development from theism and deism through skepticism and pantheism to materialism. His policy in the editorship of the *Encyclopédie* with regard to the religious problems of that day is most interestingly described by Troeltsch in the *PRE* (IV, 553 f.). Simon

---

[4] *PRE*, IV, 552 f.

[5] See the poem quoted by Durant, *op. cit.*, p. 247, printed from the *Selected Works of Voltaire* (1911), pp. 3-5.

[6] His *Treatise on Sensations* is printed in English translation in B. Rand, *op. cit.*, pp. 347-75.

[7] Writings: *De l'esprit; De l'homme de ses facultés et de son éducation.*

[8] His writings are: *Histoire naturelle de l'ame; L'homme machine.*

remarks: "Diderot kept himself from sinking into frivolity and cynicism by an ethical enthusiasm that stayed with him through life" (p. 56).

BARON DIETRICH VON HOLBACH (1723-1789) was born in the Palatinate. He lived in Paris where his home was the center of the radical liberalists in his day. Here a materialistic psychology and ethics were cultivated. Moral theories, though derived from Hobbes and Hume, lost all connection with the position of English Deism. All that exists, it was held, is matter. Holbach is without question the author of the *Systeme de la Nature* (1770) which was published under the name of Mirabeau. The contents may be described about as follows: Among the primitives, religion arose from fear and hope and from ignorance concerning the laws of nature. The different forms of religion were developed by designing social and political leaders who were prompted by egotism, ambition or led by minds of morbid enthusiasm. Thus there arose systems of metaphysics and theology, which were based upon an animalistic personification of the forces of the universe, with constant suggestion of supernatural influences. With the English Deists and with Voltaire, Christianity is taken to be a transposition of Galilean teachings into Neo-Platonic metaphysics. This was given as the reason why in the history of theology we meet both an extreme anthropomorphism and an abstract metaphysics. But Holbach dismissed the teleology of English Deism and emphasized man's dependency upon the cold causality of the laws of nature. In connection with this mechanistic materialism he saw the essence of morality in the instinct of self-preservation on the part of race and individuals. In a bolder way than Bayle he said that, by religion, ethics had become corrupted.

5. Rousseau's Naturalism. JEAN JACQUES ROUSSEAU, born in Geneva (1712-1778), gave an altogether different turn to the English Deism that Voltaire had imported into France. The constructive thought in his works of twenty-two volumes is contained chiefly in his *Emile* and in the *Contrat Social* (1762).

He turned away from Voltaire's emphasis upon the Enlightenment as an intellectual reform. Although contributing articles to the *Encyclopedie* he did not understand the comprehensive intellectual ambition of Diderot. He was fundamentally opposed to creating an intellectual aristocracy in which the common people (the "canaille" of Voltaire) were to be ignored as incapable of participating in the fruits of an age of reason. With the materialism of the Holbach circles he would have nothing to do. In the enlightenment as cultivated by Voltaire and the encyclopedists, he could see nothing but a gloss over the degradation of society.

To him, salvation was to be sought in a return to nature. Human society had taken its beginning in a garden of nature where men lived happy as children. The "war of all against all" (Hobbes) was not with the race at its beginning, but it came with civilization which developed the division of labor, the conception of property and that brutal egotism operating on the basis of the contrast between poor and rich, servants and masters. Man was good until civilization and art invaded his simplicity, corrupted his virtues and transformed him into a suffering, sinful being. So wrote Rousseau in his prize essay of 1749. In the *Emile,* he developed his program of an education that would lead back to nature. Pedagogy is to proceed on the assumption of an innate virtue (*"sentiment moral"*) which he distinguishes from the ideas *acquises.* Force is to be avoided as much as possible so that nature may have a chance to develop.

The religion of Rousseau is established not upon dogmatic knowledge but upon a certain feeling which, for the historian, is not easy to describe. He means the feeling of the naive and disinterested understanding of the uncultured people. Troeltsch [9] remarks fittingly: "With Rousseau natural religion takes on a new meaning." Nature is no longer universality or rationality in the cosmic order, in contrast to special supernatural and positive phenomena, but primitive simplicity and studied reflection (*Innerlichkeit, Urwuechsigkeit und Gefuehlmaessigkeit in Gegensatz zur Kuenstlichkeit und Reflexion*)." Although the system of Rousseau shows significant features of German idealism it was irreconcilable with a religion of revelation in which sin and grace, law and gospel occupy a central position.

Turner in his *History of Philosophy* (p. 505) remarks: "If we except Rousseau, the representatives of the age of Enlightenment were men of meager or at most of mediocre intellectual ability, who failed to leave any lasting impression on the development of speculative thought. Indeed Voltaire who certainly knew the age in which he lived pronounced it to be an age of trivialities." But more than of the English Deists it must be said of the French Naturalists that they furnished to the radically irreligious minds of Europe in the eighteenth century and succeeding ages the thoughts and ideas with which the religion of the Reformation, as incorporated in the great historic confessions of Protestantism, was combatted and ridiculed. Frederick the Great of Prussia, Joseph II of Austria, Thomas Paine and later Robert Ingersoll in America, with their followers in all lands, were pupils of this school. German Rationalism, in the first vulgar forms of expression, was of a little later date. Notwithstanding its shallowness it was far more religious in its points of emphasis. It had its own history and must be discussed in a chapter by itself.

---

[9] *PRE*, IV. 557 f.

Chapter Seven

GERMAN RATIONALISM

Literature: The standard church histories, especially of German authorship; see also the histories by PH. SCHAFF and W. WALKER. The article *"Aufklaerung,"* by E. TROELTSCH, in the third edition of the *Protestantische Realencyklopaedie* (*PRE*), II, 225 ff.; cf. the article "Enlightenment" in the *New Schaff-Herzog Encyclopedia* (*NSH*), IV, 141 ff. See also the article *"Rationalismus und Aufklaerung,"* by O. KIRN in the *PRE*, XVI, 447 ff.; cf. the same article in the *NSH*, IX, 393 ff., also the article on *"Rationalismus"* in *RGG*, IV, 1712 ff. A SAINTES: *Historie Critique du Rationalisme en Allemagne,* 1841; the same in English translation, *Critical History of Rationalism in Germany,* 1849. The writings of F. A. G. THOLUCK on Rationalism: *Vermischte Schriften,* II (1839), 1-147; his *Vorgeschichte des Rationalismus,* in four volumes, 1853-62; finally his *Geschichte des Rationalismus,* Vol. I, 1865. K. F. A. KAHNIS: *Der innere Gang des deutschen Protestantismus,*³ 1874, II, 101-123. F. LICHTENBERGER: *History of German Theology in the 19th Century* (translation from the French, T. & T. Clark, Edinburgh, 1889), 18-45. R. SEEBERG: *Die Kirche Deutschlands im neunzehnten Jahrhundert,* 4th ed., 1903. E. C. MOORE: *History of Christian Thought Since Kant,* 1912. K. GIRGENSOHN: *Geistesgeschichtliche Lage der Gegenwart,* 1924. I. KANT: *Religion innerhalb der Grenzen der reinen Vernunft,* 1793; cf. an English translation. The essay just named is of special importance for the subject here under discussion; see the topical sketch of it by R. H. GRUETZMACHER: *Textbuch zur systematischen Theologie und ihrer Geschichte,*² 1923, pp. 162 ff. F. ROEHR: *Briefe ueber den Rationalismus,* 1813, on this particular exponent of the old German (vulgar) rationalism compare the works of K. A. VON HASE, especially his *Anti-Roehr* (1837), 35-414.

INTRODUCTORY OBSERVATIONS

By "Rationalism" in this chapter we do not mean, of course, the well known philosophical principle in the field of the theory of knowledge; but we mean the specifically German movement in the history of Protestant theology which we are accustomed to consider in line with Deism in England and with Naturalism in France. In English these three movements are spoken of as the "Enlightenment."

We might speak of Rationalism in a number of respects. E. Troeltsch in his article on *Aufklaerung* in the *Protestantische Realencyklopaedie,* (II, 225 ff.)[1] and E. C. Moore, on the basis of this article, in his book, *Christian Thought Since Kant* (pp. 27-29) have shown us the influence of Rationalism in various spheres of human life. Girgensohn in a brilliantly conceived lecture, *Geistesgeschichtliche Lage der Gegenwart* (1924), refers to four other fields of operation of the rationalistic principle: Mathematics and the natural sciences, politics, practical economics, and ethics. Here we shall deal with theological Rationalism. In the history of all positive religions we observe theological Rationalism in the most varying forms. There was Rationalism in the Church long before it appeared in the Renaissance and the theology of the Enlightenment in the eighteenth century. One needs only to think of the Monarchians and the Gnostics in the ancient Church, of Duns Scotus in the middle ages, and of the Socinians in the age of the Reformation.

1. All through the history of doctrine there has been *the problem of properly relating reason and revelation.* Both revelation and reason had been accepted as sources of Christian truth. This was also the case in the theological systems of the Lutherans

---

This chapter was first published as an article in the *Biblical Review,* New York, April, 1931, and is here reprinted by courtesy of the publishers.

[1] Cf. article, Enlightenment, *NSH.*

and Reformed in the seventeenth century. The Lutherans distinguished between articles of faith which have their source in both reason and revelation, like the general belief in God and immortality, and such articles as rest purely on revelation. The dividing line between these two sources, however, was never absolutely defined, and reason succeeded more and more in gaining ground in the foundation of Christian doctrine.

2. In this direction moved that peculiar type of *Supernaturalism* into which orthodoxy had issued at the beginning of the eighteenth century. It maintained itself along with Rationalism during the whole of the eighteenth century and even during the first part of the nineteenth.[2] This Supernaturalism labored to prove by rational means the possibility, necessity, and reality of the leading contents of supernatural revelation. Representatives of the older type were men such as STORR, REINHARD, PLANCK, KNAPP, and STAEUDLIN. It was a type of theology that bore the marks of a period of transition. Truth was to be proved by Scripture. But in the conception of the Scriptures these Supernaturalists were much guided by TOELLNER'S ideas of inspiration, by SEMLER'S criticisms, and by ERNESTI'S exegesis. The idea was that, not reason, but Scripture was to decide in matters of religion; but, as to what is the teaching of Scripture, reason was taken to be the most important guide. If Rationalism reminded us of Socinianism, Supernaturalism had a resemblance to Arminianism. The Trinity, the two natures of Christ, and the mystical union were not denied, but neither were they emphasized. Christ was the Redeemer, but He was subordinated to the Father. The fall of man was replaced by a mere inclination to evil and correspondingly there were Pelagian elements in the teachings about the way of salvation. There was variation in the teaching on the work of the Holy Spirit.[3]

Thus reason was given the decisive influence in establishing the reality and the content of revelation, but in such wise that the rational principle had been gaining more and more the upper hand over the supernatural. Supernaturalism was moving unconsciously in the direction of Socinianism. So it can be said of this older Supernaturalism that it became more and more a feeder of Rationalism. The Supernaturalism here described must not be confused with the so-called "Pietistic Supernaturalism" of the middle of the nineteenth century, with representatives such as Neander, Tholuck, and Hengstenberg, in which we have a determined aim at the overthrow of Rationalism.[4]

3. To describe the *essential features of this theological Rationalism* we may say that it was for Germany the result of the *Aufklaerung* as a general movement, that recrudescence of the tendencies that characterized the Renaissance, which for a time had been checked by the Reformation, but now came back again with an irresistible force.

This "Modernism of Germany was simply the working out of hegemony in modern philosophy. Since Descartes, rational thinking had been elevated to the principles of all theoretical knowledge of truth and of all practical moral action. This was applied to the doctrine of God and to ethics especially by Spinoza. In Holland, England, and France most of the thinkers aimed to arrive at all knowledge of truth, including religious truth, from the accessible sources in this world. If there was a recognition of revelation then it was a "natural revelation." Most of these philosophers, excepting Spinoza who was not yet understood, and the whole general culture still held to the faith in a personal

---

[2] Cf. Kurtz: *Church History,* English ed., III, sec. 171, 6.

[3] Cf. Kahnis, *op. cit.,* II, 119.

[4] See Kurtz, *op. cit.,* III, sec. 182.

God. In France alone we find atheism. Of course, the achievement of the God of these intellectuals was merely the creation of the world, developed on the basis of its own laws. In this "Deism," as it was called in England, there was no room for the supernatural. Still, there was an inclination to join with Christianity and revelation.

In Germany it was GOTTFRIED LEIBNITZ (d. 1716) who sought to mediate between rational Deism and the supernatural revelation of Christianity. He was of the opinion that the existence of an omnipotent and all-wise God can be positively proved by reason. This God created the best of all possible worlds. The evil in this world was not positively bad, but something negative, merely lacking the perfect good, and thus it was taken to be aiding the development of the good. Leibnitz represents a positive optimism in his estimate of the world and man. By this he blazes the trail for a fundamental trait in the modern age, especially in Rationalism. This optimism enters into a decided opposition to the pessimism produced by the doctrine of sin that had been held by conservative Protestantism. The positive dogmas of Christianity, while not forced by reason, appeared to Leibnitz as being not against reason, but rather "above reason" (*uebervernuenftig*). Thus he aimed to mediate between Rationalism and Supernaturalism and to create a kind of super-rationalism.

CHRISTIAN WOLFF (d. 1754) popularized these thoughts. He was the real philosophical founder of theological Rationalism in its first period, before Kant. It was Wolff who formulated the rational proofs for faith in a personal God and a personal immortality. He preached the need of a practical and humane morality which was to secure temporal and an eternal happiness. Theoretically he did not deny a Christian revelation above reason, but this revelation must harmonize with natural religion and can be real only in so far as this is done.

In the course of the further development the strength of this supernatural revelation was reduced and identified with the contents of a natural religion. HERMANN REIMARUS (d. 1768), in the so-called *Wolfenbuettel Fragments,* published by Lessing, declined every special revelation and made natural religion the criterion of every historical religion, including Christianity. At the same time he sought critically to dissolve the historic foundation of Christianity as we have it in the Bible. He insisted upon the late conception of the Biblical books and pointed to numerous contradictions, especially in the reports concerning the resurrection of Christ by which he wanted to make this fact incredible.[5]

4. Theology in the various branches labored concretely and consistently to carry out these principles.[6]

Biblical criticism and history of doctrine took their beginning. Exegesis became more and more grammatical (ERNESTI) and strove to find the "natural" meaning of the Scriptures. The canon lost its authoritative formation and appeared as the result of human development. Dogma appeared as a changing factor, in itself contradictory to, and in conflict with, reason. The investigations in these fields by men such as SEMLER, MICHAELIS, SACK, TELLER, SPALDING, TOELLNER, JERUSALEM, were aiming throughout at practical and moral purposes. The effect upon the pulpit, upon hymnology, and upon liturgy was soon felt.[7]

---

[5] Cf. Walker, *op. cit.,* p. 526.

[6] See Troeltsch, *Aufklaerung* (*PRE*) and "Enlightenment" (*NSH*).

[7] See the characterization of a moderate Rationalist such as Semler, by Walker, *op. cit.,* p. 529.

The dogmaticians attacked traditional doctrines such as miracle, inspiration, pre-destination, and original sin. Toellner denied the meritorious character of Christ's active obedience; Ernesti, the doctrine of His three offices, leaving only that of teacher. In the place of justification by faith there was put the ethical accomplishment. Not, however, until the end of the eighteenth century do we meet consistent work of rationalistic dog-matics. These works on dogmatics wanted to show that the moral religion of reason and Biblical revelation are identical. The aim was apologetical, namely, to prove the maintainability of Christianity. So TIEFTRUNK, ECKERMANN, and WEGSCHEIDER.

5. *The influence of* IMMANUEL KANT (d. 1804) *deserves special attention.* It is true that Kant through his *Critique of Theoretical Reason* upset the self-confidence of the Rationalists, especially their proofs of the existence of God and of immortality. But, on the other hand, through his *Critique of Practical Reason* he strengthened the confidence of the age in rationalistic moralism as the real essence of Christianity. And especially in his essay on *Religion within the Limits of Pure Reason* (1793) he set him-self the task of a complete reconstruction of religion after the principles of that rational-istic moralism. This publication became typical especially of the second form of Ration-alism and exercised an influence far beyond the age here under discussion. Its teachings are living in Germany's "Neo-Protestantism" (*Neuprotestantismus*) and in the "Mod-ernism" of today. The fundamental thoughts of this publication present a characteristic picture of Rationalism. (We shall review the contents of this essay in our discussion of Kant in Book V, Chap. 1.)

6. *The reconstruction of the Church's doctrine* after the principles of Rationalism was systematically carried out by J. F. ROEHR in Weimar in his *Letters on Rationalism* (1813).[8] On this basis we can give a brief review of the dogmatics of Rationalism in its matured form.

Roehr declares reason to be the only principle out of which the religio-moral con-victions must be developed. Reason also is the criterion for understanding and estimat-ing the old supernatural sources of traditional dogmatics. "Rationalism follows reason entirely and considers the Scriptures as a collection of religious documents produced purely by man's reason; the teachings and statements of these must be left to the critical examination and the verdict of reason." (*Letters*, p. 2).

Next to reason, morality was taken to be a determining and positively constructive principle. Kahnis thus describes the dogmatics of Rationalism: "While to confessional theology the Scriptures as God's Word is the norm of all truth, to Rationalism it was reason (formal principle); while to the Confessions, justification by faith in Jesus Christ is the fundamental principle, to Rationalism, it was virtue (material principle)."[9]

Clarity is the criterion of truth. The one thing that is absolutely clear is the duty to lead a moral life. If so, then there must be a God, and our being must mean some-thing for a future life. This was the same idea that had been expressed by the Deists in England and by most of the Naturalists in France. This was to be harmonized with Scripture which can contain no supernatural teachings, no real revelation. Roehr said: "Rationalism leaves everything to take care of itself or dismisses what does not seem to have the character of a universal teaching and does not stand in an immediate relation

---

[8] See, on Roehr, the church histories and encyclopedias.
[9] *Op. cit.,* II, 102.

with the highest purpose of morality." All supernatural traits of the Bible are dismissed as matter characteristic of the times. The teachings of the Church are either neutralized or denied. Stripped of what is local or temporary there is nothing of religious truth that the reason of man cannot find out of itself. In this connection attention must be called to the typical rationalistic exegete of the New Testament, H. E. G. PAULUS, who, a nonbeliever as to miracles, worked miracles in his art of accommodating the tenets of Rationalism to the text of the New Testament reports.[10]

The position of Christ in the dogmatics of Rationalism is formulated by Roehr negatively when he says that Jesus ceases to be the "object" of religion; he is only its "subject" in the double significance of teacher and ethical example. As soon as Roehr has made this statement, however, he proceeds at once to attribute to Jesus a singular position in the history of religion: "Rationalism reveres in Jesus a man sent by God as a teacher of truth in the customary meaning of this expression. He was a man in whose life and mission [Schicksal] Providence worked itself out in a select way." [11] "Jesus was man like ourselves in the fullest and in a comprehensive meaning of that term, a natural product of his people and his age, but in regard to spirit, wisdom, virtue, and religion excelled by no mortal of the past or future, a hero of humanity in the highest sense" (p. 26). "The historical elements of his life are not without value, but they are means to make the religious teachings real, comprehensible and interesting for the most common mind" (p. 33). The Christology of Rationalism as a whole represented a radicalism far in excess of Ebionitism and Socinianism.

To the Rationalists the death of Christ was nothing but an historical event. Wegscheider suggested that, to accommodate ourselves to the ideas of the weak, we might speak of Christ's death as a symbol of the dismission of sacrifices, or as an expression of the love of God. Never should there be a suggestion of a vicarious significance, but rather should we urge the betterment of men's lives and the need of a restitution on the part of man.

The Church is only a human institution, but a distinct proof of a divine Providence, intended to make accessible for man the Master's ethical religion of reason. The sacraments of the church are, of course, nothing but symbols.

7. *Closing observations.* Rationalism, in one respect, has been fittingly judged as a reaction to the extreme intellectualism that ruled the orthodoxy of the seventeenth century as expressed in the theology of the Wittenberg theologians at the end of the syncretistic controversies. While admitting that Tholuck's judgment of these men in his book, *Der Geist der lutherischen Theologen Wittenbergs* (1852), was one-sided, it cannot be denied that the detailed doctrinal definitions, such, for instance, as were voiced by Abraham Calovius in his *Consensus Repetitus* (1664), which went far beyond the Formula of Concord, were bound to result in the reaction that was experienced in Rationalism. The emphasis shifted from the intellect to the will.[11a] Philip Schaff calls attention to the fact that Rationalism was the natural result of an age that worked to an extreme in dogmatics, polemics, and apologetics, but neglected exegesis. The theology of the seventeenth century in its constant conflict, especially with Calvinism, bled itself to death. In the end the interest subsided, and the springs for rejuvenation of dogmatic

---

10 See Kurtz, *op. cit.*, III sec. 182, 2; Meusel: *Kirchl. Handlexikon*, V, 195 f.

11 *Letters*, pp. 16, 26, 32.

11a For reading on this subject the writer refers to his book, *The Lutherans in the Movement for Church Union*, 1921, pp. 105 ff.

theology ran dry. The stagnation was seen in the inability to detect theological problems and to employ historical methods.[12]

The chief explanation of Rationalism, of course, lies in the rise of a modern philosophy which produced a great stimulation of humanistic thought. But the application of
this humanism to the field of theology, in the vulgar Rationalism of that day, was
Pelagianism of the baldest kind, without any concession to Synergism, not to mention
Augustinianism. Man is prevailingly good by nature; at any rate he possesses the moral
powers to suppress the evil and thereby to make himself pleasing to God.

The utilitarian and eudemonistic character of this new religion was very conspicuous. The interest was in individual or social well-being, losing itself thereby in the most
absurd trivialities. We are reminded of the adulteration of the hymns and of absurdities
in the pulpit. There was little interest in moral action as such; all had to be for a
practical purpose. This called forth the criticism of Kant.

In Christology this Rationalism was "Jesus-centric," but no longer "Christo-centric."
The distinction between Christ, the God-man, and Jesus, the ideal man (*Idealmensch*),
began to be discussed. Jesus was not to be taken as the object, but just as the subject,
of our faith.

The Church ceased to be a divine institution established for leading souls to salvation through the means of grace, and it was converted into an ethical-religious school
for the moral education of man.

On the final disintegration of Rationalism, R. Seeberg[12a] has this interesting remark:
"When tendencies and schools finally have achieved the much coveted dominion over
their antagonist then, as a rule, their days are numbered." This has proved to be true
in many a case. Thus it happened with the old "vulgar rationalism." A development
set in which spelled the defeat of Rationalism all along the line. Kant, himself a con-
tributor to a religion of reason with ethical interests as the sole content, showed at the
same time the impotency of reason in dealing with problems of religion which are ever
bound to occupy the interest of the religious man. Among the philosophers it was
especially Jacobi, a man claiming to be "a pagan with his head, but with his heart a
Christian," who labored to take religion out of the confines of pure reason and to discover
it in the depth of the inner soul, thus stimulating a longing that was becoming quenched
under the cold system of Rationalism. Even a man like Lessing, if we succeed in
reducing his seemingly anti-Christian language to its real purpose and intention, wanted
simply to make clear that the truth of Christianity does not depend upon external proofs,
but must rest upon inner experience. Defective or incomplete as such a position was, it
contributed to disestablishing that Rationalism of pure reason.

The brilliant church historian, K. A. von Hase, though himself fittingly styled an
"aesthetic rationalist," wrote in 1837 his articles against Roehr, and by doing this is
credited with having dealt the deathblow to vulgar rationalism.[13] When in 1826 Tholuck
changed his professorship from Berlin to Halle it was the philosopher Hegel who, in his
speech at a farewell banquet, called to Tholuck to carry to the *rationalismus vulgaris* in
Halle a *pereat*.[14] Already before this time a revived Pietism had sprung up against the

---

[12] Cf. Schaff, *op. cit.*, I, 105 ff.
[12a] *Die Kirche Deutschlands in neunzehnten Jahrhundert*, p. 15.
[13] See in the works of Hase (12 vols., Leipzig, 1890-93) his *Anti-Roehr*, VIII, sec. 1, 35-414.
[14] Seeberg, *Op. cit.*, p. 68.

religious barrenness of Rationalism, exercising a deep influence upon many, especially upon the theologians of the younger generation. Many of them identified themselves in theology with that school of mediating theologians of which we shall hear later.

And, last, but not least, it must not be thought that the old Lutheranism as a theology was dead. At first it came back in the form of a "repristination" of the theology of the seventeenth century, as Lutheran historians of our modern times have liked to call it—Claus Harms, Hengstenberg, Guericke, Rudelbach, Philippi, Vilmar, Loehe, Kliefoth, *et al.*—and it continued in a new way in the Erlangen School. At this point it is to be emphasized that the revived Lutheranism of the second third of the nineteenth century in exegesis, Biblical introduction, and dogmatics had a great deal to do with the overthrow of Rationalism.

But is it correct to speak of a real "overthrow" of Rationalism? Are not rationalistic principles in the ascendency today? In conservative quarters there are churchmen who think and act as if Rationalism is on its deathbed and all that is necessary is to wait patiently until it breathes its last. Schaff wrote thirty years ago: "Fortunately, the power of this great modern apostasy has been broken in the nineteenth century by an extensive revival of the principles of the Reformation." [15] But it is seen more and more, and especially after every new phase in the development of Protestant theology, that this attitude is too optimistic. Rationalism will always be with us as the constantly negating element (*der Geist der stets verneint*), occasionally, it is true, with a mission for a further purification of conservative theology. But never must it become a controlling factor.

The struggles of the Church against Rationalism in the past have always yielded the conviction that its program works to a large extent with utopias which, in the form here aimed at, cannot be realized. The deepest thinkers of the ages always have arrived and always will arrive at the conviction that the world of spirit can neither be penetrated nor be comprehended by the powers of human reason. And what a failure Rationalism has been in defending, through the actual facts of life, the dogma of the innate goodness of man and the claim that by ethical education and enlightenment he can be made good and happy! What a fundamental depravity of human nature we have seen, even in this modern age, in the crushing of the men of small business by the big corporations, in the rivalry between the business interests of contending nations, in the wars of our century as a result of these conflicts, in the exploiting of all the backward peoples in their natural innocence and political helplessness. What a condition of the natural man is reflected by the atrocities of the moving armies in these wars, what cruelties by the methods of colonization and by the forcing of the natives under the yoke of their oppressors. We might go on and speak of organized avariciousness in our so-called Christian countries, of the manifestations of materialism on every hand. But let us stop. History surely has rendered a spectacle of the sinfulness of man that stands in absolute contradiction to the dream of the rationalistic moralists. We are reminded of the reply that Frederick the Great gave to a rationalistic clergyman who praised the natural goodness of man: "*Er kennt die Kanaille nicht.*" This is well translated by saying: "You do not know the beast in man." Surely, Rationalism will always be a force, but it is a force of negation bound to suffer defeat in the end, no matter what its contribution to scientific theology in its various branches at times may be.

---

[15] *Op. cit.*, I, 353.

In closing, after this critical estimate of Rationalism, we should not hesitate to point out a few matters in which this movement has done a service to theology: (1) It brought into our theological studies the *criticism of the Bible texts*. The abuse of Biblical criticism by many scholars of irreverent mind cannot do away with the use of this auxiliary branch of theology which aids us in examining the Scripture foundations philologically and historically. If there is a text which should not be quoted because of absence from the best manuscripts (cf. I John 5:7-8) we want to know. And if we find that the essentials of our Christian religion have the support of uncontested Biblical texts then we make our affirmations with an added emphasis. (2) *The History of Doctrine* also was a child of Rationalism. With MUENSCHER (1797 ff.) it came in with the aim to show that dogmas had always been subject to change and therefore lack in authority.[16] But soon the Conservatives (Thomasius, R. Seeberg, Wiegand) made this branch of theology a means of illustrating how the creeds had become the depositories of doctrinal experience for the upbuilding of the Church. (3) Rationalism had also an influence upon the shaping of *Christian Symbolics*. The outspoken humanistic trait of Rationalism in its criticism of traditional orthodoxy, had made the savage method of discussing the differences between the churches of Christendom exceedingly distasteful, and so it came that the new Symbolics with J. PLANCK (1796) and soon after him the special "father of Comparative Symbolics" laid foundations for Symbolics as a *Konfessionskunde* in which all the various traits of the churches and sects received attention. It was done with the historical approach and by observing the method laid down by PHIL. MARHEINEKE that over the critical discussion there must rest "the peace of history" (*der Friede der Historie*).[17] And (4), finally, it was through Rationalism that the *Philosophy of Religion* became a part of theological studies. This can be used in such a way that it becomes a substitute for systematic theology, which should be avoided. All these four new subjects should be kept in their place of serving Christian dogmatics as auxiliaries.[18]

---

[16] Cf. Vol. I, Introductory Matters.

[17] Cf. in our *Churches and Sects of Christendom*, Introductory Matters, Sec. V.

[18] K. Girgensohn treated of them as "border-line themes" (*Grenzgebiete*) of Dogmatics. Cf. *Greifswalder Reformgedanken*, 1921. On the history and the various types and shades of Rationalism study *Rationalismus und Supranaturalismus* in *RGG*, IV, 1713-33.

Chapter Eight

THE OLD SOCINIANS OR UNITARIANS

Literature: Bibliotheca Antitrinitariorum, 1634. F. TRECHSEL, *Die protestantischen Antitrinitarier vor Faustus Socin*, 2 vols., 1844. O. FOCK, *Der Socinianismus nach seiner Stellung in der Gesamtentwicklung des christlichen Geistes, sein historischer Verlauf und sein Lehrbegriff*, 2 vols., 1847 (I, 121-263). T. GRABOWSKI, *Literature aryanska r Polce*, 1908. W. J. KUEHLER, *Het Socinianisme in Nederland*, 1912. J. C. VAN SLEE, *De Gescheidenis van het Socinianisme in der Gesamtentwicklung des christlichen Geistes, sein mistorischer Verlauf und sein Lehrbegriff*, E. M. WILBUR, *Our Unitarian Heritage*, 1925. K. VOELKER, *Kirchengeschichte Polens*, 1930, pp. 188 ff., 247 ff. A HARNACK, *DG*⁴, III, 1910, 782 ff. his *Grundriss*, 6, pp. 445-453. The article by O. ZOECKLER in the *Protest. Realencyklopaedie (PRE)*, XVIII, 459 ff. (cf. the *NSH*). J. L. NEVE, *Churches and Sects of Christendom*, 1940, chapter 12.

I. THE OLDER SOCINIANISM AND UNITARIANISM ON THE CONTINENT

A. ORIGIN AND DEVELOPMENT.

The outstanding original characteristic of the movement here to be reviewed was the opposition to the doctrine of the Trinity. In Book One, Chapter IX, we have traced the development of this dogma in the early Church and learned of groups that were opposed to the trinitarian conception of the One God: These were the Monarchians both of the dynamistic (Samosatean) and of the modalistic (Sabellian) type. Arius offered Subordinationism as a modification of the Trinitarian conception. But all the leaders of the conservative Reformation took over the doctrine of the Trinity as it had developed in the Ancient Church and has come to confessional expression in the Niceno-Constantinopolitan Creed. Against this teaching there were determined opponents right from the beginning of the Reformation.

1. The first Antitrinitarians of the Reformation time. There were Antitrinitarians among the Spiritualists of the Reformation age, such as H. Denck and S. Franck, who either ignored or denied the Trinity. To these came men like J. Campanus (d. 1575) from the Netherlands and the Italian humanist B. Ochino (d. 1575). A man who devoted himself entirely to teaching against the Trinity was the Spaniard Michael Servetus (d. 1557), who was burned at the stake under the regime of Calvin. His leading arguments were that the doctrine of the Trinity is not Biblical and that it is a negation of monotheism.

2. The man of special significance for the organization and doctrinal foundation of Antitrinitarianism was the Italian FAUSTO SOZZINI (1539-1604). He was the nephew of Lelio Sozzini (d. 1562) who had trained him early in his own antitrinitarian views and left to him his unpublished manuscripts. These are the traceable sources of the system known in history as "Socinianism." The significance of Fausto Sozzini is that he made the antitrinitarian theme a consistent part of his system of doctrine.

3. Poland, in the sixteenth century, was the country of refuge for theologians who were persecuted because of their religious views. Thus a number of Italians with antitrinitarian convictions (Blandrata, Aliciati, Gentilis, Ochino, Lismanini) had been admitted. The Inquisition had driven them from their home country, and, failing to find a place of safety in the congregation of refugees in Geneva at the time of Calvin, they came to Poland. Favored by the nobility, they succeeded in disseminating their views especially those regarding the Trinity. The presence, however, of "Spiritualists" of the Anabaptist type with their views on Socinian reform, coupled with the whole political situation, caused the government to refuse these foreign agitators a further abode (1564) Their teachings, however, had already been creative of a considerable company of believers in Antitrinitarianism and ideas related thereto. But the group was soon split up into factions. There were conservatives who insisted upon the pre-existence of Christ, and these would naturally advocate the worshiping of Jesus. And then there were radicals who refused all adoration of Jesus, basing their position upon the conviction of His absolute and exclusive humanity. There were also Chiliasts who expected the millennium. The question whether Christians should accept office in the state and be allowed to bear arms was debated. And there was confusion over infant baptism. These last mentioned topics indicate the Anabaptist influence. It was in this situation (1579) that Fausto Sozzini appeared in Poland, coming from Transylvania (*Siebenbuergen*) where he had been called by G. Blandatra in the "Davidis conflict" (see below, sub 5). Sozzini gradually succeeded in eliminating from this disunited group in Poland "the extremes to the right and to the left," as the Unitarian reporter puts it. He opposed the pre-existence of Jesus, but taught against Davidis that He must be the object of worship. Other differences were settled by diplomatic accommodation to existing conditions.

4. The most significant event in this period of organization in Poland was the publication of the *Racovian Catechism* in its final form. It appeared in 1605, the year after the death of Sozzini.[1] This is the historical confessional document of the old Socinians. The preparatory and fundamental work had been done by Sozzini, but it was finished by theologians who were in harmony with him.[2] The introduction states that there is no intention to bind the conscience through confessional obligation; the aim is merely to present doctrinal opinions as aids for finding the way to eternal life, which is shown by God through Christ. The Catechism then discusses the Holy Scriptures, the way of salvation, the conception of God, the person of Christ in His three offices, and the Church.

5. Before proceeding to a review of the *doctrinal characteristics of Socinianism* there must be brief mention of the developments in *Transylvania* which, besides Poland, was really the first seat of historical Socinianism. It was from here that Fausto Sozzini went to Poland. In passing only we may be reminded that Transylvania was exposed to invasion from Turkey which in that day was justifying its plans for conquering the Western countries by pointing to the "polytheism" declared to be hidden in the trinitarian dogma of Western Christianity. It tended indeed to incline the governments which were exposed to the danger of Moslem invasion to favor the unitarian conception of the Deity.

The government had established the policy of tolerance for all doctrinal beliefs (1568). Encouraged by this decree the opponents of Trinitarianism, in 1600, were recognized as "*Unitarians.*" This name was accepted later. Almost all had come from

---

[1] Racov was the intellectual center of Socinianism in Poland. The Racovian Catechism and the writings of Sozzini are published in Vols. I and II of the *Bibliotheca Fratrum Polonorum*, 1656 ff.

[2] The publication of 1605 was in Polish, followed by a German edition in 1608, a Latin in 1609 (dedicated to King James I of England). A new edition with additions appeared in 1665, and an English translation followed soon after.

he Reformed Church. Their intellectual center was and continued to be the school at
Klausenburg. G. Blandatra was here the outstanding leader. But he was opposed very
persistently by F. Davidis, Director at Klausenburg, a former Lutheran, who rejected
not only the pre-existence of Jesus but insisted, logically, that He must not be addressed
in prayer. This was the "non-adorant" faction among the early Unitarians. Sozzini and
Blandrata were united in declaiming the pre-existence of Jesus, but they rejected,
illogically, the non-adorant position of Davidis and his group. It is interesting to note
that a Unitarian hymnbook in Hungary, published in 1865, omitted this adoration of
Jesus. The peculiar Christology of the Socinians must be considered in order to understand this old "Davidis" conflict. (See below, B, 5.)

Note: The cultivation of real scholarship in the schools of both Poland and Transylvania at
those seats of learning deserves to be mentioned. With the return of Roman Catholicism all this
was destroyed.[3]

B. CHARACTERIZATION OF THE OLD SOCINIANISM.

It must not be overlooked that the founders of Socinianism developed in opposition
to the Roman Catholic Church. Philosophically their type must be traced back to the
negative-rationalistic criticism of Duns Scotus and of humanism with which they were
in contact through Erasmus. In addition to this they had felt the impulses from the
Reformation. In consequence, they represented a peculiar combination of supernaturalism and humanistic rationalism. With the recognition of revelation, there is in the
background of their system a complex of ideas and views which are foreign to historic
Christianity. In the further evolution of Socinianism these ideas and views were bound
to assert themselves as this is seen in later Unitarianism and in the forms of Modernism
of today. A brief characterization of these old Socinians, doctrinally, must here be given:

1. *Revelation and Scripture.* The founders of Socinianism and their followers up
to about the middle of the seventeenth century were strict Biblicists and supernaturalists.
In this Biblicism, the Old Testament is treated with indifference, and the New Testament is taken as the only source of revelation: There is nothing of value in the Old
Testament that is not better and more clearly taught in the New Testament. The idea of
inspiration has reference only to the matters of special religious truth in Scripture. The
Socinians subjected revelation to a rational qualification: The New Testament may
contain something above reason, but it does not express anything against reason. Reasonableness, then, is a special criterion of truth in Scripture.

2. *The Socinian conception of religion* may be summarized in the following brief
statement to which we shall add a few critical observations as we go along: (1) Christians and Jews only can have religion because here only is revelation. This position
shows that the Socinians had not yet arrived at the teaching of the English Deists, namely
that general natural religion is fundamental and essential religion. (2) Religion consists in the knowledge of saving doctrine. The "Church" to the Socinians was "the
gathering of those people who hold and profess the *doctrinam salutarem.*" The element
of truth in this isolated statement betrays the intellectualism of the scholastic age.
Harnack, in a fitting remark, characterized these Socinians as a "theological academy." [4]
(3) Only what is provable by reason could be Christian truth. This "material prin-

[3] See *PRE*, XVIII, 463-496; cf. the*NSH.*
[4] *DG*[4], III, 783 ff.

ciple" of Socinianism, in which Kant was anticipated, in his essay *Religion within the Bounds of Reason,* led the Socinians to eliminate from the interest of religion such things as incarnation, Trinity, the two natures in Christ. (4) Only what can be used for moral purposes is religion. In the stress upon this position, Socinianism presents itself as a movement in which Rationalism and moralism entered into a very close and effective relation.

3. *In the doctrine of God,* Socinianism was especially interested in the attribute of unity. The *Racovian Catechism,* in its very title, calls itself "the catechism of the churches which affirm that no one except the Father of our Lord Jesus Christ be the one God of Israel." The knowledge of God's unity is necessary for salvation (*Catechism,* question 66). The Holy Spirit is nothing but God's power and influence. Where Scripture speaks of Jesus as God it is simply a recognition of His singular relation to God. The Scripture proof on the whole subject shows superficial exegesis, and it is unhistorical. The argumentation as a whole lacks in considering the question which in the conservative-progressive theology of today means so much, namely whether the dogma of the Trinity is not an expression of Christian experience and a demand of Christian piety.[5]

4. *Man,* created after God's image, was endowed with spirit and reason (*mens et ratio*). It was this distinction that gave him dominion over the rest of creation. He was created in the condition of physical mortality. The Fall is explained as follows: There was in the original man no such wisdom and knowledge as was taught by conservative theology. His knowledge was imperfect and his will untried. So it came that concupiscence which was stimulated by the divine commandment overpowered him. We hear of no temptation from the outside, which invites the charge that the Creator was the cause of sin.[6] Through the Fall neither Adam nor his descendants lost their freedom to choose between good and evil. The Augustinian distinction of the conservative Reformation between civil righteousness and spiritual righteousness (i.e., the purely moral and the religious righteousness) is not made.[7] The insistence upon absolute freedom, Socinians taught, is a truth by which the admission of an "original sin" or an acquired depravity is to be tested: The admonition of Scripture to repentance and conversion is pointed to as evidence that man can do so if he wills. The work of the Holy Spirit as a creative divine act of grace in conversion is not needed. Such was the teaching of Pelagius before Socinianism and of Kant later when he declared: "Thou canst because thou must." The Socinians would say: There may be such a thing as a concupiscence and an inclination to sin, but it cannot be proved that such a condition is universal. If this could be proved, it would still be no evidence of the Adamic origin of this condition. And even if such an origin could be proved, that would in itself be a negation of an original sin, because there can be no sin where there is no guilt. Thus went the reasoning argumentation of Socinianism on this subject. Many and great problems that have engaged the deepest and most devout thinkers of the ages in theology, philosophy, and literature are here brushed aside in favor of a position that has never been able to do justice to the real religious principle. Harnack, in a brilliant comparative

---

[5] See in our Vol. One, Bk. I, chap. 9, our discussion of the Trinity.

[6] See the writer's interpretation of Article XIX of the *Augsburg Confession* in his *Introduction to the Symbolical Books²,* pp. 292-301.

[7] Compare Article XVIII of the *Augsburg Confession* and Article II of the *Formula of Concord.* See *Churches and Sects of Christendom,* pp. 193 f.

review of the differences between the Anabaptist and the Socinian groups of the Reformation time, drops a characteristic remark concerning the Socinians: "The religious motive in the deepest sense is absent in these Italians." [8] Sin as a condition in man, irrespective of any special sinful act, the solidarity of our race coupled with the conviction of responsibility of the group for the individual and of the individual for the group, the whole matter of sin and grace as expressed in the language of piety in prayer, liturgy, and song through the ages—out of all this there rings a testimony regarding sin as a natural depravity, involving a responsibility that cannot be ignored and a divine grace needed to meet this condition.

5. On *the Person of Christ* the Socinians naturally have a special delivery. Their antitrinitarian principle made them opposed to belief in the pre-existence of Jesus, and to the doctrine of His incarnation and divinity. The divinity of Christ is the root of the doctrine of the Trinity. But was Jesus more than man? The answer of the Socinians was that Jesus was "more than just man, a man of extraordinary qualities, endowed with wisdom without measure, elevated by God to unlimited power and given immortality." For the explanation of this exceptional position of Jesus the Socinians taught a miraculous elevation into heaven (*raptus in coelum*) where God Himself had instructed Him in the truths of Christianity.[9] Still He was essentially man, not partaker in the divinity.[10] The proof is developed in this way: The object of Christianity is to communicate immortality, which Christ can give because, being man exclusively, He could die and be raised and be the mediator of immortality. This insistence upon Christ's humanity was the outstanding point in the Socinian polemics against conservative Protestantism. Against Trinitarianism the Socinians stood for "the one God and the created Christ." What Christ was beyond His mere humanity was not something divine that belonged to His essence, to His nature, but it was that above-mentioned endowment of wisdom, power, and immortality. To this the old Socinians added His virgin birth and His holiness. But He was not pre-existent, not the Logos Incarnate. Neither was He really the Son of God, μονογενής, otherwise God would be Son to Himself, but He is called Son of God, because among all the sons of God He is πρωτότοκος the most excellent and most beloved.[11] On this ground especially, because of His divine power[12] the duty to worship Him was taught—against that "non-adorant" faction (Davidis) of which we spoke in our introduction.[13]

6. *The conception of the Atonement* as the rendering of a satisfaction to God by Jesus through His suffering and death was another point of criticism and rejection of the traditional teaching by the Socinians. They stressed the death of Christ as a necessity because it is through His resurrection that the redemption takes place. His death was simply the seal upon His teaching. Among the objections of Socinianism to a vicarious atonement were these: (1) A "wrath of God" from which mankind is to be delivered would be irreconcilable with the fact of His goodness. Our reply is that Scrip-

---

[8] *Grundriss*⁶, p. 447.

[9] See *Cat. Racov.* que. 194; cf. Sozzini's *Institutio*, p. 675.

[10] *Cat.*, que. 100.

[11] *Ibid.*, que. 166. Cf. the article of Zoeckler in the *PRE*, XVIII, 474 f., who refers to the instances of Scripture perversion on this subject.

[12] *Cat.*, que. 120.

[13] Note the argumentation on this subject by the old Socinians, see *Cat.*, que. 239 ff.; 245 ff. Cf. the disputations of Sozzini against his opponents in the *Bibliotheca Fratrum Polonorum*, Vol. II.

ture speaks of such wrath even in the New Testament (cf. John 3:26; Eph. 2:3). It does not mean vindictiveness but simply the reaction of the divine righteousness against sin. The Holy One cannot be indifferent to sin. And His moral government cannot be ignored. But it is God's own Son who pays the price of redemption. (2) It is objected that even man without satisfaction can forgive a wrong that has been suffered—why not God? Vilmar replies: Man, because he is not holy, like God, not only can forgive, but, as a sinner himself, he must forgive even without condition. (3) The main objection of Socinianism was that moral guilt is not transferable and that a satisfaction can be given only by the offender himself. Answer: But the *penalty* of sin may be transferred, and this penalty Christ suffered as God-man and federal head of the human race. Here all human analogies fail. To the replies which have been given concerning the position of the old Socinians we add this remark: There are certain mysterious truths which cannot and need not be proven by cold arguments. We all feel that death lies in sin (Rom. 6:23). If we could die not only the physical but also the eternal death of absolute separation from God and still live—which would be a contradiction in itself—then we could save ourselves. But we cannot, and therefore we need Christ as Saviour. He, the God-man, was the only one who could die and still conquer death. It is in this consideration that we behold the mysterious philosophy of redemption. He who objects to this cannot be helped by rationalizing arguments; a capacity for the spiritual and for that which is truly religious is needed.[14]

7. *The Socinian soteriology* was essentially Pelagian: The Fall had left no effects of depravity upon mind and will. Now man learns of God's commandments and promises. He can accept the truth, exercise confidence and obey the divine commandment in his own natural powers.[15] It is in the actual obedience to the commandments that the Socinians saw the real saving faith. Justification, to them, was not a divine act in the declaration of grace and forgiveness, but an act of faith, evidencing itself in obedience to the divine will and in trusting the promise of eternal life. Good works, in earnest striving—though they may be imperfect—are the real justifying factor. Justification never consists in an imputation of Christ's righteousness. This they called a human invention.[16] In the soteriology of the conservative churches there is on this subject a different ring. Art. IV of the *Augsburg Confession* has these words: "Also they teach that men cannot be justified before God by their own strength, merits or works, but are freely justified for Christ's sake, through faith, when they believe that they are received into favor and that their sins are forgiven for Christ's sake, who, by His death, hath made satisfaction for our sins. This faith God imputes for righteousness in His sight. Romans 3 and 4."

In viewing the Socinian system on this point, however, we must not overlook the moral earnestness at the basis of those statements. But the cleavage from the soteriology of the Reformation is fundamental. It affects the heart of the Gospel.

8. *The sacraments* meant very little to the Socinians. They are not essentially means of grace. Baptism was held to have been meant only for the early times of

---

[14] Besides the pertinent questions in the *Racovian Catechism*, see F. Sozzini, *De Jesu Christo Savatore*. On this whole subject we refer the reader to our *Churches and Sects*, pp. 561, 608 f.

[15] With this compare Luther in his interpretation of Article III of the Apostles' Creed: "I believe that I cannot by my own reason or strength believe in Jesus Christ my Lord, or come to Him, but the Holy Ghost has called me by the Gospel, enlightened me with His gifts, and sanctified and preserved me in the true faith."

[16] Cf. *PRE*, XVIII, 478, with reference to *Cat.*, que. 416-421.

Christianity to introduce the converts from Judaism and paganism with a public profession into Christianity. Still it may be practiced as an old tradition even in the baptism of children, although there is no sense in it. The Lord's Supper is just a memorial of Christ's death. The Socinians therefore objected very consistently to the name "sacrament" for these are mere "rites" or "ceremonies" as they preferred to call them.[17]

9. *The eternal punishment* for the unbelievers and godless was taken to be annihilation. The differing language of Jesus on this subject was explained by accommodation to conceptions of the time. The believing Christians, though not born with immortality of their soul, have become immortal through union with the risen Christ. We did see what stress the old Socinians laid upon Christ's resurrection.

10. There are several points in which *the old Socinians had something in common with the sections of the Anabaptist group.* (1) Discipline was strict.[18] They followed the Augustinian principle that the handling of Church discipline may be private where the sin did not become public but must be public where offense was given. In the latter case there was, as a milder form, the social avoidance, upon which followed the formal excommunication. (2) Although very insistent upon refusing the state to interfere in matters of church discipline the Socinians were loyal to the government under all circumstances. (3) There was discouragement from seeking redress of private grievance by appealing to the civil law; also from using weapons, although there was an open mind for modification in these things. But their general attitude forced them to consider the question of whether it was allowed to accept public offices, a very practical question which threatened their organization with schism.

II. UNITARIANISM IN ENGLAND AND AMERICA

Literature: O. FOCK, *op. cit.,* I, 263 ff. J. MARTINEAU, *Unitarian Christianity,* 1881. J. H. ALLEN, *Unitarians in the United States,* 1894 (American Church History Series). J. W. CHADWICK, *Old and New Unitarian Belief,* 1894. J. E. MANNING, *The Religion and Theology of Unitarians,* 1906. E. EMERTON, *Unitarian Thought,* 1911. E. M. WILBUR, *Our Unitarian Heritage,* 1925. *PRE,* XX, 261 ff.; (cf. *NSH*). *Enc. Brit.,* XXVII, 594. *RGG,* V, 1375. Our *Churches and Sects,* etc.

In this closing part of our review the account must be brief, because soon after the influence of Unitarianism had begun to be felt it became blended more or less with the general rise of liberalism in England before and after Coleridge, and in New England in connection with the new theology which developed against strict Calvinism.[19]

1. The earliest Unitarians in England. A Latin copy of the *Racovian Catechism* had been sent to James I. By a resolution of 1614 it was publicly burned. It was, however, not until 1860 that the Socinians of the Continent came into formal and immediate negotiations with the Unitarians of England and America. The first organization of a Unitarian congregation in England (London) took place in 1774 through THEOPHILUS LINDSEY (d. 1808), who resigned his position in the state church after his unsuccessful efforts for removal of confessional obligation to the *Thirty-Nine Articles.* But long before this event there had been liberalistic influences in England preparing the

---

[17] *Cat.,* que. 334-338; cf. 346.
[18] *Cat.,* que. 509-521.
[19] As to this development see below in Book V, Section B, on England, and Section C on America. Cf. our *Churches and Sects of Christendom,* pp. 546-564.

soil. Among these we mention Arminianism and the "Rational Theology" as movements which issued into Latitudinarianism and especially English Deism. Another leader of the earlier English Unitarians was JOHN BIDDLE who had to suffer persecution. His point of emphasis was the dignity of reason in the interpretation of Scripture. JOSEPH PRIESTLEY was the influential representative of Unitarianism in another part of England (Birmingham). Their work was continued by THOMAS BELSHAM (d. 1829), LANT CARPENTER (d. 1840), and others. The years 1813, 1825, and 1844 finally brought full freedom of conscience and civil rights regarding property also for the Unitarians. In the meantime Unitarianism in England and America had developed into doctrinal positions which in many respects were quite different from those of the old Socinians. On this see CHADWICK, as referred to. The name "Arians" had come into use to describe them in their Christology—not without fitness if we keep in mind that it was generally still their position that Christ was more than just man. It reminds one of that Arian watchword of the old Socinians "the One God and the Created Christ." [20]

2. *The later Unitarianism.* It is here especially where we must guard against anticipating the developments that must be pictured in Book V, Sections B and C. Read in our *Churches and Sects of Christendom* chapter 12. For indicating the points in the development, the following may be added:

America in the first third of the nineteenth century became the scene of interesting events. Priestley had emigrated to America to the neighborhood of Boston, where he spent the last ten years of his life (d. 1804) devoting himself to a literary activity in which he rounded out 141 titles that have been published on both sides of the Atlantic.[21] In his writings he had recognized the supernatural element to an extent that, although with modifications, he was still a representative of the old historic Socinianism. But from now on through W. E. CHANNING, THEODORE PARKER, RALPH WALDO EMERSON and many others the whole development of Unitarianism shows a different complexion. This story is told in this volume, Book V, C.

In England the same new school of Unitarianism is represented in JAMES MARTINEAU, in the Hibbert Lectures and in the contacts with Otto Pfleiderer of the Berlin University.

The influences from the old Socinianism were noticeable in the Arminianism of Holland and of England. They have been very clearly observable in German Rationalism and in the succeeding forms of this movement (*Neuprotestantismus*). Thus the remark of E. Troeltsch is correct: "In stripping itself of the positivistic supernaturalism, Socinianism passed easily over into the rationalistic types of the modern enlightenment." [22]

---

[20] See Fisher, *op. cit.*, in England, 370 ff.; in New England, 417 ff.

[21] Among the last was *Jesus and Socrates Compared*, 1804; a commentary on all the books of Scripture in 4 vols., 1802-04. Among his larger works of previous years was a *History of the Corruptions of Christianity*, 2 vols., 1782 and 1793, with a German translation. It is interesting that Priestley became the discoverer of oxygen, just as another Antitrinitarian (Servetus) discovered the double circulation of the blood.

[22] *Protest. Christentum und Kirche in der Neuzeit (Kultur der Gegenwart, I, 4), 1906, p. 275.*

BOOK FIVE

New Attitudes to Religion and Christianity

In our studies so far we have observed new attitudes to the historic faith of Christendom. In tracing them historically we must distinguish between two lines of development. We may call the one the naturalistic and the other the idealistic. The origin of the naturalistic orientation is observed in the empiricism of English philosophy, while the idealistic line had its chief representatives in Germany. But soon there was a lively exchange of thought between the different countries. In the eighteenth century the Deists of England and the Naturalists of France were in a vivid contact with each other; and beginning with Coleridge, the idealistic philosophy of Germany came into vital touch with thought in England.

1) *The Naturalistic Line.* The English philosophy of hard facts as taught by John Locke in his *Essay Concerning Human Understanding* was stimulated by the new knowledge of nature (Copernicus, Kepler, Galileo, Newton). But the real triumphs of the natural sciences came in the nineteenth century. And by this time the inclination to conceive of religion naturalistically had become very general among the educated of the different countries. Elements of truth, now entirely recognized by conservative theology, were mixed with frivolous radicalism.

By an experimental study of nature, most marvelous successes were achieved. The laws underlying electricity in its relation to light and heat were discovered (Faraday, Maxwell, Foucault) and traced to the waves of ether as their common cause (Huyghens, Fresnel, Young, and later Hertz). Frauenhofer, Kirchoff and Bunsen developed the spectral analysis, and by using this discovery in the examination even of the bodies of the firmament (astrophysics) the conviction of the essential unity of all phenomena was strengthened. By the gradually enlarging insight into these things, the speculative expression of principles had been superseded by observational methods, disassociating, for instance, astronomy from the superstitions of the astrologers and their successors. In chemistry the theory of atoms had been proposed (Dalton), and their essential unity, in spite of variation, was explained by certain observable laws. The problems and mysteries of life were studied with continued persistency. The anatomy of plants and animals (Schleiden and Schwann) led to the discovery of cells as the fundamental unit of all organic life and to the observation that all these cells depend for their life upon the same fundamental substances, namely carbonic acids, ammonia and water (Liebig). This seemed to be another large contribution to the growing belief that all things existing constitute one great unit which in all its life and motion is governed by a chain of cause and effects. The microscope exposed the germs to the searching eye of the bacteriologist and led to victory after victory in the campaign against epidemics that had been looked upon as visitations of supernatural powers. Then came Darwin (d. 1882), supported along a certain line by Lamarck, who proposed the theory that the variety of species is to be explained mechanistically by an evolutionary process governing the propagation of organic life in all its forms, man himself being no exception. History was regarded as a struggle for existence in which the stronger ("superman") strives for advantage over the weaker. To some thinkers it appeared as if in the universe there was no longer any room for a transcendent God.[1]

In Germany a situation was created in which the great systems of idealism, that had inspired scholars (Kant, Hegel, Schelling), lost all credit. The names of Strauss and Feuerbach spelled the bankruptcy of a theology that had dreamed of finally having found the formula for the unity of faith and knowledge (Marheineke, Biedermann). The public turned away from philosophy and religion, from metaphysics and theology: the interest was in the "exact sciences." The idea of evolution, which Hegel had used for the construction of his idealistic philosophy, was now taken up by the natural sciences, after the prescription of Darwin, mechanistically for the formation of a monistic world-view (Haeckel). Strauss, toward the close of his life, turned to materialism. Feuerbach did the same. Vogt, Moleschott, Buechner, with Haeckel, popularized their materialism for the masses.[2]

In England there had been considerable reticence in applying the principles of Darwinism to a world-philosophy. Darwin himself had not gone further than to make the application to biology, and to history only in a very limited way. Then came Herbert Spencer, who applied evolution to all branches of science, including psychology, sociology and even ethics in a mechanistic-naturalistic conception. The idea of evolution became the controlling viewpoint for seeing historically the unity of the world. He was followed by commanding psychologists of the naturalistic and materialistic trend. To these ethics, so called, there was nothing but the fitting of an individual for life and society.

Many among the Conservatives have an open mind for the problem of development in history as long as this idea does not present itself as a theory for eliminating God, transcendent as well as immanent, from the universe.

Blended with this "naturalism" there is in theological Liberalism also,

2) *The Idealistic line of development.* Along this line the influences received have been especially strong. For a proper estimate of these we must try to give a review of theological Liberalism in Germany.

We called the empiristic philosophy of England a "philosophy of hard facts." The philosophy of the Continent from Descartes to the present has been pre-eminently a philosophy of idealism. England had the classical period of its literature at an early time when crude conceptions of religion were still dominating the minds of the common people and of most of the educated, as well.[3] In Germany, the classical period of literature came at a time when the seventeenth century theology of the old faith was losing its hold upon the intellectual representatives of a new age, when the spirit of "vulgar" rationalism had been sweeping the Church, when the writings of Kant and the men of a new classicism were read, when Schleiermacher and a left wing of his school were trying to reconstruct theology upon the basis of a new orientation of religion. There is a sense in which it may be said with Dilthey that, in reverse, this

---

[1] Compare with this brief review the fascinating description of the whole situation by W. Elert, *Der Kampf um das Christentum*, pp. 188-195.

[2] See the close of our chapter on German Idealism, p. 102.

[3] The sentiments of Deism and free thought were confined to certain circles in the higher strata of society.

movement connects philosophically and theologically with the Renaissance and with humanism, and still further back with ancient classicism (*die "Antike"*). We may call this new Protestantism a special opposition to the religion of the Reformation of the sixteenth century. At first, the representatives of this movement were not entirely conscious of breaking with the principles of the Reformers. Kant, Lessing, Schiller, Goethe thought that a proper interpretation would put Luther on their side. In this they were greatly mistaken. Their aim, then, became more and more a conscious endeavor to bring about a "new Reformation." German *"Neuprotestantismus"* is marked along the whole line of its development by contributory thoughts of Kant, Hegel, Schleiermacher, Strauss, Baur, the school of Ritschl, Rothe, the Historico-Religious School, Pfleiderer, Dilthey, de Lagarde, Troeltsch and many others.[4]

---

[4] Cf. our article on "Modernism in the History of Protestant Theology," *American Lutheran Survey*, April, 1927.

SECTION ONE

Continental Theological Thought with Special Emphasis on German Theology After 1800

Literature: For general literature of this period we mention the following books: F. LICHTEN-BERGER, *History of German Theology in the Nineteenth Century* (translated into English from the French by L. Hastie 1889); OTTO PFLEIDERER, *The Development of Theology in Germany since Kant and its Progress in Great Britain since 1825* (German edition 1891, English by F. F. Smith, third edition 1909); REINHOLD FRANK, *Geschichte und Kritik der neueren Theologie,* 4th edition 1908; REINHOLD SEEBERG, *Die Kirche Deutschlands im neunzehnten Jahrhundert,* 4th edition 1903; E. C. MOORE, *History of Christian Thought since Kant,* 1912; WERNER ELERT, *Der Kampf um das Christentum seit Schleiermacher und Hegel,* 1921; WILHELM LUETGERT, *Die Religion des deutschen Idealismus und ihr Ende,* 4 vols. and a supplement volume, 1923 ff.; FERDINAND KATTENBUSCH, *Die deutsche evangelische Theologie seit Schleiermacher,* 5th edition 1926; R. H. GRUETZMACHER, *"Alt-und Neuprotestantismus"* in *Neue Kirchliche Zeitschrift* 1915-1918; in part reprinted in book form under the same title, 1920; HUGH ROSS MACKINTOSH, *Types of Modern Theology, Schleiermacher to Barth,* 1937. Special acknowledgment is hereby expressed to the Eden Publishing Company, St. Louis, Missouri, for a series of articles by Gruetz-macher in *Theological Magazine,* 1928; which with the permission of this house, in some sections, have been freely used. For the later phases of the period here discussed we mention *Die Religions-wissenschaft der Gegenwart in Selbstdartellungen,* edited by ERICH STANGE, 5 vols, 1925 ff

Chapter One

IMMANUEL KANT: HIS IDEAS ON RELIGION

Literature: J. L. NEVE, "German Rationalism at its First Appearance" (in the *Biblical Review,* New York, April, 1931). This article with some changes constitutes Chap. 7, Book IV, of the present work. G. C. B. PUENJER, *Religionslehre Kants.* See the article *"Aufklaerung"* by E. TROELTSCH in *PRE,* II, 224 ff.; cf. the article *"Neunzehntes Jahrhundert"* in the *PRE* by the same author (XXIV, pp. 244-260). Cf. also the article *"Rationalismus und Aufklaerung"* by O. KIRN in *PRE,* XVI, 447 ff.; see the same article in the *NSH,* IX, 393 ff. On all subjects and individuals here under discussion the most up-to-date information will be found in the articles in *Religion in Geschichte und Gegenwart.*

German theology, during the nineteenth century, has developed under stimulations from three great thinkers: KANT (d. 1804), HEGEL (d. 1831) and SCHLEIERMACHER (d. 1834). Of these, Schleiermacher, the philosophically schooled theologian, has constantly attracted all the different schools of Christian thought to his right and to his left, not merely by the example of a new method, but also by certain points of emphasis in his system, through which he challenged the theologians to take certain attitudes. But the philosophers Kant and Hegel have attracted the theologians and will continue to attract them through fundamentally conflicting philosophical principles: either to a theology of the will and of action (Kant), or to a theology of unity of thinking and being through development (Hegel).

Although Kant did not do justice to religious faith by his reduction of religion to a mere appendage to ethics he must be considered as the first great philosopher to work

92

out, as the basis of religion, a metaphysics, a point of view, which is very influential today.[1]

For the purpose of our work as a history of Christian thought we shall here limit ourselves to a review of the religious ideas of Kant, and we shall not discuss his great merits as a philosopher in other fields.

In spite of Kant's violent reaction against the rationalism of Leibnitz and Wolff, and notwithstanding his discrediting of "pure reason" in arriving at philosophical knowledge concerning God, incarnation, Trinity and things supernatural, nevertheless, in common with philosophers of his age he enthroned reason as the criterion of religion. The points here to be discussed do not include his significance for the religion of German idealism; on this the reader will find comprehensive statements in the following Chapter Two.

1. *The supreme position of reason in the teaching of Kant, then, must be noted.* His criticism was not of the possibility of knowledge, as with David Hume, but on the methods of acquiring knowledge. But the critical methods which he proposed for philosophical knowledge he also applied to knowledge in the field of theology. Later he wrote that famous essay "Religion Within the Bounds of Reason" (*Religion innerhalb der Grenzen der blossen Vernunft*, 1793), which came to be recognized in matters of religion and theology as a guide for wide circles in Germany, even after the old vulgar rationalism began to become unpopular. He held, however, that the ideas of God, of "the radical evil" (*das radikale Boese*) and of immortality are necessary presuppositions to a theological system. But a theological structure on such foundations was erected solely with the aid of reason. This principle of logical reason as a function within man was to Kant the guide to his religious philosophy, the source for his thinking of God, of law and of conscience. Kant, from his rationalistic standpoint, was decidedly at variance with the principle so much stressed by the Reformation—that man's reason, unenlightened by the Spirit of God through revelation, is bound to miss the truth when dealing with the spiritual things. (I Cor. 2:14.)

2. To Kant, *the significance of Christianity does not lie in the teaching of metaphysical doctrines, but in its moral precepts.* In his arguments against an *a priori* reasoning regarding matters of metaphysics,[2] he dwelt upon the provability of a divine Being. While rejecting the traditional speculative arguments for God, Kant, in keeping with the general theological trend of thinking, assumes a friendly attitude toward the argument from *design*. Moreover, in his Inaugural Dissertation he clearly anticipates the epistemological argument for theism, later developed by Ulrici and Lotze. It was especially the ontological proof which he rejected: God, as the thing in itself (*Ding an sich*), cannot be reached by logical processes. His philosophy was one of criticism. So much of a concession he made to David Hume's philosophy of skepticism.[3] He did not deny the world of actual phenomena about us. But he turned the interest in another direction, namely to the ethical, by stressing our duty to listen to the voice of conscience. And it was on this road that he, in his *Critique of Practical Reason* (1788), arrived at an indirect proof of the existence of God: Observing that virtue does not find its reward in this world, therefore there must be a highest Being who will guarantee final reward

---

[1] Cf. W. R. Sorley, *Moral Values and the Idea of God*, 4th edition, 1930.
[2] Cf. his *Critique of Pure Reason*, 1781, 2nd. ed., 1787.
[3] Cf. above, Book IV, Chap. V, pp. 50-66.

in a life to come. So it happened that here also Kant found himself established upon the Rationalism of his day with its stress upon the moral precepts, man's duty and the certainty of reward by a just and almighty God.

3. Kant's stress upon freedom of the will was his highest interest in the teaching of religion. This freedom he based upon the conscience which voices a double proof of our freedom. The first is our consciousness of *guilt* which could not be if we did not have to reproach ourselves for a neglect of our duty. The second proof of our freedom he sees in our consciousness of *duty*: We must obey the conscience, and because we must, *therefore we can (Du sollst, also du kannst)*. In other words, we are free. The old question of Pelagius is repeated: Would parents make a demand upon their children if fulfillment were impossible? In this Pelagian and rationalistic assertion of a native freedom of the will in man lies the unbridgeable chasm between the ethics of Kant and that of the Reformation. Luther and Calvin taught with Paul a pedagogical significance of the law which leads man to see himself as in need of grace and of strength to do the will of God. *Is there a way of strengthening and supporting Kant's "categorical imperative"?* To this question Christian theology of the truly evangelical type has an answer that is out of an experience as old as revelation of Scripture and which was reaffirmed by the testimony of the Reformation in the Confessions of Protestantism. The answer is: Not the fear of God alone, as a servant's fear and originated by the statute of law, but faith in the forgiveness of sin through Christ, which begets love and a son's fear of God, which is born not out of the law but out of the Gospel, is the basis for good works. It is called a "new obedience." This is the needed support of that "categorical imperative." Read Article XV of the *Augsburg Confession* on "Faith and Good Works," and compare the thoroughgoing commentary in Melanchthon's *Apology* on "Love and Fulfilling of the Law," also Articles IV and VI in the *Formula of Concord.* Note especially the wealth of Scripture passages there referred to. The Confessions of all the conservative churches have the same teaching on this subject. Christian theology must always distinguish between religion and mere moralism.

In the case of three points which have been discussed so far Kant has spoken with a special interest in matters of religion and as a teacher of religion. Below (*sub 5*) we shall again follow him in this line of interest. But here is the place for interpolating a consideration in which he speaks as a general educator in matters of outward righteousness (*in rebus externis*): [4]

4. Kant, as a philosopher and not as a Christian theologian and preacher, in the consciousness of functioning as a public educator, had an interest in separating ethics from religion and putting ethics upon its own feet. Religion is accepted by some and rejected by many. The forms of religion differ. The French Naturalists, following Hume, were skeptics. They lost themselves in frivolity. Their philosophy became mechanistic and materialistic, tending to the ignoring of the moral foundations of society. The same danger was threatening Germany, as can be seen in the poets of the "storm and stress" period.[5] The need was felt to establish a state ethics which would be independent of the varying developments in religion and theology. This was Kant's concern, and in it he

---

[4] On the distinction between "spiritual" and "outward" righteousness it must be kept in mind that the latter is always included in the former, but the former is not also necessarily involved in the latter. See the writer's interpretation of Article XVIII of the *Augsburg Confession* on "Free Will" in his *Introduction to the Symbolical Books of the Lutheran Church*, 2nd. edition, 1926.

[5] As to the condition of morals in Germany at that time, see Luetgert, I, *op. cit.*, 247-272.

cted in harmony with the alarmed Prussian government. It was a development, let us remember, which had taken place in other countries long before. In England it was Thomas Hobbes (d. 1697) who laid foundations for a state ethics on the basis of a psychology which he took out of the hands of the Church. And before him, Hugo Grotius (d. 1645) in Holland had laid down similar principles. Such an ethics, naturally, had to confine itself to what the Reformation understood by "civil righteousness" (justitia civilis); it could not cover "spiritual righteousness." [6] This Melanchthonian distinction of conservative Protestantism lay outside of Kant's interest; ethics, to him, simply was moral precept dictated by the voice of conscience. But according to the teaching of Christian ethics, this voice is not always reliable. The guide of Scripture revelation is needed. Philip II of Spain, on his deathbed, lay praying for forgiveness because he had not killed more Protestants. The conscience can be manipulated and become misguided and perverted. Luther spoke of a "self-chosen sanctity," and the *Augsburg Confession* declares in Article VI that the "necessary good works" are those commanded by God" (*mandata a Deo*). The Church has interests beyond those of rational philosophy. Kant's special interest was in the duties of citizenship, such things as loyalty to the God-appointed superiors in government, army, school and family, the sense of duty in all relationships of life, honesty in trusted positions, unfailing justice in the courts, industry and economy, etc. But such a general, national ethics, especially in a state church, carries with it the danger of externalization of religion. The reaction, then, had to come from a Christian ethics of the Church, frequently in need of aid from the circles of Pietism.

5. Following a review of these theoretical principles in the religious system of Kant we close with a *brief summary of a few practical points in his religion.* The reader is again referred to his above mentioned essay on *Religion within the Limits of Pure Reason* (1793). Here he aimed to present those elements of religion which can be deduced from reason. In its significance for the history of Christian thought by a philosopher it is comparable to John Locke's essay on *The Reasonableness of Christianity* (1695).

a. Kant took the position that *for the needed religion a special history of redemption* is not necessary. He was, therefore, indifferent to the historicity of the Biblical accounts pertaining not only to the metaphysical doctrines such as Christ's pre-existence, Trinity, etc., but also to matters touching the way of salvation. Rationalism had no appreciation of history. In this Kant was a natural son of the Rationalistic movement in Germany. We shall see that even Schleiermacher had here one defect of his theology. The vision of a history of redemption in the manner of the Erlangen School was closed to the men of the age here under review. (Cf. below, *sub* d.)

b. On *God,* Kant was a theist: While it is impossible to know God by metaphysical speculation yet he wanted to have Him thought of in relation to man as an individual. The conscience gives evidence of such a relationship. But to Kant this was an external relation, as with the scholastics. God guarantees the validity of the moral law. There is no heart in that relationship. God, through the conscience, makes His demand; man acts in obedience and receives his reward. On the personal attitude of Kant to religion, which he regarded chiefly as needed by the state for governing the common people

---

[6] See Article XVIII of the *Augsburg Confession* and the related discussion in the *Apology.*

compare Luetgert, as referred to, I, 226 f. W. Durant remarks that he stayed away from church all his adult life, and yet, as he grew old he felt a great longing to preserve for himself and the world the essentials of religion. These, of course, were the tenets of Rationalism: God, freedom and immortality. His mother was an ardent member of pietistic circle.[7]

c. Sin. In religion, so Kant says, we are confronted with an exclusively moral problem, namely with the struggle between the good and the evil principle for dominion over man. The evil principle consists in the turning of the impulses for human action into a direction in which the sensually selfish motives crowd out the respect for the moral law. This evil principle (*radikale Boese*) has its roots in the will. The inclination of man to the evil, when there was an original and even a persevering aptitude or disposition for the good, remains inexplicable. To Kant it was a fact that needs no proof. He refuses to accept the Church's doctrine of original sin. Neither does he charge this depravity to the Creator. In one place he says that man must have sinned before his birth, suggesting that this sinful character for which we are actually responsible must be traced back to the realm of the unconscious in a condition before time. With this idea Kant connects the thought of an infinite punishment. And, peculiarly enough, he arrives at a statement which reminds one of an influence from Pietism, namely, that as a remedy for this condition, a gradual reform will not suffice, but that it must be *the conversion of a moment,* which turns his will towards the good. But these ideas of sin were out of harmony with the other rationalistic tenets of Kant's religion.

d. Christ as Redeemer. The historicity of the life of Jesus, in itself, was to Kant a matter of indifference. Just so that the example and inspiration from such a life are received. His historic life—it was not denied as was the case by David Frederick Strauss—is nothing but the symbol and the expression, or the prototype (*Urbild*) of the human race.[8] Jesus is consequently the symbolical embodiment of man morally tested in labor as well as in suffering. In this He had not vicariously suffered for our guilt, nor rendered a moral obedience in our stead; He had simply given an example which we should follow in like situations. Faith in the Son of God as a moral ideal is practical, but faith in the Son of God as a worker of miracles is, according to Kant, without any practical or religious value. Consequently, all supernatural and historical traits in the picture of Jesus are either passed by or rejected. The Bible must be interpreted in agreement with the pure teachings of reason, even where this is not its original meaning.[9]

e. Kant had also views on the *Church:* The moral regeneration or the victory of the good principle, is to be realized, not merely in the original man, but in human society. A kingdom of God or a society established upon moral laws, is to arise.[10] The visible localized church repelled him; he looked upon the historic churches as mere endeavors at the realization of the Church. They will be overtaken by movement toward something corresponding more to Christ's ideal. He saw the coming of the Kingdom in a future union for the cultivation of virtue: "The gradual transition of the *Frohnglauben* (forced faith) of the Church to the unlimited rule of the faith of pure religion is the approach to the Kingdom of God." Similar ideas were expressed by Schleiermacher, Rothe, Troeltsch, as we shall see.

---

[7] *Story of Philosophy,* p. 285.
[8] *Die Religion innerhalb der Grenzen der blossen Vernunft,* Reclam. edition, p. 69.
[9] *Ibid.,* pp. 149 ff.
[10] *Ibid.,* p. 121.

f. *Prayer,* thought of as an inwardly performed service and as a means of grace, is a superstitious delusion, the working of a fetish. Still he spoke respectfully of a spirit of prayer, which must show itself without ceasing in a desire to please God in our whole life (p. 248).

g. *Grace,* in Christianity, was objectionable to Kant. He mocks the Christians who crave to be favored instead of simply being good servants. They want the Lord to overlook something, and thus they discredit virtue. There may be an element of truth in this remark. But this also is true: Rationalism lacks in sympathy with the brokenhearted, with the "poor in spirit." Luther's chief interest was: How may I find a gracious God?

Note: After Kant the older Rationalism soon lost its hold on the minds of the spiritual leaders of the people. Yet a few names deserve to be remembered by the historian. The "Nestor" of rational exegesis was H. E. G. Paulus (1761-1851) at Heidelberg who was famous for his rational explanation of Biblical miracles. The dogmatician of the *rationalismus vulgaris* was J. A. L. Wegscheider (1771-1849). His *Institutiones Theologiae Dogmaticae* went through eight editions (first edition 1815). Post-Kantian Rationalism was at its best in the field of historical and grammatical research. Wilhelm Gesenius' *Hebrew-German dictionary* (1810 ff.) and *Hebrew Grammar* (1813) have had a wide circulation. He also started a critical *Thesaurus of Hebrew and the Chaldean* (1829 ff.).[11] The monumental *Corpus Reformatorum* was founded by K. G. Bretschneider (1776-1848). The death blow to Rationalism was dealt by the church historian Karl von Hase with his book, *Hutterus Redivivus* (1828, 12th edition 1883). By 1830 the old Rationalism was a dead issue in academic circles while it continued to be a force in church life, through the rationalistically trained pastors, till about 1870.

---

[11] Cf. Edward F. Miller, *The Influence of Gesenius on Hebrew Lexicography,* 1927.

Chapter Two

GERMAN IDEALISM AND ITS RELATION TO CHRISTIANITY

Literature: R. SEEBERG, *Christentum und Idealismus*, 1921. E. HIRSCH, *Die idealistische Philosophie und das Christentum*, 1926. H. GROSS, *Der deutsche Idealismus und das Christentum,* 1927. Note the great work of W. Luetgert as referred to. Articles by F. BRUNSTAED and H. STEPHAN on *"Idealismus"* in *Religion in Geschichte und Gegenwart²* (*RGG*), III, 51-53.

1. THE DEVELOPMENT IN LARGE PERSPECTIVE.

Many of the intellectuals had lost their faith in the teachings of the Reformation. Descartes' philosophy of selfconsciousness has been referred to. It had been interpretative of a coming age of anthropocentric emphasis in matters of religion. To this was added the message of empiricism from England (F. Bacon, the English Deists, Locke's Reasonableness, the criterion of truth. This position was followed by David Hume's philosophy of skepticism with its stimulation of the philosophy of criticism by Kant.[1] Voltaire had been following in the ways of the English Deists, and his writings on the Philosophy of Religion had many followers in Germany.

Then came the philosophers of the succeeding age, the writers and theologians of the Enlightenment.[2] This whole movement for a new view upon life included unconsciously also the groping for a new conception of religion and theology. This can be traced back to the earliest liberalists in the seventeenth century. It may be described as a revival of the Renaissance and of the humanism of Erasmus, which in the earlier age had been repressed by the powerful influence of the Reformation.[3] Kattenbusch remarks that there was about the earlier rationalists a good deal of that "consequential air" (*Wichtigtuerei*) which so frequently characterizes the pioneers in revolutionary movements.[4] But they were conscious of being recognized heralds for freedom of thought and emancipation from the Confessions of the Reformation as binding authority.

It must not be overlooked, of course, that in the circles of the Conservatives, especially in Roman Catholic countries during the seventeenth century, but also in Protestant lands, there had been much of that persecution which is bound to drive negatively inclined minds into extreme positions. It was seen in the treatment of the Socinians and the Anabaptists, in the repeated imprisonment of Voltaire, etc. All this had helped to further the movement for emancipation from the Church and her standards.

2. KANT, AS THE FOUNDER OF GERMAN IDEALISM

Although rationalist in religion, Kant was the founder of German Idealism. Without yielding to the philosophy of empiricism, which in England and France had issued into skepticism, he stressed the idea of God as necessary to thought, even though it

---

[1] See Book IV, Chapter V, on the English Deists, pp. 50-66.
[2] Cf. *PRE* II, 224 ff.; and in the *NSH* IV, 141 ff.
[3] Cf. Kattenbusch, *op. cit.,* pp. 5 f.
[4] See the closing paragraphs of our discussion of German Rationalism (pp. 77 ff.).

cannot be reached on the basis of the laws of logic. In connection with this thought there stood out for the cultured in Germany, in their critical attitude to matters of religion, the fact that this world, with man as its crown, is governed by spiritual laws, organized upon spiritual principles, and that it has a reality independent of the intellectual limitation of the individual. The idealists, the followers of Kant, men throughout who had turned from the old teachings of revealed religion and were in danger of losing themselves into pessimism and materialism, saw before them a way of ascent into the world of ideas: God, freedom, immortality. Briefly, this is what we understand by "German Idealism."

3. GERMAN IDEALISM AS A MOVEMENT.

In the description here to be given, we have in mind the classical period of German literature along the lines of philosophy and poetry in the Germany of the time between 1750 (the time of Lessing, Herder, Schiller, Kant) and around 1830 (the time of the death of Goethe, Schleiermacher and Hegel). It was the time of a remarkable originality of life. There was a new interest in the mysteries of origins and development, in the reason and purpose of all history. It was felt with Hegel that the roots of the present life are in the past. There came into the German language, in addition to that older word *"Gemuet,"* the term *"Geist,"* for which also there is no quite equal conception in other languages.[5] The impulses for this literary movement were received from the philosophers, after Descartes and Leibnitz then especially from Kant as we have seen and then from Fichte, Schelling and Hegel. Among the poets it was especially Schiller who idealized the thoughts and suggestions of Kant and Fichte. He aimed to deepen the categorical imperative of duty into a free and joyful response to aesthetic ideals. According to him, man is not a dead entity but living, active, responsible. But he went beyond Kant and also Luther in trying to reconcile freedom for the use of the natural with an overoptimistic trust in man's nature, which was idealized after the patterns of Greek antiquity. This, as an example, shows that the poets went creatively beyond the philosophers.[6]

Fundamentally, the aim was not at a religion, but at a new view of world and life. It was a reaction against intellectualism and mechanization. The leaders of the movement were, as a rule, not churchmen, but poets and thinkers. Yet religious interests were everywhere included. The groping for a new religion was unconscious. There was aversion to all form in religion and, therefore, people turned away from traditional orthodoxy. But their need for unbounded freedom of thought, together with their worldliness, kept them from identifying themselves permanently with movements like Pietism, or Moravianism. Some interested themselves in religiously tinged forms of Romanticism.[7] The positively evangelical features of the Reformation were objectionable to them. They did like the ideas of "Protestantism" in religion, and on this ground— *mirabile dictu*—they admired Luther! Kant, Lessing, Fichte, Schiller, Goethe all thought that a proper interpretation would put Luther on their side. But they and their followers in the field of theology soon found that the Lutheran Reformation was hopelessly

---

[5] See on this point *RGG*, II, 94.

[6] The peculiar traits of this age may be studied by reading Luetgert, *op, cit.*, I, 260.

[7] On German Romanticism see *RGG*, V. 2096. Cf. Luegert, *op. cit.*, I, 257, 259, and also Selbie in his work on Schleiermacher, p. 20, which we quote in Chapter III, pp. 103-118, below.

against them. So they felt that their new movement had to complete the Reformation by setting up new and independent fundamentals. This was the beginning of the so-called "religion of German Idealism," to which the above quoted literature has devoted special attention.

This peculiar Idealism was characterized by a great variety of interests: Ancient classicism, a new humanism, features of mysticism, and religious aestheticism. In addition to these interests of the poets there came the conflicting systems of the philosophers. But there was missing in all of those profound and brilliant views a religious unity that would connect the movement with at least the leading ideas of historic Christianity. The Bible and Luther were misinterpreted or ignored. It soon became evident that Christianity had not been able to permeate this movement of national classicism. It is true that Lessing's early criticism of traditional Christianity is to be explained by his conviction that the truth of the Christian religion is not proved by logical arguments. But the moment came when he yielded to Spinoza's pantheistic conception of God. Goethe who in his younger years was open to Pietistic influences[8] soon settled upon views concerning God which committed him also to Spinozian pantheism. It furnished to him the basis for his philosophy of nature. Spinoza wanted to understand nature; Goethe wanted to enjoy it. Goethe was a realist and as such opposed to Kant's idealism. In *Faust* he speaks of Mephisto and of sin, but the meaning of sin was brushed aside; it was to him nothing but a pantheistic principle. Redemption was auto-redemption which takes place in man living himself into the working of nature. The ethical principles held by Goethe were fundamentally to some extent in harmony with the ethics of Schleiermacher, as expressed in his *Monologues,* to which we refer in the next chapter. Here again, Goethe was motivated by his intense naturalism.[9] Schiller came close to historic Christianity, but he did not accept it.

4. FAILURE OF THE MOVEMENT.

From the standpoint of the Christian who accepts revelation and is living a rich spiritual life by faith, this religion of German Idealism was a very poor substitute. History will have to record the fact that it was brilliant and a powerful movement. And all who have had the privilege to live in the productions of that age will say that it represents classical literature. S. T. Coleridge, as a student in Goettingen, came under its influence and took its thoughts and principles to England, which brought to that country great impulses for philosophy, history of literature and theological criticism (cf. Thomas Carlyle). But one must read the four volumes of W. Luetgert, *Die Religion des deutschen Idealismus und ihr Ende* and compare with it the articles by F. Brunstaed and H. Stephan on "Idealism," as referred to, in order to realize fully the tragedy of the final bankruptcy of his brilliant movement.

After the classical period had spent its force (about 1830) the process of a gradual dissolution is observable. Strauss, Feuerbach, Marx, Schopenhauer indicate stations of the downward grade. Pantheism dissolved the facts of Biblical history. The development led to materialism. And this materialistic philosophy became the basis for the revolutionary economic and social theories of the age. The fundamentals of historic Chris-

---

[8] Through the Moravian Fraeulein von Klettenberg. Cf. his "Confessions of a Beautiful Soul."
[9] See Luetgert, *op. cit.,* I, 98-100.

tianity were present in Shakespeare, but absent in Goethe. To be fair in this comparison, however, we must remember that England had the Shakespearian height of its classicism before the Enlightenment; Germany had its period after that experience. It was a movement out of harmony with the program of Paul (I Cor. 1:18—2:16), and out of harmony also with the program of the most fundamental principles of Luther. So modern a scholar as Horst Stephan (Leipzig) calls the final issue of German Idealism *"eine tiefe Tragik."* We add: It stands as an epitaph to the lesson of history that the religion of modern humanism, in which Christianity is stripped of the Biblical religion of redemption, is bound to fail in the end—in any country.

5. POST-KANTIAN IDEALISTS.

There was objection to Kant's *"Ding an sich."* The aim was to arrive at a consistent idealism by dissolving all the phenomena into elements of consciousness, as necessary productions of the mind, as a system of reason.

From this standpoint J. F. FICHTE (d. 1814) declared that the truth is in the inner sanctity of our own being. The "I" is the point of certainty. All else is the "non-I" which is posited by the "I" which through a reaction from the "non-I" arrives at certainties. This philosophy was made use of by Schleiermacher and later also by F. R. H. Frank of the Erlangen School as a foundation for subjectivism in theology: The subject posits itself as object. In this way the subject receives impressions through its own object, which contributes to assuring the subject of truth. Frank made use of this philosophy to defend his theory of certainty as being established not upon Scripture but upon the religious selfconsciousness of the theologian. With this philosophy there was no room any more for the theistic conception of God. God was to Fichte merely the "moral law of the universe" (*moralische Weltordnung*). When this brought him the accusation of atheism he receded to speaking of God as "absolute being" after the Spinozian pattern.

F. W. SCHELLING (d. 1854), a predecessor of Hegel's pantheism, identified "nature" and the "I," objective and subjective reason, or realism and idealism, and then he subsumed both under the conception of an *absolute reason* which he called God and which he saw moving through history. In this we have already a prefiguration of Hegel's "Phenomenology of the Mind" (1807). To Hegel's philosophy and Hegelian theology we devote Chapter IV.

In connection with these men who started with Kant but were moving away from him in the direction of mysticism and pantheism the following two must be added, who also aimed at deepening the concepts of Kant:

F. H. JACOBI (d. 1819): He agreed with Kant that neither God nor freedom can be established by reason. But this certainty comes through faith. We can feel God. He can be divined (*geahnt*), and experienced. For this, however, an inner faculty (*Gemuet*) is needed. It was Jacobi who claimed to be a "pagan with his head, but a Christian with his heart." It reminds one of the double truth in the system of Duns Scotus.

J. F. FRIES (d. 1843) criticized Kant's definition of faith as something less than knowing (reminding of the New Alexandrian School). Kant was unable to think of religion as a peculiar function of the mind.

6. DIASTASIS OR SYNTHESIS?

Elert, in his *Kampf um das Christentum,* makes the remark: The Kantian age is sinking . . . The more Christianity will stress its distance from this sinking civilization, the less is the danger of going down with it (p. 7). He raises the question of "diastasis" or "synthesis," that is the question whether Christianity and non-Christianity shall combine or be exclusive (p. 3). It is an old problem. Irenaeus and Tertullian in the early church advised diastasis; Clement and Origen were the idealistic advocates of a synthesis with philosophy.[10]

Elert sees, of course, that Christianity, as placed historically in the environment of non-Christianity, cannot and must not keep itself aloof from the natural and necessary contact. We inhale its influences but then we energetically exhale them, and in this physical action we always again free ourselves from them. This he calls the rhythm of Christian history in the constant motions between synthesis and diastasis. But aim and ideal must be in the diastasis.

In the modern Germany, particularly since Schleiermacher, the danger has always been in the inclination of theological scholarship to effect a combination, even an actual union, between Christianity and its non-Christian environment. The first endeavor at such an unnatural synthesis, so Elert observes, appeared at the beginning of the eighteenth century. Under influence of the new philosophy of Lessing, Kant and Idealism, Christianity came near losing altogether its selfconsciousness. Reaction then appeared, in a revival of Pietism which steered in the direction of the diastasis. Then followed the endeavor of the Hegelian theology in a new attempt at a synthesis between philosophy and Christianity—a complete failure, as we shall see in Chapter IV.[11] The Neo-Kantian excursion in the Ritschlian movement, another endeavor at the synthesis, brought no relief. In the Historico-Religious School and in the Christian sociology of today the independence of Christian theology has entirely disappeared. It is forced to accept dictations which it could not follow without denying the foundations upon which it is built. We must have a theology in which the foundations for Christian certainty are taken not from the outside, but from itself, that is, from Christian revelation.

---

[10] See our discussion in Book I, Chapter VIII, 1, 2: II, 4, 5, and III, 1.

[11] Cf. below, pp. 119-127.

Chapter Three

SCHLEIERMACHER (1768-1834)

Literature: T. SIMON, *Grundriss der Geschichte der neueren Philosophie in ihren Beziehungen zur Religion,* 1920, pp. 108 ff. O. KIRN in *PRE* XVII, 587-617; English in *NSH.* Compare the article by WOBBERMIN, *RGG,* V., and the article in MEUSEL, *Kirchl, Handlexikon.* For fundamental investigation: W. DILTHEY, *Leben Schleiermachers,* 1870. H. MULERT, *W. Diltheys Leben Schleiermachers I,* 1922. G. CRESS, *The Theology of Schleiermacher,* 1911. W. B. SELBIE, *Schleiermacher, a Critical and Historical Study,* 1913. RICHARD B. BRANDT, *The Philosophy of Schleiermacher,* 1941. DILTHEY-JONAS, *Aus Schleiermacher's Leben in Briefen,* 4 vols., 1858ff. (*Life and Letters of Schleiermacher,* translated by MISS ROWAN, 1860). The sermons constitute 10 volumes in O. REIMERS' publication of the *Works,* 1836-64. This edition by *Reimers* is insufficient because the majority of the included writings were not prepared for publication by the author. *A new critical collection is needed.* The review here given is confined to (1) the *Reden uber die Religion,* (2) the *Program for Theological Study,* (3) the *Christliche Glaube* and (4) the *Monologen* and related matters on ethics. There are piece-meal translations of his Works by various British and American scholars. We mention: W. FARRAR, *Brief Outline of the Study of Theology,* 1850; MARY WILSON, *Selected Sermons,* 1890; W. HASTIE, *Christmas Eve,* 1890; JOHN OMAN, *Discourses on Religion,* 1893; H. L. FRIES, *Monologues,* 1926; H. R. MACKINTOSH and J. S. STEWART, *The Christian Faith,* 1928.

INTRODUCTORY REMARKS

Protestant Theology in Germany of the nineteenth and twentieth centuries is characterized by a double line of development, the liberalistic and the conservative. Theological liberalism proceeded upon the presumption that the theology of the Reformation was fundamentally unmaintainable.[1] There was the determination to reconstruct religion and theology independent of the confessional heritage after the ideals that had developed in connection with Rationalism, by ignoring the revelation in Scripture and by working with thoughts offered by the new philosophy. Outstanding schools along this line are (1) the group following the Hegelian philosophy of development, (2) the Ritschlian theology, and finally (3) the Historico-Religious School. The other line was represented by successive or contemporaneous schools of conservatism which were resolved to hold to the fundamentals of the Reformation: (1) The old Confessional Theology, (2) the Erlangen School, (3) the Mediating Theology, (4) the Biblicists. The position of the Conservatives was one of apologetics and polemics against the liberals, denying them the right to alter, within the Church, the fundamentals of historical Christianity.[2]

The special study in this chapter is Schleiermacher. With his peculiarly dualistic world of thought, he stands at the beginning of the new age as it was set for that conflicting development of liberalism against conservatism. One has to admire in this "modern Origen" the universality of interest, the strong mental powers to organize and to systematize, the mind so creative in the pouring out of thought. He left no school of his own. But the schools of theology after him, to his left and to his right and through the generations, received impulses and stimulations from this genius of thought. The question all through Germany's history of Protestant theology on practically every point of orientation and in almost all branches of theology has always been: What did

---

[1] In order to show what is meant the writer must refer to his estimate of A. Harnack's *History of Dogma* in Vol. I, Bk. I, Chap. I.

[2] On the situation, cf. Neve, *Story and Significance of the Augsburg Confession,* pp. 116-121.

Schleiermacher say? The admiration of a genius easily runs into overstatements. Schleiermacher has many very serious shortcomings. They must be pointed out on the pages of this chapter as occasion offers.

I. INFLUENCES IN THE DEVELOPMENT OF SCHLEIERMACHER

The peculiarity of Schleiermacher lies in the many ideas that were combined in him. It is not only interesting but it is necessary to trace the influences which contributed to his development.

FRIEDRICH DANIEL ERNST SCHLEIERMACHER came from a family of Reformed preachers. His grandfather, Daniel, was an adherent of a peculiar apocalyptic sect (Roonsdorfer Sect).[3] His father, Gottlieb, was a chaplain in the army of Frederick the Great. In consequence of the influence from that sect the father became confused on matters of faith. Later he found his way back to the Church through relationships with the Moravians at Herrnhut. So it came that our future theologian received his first higher training in the *Paedagogium* of the Moravians at Niesky and, following this, in their seminary at Barby. But doubt pertaining to the fundamentals of the faith troubled him. In this situation his teachers and his father also failed to meet him with helping sympathy.[4] His doubts were of a peculiar persisting sort: How can Christ who calls himself the Son of Man be of God? The idea of an atonement was objectionable to him. He related that at the age of ten the question came to him whether the whole of ancient history might not be a fraudulent transmission. When he was eleven the question of eternal punishment troubled him. Criticism was his natural trait. His father allowed him to continue his study in the Halle University (1787-89).

His descent from the Reformed Church and the influence from the Moravians explain certain characteristics about him: The Christocentric character of his theology, his warm subjectivism, his non-Lutheran type, and, confessionally, his stand for the union of Lutherans and Reformed.

The philosophical influences upon Schleiermacher especially point to outstanding traits in his picture as a theologian. In Halle he studied Kant. The impressions from Hegel, his contemporary, who himself was at that time just developing, were naturally sporadic. Neither of these two philosophers could hold him in a continued interest. But Aristotle first and then Plato attracted him to Greek philosophy, the latter to such a degree that he became a translator of his writings. Among the modern philosophers he had an especial liking for Spinoza, whose influence upon his conception of God and upon his theories concerning ethics shall soon engage our attention.

Next, it was Romanticism which made a deeper impression upon Schleiermacher than any of the factors that have been mentioned. He was now in Berlin (1796-1802). Here he came into close friendship with F. Schlegel, the brilliant but unbalanced representative of the Romantic movement, with his contempt for the "grammar of virtue." Both were members of that literary circle which had its members chiefly among the liberal Jews of Berlin with Moses Mendelssohn as leader. Here he met some of those highly cultured women such as Dorothea Veit, daughter of Mendelssohn, and Henriette Herz, wife of a physician. All were interested in the classical movement of German

[3] *PRE*, XVII, 131 ff.

[4] Read Seeberg, *Christentum und Idealismus*, p. 38 f.

Idealism. In a society of this sort he found channels for an education which he needed for his individual world of feeling and thought.[5] Regarding friendships he admitted: "It lies deep in my nature always to attach myself more closely to women than to men."[6] He felt a peculiar need for self-communication and a pleasure in seeing and feeling the soul of another individuality. This was a specific trait of Romanticism. But considering the mixed composition of these circles—in Weimar, around Goethe, we find a similar group, the "Olympians"—there was much occasion for compromise along ethical lines. Schleiermacher laid himself open to criticism when he undertook, in his *Confidential Letters on Schlegel's "Lucinde"* (1800), to find points of beauty and truth in this questionable novel of his friend. J. C. Gass regretted that such "beautiful commentary" was written on "so bad a text." The time came soon when Schleiermacher looked upon that apology as an aberration. Luetgert, in his work on German Idealism, closes the first volume with an account of the relations between the men and women in that cult of classicism. There he also analyzes Schleiermacher in the Lucinde affair.[7] That whole account by Luetgert on those relations and correspondences,[8] shows how, under the pretense of free play for the genius, spirit and flesh entered into dangerous combinations. The point of interest here is that in Berlin, through all these associations, Schleiermacher "became a modern man."[9] The impressions received explain much in his first writings (*Reden* and *Monologen*) which made him famous. Schleiermacher, whose theological writings, sermons, and lectures reveal a high standard of ethics, especially also in his family life, was fully aware of the danger referred to. In a "catechism for noble women" he wrote: "Thou must be able to be friend without letting this attitude run into love."[10] But the insufficiency of even such advice can be seen in his own relation of friendship to Eleonore Grunow, the unhappily married wife of a pastor in Berlin.[11] But Schleiermacher, although failing occasionally in the proper distinction between the ethical and the aesthetical, never became a victim of what is mean and low. He spoke his final word on marriage in his sermons on the *"Christlicher Hausstand"* (1818). There he also expressed himself decidedly against the Romantic encouragement of divorce.[12]

Note: Here will be the place for a brief characterization of German Romanticism, which should be considered together with the previous chapter on "German Idealism." The description may be given in the following lucid and comprehensive definition of W. B. Selbie, the successor of Fairbairn in Mansfield College at Oxford, in his work on Schleiermacher (p. 20): "Romanticism must be regarded as a tendency or fashion of thought rather than as a school. It is elusive, complex and very difficult to describe. It stands for a kind of culture touched with emotionalism. It involves an aesthetic view of life, the attempt to see the unknown and mysterious in the most familiar things of life. It means mysticism in religion and subjectivism in art. At its worst it is individualism run mad, divorced from all obligations of morality and knowing no standards save those of a rather sensuous taste. At its best it became the source of a most fruitful literary reflection and criticism, and of a counter movement to the rationalism of the enlightenment which in the end deprived it of all real influence. It helped to deliver both art and literature from the deadening grasp of conventionalism and gave to its creative genius the freedom and range needed for its full development. It brought imagination to bear upon life, turned prose into poetry and

---

[5] Cf. Seeberg, p. 40 f.; also Kirn in *PRE*, XVII, 590, line 57 with reference to the *Monologues*.
[6] Quoted by Luetgert, *op. cit.*, I, 257.
[7] *Ibid.*, pp. 263 ff.
[8] *Ibid.*, pp. 257-271.
[9] Seeberg, *op. cit.*, p. 41.
[10] Luetgert, *op. cit.*, I, 260.
[11] See *PRE*, XVII, 592; Meusel, Meusel, VI, 37; Luetgert, *op. cit.*, I, 259.
   Goethe did the same toward the close of his life in his *Wahlverwandtschaften*.

evoked the deeper hidden meaning of things." The German movement had within it the seeds of its own decay. In England the poetry of Wordsworth represented it at its best. Among the German representatives there should be added the name of the noble and deeply pious "Novalis" (F. von Hardenberg, originally Moravian, then Pietist), the singer of the most beautiful religious hymns of the Goethe age: "Wenn alle untreu werden," "Wenn ich ihn nur habe," and many others.[13]

II. SCHLEIERMACHER'S DISCOURSES ON RELIGION

1. INTRODUCTORY REMARKS.

In the year 1799, in the midst of his Romantic enthusiasm,[14] Schleiermacher published anonymously his famous *Discourses on Religion Addressed to the Cultured Among its Despisers*.[15] These were in themselves a symptom of the age in which he lived. It was the age of German Idealism when the spirit of classicism was spreading its wings in an atmosphere of a new culture. And many of these cultured spirits were groping for new forms of expressing religious ideas and attitudes. Schleiermacher, with a deep susceptibility for contemporary piety, and now stimulated by Greek classicism and modern Romanticism, was fundamentally opposed to an attitude of a "diastasis" and was bent upon creating a "synthesis" of culture and religion. Here and in his succeeding writings he emphasized the need of a union of theology with the scientific spirit.

Outstanding, however, among the impulses for Schleiermacher's reconstruction of theology was his reaction against the traditional dogma. Many have praised him for breaking with the old Protestant scheme of dogmatics. But he also broke with the analogy of faith (Rom. 12:7). In the teaching of Irenaeus, of Tertullian, of Augustine, of the best among the scholastics and mystics and especially of the Reformation, there is in the trinitarian position regarding the person of Christ and His redemption, in the evangelical features of the teaching on sin and grace and on the way of salvation as taught in a document such as Melanchthon's *Loci*, and in the catechism of the Reformation—in spite of differences—a gradually growing consensus of fundamentals which may be called the "analogy of faith." Schleiermacher ignored this heritage and broke the ground for a new theology.[16] So modern a theologian as Horst Stephan of Leipzig puts his judgment into the sentence: "*Er hat die Theologie an Luther vorbeigefuehrt.*" Schleiermacher's reinterpretations of Reformation ideas fail to do justice to the historical substance of that heritage of the Church. This must be the verdict even though it is not to be denied that in the wealth of his suggestions he gave important stimuli also to a conservative theology needed in a modern age which is tuned to problems that could not yet exist in the mind of the Reformers.

---

[13] Given in English, side by side with the German text, edited by B. Pick (Open Court Publ. Co., 1910). See the article on "Novalis" in *RGG*, IV, 599 f. For the literature on German Romanticism consult the same volume, 2096 ff.

[14] Cf. *PRE*, XVII, 592, lines 10 f., 20 ff.

[15] *Reden uber die Religion an die Gebildeten unter ihren Veraechtern*. In a second edition the author incorporated certain changes and explanations. G. C. B. Puenjer published a critical edition which shows the variations (1879). All editions after the 2nd (1821) are reprints. The historical effect of these "Reden" attaches itself to the first publication. Our few references are to this edition. The writer has used for his readings the text in volume four of the *Bibliothek Theologischer Klassiker* with its valuable introduction of 64 pages by S. Lommatzach, and has compared this first edition with the text of the 2nd. ed. in the reprint by Reimers in the 6th ed. (Berlin, 1859) which contains the author's added notes of explanation. The reader will find many of the sentences of special interest in R. G. Gruetzmacher's *Textbuch zur systematischen Theologie*, 2nd edition, 1923 pp. 35-38. These as well as the references to the other writings of Schleiermacher will be read with profit in connection with our discussion. English readers should use the translation by J. Oman, 1893.

[16] The first lesson in the possibility of reconstructing the old-time religion he had received from Kant's essay on *Religion within the Limits of Pure Reason*. See the remarks of Kattenbusch, *op. cit.*, page 21.

2. ANALYSIS OF THE "DISCOURSES"

After an introduction in the *First Discourse,* the author discusses in his *Second Discourse*—the most important of the five—the nature of religion. It is not a knowledge of principles and doctrines, nor is it the action after the commandments of morality; but it is an immediate "intuition and a feeling" of the "Universe," and this "is the most universal and highest form of religion." In place of the "universe" Schleiermacher employs also terms such as "the one and the whole," "the infinite in the finite," the "heavenly," "eternal and holy," "fate," the "eternal providence."

a. Here the question has been raised as to *Schleiermacher's conception of God.* He was charged with Spinozian pantheism. There was ground for this charge in the text of the first edition in the way he seemingly identified the universe with God. He modified his language in the second edition. What then was Schleiermacher's conception of God? The fact is that he had little interest in this question apart from the appearance of the divine in nature, in man and in history. Even an unbeliever may have religion. He says there can be religion without God, and such a religion may be better than one with God. And while concerning man he stressed the need to emphasize individual personality, yet in his conception of God he was and he remained a consistent pantheist, even in his *Christliche Glaubenslehre.* This is also the judgment of so keen an observer as T. Simon.[17] This does not mean that he accepted the whole of Spinoza's system.[18] Toward the close of the *Second Discourse,* in the second edition, Schleiermacher gives an account of his conception of God. He opens this apology with the question, "How can anybody say that I have pictured to you a religion without God when I have been exhibiting nothing but the immediate and original being of God in us through feeling?" Such statement does not absolve from pantheism.[19] The indifference of Schleiermacher to the personality of God extends to a like indifference to personal and individual immortality, another feature of Spinozianism: "In the midst of the finite to become one with the infinite and to be eternal in every moment—this is the immortality of religion." [20]

b. What is Schleiermacher's conception of religion? The intuition of the universe creates in the religious individual a "feeling of dependency." The universe is active, the religious individual passive. Religious feelings are produced such as "reverence for the eternal and invisible, humility, gratitude, joy, confidence, trust." "The intensity of these feelings determines the degree of religion." These feelings and individual attitudes are spoken of as the real essence of religion. This tends to make his theology practically a psychology. On this subject compare our closing observation (2).

How does religion arise in the details of Schleiermacher's description? It starts with a view upon nature, its laws and its anomalies. But nature is only the vestibule. The clearest and deepest objectivation of the universe is in the inner life of man. The individual "is a compendium of humanity." It is here, in the wealth of the individual and in the place of each for the harmony of the whole that religious intuition rises to a contemplation of the universe culminating in man and reflecting God.

---

[17] See his *Grundriss der Geschichte der neueren Philosophy in ihren Beziehungen zur Religion,* 1920, p. 111.
[18] Cf. S. Lommatsch, Intr. to the *Reden* in vol. 4 of *Bibliothek Theol. Klassiker,* 14 f.
[19] For a weighing of argumentation on the other side, see Kattenbusch, *op. cit.,* pp. 21-23.
[20] See the closing statements of the second discourse. Cf. Luetgert, *op. cit.,* II, 200 f., also our reference to this point in Schleiermacher's *Glaubenslehre.*

In one of his letters to the Jewess Frau Henriette Herz, Schleiermacher expressed the need of seeing her for the purpose of beholding in her the universe. When man is able to watch the springing up of his own individual existence out of the original source of all being, then, and in as far as this is given to him, has he religion.[21] One can understand that Kant's rationalistic and semi-deistic conception of God repelled Schleiermacher. In the "act" of his religion of feeling he was through and through a mystic of the pantheistic type. To this study of humanity is added the intuition and contemplation of the *Weltgeist* in history. Here is the real sanctum of the universe, because here the pious beholds the functioning of eternal love. There are other spheres for religious observation although these may be beyond our present knowledge so that for the present we cannot do more than to divine. What is revelation? "Every original and new intuition of the universe." What is inspiration? "Every reproduction of a religious intuition in such a way that others also can participate in it. And every anticipation of the other half of a religious event after the first has been given." What is a miracle? "Every natural event which reveals to the soul (*Gemuet*) the infinite; not necessarily that which appears to be miraculous." Who is a believer? Not he who adopts the teachings of another in thinking and feeling, but he who has an experience and an intuition of his own: This means "that not he has religion who believes in a Holy Scripture, but he who needs no Scripture and himself might be able to make one."

Note: One sees in the genius of Schleiermacher the urge to abandon what he felt to be "outworn categories" and to substitute new categories. But it was these *old* categories, vivified by the pietistic movement, that attracted Schleiermacher's own devoted wife to the Gospel sermons of Gossner instead of to those of her own husband. The young Claus Harms, a seeker of saving truth who was helped by the *Reden,* was disappointed when he turned to the reading of Schleiermacher's sermons. These sermons (10 vols. have been published) missed the "analogy of faith"—that sacred heritage from the history of Christian thought! The complaint of Claus Harms was: "He who had begotten me had no bread for me." [22]

In the *Third Discourse* the education for religion is discussed: All men have from birth the religious aptitude. The age of Rationalism, however, was not favorable to its development, he observed. But the improvement in philosophy and art prophesy the coming of a time when the soul will find its relation to the universe.

The *Fourth Discourse* deals with the social features of religion in the Church. Religion creates the most perfect forms of human society. The imperfections in the present empirical Church have their root in its connection with the state. The aim must be at free associations of the pious with no hierarchy and with no dictation from the state.

In his *Fifth Discourse,* Schleiermacher speaks of the relation of the so-called "natural religion" to the historical forms of religion. He observes that the natural religion has "very little of the specific characteristics of the Christian religion," that religion must individualize itself as has been done in the specific positive religions. Here Schleiermacher gave utterance to a very correct observation. In our interpretation this is what he wanted to say: The real inner essence and life of the genus finds expression in its species. Apple as the genus, in the form of an abstract conception, furnishes no food for the table; it is only in the form of a species that it can be enjoyed. This was a word

---

[21] So remarks Kattenbusch in his endeavor to interpret Schleiermacher on this point; *op. cit.,* p. 22.
[22] *PRE*, VII, 434.

necessary to be spoken against that "natural religion" of the English Deists, which tended to perpetuate its life in that general religion of "God, virtue and immortality," which later was promulgated by the German Rationalists.

This individualization of religion is undertaken by producing "out of free choice, an individual intuition of the universe" and making this "the central point of religion and by relating everything to this intuition." In the study of the specific religions, this point is to be found. Through this thought Schleiermacher gave an impulse to the comparative study of religions. In this particular study he saw the special root of theology.[23]

It was in this *Fifth Discourse,* in the closing pages of the book, that Schleiermacher took occasion, for the first time as a public writer, to express himself on the person of Christ: The truly divine in Jesus lay "in the exhibition of the wonderful clarity of the great idea that in order to unite with divinity all the finite beings are in need of higher mediations." He was conscious of having "the office of mediation"; but he "never claimed to be . . . . . . the only mediator." Schleiermacher refused to accept the divinity of Christ on the basis of the incarnation. In the second edition of the discourses he calls Christ a "mediator without parallel." [24]

There is one more suggestion of interest which Schleiermacher expressed in the last few pages of his *Reden.* It is the idea that Christianity does not claim to be the only form of religion and to rule alone in humanity. Christ "has always pointed to the truth that was to come after him." This abandonment of the absoluteness of Christianity, which then was repeated with more seriousness by F. C. Baur, R. Rothe and E. Troeltsch (see below) was with Schleiermacher more a theoretical idea than a practical experience.[25]

3. THE EFFECT OF THESE DISCOURSES.

There were those among the great men of that age who confessed that these *Reden* had shown them the way to a new life. Neander gave such testimony. Claus Harms in his autobiography dated his birthday for a higher life from a reading of Schleiermacher's *Reden.* He confesses to have learned from them that there is nothing in Rationalism, that our own knowledge and our own conduct do not help us, but that man's salvation must have altogether different causes. Many—perhaps most—of the first readers did not understand the book. It is one of those classical writings full of original and prophetic thought that cannot simply be read but must be studied and restudied. Kirn is right when he speaks of the long *Nachwirkung* of this book.[26] One effect lay in this, that the new scientific spirit of that age found itself forced to recognize religion as a constituent factor of civilization and as an independent force.

III. SCHLEIERMACHER'S CONCEPT OF THEOLOGY

The very interesting history connected with Schleiermacher's changing from place to place in the earlier part of his career must be read in the biographies and in the encyclopedias. Here we need to remember that in 1804 he was called to Halle as professor

---

[23] See his *Kurze Darstellung des theologischen Studiums,* a program for the study of theology, presently to be reviewed.

[24] Cf. *PRE,* XVII, 596, line 7.

[25] Seeberg, *op. cit.,* p. 47. R. G. Gruetzmacher, *Theol. Magazine,* Jan., 1928, p. 33.

[26] "Und doch war den Reden mehr eine lange Nachwirkung als eine starke Erstwirkung beschieden." *PRB* XVII, 595, lines 15 f.

and that in 1807 he was again in Berlin, first as preacher and soon as participant in the foundation of the new university and as its professor.

His program appeared in 1811 in a "Brief Outline of Theological Study." [27] This brief writing shows the remarkable ability of Schleiermacher as a systematician. He was the first to conceive clearly the idea of a theological encyclopedia: Guided by a conception of Christian Theology as an organism he defined the relation of the individual branches of theology as to their place in the system. In this there is a lesson of method also for those who cannot agree with his conception of theology. The details of Schleiermacher's suggestions in this writing invite a series of critical remarks along the following lines:

1. Schleiermacher demanded a "philosophical theology" (paragraph 24) with starting points above and before Christianity (par. 33). This recalls the Fifth Discourse in his *Reden* where he spoke of religious truth outside of Christianity in forms of religion against which Christianity must not be exclusive. In the language of today, this would be called religious philosophy. Apologetics and polemics especially were to be used as the channels for this discussion (par. 67). Independent of the Christian faith, entirely upon the basis of principles of its own, this "religious philosophy" or "philosophical theology" determines contents and truth in all the leading conceptions of Christianity and Church. The intra-theological disciplines, such as dogmatics and ethics, have nothing to do with the finding of Christian truth except to give a report of what religious philosophy has found (par. 41). To this we have to reply that Christian theology cannot accept the determination of its principles for the exposition of dogmatics by such a universalistic entity as religious philosophy. Whatever may be needed in the way of prefatory principles, a Christian theology must demand that such a *"Prinzipienlehre"* rests upon the admission of the absoluteness of historic Christianity. By admitting the authority of such a philosophical theology Schleiermacher prepared the way for the present-day conversion of theology into a philosophy of religion in which the truth of Christianity is made dependent upon general speculations.

2. In his program Schleiermacher sees the essence and purpose of theology in the things that are called "practical theology" (par. 5 and 26). This is to him the "crown of theology." Outside of this practical purpose and interest, these same matters of knowledge do not belong to theology but to that "philosophical theology" of which we have spoken (Cf. par. 6). What is the meaning of this distinction? There are those who interpret it to mean that theology as such must serve the Church; to the degree that it does not serve the Church it is not theology but philosophy. In other words: Theological science is denied the right to be an end in itself.

3. It is interesting to observe that Schleiermacher divided historical theology—in its wider conception—into three parts: Exegetical theology, including symbolics and statistics, and ethics. The lesson for us from this strange division is that the need of the historical approach and interest was seen to be governing the whole of theology.

IV. SCHLEIERMACHER'S DOGMATICS

The application of the program which has been discussed was made in Schleiermacher's work on dogmatics, which appeared eleven years later: "The Christian Faith

---

[27] *Kurze Darstellung des Theologischen Studiums*, 2nd ed. by H. Scholz, 1910. English readers may use Farrar, *Schleiermacher's Brief Outline of the Study of Theology*.

According to the Principles of the Evangelical Church, Presented under an Organizing Principle." [28] It represents a new method in the history of dogmatics. Seeberg writes: 'This book was the teacher of theology to the church of the nineteenth century. All theologians have been influenced by it, and who could imagine the theology of today without it?" [29] In this remark Seeberg has no intention of recommending Schleiermacher as a doctrinally reliable guide on the individual topics of dogmatics. His reference is to the work as an organization, as a plan, to the new method in the building of dogmatics as a system. Note the expression in the title: *"im Zusammenhang dargestellt."* (And compare with it par. 19.)

1. This *difference of method* will become clear by a review of the history of dogmatics as a science:

The type that had ruled since the Reformation was that of the *Loci.* Melanchthon gave us the first Dogmatics of Protestantism in his *Loci Communes Rerum Theologicarum,* 1521. Guided by the "topics" (*Loci, Leitbegriffe,* leading conceptions) in Paul to the Romans Melanchthon sought for the verification of these topics in the Scriptures. Chemnitz and then all the seventeenth century theologians wrote their *Loci.* They searched the Scriptures for outstanding doctrines (*sedes doctrinae*), and then they grouped these after their reference to the traditional topics: God, Trinity, soteriology, the means of grace, the Church and eschatology—much like Melanchthon and like Calvin (in his *Institutes*). With little variation this method has ruled up to the age of Rationalism.[30] There was a craving for more subjective discussion. With concessions to this demand Schleiermacher now created an all-around logical system erected upon a controlling fundamental principle.[31]

The actual forces of the religious life of the Christian fellowship are to be studied in order to find what is religion and what are the contents of religion.

Such a development of dogmatics (1) upon the basis of a fundamental principle, (2) with the description of its contents in terms of the life of the Church and, (3) the demand that in it all, the dogmatician must express his own religious consciousness—all this proved to be very fascinating to the theologians of the new age in Germany.

Schleiermacher made the statement that the truth of the findings "must be approved by agreement with the evangelical Confessions, and, in the absence of such, partly by the New Testament writings and partly by the connection of a doctrine with other already recognized doctrines." (Cf. par. 27.)

It is at once clear that these seminal principles of Schleiermacher's mind would offer challenges for theologians to the right as well as to the left to build speculative systems of their own upon very differing foundations. There were those who followed the evolutionism of Hegel, as we shall see in Chapter IV, and others who followed the ideas of Kant and their modifications. (See Chapter I.) Among the conservatives we mention especially F. H. Frank, who created a much discussed "system" in which he demanded

---

[28] *Der Christliche Glaube nach den Grundsaetzen der evangelischen Kirche im Zusammenhang dargestellt;* 1st ed., 1821 and 1822; 2nd revised edition, 1830, which the writer has before him as Vols. 13 to 16 in the *Bibliothek theologischer Klassiker,* 1889.

[29] *Kirche Deutschlands,* 2, p. 84

[30] Cf. K. F. A. Kahnis, *Der Innere Gang des deutschen Protestantismus* [3], II, 99; also *RGG* on Dogmatik I, 1966.

[31] Here we have tried to put into one statement what Schleiermacher says in paragraphs 3, 4, 15, 19, 29-31 of his *Dogmatics,* 2nd revised edition. On the meaning of the terms employed compare Kattenbusch, *op. cit.,* pp. 22, 29 ff., and especially Wobbermin in *RGG.* V. 171 ff.

that "Christian certainty" is to be explained out of the pious selfconsciousness of the individual theologian.

2. *The Special Topics:* The strong inclination of Schleiermacher to Spinozian pantheism in the *conception of God* was discussed in connection with the second of his *Discourses on Religion*. While in the *Glaubenslehre* there is no theoretical reaffirmation of pantheism (cf. par. 8, note 2) yet it is this sentiment that forms the background of the discussion.[32] It is observable in his writing on creation, on God's omnipotence, on preservation and miracle. Kattenbusch remarks: "There is something painful in the observation how uncertain Schleiermacher remains with regard to the ultimate relation of knowledge and religion. . . . Again and again, up to his end, he has statements that make problematic and unsatisfactory the religious thoughts regarding the distinction between God and world, for which the theologians must stand" (p. 27)

Special note must be taken of the central place which Schleiermacher gave to *Christ as redeemer from sin*. In this he is credited with having paved the way for the Christocentric trend of the conservative theology of the nineteenth and twentieth centuries. The example of a great thinker will always have an encouraging effect, of course. But the fact of the Reformation in itself, as it spoke through the confessional writings, surely was strong enough to resurrect that deep Christological interest which has permeated Christian theology from the beginning of the history of the Church up to the time of the apostasy in Rationalism. It may be admitted that the "Mediating School" was noticeably helped by the bridge which Schleiermacher furnished in his emphatic though peculiar emphasis upon the person of Christ and the redemption through Him.

In order to arrive at an estimate of Schleiermacher's final conception of the work of Christ, the beginning of our examination may be made with an enquiry as to his teaching on *sin*: It was to him the positive antithesis of sensuality against the spirit by which we are hindered in the consciousness of our absolute dependency upon God. (Cf. par. 66 and 67.) Sin, therefore, is not as with the Reformation the opposition of the will to God, but it is, Platonically, a disturbance of the harmony between man's natural powers, which hinders within him the assertion of his relation to God.[33] Redemption, then, means an ethical influence of Christ upon the believer, by which he is received into Christ's own energy (*Kraeftigkeit*) of the divine consciousness (par. 100 and 101). In this fellowship with Christ the believer experiences justification and conversion (par. 107 and 109). But all these terms are reinterpreted. The forgiveness of sin as guilt and an objective atonement drop into the background. God does not change His attitude, but man's relation to God is changed (Cf. Abelard). All this must be held in view when the fundamentally Christocentric trait in Schleiermacher's theology is spoken of. The great merit of Christ consisted, as was stated, in this that He was the first to conceive of the thought that the infinite and the finite are in need of a higher mediation. The way He effected this made Him a "mediator without parallel" (Cf. the fifth of the *Reden*). Although seeing Christ as man like ourselves and not really God, Schleiermacher seeks terms that might serve as substitutes: He was without sin; in no need of redemption; His origin different from all others; His personality not to be explained out of His environment. He represented a new creation, like a second Adam. The constant energy

---

[32] See Kattenbusch, *op. cit.*, pp. 27, 28.
[33] See Gruetzmacher, *Textbuch*, pp. 45 f.

of His divine consciousness was identical with a real being of God in Him.[34] Because
Schleiermacher refused to accept the divinity of Christ on the basis of the historical teaching of the incarnation (which he reinterprets), he was at a loss as to what to do with
the *Trinity*. On this topic he offers remarks to the close of his work (par. 170, 172). He
inclined to Sabellianism but suggested a reconstruction of the ancient formulations. The
Holy Spirit was to him merely the *"Gemeindegeist,"* proceeding from Christ, "a working,
spiritual force." And because of his conception of sin as a disharmony of the natural
powers, instead of an attitude of the will against God and consequently a guilt to be
blotted out and to be forgiven on the basis of an objective atonement as basis for the
subjective, therefore redemption is given a merely mystical significance, and Christ
ceases to be Saviour in the meaning of the Reformation.

Opposed, as Schleiermacher was, to the "metaphysics" in matters such as the Trinity,
so he also declined to give to *eschatology* a place among the fundamentals of Christianity
(par. 159). On the question of *personal immortality* which was denied in the *Reden*
Schleiermacher gave a dualistic answer in the *Glaubenslehre*. Acceptable from the standpoint of our relation to Christ; no root of necessity for it in man's relation to God.[35]

3. For an estimate of Schleiermacher's theology, it is necessary to remember, as was
pointed out in our discussion of his "Brief Outline for Theological Study," that the
*determinative principles for a system of the Christian Faith were sought outside the
field of theology.* He speaks of "ethics," by which he means a kind of a sociological
philosophy of history. He also includes in that a philosophical theology which we called
a "religious philosophy," that is, a kind of comparative religion. He calls those determining principles *"Lehrsaetze"* (guides for the theological discussion). Thus there is a
foreign philosophical criterion which constantly shapes or influences the subject matters
of Christian theology. True, he aims at the establishment of a certain agreement with
Scripture and the Confessions. These, however, are not to be used as sources of theology
but just as confirmation of what has been found. His interest is in the agreement of
theology with his *Dialektik* (1838) and with his *Draft of a Philosophical Ethics* (1835).
Here were the real foundations of his theological views.[36]

V. SCHLEIERMACHER'S ETHICS

From the beginning of his career Schleiermacher had a deep interest in the study
of ethics. As early as 1790, about the time of his examination as a candidate for the
ministry, he wrote with penetrating insight on the problem of freedom and determination.[37] His sermons at that time show the moralistic trait in rationalistic fashion. The
significance of Christianity is seen in its being the source of a higher morality. Then
followed his first six years in Berlin, up to 1802, as a preacher, and here, immediately
after his *Reden,* in 1800, he published his *Monologen* on the problems of general ethics,
which, later, he developed in a *Draft of a System of Ethics* published after his death
(1838). His university lectures on *Christian Ethics* were published in 1843.[38]

---

[34] On all these points compare his *Glaubenslehre;* 2nd ed., pars 35, 93, 94, 98.

[35] Read Kirn in *PRE,* XVII, 607.

[36] R. Locke, *Die Quintessenz der Theologie Schleiermacher's,* Sect. II; *Schleiermacher's Psychologie und
Dialektik in ihrem Zusammenhang mit der Theologie,* 1885. Cf. also Simon, *op. cit.,* pp. 108 ff.

[37] See the fragment quoted by Dilthey, *op. cit.,* pp. 19-46.

[38] This enumeration of Schleiermacher's works on ethics does not include his *Grundlinien einer Kritik der
bisherigen Sittenlehre* (1803), because that deals pre-eminently with technical questions, moving in abstract
discussion, for which reason it has never been much read. Cf. *PRE* XVII, 596, line 48 ff.

The strong interest of Schleiermacher in ethics indicates his ethical approach to Christianity as a religion. It is another symptom of the anthropocentric emphasis in theology of which Schleiermacher was making himself the spokesman. The *Monologues*, written in 1801, announce the leading thought of his ethics: Development of our own self into a distinct individual form of humanity. "To become more and more what I am—this is my only will; every action is a distinct development of this One will." [39] Kirn calls him the "philosopher of individuality": In the inner soul of man he discovered the law of individuality, which man is in duty bound to follow. This principle placed Schleiermacher in ethics on the side of Goethe and removed him from Kant.

Ethics, in the definition of Schleiermacher, is development of the individual in loving union with humanity, especially in friendship and in the married state. The whole tendency of Schleiermacher to a union of theology with philosophy colors also his Christian ethics. The aim is at a *"Kulturethik"* such as is developed in a system by R. Rothe. Sin, redemption, regeneration lose their Christian meaning. They are Platonized. Neither is there an appreciation of the fact that between the Church and the world there is not merely a difference, but an antithesis.[40] The fact is that the "Christian" ethics of Schleiermacher is strongly influenced by his conception of a generally humanistic ethics. This is true to such an extent that, in the judgment of very progressive conservatives, he actually "Hellenized Christian ethics." The Christian and the truly human were identical to him. As to his writings on ethics in general the student must keep in mind, that his life came to a close before he could give to these the form which he desired for their publication.

VI. CLOSING OBSERVATIONS ON THE SIGNIFICANCE OF SCHLEIERMACHER

In the following notes there is no aim at systematic presentation. The reader will find that some of the points were already referred to in the discussion. Here we shall try merely to enumerate the various features in the picture of Schleiermacher as a theologian.

1. *Schleiermacher combined in his theology the scientific, or let us say, the philosophical interests with those of the Church.* The union of these two factors was his special concern. In principle he was opposed to mixing theology with philosophy. But he did not succeed in his intention of keeping the two fields separate. Kattenbusch remarks: "Schleiermacher fails to overcome the disunion (*Zwiespalt*) of the philosopher and the theologian in one person." And again: "The philosopher and the theologian in him did not find each other." [41] He himself said "I would not have permitted my own amateurishness in philosophy to influence the contents of the Glaubenslehre. How I have succeeded in my intention—this, of course, is another question." Once more we recall the demand in his program for the study of theology to look for leading principles to philosophical ethics. It was by this that Schleiermacher laid foundations for converting Christian dogmatics into a philosophy of religion. Thus he set the example for the speculative theology of the nineteenth century. Further stimulation was then received from Hegel and the Hegelians, as we shall see in the next chapter.

---

[39] Critical edition by F. M. Schiele; 2nd ed. by Mulert, 1914.

[40] Cf. John 5:19 "And we know that we are of God, and the whole world lieth in wickedness." Gal. 1:4 "Who gave himself for our sins that he might deliver us from this present world."

[41] *Der Philosoph und der Theolog in ihm fanden sich nicht, op. cit.* p. 28.

2. *The strong emphasis by Schleiermacher on feeling, on the Christian's dependency upon God, as the unifying principle of his Glaubenslehre, on Christian experience and the movements of the soul, makes his theology a religious psychology.* It may be admitted that it was through this act of positing the essence of theology in feeling, in the heart, instead of in the intellect or in the will, that he secured for theology a province of its own. Theology again became respected. The contempt in which it had been held is reflected in the treatment of Pfarrer Goeze by Lessing. Kattenbusch remarks that outstanding minds (*"Koepfe"*) among the young theologians in the age of Schleiermacher practically all passed from theology to philosophy, as witness Fichte, Schelling, Hegel. But it was also upon this basis of psychological orientation that Schleiermacher brushed aside the theocentric interest in theology and replaced it by the anthropocentric. He declares "the description of human conditions as the *dogmatische Grundform.*" (See especially par. 30.) Man, in the conditions of his soul instead of God and His work which was the leading interest of the Reformation, becomes the center of theological thought. Here Schleiermacher committed dogmatics to the trend which had been created by modern philosophy since Descartes. This as an instance shows how he labored for a compromise between the traditional metaphysical and the historical components of Christianity and his own pantheistically modernized world-view in which subjectivism and psychological orientation received the stress. Among the conservatives it was in the men of the "Mediating School" that the principles of Schleiermacher found special appreciation.

3. *There is no school that has accepted Schleiermacher's theology.* The conservatives of the pietistic and of the professedly orthodox type, while permitting themselves to be stimulated by this and that principle, refused to follow his theology, and they re-established the thought-categories of the Reformation. They were convinced that he had departed from the analogy of faith. The confessional theologians of the earlier period were his determined opponents. Philippi, in the four large volumes of his *Dogmatics,* wrote much against him. The Lutherans in America generally refused him, not only as to the substance of his teaching, but also as to the speculative type of his method. The remark of Horst Stephan, an admirer of his method, quoted above (II, 1), characterizes an actual situation: *"Er hat die Theologie an Luther vorbeigefuehrt."*

4. On the example of Schleiermacher *to develop Dogmatics upon the basis of one controlling and unifying principle* there need to be only a few remarks. The principle upon which he built was the feeling of dependency of the pious soul upon the infinite. Others have chosen different principles. Such as the "theocentric" (Schaeder), or the "soteriological" (A. von Oettingen) may prove to be practical for a presentation of what is fundamental. But when Schleiermacher chose religion as "feeling," and when a Hegelian chose the unity in the movement of "thought" (Marheineke, Twesten), and again another the movements of the "will" (Roehr), then W. Elert is surely right when he points to the fragmentary character of a theology that follows either Kant, or Hegel or Schleiermacher. Surely, there must be a synthesis of all that is vital to the life of the Church on the basis of Scripture and Confession. This leads us to consider whether the heritage of method from Schleiermacher has been so great a benefaction as his eulogists have led many to think. A reasonable combination of the old objective and the modern subjective method will be the best method for serving the Church in its need of a theology for the guidance of souls to their salvation. The purpose of dogmatics

is not to exhibit a field for mental gymnastics and brilliancy of new thought but to be helpful to the preacher of the Gospel. In this statement we are conscious of having many opponents.

5. The most delicate point among the suggestions for reform from Schleiermacher's *Glaubenslehre* is *the practice of developing the contents of Dogmatics out of the "pious self-consciousness" or out of Christian experience.*

a. A positive Christianity cannot accept a theology which does not make the testimony of Scripture, God's revelation to us, in a special sense the primary source of truth and its authority. A "standard dogmatics of the Church for all time," such as some are craving, is unacceptable for the simple reason that Christian dogmatics must constantly renew itself out of a growing understanding of Scripture. There are pages—not many—in the four volumes of Schleiermacher's *Dogmatics* where he does point to Scripture passages, but mostly he uses them just as references or illustrations. He does not draw from them as real sources. Yet it does occur that he uses them as means for proof. He says there are cases "where necessarily other Scripture passages must be applied *als Beweismittel,*" and on page 242 he speaks of a *"schriftmaessige Dogmatik"* (par. 27, 1. Vol. I, 237). Thus we see that Schleiermacher himself found that in the application of his principle he could not be consistent. It is very interesting to observe that for proof purposes Schleiermacher put the Confessions of the Church *before the Scriptures.* This was in keeping with his position that the Confessions must be valued as Christian experience of the churches. The conservative theologians know, of course, that as a matter of fact the average Christian theologian *starts* his work in dogmatics not anew in every case as a pioneer in the erudition of Scripture facts, but he begins his theological thinking on the basis of a heritage deposited in the confessional experience of the Christian Church. It was this fact upon which Schleiermacher psychologically built his emphasis upon Christian experience as the primary source of dogmatic truth.

He ignored the significance of the Scriptures for dogmatics. Every new topic in his work is introduced by the statement of a principle. Among these is not one in all four volumes that begins with the Holy Scriptures. In par. 15 he formulates the principle: "Christian statements of faith are conceptions of the Christian pious conditions of the soul (*Gemuetszustaende*), exhibited in the form of speech." Wobbermin, follower of Schleiermacher in many things, remarks: If he now had added an answer to the question as to which of these *Gemuetszustaende* are Christian then that would have led him to the historical contents of the religious life, and from there to the relation of faith to the Holy Scriptures. True, Wobbermin adds that the Scriptures can be understood only by means of the individual experience of faith. But on the other hand, the really Christian experience of faith must constantly orientate and legitimate itself on the Holy Scriptures as its real norm.[42]

b. In the above quoted statement (VI, 5) and by example in his whole work, Schleiermacher established the practice for writers in dogmatics to develop the *subject matter* out of their own Christian selfconsciousness. The attitude of the theologians to this innovation has been varied. One must read Schleiermacher's work in order to understand this method. He has had followers also among the conservatives. F. H. Frank, the first great systematician of the Erlangen School, wrote after this method in his

---

[42] *RGG*, V. 174 f. See also Kirn *PRE*, XVII. 595. line 34.

System of Christian Certainty (1870 ff.). We ask: Does this method do away with the Scriptures as source and authority? If it did to a considerable extent in the case of Schleiermacher, must it do the same in the case of dogmaticians who make moderate concessions to this method? Frank was not fortunate in his expression on the subject. Philippi subjected him to much criticism. But the best theologians among Frank's successors have followed him and have made use of the principle in loyalty to the other principle that in all cases the Scriptures must be the real source of truth and constitute the final court of appeal (Luthardt, von Oettingen, Ihmels, Girgensohn, et al.). When they have spoken of Christian selfconsciousness and experience as a creative factor in dogmatics, they were not theorizing on the Bible and putting Scripture into contrast with Christian experience, but they merely wanted to explain how the conviction of Christian truth, on the basis of communicated Scripture revelation, originates and takes shape in the mind of the individual, particularly in the mind of the theologian when he is writing dogmatics. Schleiermacher, in this case, wrote and acted as an observer of psychological facts. The fact is that the Christian dogmatician, when writing his work, does not first make his mind a blank and then go to Scripture for thought upon thought. No, he is a Christian. The influences from a Christian home, from a Christian environment, from Christian teachers and preachers of varying personalities, from inner experiences in struggles for forgiveness of sin and for Christian certainty, from all the Scripture truth accompanying such a development—these are the things which start him in his writing, and the meditation over these things furnishes him the organization of his material. Then he considers and reconsiders his thoughts in the light of Scripture, Confession, history and the influences about him. Agreement with Scripture and the testimony of the Church are his chief concern. Every leading statement is examined and re-examined in this light. It is in this sense that one can speak of the dogmatician as drawing from his own Christian consciousness. The subjective element, which had an overemphasis with Schleiermacher, cannot be dismissed altogether. Even if we should want to draw with strictest objectivism from Scripture, the element of interpretation would still be the subjective factor which we cannot deny.

Does this place us upon common ground with theological liberalism? (1) In liberalism, the Scriptures are estimated merely as a commentary on the Christian life, or as a reflector of Christian experience. Even as a factor in creating the Christian consciousness, they are not source and authority of truth, and, therefore, have no proving value. (2) Here the conception of revelation extends to the gems of truth and beauty in all thought. Thus the philosophizing mind of the individual, autonomous and under no authority, is in reality the revealing source of truth. The singular significance of Scripture is completely sacrificed.

. . . .

We have come to the close in our characterization of one of the most remarkable theologians of history. Schleiermacher was a man of a penetrating intellect, a philosopher and a theologian, a universal mind of remarkable insight into psychological facts, a creative genius, an organizer of thought, endowed with a wonderful power in systematizing his materials, a seminal mind, a prophet at the portals of a new age, inexhaustible in suggestions even where his leading position is not acceptable. He was the father of modern theology along two lines of conflicting tendencies. At the news of his death

A. Neander declared to his students: With the passing of this man history will record the beginning of a new period in theology. The theologians of more than a century have been working on his thoughts. Kattenbusch remarks, however, that by this time the suggestions from him have been exhausted. Much was to be supplemented that he particularly was unable to give. Theology must not return to Schleiermacher.

In recent times Schleiermacher has met with the most bitter criticism of Karl Barth and his school. The Barthians regard Schleiermacher as the arch-heretic of the nineteenth century because it was he who put theology on a definite anthropocentric basis.[43]

---

[43] Cf. the trenchant criticism of E. Brunner in *Die Mystik und das Wort*, 2nd Ed., 1928.

Chapter Four

THEOLOGY AND THEOLOGIANS UNDER THE INFLUENCE OF HEGEL'S PHILOSOPHY

Literature: We shall hold in mind the following authors, referred to at the beginning of Book Five: LICHTENBERGER, PFLEIDERER, SEEBERG, ELERT, KATTENBUSCH, GRUETZMACHER. We add: G. P. FISHER, *History of Christian Doctrine*, 1896-1906, pp. 531 ff. E. OTT, *Die Religionsphilosophie Hegels*, 1904. CUNO FISHER, *Hegel*, 2nd ed., 1911. T. SIMON, *Grundriss der Geschichte der neueren Philosophie*, 1920, pp. 116 ff. K. LEESE, *Die Geschichtsphilosophie Hegels*, 1922.

I. GEORG FRIEDRICH WILHELM HEGEL

Hegel (1770-1831), philosopher at the University of Berlin, aimed to reconcile religion with reason, or, what is the same, theology with philosophy. He, therefore, incorporated into his philosophical system an extensive treatment of the history of religion and Christianity, which had a great influence upon at least two generations of theologians. It may be repeated that Germany's theology of the nineteenth century, in addition to the influence it received from Schleiermacher, moved in an alternative way between the strong impulses from Hegel and Kant.

1. It is interesting to observe the development *from Kant to Hegel.* There was the aim at a complete comprehension of reality and the growing conviction of the possibility of its accomplishment. In the terse statements of T. Simon, the development was as follows: Kant found his limit in the *Ding an sich.* Fichte's *I* did produce the *Non-I*, but only unconsciously, so that after all it had not been done by the powers of thought. And, furthermore, in this *Non-I* of Fichte there remained a remnant of an impenetrable matter needed as object for the stimulation and exercise of freedom (pp. 89, 116). Schelling's philosophy of identity was just a statement which brought no complete penetration of reality by the mind. Then came Hegel with a philosophy of a peculiar appeal also to many theologians.

2. The ideas of Hegel. Here we can be expected to speak of the Hegelian ideas only in so far as they became a guide for thinkers in the field of theology.

Hegel identified being with thinking. In thinking we grasp reality to the extent of objectifying it. He does not mean that the thinking of an individual necessarily is identical with the objective being; its errancy and accidentality are admitted. But *absolute* thought, *absolute* reason and *objective* reality are the same. It must be kept in mind, however, that the thinking of an individual shares in this identity with reason and reality only in so far as his thinking is a part of absolute thought. In Hegel the "substance" of Spinoza becomes subject or mind, and its reality consists in the participation of absolute thought. In contrast to Schleiermacher, Hegel stands for intellectualism in religion and theology.

God, the reality in the background or at the foundation of this thought, is objectively comprehensible by human thinking. Philosophy and theology, therefore, have the same contents, namely God as the absolute mind. In this, however, they are different according to Hegel: Religion and theology can see and comprehend God only symbolically and mythologically, as in the teachings of the Bible. The Church's dogma, therefore, could not help but include matters contradictory to reason. But philosophy furnishes the intellectual and rational formulas in which those contradictions are harmonized and reduced to unified expression.

3. *There is a difference between Spinoza and Hegel* that qualifies materially the latter's conception of God. Spinoza conceived of God and world as "substance" at rest. In oriental fashion (Spinoza was a Jew), that absolute Being is thought of as the mass of waters in the ocean, out of which the waves rise eternally and recede into that "substance," ever the same in eternal stagnation. (In an up and down movement; never in the manner of a flowing stream.) Spinoza had predicated real existence to substance only as that in which individual things are contained as modes. Thus he did away with the individual life of personality. The ego was to him no individual reality. But according to Hegel, with his emphasis upon mind and the spiritual phenomena, we see God and world in a process of continuous development. It is in this development that reality must be seen. It is the doctrine that man is the end and aim of all expressions of life in the universe (*Geistesphilosophie*). The divine selfconsciousness is unfolding itself from non-being to being, from something potential to something actual. As Schelling had already pictured it in his *Naturphilosophie,* the development of that absolute being in God and world begins with the appearance of life in nature and then moves through the realms of the mind. The actual movement is thus defined as a revelation upward, from art to religion and from religion to philosophy. The method after which this dialectical movement proceeds is indicated by the famous three stages: thesis (assertion of the idea), antithesis (its critique), synthesis (its harmonization)—an old thought, indicated by Empedocles and embodied in the "golden mean" of Aristotle (W. Durant). In the history of religion especially we behold that upward development in which God reveals himself to an ever clearer selfconsciousness. In paganism, Judaism and Christianity we have these progressing stages of development in the process of unfolding the divine. In the Hegelian observation historical development is the constant representation of the absolute. In this historical process there is no permanency: God Himself, indistinguishable from the phenomena, is in a constant process of change. He has no real existence. The absolute is always only on the way of becoming real, but never reaches that end as a completed process.[1]

4. *Hegel's pantheism has greatly influenced the study of history.* Before Hegel, the historian saw but isolated historical facts which he at best succeeded in explaining by a so-called "pragmatism of individual motives." Before Hegel, history was always written in this way: There once was a man who did so and so. Hegel taught the historian to see in all historical development the rule of an objective and universal reason. This thought took hold of many theologians, as we shall see: The movements of individuals and groups were taken to be the acts of God as the "absolute" which is realizing itself in the acting individuals and groups.

There is truth in this, of course. The representatives of development in history are not altogether independently the makers of history. In the realization of their ideas they are in many cases in the service of a higher reason, namely of God who is either directing

---

[1] Different from Spinoza whose "substance" had existence.

or overruling. Critically the following observations will be in place: (1) It must not be overlooked that the individual for himself, or by his influence upon a group, acts with personal responsibility. (2) The reason which we see in the universe is not God Himself, but something from God. It is His laws, His order, His system of relations; but back of it all is Himself as the personal God. Pantheism fails to press through from the effect to the cause, from the laws to the One who established them, from the order in the universe to the One from whom it originated.[2]

5. *Christianity*, Hegel said, is the highest, most perfect of the religions. It is the absolute religion which cannot be excelled for the reason that in the historic Christ as the God-man the conception of religion as the selfconsciousness of God in the mind of man comes to the clearest expression and the fullest reality. This revelation, however, has its existence only in representation—symbolically, as was remarked. This thought made followers among the theologians who stood under the influence of Schleiermacher.

What becomes of the historic Christ in this way? His significance is reduced to a philosophical idea, the same as with the modalistic Monarchianism of the ancient Church, of which Sabellianism was a clear type. Here Christ was chiefly an idea, with no tangible existence (Docetism).

There were a number of religious conceptions belonging to the faith of historic Christendom, which contained the suggestion that as "representations" they needed not to be established upon historical facts. We shall here mention only two: (a) *Sin*: In the purely natural world there was no possibility of sinning. But in the spiritual world, among men who in the above described development from the purely natural to the personal have come into an existence of being themselves (*"Fuersichsein"*), there is the possibility of independence and freedom. Man, as part of God, must decide for God. Then he is good. If he decides for himself and serves himself he is evil. All men have to make this decision. The Biblical record puts this experience of every individual at the beginning of man's history, and the Church explains the universality of sin through the idea of an "inherited evil." But what the conservatives have criticized in Hegel is this: His idea of an absolute unity in the universe necessitated the rejection of a moral and rational dualism. Man's fall and sin in general consequently became to Hegel not only a necessary stage of development for striving toward the higher, but even a needed impulse for that end. The "fall" in Christian "mythology" made man the real man. It was a fall upward. The dualistic conception disappears. (b) *Atonement:* The consciousness of his sinful condition made man long for reconciliation. But he could not find that reconciliation if it were not already actually existing in the unity of the divine and the human. The mission of Christ as the God-man, therefore, was to be an objective visible representation of the existing reconciliation which we must accept in faith. There is no real chasm to be bridged. In both of these conceptions (sin and atonement) the *necessity* of the Biblical accounts as facts did not appear, although Hegel himself had no intention to question the historicity of the person of Christ and His work. But among the theologians who followed him were men who made much of the mythological character of Biblical history.

We shall here content ourselves with passing reference to Hegel's conception of the relation between Church and state. We know how he stressed the importance of the

---

[2] On this subject compare the criticism of Pantheism by C. E. Luthardt, *Die christliche Glaubenslehre,* 2nd edition, 1906, pp. 133-37.

state as the goal of historical development. Here ethics and religion were to find their highest form. The Church is only a means to accomplish it. This is an idea that has had outspoken successors in theology (Strauss, Baur, Rothe, Dilthey, Troeltsch).

The significance of Hegel for theology may be described as follows: (a) Hegel paved the way to reduce historic religion to philosophical ideas and rational conceptions. In this he was followed by a strong school of liberalistic theologians of which we shall treat below. There were also conservative theologians who made use of the Hegelian categories in order to present an orthodox system of theology, in which the old conflict between "faith" and "knowledge" (*Glauben und Wissen*) was imagined to have been ironed out. (Ph. Marheineke.) (b) Through Hegel the tendency to pantheism in theology, which had already been observed with Schleiermacher, was much augmented.

II. HEGELIAN THEOLOGIANS

1. A. E. BIEDERMANN. A clear case of Hegelian influence upon theology is observed in the liberal Swiss theologian A. E. Biedermann (1819-89). The starting point in his *"Christliche Dogmatik"* (first edition in 1868) is the dogma of the Church, but in all of its topics he labors to show the mythical character of its historical foundations as well as the logical contradictions of its formulations. His own positive contribution consists in the reducing of the religious contents in the foundations of the dogma to philosophical formulas. The belief in God as person is declined and replaced by Hegel's idea of the absolute mind. Individual immortality is declared to be indifferent; the truth in this teaching is the continuance of life in the universal mind back of objective reality. The Christian idea of redemption is a representation of the ideal thought of redemption, which for the first time in history arrived at selfconsciousness and realization in the person of Jesus.

2. Application to the history of the Old Testament. Hegel, from his standpoint of an evolution of the divine mind in history, could not admit the teaching of the English Deists that originally religion was pure and that only gradually it became corrupted. David Hume had already taken the opposite position and taught a development from the imperfect to the more perfect. This had also been the teaching of Voltaire in France. Hegel accepted this thought, but he gave it the idea of an absolute progressive mind as the moving factor in this evolution. VATKE, pupil of Hegel and professor of Old Testament literature in the Berlin university, published in 1835 his *Religion des Alten Testaments.* Here, for the first time, Hegel's conception of evolution is applied to the history of the Old Testament. The Jahvistic monotheism of the Old Testament prophets is the result of a gradual evolution from the old crude Semitic worship of nature to the purer conception of a personal God. Not much notice was taken of this book when it appeared. But here already we have the teachings and principles of the WELLHAUSEN'S school and its successors, all dominated by the Hegelian idea of evolution.

3. Hegelian ideas applied to the New Testament. (a) When Hegel died (1831), the "left wing" of his school which comprised most of his followers (the so-called "Young Hegelians"), developed more and more into religious radicalism. It appeared that the hope that in Hegel's philosophy the formulas for the union between *"Glauben und Wissen"* had been found was nothing but a dream.

a. The chief representative of the Hegelian left was DAVID FREDERICK STRAUSS (d. 1874). He began as teacher of theology in Tuebingen. But his radicalism was the cause of his removal from theology into a position as teacher of classical subjects. Declining to do this work he accepted a call as professor to Zuerich. But protests from the Church soon caused him to be pensioned after which he lived the life of a private scholar.

It was Strauss who with one act, namely in the publication of his *Leben Jesu* (1835-36), tore to pieces that phantom of an agreement between Hegelian philosophy and the faith of the Church. His starting-point was the miracles of Jesus, which he did not regard as authentic. But they are reported as historic in the Gospels of the New Testament. These Gospels, consequently, cannot be accepted as history. The stories of Jesus, therefore, must be legends which gradually came to be believed and which were woven about the head of the Master by the devoted disciples.

They may be used as truth, but only in a certain sense. What is here attributed to the individual can be claimed only by humanity as a whole. Hegel had taught that in the individual person of the God-man Jesus we have an expression of the universal idea. But Strauss objected that the "idea" does not exhaust its fullness in one individual, but distributes it over the whole race. So he argued that "Christ can neither be the perfect revelation of the divine nature, nor the perfect revelation of human nature. For God can only be perfectly revealed by the entire kingdom of spirits; and the full idea of man can only be perfectly revealed by the entire human race." (Cf. Bishop Martensen in his *Dogmatics,* p. 248.) The truth and lesson in the Gospel stories of Christ according to Strauss is simply that the human race lives, suffers, dies, is risen from the grave and ascends to heaven.

In the Gospels, then, we have myth and fiction. Strauss sees the starting-point of the development as a rule in stories of the Old Testament, occasionally also in legends of the pagan religions: the virgin birth of Christ in Isaiah 7:14; the star of Bethlehem in the star of Bileam (Numbers 24:17); the feeding of the five thousand in the wonderful feeding of the widow at Zarepta, and so on. According to earlier statements these myths developed spontaneously, without intention, stimulated simply by the powerful impression of Jesus upon His followers. But in a fundamentally reconstructed "Life of Jesus for the German People" (*Leben Jesu fuer das Deutsche Volk,* 1864), these mythological representations were unconsciously created by the disciples for the purpose of presenting the life of Jesus in romances.

Strauss had gradually become very radical. In his *Christliche Glaubenslehre* of 1840 he had already subjected the faith of the Church to a destructive criticism. He ridiculed the theistic conception of God as an impossible dualism. Man, the unity of the finite and the infinite, feels his limitations and produces God as a person in opposition to himself. In clear thinking we must learn to conceive of God as the infinite who arrives at personal representation in the finite spirits. In death, personality is lost, and we return to the divine unity. This was outright pantheism. Upon this basis there was no room any more for the Biblical and traditional faith of the Church.

Still, there was a certain seriousness and dignity about Strauss even in this impossible theory. But in succeeding writings, already in the above-mentioned second *Life of Jesus* (1864), but especially in his last book *Der alte und der neue Glaube* (1872), he moves noticeably on the downward grade as a theologian. He asks the question: "Are we still

Christians?" His answer is in the negative. He characterizes Christianity as a modified Judaism. Christ's resurrection is spoken of as mere "humbug." Our religion is seen in our relation to the universe in which there is order, law, reason, and kindness; but this universe is to him a blind mechanism without a purpose. Strauss turned to materialism. There is no hope for a life to come. He praised Darwin's discoveries as the bible of the new religion, with all theology removed. The Church was to disappear. The national classics were recommended as the books of devotion, the church buildings to be replaced by concert halls and theaters and to serve as the places of worship.

The last years of Strauss revealed more and more his degeneration as theologian and as a Christian. Seeberg in his *Theologie Deutschlands in neunzehnten Jahrhundert* (p. 88) publishes a poem which Strauss wrote in these outgoing years of his life. In this he mocks his own funeral. He wants two cats to be present to make music, etc.

And this was the end of David Frederick Strauss who with his "Life of Jesus" had succeeded in putting whole generations of theologians to work on the problems of Christology.

b. FERDINAND CHRISTIAN VON BAUR *and the Tuebingen School.* We turn to another very remarkable representative of Hegelian philosophy in theology, F. C. BAUR (1792-1862), the founder of the Tuebingen School (ZELLER, SCHWEGLER, VOLKMAR. HILGENFELD, HOLSTEN, and for a time RITSCHL).

Baur was a remarkable man. He is the only one in the first part of the nineteenth century who in mental endowment and in power of criticism can be compared with Schleiermacher. Schleiermacher devoted himself chiefly to the dogmatic interests of the new century. Baur raised the historical questions: the problem of the history of dogma, the history of Christianity in the first centuries, and, subsidiary to all this, the history of the origin of the New Testament Canon, to which he devoted his special attention. In these labors, as a critic of history, he showed a persevering diligence and a learning that was the marvel of the age. Lichtenberger describes him as not especially attractive in personality, as by nature "concentrated, substantial, historical and in a certain way objective; and he remained confined within the domain of intelligence. For him it is the world of thought and of science that alone exists, while the world of practical activity, of moral struggling and suffering, seems closed to him. But purely as a scholar he was one of the most eminent representations of the intellectual nobility of Germany in the university of the world."

His research was governed altogether by Hegelian ideas. Christianity is not a finished product expressed in the person of Christ and in the New Testament, but it is the expression of an idea in progressive development. With this thought before him, Baur wanted to explain Protestantism as a functioning principle through the history of the Christian Church. The Reformation, to him, was beset with the transcendental limitations of Roman Catholicism. But the "idea" or "principle" is constantly pressing forward to spiritualization. The Anabaptists and Socinians did special pioneer work in this direction. The "new reformation" is declared to have come with the age of Rationalism as it was born out of the new philosophy. But even in the most advanced religion of the present day, Baur said, there are still too many remnants of supernaturalism, irrationalism and mysticism, which must be overcome by a religion more humanized, rationalized, subjectified and spiritualized.

In the pursuit of discrediting traditional religion and for furnishing the foundations for the new religion, Baur reconstructed the whole history of doctrine upon the basis of Hegel's scheme for historical development. First, there is a period when in the form of a "thesis" a new one-sidedly expressed idea is proposed in a comparatively crude and simple condition. To this elementary attitude of the "idea," an antithesis arises, which contains corrective and supplementary elements, promising larger perfection, but which also is one-sided because it carries the opposition too far. After a time of controversy between these two extremes a happy middle position, a "synthesis," is found, which represents clarified truth or at least is a compromise.

In a large way, Baur saw an illustration of such stages in the unfolding of the idea in the history of doctrine; (He wrote a *History of Dogma*, 1847, 3rd ed. 1867. Cf. his *Lectures* on the same subject in three parts, 1895 ff.; also his large monographs on *Atonement* (1838), *Trinity and Incarnation*, 3 parts (1841 ff.). Catholicism is succeeded by the Old Protestantism, and this is followed by the New Protestantism. But the field in which Baur and his followers spent their special efforts was that of New Testament writings. The interest was in this: Does the authorship of these writings entitle them to be standards of truth? Following the just mentioned Hegelian scheme he finds the "thesis" in the period of Ebionitism, the primitive Christianity, or Judaeo-Christianity, or the Petrine Christianity, where the faith of the first Christians may be summed up in the single proposition: Jesus, the Messiah in whom the prophecies of the Old Testament are fulfilled. The representatives of this position are mostly Peter, James and "John." The literary documents are found in the legendary narratives such as the Gospel of the Hebrews, of Peter, of the Ebionites, of the Egyptians; especially in Matthew; also in the Apocalypse of John. Here Baur finds a narrow particularism which maintained itself with great tenacity in the early Christian Church. Against this "thesis" the opposition or "antithesis" came by Paul who opposed "a new principle of life with a universal character, in open rupture with Judaism, the temple and the Mosaic Law." The four great Epistles of Paul (Romans, Galatians, and both Corinthians), the only ones authentic, give evidence of his struggle against this Judaeo-Christianity. The conflict lasted beyond the lifetime of Paul into the middle of the second century. Then the inroads of Gnosticism and the persecutions of the Roman emperors made a union necessary, and a compromise took place. This event is reflected particularly in the "pseudo-Pauline" epistles to the Thessalonians, Ephesians, Colossians, Philippians, Philemon, Timothy, Titus, and in Luke with Mark in retouched form.

The Gospel of John has not yet been mentioned. Baur and his school decided that while the disciple of Christ was the author of the Apocalypse, he had not written the Gospel; it was declared to be a work written in the second century of high metaphysical speculation, relating no actual history. The facts and acts attributed to Christ are only starting-points, as we might say, pretexts for his discourses, attuned to the program contained in the prologue.

We close this review of the Tuebingen School with a few critical remarks. Baur's fundamental mistake lay in the preconceived ideas of Hegelian categories. He built his work upon a discovery which was found as if by divination, and so he failed to be critical where criticism should have started. His work in its positive features has gone up in consuming fire. A critic like Harnack has rendered the following often-repeated verdict: "The work of the Tuebingen School was an episode in which we have learned much, but after which we must unlearn more." (In his *Chronology of the Old Catholic Age*)

Still, for a full generation his "Tendenzgeschichte" dominated in the field of the New Testament research to such an extent that all who refused to fall in line had to submit to the stamp "unwissenschaftlich." R. Seeberg remarks of Baur: "He gave work for two generations of theologians. One generation he forced to accept his views, the other he forced into the work of refuting them." [3] If we think of how completely this Tuebingen School broke down then we have an illustration of how thoroughly an age can be deluded by a "scientific" system. F. Lichtenberger characterizes Baur's *History of Dogma* as an intellectual mechanism moved by a special force, a purely logical movement which receives no impulses from without and which notably remains without relation to the history of Christian life and morals." [4] Baur takes too little account of the person of Christ. He wanted to explain the historical origin of Christianity, in which he was unable to see anything of its supernatural character. For this reason he could not explain the resurrection of Christ and the conversion of Paul. As Strauss so Baur also, to the end of his life, discussed the question: "Are we still Christians?" which he had to answer negatively.

We admire his great scholarship. He had a vast knowledge, and with it he possessed constructive power. There was method in his criticism. Endless were the fact-materials that he dug up or which were brought to light by opponents as well as followers. He gave powerful impulses to the study of the New Testament introduction. But this must be said: While Baur's failure amounted to a complete vanquishment, he left a dangerous heritage to theological research in Germany. It was the temper of his criticism, the manner of treating the New Testament Scriptures like any other literature. He could see in the facts, in the voices and principles of the *"Urchristentum"* nothing of the forces that regenerated the degenerated pagan world of that day. The history of the early Church can be reliably interpreted only by one of a sympathetic attitude of mind to the spiritual factors of Christianity. Luther once said that the true theologian must be a *homo renatus.* A. Neander of Berlin university put it into the words: *Pectus est quod facit theologum.*

4. OTTO PFLEIDERER (d. 1909) *of the Berlin university also worked upon an orientation from Hegel and Baur.* He was a systematician and wrote on the basis of evolution.[5] He was a frequent visitor in England and America where he gave cycles of lectures. It is of interest that through him the way was paved to the Historico-Religious School. This is not difficult to understand. His fundamental orientation had been received from Hegel and Baur, and he had always refused to recognize Ritschlianism. He wrote as an historian on the background of a philosophico-religious conception of things. His larger works are: *Die Religion, ihr Wesen und ihre Geschichte,* 2 vols., 2nd edition 1883; *Grundriss der christlichen Glaubens—und Sittenlehre,* 5th edition 1893; and *Religions-philosophie auf geschichtlicher Grundlage,* 2 vols. 3rd edition 1893, translated: *The Philosophy of Religion,* 1886.

5. LUDWIG FEUERBACH, 1804-1872, *like Strauss, began with Hegel and ended in materialism.* Works: *Das Wesen des Christentums* (1841) and *Das Wesen der Religion* (1845). He converts the Biblical statement "God created man in his own image" into

---

[3] *Die Kirche Deutschlands in* 19. *Jahrhundert,* p. 145.
[4] *Op. cit.,* p. 380.
[5] *Christentum und Religion,* 3 vols., 1906 f. To this larger work he added a number of popular writings: *Entstehung des Christentums,* 2nd edition, 1907; *Religion und Religionen,* 1906, translated: *Religion and Historic Faiths,* 1907; *Die Entwickelung des Christentums,* 1907.

ts opposite: "Man created God in his own image." He saw the essence, the origin, of religion in man's wish. That which makes man happy is to him his God. His own thinking, willing, feeling, his selfconsciousness, is to him his highest, his God. Thus the consciousness of God is nothing but man's own selfconsciousness. What man is not, but wishes to be—that he sees as reality in his gods. The gods, therefore, are nothing but the wishes of man. As such the idea of "God" is a delusion, and a harmful delusion, because it takes from him the power of the real life. The body belongs to man's real life; in fact it is the "totality of his I." The reality is what we see. From theology we must come to anthropology. Instead of candidates for the beyond we must be students of the present real life. He describes his own development in the sentence: "God was my first, reason my second, man my third and last thought." He coined that well-known motto of materialism: "What man eats that he is." On this position all theology is lost.

6. BRUNO BAUER (1809-1882) *disposed altogether of the historicity of Jesus* by making him a mere idea produced by the Graeco-Roman world in the closing years of the second century. In proposing this view, he gives an interesting anticipation of ideas which were later developed more in detail in the Historico-Religious School where Christ appears, so to speak, as "a working hypothesis of God's character." From Strauss' mythical character of the Gospels, then, it has gone to the position that Christ himself was a myth (A. Drews, W. von Schnehen, K. Klathoff, P. Jensen). Of this we shall hear later (Chapter VIII).

Chapter Five

CONFESSIONAL THEOLOGY

1. During the first half of the nineteenth century *a revival of religion* came about in all parts of Germany. This religious movement was intimately connected with the Romantic school in literature and the rebirth of German nationalism during the years of the Napoleonic oppression. It had a marked pietistic character, for it was primarily concerned with the salvation of the individual. Sin and grace were considered the fundamental facts and experiences in the religious life. Although the tercentenary of the Reformation in 1817 brought with it only a very limited emphasis on the religious character of the Reformation, there were even as early as in 1817 some individuals who conscientiously turned back to the Reformation and united the subjective revival of the religious life with the objective content of the Reformation theology. This was especially the case in the Ninety-Five Theses of Claus Harms (1778-1855) with their uncompromising attack on Rationalism and the Union to be established in Prussia. HARLESS and THOMASIUS, the founders of the Erlangen School, likewise harked back to objective Lutheranism. They said, "We were Lutherans long before we knew it. We finally discovered that the content of our personal experience was also the content of the Lutheran Confessions." Thus the way was not from the objective Confessions to religion but from a personal religious experience to the Confessions of the sixteenth century. This new attitude toward the Reformation was not limited to the Symbolical writings but also included Luther's works,[1] the hymnbooks, the liturgical forms, and the church orders of the same period. Thus the Lutheran church awoke to a new life. Here the influence of TH. KLIEFOTH of Mecklenburg was particularly in evidence.[2] Above all a new relationship to the state was sought: one that would give greater independence to the Church. The theological periodical of this revived Lutheranism was named *"Zeitschrift fuer Protestantismus und Kirche"* (Journal for Protestantism and the Church). This title was explained as meaning: "We do not want Protestantism without the Church nor the Church without Protestantism."

On the basis of this religious revival and ecclesiastical reorganization there arose a Lutheran theology that sought to express its content in scientific form and which consisted of two main types: The orthodox theology which became best known under the somewhat misleading term "Theology of Repristination," and the more progressive Erlangen theology.

2. We shall first describe briefly the *Theology of Repristination*. This school sought not only to restore the treasures that had been cast aside by Rationalism but also aimed to revive the scientific methods of the Lutheran theology of the sixteenth and seventeenth centuries. A statement of its aim is found in *Die Theologie der Tatsachen wider die Theologie der Rhetorik* (A Theology of Facts Against a Theology of Rhetoric) that was published in 1856 by AUGUST VILMAR (1800-1868), Professor in the Marburg Univer-

---

[1] The Erlangen Edition of Luther's works was started in 1826.
[2] *Liturgische Abhandlungen*, 8 vols., 1854 ff.

sity. "Theology," he says, "must know that she has nothing new to say, nothing new to discover, but that her task is to preserve the spiritual treasure that has been given in Holy Scripture and received by the Church, in such a form that it may be transmitted to future servants of the Church undiminished, certain, and in its most useful form" (p. 16). Vilmar's demands were, in fact, only the application of the program of Romanticism to theology.[3] Just as Romanticism saw all perfection and light in the Middle Ages and turned back to them, so Lutheran theology was to return to the treasures inherited from the Fathers, to treasure them and to transmit them to coming generations in the most practical form. The attempt was made to carry this out in all the departments of theology.

First came the *Biblical disciplines* with a series of Old Testament studies by E. W. HENGSTENBERG (1802-1869) and a number of his pupils. He defended the genuineness of all the Biblical writings according to the understanding of the churchly and rabbinical traditions. The Old Testament in its entirety was regarded as a prophecy that contained all the essential Christian doctrines.[4] Hengstenberg arrived at his conclusions through the use of a markedly allegorical-spiritualizing exegesis. The attitude toward the writings of the New Testament was the same. The greatest stress was laid on the proof of their genuineness and authenticity. He tried to read back into the New Testament the terminology of the later dogma. As regards New Testament prophecy, he was an exponent of the so-called "continuous-historical method."

A pupil of Hengstenberg was C. P. CASPARI (1814-1892). Born in Germany, he held, after 1847, a theological chair in the University of Oslo, Norway. Caspari used to refer to himself as a "hard boiled Hengstenbergian." He wrote an *Arabic Grammar* (1844 ff.) which was later translated into German (1859), English (1862), and French (1879 f.). He also was a pioneer in the science of comparative symbolics.

3. A similar attitude towards Scripture became the basis for the dogmatic representation of *systematic theology*. Its chief exponent was F. A. PHILIPPI (1809-1882) of Dorpat and Rostock, who published an extensive *Kirchliche Glaubenslehre* (6 vols. 1854 ff.) which was widely read. This work seeks to present the ideas of the old Lutheran teachings together with a refutation of the attacks made on them in later times. Following the impulse given by Schleiermacher, he regards as the source of systematic theology "the experimental consciousness of the believers," but in practice the only determining source of it is the logical use of the content of Scripture. "The source from which dogmatics must draw is the dogmatician's reason enlightened by revelation." [5] Consequently he begins his *Glaubenslehre* with a declaration concerning the inerrant, inspired Scriptures, in which he teaches an inspiration not of words but of the Word. "The Apostles, and Prophets, immersed in the Spirit of God, living and laboring under His impulses, could only speak with words filled with the Spirit." While claiming inspiration for the sacred writers, he explicitly denies verbal inspiration. "The single letters, syllables, and words, apart from their content and connection, are not to be regarded as something to be dictated from without, for Scripture is not the words but the Word of God; if it were, divine providence would not have permitted these sacred words to have been transmitted to us in variant readings" (I, 251).

---

[3] P. 16. Vilmar also was an ardent student of Germanistics and the author of a remarkable *History of German Literature*, 1845.

[4] *Christologie des Alten Testamentes*, 3 vols., 1829 ff.

[5] *Op. cit.*, 3rd edition, I, 125.

Philippi became involved in a vehement controversy with Hofmann of Erlangen University (see below) over the orthodox Protestant statement of the doctrine of the Atonement. "It is only," said he, "because of reconciliation and justification, as taught in the Confessions, that I am a Lutheran theologian, a Lutheran Christian, or a Christian at all." Whoever therefore, he continues to argue, belittles the comfort of faith in the atoning blood of Christ and in the imputation of Christ's righteousness, "robs me of Christianity itself." "Then I might as well have remained in the religion of him who was my father according to the flesh, Abraham." [6]

In this connection we must not forget ERNST SARTORIUS with his great work on Christian ethics, *Die Lehre von der heiligen Liebe* (1840 ff.), translated into English under the title *Doctrine of Divine Love* (1884). His book on Christology, *Lehre von Christi Person und Werk,* went through seven editions (1831; 7th edition, 1860).

4. Although this school aimed to return completely to the theology of the seventeenth century, we nevertheless discern in its teaching influences emanating from the thought world of the nineteenth century. THEODOR KLIEFOTH (1810-1895) in his first large work, *Einleitung in die Dogmengeschichte* (1839) clearly portrays the influence of Schleiermacher and Hegel. Here the development of dogma appears as a development divinely guided, as an actual progressive incarnation of Christ. The development of dogma comes about as one doctrine after the other enters into the dogmatic consciousness. When one group of dogmas has been scientifically developed in all its aspects, another group demands consideration. But this rationalistic and optimistic conception is corrected by Kliefoth himself through the recognition both of the supernatural and also the sinful element involved. In his work, *Acht Buecher von der Kirche* (1854), he speaks of the Church as a living organism, constituted by God, consisting of "articulated institutions and callings, offices and stations." In regarding legal order as a part of the essence of the Church, Kliefoth has been accused of Roman and Reformed tendencies. Vilmar held similar views, especially in his teaching of ordination as the means by which the office of the ministry is perpetuated. Another exponent of this high church conception was WILHELM LOEHE (1808-1872), the spiritual father of the former Iowa Synod. Furthermore, the teaching of these men of the sacraments clearly marks a deviation from the traditional Lutheran conception. The office of the ministry, according to Kliefoth, safeguards the efficacy of the sacraments. And while the Word, as Vilmar says, affects man, through the Spirit from above, the sacrament is a "physical action" (*leibliche Tat*) of God with a gracious effect through matter, both on man's body and spirit.[7] Here the influence of Schelling's *Naturphilosophie* is evident in a manner that cannot be mistaken, and in their teaching these men form an interesting parallel to the Oxford theologians of the nineteenth century.

Vilmar also criticized the young Luther. "It is now admitted," he says, "that the book, *An den Adel,* is not properly speaking a reformation writing, that Luther here overstepped his own appointed bounds." [8] Vilmar seeks to remove everything revolutionary from Luther. Luther was to him essentially the preserver of a purer antiquity, and of the true Catholic Church from which the Roman Church, especially at the close of the Middle Ages, and later defined in the Tridentine Council, had erred. In Vilmar's view

---

[6] *Herr Dr. von Hofmann gegenueber der lutherischen Versoehnungs und Rechtfertigungslehre,* 1856, p. 56. Philippi was born of Jewish parents and had accepted Christianity at the age of twenty.

[7] *Theologie der Tatsachen,* p. 68.

[8] *Luther, Melanchthon, Zwingli,* posthumously edited in 1869, p. 51.

Luther is the pattern of a political conservative and of a citizen of a legitimate monarchial state. Consequently, Vilmar denounced bitterly the annexation of his native Hesse by Prussia in 1866. In the same way, the Jewish convert, JULIUS STAHL (1802-1861), a jurist, regarded Lutheranism as a pillar for the support of a Christian monarchy. Thus it followed that this school of theology had a close connection with the conservative and reactionary political movement in Germany during the time of Metternich, and most of its non-Prussian followers remained in opposition to Bismarck even after the unification of Germany in 1871.

5. We now shall discuss the *Erlangen Theology*. This school is also rooted in the religious revival of the nineteenth century. In contrast, however, to the "Repristination" theology it aimed at a healthy synthesis of the Lutheran heritage with the new learning: *eine alte Weise, neue Wahrheit zu lehren* (to teach the old truth in a new garb). The Repristination theology interpreted the sixteenth century in the light of the seventeenth century; the Erlangen school, on the other hand, wanted to make a careful distinction between the Reformation and the post-Reformation theologies, trying to uphold, at many points, Luther and the Confessions against the dogmaticians of the seventeenth century. Even the Confessions are to the Erlangeners not external law but the expressions of the religious experience of the Church in its conflict with error and in its search for truth. 'Regarding the reproach of repristination, it is true that we have held fast faithfully to the Confessions of the Church, and have defended them on many sides when they were assailed. But it is not true that they have ever been a mere external law or bond for us. We have confessed them from within because we found in them the expression of our own convictions and because we have been convinced of their scripturalness." [9] This distinction between the intentions of the Confessions and the mere wording of them opened up a new vista before the eyes of the Church: confessional theology must not needs be something static but a dynamic force in the life of the Church. This new approach to the formulas of the past accounts for the original and progressive element in the Erlangen theology. In the second place, this attitude explains that trend toward a Biblicism which we find in the Erlangen school. The Scriptures, the Confessions, and religious experience, these are the three great principles upon which it established itself.

The Erlangen theology also differed in principle from Vilmar and Kliefoth, and Loehe as regards *the nature of the Church*. Fr. Hoefling in his book, *Grundsaetze evangelisch-lutherischer Kirchenverfassung* (1850) rejects what he calls the "manifestly Romanizing hierarchical position" of his times, stating that "the nature of the Protestant idea of the Church forbids the acceptance of all external legal forms as a part of the essence of the true Church. It is rather a gathering of believers whose active instruments are the means of grace and the office of their administration which is included in their institution." This ideal of the essence of the Church, which was also defended by ADOLF VON HARLESS, professor and president of the Lutheran Church of Bavaria (1806-1879), as a purely religious fellowship has remained the common position of the whole Erlangen school. It was not only accepted by the leading theologians, Thomasius, Hofmann, and Frank, but also by a number of teachers of church law, particularly, in its extreme form, by RUDOLF SOHM (1841-1917).

The ethical peculiarity of the Erlangen theology is marked by the attempt to find a

---

[9] G. Thomasius, *Des Wiedererwachen des evangelischen Lebens in der lutherische Kirche Bayerns*, 1867.

purely religious and Christian foundation for ethics. In contrast to the combination of theological with philosophical ethics in Neo-Protestantism, Hofmann declared: "How can the science of Christian morality be derived from the idea of morality in general or from man's ethical disposition, when for Christians the reality of ethical goodness is revealed only in Jesus Christ? There is no other starting point for theological ethics except one that at the very beginning is distinct from philosophical ethics." [10] As the source and motivation for Christian ethics we find that Hofmann refers to justification, Harless[11] and Frank[12] to regeneration. In regard to the relation of Christian ethics to the world, the Erlangeners hold a middle position. As Lutherans they value the world and its natural order as a gift of the Creator. On the other hand, they are of the conviction that sin has infected all creation and that communion with God surpasses all earthly values. As a result, a double asceticism is required of the Christian: he is to disregard all temporal goods as a means of attaining to the highest good, and is to eliminate all influences of the world that might affect the personality. The immediate and paramount subject of ethics is the individual Christian. But since the individual is conditioned by his various social relationships and he in turn is to influence others, Christian ethics must extend its influence to society.

6. *We now proceed to a brief discussion of the leading theologians of this school.* Its real founder and greatest genius was JOHANN CHRISTIAN KONRAD VON HOFMANN. He was born of poor parents in 1810. In 1827 he entered the University of Erlangen. Here he came in close contact with Christian Krafft, pastor of the German Reformed congregation at Erlangen and professor at the University, and with Karl von Raumer, professor of natural sciences. Both became instrumental in his conversion to a genuine evangelical piety. In 1829 Hofmann went to Berlin where the historian Leopold von Ranke attracted the young student far more than either Schleiermacher or Hengstenberg. In 1838 he established himself as *Privatdozent* in Erlangen. Four years later he went to Rostock University in Northern Germany. Returning to Erlangen in 1845, he held a commanding position in the theological faculty till his death in 1877.

Hofmann's approach to theology is primarily historical. He originated the idea of the *heilsgeschichtliche Theologie* (theology of redemption). In his first publications, a text book of universal history and a historical monograph, he treated his subject both as a historian and theologian who sees the manifestations of God's activity in history. The idea of a history of redemption goes back to the "federal theology" of John Coccejus which was represented in Erlangen by Christian Krafft, and to the Suabian pietist A. Bengel. This close union of history and metaphysics is also found in the philosophy of Schelling who exerted the most direct influence on Hofmann.[13]

Note: In his *Vorlesungen ueber die Methode des akademischen Studiums* (1803), Schelling had discussed the connection of history and metaphysics, which was to be accomplished through theology. "Theology is the highest synthesis of philosophical and historical knowledge." "Chris-

[10] *Zeitschrift fuer Protestantismus und Kirche,* 1863.

[11] *Ethik,* 1842.

[12] *System der christlichen Sittlichkeit,* 1884 ff.

[13] The influence of Coccejus and his school is also evident in the Reformed theologians Ebrard and Menken as well as in Beck of Tuebingen. This fact accounts for the Biblicism in the theologies of these men. The material and arrangement of dogmatics is with them subordinate to the content and historical development in the Scriptures. It also explains their intense interest in the eschatological features of the Bible (world mission, conversion of Israel, the Anti-Christ, millennium). Hofmann was first of all an exegete; Menken followed conscientiously the purely analytic method of preaching. Even Ritschl, like Hofmann, presented his theology in form of a Biblical study, *Rechtfertigung und Versoehnung.*

ianity in its inmost spirit is historical in the truest sense." History for Schelling is not merely he succession of a number of empirical facts bound together by the law of causality but it is also he manifestation of the eternal and absolute. In his later work, *Philosophie der Offenbarung* (posthumously edited in 1858) Schelling states: "The content of revelation is nothing more than a higher form of history that reaches back to the beginning of all things and forward to their end." Christ as an historic figure, according to Schelling, reveals eternity in Himself. "The real content of Christianity is Christ Himself." Christ is not the teacher, He is not the founder, He is the content of Christianity. "Anyone who does not know of a superhistorical history has no place where he can locate a personality like Christ." Though Schelling emphasized the peculiar character of the history of Christianity, he, nevertheless, saw an intimate connection with the universal history of religion. Christ Himself was present in all history, only concealed, "in heathenism by a double, in Judaism by a single veil."

It was particularly in Hofmann's *Weissagung und Erfuellung im Alten und im Neuen Testament* (Part I, 1841; Part II, 1844) that this influence of Schelling is most noticeable. Prophecy is fulfilled in the first place not in words but in related facts whose significance is subsequently made clear by the word. The history of Israel is a related chain of actions that lead up to and prepare for Jesus Christ. "In the holy and blessed man Jesus the history of the relation of God and man has reached its preliminary consummation" (I, 32). But the history of Christ is to Hofmann again the starting point of a further history which in itself includes another prophecy concerning the completion of communion between God and man. "In Christ's self-manifestation to the world we have both history and prophecy: history of the continued establishment of the communion between God and man, prophecy in the continual pointing to the final form of that communion" (I, 40). The heathen religions are included in this prophetic view of history: "The heathen felt His presence in creation but did not differentiate between Him and created things, and they so mourned over Him when they mourned over the death of their religious heroes: Cadmilus and Dionysos and Adonis they call Him, and they wept over Him all too early, long before He died on the cross . . . The heathen knew of sons of God all too early, long before Jesus Christ, the Son of God, was exalted and made the Lord over all things" (I, 39).

Hofmann made this so-called prophetic conception of history, the basis also of his second great work, *Der Schriftbeweis* (2 vols., 1852 ff.). Prior to any scientific investigation, he says, Christianity has its independent existence (1) in the experience of regeneration of the individual, (2) in the history and fact of the Church, (3) in the Scriptures. And the soundness of a man's theology, he holds, is conditioned by its agreement with this threefold testimony of the Holy Spirit (I, 23 f.). Hofmann is wrestling with two main problems in the *Schriftbeweis:* (1) the method of dogmatics, (2) the form of Scriptural proof.

By the experience of regeneration, the individual is made conscious of his being a member of the Church. As there is but one faith, the Church's faith, the individual has his faith in common with all. Faith is the primary constituent factor of Christianity which he defines as "a personal communion between God and man mediated through Christ Jesus" (I, 7). From faith, Hofmann clearly distinguishes theology, the scientific interpretation of Christianity. In contrast to faith, a man's theology is conditioned by his own individual personality. In writing therefore, a book on theology, a theologian, according to Hofmann, must write a kind of an autobiography. "I as a Christian am the primary object of my scientific investigation as a theologian" (I, 10).

This emphasis on the psychological element in the Erlangen theology is unquestionably due to the influence of Schleiermacher. However, we must not overlook the principal differences between Schleiermacher and Hofmann. While Schleiermacher developed his dogmatics out of his religious self-consciousness, Hofmann intended to describe the divine fact in his life by which he was made a Christian. Schleiermacher's conception of God is conditioned by his monistic philosophy; Hofmann's is determined by the revelation of God embodied in Scripture. Schleiermacher was a religious intuitionist interested in the universal truth of religion; Hofmann was a confessional Lutheran with the Scriptures and Confessions as his starting point. In brief, religious self-consciousness is for Schleiermacher the source of dogmatics, for Hofmann the means by which he has become certain of the truth of the Bible.

As to the second problem, Hofmann rejects the form of scriptural proof that was in use among the old dogmaticians and by writers of the orthodox Lutheran revival. These accumulated a mass of single passages without regard to their place in the history of redemption. He demands that proofs be derived from the whole of Scripture and that each single portion of the Bible be interpreted in the light of the whole. Above all the recorded facts, the historic events are to furnish the proofs. "We have to receive everything in Scripture in its historic place and in the setting of its historic connection" (I, 25).

The new understanding of history also had a bearing on the teaching of inspiration in the Erlangen theology. Actual revelation is, according to Hofmann, accomplished by historical events whose meaning is disclosed by the spoken, inspired word. Scripture is the record of these historical events and words. In *Weissagung und Erfuellung* there is the statement, "The word concerning Christ is not doctrine but history. Teachings that have not grown out of historic soil are found as little in the New Testament as in the Old" (I, 42). "In the Bible we have not mere textbooks but history and its application" (I, 47). In other places Hofmann calls the Scriptures, "The monuments and sources of the history of redemption." Hofmann does not regard Scripture and revelation as identical but neither are they in opposition to each other or without relation to each other. Scripture is rather the conclusion and result of the history of redemption. Just as other historic happenings, *e.g.,* an election, are completed when the minutes concerning them are adopted, so the history of redemption is terminated only by the Scriptures that are its certification. The inspiration of Scripture is derived from the working of the God of revelation Who through it wills to maintain the living and efficient power of His revelation. Consequently, Hofmann views the composition of the Biblical books and the creation of the Canon a divine necessity. The older dogmaticians, in his opinion, had simply applied the authority which belonged to the Scriptures itself to the existing collection of the canonical books; while the newer critical school had excluded a number of books from those it regarded as a part of the trustworthy and primitive Christian tradition. As a substitute for the older view and in opposition to the newer critical attitude, Hofmann began his gigantic commentary on the New Testament, *Die heilige Schrift neuen Testaments zusammenhaengend untersucht* (1862 ff.). He proposes two problems for solution: (1) to determine by a historical investigation whether and to what extent the Bible really is a source of the historic revelation of redemption; (2) to write a history of the testimony of the Church to the Scriptures. Death, however, did not permit Hofmann to carry out his second task. (It was carried out later by M. Kaehler). Hofmann himself, in the work just referred to, dealt with the first problem showing the internal connections of all the writings in the New Testament and the necessity of collecting them into one book. As in a cathedral each stone is in its appointed place and on that account its removal would endanger the entire building, so it is with the structure of the Bible. This consideration, moreover, determines the character of his exegesis which is concerned with proof for the inner connections between verses and verses, chapters and chapters, so that Scripture is seen as a completed whole from which it is not possible to remove at will this or that section on the ground that it is not genuine.

In Christology Hofmann adopted the modern kenotic theory. His view of Christ's work of reconciliation caused considerable resentment in the Lutheran church. He rejected the vicarious sacrifice of Christ and the thought of His suffering the wrath of God. He interpreted the work of Christ in the sense of Greek theology and Schelling's philosophy as a contest with the devil. Christ, the Holy One, suffered all the torments of evil but overcame it by preserving, in life and death, the purity desired by God in fulfilling His calling.[14] In eschatology Hofmann maintained for the teaching of premillennianism a place in nineteenth century Lutheranism.

For literature on Hofmann we refer to J. Haussleiter, *Grundlinien der Theologie Hofmanns* (1910), Ph. Bachmann, *J. Ch. K. von Hofmanns Versoehnungslehre und der ueber sie gefuehrte Streit* (1910); P. Wapler, *Das Leben J. Ch. K. von Hofmanns* (1914), Martin Schellbach, *Theologie und Philosophie bei von Hofmann* (1935).

7. *Next to Hofmann*, FRANZ HERMANN REINHOLD VON FRANK stands out as the most original theologian of the Erlangen school. Frank was born in 1827. In 1857 he was called to Erlangen. He died in 1894. Though in point of time Frank belongs to the second generation of the Erlangen theologians, it was he who most fully developed the subjective starting point in the Erlangen theology. In contrast to Hofmann, Frank was not a historian. His chief interest lay in the psychological element of religion. He takes the theme of his greatest and most independent work, *System der christlichen Gewissheit*[15] from the characteristic attitude of the religious life of the Reformation, which, while it was bound by its conscience to God, yet broke with the authority of the Roman Church. Then there was also a second motive that influenced him in the adoption of the method followed in the teaching concerning Christian certainty and that was the analogy to the methods of the natural sciences. When Frank published the first edition of his work referred to, natural science was at the peak of its intellectual influence. In it Frank saw the fundamental principle of empiricism. The natural sciences deal with facts, and the accurate observation of these facts is of fundamental importance. As natural science uses the principle of causality as it observes actions and from them argues back to their efficient causes, so theology should pursue a similar method. From the facts of the new spiritual life it was to recognize the causes that occasioned them. In the newly applied methods of Hermann Helmholtz, professor of physiology and physics, that were used in the spectroscopic analysis of the sun, Frank saw a type of the proper method for the theologian. "If spectrum analysis has succeeded to a certain extent in determining the chemical composition of the sun by breaking up its light into its component parts, because the daylight that we see is the same as the rays that radiate from it,

---

[14] *Schutzschriften fuer eine neue Weise, alte Wahrheit zu lehren*, 4 vols., 1856 ff.

[15] First edition 1870 ff.; 2nd edition, 1881 ff., translated into English under the title *System of the Christian Certainty*, 1884; 2nd edition, 1886.

why should it be contradictory or improper to discover in the spectrum of the regenerate human personality the nature of that Sun from which have emanated the rays that are reflected from that personality?"

In his *System der christlichen Gewissheit* Frank begins with a universal psychological definition of the nature of certainty: "Certainty is the becoming sensible of the harmony of the being with the notion, or of experience with knowledge." [16] Certainty is a condition of the subject which at the same time is related to an object. Christian certainty has the same formal character, but in its content Christian certainty is distinguished from ordinary certainty by its peculiar moral experience which consists in regeneration and conversion. This experience produces a transformation of the moral life. As the result a new ego asserts itself as the determining factor of the new ethical existence over against that which had previously governed man's personality. This moral transformation is called in the language of dogmatics "regeneration" and "conversion." By regeneration we describe it as determined by external factors; by conversion we refer to that part which has been played by man in the transformation of his own self.

Out of this fundamental experience of regeneration Frank deduces the certainty of all the important truths of Christianity as a religion of redemption. He distinguishes between three classes of such truths which he describes as immanent, transcendent, and transeunt. The "immanent" truths are the experience of regeneration, sin, righteousness, *etc.* From them he proceeds to the active factors that have produced them. The "transcendent" objects of faith are those whose nature and being lie in the beyond, outside the human subject, and which, because of their causal relationship, do not remain transcendent but with their activity enter into the subject and thus become a part of his experience.[17] Among the objects of faith so classed is included first of all God and His personality, the Holy Trinity, the God-man and His work of redemption. The "transeunt" objects of faith are the channels through which the transcendent factors pass in order to effect their connection with the immediate actions of the Christian life. Here the Church, the means of grace, and Scripture enter into the picture.

On the basis of Christian certainty Frank carries on a controversy with the worldview that is opposed to Christianity. He maintains that an apologetic in the sense of an unprejudiced comparison of Christian and anti-Christian views is worthless. He only wants to show that a Christian who is really a Christian is not disturbed by these contrasts and looks upon them as something inevitable. The one who experiences no miracle must be a rationalist, the one who does not experience the powerful working of the Word of God must destroy it by criticism, the one who does not grasp the personal opposition between the Holy God and sin must unite God pantheistically with the world. So Frank shows how, in principle, and in a certain sense historically, it is necessary for these opposing tides of rationalism, pantheism, criticism, and materialism to develop but that they are unable to rob the Christian of his certainty.

Frank's system is a really grandiose production in which he seeks independently to establish the old truth by new methods. His opponents have derisively said that he tried to deduce the whole theology of the Formula of Concord, which he had discussed in his first great book, *Die Theologie der Concordienformel* (4 vols., 1858 ff.) from Christian experience. By the men of the Lutheran orthodox revival, and lately by Karl Barth and

---

[16] Engl. translation, 2nd edition, p. 74.
[17] Cf. *Op. cit.,* p. 188.

is school, Frank's theology has been branded as anthropocentric. But in spite of the subjective starting point in his system, we must not overlook the fact that Frank's subjectivism, unlike that of Hofmann, does not have a realistic character in the sense of those epistomologies and cosmologies that only admit a subjective knowledge and regard this as the final reality. His subjectivism is purely epistemological beginning with the selfconsciousness of the subject but proceeding from it to the perception of the object. From the standpoint of the old truth, little objection can be raised to the content of Frank's system, but the question must be raised as to whether the method pursued by him is the correct one, and as to whether it really can prove what it is meant to prove according to Frank.[18]

8. *The Erlangen theology also did valuable service in the field of church history and the history of doctrines.* Here we must mention especially GOTTFRIED THOMASIUS (1802-1875). In his work, *Die christliche Dogmengeschichte als Entwickelungsge-chichte des kirchlichen Lehrbegriffs* (2 vols., 1874 ff.), he shows, as the title indicates, that he was influenced by the Hegelian conception of history. He recognizes in the history of doctrine a distinct pattern and its working out of distinct tasks. "The first period deals with the development of the great central dogmas which were to form the basis for further progress. It was the task of the second period in part to apply this material logically, and in part to further develop it. But since during this period the doctrinal content of Christianity suffered, under the influence of Scholasticism, a deformation, it became necessary for the third period to bring back what had become abnormal into the old sound paths, to deepen the understanding of the ancient dogmas and to develop them according to the doctrinal conception of the evangelical church." Thomasius also regarded the history of doctrines as essentially the organic development of the doctrinal position of the Lutheran church.

In dogmatics Thomasius followed Schleiermacher's Christocentric method.[19] He also applied the speculative ideas of German idealism to the treatment of dogma itself. He conceived of the Trinity as a volitional process within the Godhead. In the sphere of Christology he developed the speculative tendency in the doctrine of the kenosis. He referred the kenosis not like the old Lutheran theologians to the incarnated Christ but to the act of the incarnation itself. Christ in His incarnation, he taught, laid aside the so-called transcendent divine attributes, namely, omnipotence, omniscience, omnipresence, while he retained the so-called immanent attributes of absolute power, truth, holiness, and love. Thomasius regarded this far-reaching surrender, not to say transformation, of divinity necessary so that the divine might be united with the human in a real historical existence. With various modifications this kenotic theory was advocated by other theologians, especially by Frank, while in still other quarters it was vigorously assailed.

9. *The Erlangen theology was not limited to the University of Erlangen.* For a time it was an influential factor also at the universities of Rostock, Dorpat, and especially in the theological faculty of Leipzig. At Dorpat its best known representative was THEODOSIUS HARNACK (1817-1891), the father of the great liberal Harnack of Berlin. While professor at Erlangen from 1853-1866 he wrote the first volume of his *Luther's*

---

[18] See Ihmels, *Die christliche Wahrheits gewissheit*, p. 165; also *Neue Kirchliche Zeitschrift*, March, 1927, with articles on Frank by Seeberg, Ihmels, Bachmann, and Hofstaetter.

[19] *Christi Person and Werk, Darstellung der evangelisch-lutherischen Dogmatik vom Mittelpunkte der Christologie aus*, 2 vols., 1852 ff.

Theologie (1862).[20] It was a forerunner of the modern Luther Renaissance. Also at Dorpat we have JOHANN HEINRICH KURTZ (1809-1890), author of the widely used textbook on Church history.[21] As a Biblical scholar he held a mediating position between Hofmann and Hengstenberg. At Leipzig the Erlangen school was represented by FRANZ DELITZSCH (1813-1890), F. A. KAHNIS (1814-1888), and ERNST LUTHARDT (1823-1904). Delitzsch was a scholar of the Old Testament. His commentaries have received a wide reading. He also translated the New Testament into Hebrew. Kahnis was both an historian and a systematician. Though Luthardt was a student of Hofmann, the peculiarities of the latter have mostly disappeared in his own dogmatics, *Kompendium der Dogmatic.*[22] The greatest importance of Luthardt, however, lies in the field of personal influence and practical work. He is the founder of the *Allegemeine evangelisch-lutherische Konferenz* (1868) as a unifying organization of German Lutheranism against the encroachment of unionistic tendencies in German Protestantism. After the First World War, this *Konferenz* developed, under the leadership of Bishop Ihmels, into the Lutheran World Convention with Dr. John Alfred Morehead (1867-1936) as its first president.

10. *The last consistent representative of this school at the Erlangen University* was PHILLIP BACHMANN (1864-1931), outstanding as teacher and preacher of the university church. He wrote, among other volumes, *Grundlinien der systematischen Theologie* (1908), and a commentary on First and Second Corinthians (in Zahn's great commentary on the New Testament).

Also HERMANN VON BEZZEL should not be passed by. Though he never held a chair in a university, his influence far extended beyond the boundaries of his native church of Bavaria of which he was bishop from 1909 till his death in 1917. The central point of his theology is to be seen in his emphasis on the gracious condescension of the Eternal into the finiteness of time and space.[23] His sermons are real gems of German prose.[24]

11. *A unique character among the Lutherans of the nineteenth century* was NICOLAI FREDERIK SEVERIN GRUNDTVIG (1773-1872), theologian, poet, historian, and educator of his beloved Danish people. He was a genuine son of the Romantic movement and Lutheran revival. It was his cousin, Henrik Steffens, in his lectures on Schelling and Fichte, who led him to see Christ and to a new meaning of history.[25] Grundtvig's position is marked by a close synthesis between Christianity and the nation. In his theology he at first accepted the orthodox view as regards the authority of Scripture. Later he substituted the authority of the "living" Word for that of the written Word, for in the pursuit of historical studies he came to the conviction that the written Word was not the original source and norm of the Christian faith. The Gospel was spread by the living power of

---

[20] The second volume was published in 1886. The whole work was re-edited in 1927 by W. F. Schmidt and O. Grether.

[21] Latest German edition (the 14th), 1906, by N. Bonwetsch and P. Tschackert; English edition in three volumes, 1888 ff.

[22] 14th edition, 1937, by R. Jelke with references to theological thought of Scandinavian, British and American scholars.

[23] *Der Knecht Gottes*, 1921.

[24] *Auf ewigem Grunde*, sermons on the Gospel lessons of the church year, 1914; *Dienst und Opfer*, sermons on the Epistle lessons, 2 vols., 1916, et al. Cf. J. Rupprecht, *H. Bezzel als Theologe*, 1925.

[25] Later Steffens became instrumental in organizing the Altlutheraner, the Lutheran seccession from the church of Prussia in protest against the Union.

he Apostles and the Church, and independently of the written Word. The source and orm of Christianity, so he taught, is to be found in the life of the Church. As to an arly and basic expression of this, Grundtvig set forth the peculiar idea that we have in he Apostles' Creed the earliest confession of faith which preceded the Bible and is Christ's own confession imparted to the Apostles during the forty days after His resurction. This view of the Apostles' Creed is what Grundtvig called his "discovery" (*kirkelige Anskuelse*) and which remained basic and central for him during his long nd influential career. The importance of Scripture, therefore, is to him only secondary; he Church, he claims, does build on history. The "living Word," Grundtvig teaches, is riven to each successive generation in the sacraments. Baptism and the Supper are the life fountains" of the Church in which we meet the living Christ. Consequently, he ays special emphasis on growth in faith instead of conversion and on the corporate coneption of religion over against the extreme individualism of pietists and Kierkegaard. His conception of ethics bears an anti-nomistic stamp. Though fundamentally a Lutheran, Romanizing tendency is quite obvious in the theology of this great follower of the Romantic movement because tradition, not Scripture, is to him the foundation of docrine and practice. In his opposition to Pietism he stood too close to the *Kulturrotestantismus* of the age of Hegel.[26] A selection of Grundtvig's works has been published by Holger Begtrup (10 vols. 1904 ff., supplemented by the same editor in 909 ff.). The most notable exponents of Grundtvigianism in Denmark are at present . P. Bang, professor of Systematic theology in the University of Copenhagen, 1910-1924 *Troen og Livet,* 1917 ff.), and A. Noergaard with his book *Protestantismens Grundkade* (1936).

Note: The protest of the Lutherans against Grundtvigianism has been on account of that overmphasis on the preached Word of Christ and the Apostles and a corresponding depreciation of cripture or the Bible. It was natural that the preached Word had to precede the New Testament vritings in its individual parts and as a whole. But essentially the two—preached and written—elonged together: the former needed the latter and the latter gave content and permanency to the ormer, in connection with the work of the Holy Spirit in the Church of Christ. Chronologically he Bible is second, but as contemporaneous factors, in ontological economy, the relation between he two expresses itself in a kind of *perichoresis* or *permeatio,* under the Holy Spirit's *directio ivina.* And to this should be added that this whole divine-human economy is an integral part of he Church's history pertaining to its work on the congregations of believers. The search for "the Gospel before the Gospels" is always, in Grundtvigianism as well as in modern Form-Criticism, raught with dangerous subjectivism.

Though the Danish Church was, for a long time, not in sympathy with Grundtvig's principles, he always was opposed to the idea of secession. His followers organized themelves as self-governing congregations within the Establishment. After his death the novement as a whole was considerably diluted because many of his followers showed nore interest in his political, educational, and democratic ideas than in his central Chrisian emphasis.[27]

Grundtvig's influence also extends into our own country. The Danish Evangelical Lutheran Church in America is basically Grundtvigian in character. Grundtvig also had his followers among the Norwegian Lutherans of America especially at the beginning of their history.

Of English literature on Grundtvig we refer to the articles in the *New Schaff-Herzog*

---

[26] Cf. the discussion of Rothe, below, pp. 144 f.
[27] Cf. W. M. Horton, *Contemporary Continental Theology,* 1938, p. 151.

Encyclopedia, and in Hastings' *Encyclopedia of Religion and Ethics.* Compare also J. P. Bang, *The Nature and the Function of the Church,* translated by E. D. Nielsen (Cedar Falls, Iowa, 1940), and the discussion of this little book by G. M. Bruce in the *Journal of Theology of the American Lutheran Conference* (November, 1940), and in the *Concordia Theological Monthly* (January, 1941), and by J. O. Evjen in *The Trend* (March, 1941). See also the article by J. Knudsen, "Beyond the Sacred Page," *Journal of Theology of the American Lutheran Conference* (September, 1940).

12. *The anti-nomistic tendencies* Grundtvigianism shared with another theological movement in the Scandinavian countries. Our reference is to the theology of the *Bornholmers.* This theology was not an academic but a practical movement. It took its inception among the pietists of Sweden about the year 1805. A few decades later the movement gained momentum through the work of the Finnish theologian F. G. HEDBERG. Its greatest genius, however, was KARL OLAF ROSENIUS (1816-1868) of Stockholm while, for a time, it gained a special foothold on the Danish island of Bornholm. The pioneering leader here was P. C. TRANDBERG who later migrated to Chicago where he was on the faculty of the Chicago Theological Seminary of the Congregational Church until 1890. He then withdrew and founded the Evangelical Lutheran Free Church Seminary, Chicago.

The theology of Rosenius and the Bornholmers is marked by a *one-sided emphasis on the gospel of free grace.* Reconciliation and justification are to them practically identical. *Verden i Kristo redfaerdig er vorden!* Since the death of Christ, they say, it is a sin to ask for forgiveness, for the sin of every man is forgiven through Christ before man comes to faith in Him. Even the sins of the lost in hell are actually forgiven through the Cross. They conceive of faith as a mere acknowledgment of the historical redemption. While the Bornholmers set forth passionately the riches of God's grace, they, on the other hand, condemn violently the preaching of good works as detrimental to Christian piety. One of its representatives is reported that he went so far as to assert: The drunkard in the gutter and the prostitute in her vice are just as close to the fatherly heart of God as the pious on his praying-chair! Nevertheless, in actual life the Bornholmers were a group of pious people. While the Swedish followers of Rosenius remained within the established church, the Danish group, under the impact of Kierkegaard's severe criticism of the Church of Denmark, developed a rather hostile attitude toward the Establishment.

The chief literary source of the movement is Rosenius' volume *Geheimnisse in Gesetz und Evangelium* (1870). For a brief selection of his writings in English we refer to *The Believer Free from the Law* (1923), translated by A. Hult, and *A Faithful Guide to Peace with God* (1923), edited by G. T. Rygh. Both volumes are prefaced with an introduction on the life and significance of Rosenius. Compare also the orientating article in *Protestantische Realencyklopaedie* (III, 326 ff.).

During the second half of the last century the teaching of PAUL PETER WALDENSTROEM (1838-1917), theologian and political leader, created much discussion among the followers of Rosenius when he began to attack, since 1873, the orthodox conception of God and of the Atonement. His theology bears a close resemblance to the teaching of A. Ritschl. For this reason he is a striking example of the fact that a pietistic way of life and theological liberalism may go a long way together.[28]

---

[28] See E. Newman, *Den Waldenstroemska foersoningslaeran i historisk belysning,* 1931.

The movement caused by Waldenstroem resulted in the organization of a new ecclesiastical group, the so-called Mission Covenant which has a branch also in our country with a college and seminary in Chicago).

13. A passing remark may be in order on *Reformed theology* during the period under discussion. As to Germany we venture to say that it almost passed out of existence during the nineteenth century. The few still existing theological schools were suspended and most of the Reformed territories were swallowed up by the union movement. Virtually the only representatives of high Calvinism were the two brothers KRUMMACHER, FRIEDRICH ADOLF (1767-1845) in Bremen and GOTTFRIED DANIEL (1774-1837) in Elberfeld. In Bremen also we have GOTTFRIED MENKEN (1768-1834), a pupil of the lay theologian SAMUEL COLLENBUSCH (1724-1803). Menken's conception of the Atonement shows a striking similarity to that of Hofmann's. In Erlangen the Reformed faith was represented by CHRISTIAN KRAFT, whom we have mentioned above, and J. H. A. EBRARD (1818-1884). While Ebrard laid stress on the Calvinistic conception of Church order and worship, he openly opposed Calvin's teaching of a double predestination. At heart he was a mediating theologian. As a member of the consistory at Spires, he promoted the cause of church union in the Palatinate. The same holds true of H. HEPPE (1820-1879) at Marburg, the great opponent of the Lutheran confessionalists in Hesse. Among German-speaking Swiss, HANS VON ORELLI (1846-1912) deserves to be mentioned with his commentaries on the Old Testament, and the French-Swiss scholar FR. GODET (1812-1900) for his work on the New Testament. His commentaries, translated into German, have been used extensively by German theologians. In more recent times the Reformed Confession had two able representatives in the theologians AUGUST LANG, of Halle, and KARL MUELLER, of Erlangen. Lang wrote several volumes on Calvin and the Heidelberg Catechism. In 1920 he was made moderator of the *Reformierte Bund* in Germany. Mueller published among other volumes a *Symbolik* (1896) and *Die Bekenntnisschriften der Reformierten Kirche* (1903), until recently the standard collection of the Reformed confessions.

In the Netherlands ABRAHAM KUYPER (1837-1920) figured during the last generation as one of the most outstanding Reformed theologians. As a scholar he brought about a revival of historic Calvinism in Holland, and as a statesman waged a determined battle against the revolutionary forces which threatened to undermine the Christian civilization of his country. He was a very prolific writer.[29] In 1898 he delivered the Stone Lectures at Princeton, published under the title *Calvinism*. J. H. de Vries has translated a number of his best writings into English (*The Work of the Holy Spirit* (1900), *et al*).

---

[29] Cf. *RGG*, III, 1443.

Chapter Six

THE MEDIATING THEOLOGY. THE BIBLICISTS

1. Besides the confessional theology there was in the nineteenth century another form of Protestant faith, the so-called *Positive Mediating Theology.* If the former could appeal to Luther, this was Melanchthonian in its scientific and ecclesiastical tendencies. As in the case of Melanchthon, it endeavored to reconcile reason and revelation, philosophy and theology, and advocated unionism in the ecclesiastical sphere.

We must first consider its mediating position in the sphere of *Biblical and historical theology.* On the one side were Strauss and Baur who attacked the reliability and genuineness of the New Testament writings; on the other side were the orthodox Lutherans as well as the older theologians of the Erlangen school. Between them a number of Old and New Testament scholars, chiefly in the Prussian universities, especially in Halle and Berlin, men like AUGUST NEANDER (1789-1850), WILLIBALD BEYSCHLAG (1823-1900), and BERNHARD WEISS (1827-1918), sought to mediate between the critical and traditional views. By strictly scientific and historical methods the genuineness of most of the New Testament writings was demonstrated, with the possible exception of the Pastoral Letters and II Peter. On the basis of these sources a number of *"Lives of Jesus"* were written in which most of the miracles and facts of redemption were regarded as credible.[1] As to the Confessions, the Apostles' Creed was maintained, with the elimination, however, of some of its statements, particularly of the Virgin Birth and Christ's descent into hell. The Nicene and Athanasian Creeds did not receive even such a favorable treatment. Among the Confessions of the Reformation, the Augsburg Confession was preferred, especially the ungenuine *Variata,* while the Formula of Concord was rejected. Luther was interpreted via Melanchthon, and consequently misunderstood while his uncompromising positions concerning the Supper and predestination were modified to suit the writer's taste. This position was especially maintained by JULIUS KOESTLIN (1826-1902) in his *Luthers Theologie* (1862)[2] and in his biography of the Reformer, *Martin Luther, sein Leben und seine Schriften,* 1875. Almost all the mediating theologians were adherents of the Prussian Union of 1817 or of similar morganetic unions between the Lutheran and Reformed communions in other German states. As a result their theology was chiefly concerned about the teachings common to both confessions.

In *systematic theology* the attempt was made to establish a synthesis between theology and philosophy, between reason and revelation, between Christian ethics and human culture. Its basis, in addition to Schleiermacher, Hegel, and Schelling, was provided by the so-called "theistic philosophy." This was taught by a number of philosophers, like the younger Fichte (1797-1879), H. F. Chalybaeus (1796-1862), and Ch. H. Weisse (1801-1866), all of whom had only a limited place in philosophy, and who for that very reason, sought to make their influence felt in theology. These men

---

[1] B. Weiss, *Das Leben Jesu,* 2 vols., 1882, translated in 1883, *The Life of Jesus;* W. Beyschlag, *Das Leben Jesu,* 1885.

[2] Translated by Charles E. Hay. 1897.

pposed the pantheistic tendencies of German Idealism, and confessed a personal God, idependent of the world. They developed the doctrine of the Holy Trinity in a specu-tive way so that they assured the personal existence of God apart from the world. In iis way they sought to provide theology with an assured philosophical foundation. The iediating theology accepted it and believed that by union with this philosophy it had icceeded in harmonizing faith and knowledge. The leading literary organ of the medi-ting theology, the *Theologische Studien und Kritiken,* which began its appearance in 828, formulated its program thus: "As little as there can be a true Christian theology ·ithout Christian faith, even so a theology that ignores the noble, divine gifts of reason nd science, is a monstrosity. All true results in theology depend on the co-operation nd intermingling of faith and knowledge."

2. *As the greatest contribution of this school to theology lies in the field of system-ic studies,* we shall now present a brief discussion of its leading systematic theologians.

The successor to Schleiermacher in the chair of systematic theology at Berlin was UGUST TWESTEN (1789-1876), representing the conservative, Lutheran element among ie followers of Schleiermacher. He wrote an (incomplete) *Dogmatik der evangelisch-utherischen Kirche* (1826 ff.). In Berlin we also find KARL IMMANUEL NITZSCH 1787-1868) and ISAAK AUGUST DORNER (1809-1884). While Twesten believed only n the confederate nature of the Prussian Union, Nitzsch was a staunch defender of its bsorptive character. In 1846 he proposed a new creed for subscription of theological andidates at their ordination containing, as it was claimed, all the basic truths of Chris-ianity. No mention, however, was made of such doctrines as original sin, Christ's descent o hell, His ascension, the resurrection of the body, eternal life and eternal condemnation. Nitzsch's opponents derisively called this creed, in distinction from the *Nicaenum* of he fourth century, the *Nitzschenum* of the nineteenth century.[3] Dorner was a great peculative genius striving at a close synthesis between philosophy and theology, faith nd knowledge. In the introductory part of his *System der christlichen Glaubenslehre* 2 vols., 1879 f.)[4] he discusses at length the quest for religious certainty. Man, he argues, uzzled at the historical in Christianity, will turn for truth to purely timeless ideals. But these cannot satisfy him nor give him real religious certainty. At this he will arrive, Dorner continues, only when he turns to Christianity in which the ideal is united with he historical.[5] This theoretical approach is coupled, according to Dorner, with the ·thical and practical, for the content of the Gospel implies the self-condemnation of man nd his justification through faith in Christ. However, Dorner is remembered in the iistory of doctrine chiefly for his discussion of the Christological problem. The union of God with man in Jesus, Dorner regards as the ultimate goal and climax of the divine vorld order. The incarnation, therefore, he holds, was planned by God even apart from he fact of sin. The Logos was to him merely a divine principle. In order that real ersonal unity of life may be comprehensible in Jesus, it is said that the union of the wo natures in Christ gradually took place during His earthly life. In conformity with he increasing receptivity of the human nature of Jesus to the divine, the Logos ecame more and more indwelling in Him, so that the process of the union between

---

[3] For orientation on the Union in Prussia and other German states, we refer the reader to the orientating rudy of J. L. Neve, *The Lutherans in the Movements for Church Union,* 1921, pp. 110 ff.

[4] English translation in 4 vols., 1880 ff.

[5] I, 101, 2nd edition of 1886.

the divine and human is not completed until the end of the earthly life of Jesu (II, 412 ff.). "This theory," Gruetzmacher says in the article referred to, "places along side the kenotic theory, which Dorner vigorously attacked, the most original speculativ attempt to rationalize the God-manhood of Jesus that is found in the newer theology.'

The most original theologian of this school was RICHARD ROTHE, born in 179? died as professor at Heidelberg in 1867. He was a speculative genius of first magnitud wholly devoted to the program of the mediating school to harmonize Christianity wit philosophy. He combines in his system the formal principle of the Hegelian school, it dialectical method, with the theosophical tenets of Schelling and peculiarities of Schleier macher's theology. Rothe holds man to be a microcosmos who comprehended and recapit ulated in himself the whole universe. Philosophical speculation, he says, must start fron the consciousness of the ego, from the act of the thinking self; theological speculatior on the other hand, must start from the consciousness of God. God is to him the Absc lute. Rejecting the Church's doctrine of the Trinity, he holds to a threefold form o divine Being: God's hidden nature, the I; matter, the non-I; and personality in whic' God arrives at consciousness of Himself. This fashioning of matter into the organ of th divine spirit, Rothe conceives as a continuous process of creation (*Weltwerdung*) or, i viewed from the aspect of its goal, as the incarnation (*Menschwerdung*) of God withi the limits of material existence. Christianity is to him strictly supernatural, grounde in the "manifestation" of God in history. From this divine manifestation he distinguishe "inspiration," *i.e.,* the immediate enlightenment of the Biblical writers to receive an interpret the historical manifestation of God. From his abnormal sinful depravity ma is delivered by the Second Adam who marks the beginning of the normal developmen of man. Jesus came into the world by a miraculous act of God: He was born of woman though not begotten by a man. He was not from the first a divine being. Th incarnation was, according to Rothe, a continuous process in which God became man an man became God. This process was completed in the resurrection and elevation of Jesu to the divine sovereignty of the world. At the end of time, Christ will visibly appea with all the saints. The pious will then be clothed with a spiritual body while th wicked will be given over to complete annihilation. "Finally the terrestrial world wi also be spiritualized and placed in communion with the heavenly spheres. Thus th kingdom of earth becomes the kingdom of heaven." In keeping with this view, Rothe' interest was centered in a "Christian civilization" which is to express the unity of natur and spirit. The Church can have temporary significance only, because it is merely th means of bringing about a new order, in which a general humanized Church will b absorbed by a State (society) established upon the principles of general ethics.

It goes without saying that Rothe's theology contains many contradictory elements His conception of God, for example, is in part strictly theistic while, at the same time he holds to the Hegelian teaching that God arrives in man at consciousness of Himself In the same way, sin is to him an unavoidable passage in the development of man Nevertheless, he also speaks of sin as guilt and considers the sinful depravity of man t be abnormal. Little wonder, that, on the one hand, Rothe's theology could appeal t such a scholar as Martin Kaehler, and that, on the other hand, the liberals may look t Rothe as a percursor of Neo-Protestantism in Germany.

---

[6] Cf. also Dorner's *History of the Development of the Doctrine of the Person of Christ;* first German edition 1839, English edition, 1861 ff.

His *magnum opus* is *Theologische Ethik* (3 vols., 1845 ff.; 5 vols., 1867 ff.). For literature on Rothe we refer to the very instructive article in *Protestantische Realency-klopaedie*, XVII, 169 ff.

Another systematic theologian of the same school was JULIUS MUELLER of Halle (1808-1878) who, in his work, *Die christliche Lehre von der Suende*[7] set out to investigate the nature and origin of sin. Sin is to him selfishness and as such a freedom that destroys itself. Its origin is to be sought in a tragic misuse of freedom which had its beginning in the sphere of the extra-temporal. He thus adopts the theory of a pre-mundane fall of man as taught in the ancient Church by the Gnostics and Origen. Yet, in the end, Mueller is compelled to admit that "evil in its essence is incomprehensible; it is the inescapable mystery of the world."

The attitude of this school regarding Christian ethics in its relation to human culture is best illustrated in the writings of the Danish professor and bishop HANS LARSEN MARTENSEN (1808-1884). His *Den kristelige Dogmatik* (1849) and *Den kristelige Ethik* (1878) were widely read both in a German and English translation. Martensen followed largely in the line of the cultural ethics of Schleiermacher and Rothe. He also stood very close to Dorner. He sees in Christianity the means to purify and complete all the intra-mundane accomplishments of human culture. This easy-going attitude caused the resentment of Kierkegaard and his (unparalleled) bitter attack on the Danish Church.

3. *While all these theologians were friends of a speculative development of Christian doctrine*, we must include here two other men whose mediating theology bears a different stamp. Our reference is to AUGUST NEANDER of Berlin, whom we mentioned above, and AUGUST THOLUCK of Halle (1799-1877). The theology of both is rooted in the revival of religion during the earlier parts of the nineteenth century. Starting with Schleiermacher's *Gefuehlstheologie*, Neander developed it into what is called the "pectoral theology." *Pectus est quod facit theologum.* He was bitterly opposed both to the speculative Hegelians as well as to the orthodox Lutherans. His chief contribution lies in the field of historical studies. He also wrote a *Life of Christ*, 1837, in reply to the destructive work of Strauss. In Tholuck the strict pietism of his earlier days was later blended with certain Latitudinarian tendencies. His works, including exegetical, historical and apologetic studies, are edited in eleven volumes (1863 ff.).[8]

This school was for a time very influential in practical life of the Church with the royal consistories in the Union, recruiting its higher personnel from the ranks of the mediating theologians. It also was represented in the pulpit by a number of outstanding preachers such as E. FROMMEL (1828-1896) and R. KOEGEL (1829-1896), for example.

4. *Another type of mediating theology* was taught by the *Groningen school* in the Reformed church of Holland with L. G. PAREAU (1800-1866) and PETRUS HOFSTEDE DE GROOT (1802-1886) among its most prominent leaders. The Groningers were pupils of Ph. W. van Heusde (1778-1823), philosopher and theologian at Utrecht. Tenets of Lessing, Herder, Schleiermacher, and the German mediating theology are traceable in the teaching of these men. They inclined toward a humanistic interpretation of Christianity.

---

[7] First edition, 1837 ff., followed by five other editions, also one in English, *Doctrine of Sin*, 1868.

[8] Cf. G. N. Bonwetsch, *Aus A. Tholucks Anfaengen*, 1922.

Van Heusde regarded it as the highest revelation of God, and history as the education of humanity for an understanding of the divine. The importance of sin was minimized, education taking the place of regeneration. The Groningers denied the Trinity and deity of Jesus, though they maintained the supernatural in religion. In eschatology they taught the restoration of all. They had a special liking for Erasmus and took pride in calling themselves the "genuine" Dutch theologians over against the strict Calvinists. It was a theology "warmly pious"—after 1867 they were known as the Evangelicals— "frankly heterodox, but thoroughly supernaturalistic," [9] showing a striking resemblance to the older type of Unitarians. In ecclesiastical politics they sided, as Vanderlaan says, with the Modernists, "but in theological controversy they bitterly opposed the Modernists as deniers of the supernatural."

5. *The Biblical Theology.* This type rejected in principle every connection with any philosophy, whether of Kant or Hegel or Schelling or of philosophical theism. It was averse to speculation as to the formation of a Christian world view or, in the ethical field, to the creation of a Christian civilization. Nor did it care to consider the dogmatic development in so far as it goes beyond the Bible and is conditioned by philosophy. It therefore regarded with indifference the contrast of the confessions of Lutheranism and Calvinism, it objected to Romanism only because of its insufficient Biblical foundation. Finally it rejected experience as a source of Christian knowledge in the sense of Schleiermacher and the Erlangen school. It put the Bible as an objective norm in the place of this subjectivism. In its positive tenets it was influenced by the same theological forces which are essential in Hofmann's theology of redemption, and it shared with the Erlangen theology its intense interest in the eschatological teachings of the Bible.

The most original exponent of this school, TOBIAS BECK of Tuebingen (1804-1874), has expressed its underlying principles most clearly. He wrote an *Einleitung in das System der christlichen Lehre,* 1837, and *Die christliche Lehrwissenschaft nach den biblischen Urkunden,* 1840. His lectures on dogmatics (*Christliche Glaubenslehre*) and on ethics (*Christliche Ethik*) were published posthumously in 1886 f. and 1882 f. respectively. In his *Glaubenslehre* (I, 583) he states that "all true Christian knowledge is essentially conditioned by the fact that it has as its exclusive material the perfect and perfecting truth of doctrine laid down in Holy Scripture which constitutes the entire field of religious knowledge for the Christian and provides the positive content of doctrine for all Christian knowledge and science. Everything that is not given scripturally has no objective significance for Christian knowledge in the religious field." His conception of the Bible is essentially that of the seventeenth century: the Scriptures are regarded as identical with revelation. In exegesis he insisted on the "pneumatic" interpretation of the text. The real content of the Bible is for him the Kingdom of Heaven. This Kingdom, however, does not designate an ideal condition of the Christian community, nor an ecclesiastical organization, nor any other historical product. On the contrary, the Kingdom of God, rather, has existed with God before the creation of the world as "an organized system of life" (I, 135). It entered into history particularly in Christ to effect through Him a regeneration, first, of the individual and, finally, of the whole universe. Christianity brings in "a new type of life" (I, 398). With this formula Beck expresses his moral conception of Christianity. The new life is imparted to the

---

[9] E. C. Vanderlaan, *Protestant Modernism in Holland,* 1924, p. 16.

individual through justification. This establishes, as Beck says, "a righteous personal relationship to God in Christ which is at the same time a natural disposition for a corresponding righteous action" (II, 603). Justification is, therefore, for Beck not simply identical with moral regeneration, but the real goal of justification, nevertheless, remains regeneration. These views of Beck, as the student will note, are not simply a reproduction of Biblical ideas. On the contrary, they portray the influence of Jacob Boehme and such Suabian theosophists as Fr. Ch. Oetinger, with their insistence on a mystic transcendental realism. In ethics Beck held that it is impossible to Christianize the world and its social forms. These are only "institutions of law and discipline for the regulation of life during the earthly development of mankind to serve as a protection against the destructive power and influence of sin." [10] Only the eschatological transformation will bring with it the forms of society that are in conformity with the Christian ideal. So Beck stands in most pronounced opposition to the Neo-Protestant ideas of an intra-mundane ethical culture.

This type of Biblicism was also represented by KARL AUGUST AUBERLEN (1824-1864), professor at Basel, and by ROBERT KUEBEL (1838-1894) who succeeded Beck at the University of Tuebingen.

6. *Another Biblicist was* HERMANN CREMER *of Greifswald* (1834-1903). He likewise regarded justification as the content of Biblical Christianity. But in contrast to Beck, he understood that doctrine in its genuine Pauline sense: Justification is the utterly paradoxical imputation of righteousness to the sinner, in contrast to his moral condition, and without regard to the moral alteration in him. On this faith Cremer also bases the proof of religious certainty. As the natural man experiences God as the Judge in his conscience, Christianity confirms this impression, teaching men the paradox that they shall recognize the redeeming God in the condemning God.[11] In refutation of Harnack's *Essence of Christianity,* Cremer defined Christianity "not as the religion which Jesus Himself had taught, believed or practiced, but as the religion which establishes a personal relationship of the believer with Jesus, a religion which is communion with Jesus and through Him with God." The New Testament does not proclaim the religion of Christ (*ein Christentum Christi*), but the religion about Christ (*das Christustum Christi*). "These two religions," he says, "are altogether different, contradicting and excluding each other, the one in which, as in the teaching of Jesus Himself, the forgiveness of sins is conditioned by His death and resurrection, the other in which man absolves himself." [12] With his *Biblisch-theologisches Woerterbuch zur neutestamentlichen Graezitaet* (1867), Cremer laid the foundation for a comparative study of the religious connotation of the New Testament Greek vocabulary. The work of Cremer was continued by JULIUS KOEGEL (1871-1928) who prepared the tenth (1910 ff.) and eleventh editions (1923) of this lexicon. The work of these two men in turn inspired G. Kittel and his more than fifty co-laborers to start the publication of the gigantic *Woerterbuch zum Neuen Testament,* published since 1932 by Kohlhammer, Stuttgart.

---

[10] *Christliche Ethik*, p. 159.

[11] "*Dogmatische Prinzipienlehre*" in Zoeckler's *Handbuch der theologischen Wissenschaften*, 3rd edition, 1890, Vol. III.

[12] *Das Wesen das Christentums*, 1902. The book went through three editions in one year. The quotations are from the 3rd edition, pp. 220, 228.

Chapter Seven

NEO-KANTIANISM AND THE RITSCHLIAN THEOLOGY

1. *The middle of the nineteenth century was marked by a great spiritual revolution.* Philosophical idealism was discredited and men no longer followed those theologians who tried to establish the metaphysical meaning of the world, or even God's nature, through speculation. The mystical experience of Schleiermacher's school was going out of fashion. Practical religious life was declining because the religious revival of the earlier part of the century had spent its force. Popular interest was diverted from philosophy and religion to the natural sciences, sociology, and kindred subjects. Practical social and political movements came to the fore, socialism and communism gained ascendency, and a materialistic philosophy seemed to satisfy every need. The idea of evolution, first a philosophical tenet, was taken over by the natural sciences, transformed into a mechanical operation, and made the basis of a monistic view of the world. Darwin, with true English caution, was slow in turning his theories into a philosophical system, but in Germany Ernest Haeckel (1834-1919) thought he could find in it a solution of all the riddles of the universe.[1] This monism soon passed into pure materialism. We have already seen (Chapter Four) how Strauss and Feuerbach had gradually turned to materialism, while the popular writings of J. Moleschott (1822-1893), Karl Vogt (1817-1895),[2] and Ludwig Buechner (1824-1899) helped to diffuse the same ideas. So materialism soon became the socialistic philosophy of history and was made the explanation of the forces that motivated all religions, including Christianity.

With these changes in spiritual attitude, the theology of experience had completely lost the props of an idealistic philosophy and the whole speculative theology that had been tied up with it was carried along to destruction. Materialism even excluded the very idea of religion and with it of theology as the science of religion. Then came a reaction in philosophic thought that seemed to offer new possibilities for religion and theology. Its cry was "Back to Kant," and that cry found a ready response. A *Neo-Kantianism* came into existence. It interpreted Kant in the manner of a Positivism which theoretically rejects every form of metaphysics and denies the possibility of knowledge of God. God is an entity with which neither philosophy nor science has anything to do. A philosophical view of God and the world is theoretically impossible. Besides this theoretical reason, Neo-Kantianism recognizes the practical reason that deals with moral problems. Its content is defined in the sense as Kant defined it: every human being has been endowed with the consciousness of a categorical imperative which demands unconditional performance of duty. This obligation of duty is universal, as the principles guiding the individual in his actions must be of the sort that are binding on all. Consequently, our duty has a double content: (1) that we assert our spiritual

---

[1] *Weltraetsel,* first edition, 1899.

[2] In his book *Koehlerglaube und Wissenschaft* (1855) he says that the thoughts of man stand in relationship to the brain like the gall to the liver and the urine to the kidneys.

personality over against nature, and (2) that we unite in mutual regard with all other men in a spiritual kingdom. The individual is not only aware of this imperative, he also possesses the ability to realize its demands. In spite of natural limitations, man possesses free will and self-determination in moral action. Ethics therefore is autonomous, it has no need of religion. God and immortality are, as with Kant, merely ethical postulates; their existence as metaphysical entities is left an open question. In the most extreme development of Neo-Kantianism, the religious concepts are treated as practical values though they may be theoretically false.[3] The University of Marburg became the center of the Neo-Kantian school with Hermann Cohen (1842-1918) and Paul Natorp (1851-1924) as its recognized leaders.

2. It was under the influences of this spiritual and intellectual situation that *the Ritschlian theology was developed*. Its exact relation to Neo-Kantianism varied greatly and was less pronounced in the master himself than in some of his pupils.

ALBRECHT BENJAMIN RITSCHL was born at Berlin in 1822. Educated at Bonn, Halle, Heidelberg, and Tuebingen, he was at first a follower of Hegel and Baur. Early, however, he sensed the new trend in thought. His break with the Tuebingen school became known when he published in 1857 the second edition of his historical monograph, *Die Altkatholische Kirche,* in which he refuted the Tuebingen construction of the Apostolic and post-Apostolic Church. In 1864 he was called to Goettingen where he remained till his death in 1889. Here he wrote among other books his *magnum opus, Die christliche Lehre von der Rechtfertigung und Versoehnung.*[4]

Ritschl's position may be said to be a "negative" mediating theology, i.e., Ritschl does not attempt to secure a place for religion and Christianity by pointing out the identity of reason and revelation, faith and knowledge; he rather insists on the otherness of faith and Christianity. If philosophy and sciences move in the sphere of intellectual truths, religion has its place in the realm of practical values. Both religion and sciences can peacefully exist, side by side, if neither one oversteps its own limit. With Hegel the emphasis rests on synthesis, with Ritschl on diastasis.[5]

Just as Ritschl tried to exclude the intellectual element from Christianity, so he strove to banish everything that was emotional and mystical. He severely criticized these elements in his *Geschichte des Pietismus* (3 vols., 1880 ff.), and even rejected such elements as the *unio mystica* which had found a place in all orthodox theology. While Schleiermacher had given the first place in religion to feeling, Ritschl placed the emphasis entirely on the will. As a result he accomplished a moralizing of Christianity according to the Kantian tradition. Accordingly, Christian theology, when limited to itself, has to describe the Christian idea of God and of man's salvation from a practical ethical viewpoint. Consequently, all the elements of dogma that have no immediate significance of that sort are to be excluded. Theology is, as with Schleiermacher, a *Heilslehre,* not a science offering a comprehensive world view.

---

[3] Cf. the "As-If Philosophy" of Hans Vaihinger and the Pragmatism of James and Dewey.

[4] 3 vols., 1870 ff.; 3rd edition, 1888 f. The first volume was translated into English by John J. Black, *A Critical History of the Christian Doctrine of Justification and Reconciliation,* 1872; the third volume was edited by H. R. Mackintosh and A. B. Macauly, *The Christian Doctrine of Justification and Reconciliation,* 1900.

[5] Pfleiderer discusses Ritschl under the heading Elective Mediating Theologians (English edition, pp. 183 ff.). Elert, on the other hand, assigns to him first place in the section, *Die theologische Verselbsstaendigung des Christentums (The Declaration of Theological Independence of Christianity,* pp. 258 ff.). There is something to be said for the arrangement of either scholar. Ritschl's theology is mediating in that he declined, in deference to the skeptical trend of his time, the metaphysical in the Church's doctrine. Yet by doing so, he wanted to put Christianity on its own basis; its right and verity are conditioned, in his judgment, by the practical values of religion.

In dealing with the metaphysical problem of theology, Ritschl established himself on the distinction between *Seinsurteil* (a merely intellectual statement about the exist-ence of a thing) and *Werturteil* (an "emotional" statement about the existence of a thing) eliminating the "judgments of being" entirely from the scope of theology. Restricting, however, theology to "judgments of value," Ritschl did not reject the meta-physical nature of God, he only denied to human reason the possibility of a theoretical knowledge of God. His "judgments of value" therefore, stand in opposition not to the existential verity of the metaphysical world but to a purely theoretical knowledge of the intellect concerning God.

The sources for a genuine understanding of the Christian religion are for Ritschl to be found only in the Biblical books which are closest to the time of the founding of Christianity. In his judgment concerning the genuineness of the New Testament sources, he was quite conservative. As a criterion of the canonicity of the New Testament Scrip-tures, he cites their close connection with the Old Testament as contrasted with the post-Apostolic writings which already show the influence of pagan thought. Ritschl connects Christianity only with Judaism. He isolates it from the general history of religion and from natural revelation far more completely than was the case in either Catholic or Protestant theology, to say nothing of the school of comparative religion. Thus in prin-ciple Ritschl is always a Biblicist; he did not consider religious experience as a source of religious truth.

In his concept of God, Ritschl is strictly personalistic. But he removed from the consideration of the nature of God not only the concept of divine wrath, which he calls an "unrelated and formless theologumenon." [6] Even the attribute of holiness is rejected by him. The only adequate concept of God is expressed, as he says, in the concept of love. *God is only Father.* His disposition has not been changed by man's sin, but as the loving Father He has always been ready to forgive man unconditionally and to readmit him to His fellowship. But where man in his sin had refused to revere and trust God, he con-structed a false picture of the holiness of Him whose wrath he feared. As a result man no longer ventured to draw near to God. To remove this false idea and to impress man with His never-changing paternal love, God revealed Himself in Christ. The revelation in Christ never had the purpose of establishing a new relationship between God and man but was only to reveal to man the never-changing attitude of divine love. At the same time Christ appeared as the perfect moral man who, by His trust in God, over-came the world. Above all in His efforts He preserved a moral fidelity to His mission. For Ritschl Christ is "the perfect Revealer of God and the *Urbild* of a spiritual dominion over the world." [7] The example of Jesus, he says, inspires men with a believing convic-tion of the love of God and of their forgiveness and justification by Him. They then give up their mistrust of God or, to put it in other words, they are reconciled, on their part, with God. As it is shown by the inversion of the two words in the title of his *magnum opus, Justification and Reconciliation,* Ritschl does not regard reconciliation as a prerequisite of justification but as its consequence. Justification is the forgiveness that, through the revelation made in Christ, is accessible to every believer; reconciliation is the subsequent conciliation between man and God (III, 61 ff.). Reconciliation expresses the idea that those who previously were in active opposition to God, have been

---

[6] *Rechtfertigung und Versoehnung,* 3rd edition, II, 155.
[7] *Op. cit.,* III, 367.

placed in accord with God (III, 503 ff.). The purpose of this divine forgiveness is to produce in the Church and individual the ethical life exemplified in Christ. Both the Church and the individual, through their communion with God, become lords over nature and its inherent limitations. The Christian exercises the religious dominion over the world, which is the direct aim of reconciliation with God through Christ, through faith in the loving providence of God, through the virtues of humility and patience, and finally through prayer (III, 634). In prayer, according to Ritschl, the act of thanksgiving must predominate in the Church. Petitions are only a modification of the prayer of thanksgiving (III, 608). The individual Christian realizes this ethico-religious life in his worldly calling, the Church in close co-operation with the state. There is no room for ascetic ideals after the manner of Catholicism and Pietism in the ethics of Ritschl. The Kingdom of God is for Ritschl mankind organized according to the principle of neighborly love. The Kingdom, completely stripped of its eschatological significance, is with him, as with Kant, ethical through and through (III, 12). Ritschl's teaching of sin bears a sociological stamp. The Church's teaching of original sin he replaced by the corporate conception of a "kingdom of sin" (III, 326).

Ritschl's Neo-Protestant conception of Christianity is still more evident in his conception of the Reformation as developed in the *Geschichte des Pietismus* and in his anniversary address on *Dr. Martin Luther* (1883). Here the assertion is made that the teaching of the Reformation remained essentially on a Roman Catholic level, so that the real meaning of the Reformation "is more concealed than revealed in the works of Luther and Melanchthon" (p. 14). It was only in their ethical ideas that the Reformers offered something new. "If the Reformation of the sixteenth century did not display an ideal of a Christian life we would be in great embarrassment when trying to assign to it any epoch making significance and a permanent place over against the Catholic conception of Christianity. In the ethical ideals of our Reformers, faith in God's providence, and prayer, and the valuation of a worldly calling, as the domain for the exercise of love towards our neighbor, all stand in mutual relationship." [8] With such an appraisal of the Reformation it is quite comprehensible that Ritschl desired a new Protestant reformation and wanted to accomplish it through his teachings. Thus in spite of his Biblical *Ansatz*, Ritschl effected a marked alteration of historical Christianity into the form of an ethical Neo-Protestantism. Through his opposition to metaphysics, he effected the transfer of Christ into an ideal man who was made by divine providence to be the perfect revealer of God's love, and the transfer of the Person of the Holy Spirit into the conception of an impersonal power emanating from God and dwelling in the Church.[9] For faith in the reconciliation of a holy God through the work of Christ, he substituted a trust in divine paternal love that was always present and was only revealed more impressively by Christ. In place of a specifically Christian faith in reconciliation came a general faith in divine providence. The chief purpose of Christianity became the realization of an ethics in the Kantian sense. Frank of Erlangen and other conservative Lutherans, therefore, hurled against Ritschl the charge of "counterfeiting" Christianity. In fairness to Ritschl it must be said that some of these alternating tendencies were more of the kind

---

[8] *Geschichte des Pietismus* I, 41. The same conception of the Reformation is held by Harnack and Loofs in their *History of Doctrine* and by such men as Theodor Brieger, *Der Glaube Luthers und seine Freiheit von menschlichen Autoritaeten*, 1892, W. Hermann, *Der Verkehr des Christen mit Gott im Anschluss an Luther dargestellt*, 1886, and other scholars.

[9] *Rechtfertigung und Versoehnung*, III, 444.

of a hidden force than an open statement in his system. As for himself, he never denied the metaphysical sonship of Christ; he only claimed that it cannot be an object of theological inquiry.[10] And as Otto Ritschl tells us his father had requested him beforehand to comfort him at the hour of his death with reciting the closing verses of Paul Gerhardt's famous hymn, "O Sacred Head, Now Wounded," which clearly expresses the idea of the vicarious death of Christ.[11] This is the more significant because of Ritschl's adverse criticism of this hymn in his *Geschichte des Pietismus* (II, 65).

By resting in agnosticism, however, Ritschl opened the door for a further assault on Evangelical Christianity by some of his pupils as we shall see.

Note: When Ritschl looked to Kant as the philosopher of Protestantism *par excellence*, he revealed a deplorable lack of insight into the heart of the Reformation. True, Luther, like Kant, voiced his protest against the pride of human reason to reach God by speculation. Religion was to Luther a practical matter. *Hoc est Christum cognoscere, beneficia eius cognoscere* (Melanchthon). But "what concord has Luther with Kant?" Kant's religion is moralism through and through, while Luther stands out as the champion *par excellence* of a religion of grace. Besides, when Luther opposed speculation, he was contrasting speculation with revelation. He was not a historical positivist, like the Neo-Kantian theologians.

For *literature on Ritschl* we refer the reader to the biography just mentioned (2 vols., 1892, 1896); also to a publication by his son *Ueber Werturteile* (1895). Next we mention R. A. Lipsius, *Die Ritschlsche Theologie* (1888), and O. Pfleiderer, *Die Ritschlsche Theologie* (1891), both offering a trenchant criticism from the standpoint of Hegelian liberalism. R. Frank, *Ueber die kirchliche Bedeutung der Theologie Albrecht Ritschls* (1888), and L. Lemme, *Die Prinzipien der Ritschlschen Theologie* (1891), adding two critical German studies from the conservative point of view. In English we have James Orr, *The Ritschlian Theology and Evangelical Faith* (1898); *Ritschlianism* (1903); A. E. Garvie, *The Ritschlian Theology Critical and Constructive* (1899); J. K. Mozley, *Ritschlianism* (1909); E. A. Edghill, *Faith and Fact, a Study of Ritschlianism* (1910); Robert Mackintosh, *Albrecht Ritschl and His School* (1915).

3. *Among the followers of Ritschl,* WILHELM HERRMANN (1846-1922) developed most drastically the anti-metaphysical and moralistic ideas of the master. Because of his magnetic personality and the opportunities afforded him by his long career as a professor at Marburg (after 1879), Herrmann exercised a widespread influence. In *Die Religion im Verhaeltnis zum Welterkennen und zur Sittlichkeit* (1879) he says of himself, "I have adopted the teaching of Kant in its separation of theoretical from ethical knowledge because I see in it the liberation of theology from the fetters of a philosophical world view" (p. 14). In his lectures on dogmatics[12] he sets before himself the task to describe religion as a historical reality perceived by those who experience it.[13] Since Evangelical Christianity cannot have dogmas in the old sense of the term (p. 16), "religion means seeing the working of a God in the events of life" (p. 20). Kant, therefore, was wrong when he simply identified religion with ethics, although religion "is always bound up with morality" (p. 27). "We possess it (religion) only when we come to the consciousness that God is working upon us in some particular situation as

---

[10] Compare the very sound and reserved criticism of Ritschl by H. R. Mackintosh. The late Scottish theologian is right when he warns the student of Ritschl "to guard himself against the mistake of hastily identifying 'the theology of Ritschl' with what is known, more generally, as 'the Ritschlian theology.'" (*Types of Modern Theology*, pp. 179 ff.). Besides, in the study of Ritschl, he says, as so often, "we are confronted by the possibility of divergence between a writer's personal convictions and the logical implications of his actual words" (*Ibid.*, p. 165).

[11] O. Ritschl, *Albrecht Ritschls Leben*, II, 524.

[12] Posthumously edited by Martin Rade, 1925, translated into English by N. Micklem and K. A. Saunders, *Systematic Theology*, 1927.

[13] Engl. transl., p. 18. Quotations by permission of The Macmillan Company, publishers.

the Power which saves us" (p. 40). This experience Herrmann calls "revelation," for the communication of religious forms and content of the past is no revelation at all, he says, "till religious conviction is created in ourselves; and only that which effects this in us ranks for us as revelation" (p. 39). Obedience to the Scripture, therefore, "should be required of no man as regards those passages in which he personally does not hear God speak to him" (p. 72). In the person of Christ we find "what only God Himself can give," and He is to us "what only God Himself can be" (138), and this is, according to Herrmann, the meaning of His divinity. Christ's work was to open men's eyes for the goodness of God, not to effect a change in God's attitude to sinners (p. 121 f.). Thus for Herrmann, as for Ritschl, Christianity is still intrinsically bound up with the "historical Jesus." Since Biblical criticism, however, has rendered the tradition about Jesus quite uncertain as to many details of His life, Herrmann wants to become independent of them in his appraisal of the Lord. He, therefore, singled out the "inner life of Jesus" as a plank unassailable by historical criticism, from which we may learn the ethico-religious significance of the Lord's earthly life. This "inner life of Jesus" is said to have as its essential content the universal ethical ideal of a spiritual personality and the founding of a spiritual brotherhood. And when we unite our imperfect moral life with the moral life of Jesus, we receive the ability to do good. These tenets of his theology, Herrmann has discussed more fully in his most widely known book, *Der Verkehr des Christen mit Gott*.[14]

Thus Herrmann has consistently reduced Christianity to a subjective system. The Scriptures mean less to him than to Ritschl. Emphasizing the psychological element in religion he has, in no small degree, altered the original Ritschlian theology by a retrogression to Schleiermacher. While Ritschl's thought revolves about the impersonal idea of the Kingdom of God, Herrmann's religion, by a concentration upon and devotion to the Person of Jesus, as he had learned it from his teacher Tholuck, is warmer because it is more personal.

4. *The greatest historian of the Ritschlian school* was ADOLF VON HARNACK (1851-1930), professor at Berlin since 1888. He published a great number of notable historical studies, especially in relation to the Ancient Church and the New Testament. In his widely read book, *Das Wesen des Christentums*[15] he writes "What is Christianity? We will seek to answer this question solely in a historical sense, that is, with the method of historical science and with the personal experience gained in life" (p. 4). However, a dogmatic position lies concealed in this added personal experience which has been determinative for Harnack's historical conclusions. It is marked by a rationalistic religion of an ethical character. His rationalism is expressed, as it was in the case of Strauss, by the statement: "Miracles, of course, do not happen, but there is plenty that is marvellous and inexplicable" (p. 18). The content of the Gospel he reduces to the formula: faith in God the Father, His providence, the divine sonship of man, and the infinite value of the human soul (p. 44). This is practically the same as Ritschl's religion. Then, on the negative side, he rejects the communion of Jesus with God in the metaphysical sense and affirms that "we can have the Easter faith without the Easter message" (p. 101). In the first edition he even said: "Not the Son but only the Father belongs in the Gospel

---

[14] First edition, 1886; 7th edition, 1921; translated into English from the second German edition, 1895, and from the fourth German edition, 1903, under the title *The Communion of the Christian with God*.

[15] First edition, 1900, translated into English *What is Christianity?* 1901, and subsequent editions.

that Jesus preached" (p. 19). In his great *Lehrbuch der Dogmengeschichte* (1885 ff.; 4th edition, 1909 ff.) Harnack follows the antimetaphysical tendencies of Kant and Ritschl. He fears danger that in the Church's dogma religious knowledge would supplant faith, and in his opinion, dogma, in all its forms, contradicts the very principles of Christianity and belongs to a stage of development that has been or should be passed. On the other hand, he recognizes the fact that even with Jesus the Gospel already possessed a clearly defined content which could not be formulated otherwise than in definite conceptions, that is in dogmas. As a result he rejects only the dogmas of the ancient Church, because he believes that here the Greek spirit had been the determining factor. So he arrives at his famous definition: "Dogma in its conception and development is the work of the Greek spirit on the basis of the Gospel" (4th edition, p. 19). Yet he has to admit that the Reformation not only permitted the dogma to continue but even filled the ancient formulas with a new religious significance for the Church. He, therefore, attributes a double character to the orthodox Protestant Reformation: "The Reformation, as it appears in the Christianity of Luther, is in many ways a catholic or more specifically, a medieval phenomenon, while judged by its religious essence, it rather is a revival of Pauline Christianity in the spirit of a new time" (p. 809). So, historically, Harnack prepared the way for a distinction between an Old and New Protestantism. To the latter he gave a popularized Ritschlian interpretation that became normative in wide circles.

Another historian of reputation was FRIEDRICH LOOFS at Halle (1858-1928) whose writings are outstanding because of the abundance of quotations from the original sources and a concise and up to fact presentation of the material.[16]

5. *A combination* along broad lines of Ritschlian theology with the philosophical ideas of Kant was undertaken by JULIUS KAFTAN of Berlin (1849-1926). In his book, *Philosophie des Protestantismus* (1917) he agrees with Ritschl that Kant's most important contribution to Protestantism lies in the limitation of the theoretical knowledge and the exaltation of practical reason. In his *Dogmatik* (7th and 8th editions, 1920) Kaftan espouses in principle the positivistic conception of revelation held by Ritschl, but in fact, in many doctrines, for example the doctrine of God and the deity of Christ, he approaches so closely to the doctrinal statements of the Church that it is not possible to call this theology Neo-Protestantism.[17] The same thing is true of other exponents of the Ritschlian right, for instance THEODOR HAERING (1848-1920), successor to Ritschl at Goettingen, and later at Tuebingen, OTTO KIRN (1857-1911) at Leipzig, and FERDINAND KATTENBUSCH (1851-1936) at Halle. On the other hand, the radicals of the Ritschlian school, E. TROELTSCH, for example, were in time attracted by the rising fame of the historico-religious school.

Over against these various modifications of the Ritschlian theology, Ritschl's son Otto, till his recent death professor at Bonn, tried to emphasize the original, genuine tenets in the theology of his father.

6. *The literary organs of the school* were the *Theologische Literaturzeitung, Zeitschrift fuer Theologie und Kirche,* and *Die Christliche Welt,* the "Christian Century" of Germany whose able editor, for a long time, was Martin Rade of Marburg.

---

[16] *Leitfaden Zum Studien der Dogmengeschichte,* 1889; 4th edition, 1906, and many other monographs.
[17] Cf. C. Stange, *Der Dogmatische Ertrag der Ritschlschen Theologie nach J. Kaftan,* 1906.

Chapter Eight

FROM RITSCHL TO BARTH

Literature: JOHN L. NUELSEN, *Some Recent Phases of German Theology,* 1908; W. PETERS-
ANN, *"Die Wende in der Modernen Theologie"* in *Theological Magazine* (Baur Jubilee Number,
929, pp. 32 ff.; J. L. NEVE, "Modernism in Protestant Theology," in *American Lutheran Survey,*
pril, 1927; and "Points of Differences between Theological Liberalism and Conservative Theology,"
 his *Churches and Sects of Christendom,* 1940, pp. 601 ff.

When Ritschl died in 1889, the young emperor, Wilhelm II, had just ascended the
rone; when Karl Barth's famous commentary on Romans made its first appearance in
e fall of 1918, the German empire, the Second Reich, was doomed to destruction and
ith it was buried the nineteenth century with its optimistic belief in progress and
volution.[1] Ritschl began as professor in Bonn, and, as we have seen, he developed the
nal phase of his system at Goettingen. His school, therefore, is sometimes referred to
s the Goettingen school. Karl Barth, on the other hand, began his academic career at
oettingen and concluded it, as far as Germany was concerned, at Bonn. *Difficile est
atyram non scribere,* for the Ritschlian theology found in Karl Barth its greatest rival
nd most formidable opponent. Ritschl believed in a harmonious co-operation between
hurch and state, in a progressively Christianizing and ethicizing of society. He even
resented Jesus in accordance with this ethico-religious ideal like a respectable Goet-
ingen citizen in the "gay nineties." While this *Kulturprotestantismus* continued to
ppeal to most of the Ritschlians as the great aim of Church and theology, some keen
nd honest thinkers soon discovered the injustice which the "historical Jesus" had
uffered under the hands of Ritschl. And strange as it seems, the reaction against the
ourgeois Christ of Ritschl started within Ritschl's own family. In 1892, Ritschl's son-
n-law, Johannes Weiss (1863-1918), published his little volume *Die Predigt Jesu vom
Reiche Gottes* (The Preaching of Jesus concerning the Kingdom of God). This publi-
ation has, in the words of Albert Schweitzer, "on its own lines, an importance equal to
hat of Strauss's first *Life of Jesus."* [2] In a consistent manner the author lays bare the
schatological thought of Jesus which had been completely pushed into the background
y Ritschl, thus opening up new vistas for the eyes of theologians.

In this Chapter we shall, first, enlarge upon the development of liberal thought
fter Ritschl, which goes under the name of the Historico-Religious School, and, second,
e shall give a brief sketch of the more important conservative theologians who tried
ard to uphold during this period, the faith of Evangelical Christianity.

I. THE HISTORICO-RELIGIOUS SCHOOL

1. As the name of the *Historico-Religious School* indicates, theologians now began
o lay special stress upon the development of Christianity as seen in the light of its
istorical and geographical environment. Ritschl had isolated Christianity and had

---

[1] In the Western hemisphere the false optimism of the nineteenth century extended well-nigh into the
arly thirties till we began to realize that our optimistic creed was a dream also.
[2] *The Quest of the Historical Jesus,* 2nd English edition, 1931, p. 237.

recognized a connection only between Christianity and Judaism. Others before him however, Schelling for example, had viewed the doctrinal content of Christianity in th light of the pagan religions of the ancient East. This emphasis on the general cultur background of Christianity received a new impetus in the work of Paul de Lagard (1827-1891), a colleague of Ritschl in the University of Goettingen. He insisted th theology is a historical not a philosophical science; its aim should be the study of com parative religion. The same demand was voiced by the philosopher Wilhelm Dilthe of Berlin (1833-1911). Equally important for the origin of the historico-religiou school was the work of Otto Pfleiderer who served as the connecting link between and the older evolutionary (Hegelian) theology. A number of the younger theologian were soon attracted by this new program. Also a goodly number of classical schola began to devote their time to a study of the religious environment of the primitiv Church, such as Hermann Usener,[3] Richard Reitzenstein,[4] Eduard Meyer,[5] and other

2. These German scholars, to some extent, were supported by the Dutch liberal *The Leyden School,* as these are called, had kept well abreast of the critical work i Germany. J. H. SCHOLTEN (1821-1892) leaned toward Hegelian monism, and C. V OPZOOMER was the leader of a new school in empiricism. In the field of the Old Testa ment ABRAHAM KUENEN (1828-1891) was prominent. He was a pupil of K. H. GRA (1815-1869). Kuenen wrote a critical *Introduction into the Old Testament* (3 vols 1861 ff.). The first compendium of comparative religion was written by CORNELIU PETRUS TIELE (1830-1902). This book was later revised through several editions b NATHAN SOEDERBLOM. At Leyden there was also P. D. CHANTEPIE DE LA SAUSSAY (1848-1920) who published the first compendium of comparative religion in the Ger man language (2 vols., 1887).[6]

3. Under these influences the Biblical writings both of the Old and New Testamen were subjected to *a new method of study.* In the Old Testament JULIUS WELLHAUSE (1844-1918) and his school dominated the field. Wellhausen, the special leader o higher criticism, tried to trace the evolutionary development of Israel's religion from a early crude polytheism to a pure ethical monotheism. Most startling had been his bol assertion that, contrary to the traditional view, the great prophets of the Old Testamen religion had preceded in time the codification of the Mosaic Law.[7]

The real explorer in the field of a historico-religious interpretation of the Ol Testament was HERMANN GUNKEL (1862-1932). In his book, *Schoepfung und Chao in Urzeit* (1895) he sets out to show that the Biblical narrative of the beginning an end of time are based on extra-Biblical legends of the oriental peoples. Concerning th origin of Christianity, he boldly stated, in a later volume, *Zum religionsgeschichtliche Verstaendnis des Neuen Testaments* (1903): Christianity is a syncretistic religion (p. 95); the essentials of the Church's Christological doctrine are not derived from th historical Jesus (p. 64).

---

    [3] *Religionsgeschichtliche Untersuchungen:* I. *Das Weihnachtsfest,* 1889; II.   *Christlicher Festbrauch,* 1889 III. *Die Sintflutsagen,* 1899.
    [4] *Poimandres. Studien zur griechisch-aegyptischen und frueh-christlichen Literatur,* 1904; *Die hellenistische Mysterienreligionen,* 1910; *Weltuntergansvorstellungen,* 1924; *Die Vorgeschichte der christlichen Taufe,* 1929, et al
    [5] *Urspruenge und Anfaenge des Christentums,* 3 vols., 1921 ff.; et al.
    [6] See E. C. Vanderlaan, *Protestant Modernism in Holland,* 1924.
    [7] *Geschichte Israels,* 1878; in a second edition *Prolegomena zur Geschichte Israels,* 1883; translated a *Prolegomena to the History of Israel* by J. Sutherland Black and Allan Menzies. With Preface by W. Robertso Smith, 1885.

Gunkel's view was further developed by HUGO GRESSMANN (1877-1927). He
laid down the axiom of the historico-religious school when he said in *A. Eichhorn und
die religions-geschichtliche Schule* (1914): "There is in the world no material that
does not have its history, no conceptions of thought without its connections with previous conceptions. This maxim holds true not only in the small and trivial things of life,
but also concerning the prophetic religion of Israel and the origin of Christianity"
(p. 35). The study of history is conditioned by the axiom of development. He who
rejects evolution, can make no claim to scientific knowledge (p. 37). Thus evolution
in the field of Biblical studies is an established fact and has supplanted a Biblical history
based on supernatural forces. Such prophetic elements, as for instance, the idea of the
Messiah and eschatology, are conditioned, according to Gressmann, by similar extra-
Biblical notions, not by supernatural revelation and inspiration.

4. Other scholars, WREDE, WEINEL, HEITMUELLER, and BOUSSET, for example,
applied this method to study of the New Testament. According to WILHELM WREDE
(1859-1906) it was Paul and not Jesus who founded the Christian religion (*Paulus,*
1905). Jesus Himself held no Messianic claims. The impulse to give a Messianic form
to the earthly life of Jesus has arisen, according to Wrede, within certain circles of His
followers among which Mark, very likely, held a prominent place.[8] The supernatural
tenets in the Gospels are dismissed by this school as accretions from the mystic religions
of the ancient Orient which, with their legends of a dying and rising god, have supplied
the primitive Christian community with such ideas as the virgin birth, resurrection and
ascension of the Lord. Likewise, the sacraments are held not to have been instituted by
Jesus. As to their origin, usually a distinction is made between a primary Jewish and a
Hellenistic element representing the second stage of development. The conception of
baptism unto repentance is said to be a Jewish notion in the New Testament; baptism
as a washing of regeneration shows the influence of the mystic religions upon Christianity. In the same way, the Lord's Supper was for Jesus simply a farewell meal, the
Pauline interpretation of it as a supper in which Christ gives the Church His body to
eat and His blood to drink, is again relegated to the domain of the mystery cults.[9] On
the other hand, it was held that in order to discover the "essence of Christianity" we
must only concentrate on stripping off in the New Testament everything which might
have conceivably come out of the experience or reflection of the primitive church.
We would then be face to face with the "historical Jesus" whose features, broadly speaking, according to this school, are as follows: Jesus was the cheerful lad of a Galilean
village. Attracted by the message of John and being conscious of sin, He came to the
Jordan for baptism by John. He then gathered a company of disciples and went about
with them to preach the kingdom of God. His chief significance for faith lies in that
He realized in His life the ideal of a universal religion, i.e., belief in God, virtue, and
immortality. What Jesus thought of Himself, and what significance, if any, He attached
to his death, we shall never know. It is likely that at some moments of His life He had
visions of becoming the Messiah and the Son of Man. By His criticism of the legalistic

---

[8] *Das Messiasgeheimnis in den Evangelien. Zugleich ein Beitrag zum Verstaendnis des Markusevangeliums*
(The Messianic Secret in the Gospels. A contribution to the understanding of the Gospel of Mark), 1901; cf.
A. Schweitzer, *Op. cit.,* pp. 328 ff.

[9] A. Eichhorn, *Das Abendmahl im Neuen Testament,* 1898; W. Heitmueller, *Taufe and Abendmahl bei
Paulus,* 1903; cf. also his article on the Lord's Supper in the first edition of *Die Religion in Geschichte und
Gegenwart,* I, 20 ff.

tenet of Judaism He encountered the suspicion and hostility of the Pharisees and scribes. They set traps for Him and endeavored to cause Him to fall. When, at last, He showed Himself in Jerusalem, He was arrested by the Jewish authorities. He remained passive and was condemned to death, the Roman government supporting the claims of the Jews.[10] The Jerusalem Church, being convinced that He was still alive after his crucifixion, envisaged this "Jesus of history" as the Messiah who would soon return in glory to inaugurate the final rule of God. This Judaistic Christology, it is said, underwent further change in the Greek Churches. Here the eschatological belief of the former gave way to the Hellenistic conception of Jesus as a divine *Kyrios,* the Lord of mystery cult.[11]

5. This school, as we have seen, tried to explain the rise of Christianity by an intramundane *evolutionary process of religion.* It made theology a historical science and established itself upon the historical Jesus as its scholars saw Him. But soon its leaders became painfully aware of the insufficiency of their religious foundation. Neither faith nor history could be satisfied with it. For the historian "the quest of the historical Jesus" seemed to be a hopeless undertaking since the documentary evidence in the New Testament seemed too scanty for writing a biography of Jesus and the differing scholars of this school held too sharply conflicting views as regards the details of the life of Jesus. It was also felt that faith cannot live by a person of history. Because of its very nature it seeks contact with an ever-present Reality. As a result, the Historico-Religious School underwent a great transformation. Turning away from history and "the historical Jesus," it began to concentrate its efforts on the philosophy of religion and to replace "the historical Jesus" by a religious symbol rooted in human reason. This change of attitude was expressed by WILHELM BOUSSET in a lecture at the Fifth Congress for Christianity and Religious Progress at Berlin (1910). Said Bousset: The serious and persistent pursuit of history points us to something that lies beyond its own boundaries and forces us to look for another foundation of faith, i.e., reason (p. 10). Continuing his argument, Bousset predicates a religious *a priori* in the soul of man. The great creative personalities of religion not only create religious symbols, but they are themselves symbols for their followers (p. 16). On account of this new attitude, "the quest of the historical Jesus" has now lost its significance. We need not be alarmed, says Bousset, by the obvious failure of this quest, for we are concerned with Jesus as a religious symbol not with the details of His life! For this reason, the Gospels, though they are a veritable mixture of fiction and truth, will always have a greater appeal to man than the most exact reconstruction of the life of Jesus by a modern historian (p. 17).

While Bousset and others with him were indifferent to the details of the life of Jesus, some went a step further and flatly denied the historical existence of Jesus altogether. Here we must mention ALBERT KALTHOFF, pastor in the free city of Bremen which for a time was the very hotbed of theological radicalism. According to Kalthoff,[12] the origin of Christianity is rooted in a communistic movement in the Roman empire. "The crude social ferment at work in the Roman empire amalgamated itself with the religious and philosophical forces of the time to form the new Christian social move-

---

[10] W. Wrede, *Op. cit.;* W. Bousset, *Jesus,* 1904; W. Heitmueller, *Jesus,* 1913.

[11] W. Bousset, *Kyrios Christos,* 1913; *Jesus der Herr,* 1916; cf. our article "The Fifth Gospel: the Gospel according to Saint Paul," *The Lutheran Church Quarterly,* (XIII, 3) July, 1940, pp. 223 ff.

[12] *Das Christusproblem,* 1902; *Die Entstehung des Christentums,* 1904.

ent." In the late-Jewish literature, on the other hand, the principle of "personifications" d long been at work. This principle the early Christian writers applied to invent the storical person of Jesus. "From the socio-religious standpoint the figure of Christ is e sublimated religious expression for the sum of the social and ethical forces which ere at work at a certain period." [13] We might add as a special sample of this view e book of P. Jensen, *Das Gilgameschepos in der Weltliteratur* (Vol. I, 1906) in which e author makes the whole life of Christ a Jewish version of the contents of that bylonian epos.

The monistic and unhistorical view of Kalthoff was also shared by the philosopher, RTHUR DREWS, who in public lectures and writings tried to disseminate his ideas nong the common people.[14] This shift of interest from history to philosophy was ite general in German thought after 1900. It thus happened that the Historico-eligious School was transformed into a philosophico-religious school and that its vn greatest exponent came to be not a historian but a systematic theologian: Ernst oeltsch.

6. ERNST TROELTSCH, born in 1865, *was a pupil of Ritschl*. He held theological ofessorships at Goettingen, Bonn, and Heidelberg. The plan of the Prussian minister culture to appoint him in 1908 as successor to Otto Pfleiderer in Berlin was frus-ated by the opposition of the theological faculty of that university. In 1914, however, was called to Berlin as professor in the philosophical department. From 1919 to 1921 held a position in the revolutionary government as church secretary. He died in 1923.

At first Troeltsch established himself on a synthesis of Ritschl and Schleiermacher. rly, however, he became dissatisfied with the isolation of religion into a special com-rtment. Realizing the need of a metaphysical foundation of religion, he went back Hegel and the older liberal theology. Considering the structure of the human mind, maintained that we are justified to speak of a "rational (though not intellectual) priori of religion" and of a "rational kernel of religion." With great mental acumen began to investigate the absoluteness of Christianity. Christianity, so he begins, is historical religion, yet it has always made the claim of offering religious absolutes. it can these two things be reconciled: the historical nature of Christianity and its aim of religious absoluteness? Troeltsch answered the question in the negative. istory is an ever-moving process involving change of form and thought. Whatever, erefore, is historical cannot be absolute. "To be historical and relative is identical." [15] esides, everything historical is conditioned by the principle of causality. Consequently, iristianity as a historical phenomenon is subject to that same principle. Thus no room left, in the modern mind, for the supernatural in the origin of Christianity. We, erefore, are forced to dismiss the idea of the absoluteness of Christianity. What we ay uphold, then, is only this: that Christianity thus far represents for the European-merican mind the highest type of religion. "Christianity is indeed among the great ligions the most potent and complete revelation of a personalistic religion" (p. 86). it, we may ask, what is the criterion for such an evaluation of our Christian religion? answer this question, Troeltsch appeals to the subjective personal yet unbiased and

---

[13] The translation of these quotations is taken from A. Schweitzer, *The Quest of the Historical Jesus*, pp. 3-318, which the English student may use as a convenient source of information on Kalthoff's view.

[14] *Die Christusmythe*, Vol. I, 1909; Vol. II, 1911.

[15] *Die Absolutheit des Christentums und die Religionsgeschichte*, 1902; revised edition, 1912, pp. 52, 86.

objectively minded conviction of the individual, i.e., Troeltsch admits that there is ⲛ
objective-scientific criterion to settle the question. Not even the study of comparati⥀
religion can answer it. Religion always is a matter of personal conviction. This is,
Gruetzmacher rightly remarks, the same solution which the Church has always set fort⥀
Troeltsch does not follow here a modern scientific method over against an antiquat⥀
dogmatic method of the Church. Rather we are here face to face with two dogmat⥀
principles both of which are based on a preconceived axiom.[16]

The "essence of Christianity" Troeltsch has discussed in *Zur religioesen Lag⥀*
Religionsphilosophie und Ethik (1913). Here he says: "The Christian position
maintained when we are conscious of the Father of Jesus Christ as a living present
our daily conflicts, labors, hopes, and sufferings, and when we arm ourselves, in tʰ⥀
power of the Christian spirit, for the weightiest decision in the world, the final victo⥀
of all eternal and personal values of the soul (p. 440). The faith of the Christi⥀
religion is faith in the regeneration, the rebirth on a higher level, of a culture which
this world is alienated from God, by means of the knowledge of God in Christ, th⥀
achieving the Kingdom of God by bringing culture into union with God (p. 512⥀
Thus Christianity becomes the gospel of the attainment and preservation of the Go⥀
filled soul. . . . We do not ask: How can I obtain a gracious God? But rather: Ho⥀
can I find my soul again, how can I learn to love again?" (p. 522). In brief, for tʰ⥀
Christian faith in a divine Redeemer Troeltsch substituted belief in an evolutionist
development of human personality. Thus the distinction between true and false, natu⥀
and revealed, religion disappears. The attack of Troeltsch was mainly directed again⥀
Ritschl and his school because the latter declared the person of Jesus to be the su⥀
total of redeeming truth, while it held the other religions to be burdened with so mu⥀
error and uncertainty that without Jesus one would finally end up in atheism. For tʰ⥀
religion of Troeltsch, on the other hand, the person of Jesus is not absolutely necessa⥀
In an address, delivered at the fifteenth meeting of the Christian Students' Conferen⥀
in Aarau, Switzerland, 1911, he declared that it is, however, desirable for sociologic⥀
and psychological reasons to maintain the person of Jesus as the focal point of worsh⥀
and as the unifying factor in the community.

Christianity, according to Troeltsch, has produced three distinctive social type⥀
(1) the church, inclusive, and possessing the indispensable and inalienable charact⥀
of holiness by virtue of the means of grace administered by her, (2) the sect, as ⥀
exclusive association of truly regenerate people, and (3) the religious mystic intereste⥀
only in the development of his inner life. The Middle Ages did not end with tʰ⥀
Reformation of the sixteenth century but with the period of enlightenment in the eigʰ⥀
eenth century which issued into a Neo-Protestantism whose "symbolical books are Go⥀
freedom, and immortality and whose Christology is the earthly life of Jesus."[16a] Tʰ⥀
Lutheran Church, in the eyes of Troeltsch, represents the most antiquated form of Prc⥀
estantism while Calvinism, by virtue of its alliance with humanism, is more modern a⥀
progressive. Still more progressive are the spiritualistic sects which have abandon⥀
altogether the supernatural and historical foundation of Christianity.

---

[16] Cf. H. R. Gruetzmacher in *Theological Magazine*, September, 1928, pp. 346 ff.
[16a] *Protestantisches Christentum und Kirche in der Neuzeit* in *Kultur der Gegenwart*, IV, 696, 2nd editi⥀
1909; cf. also the lecture, *Die Bedeutung des Protestantismus fuer die Entstehung der modernen Welt*, 1911.

As the Christian dogma, so Christian ethics are relativized by Troeltsch. The ethical outlook of the primitive Church was purely ascetic and eschatological. The historic churches in their pursuit of a Christian civilization have turned down the ethical requirements of the New Testament. The pietistic sects, in turn, trying to enforce the rigid otherworldliness of the New Testament, have forced themselves into cultural inactivity. As to the ethical duties of the present, Troeltsch had no solution to offer. The social work of the Churches was to him highly problematic. Christian ethics in itself is unable to satisfy the needs of the time.[17] Little wonder that Troeltsch exchanged his theological professorship for a chair in the philosophical faculty. His theology attempts to destroy the very basis on which alone it can rest. Troeltsch's works have been edited in four volumes (1912-1925). For literature on him we refer the reader to W. Guenther, *Die Grundlagen der Religionsphilosophie Ernst Troeltschs* (1914); E. Vermeil, *La pensée religieuse de Troeltsch* (1922); R. S. Sleight, *The Sufficiency of Christianity* (1923); G. Ritzert, *Die Religionsphilosophie Ernst Troeltschs* (1924). For further literature compare the article on Troeltsch in *Religion in Geschichte und Gegenwart*.

7. *Three other German theologians deserve attention here*. First is ADOLPH DEISSMANN (1866-1937), professor at Marburg, Heidelberg, and Berlin. By providence it became his task to liberate the New Testament from the straightjacket of a narrow conception of "Biblical Greek" as being unique in vocabulary, inflexion, and style. He devoted all his efforts to interpret the New Testament Greek in the "light from the ancient East." His word was hailed with delight by the scholars of the Anglo-Saxon world as witnessed by the translation of most of his writings and his many lectures in English and American institutions. This pupil of Herrmann, Wellhausen, and Cohen sought to explain the "essence of Christianity" in terms of a cult-worship and *Christusmystik*. His *Bible Studies* have been edited in English by Alexander Grieve in 1901 (3rd edition, 1923). *Light from the Ancient East* was published in English in 1910 (3rd edition, 1926). *Paul, a Study in Social and Religious History* has gone through two editions in German and one in English (1912).[18]

In contrast to Deissmann, RUDOLPH OTTO (1869-1937) stands out as a man of many diverse interests, being well versed in philosophy, the natural sciences, comparative religion (studies in the religions of India), and theology. Out of his religious-psychological and religious-historical investigation has come the widely read monograph *Das Heilige*.[19] Here the conception that had been completely set aside by Ritschl appears as the actual center of all religion. The "Holy" is the numinous, the mysterious, the "wholly other" which fills the soul of man with wonder and awe. On the other hand, the Holy possesses something fascinating and attractive that gains the confidence of man. It is composed of both super-rational and rational elements. Consequently, the doctrines of the Church contain both rational and super-rational statements. With this — though proponderately aesthetic — conception of the Holy, Otto approached decidedly towards one of the fundamental positions of orthodox Protestantism and helped to prepare the way for the Barthian reaction against the Ritschlian, Neo-Protestant depravation of faith. Of other works by Otto translated into English we mention *Naturalism*

---

[17] *Die Soziallehren der Christlichen Kirchen und Gruppen*, 1912; English edition, 1931.

[18] Cf. Deissmann's autobiographical sketch in Stange, *Selbstdarstellungen*, I, 43 ff.

[19] First edition 1912, with many subsequent German editions and translations; in English known under the title, *The Idea of the Holy*, first edition, 1923.

and Religion (1907), *Life and Ministry of Jesus* (1908), and *The Kingdom of God and the Son of Man* (undated).

On several occasions we have referred to ALBERT SCHWEITZER (born 1875), theologian, philosopher, physician, noble missionary, and church musician. Following in the footsteps of Johannes Weiss, he has become the most consistent exponent of the eschatological interpretation of the life of Jesus.[20] His endeavors to interpret also the religion of Paul from a purely eschatological point of view have met with less success.[21] As to his world view, Schweitzer does not share the naive, evolutionary optimism of the last century. A planned evolution can nowhere be discovered, he says. The good is always opposed by the evil. Yet, he still holds to the ethicizing conception of Christianity in Neo-Protestantism when he lays down as an ethical imperative the principle of "reverence for humanity" (*Ehrfurcht vor dem Leben*). "It is good to sustain and further life; it is evil to destroy and thwart life." This "reverence for humanity" he holds to be identical with the ethics of the Sermon on the Mount and therefore the absolute ethic. And in proportion as we have the spirit of Jesus, he says, we have the true knowledge of Jesus! [22]

8. For the first time in modern German theology, the Historico-Religious School *undertook to disseminate its ideas* among a wider reading public. For this reason its scholars issued a series of semi-popular monographs called *Die religionsgeschichtlichen Volksbuecher*. Likewise, *Die Schriften des Neuen Testaments, neu uebersetzt und erklaert,* a New Testament commentary with translation, edited by Johannes Weiss and published by Vandenhoeck und Ruprecht at Goettingen (1905 ff.), was intended for the same purpose. The first edition of *Die Religion in Geschichte und Gegenwart* (1909 ff.) was written and edited exclusively from the standpoint of this school. The many contributions of more conservative scholars have, however, given the second edition of this work (1927 ff.) an entirely different character.

9. Last *but not least* we must say a word about NATHAN SOEDERBLOM (1866-1931), the late Archbishop of Upsala, Primate of the Church of Sweden. By placing Soederblom at the end of this section, immediately preceding our discussion of the contributions made by conservative theologians, we have indicated to the observing reader that Soederblom held such a mediating position in his day. He was a liberal scholar but conservative churchman, an exponent of the Historico-Religious School. (Prior to the appointment as primate of his church he held the chair of comparative religion in Upsala and Leipzig.) He had a pronounced leaning toward Luther. As scholar, churchman, and linguist he was of first magnitude, and what is still more, he was a simple Christian with a heart of love for all mankind. He was the spiritual power behind the first ecumenical council of Christendom in modern times when it met in Stockholm in the summer of 1925 ("Life and Work"). His theological interest was centered in the idea of "general revelation." "No religion is a product of culture, all religion depends on a revelation." [23] With an untiring effort he tried to prove that God is active in nature, history, and the consciousness of His prophets. Divine revelation

[20] Cf. his famous work, as referred to; also *Das Messianitaets-und Leidensgeheimnis,* 1901.

[21] *Geschichte der paulinischen Forschung von der Reformation bis zur Gegenwart,* 1911; *Die Mystik des Apostels Paulus,* 1930; English: *The Mysticism of Paul, the Apostle,* 1931.

[22] *Kulturphilosophie,* 2 vols., 1923; in English *Philosophy of Civilization.* For a brief introduction into the philosophy and writings of Schweitzer see the little book by Ch. E. B. Russell, *The Path to Reconstruction,* 1942.

[23] *The Nature of Revelation,* 1933, p. 8.

therefore was to him a "continued revelation." It reached a climax in Christianity. Jesus is unique, he held, because He is the historical revealer of God. In Him "the eternal reason and will of God, the Logos, became very flesh." [24] Soederblom quite definitely rejected the ethicizing of religion in Ritschlianism, "for the final question put to religion is not: How will you shape my life, what ought my life to be? It is rather this: How can you rescue my life and sustain it, so that I may not be engulfed in a meaningless existence or lost in despair?" [25] Religious experience was to him an experience of the infinite majesty and holiness of God coupled with an experience of "terror and anguish, of death and hell" (Luther) as the natural reaction of the whole human personality, although he was willing to grant that "it is wrong and unpsychological to make the experience of the great hero of faith the standard for all." [26] We thus see that the "otherness" of God and the *sola gratia* of Paul and Luther are foremost in his conception of Christianity. In this respect Soederblom was a genuine Lutheran. However, when we inquire about the *propter Christum* in the act of justification, we find that many Evangelical Christians will register their protest. When the incarnation is limited to a personal embodiment of the character of God in the man Jesus and the Cross is merely seen to be "the strongest testimony that God has been seeking man," [27] pupils of Paul and Luther will deplore that Soederblom has allowed Ritschl to obscure his vision of the meaning of Christ.

Note: This statement, we believe, will stand in spite of the many fine remarks of Soederblom about "vicarious suffering" in his little book *The Mystery of the Cross* (1933), translated from the larger original *Kristi pinas historia* (1928). The meaning of the Cross, as set forth in these pages, is, in all essentials, that of Ritschl tinged with the conception of the Atonement as found in the theologies of the Greek Fathers and of Hofmann: recognizing His solidarity with the human race, Christ unmasked the evil and manifested God's love.
This one-sided emphasis on the conquering love of God also prevails in the little book by E. Eidem, successor to Soederblom as Primate of Sweden, *The Suffering God* (1938). Also the view of G. Aulén, pupil of Soederblom, is interesting in this connection. Compare our discussion of Lundensian Theology (pp. 184 ff.). In addition to the volumes referred to, Soederblom wrote, among many other books, *Gudstrons uppkommst* (*The Development of the Idea of God*, 1914), and *Religionsproblemet inom katolicism och protestantism* (1910) which contains a critical discussion of the Modernist movement in the Church of Rome. For his studies in Luther compare p. 184.

10. *A great admirer of Soederblom* is Friedrich Heiler of Marburg. Reared and educated in the Roman Church, he early was attracted to the principles of the Catholic modernists and Protestant liberals. In 1919 he was received by Soederblom into the Lutheran communion without renouncing his membership in the Church of Rome. Heiler has addressed himself to promoting the cause of an "evangelical catholicism" (a synthesis of the Catholic ideal of the Church and the Protestant emphasis on the *sola gratia* in piety). In his books we discern that same comprehensive view of religion as in the writings of Soederblom. The most important books are: *Das Gebet* (1918); *Luthers religionsgeschichtliche Bedeutung* (1918); *Der Katholizismus. Seine Idee und seine Erscheinung* (1923); *Evangelische Katholizitaet* (1926).

11. In conclusion a *word of criticism* will be in order. We do not intend to minimize in the least the chasm that exists between such theologians as, for example, Ritschl

[24] *The Living God*, The Gifford Lectures, 1931, published posthumously in 1933, p. 319.
[25] *The Nature of Revelation*, p. 3 f.
[26] *Op. cit.*, p. 93.
[27] *The Living God*, p. 344.

and Soederblom. Yet, nevertheless, as a matter of fact, the chief concern of all these scholars is not the *revelatio specialis* but "religion in general." The "essence" of Christianity to them is to be sought in the general history of thought and religion. The truth that breaks forth in the Gospel is not a new truth which did not exist before Jesus; it is a truth that always existed, the "immanent purpose" of the cosmological drama. Only this purpose was not clear until Jesus came. Christ, therefore, is to them the "Archetype" (Schleiermacher), the "Revealer," the "Bearer of a moral idea," the "Founder of a religion in whom the ethico-religious ideal was realized for the first time." This is all they mean when they speak of the "uniqueness" of Christ. His relation to Christianity they regard of course as "factual and causal," but not as positive and absolutely necessary.[28] To believe is to them not to believe in Christ, but to have faith like Christ who is to them not the object of faith, but rather an "exemplification of faith and love."

The effect of Neo-Protestantism on the life of the churches in Germany, for example, was definitely destructive. Under its message church attendance dropped to a minimum. Its theologians were swept off by the current of a general individualistic religiosity,[29] or of a religious and political socialism.[30] But they could regain for Christ neither the educated nor the proletariat. The way for a restoration of Biblical Christianity was prepared in the theologies of such men as Ihmels, Kaehler, Schlatter, and Schaeder, and accomplished in the Barthian and Neo-Lutheran revival of the next period.[31]

II. Conservative Theologians

1. *During these years* when the historical and rational aspect of religion commanded the interest of theologians, German Protestantism was not lacking of men who not only strained themselves[32] to confess the creeds of Evangelical Christianity but who with great scholarship and genuine piety waged a courageous fight for the faith "once delivered to the saints."

2. In *Biblical studies,* THEODOR ZAHN (1838-1933) stands out as the great authority on the New Testament and the literature of the ancient Church. He was a pupil of Hofmann and his successor in the chair of New Testament at Erlangen. Being unhampered by the preconceived dogmatic theory of his teacher, Zahn endeavored to prove the authenticity of the early Christian tradition by a thorough historical investigation of all the extant literature of that period. With this in mind he wrote an *Introduction to the New Testament.*[33] We note also his *Forschungen zur Geschichte des neutestamentlichen Kanons* (9 vols., 1881 ff.). At the advanced age of sixty-five he began his great *Commentary on the New Testament* to which he contributed the exposition of Matthew, Luke, John, Acts, Romans, Galatians, and Revelation.

The position of Zahn was, broadly speaking, shared by his collaborators in the Commentary, PH. BACHMANN (died 1931), G. WOHLENBERG (died 1917), P. EWALD

---

[28] Cf. E. Brunner, *The Mediator,* 1934, p. 97.

[29] Cf. for instance, the position of Johannes Mueller's *Blaetter zur Pflege persoenlichen Lebens* and other works of his; also Karl Koenig, *Gott, warum wir bei ihm bleiben muessen,* 1901; *Der moderne Mensch auf dem Wege zu Gott,* 1904, *et al.*

[30] Fr. Naumann, *Briefe ueber Religion,* 1903.

[31] Cf. Neve, *op. cit.*

[32] A Schweitzer of Zurich is credited with the significant saying that as once the fathers confessed their faith, so now theologians sometimes endeavor with might and main (*sich abmuehen*) to believe in the confessions of their fathers. Cf. F. Kattenbusch, *op. cit.,* p. 57.

[33] 2 vols. 1897 ff.; 3rd edition 1905 ff.; published in English by T. and T. Clark, Edinburgh, 1909, 3 vols.; and by Scribner's, New York, 1917, 1 vol.

(died 1911), and the blind scholar E. RIGGENBACH (died 1927), and by P. FEINE (died 1933) of Halle University, and A. SCHLATTER (see below); in the field of the Old Testament by such men as R. KITTEL (died 1929), E. KOENIG (died 1936), and E. SELLIN at Berlin. All these scholars give due regard to the literary and critical problems and to those of comparative religion. But they do not regard the relatively late composition of a book as militating against its reliability. While rejecting the evolutionary conception of Christianity, as held by the Historico-Religious School, they follow the method of comparative religion not to destroy but to disclose more clearly the unique character of the Biblical religion.

3. As to the *origin of Protestantism,* the conservatives conceive of the Reformation of the sixteenth century as a revival of the Biblical religion of redemption. This Christianity as it is given in the Scripture, in the historic Confessions, and in the living religious experience of the Evangelical religion, they seek to understand and establish with the scientific methods of the present, without permitting it to be destroyed in content by the so-called modern spirit. In 1883 the great *Weimar Edition of Luther's Works* was started. Prominent in the field of Luther research are W. Walther (died 1924), K. Holl (died 1926), H. Boehmer (died 1927), and H. Preuss.

4. In *Systematic Theology* we have LUDWIG IHMELS (1858-1933), professor at Erlangen and Leipzig, Landesbischof of Saxony, as the recognized leader of Lutheranism. He was a pupil of Frank whose theology, however, underwent in his work a noteworthy correction along more conservative lines. Ihmels agrees with Frank that the ultimate basis on which[34] Christian certainty is founded is a subjective one. "All certainty of the individual bears of necessity a subjective character." It can come to pass only through a personal experience of salvation. The question then arises as to whether I can deduce the knowledge of objective Christianity from my subjective experience or whether this does not have to be given me in some other way. Ihmels is of the opinion that we have to adopt the second of these two alternatives. He says it is the divine Word, with its message of sin and grace which, when preached, exercises its influence upon me. In this manner, he argues, I may become certain of divine realities. Religious experience is always secondary, arising from the objective knowledge of the Word. Thus the way leads from the objective to the subjective, from history to psychology. A further difference between Frank and Ihmels consists in the definition of the fundamental religious experience. While Frank was in danger of permitting the ethical interpretation of Christianity, which was so predominant in the theology of Ritschl, to obscure the central message of the New Testament, Ihmels remained much closer to the Scriptural truth when he designated this experience as justification. In fact, during the last twenty years of his life, Ihmels was the most forceful preacher in German Lutheranism, with the Fourth Article of the Augsburg Confession, on Justification at the basis of all his sermons:

"I build on this foundation
That Jesus and His blood
Alone are my salvation,
The true, eternal good;

---

[34] *Die christliche Wahrheitsgewissheit,* 1901, 3rd edition 1914.

Without Him all that pleases
Is valueless on earth;
The gifts I owe to Jesus
Alone my love are worth."[35]

5. *Another scholar* who, like Ihmels, owes much of his theology to the Erlangen school is OLE HALLESBY, professor at the Independent Theological Seminary, Oslo, Norway. Through personal contact and translation of several of his writings he has become well known to his American co-religionists. He wrote a dogmatics in two volumes, *Den kristelige troslaere* (1920 f.). His translated works include *Why am I a Christian?* (1930), *Prayer* (1931), *Conscience* (1933), *The Christian Life* (1934), and *Religious or Christian?* (1939). Through all these writings runs a deep devotional spirit.

6. *We now come* to REINHOLD SEEBERG (1859-1935), the eminent scholar of the Berlin University who held doctoral degrees in theology, philosophy, jurisprudence, and even medicine. Seeberg was a Lutheran by birth and education coming from the Baltic countries with their strong Lutheran consciousness. Frank of Erlangen had a considerable share in shaping his theological thought. But unlike L. Ihmels, Seeberg further liberalized the Erlangen theology. Thus he became known as a mediating theologian. These tendencies moved him to accept a call from the historically Lutheran University of Erlangen to the Union University of Berlin. His main contributions lie in the field of historical and systematic theology, but he also was an expert in higher Biblical criticism as much as any specialist in the field. As a marvel of scholarship he stands before us in his five large volumes of together 3,166 pages on the history of Christian Thought (*Lehrbuch der Dogmengeschichte*) which, during the years of abject depression in Germany, after the First World War, went through several editions—a work that is bound to hold first place for a long time. Seeberg's usefulness for the Church is much greater than that of his brilliant contemporary and colleague, A. von Harnack. He is particularly original in the field of Medieval Thought, the significance of which for the interpretation of the Reformation he has demonstrated. Dogmas he defines "as a special form of expression for the understanding of the truths of salvation on the part of the Church, dealing in matters which the Church regards as necessary for its historical existence and, therefore, . . . made a permanent part of its existence through public definition" (I, 4, 3rd edition). He considers the Reformation as a definite stage of the development of Paulinism and Augustinianism.

In the book *Die Kirche Deutschlands im 19. Jahrhundert* (1900, 3rd edition 1910) he stressed the need of a "modern positive theology," that would meet the spiritual situation of the times. He sought to meet this in a popular book, *Fundamental Truths of the Christian Religion* (German 1902, English 1908), and later in a more developed and different way in his *Christliche Dogmatik* (2 vols., 1924 f.). Here he describes the fundamental principle of his new dogmatic formulation as a "voluntaristic transcendentalism." In contrast to the old "substantial" conceptions of the divine and human being, the will is regarded as the characteristic element in the human and divine being,

---

[35] Cf. his sermons, *Eins ist not*, 2nd edition 1907; *Aus der Zeit fuer die Zeit und Ewigkeit*, 1921. He also wrote, among other books, *Zentralfragen der Dogmatik*, 4th edition 1920, and *Die Selbstaendigkeit der Dogmatik gegenueber der Religionsphilosophie*, 1900.

and so the relationship between them must be described as a relationship of the will.[36] The "essence of Christianity," according to Seeberg, is expressed in the two concepts of the redemptive supremacy of God and of faith, and of the Kingdom of God and of love. This sovereignty of God is mediated by Jesus Christ. Christianity is the absolute religion "and all other religions are only religions in so far as their center is related to Christianity" (I, 195). The source of Christian dogmatics for Seeberg is neither subjective experience nor the teaching of the Bible but "the revelation that is believed" (*die geglaubte Offenbarung*). In dealing with the individual doctrines he adopts a more or less extensive modification of traditional dogmatics, especially in discussing the doctrines of the Holy Trinity, Christology, and eschatology. Since the essence of a person is nothing but will, the Trinity consists of three wills in God: "The Father wills the world; the Son wills the Church by overcoming the sinful antagonism of mankind; the Spirit wills myself as a member of the Church and for labor within it (I, 381 f.). Jesus had His origin as a man, with whom, at His baptism,[37] the Logos, or the Spirit, united which union was made perfect by Christ's resurrection." Thus Jesus became the Son of God, i.e., the historical organ through whom God accomplished the redemption of mankind.[38] The traditional eschatology with its many "open questions" Seeberg recasts, on the basis of deeply devotional studies in Paul and John, and published the result of his thought in a little volume under the title *Ewiges Leben* (1915, and subsequent editions), which was dedicated to the many mourners of the young men fallen in the World War. This book together with his other systematic studies makes it very plain that some of the fundamental ideas of Christianity have been distorted by his leaning toward German Idealism. Little wonder that he held to an "analytical conception" of justification involving a successive purification of man in a "purgatory of grace." [39] In this connection his under-rating of God's wrath in the theology of Luther is highly significant. Paul Althaus says of him: "Seeberg showed no appreciation for a 'theology of faith.'" Yet Seeberg was far removed from "Modernism" as a system. His heart was with the Lutheran Church. In his *Christian Dogmatics* we see nothing of the stressing of the claim of science against the religion of faith; no urging of a naturalistic philosophy upon theology; no denial of the supernatural. Seeberg was a man of the nineteenth century who wanted to help the modern man in his difficulties, particularly his students of the Ritschl-Harnack-Troeltsch age.

7. For a time it was believed that Seeberg would succeed in establishing a *"modern-positive school."* And even after it had become evident that this could not materialize, men continued to speak of *die Kreise um Seeberg herum,* meaning by it that there was a group of mediating theologians which was aiming to steer between the old Erlangen theology on the one hand and theological liberalism on the other (Karl Beth, R. H. Gruetzmacher and others).

The most original of these scholars was THEODOR KAFTAN (1847-1932). In contrast to Seeberg's speculative idealism, Kaftan's "modernism" was conditioned by the Neo-Kantian opposition to metaphysics. He made a sharp distinction between faith and theology. The substance of faith cannot change; it must be the old or no Christian faith

---

[36] Preface to Vol. II.

[37] Seeberg made much of the "Spirit" of Christ as Kyrios through the Logos Who had joined Himself to the Lord Jesus (referring to II Cor. 3:17, "Now the Lord is that Spirit."

[38] *Der Ursprung des Christusglaubens*, 1914.

[39] *Christl. Dogmatik* II, 568 f.

at all. But theology as the science of faith must develop according to the spiritual progress of mankind. Kaftan did not hold a theological chair but was the titular head of the Lutheran Church of Schleswig. His heart was so much with the Lutheran Church that even as emeritus he served a small independent Lutheran congregation in the Union of Baden.[40]

8. The *Biblical tradition* at its best was represented during this period (1) by KAEHLER and (2) SCHLATTER.

MARTIN KAEHLER was a pupil of Rothe, Tholuck, and Beck. He also shows the influence of Hofmann. Thus there is combined in his system a threefold heritage: pietistic, Biblical, and churchly. Like the other great Biblicists before him, Kaehler made justification the center of Christianity. He even includes this idea in the title of his great work, *Die Wissenschaft der christlichen Lehre von dem evangelischen Grundartikel aus im Abriss dargestellt.*[41] In this work Kaehler presents a great wealth of Biblical ideas which, after the example of Hofmann, he presents in the order of the history of redemption. In a somewhat limited way he provides a place for the Confessions of the Church,[42] but he strongly emphasized the "proof of religious experience in the personal life." Thus he goes beyond the bounds of a strict Biblicism as he finds value in the teaching of the Church, in experience and speculation for the Christian recognition of the truth. But it was Kaehler who particularly furthered an understanding of the significance of the Bible. For him the central content of the Scriptures is the Biblical Christ, and he contends for this content over against the popular "lives" of Jesus and the "historical Jesus" type. This he did particularly in the book, *Der sogenannte historische Jesus und der geschichtliche biblische Christus.*[43] In the Apostolic message concerning Christ, the "superhistorical (*das Uebergeschichtliche*) and the historical are intertwined inseparably. The whole Biblical Christ is truly and deeply the historical Christ. In the search for the true Jesus we cannot go beyond the Gospels of the New Testament. We can know Christ only in the Apostolic mind as a mirror of his personality. The Christ as such—*das Ding an sich*—cannot be an object of our scientific investigation. "The Risen Lord is not the historical Jesus underlying our Gospels, but the Christ of the Apostolic message, in fact, of the whole New Testament" (p. 64). "Christ Himself is the source and author of the Biblical picture (p. 87). Kaehler must be credited with the important accomplishment of having shown the untenable nature of the Neo-Protestant picture of Christ.

ADOLF SCHLATTER (born in 1852), a native Swiss, taught at Bern, Greifswald, Berlin, and Tuebingen. Having resigned his chair in 1922, he continued to be productive in literary work till his death in 1938. Schlatter's method is empirical in the best sense of the word. "Learn how to see and how to hear." He was strenuously opposed to the "Greek" spirit which tries to master the world by means of ideas, to the use of syllogism as a way to knowledge, and to "pure reason" with its power of giving form to the thing perceived. True knowledge, according to him, is "to see that which presents

---

[40] *Moderne Theologie des alten Glaubens,* 1905; *Zur Verstaendigung ueber die moderne Theologie des alten Glaubens,* 1909. For a brief review of the movement see *RGG,* IV, 126 f.

[41] *An Epitome of the Christian Doctrine written from the Standpoint of the Basic Article of Evangelical Faith,* 1883; 3rd edition, 1905.

[42] His conception of the Church is consistently non-confessional. He taught at Bonn and Halle both of which are universities of the Union.

[43] *The So-called Historical Jesus and the Historical Biblical Christ,* 1892; 2nd edition, 1896.

tself to us" by a "determined affirmation of the spiritual constitution given to us, and
performance, in conformity with their inherent laws, of the functions implanted in us,
performing them not only without reluctance but with concentrated will. Then we are
no longer permitted to isolate our thinking from the objective reality that presents
tself to our view, and every autonomous production of ideas becomes a sin for us. Over
and above our self-made images there is now placed that which we have received, the
process which we call 'seeing.' " [44] In conformity with this theory of knowledge he
defines as the task of theology the observation of man. "For we can arrive at a doctrine
of God only by observing those events (*Vorgaenge*) which transmit to us the knowledge
of God, and these events occur within us. . . . In so far theology, especially when it
seriously considers God, is anthropocentric because it has its place not above man but
in man." [45] Devoting the first 279 pages of his *Dogma* to anthropology, however, he
does not want to reproduce the scholastic teaching of a "natural theology," rather to
describe man as a creature of God, the Creator. Man in the state of sin is still the
creature of God and capable of knowledge of God. In so doing, his method marks a
sharp deviation from the theological tradition of both Schleiermacher and Ritschl who
had reduced theology to a *"christozentrisch verengte Heilslehre,"* a narrow soteriological
doctrine. This notion led Schlatter to reject certain tenets of the Augustinian-Lutheran
tradition. The axiom that man and nature after the Fall are nothing but sin, Schlatter
opposed as implying a denial of the creative work of God. Man's condition, Schlatter
asserts, is a "mixed" one; there is good and evil in him, and nature still reflects the glory
of God. Upon this background, Schlatter has maintained a critical attitude toward the
Reformation claiming that Protestantism has never fully appropriated the whole message
of the Bible. By its one-sided emphasis on the forgiveness of sins, it has failed to understand that man is called by Christ to serve God. The preaching of the churches has led
the people to faith but seldom to the new obedience and work.[46]

Schlatter's greatest achievement lies in the field of New Testament studies, although
he emphatically objected to being called a "Biblicist." Pure Biblicism is "senseless" in
the eyes of Schlatter, for God was operative not only in the men of the Bible but still
is active in history through His Spirit. "Theology dare never remain solely exposition,
whereby the Scriptures are opened to our understanding, but the Church always has
need of the dogmatician, especially at such times when she is shaken and confused and
buffeted about by religious controversy." [47] Having at his command an excellent knowledge of Palestinian Greek and Rabbinical language and theology, he followed the method
of comparative religion not to destroy but to establish the uniqueness of Christianity.
Most decisively he turned against any attempt to establish a cleavage between Jesus and
the Apostles. "The picture of Jesus," he says, "was not transmitted to the Church in a
mechanical fashion, neither photographically nor stenographically. If we were to lament

---

[44] In E. Stange's *Religionswissenschaft*, I, 11.

[45] *Das christliche Dogma*, 2nd edition, 1923, p. 14.

[46] Althaus and other recent Luther scholars deny that Schlatter's polemic against Luther really strikes Luther.
Schlatter is simply confusing Luther with the dogmatics of the seventeenth century. See Althaus in *Adolf
Schlatter, Gedaechtnisheft der Deutschen Theologen*, 1938, pp. 32 f.; and developed still further in *Paulus and
Luther ueber den Menschen*, 1939. In fact, Schlatter's teaching of the "mixed condition" of man has met with
much opposition from the Lutheran side. It would lead the Church back into semi-Pelagianism and perfectionism
as is evident from the perfectionistic tendencies in the teachings of Schlatter's son, Theodore, Prelate in
Wuerttemberg.

[47] In Stange's *Selbstdarstellungen*, p. 12; cf. also Schlatter's *Die Theologie des Neuen Testaments und die
Dogmatik*, 1909.

this, we should thereby prove that we had not yet comprehended that God is Spirit and Truth. Jesus speaks to humanity through His Apostles, and He does this by making His word and His picture the governing center of their life. To be sure the Evangelists report things really heard and seen; but the seeing and hearing are by eyes and ears, and the reproduction of what eyes and ears have received is achieved by means of intellectual faculties by which the Evangelists give form to what they say. Thus the Evangelist while he is showing us Jesus, simultaneously permits us to share his own innermost possession. The Gospel, therefore, reveals the Evangelist also, after the manner of an overtone which accompanies the principal tone and gives to the latter its peculiar coloring." [48]

In his commentaries on the Gospels, Schlatter "proves with a clarity that leaves nothing to be desired," that both Matthew and John, as well as the "New Narrator," introduced by Luke, belong to the bilingual Palestinian circle, while Luke himself was a Hellenist employing a Greek diction that was current in Syria. Romans, Schlatter says, was not written to answer Luther's question, "How may I find a gracious God?" but set forth the righteousness of God by which man is redeemed 'to walk in the newness of life.' " In Corinthians, he maintains, Paul combats not Greek Gnosticism, but a perfectionism and enthusiasm rooted in the erroneous Jewish ideas: "Onward and upward over that which is written" (I Cor. 4:6). The Letter of James, he says, is not a polemic against Paul but the message of a Jewish "sage" who wrote as a Christian at a time when there still existed a mutual toleration between Christians and Jews. And the Pastorals on whose Pauline authorship Schlatter had looked with suspicion in his former years he has interpreted in 1936 as letters of Paul under the significant title, *Die Kirche der Griechen im Urteil des Paulus*.

In his *Christliche Ethik* (3rd edition 1929) Schlatter insists with all the vehemence of the Reformed Confessions on the application of the motives arising from religion to an active service in the Christian fellowship and in the secular calling.[49]

9. As Schlatter gave expression of his *grievances against the theological trend* of the nineteenth century, so likewise ERICH SCHAEDER (1861-1936) complained that the whole theology of the last century, not only in the case of Schleiermacher, Ritschl, and the school of comparative religion, but even the Erlangen school was too anthropocentric. They all placed man and his need of salvation in the forefront and only understood the love of God as a means for attaining man's salvation. In contrast Schaeder wanted to sketch a theocentric religion and theology.[50] Here the majesty of God which has revealed itself in nature and history as well as in Christ, occupies the center of consideration. Our existence for God as serving instruments of divine governance is emphasized above God's work for us and His pardoning grace given in Christ. Schaeder himself admits that in such an orientation it is evident that certain teachings of Calvinism have been made fruitful for the Christian and churchly teaching of faith

---

[48] *Gesunde Lehre*, 1929, p. 201.
[49] Most of my English references are quoted from W. Strunk, *"The Theology of Adolf Schlatter"* in *The Lutheran Church Quarterly*, 1938, pp. 395-402.
[50] *Theozentrische Theologie*, 2 vols., 1909, 1915.

Chapter Nine

THEOLOGICAL THOUGHT BETWEEN THE
TWO GREAT WARS

Literature: P. TILLICH, *The Religious Situation* (English by R. Niebuhr), 1932; O. PIPER, *Contemporary German Theology*, 1935; WALTER M. HORTON, *Contemporary Continental Theology*, 1938; NELS F. R. FERRÉ, *Swedish Contributions to Modern Theology*, 1939. C. G. CARLFELT, Recent Theology and Theologians in Sweden," in *The Augustana Quarterly*, January, 1935, "Some Impressions of Recent Theological Tendencies in Sweden," as referred to, January, 1940.

INTRODUCTION

The most striking feature in present-day Continental thought is a marked swing toward theological conservatism. With the collapse of civilization at the end of the first World War, liberal thought lost the very props on which it was constructed. The great triumvirate of theological liberalism, Schleiermacher, Ritschl, and Troeltsch, fell into profound disrepute among German-speaking theologians, especially among the younger generation. This does not mean, however, that Continental scholars have abandoned liberalism as a methodological principle. They are a long way removed from the literalism of American Fundamentalism. On the contrary, they endeavor to promote the cause of true evangelical religion by means of an unbiased, scientific approach to the problems of theology. Theology with them must be strictly scientific as well as true to the essence of the Biblical religion. Consequently, the two "classical periods" of the Church, the period of the New Testament and of the Reformation, have attracted the special interest of these scholars. Through the great Weimar edition of Luther's Works (1883 ff.) theologians were offered a new opportunity to study the thoughts of Luther and especially of the young Luther. To this must be added the startling discoveries of a number of manuscripts containing Luther's lectures on Romans, Hebrews, and some other material.[1] All this tended to cause a revolution against the Ritschlian interpretation of Luther. As early as 1900 JOHANNES VON WALTER, in his book *Das Wesen der Religion nach Erasmus und Luther,* had charged the Ritschlians with having established themselves not on Luther but on Erasmus. The honor of having effected a real turning of the tide belongs to CARL STANGE of Goettingen,[2] and KARL HOLL of Berlin.[3] These scholars again brought the theocentric character of Luther's theology to light. Luther is considered as the great antagonist of ethical idealism with "the justification of the ungodly" at the center of his theology. This anti-idealistic conception of Christianity

---

[1] The Lectures on Romans of 1515-1516 were edited by Johannes Ficker, *Luther's Vorlesung ueber den Roemerbrief,* 1908, translated into German by E. Ellwein, *Roemerbriefvorlesung,* 1927, and subsequent revised editions. The lectures on Hebrews of 1517-1518 are now available in two editions: Johannes Ficker, *Luther's Vorlesung ueber den Hebraeerbrief,* 1929, based on all available material and translated by George Helbig, 1930; E. Hirsch and H. Rueckert, *Martin Luther, Vorlesung ueber den Hebraeerbrief,* 1929, based on the Vatican manuscript and translated by E. Vogelsang, 1930.

[2] *Die aeltesten ethischen Disputationen Luthers,* 1904; *Die Heilsbedeutung des Gesetzes,* 1904; *Studien zur Theologie Luthers,* 1928. Stange has also contributed much to the discussion of philosophy, ethics, and general dogmatics. All his writings portray the keen mind and deep Lutheran piety of the author. Of his other books we may mention: *Die Christliche Ethik in ihrem Verhaeltnis zur modernen Ethik,* 1892; *Der Gedankengang der Kritik der reinen Vernunft,* 4th edition, 1920; *Moderne Probleme des christlichen Glaubens,* 2nd edition, 1923; *Christentum und moderne Weltanschauung,* 2 vols., 1911 ff.; *Dogmatik,* 1927. *Das Ende Aller Dinge,* 1930.

[3] *Gesammelte Aufsaetze zur Kirchengeschichte,* Band I, *Luther,* 1922, and subsequent editions.

is also evident in many of the more recent New Testament studies. In Kittel's gigantic lexicon, as referred to in Chapter Six, the attempt is made to indicate and emphasize the unique character of the New Testament in comparison with Greek thought, the Old Testament and contemporary Judaism (Josephus, Philo, and Rabbinical studies).[4]

As our interest is focused on the revival of conservative theology, we must not lose sight of the fact that theological liberalism, though much discredited since the World War, is by no means a dead issue in the Continental churches. It has in fact gained new momentum by the rise of National-Socialism in Germany since 1933, for the theology of the German Christian Movement is a texture whose warp shows all the trade mark of Harnackian liberalism to which is added a strong weft of ideas of a dogmatized nationalism.

In the present Chapter we shall discuss the different movements in the order indicated above and then conclude our study with a brief reference to a few important theologians who have maintained a more or less independent position.

I. THE BARTHIAN THEOLOGY

1. The recognized leader of this movement is KARL BARTH, born in Basel, Switzerland, in 1886. He was educated at Bern (where his father held a theological chair) Berlin, Tuebingen, and Marburg. During the first World War he was engaged in pastoral work in Geneva and Safenwil, Switzerland. In 1921 he was appointed professor of Reformed theology at the University of Goettingen. Afterwards he taught at Muenster and Bonn. In 1934 he was expelled from Germany. At present he is professor in the University of Basel. While a student at Berlin and Marburg he came under the influence of the two great Ritschlian scholars Harnack and W. Herrmann. Before entering the ministry he even was for a short time (1908-1909) associate editor of the Ritschlian journal *Die christliche Welt*. But "in Karl Barth liberal theology brought forth its own conqueror. He could overcome the liberal theology because he was bone of its bone and flesh of its flesh." [5]

In writing on the Barthian theology we shall proceed historically, describing briefly the different phases of its development, for there is hardly any other theologian of recent times who has changed his position as often and as drastically as Karl Barth has done. Nevertheless, his name will go down in history as the great conqueror of liberal theology, as a prophet of a new Christianity, for it was he who has held first place in interpreting the crisis of Western civilization in the light of the Word of God. As a "preacher in the wilderness" he stands before us proclaiming relentlessly the divine yes over against our human no, and the divine no over against our human yes.

2. Barth began his literary career with an article published in the *Zeitschrift fuer Theologie und Kirche* (1909, pp. 317-321), *"Moderne Theologie und Reichsgottesarbeit."* In this article Barth speaks of the predicament in which a theologian finds himself who has been trained in the religious individualism and historical relativism as taught in Marburg and Heidelberg. Nevertheless, as a faithful pupil of Herrmann, he

---

[4] In this connection reference should be made to H. Strack and P. Billerbeck, *Kommentar sum Neuen Testament aus Talmud und Midrasch* in four large volumes, 1922 ff., and to the exegetical studies of C. Bornhaeuser, *Das Wirken des Christus*, 1921; *Das Johannesevangelium, eine Missionsschrift fuer Israel*, 1928; *Die Geburts-und Kindheitsgeschichte Jesu*, 1930, etc. Bornhaeuser is famous for his consistent approach to New Testament interpretation from the standpoint of contemporary Judaism.

[5] H. Sasse, *Here We Stand*, translated by Th. G. Tappert, 1938, p. 155.

defines religion as a strictly individual experience, and it is the task of the theologian, he claims, to set forth this conception of religion with reference to the general human *Kulturbewusstsein* in its scientific aspect.

3. *A change of outlook* became noticeable when in 1911 Barth moved to Safenwil, where he became interested in the *Swiss Religio-Social movement* of Hermann Kutter and Leonhard Ragaz.

Note: This radical movement owed much of its enthusiasm to the teaching of the Suabian pastor CHRISTOPH BLUMHARDT (1842-1919). Having been brought up in the Biblical realism of his father Johann Christoph (1805-1880), Blumhardt, the son, proclaimed, in a manner not heard before, the advent of the Kingdom which he conceived as truly God's Kingdom not as a product of human endeavors. Jesus was to him the Son of Man, the Man of all men, the Saviour of mankind, the Conqueror of all evil powers. He rejected the asceticism of the Suabian Pietists and associated himself with the political Social Democrats. This step, however, he did not take because he held Marxism to be identical with Christianity but because it meant to him a demonstration of the fact that God's love truly extends to all men.[6] In keeping with this view, H. Kutter published in 1904 his epoch-making book, *Sie Muessen.*

The effect of this movement on Barth is seen in a paper entitled *"Der Glaube an den persoenlichen Gott,"*[7] in which he interpreted the Kingdom in terms of God's lordship, and not in terms of human achievement and progress.

4. *The next step* in the development of Barth is marked by the effect which the first World War had on him. Seeing that Socialism was unable to check the hostilities and cruelties of the War, he discarded religious socialism as well as the "bourgeois Christianity" of theological liberalism. He and his friends, as Thurneysen says in an article of 1927,[8] learned to be *"ganz neu aufmerksam auf die Bibel."* Over against the conception of an immanent evolution, Barth begins to lay stress on the transcendent dynamic principle in religion. A definite turn toward the Reformation theology is noticeable. In an address delivered in 1916 he said: "His (God's) will is not a corrected continuation of our own. It approaches ours as a *Wholly Other (ein gaenzlich Anderer)."*[9] And again in another lecture of 1916 on "The Strange World in the Bible" the idea of God as the Wholly Other is set forth with new emphasis. The thought of this period had its climax in the first edition of the *Roemerbrief* in 1919. It is the divine, *das ganz Andere,* the eternal world, however, present as a reality in this life of ours.

5. *When the second edition of the Roemerbrief appeared in 1921,* we see that Barth once more had undergone a thorough metamorphosis. He now has reached that stage in his development which will be remembered in history as the "theology of the crisis." In the Preface to the revised edition he informs the reader that of the former structure "no stone is left upon another." As to the main factors that have influenced him, Barth mentions (1) a further study of Paul, (2) the teachings of Overbeck, (3) a better understanding of Plato and Kant due to the work of his brother Heinrich, (4) an increased notice of what is to be gained from Kierkegaard and Dostoievski, and (5) the reception and criticism of the first edition by the reading public.

---

[6] E. Thurneysen, *Christoph Blumhardt,* 1926.

[7] *Zeitschrift fuer Theologie und Kirche,* 1914, pp. 21-32, 65-95; cf. Peter Haman Monsma, *Karl Barth's Idea of Revelation,* 1937, pp. 44 ff.

[8] *Zwischen den Zeiten,* 1927, pp. 513-522.

[9] *Das Wort Gottes und die Theologie,* 1925, translated by Douglas Horton, 1928, p. 24.

Note: FRANZ OVERBECK (1837-1905) was professor at Basel and an intimate friend of Fr. Nietzsche. He held, like A. Schweitzer, that primitive Christianity was an ascetic-eschatological movement through and through. On account of its constant endeavors to arrive at a harmonious synthesis between Christianity and human culture, the Church's theology is, in his eyes, the "Satan of religion." Overbeck's thought revolves, according to Barth, around the two main ideas of *Urgeschichte* and death. *Urgeschichte* is the supertemporal, the impenetrable beginning from which we come, death the *unausdenkbar* meaningful moment for which we are headed. Whatever lies between these two is the world, the historical, the relative. Christianity, therefore, as a historical religion, can hold no claims to religious absolutes. *"Wenn Christentum, dann nicht Geschichte; wenn Geschichte, dann nicht Christentum!"* (If it's Christianity, it cannot be history; if it's history, it cannot be Christianity.) Overbeck had actually severed all ties with Christianity. He spoke merely as a historian. As a theologian he expected nothing but *ein sanftes Verloeschen* (peaceful extinction) of the Christian religion.[10]

SOEREN KIERKEGAARD, the "Socrates of the North," was born in Copenhagen in 1813. His thoughts must be studied in the light of his tragic life as well as from the standpoint of his opposition to the Hegelian philosophy. From his father he had inherited a deeply melancholic nature. His early religious training centered exclusively on the cross of Jesus which the father held, onesidedly, to be an expression of man's wickedness. In 1840 he became engaged to Regina Olson, a respectable young lady. But soon Soeren found out that he had made a great mistake in asking Regina to become his wife. He renounced his engagement. The mysteries surrounding his decision have never been fully explained. Two more incidents added to the miseries of his life. Beginning with 1846 he became the target of the scurrilous weekly, *The Corsair,* which made life in Copenhagen very unpleasant for him. In 1854 Bishop Mynster died, and when Martensen, the great Hegelian theologian, as successor to Mynster, preached a panegyric in which he called Mynster a "witness of truth," Kierkegaard began his bitter assault upon the church of Denmark and "official" Christianity. This controversy lasted till his death in 1855. In contrast to Hegelian pantheism, Kierkegaard insisted on "the infinite qualitative difference" between time and eternity, the unbridged chasm between the infinite and the finite, faith and reason. In epistemology he was opposed to abstract speculation and developed what now is called the "existential thinking" according to which, in a series of life's alternatives, man must make a serious responsible decision that enslaves the whole man, for man's existence as an individual is at stake in every crisis of his life. Closely associated with this "either-or" conception is the paradoxical method, i.e., stating the truth in a contradictory manner, in a series of dialectical yeses and noes. In modern contemporary German philosophy the influence of Kierkegaard is quite pronounced on some representatives of the Heidelberg school (an offspring of the revival of Kantianism), especially on M. Heidegger.

The greatest Kierkegaard scholars in recent times are T. Bohlin, a Swede, and the late Danish theologian E. Geismar. For English literature on Kierkegaard see E. L. Allen, *Kierkegaard, His Life and Thought,* (1935); J. A. Bann, *Soeren Kierkegaard, His Life and Religious Teaching,* (1935); Geismar, *Lecture on the Religious Thought of Soeren Kierkegaard,* (1937); Walter Lowrie, *Kierkegaard* (1938); M. Channing-Pearce Routledge, *Terrible Crystal* (1940); W. Riviere, *A Pastor Looks at Kierkegaard* (1941); and D. F. Swenson, *Something about Soeren Kierkegaard* (1941). Piecemeal translations of Kierkegaard's writings by American and British scholars have been published in recent years by the Princeton University Press, the Oxford University Press, Harper Brothers, and the Augsburg Publishing House, Minneapolis, Minnesota.

Kierkegaard's disclosure of the "ultimate potentialities of the human soul" has found ample illustration in the writings of the Russian novelist F. M. DOSTOIEVSKI (1821-1881) with his strong emphasis on the otherness of God, the apocalyptic nature of the Kingdom, the wickedness of the individual and society, the paradoxical character of forgiveness, and the new life by virtue of the resurrection. The quintessence of Dostoievski's thought is best set forth in the legend of the Grand Inquisitor, in which the Grand Inquisitor, representing the principle of regimentation both in Church and state, is put to shame by the silent figure of Christ. "Tragic freedom is better and nobler than compulsory happiness and leads at last, through purgatorial suffering, to the feet of Christ."[11] The chief writings of Dostoievski in English translations are: *The Brothers Karamazov* (1910); *Crime and Punishment* (1911); *The Idiot* (1912); *The Possessed* (1913); *House of the Dead* (1914); *The Insulted and the Injured* (1915); and *A Raw Youth* (1915). For an interpretation of his thought consult E. Thurneysen, *Dostoievski* (3rd edition, 1925); N. Berdyaev, *An Interpretation of Dostoievski* (1936).

6. *Barth's aim in the revised edition of the Roemerbrief* is to refute the relativism in the theology of the Harnack-Troeltsch age. As we have seen in the preceding

---

[10] Karl Barth, *Zur inneren Lage des Christentums,* 1920, pp. 1-24; cf. the analysis of Barth's article in Monsma, pp. 69 ff., also the article on Overbeck in *RGG,* IV, 843 f.
[11] Horton, *op. cit.,* pp. 12 f. By permission of Harper & Brothers, publishers.

chapter, the Historico-Religious School had fully discarded the historical foundations of religion. In this dilemma, W. Hermann had resorted to a psychological phenomenon, "he inner life of Jesus," as the staying principle in theology. The conservatives, in their apologetic endeavors, had usually arrived at some sort of a compromise between the results of Biblical criticism and the religious finality of the Bible. Trained as a liberal, Barth could not accept the position of the fundamentalists. On the contrary, he set out to overcome the historism and psychologism in theology by establishing himself on the theory that revelation and redemption are phenomena which are wholly outside of the reach of history and psychology. Under the influence of Kierkegaard, he had already made much use of the dialectical method before 1921; but in the revised edition his dialectics received an altogether new twist. Having found out that "Paul and Plato can go quite a ways together," dialectics now became for Barth an *ontological* verity over against the mere *logical* dialectics of the former period. A cosmic dualism underlies the religion of the revised *Roemerbrief*. God and man, eternity and time, are viewed as metaphysical opposites. "God is in heaven and thou art upon earth!" God is known as the unknown God. The Absolute, the *Ding an sich,* cannot be reached by man. *finitum non est capax infiniti!* A history of redemption is a *contradictio in adjecto.* History may be a predicate of revelation, but revelation can never be a predicate of history. Revelation is something superhistorical and transhistorical, *ein Augenblick zwischen den Zeiten* (a moment between the times; p. 481). Historical facts are nothing more than parables and demonstrations of the divine. The center of theology is Christ (the superhistorical), not Jesus (the historical).[12] In keeping with this, Barth holds the Fall to be not a historical incident but a superhistorical verity. It is the realization of two metaphysical opposites, the cause of a distinction between the infinite and finite, time and eternity, God and creature. The teaching of supralapsarian predestination, therefore, is the only key for an understanding of the universe. This conception of the Fall, furthermore, involves the simultaneity on the part of every individual! We are not separated from the Fall by generations preceding us, but every moment of time stands in an immediate relation to it. Consequently, the conception of sin receives a metaphysical twist. Time, creature, and sin, all belong to one and the same order of things. Likewise, the Second Coming is not a spectacular phenomenon at some distant future, but rather the superhistorical, ever-present annihilation of time.[13] Salvation is never realized on earth, we do not possess it but can only hope for it. Whenever men take the law in their own hands they do not build the Kingdom but the Babylonian tower (p. 417). The problem of ethics is identical with that of dogmatics: *Soli Deo Gloria.* Man is not a divine instrument through which God may achieve His purpose: the ethical life is nothing but a demonstration for the honor of God (*ibid.*).

These are in brief the salient features of "the theology of the crisis." A caustic critic, like W. Schmidt, does not go amiss when he says: "The 'dialectic theologians' may well jot down their dogmatics on a scrap of paper: God is not man, revelation and redemption are not history, eternity is not time. Whatever else they may have to say, can only be a repetition of these sentences." [14] In his address *"Not und Verheissung*

---

[12] For an able presentation of the Lutheran conception of history compare Otto Piper, *God in History,* 1939.
[13] Cf. Barth's interpretation of the well-known passage, Romans 13:11-14.
[14] *Zeit und Ewigkeit,* 1927, p. 285.

der christlichen Verkuendigung," [15] Barth remarked that his theology should not b considered as a new system but only as a "marginal note," *das bisschen Zimt zur Speis* a pinch of spice in the food. However, his revised *Roemerbrief* is indeed a new system a textbook of "the theology of the crisis." The Barthian theology had come into exist ence. As time went on, this fact became still more pronounced with the publicatio of Barth's *Dogmatik* in 1927 and 1932.

7. *The first edition of the dogmatics* appeared under the caption, *Die Lehre vor Wort Gottes, Prolegommena zur christlichen Dogmatik.* In the second edition the wor *kirchlich* (churchly) has replaced the adjective *christlich.* This change is significan Barth wanted to give renewed weight to his claim that theology is not a "free" scienc but "bound to the realm of the Church." In the revised edition he also states *express verbis* his denial to grant philosophy any part in the occurrence of revelation. The Wor he says, is the only criterion of dogmatics. It has, according to Barth, a threefold form the *spoken word* in the preaching of the Church, the *written word* of Scripture, an the *revealed word* to which the other two forms of the Word bear testimony. The con tent of the Word is Jesus Christ, the Immanuel, revelation is *Dei loquentis person.* In the Logos the *Deus absconditus* becomes for us the *Deus revelatus.* In this fact Bart sees the root of the doctrine of the Trinity. But everywhere Barth protests against th idea that in the act of recognizing the Word, it becomes a part of man. It is the Wor only by a divine occurrence and as long as it is used divinely. The Bible is not a infallible book, as regards any rational subject, such as scientific or historical dat: it is not a document on a level entirely different from other religious literature. Highe criticism holds a legitimate place in theology. As to the epistemological problem, Bart rejects the Cartesian maxim: *Cogito ergo sum* (I think therefore I am), and holds, o the contrary, that *Selbsterkenntnis* (knowledge of self) is based on the *Gotteserkenntn* (knowledge of God): *Cogitor ergo sum* (I am thought therefore I am). As a believe man is wholly the result of the object of faith, i.e., of God. In faith, moreover, man made conformable to the Word, adapted to hear God speaking.

On the supposition that God is revealed to us only in His Word, i.e., God speakin to man, Barth was led to reject emphatically the Roman doctrine of a *theologia naturali* the natural knowledge of God, as well as the modern Protestant teaching of a religiou *apriori.* This principle caused a painful breach in the ranks of his close friends and w; the reason for his persistent opposition both to the German Christian Movement an the confessional Lutherans who, on the basis of the Reformation doctrine of a *revelati generalis,* were prone to interpret the national revival of 1933 as "the Lord's doing an marvelous in our eyes." [16]

Barth has given us his latest comprehensive exposition of the Christian faith sixteen lectures on the Apostles' Creed delivered at the University of Utrecht in Februar and March, 1935, published under the title *Credo* (English edition, 1936). That whic strikes the reader of these Lectures most is the fact that the vehement eloquence of th Barthian language is notoriously absent from this book. If the caustic remark c G. Heinzelmann was justified that Barth should have apologized to the reader in th revised *Roemerbrief* for having so grossly misinstructed him about God and the worl

---

[15] *Das Wort Gottes und die Theologie,* English edition, p. 198.

[16] The quarterly *Zwischen den Zeiten* was discontinued and Barth, with the co-operation of Thurneysen, w sided with him, began the issue of a series of pamphlets, *Theologische Existenz heute.* On Barth's dogmat compare the thorough discussion in Monsma, *op. cit.*

n the first edition of the *Roemerbrief*,[17] the same remark is true as regards the *Credo* n comparison with the revised *Roemerbrief*. It is difficult to recognize the author of hese two writings as one and the same man. The specific tenets of the crisis theology ave disappeared. Whereas in 1921 Barth virtually heaped ridicule on those who look or a Second Coming at some distant future, he now speaks of Christ as our "future," ur "hope." "The Second Coming of Christ is the restoration, but at the same time the niversal and final revelation, of the direct presence of Jesus Christ as 'God-man,' as that /as the content of the forty days after Easter" (p. 121).[18] The emphasis which Barth ays on the historic Jesus is in keeping with this temporal conception of the Second Coming. Pontius Pilate now holds a legitimate place in the Creed. And while he ormerly denounced the Church as the "annulment of the Gospel," he now writes that the Church is indeed the Kingdom of God in the interim period" (p. 141). Only at ne fundamental point Barth remained the same: he still rejects each and every acknowl- dgment of a *theologia naturalis.*

The rejection of a Natural Theology put Barth in a peculiar position when he was nvited by the Senatus of the University of Aberdeen, 1935, to deliver the Gifford .ectures on Natural Theology. In loyalty to his calling as a Reformed theologian, Barth elt, as he says, that he could not do justice to the requirements of the Gifford founda- ion, "to promote, advance, teach, and diffuse," the study of Natural Theology "among ll classes of society," and "among the whole population of Scotland," in *direct* agree- nent with the intentions of the late Lord Gifford. He could make this task his own only *indirectly,* namely, "to confer on Natural Theology the loyal and real service of eminding it of its partner in the conversation." Barth delivered the lectures in 1937 nd 1938. Their title is *The Knowledge of God and the Service of God to the Teaching of the Reformation* (published 1939). They are based on the articles of the Scottish Confession of 1560. The author is very frank as regards his rejection of any sort of Natural Theology. As regards the general tenor of the lectures, the student who is wont to identify Barth with the theology of crisis will be as much surprised as in the study of his *Credo.* In direct opposition to his former emphasis on the "infinite differ- ence between time and eternity," Barth now says, "While it is beyond our comprehension hat eternity should meet us in time, yet it is true because in Jesus Christ eternity has become time" (p. 72). And again: "Eternity is here (in the stable at Bethlehem and n the Cross on Calvary) in time" (p. 78).[19] In agreement with this attitude toward he reality of God in time, is the emphasis which Barth now puts on the reality of the Christian life and the divine mission of the empirical church.

Note: In his contribution of *The Christian Century's* series "How My Mind Has Changed" (September 13 and 20, 1939) Barth contended that he had undergone no significant change of mind. "All my thinking," he wrote, ". . . remains at one point the same. It is unchanged in his that *not* so-called 'religion' is its object, its source and criterion, but rather, as far as it can be my intention, *the Word of God.*" This assertion may be correct as far as it goes. True, his thought has always revolved about the Word and not about religion. Since, however, in his opinion, the Word is not an objective entity because it is not to be identified either with the Jesus of history or with the Bible, no argument can do away with the fact that he had undergone, more than once, a thorough metamorphosis as to the understanding, interpretation, and application of the Word.

---

17 See W. Schmidt, *Zeit und Ewigkeit*, p. 14.
18 *Credo*, pp. 121, 141; quotation by permission.
19 *Knowledge of God*, pp. 72, 78; quotation by permission.

As to his changed attitude in the field of Christian ethics, compare his booklet *The Church and the Political Problem of Our Day* (1939), also *This Christian Cause* (1941). Under the impact of the political upheaval of recent times, Barth has virtually become an "activist of first rank."

8. *And now a word of criticism.* Over against the theological tradition of the past, Barth has come out with the claim that his theology is a corrective which is bound to mark a new departure in theological thought. Of course, no one will deny that there is truth in this statement. Nevertheless, it is not difficult to show that Barth is laboring under a self-deception when he makes such a claim. Fundamentally, he has remained within the tradition of the past. In fact, the theology of the past is climaxed, at many points, in Karl Barth.

Like Kant, Barth limits revelation to the sphere of reason; nature and history are meaningless to him. As with Schleiermacher, theology to him is identical with soteriology. With German Idealism he shares the mystical, unhistorical conception of the time-eternity relation. Consequently, sin is for him more a sort of fate than personal guilt. With Ritschl he shares the Neo-Kantian agnosticism as to our certainty of the metaphysical. In his surrender of the historical to skepticism, he is in keeping with Bousset and Troeltsch. At heart he always has remained a Reformed theologian: *finitum non est capax infiniti.* This Reformed position is evident everywhere, in his teaching concerning revelation, the Incarnation, the means of grace, and in his inability to distinguish properly between the Law and Gospel.[20] With all his emphasis on Luther and Calvin, he comes painfully short of Luther's conception of faith as *fiducia* (trust). His conception of ethics is, as in the case of Kant, coldly formalistic. Not without good reason has it been said that Barthianism is a system without an ethics.

Note: We have limited ourselves mainly to a criticism of the "theology of crisis," for in the eyes of most scholars, especially in the Anglo-Saxon world, "Barthianism" is identical with the dialectical theology. And there is some justification in this position. Though Barth has developed, as we have shown, considerably beyond the former radical separation of time and eternity, all his later writings should be interpreted against the background of the Reformed maxim: *finitum non est capax infiniti.* Besides, Barth has never withdrawn his earlier books.

As a whole, Barth's theology bears an eclectic stamp. Consequently, he could hold the confidence of neither the Reformed nor the Lutheran confessionalists. This experience explains his veering toward church union since 1933 in spite of his earlier sarcastic remark about those who say "in happy generality, covering so much and yet so little!" that they belong to the Evangelical, not Lutheran nor Reformed, Church.[21]

In spite of these critical comments we do not want in the least to minimize the importance of Barth's message. H. R. Mackintosh has a fitting remark; his words deserve to be quoted: "The theology of Karl Barth, criticize it as we may, is the Christian thinking of a great Christian mind, explosive and often unduly emphatic, but none the less of

---

[20] Cf. H. Sasse, *Op. cit.*, pp. 112, 159 ff.

[21] *Das Wort Gottes und die Theologie,* English edition, p. 225. When W. M. Horton in *Continental Theology* (p. 94) holds that the Confessional Church in Germany is Lutheran, not Barthian to any degree, he has not carefully distinguished between the *Bekenntskirche* and *Bekennende Kirche.* The former is Lutheran with the bishops Marahrens of Hanover, Wurm of Wuerttemberg, and Meiser of Bavaria as its leaders. But the *Bekennende Kirche* is Barthian through and through. Its stronghold is the Prussian Union with Niemoeller and H. Assmussen among their prominent leaders. Note the difference in terminology: *Bekenntnis* is a *nomen qualitatis* by which this group wants to emphasize the Lutheran character of the church; *Bekennende* is an active participle. Stress is here laid, under the impact of existential thinking, on the act of confessing irrespective of the nature of the confessions of the church.

ncalculable import for the Church of our time." "To a humanism which understands tself, the ideas of God, sin and death have lost all importance, except as symbols which proved of temporary advantage in the past. Barth replies that there is a living God, and hat God has spoken. With a volcanic vehemence—feeling that passion alone is suited o the occasion—he is endeavoring to draw the Christian mind of his generation back o the truth in which all other truth that counts is embraced, viz., that in the Bible God as uttered His absolute and ineffably gracious will." [22]

9. *The English translations* of the principal works of Barth are as follows: *The Word of God and the Word of Man* (1928); *The Christian Life* (1930); *The Resurrection of the Dead* (1933); *Come, Holy Spirit*, a collection of sermons by Barth and Thurneysen (1933); *The Epistle to the Romans* (1933); *God's Search for Man* (1935); *God in Action* (1936); *Credo* (1936); *The Doctrine of the Word of God* (second edition of his dogmatics, 1936).

W. Schmidt's *Zeit und Ewigkeit* (1927) was the first comprehensive study of Barthianism in German. Of English works we may mention: R. B. Hoyle, *The Teaching of Karl Barth* (1930); A. S. Zerbe, *The Karl Barth Theology* (1930); John McConnachie, *The Significance of Karl Barth* (1931) and *The Barthian Theology* (1933); W. Pauck, *Barth, Prophet of a New Christianity* (1931); H. Rolston, *A Conservative Looks at Barth and Brunner* (1933); P. H. Monsma, *Karl Barth's Idea of Revelation* (1937).

10. *On the associates of Karl Barth* we must be very brief. The most renowned among them are: EDUARD THURNEYSEN of Basel; EMIL BRUNNER of Zurich, and FRIEDRICH GOGARTEN of Jena. Gogarten has done valuable work in the field of epistemology. His own theology has always borne a Lutheran stamp: *finitum capax infiniti*. Both Brunner and Gogarten have openly deserted Barth when he began to launch his attack upon the *theologia naturalis*. In harmony with the Reformers and the New Testament both scholars hold to the idea of revelation also apart from the Bible. For both, institutions like the state and marriage are rooted in the "divine order" either of creation or of conservation. From Gogarten's pen we have *Von Glauben und Offenbarung* (1923), *Ich glaube an den dreieinigen Gott* (1926), in which he discusses the relation between faith and history; *Glaube und Wirklichkeit* (1928), which is a discussion of the Word and faith; and *Gericht und Skepsis* (1937), a controversial treatise against Barth. Brunner's stimulating volume *Der Mittler* (1927), translated as *The Mediator* (1934), offers an elaborate discussion of the "once-for-all" revelation in the historical Jesus *versus* the aspirations of a mystic-idealistic-moralistic universal religion, which lays no claim to a concrete factum of history. In *Natur und Gnade* (1935), and *Der Mensch im Widerspruch* (1937), translated as *Man in Revolt* (1939), Brunner has wrestled with the problem of Christian anthropology. He holds that man is to be understood as a *unity* against the Catholic distinction between the *imago* (rational soul) and *similitudo* (supernatural endowment), but that the "relic" (Luther) of the divine image is not a *profanum* nor a "trifle" (Barth). Rejecting both the solution of Flacius and of the synergists, he insists that the Bible always regards man as a responsible subject over against the divine Word. Yet, says he, the *activity* of man in the process of faith is *passio* (not in its psychological form), i.e., to surrender oneself.[23] Brunner reverts to a dialec-

---

[22] *Op. cit.*, pp. 319, 317 f.
[23] Cf. especially *Man in Revolt*, pp. 527 ff.

tical solution of the problem of human responsibility. In his view the monergism of grace and the responsibility of man do not exclude each other, they are rather *dialectically* related to each other. *Die Mystik und das Wort* (2nd edition, 1928) and *Das Gebot und die Ordnungen* (English: *The Divine Imperative*, 1937), are also important.

The greatest exegete of the Barthians is RUDOLF BULTMANN at Marburg. His book *Jesus* (1926) is a classical example of an alliance between Barthian existential thinking and a critical radicalism based on the exegetical method of "form-criticism" (see below).

II. NEO-LUTHERANISM IN GERMANY

1. By the term *"Neo-Lutheranism"* we refer to the work of a number of younger scholars such as Werner Elert, Paul Althaus, Jr., and Hermann Sasse, all of Erlangen; Karl Heim, Gerhard Kittel, and Adolf Koeberle of Tuebingen; Ernst Sommerlath of Leipzig, Walter Kuenneth of Berlin, Joachim Jeremias of Goettingen, and a number of others. In keeping with the Luther Renaissance the interest of this group is centered in a new and exhaustive study of Luther's works and the New Testament. They try on one hand to combat theological liberalism of the Ritschlian-Harnackian age, and on the other hand they reject the scholastic intellectualism in traditional orthodoxy. Elert made a name for himself by his excellent study *Die Morphologie des Luthertums* (2 vols. 1931 f.) and earlier *Der Kampf um das Christentums seit Schleiermacher and Hegel* (1921). His *Die Lehre des Luthertums im Abriss* (1924) is also available in an Hungarian and an English translation.[24] Althaus gained recognition in the theological world by his study of eschatology in *Die letzten Dinge* (1922; 4th edition, 1933); Koeberle through his volume *Rechtfertigung und Heiligung* (1929), translated from the third German edition by John C. Mattes, *The Quest for Holiness* (1936); and Sasse by a small volume *Was heisst lutherisch?* (1934, translated and enlarged from the second German edition by Theodore G. Tappert, *Here We Stand*, 1938). On Heim compare our discussion below.

2. In the *problem of epistemology* the Neo-Lutherans follow, on the whole, the general trend in recent theology toward the "existential thinking." God is to them not an intellectual problem but an existence problem. Theology is not, as in Greek intellectualism, a study of defining the essence of God, nor an attempt to control rationally the object of its investigation. On the contrary, it should concern itself with the relation in which man stands to God, letting God give His understanding of man. "Existential thinking," therefore, is not limited to the human intellect, rather it lays claim to the whole man. Consequently, faith is not an intellectual faculty of man but a personal decision, engaging man as a whole.

3. These scholars are not apologists. They are not afraid to stress the *"otherness" of the Bible,* even at the risk of giving offense to the modern mind. Nor are their Biblical studies apologetic in the old meaning of the term. To them the Bible is entirely divine and entirely human. With respect to introductory problems of the New Testament, they are far more critical than were their two great teachers in this field, Zahn and Schlatter.[25] Though it is evident from their Biblical studies that the method of "Form-criticism" has

---

[24] The latter was made by C. M. Jacobs, 1927.

[25] Cf. *Das Neue Testament Deutsch,* the New Goettingen Commentary, edited by P. Althaus and J. Behm, 1923 ff., which is both truly evangelical and strictly critical.

xerted some influence on their conception of the Gospel narratives, the Neo-Lutherans eel that they cannot dismiss as lightly as the Barthians the question concerning the uthenticity of the New Testament records. In keeping with the Lutheran maxim, *initum capax infiniti* or better, *infinitum capax finiti*, they reveal a deeper appreciation f the incarnation than the Barthians, and they cling tenaciously to the great principle f Martin Kaehler that "the whole Biblical Christ is truly and deeply the historical Christ." "God in history!" Therefore they refuse to follow skepticism in its demands egarding the Biblical records. They likewise were unable to follow Barth in his radical pposition to the new German state, taking a sort of a mediating position. Althaus, for xample, rejects both extremes: the illusion of the so-called German Christians (see)elow) as if the Christian could hear in the voice of the people the very voice of God, s well as the "nihilistic" attitude which considers the state and the other "orders" of ife so completely sinful that it attempts either to withdraw from the "world" or aban-lons all ethical judgment in the realm of the natural.[26]

4. As to the *question of anthropology,* the Neo-Lutherans seek to follow Luther's onception that the Pauline terms "flesh" and "spirit" are not psychological distinctions. hey do not refer to a lower or higher quality in man; but rather have a theological onnotation: "flesh" designating man in his state of opposition to God, and "spirit" signi-ying man as a regenerated child of God.[27] Man as a whole, including his so-called igher nature, is under the curse of sin; likewise, redemption pertains to man as a whole, ncluding the body. This has brought in a new interest in the holiness of life; in con-ersion and regeneration the sinner is saved not only from the guilt of sin (justification))ut also from the power of sin (sanctification).[28] This rejection of an anthropological lualism also implies a new emphasis on the Biblical message of the resurrection of the lead over against the Platonic idea of immortality as an inherent quality of the human oul.[29]

5. After the manner of the dialectic theologians, ALTHAUS conceives of *revelation s an act of divine kenosis.* The divine kenosis does not materialize in history; history tself is an act of divine kenosis. Revelation of divine majesty and glory, therefore, is nthinkable and impossible in the course of history. Consequently, he rejects the ortho-lox view that the supernatural character of the Bible can be demonstrated to reason. Ie likewise rejects the idea that the Christian experience of regeneration carries weight o prove rationally the truth of the Bible to the unbelieving. A Word, demanding)bedience, constitutes revelation. Through this Word, which was incarnate in Jesus, :ternity reaches into time. The only human corollary to divine revelation is faith. In his way Althaus arrives at defining his theology as "a theology of faith."[30] History,

[26] See Althaus, *Theologie der Ordnungen,* 1935; W. Elert, *Karl Barth's Index der verbotenen Buecher,* 1935. Cf. Horton, *op. cit.,* pp. 139 f.

[27] C. Stange, *Luther und das sittliche Ideal,* 1919; reprinted in *Studien zur Theologie Luthers,* as referred to.)p.159 ff.

[28] Cf. the German title of Koeberle's famous book: *Rechtfertigung und Heiligung.*

[29] Stange, *Die Unsterblichkeit der Seele,* 1925; cf. also *Studien zur Theologie Luthers,* pp. 287 ff., *Luther und las fuenfte Laterankonzil,* 1928, a number of articles in *Zeitschrift fuer systematische Theologie,* and *Das Ende iller Dinge,* 1930. In these studies Stange has advanced the teaching of annihilation for the wicked. He also 1as tried to show that Luther rejected belief in the immortality of the soul. This was a matter of conflict between 1im and P. Althaus. The latter agrees with Stange in declining the Platonic conception of immortality, but the :ternal "existence" of all men he sees warranted by the *Gottesverhaeltnis* in which all stand to God. From the *Gottesverhaeltnis* he distinguishes the *Gottesgemeinschaft* pertaining only to the pious. *"Die Unsterblichkeit der Seele bei Luther"* in *Zeitschrift fuer systematische Theologie,* III, 725 ff.; *Unsterblichkeit und ewiges Leben bei Luther,* 1930; *Die letzten Dinge,* 4th edition, pp. 92 ff.

[30] *Grundriss der Dogmatik,* 2nd edition, 1936, I, 49 ff.

death, and faith belong to one and the same order of things. Death is not a mere acci
dent in historical life; it is a natural part of historical existence. The story of the
Original State and of the Fall does not mean a historical day of the human race, it is
a mere reflection of human sin and guilt. The beginning and end of the universe as a
physical entity is immaterial to a religious interpretation of life, Althaus holds. This
attitude removes at once all friction between Christianity and natural sciences. The
Church needs no longer to harmonize the book of Genesis with modern science.
Althaus' conception of the end is in keeping with this view of the beginning of life.
The idea of the Millennium is to him an idle fancy of pietistic Judaism (cf. Article XVII
of the Augsburg Confession). The kingdom of Jesus is never of this world, not even
at the end. The apocalyptic material in the New Testament must be interpreted
"existentially" as a word of comfort and warning to the Church at any time. It is given
to us in order that every generation may derive from a spiritual interpretation of the
past a true impression of the present in the light of the final judgment.[31] Under the
impact of severe criticism from other Lutheran scholars such as Karl Heim, E. Sommer
lath, Ph. Bachmann, H. W. Schmidt, and especially Kuenneth (*Theologie der Aufer
stehung,* 1933) and others,[32] Althaus has relinquished the radical dialectic conception
of the Second Coming as a mere metaphysical antithesis to historical existence. In the
fourth edition of *Die letzten Dinge* he writes: "The Second Coming marks the end of
history. History moves in the course of time toward its end, and the end will come at
its appointed time, day, and hour. In this respect the Second Coming is an historical-
temporal occurrence. But the end of time is not to be identified with the Second
Coming. The very nature of the Second Coming, the manifestation of glory, is impossible in history. The revelation of the Son of Man is no *endgeschichtliches* but a
geschichtsendendes occurrence" (pp. 242 f.). This means that Althaus now recognizes
a march of time towards its appointed end, but he again reaffirms his view that history
and manifestation of glory are metaphysical opposites.

6. *By way of the exegetical findings* of Schlatter and the existential thinking, which
is interested more in the *agere* than the *esse* of a thing, Althaus also has tried to modify
the Lutheran conception of the *Lord's Supper.* In *Die lutherische Abendmahlslehre in
der Gegenwart* (1931) he says that the teaching of a presence of the *glorified* body and
blood of Christ in the sacrament has no foundation in the New Testament. The interpretative words over the bread and wine are not a definition of what the elements of the
Supper are but of what Christ is doing. Body and blood in separate form signify life
which is given over to death. "You live by my death." The sacrament is a *Tat-Gleichnis,*
a parable in action. The Real Presence is to be understood in the wider sense of divine
revelation and the incarnation of the Logos which is perpetuated in His Church. Christ's
presence, therefore, Althaus holds, is not confined to the sacramental elements, rather
the action of the Church warrants His Real Presence and His grace. This modification
of the Lutheran view does not imply, however, that the author is veering towards the
Reformed conception of the Supper. *Expressis verbis* he rejects Calvin's view and insists
on the Lutheran teaching of the *manducatio oralis* and *manducatio indignorum.* A
similar view of the Supper is held by C. Stange in his book, *Die Bedeutung der Sakra-*

---

[31] Cf. Althaus' articles on *"Eschatologie"* in *RGG*, II, 345 ff., *"Ewiges Leben,"* 459 ff., and *"Wiederbringung
Aller Dinge,"* V, 1908 ff.

[32] Cf. on the whole complicated discussion Folke Holmstroem, *Das eschatologische Denken der Gegenwart,*
1936, pp. 279 ff.

mente (2nd edition, 1927). Not the elements, but the action of the Church, warrant, according to Stange, the Real Presence of the Lord. In contrast to Althaus and Stange, E. Sommerlath has maintained the Lutheran view in a little volume entitled *Der Sinn des Abendmahls nach Luthers Gedanken 1527-1529* (1930), and especially H. Sasse has taken sharp issue with his colleague's view in his book *Kirche und Herrenmahl* (1938) and in the composite volume *Vom Sakrament des Altars* (1941), defending staunchly the orthodox Lutheran position. From a review in the *Kirchliche Zeitschrift* (February, 1941) we learn that Elert has published a book on dogmatics, *Der christliche Glaube* (1940) in which he also registers a sharp protest against what he calls the "crypto-Calvinistic" tendencies in the teaching of Althaus and other contemporary theologians. Compare also the orientating booklet by M. Reu, *Can We Still Hold to the Lutheran Doctrine of the Lord's Supper?* (1941).

7. *It may seem daring* to classify KARL HEIM of Tuebingen with the Neo-Lutherans. He was born in 1874 and is Stange's junior by only four years. Many of the younger scholars are his pupils just as they are students of Stange. But Heim did not, as Stange, altogether disown dialetics in theology and he has kept unusually well abreast of the changing mood of thought in Germany since 1918. He has always maintained the Reformation position which places the forgiveness of sins at the central place, springing, as Horton well says (p. 127),[33] "from that Pietist tradition in German Lutheranism which has always kept in close touch with British Methodism and American evangelism." He is indeed the "evangelist" among the academic theologians of Germany. Up to 1902 he served as one of the chief assistants of John R. Mott in the Christian Student Movement and he has always kept this objective in view: "Confronting young men with the Living Christ." The origin of faith, he holds, is completely independent of philosophical thought.[34] Nevertheless, he includes in his writings very elaborate epistemological propositions but only for the purpose of meeting the modern man where he is and confronting him with the necessity of deciding for Christ. In the decade before the first World War the Ritschlian distinction between faith and reason held Heim's interest. In his *Leitfaden zur Dogmatik* (1912) he said: "The all-comprehensive theme of dogmatics is the delineation of the infinite misery of sin as it is removed by Christ" (II, 20). After the World War he turned to a critical investigation of problems suggested by Einstein and the *"Existenzphilosophie"* of the Heidelberg School.

The new thoughts of Heim were gathered in *Der Glaube und das evangelische Denken der Gegenwart* (3 vols. 1931 ff.). In the first volume *Glaube und Denken* (translated under the title *God Transcendent*, 1936), Heim grapples with the question, "What does faith imply, when, in an age which is aware of the consequences of the Copernican revolution, it continues to speak of the Transcendence of God?" (p. 237). In our day we know the world to be an infinite universe. The idea of the transcendence of God, therefore, has lost its original "spatial" sense. Heim enters upon an elaborate discussion of the three dimensional world of human experience: "my objective world" and "thy objective world"; the "I world" and the "It world" (the dead "Already-become"); and the living "I World" and "Thou World." Each of these worlds is marked off from the other only in the "dimensional" mode, not by a "boundary of content." Now the question arises, Is the Beyondness of the omnipresent God to be compared

---

[33] *Op. cit.*, p. 127; quotation by permission.
[34] *Glaubensgewissheit*, 1916.

with any of these intra-mundane forms of transcendence? The answer must be: No! for God is not an aspect of this world, accessible to our dimensional mode of cognition If He were, then we would be forced either into "Idolatry," i.e., giving absolute value to some thing which has only relative reality, for example, race, blood, and soil; or into Pantheism "by deifying the infinite Whole of things." God simply transcends our thinking and observation. For a knowledge of God we are thrown back on His own revelation.[35]

In the second volume of the work under discussion, *Jesus der Herr,* Heim supports the conception of Christ's work in the ancient Church as an overpowering of Satan. In the third volume, *Jesus der Weltvollender,* he is set to uphold the realistic eschatological drama of the New Testament over against the spiritualizing, explaining away of its importance in the thought of the liberals, old and new (Harnack and the German Christians) and the purely axiological, Platonizing conception of eschatology in Barth's revised *Roemerbrief.*

Heim's emphasis on Christ's victory over Satan in the work of the Cross is very significant. For this aspect of the redemptive work of the Saviour is also much discussed in contemporary Swedish thought to which we shall now turn.

III. LUNDENSIAN THEOLOGY

1. *Sweden is a Lutheran country* whose theologians have always kept well abreast of the theological development in the homeland of the Reformation. Little wonder therefore, that the new *Lutherforschung* in Germany met with an enthusiastic response in Sweden. In the pre-war age Archbishop Soederblom took the lead. The first book from his pen dealt with Luther's religion (1894) while the result of his life-long study of Luther is contained in *Melankoli och humor och andra Luther-studier* (1919). Next to the late Archbishop, Einar Billing's (1871-1939) name will loom large in Swedish thought as a pioneer in Luther studies: *Luthers laera om staten* (1901); *Ett bidrag till fragen on Luthers religioesa och teologiska utvecklingsgang* (1917). The fire which was kindled by these men at Upsala is being kept alive by Arvid Runestam, the son-in-law of Soederblom, and by Torston Bohlin and Tor Andrae, both of them disciples of Soederblom.

2. In recent years the University of Lund has become the *seat of a new theology* which owes its best to Luther with GUSTAV AULÉN, ANDERS NYGRÉN, GUSTAF LJUNGRÉN, RAGNAR BRING, HJALMAR LINDROTH, now at Upsala, as its chief exponents.

"Lundensian thought," in the words of Ferré (p. 23), "is best understood as the resurgence of historic Christianity, as a reaction to the indefiniteness of a confused liberalism which never won much more than the minds of its converts, and that only partially, as an affirmation of the absolute assurance of religion in the face of a bewildered relativism." It is "a return from all relativism to the absolute assurance of religion, but not to the Biblical literalism of the past" (p. 29). In other words, the Lundensians, like their contemporary German colleagues, endeavor to assert the religious absolutes by means of modern scholarship. Religion and theology must be to them both Evangelical in content but strictly scientific as to its method. The Lundensians draw a sharp line of demarcation between the subjective nature of faith and the objective

---

[35] God Transcendent; quotation by permission; cf. Horton, *op. cit.,* pp. 130 ff.

nature of science. Faith, they say, must be respected "in its claim to be an independent and unique category" supplying its own self-originated material as well as its own principle of interpretation. Religion as faith is never knowledge; it is alogical in nature. It is immediate commitment (existential thinking!) a value judgment (Ritschl). But the faith-state, they claim, is never devoid of intellectual content. In fact, something is comprehended in the faith-state. This alogical content of faith is transmitted in logical forms, for that which is comprehended is also capable of expression. For an illustration Nygrén and Bring, as Ferré says, often refer to pain. As an experience, pain is far from logical in nature, but when it is comprehended by man, it may be expressed in logical categories.[36]

3. A *positivistic bent* is evident in all Lundensian theologians. With the Swedish philosopher Axel Haegerstroem they are agreed that no science is ever normative; all knowledge, they hold, is descriptive. Theology, therefore, is only a logical-descriptive discipline with its object to be investigated and received objectively from history.[37]

The *method of theology* "must be typological, a non-normative analysis of the field of investigation with a view to the synoptic unity of the object" (Ferré, p. 61). In this way they arrive at what they call the *"motivforskningen."* In the analysis of dogma, they claim, the theologian must go deeper than the outward form and dress of a given doctrine, he must penetrate behind the outward form to the underlying motive. All basic motives, however, it is said, are not more than "approximations," a "general notion" or "fundamental attitude," *ein Lebenstrieb* ("vitality").[38] For this very reason Aulén refuses to speak of the "idea" of God, but speaks in terms of the "picture" of God.[39] In *Die Dogmengeschichte im Lichte der Lutherforschung* (1932), the same author says: "The history of doctrine aims at an understanding of the inner history of Christianity. It is concerned with the originality of Christianity" (p. 15). This *motivforskningen* the Lundensians have applied mainly to three great problems of doctrine, Aulén to the concept of God and of the Atonement (*Den kristna gudsbilden*, 1927), and *Den kristna foersoningstanken,* 1930 (translated under the title *Christus Victor* 1931), Nygrén to the Christian idea of love in his work known in English as *Agape and Eros* (3 vols., Swedish edition, 1930 ff.; English, 1932 ff.). To these may be added the study of eschatology in German and Swedish theology by Folke Holmstroem, *Det eskatologiska motivet i nutida teologi* (Swedish, 1933; German, 1936).

4. In *Den kristna gudsbilden* Aulén points to the fact that hitherto theology has failed to concentrate its efforts on the Christian concept of God: theologians, in most cases, busied themselves with an investigation of single loci in dogmatics. Consequently, they failed to set forth the organic unity of the Christian faith, for every doctrine, the Christological, for example, is ultimately a problem of one's "picture" of God. Aulén traces the "picture" of God through the course of history beginning with the Biblical age, through the ancient Church, the Middle Ages, the Reformation, down to modern theology in Sweden, Germany, and England. Thus Aulén arrives at the conception that

---

[36] Cf. the chapter on "Theological Methodology" in Ferré, *op. cit.,* p. 34 ff. Quotations by permission of Harper & Brothers, publishers.

[37] Nygrén: *Religioest apriori dess filosofiska foerutsaettninger och teologiska konsekvenser,* 1921. *Filosofisk och kristen etik,* 2nd edition, 1932; *Dogmatikens vetenskapliga grundlaeggning,* 1935; Bring, *Till fragen om den systematiska teologiens upgift,* 1933.

[38] Aulén, *Den kristna gudsbilden,* German translation *Das christliche Gottesbild,* 1930, p. 54.

[39] *Op. cit.,* pp. 3 f. Cf. Vol. I, 13 ff.

God is sovereign love who condescended to men in Christ Jesus. There is only one way for man to God and that is God's way to man and never man's way to God.

5. In *Christus Victor* Aulén takes sharp issue with the lack of understanding which modern theologians have shown as regards the Atonement in the patristic age. He distinguishes between three main types of the Atonement: the patristic which he calls the "classical," the objective Anselmic, and the subjective Abelardian type. The negative attitude of modern scholars toward the "classical" type, Aulén claims, is a clear indication that they have failed to penetrate behind the crude language of the Greek Fathers into the very motive by which they were guided. On the contrary, the "classical" teaching deserves, in the eyes of Aulén, the most careful attention. According to this view, the Atonement is a cosmic drama in which "Christ—*Christus Victor*—fights against and triumphs over the evil powers of the world, the 'tyrants' under which mankind is in bondage and suffering, and in Him God reconciles the world to Himself" (English edition, p. 20). The work of the Atonement is, according to this view and according to this view only, what it must be: "from first to last a work of God Himself a continuous divine work" (p. 21). It is, moreover, the view espoused by the New Testament and Luther who always held that "the satisfaction is made by God, not merely to God" (p. 135).

In criticism it must be said that Aulén's view tends to underrate the religious significance of the Anselmic doctrine of Christ's work as an expiation for human guilt. He likewise seems to miss the real views of Luther. The Reformer did not one-sidedly follow the Greek Fathers. His own teaching rather is a wholesome synthesis of the best that is contained in both the teachings of the patristic age and the Middle Ages.

6. NYGRÉN in his *Agape and Eros* strikes *essentially the same note*. To him also the interpretation of Christianity in the whole Neo-Protestant school is altogether false. The Gospel does not, as Harnack claimed, deal with "the infinite value of the human soul." On the contrary, "when it is said that God loves man, this is not a judgment on what man is like, but on what God is like" (Vol. I, 52). Agape is altogether "*spontaneous*" and "*uncaused*," "*indifferent to human merit*." Its meaning can only be rightly grasped "when it is seen that human goodness or worthiness is left clean out of the reckoning" (p. 54). "It is not that God loves that which is in itself worthy to be loved; but, on the contrary, *that which in itself is without value acquires value by the fact that it is the object of God's love*" (*ibid.*). Agape is a creative power opening the way of fellowship with God (p. 56). The conclusion then follows that *there is no way, from man's side, by which he can attain to God* (*ibid.*). Having traced the meaning of Agape as it is seen in the Gospels, the Pauline and Johannine writings, Nygrén turns to a discussion of the "Eros motif" as it is found in Plato, Aristotle, and Neo-Platonism. The Platonic conception of love, he says, may be summed up in three points: "Eros is the love of desire, it is man's way to the Divine, and it is egocentric" (p. 133). In short, it is man's way to God.

"During the early period of Church history," Nygrén says, "the contrast between the religions of Agape and Eros remained relatively sharp" (p. 38). "It is in Augustine that a real union of the two is first reached" (p. 39). The result of this emergence, Nygrén says, may be summed up in the word "*caritas*." "Medieval Christianity is throughout *caritas-religion*" (*ibid.*). After a thousand years the two streams that had flown together again separated. The Renaissance makes a new revival of the Eros-

onception while in Luther the idea of Agape breaks out again, "with a force com-
arable to that of its first appearance in the Apostolic Age" (*ibid.*).

From his stress on Agape, however, we should not infer that Nygrén, after the
manner of Barth, sees no value in the world of Eros, the world of man. The translator,
.. G. Herbert, in an important prefatory note, makes it clear that Nygrén always
ndeavors to maintain a balance between creation and redemption: "It is fundamental
o Christianity that God is both Creator and Redeemer. The God Who created the
orld is the God of Agape. As Creator, He is the author of the natural world and of
uman life, with its upward movement of human life, which Aristotle describes in terms
f Eros, and in this natural world, and in the natural goodness of human life, God is
resent and His glory is manifested. But it is only in redemption, that is, by Agape,
aat He is personally revealed, both in the incomplete revelation of Agape in the Old
'estament, and in perfect manifestation in Christ" (p. XII).

7. There can be no doubt, that Lundensian theology represents a serious attempt
o *return to Luther and the New Testament.* It strikes without mercy at the humanistic
erversion of the Gospel in Neo-Protestantism. If further evidence should be required
re may quote from Ljungrén: "Moral idealism is the very incarnation, as an approach
o religion, of man's rebellion against God." [40] Lundensian thought is a great eulogy
f the *sola gratia* and *sola fide* in religion. However, it should not be left unsaid that
: does not take long to discover the remains of Ritschlianism in the Lundensian
nought. We referred above to its positivistic bent. Moreover, there is always that
rucial problem of authority in religion, whether it is seen in Christ together with the
rophets and apostles and mediated through the Scriptures or whether it is found in
xperience. On this point the Lundensians will not meet with the approval of many
utherans. From Aulén's discussion in his dogmatics, *Den allmaenneliga kristna tron*
1931), the conclusion seems to be justified that he is in danger of minimizing the
uthority of the Written Word and to exalt what he calls the "spirit complex" controlled
y the glorified Christ.[41]

Note: A brief note about *theological thought in Finland* may find its place here. As else-
here on the Continent, the Lutheran Church of Finland went through a period of orthodoxy,
ietism, and rationalism. Then came the religious revival of the nineteenth century with such men
s P. RUOTSALAINEN (died 1852), H. RENQUIST (died 1866), F. G. HEDBERG (died 1893),
hom we have mentioned in connection with the Bornholmers in Chapter Five, and L. L. LAES-
ADIUS (died 1861) as leaders. Among the prominent scholars were F. L. SCHAUMAN (died
877), professor at Helsinki and bishop of Borga, and A. W. INGMAN (died 1877), who portrays
n his writings the influence of Beck of Tuebingen. Next we mention G. ROSENQUIST who wrote
n Lotze and Ritschl. Current theological thought in Finland is characterized by a remarkable new
itality and productivity. The most influential of the twentieth century theologians is A. G.
IETILAE (died 1932), professor of dogmatics at Helsinki, the author of a three-volume *Christian
)ogmatics* and a score of other doctrinal works. The richness and originality of his thought is
xplicable in part in terms of his Laestidian background. His successor at Helsinki, now bishop,
INO SORMUNEN, is Finland's most outstanding representative of the new Luther-research. Two of
is works have appeared in German *Die Gnade Gottes* (1932), and *Die Eigenart der lutherischen
'thik* (1932). Sormunen represents the Evangelical movement in Finland. Other Finnish the-
logians of note are E. G. GULIN, professor of New Testament at Helsinki, and author of *Die
'reude im Neuen Testament* (1934), Y. J. E. ALANEN, Sormunen's successor at the University of
Ielsinki, known for his works in relations of theology and cultural philosophy, and Bishop ALEXSI
EHTONEN, a prominent figure in the Ecumenical Movement. The work of all these men is

---

[40] Quoted by Ferré, *op. cit.,* p. 149.
[41] Cf. Carlfelt, *op. cit.* Cf. also the critical article by Floreen in *The Lutheran Companion,* February 9, 1939;
eprinted in the *Kirchliche Zeitschrift,* April, 1939.

marked by a deep loyalty to the Lutheran Confessions combined with a determined effort to express that spirit in the language of current thought.[42]

IV. ARYANISM IN THE THIRD REICH

1. In Chapter Eight we had occasion to quote from Gressmann *the maxim for all historico-religious investigation:* "There is in the world no material that does not have its history, no conceptions of thought without their connections with previous conceptions." This certainly holds true also in regard to the Aryanism and Aryan interpretation of Christianity in the Third Reich. This religious movement did not spring up over night with the rise of National Socialism in 1933. "It has its root," as Aulén says correctly "in the previous age; it is a child of the humanistic religiosity that during the last century has been confused with Christianity." [43] Aryan Christianity is a child of that extreme humanism which would limit revelation "to what man discovers whether through experience or social progress." It is a dogmatized nationalism, the veneration of race, blood, and soil engrafted upon theological liberalism. Liberal theologians have furnished the German government with its weapon against the "political clergy." The situation abroad should be understood in the light of teachings in the preceding age. According to various pronouncements of the German government, religion and Christianity are to be looked upon as a purely inward attitude of man. But this is just what Ritschl and Harnack taught when they defined religion as an individual, inward disposition of the soul and when they limited the Lordship of Jesus to a rule in the spiritual realm for which the Church, as an organized society, with an ethics of its own, is of little, if any, importance. It is of interest to note that this purely spiritual conception of the Church was also held by such a conservative Lutheran as the late R. Sohm (referred to p. 131). According to this view the "Church" cannot be persecuted; that which suffers persecution is only a man-made religious organization.

As regards the National Socialist ideology, philosophers, such as SCHOPENHAUER (1788-1860), EDUARD VON HARTMANN (1842-1906), and FR. NIETZSCHE (1844-1900) led the way. They all were agreed in rejecting the humility and submissiveness as taught in Christianity and looked upon the religion of the future as a new creation of the Indo-Germanic genius over against the Semitic traits in Christianity. The views of these German writers found support in the writings of the Frenchman, ARTHUR GOBINEAU (1816-1882) who regarded religion "as essentially a product of the racial and biological impulse," and of the English writer, HOUSTON STEWART CHAMBERLAIN (1855-1927), the prophet of the Wagner circle, who in his *Foundations of the Nineteenth Century* looked upon Greek art, Roman law, and the Personality of Christ, as the basis of all European culture. But Jesus, according to his theory, was an Aryan because He came from Galilee, "land of Gentiles."

2. As the real precursor of such men as *Reichsbischof* Mueller and A. Rosenberg, we may look to PAUL DE LAGARDE (1827-1891).[44] He was bitterly opposed to the liberal trend in the life of his time. All his thought revolved about Christianity and the

---

[42] For acknowledgment compare the Foreword herein. Cf. the little valuable book by Lehtonen, *The Church of Finland*, 1927.

[43] John Baillie and Hugh Martin, eds., *Revelation*, 1937, p. 284. By permission of The Macmillan Company, publishers.

[44] Cf. our remark on him in Chap. VIII, 1. Cf. also L. Schmid, *Paul de Lagardes Kritik an Kirche, Theologie und Christentum*, 1935.

German fatherland. He wanted to purge the religion of the Germans of all its Judaic characteristics. Paul and Luther found little favor in his eyes. A divine revelation in the past, he declared to be insufficient. "We need," he said, "the presence of God and the divine, not its past." [45] Parallel with the philosopher's protest against the domination of historical Christianity went the Germanization of the life of Jesus in the work of some New Testament scholars.[46] Von Soden, for example, in his *Die wichtigesten Fragen im Leben Jesu,* 1904, endeavored to explain away the ecstatic and apocalyptic in Christ, saying that His nature "was sound to the core." A picture of such a Germanized Jesus was brought to life in Gustav Frenssen's "The Manuscript" incorporated in his novel, *Hilligenlei* (1905).[47]

3. *The "Bible" of the Aryan cult in Germany* is ALFRED ROSENBERG'S *Mythos of the Twentieth Century.* The author holds that all religions live on myths which are an indigenous creation of the race. As Christianity grew out of the Semitic race, it has adulterated the German myth with its emphasis on honor, duty, and freedom, by its stress on love, and passive virtues. The chief end of men, according to Rosenberg, is the good of the nation, not of the individual, and the devotion to honor, duty, and freedom is the religion that will give power to achieve this supreme objective. The religious hero for Rosenberg is not Luther but Meister Eckhart, the German mystic of the closing Middle Ages, with his emphasis on the identity of man and God.

4. *Less passionate in language* is W. HAUER of Tuebingen, a former missionary of the Basel society to India in his *Deutsche Gottesschau* (1934). Hauer is the scholarly leader of the German Faith Movement (*Deutsche Glaubensbewegung*) which in turn shows a striking resemblance to the Anthroposophy of Rudolph Steiner (1861-1925). Like Rosenberg, he insists that religion must provide the means to meet God in 'unmediated Reality." "Once upon a time that focus (of religion) may have been the person of Jesus and the community of believers, but for us today it is the nation and German history . . . " "We can see God advancing over German soil, seeking his instruments and, in spite of all opposition, molding events according to his purpose."

5. While Rosenberg and Hauer, and such men as E. Bergmann, and Count Reventlow do not hesitate to renounce allegiance to historic Christianity, we see *another party* at work which aims to mediate between the new religion and Christianity. Our reference is to the GERMAN CHRISTIANS (*Deutsche Christen*). They represent scientific liberalism in present-day theology interpreting Christ as "approved" by critical scholarship of previous decades. This is the position as held by the Reichsbischof Mueller and his former associate J. Hossenfeld. In academic circles this view is best represented by IMMANUEL HIRSCH, professor at Goettingen. Hirsch is a truly tragic character. As a pupil of K. Holl, he ranked in the twenties as one of the leading Luther and Kierkegaard students.[48] But he could never overcome a pronounced leaning toward philosophical idealism,[49] and this fact will best explain his veering toward his new position.

---

[45] *Deutsche Schriften,* 4th edition, 1904.

[46] Observe also the fact that German painters, especially since 1850 (Richter, Thoma, Uhde, Steinhausen, von Gebhardt, and Rudolf Schaefer) made Jesus live and move in a German environment. This trend in art is perfectly legitimate even from the orthodox point of view. Art, in this respect, shares with theology the task of making the wall transparent which separates us from the first century. Biblical piety, however, must voice its protest when such tendencies try to obliterate the uniqueness of the historic Christ.

[47] Cf. A. Schweitzer, *The Quest of the Historical Jesus,* pp. 307 ff.

[48] *Luthers Gottesschau,* 1918; *Luthers Deutsche Bibel,* 1928.

[49] *Die idealistische Philosophie und das Christentum,* 1926.

In his studies on the Fourth Gospel [50] he proved himself to be a follower of F. C von Baur and of that critical-mystical approach to religion as demonstrated in the worl of Soederblom, von Huegel, and Heiler. In his polemical writings[51] we see him tryin; earnestly to hold a middle ground. He does not deny that the Old Testament peopl "had dealings with the living God under the mantle of the Yahveh faith . . . a deepe (and that means also a more terrible) knowledge and experience of what it means to deal with the living God than other men in non-Christian religions, who also unde their mantle had dealings with the living God." [52] But the Old Testament religion, he holds, is abrogated by the revelation of the New Testament.[53] However, Hirsch want to guard himself carefully against the deification of race, blood, and soil. The God is contemporary history is to him only a hidden God whereas only in the New Testamen we are face to face with Him as revealed in Jesus Christ.[54]

V. Some Independent Theologians

1. In the final paragraph of our investigation we shall discuss a number of the ologians who are *representatives of theological side-currents in Continental thought* Our first reference is to the exponents of the method of *Form-Criticism* in the field o the New Testament. The movement was inaugurated in 1919 by Martin Dibelius and Karl Ludwig Schmidt, both writing independently of each other, the former with hi book *Die Formgeschichte der Evangelien* (translated from the second edition under the title *From Tradition to Gospel,* 1933), the latter with his discussion of *Der Rahmer der Gerschichte Jesu.* In 1921 R. Bultmann followed suit with his *Die Geschichte de synoptischen Frage.* The interest of these scholars is centered in such questions as "What has taken place between Jesus and the Gospels?" [55] What was the form of the Gospel stories before they received literary form? and What were the motives that lec to their selection and preservation? The exponents of this method regard the Gospel and Acts and to some extent also the epistolary literature of the New Testament [56] a mosaics of tales, legends, sermons, and paradigms which had become traditionally fixed by the preaching of the Church. These fragments then were collected and loosely pu together by the later evangelists. The *Rahmen* (framework), and in part also the stories of the Gospels are altogether unhistorical, being the result of the missionary zea of the Church.

This method has its immediate precursor in Gunkel's and Gressmann's *gattungsge schichtliche Forschung* of the Old Testament. The *Gattung* (form, style), these scholar

---

[50] *Das vierte Evangelium in seiner urspruenglichen Gestalt verdeutscht und erklaert,* 1936; *Studien zum vierte Evangelium,* 1936.

[51] *Deutsches Volkstum und evangelischer Glaube,* 1934; *Die gegenwaertige geistige Lage,* 1934; *Das Alt Testament und die Predigt des Evangeliums,* 1936; *Der Weg der Theologie,* 1937.

[52] The translation follows Horton, *op. cit.,* p. 121. By permission of Harper & Brothers, publishers.

[53] Compare again the liberal Harnack: "To reject the Old Testament in the second century, was a mistak which the Church rightly opposed; to retain it in the sixteenth century was a fate (*Schicksal*) which the Reforma tion could not yet avoid; but to conserve it as canonical in nineteenth century Protestantism is the result of religious and ecclesiastical paralysis!" (*Maricon,* 1921, p. 243.) The revolt against the Old Testament is onl the natural result of an unbalanced emphasis on God's revelation in Jesus which is so characteristic for the whol nineteenth century and also for Barth's revised *Roemerbrief.*

[54] Cf. Horton, *op. cit.,* 113 ff.; John Aberly, "*Religion in the Third Reich,*" The Lutheran Church Quarterly 1938, 385 ff.

[55] Cf. H. J. Cadbury, in *Harvard Theological Review,* 1923, pp. 81 ff.

[56] Cf. Werner Straub, *Die Bildersprache des Apostel Paulus,* 1937.

claimed, is determined by a sociological factor, the *Sitz im Leben,* i.e., it bears the color of its historical environment. And the criterion by which a datum is identified as authentic, it is said, is "agreement with a known environment." For the Gospels this *Sitz im Leben,* is, according to Schmidt, the Christ-cult of the primitive Christian community. The Gospels, therefore, are not human biographies, they rather reflect in a very great variety of fragments the central theme of the Church: the incarnation of the Logos.[57] It was on the background of this method that Dibelius wrote his little book on *Jesus* (1939). *A Fresh Approach to the New Testament and Early Christian Literature* (1941) applied this method, for the first time, to a wider field of research.

For a word of criticism we may refer to such an eminent Biblical scholar as A. Schlatter. The method of Form-criticism, in his judgment, is but another modern manifestation of the "Greek spirit" which limits the work of Jesus to a revelation of divine ideas (Plato). But the actual meaning of the words of Jesus is lost, Schlatter said, if, divested of their historical setting, they are turned into timeless maxims.[58]

2. GEORG WOBBERMIN, now at the University of Berlin, *follows in the footsteps of Schleiermacher and Ritschl* when he lays down for theological methodology the axiom that it has to strive toward reaching an equal balance between the personal religious experience and the emphasis on the historical in Christianity, eliminating abstract speculation. Wobbermin is not an exponent of psychological experimentation in religion though he made an endeavor to interpret the work of W. James to German scholars.[59] Yet a personal religious experience is to him indispensable for a scientific investigation into the essence and verity of Christianity. Schleiermacher's definition of religion as a "feeling of dependency" he regards as insufficient; it should be supplemented, he holds by a "feeling of security" (*Geborgenheit*), and of "yearning" (*Sehnsucht*). Taking his stand with the right wing of the Ritschlians, Wobbermin always addressed himself to the task of overbridging the chasm between liberal and orthodox thought and, in this way to promote the ecumenical work of the churches. His *magnum opus* is *Systematische Theologie nach religions-psychologischer Methode* (3 vols., 1913 ff.).

Schleiermacherian and Ritschlian tendencies are also at work in HORST STEPHAN of Leipzig, as is evident in his *Glaubenslehre* (1920).

3. To these names we may add *two other scholars* whose hearts are truly with historic Lutheranism: KARL GIRGENSOHN, a native son of the Baltic countries who held for a short time, till his premature death in 1925, the chair of systematic theology in the Leipzig University, and HERMANN BRUNSTAED of Rostock. Girgensohn did the pioneering work in religious experimentation in German theology: *Der seelische Aufbau des religioesen Erlebens.* (1921), and *Religionspsychologie, Religionswissenschaft und Theologie* (1923). (A pupil of his is Carl Schneider of Koenigsberg.) Brunstaed, who exchanged his philosophical chair for a chair in theology, aims at an harmonious synthesis of German idealism with a Lutheran (Erlangen) conception of Christianity. Idealism purged from its Kantian phenomenalism and Hegelian ontology, he holds, can be of real service for a scientific interpretation of Lutheran theology (*Reformation und Idealismus,* 1925).

---

[57] Cf. his article in *RGG*, II, 836 ff.

[58] Cf. our article, *"Recent German New Testament studies, 1933-1937," The Lutheran Church Quarterly,* 1938, pp. 159 ff.

[59] He edited in translation, William James, *Die religioese Erfahrung in ihrer Manigfaltigkeit,* 1907, and subsequent editions.

4. At this place we must mention also PAUL TILLICH, now at Union Theological Seminary in New York. Born in Germany (1886), he is one of the theologians who were forced to leave the Fatherland when the present regime began to purge German life from all alleged Marxian influence.[60] He is, broadly speaking, rooted in the same tradition of existential thinking with which we became familiar in our study of Barth. On the other hand, he shows a close affinity to the speculative philosophies of Jacob Boehme and Schelling. The unconditioned reality of God, according to Tillich, infinitely transcends the natural world. Religion is not from without, it is not "heteronomous." Nor is man an "autonomous" being in religion. On the contrary, the true state of religion is understood when we see in every human desire, achievement, or event, a pointing to an infinitely vaster reality. In other words, man's condition is "theonomous," his being is grounded in God, his life is akin to divine Reality. Grace is not an irresistible force from without. His German writings include *Ideen zu einer Theologie der Kultur* (2nd edition, 1924), *Das Daemonische* (1926), *Kairos* (2 vols., 1926, 1929), and *Die religioese Lage der Gegenwart* (1926, English edition, 1932).

5. Another refugee theologian is OTTO PIPER (born 1891), successor to Barth in the chair of systematic theology at the University of Muenster (1930), now in the same chair at Princeton Theological Seminary. In philosophy Piper holds to a strictly realistic interpretation of reality. The prevalent nominalistic view, in his opinion, has not only made Protestant theology incapable of coping with the materialistic and biologic realism of modern science, it also has impoverished theology itself. Piper refers to the fact that the concepts of angels and of Satan were dropped in modern theology or given an insignificant place. Compare in his *God in History*, which we had occasion to mention before, especially on the "Supra-Historical and the Historical" (pp. 53 ff.). In theology he rejects the static conception of God as the Absolute and stresses the dynamic aspect in religion: God is a personal God with unlimited power. Consequently, in the field of ethics, it is not possible for the Church to offer a so-called Christian program to the world; she rather ought to make known the power of God in every concrete situation of life (the dynamic and existential *versus* the static and doctrinal).

During his German period, Piper published, among other volumes, *Das religioese Erlebnis* (an analysis of Schleiermacher's *Reden, 1920*), *Theologie und reine Lehre* (1926), and *Die Grundlagen der evangelischen Ethik* (2 vols., 1928 ff.).

With these scholars we may fittingly close our discussion of Continental Theology. Tillich's idea of the "theonomous" nature of man is not simply an isolated phenomenon in present-day theology. It rather underlies all the theologies from Karl Barth to the Niebuhr brothers in America. Against this "neo-supernatural" background we must study and evaluate the pronouncements of these men on revelation and on Scripture, the Church, and reason and experience as a road to God. True, they are Supernaturalists, but not in the older meaning of the term. They endeavor, with greater consistency than the older Supernaturalists, to uphold the "otherness" of God, trying to extricate Him from all entangling alliances with the natural world. Nothing natural, they claim, can be a direct or "unbroken" manifestation of God, neither a book (the Bible), nor an

---

[60] In 1919 Tillich founded, with other theologians, the party of the Religious Socialists. The party sought to arrive at an understanding between Christianity and the economic and cultural program of Marxism. Prominently identified with the movement was also G. Wuensch of Marburg *Religion and Wirtschaft*, 1925, *et al.*

nstitution (the Church), nor the so-called "Jesus of history," as mirrored by a liberal-
stic theology of the past (compare especially R. Bultmann), nor mystical experience, nor
dialectical reasoning. All of these, they say, are subject to the historical and psychological laws of nature. God is known only by revelation which is apprehended only by
faith.[61] The "Word" they hold, should not be equated with the Bible. The Bible, in
their estimate, is "secondary," it may have all the faults of historical development. But
God Who completely transcends history is not hereby affected, nor is His Word to man
thereby impaired. As we have seen, Barth and Althaus, for example, vary greatly as to
their view concerning the historical reliability of the Written Word; nevertheless, they
are all agreed as to the underlying principle.

What shall be our criticism? True, the Bible is the Word of God, cast in human
speech.[62] The Biblical writers were conscious that human speech is in many cases but
an inadequate vehicle of divine reality. Compare, for instance, the designation of Jesus
as the "Son" or the "Word" or the symbolical language of the apocalyptic writers, also
such passages as John 3:12, II Corinthians 12:4, and I Corinthians 13:12. Luther also
was fully aware of the fact that the doctrinal formulas of the Church are not always
adequate expressions of the thing which they signify.[63] But it must not be overlooked
that the current distinction between the Word and the Bible, especially in the manner
in which this is frequently applied, may easily lead the Church and the individual Christian into unbelief, subjectivism and despair. It is the Word of Scripture, written and
preached, that conducts to us God's revelation, His message of salvation and the certainty
of His grace! And from Luther we must learn to think of the organic relation between
Scripture and the Word, the Spirit and the letter, in general, of the human and the
Divine. Thus with regard to many other things in sacred theology.

Note: Among the independent theologians in this section we mentioned the late Karl
Girgensohn. Here our reference is specially to his *"Geschichtliche Offenbarung"* in *Biblische Zeit
und Streitfragen* (1910), and to *Die Inspiration der Heiligen Schrift,* reprinted from the *Pastoral-
blaetter* (1926). See also his brief *Grundriss der Dogmatik* (1924, paragraphs 18 f. And compare L. Ihmels, *"Das Wesen der Offenbarung im Licht der neueren Dogmatik"* in *Jahrbuch der
Pastoral-theologischen Konferenz fuer Westfalen* (1910). See also Neve on "Revelation" and
"Source and Authority of Truth" in his *Churches and Sects of Christendom* (pp. 602 ff.).

[61] The importance which the problem of revelation holds in modern thought is well brought in the composite volume of Baillie and Martin, as quoted above. See also *The Meaning of Revelation* by H. R. Niebuhr
(1941).
[62] On the *Inspiration of Scripture* and the history of the types of this doctrine in the post-Reformation age
and—proleptically—into later and present-day dogmatics, see Vol. I, 322 ff.
[63] Erlangen edition 12, 378; 61, 230 f., Weimar edition 45, 89; 46, 436.

APPENDIX

A brief reference to Catholic thought on the Continent should be added here. The decrees of the Vatican Council have been discussed in Volume One (pp. 333 f.) The pre-War Modernist Movement in the Church of Rome receives attention in Section II of the present volume (pp. 241 ff.). Here we are chiefly concerned with the *revival of Thomism in the Roman communion* and with the *rediscovery of the Eastern Church* by Western Protestantism.

I. *It has been the customary policy of the Roman hierarchy* to lay the loss of spiritual coherence and unity to the charge of the Reformation. Little wonder, therefore, that Pope Leo XIII, in the bull *Aeterni Patris* (1879), recommended to the world "the precious wisdom of Saint Thomas" and its propagation as a cure for the religious and social evils of the time. However, the then powerful historical and psychological approach to religion greatly disturbed the tranquility of the Roman Church in the decades preceding the first World War. It was the breakdown of nations and morals through the War which gave new momentum to the Catholic cry: Back to authority. The prestige of the hierarchy was considerably enhanced by the shift of emphasis in the philosophical world from abstract Idealism and Monism to a new ontological Realism. Catholic schools such as the Institute Supérieur de Philosophie at Louvain in Belgium, the Institute Catholique at Paris, and the universities at Freiburg, Switzerland, and Innsbruck, Austria, became the leading centers of Thomistic studies. (On the North American continent the Catholic universities at Washington, D. C., and Ottawa, and Laval University formerly at Quebec, now at Montreal, are promoting the cause of Neo-Thomism.) Among the leading men we find such as Désire Joseph Mercier (1851-1926), the late primate of the Church of Belgium, Count von Hertling, wartime chancellor of Germany (1843-1919), Clemens Baeumker, successor to von Hertling in the chair of philosophy at the University of Munich (1853-1924), and Peter Wust, at one time colleague of Barth at Muenster. The most accomplished scholars of the present time are the French philosopher JACQUES MARITAIN and the German Jesuit ERICH PRZYWARA at Munich.

As a scholastic, Maritain is unrelenting in his opposition to Luther, Descartes and Kant. Luther's conception of the certainty of salvation, according to Maritain, has led to a metaphysical egotism which makes man, not Christ, the center of religion. He sees in the teachings of Thomas the specific antidote against all the evils resulting from the philosophies of Descartes and Kant, i.e., modern agnosticism, naturalism, and individualism. Among his principal works in English translation are *The Things That Are Not Caesar's* (1931), *Religion and Culture* (1931), *Freedom in the Modern World* (1936), *True Humanism* (1938), *Scholasticism and Politics* (1940), *Science and Wisdom* (1941), and *Ransoming the Time* (1941). With Ch. Dawson and P. Wust he edited *Essays in Order* (1930). He also is editor of the composite volume *Religion and the Modern World* (1941).

Over against the Barthian dislike of the intellectual element in religion ERICH PRZYWARA stands out as a staunch defender of scholastic rationalism. God in Catholic thought, he says, is both like and unlike the world. He is in the world but also forever above the world. He is neither to be equated with the world nor is He the "Wholly

)ther." Catholic theology stands aloof from pure immanentism as well as from pure ranscendentalism. It maintains that the way upward from man to God is closed to us, nd that we shall never be able to reach in this world a perfectly harmonious solution f our problems. This doctrine is in all its essentials a revival of the scholastic conception of an Analogy of Being (*analogia entis*). His book *Unsere Kirche* (1915) has gone through many editions. He also wrote *Gott* (1926), *Religionsphilosophie katholischer Theologie* (1926), *Analogia Entis* (1932), *et al.*

An historian of international reputation is E. GILSON of Paris to whose historical writings we had occasion to refer in Volume One (pp. 186, 188). Here we may refer to his recent book *God and Philosophy* (1941), written to vindicate Thomistic philosophy.

Two other church historians deserve to be mentioned: H. DENIFLE (died 1905), and H. GRISAR (died 1932). The writings of Denifle on Martin Luther[1] caused much resentment in the Protestant world. Grisar's works on Luther,[2] though they are less polemical, reveal the same unrelenting attitude toward the great Reformer.

For a good illustration of a loyal Catholic's wrestling with the problem of higher Biblical criticism we may refer to NORBERT PETERS. The Catholic Church, he says, does not equate revelation with the Bible. The Bible is not the revelation, but contains it. A distinction ought to be made between that which the sacred books assert and that which they record. Biblical inerrancy is, in Catholic thought, strictly limited to the former. Beliefs recorded as to natural science, for example, are not a part of Catholic doctrine.[3]

II. The disastrous consequences of the war of 1914-18 led to a *new discovery of the Greek Orthodox churches* by the Protestantism of the West. While the Anglican Church succeeded in gaining recognition for the validity of its orders from the Eastern sees, Continental scholars became engaged in a series of theological conferences with Orthodox theologians. The mutual *rapprochement* was much facilitated through contact with the Russian refugee church, having Paris as its theological center. By approving Evangelical means of fostering spiritual life, such as preaching and Bible reading, the Orthodox churches seem to be revitalized in no small degree.[4] Their two most renowned contemporary scholars are the Russian lay theologian NICHOLAS BERDYAEV and his friend Father S. N. BULGAKOV.

Both have gone through a spiritual metamorphosis which led them from Marx through Kant and the German idealists to Christ and the Orthodox Church. Both are also deeply influenced by the two great Russian writers Dostoievski and Vladimir Soloviev (1853-1900).

BERDYAEV'S thought revolves mainly about God, man, and freedom. History is to him a product of three factors: natural necessity, human freedom, and divine Grace. He concurs with Oswald Spengler in the opinion that civilizations pass through "life-cycles." But, unlike Spengler, he is not a fatalist. Civilization must not inevitably revert to barbarism. It may be reborn and pass through a "religious transfiguration." Its ultimate meaning is not on the temporal but on the metaphysical plane. Of his works in

---

[1] *Luther and Luthertum*, 2 vols., 1904 ff.

[2] *Luther*, 3 vols., 1911 f.; English in 6 vols., 1913 ff.; *Lutherstudien*, 1920 ff.

[3] See the autobiographical sketch in Stange's *Selbstdarstellungen*, III, 90 ff. Cf. with this approach that of so staunch a Calvinist as Charles Hodge, p. 292.

[4] Cf. the *Zoe Movement* (New Life) in Greece which owes much to the work of the lay theologian Apostolos Makrakis (1831-1905).

English translation we mention *The End of Our Time* (1933), *Freedom and the Spirit* (1935), *The Meaning of History* (1936), *The Destiny of Man* (1937), and *Spirit and Reality* (1939).

Father BULGAKOV'S thought-world is much akin to that of Berdyaev's. In a search for a metaphysical basis of human existence, he too turned to the Biblical, or rather Orthodox-Platonic, view of man as created in the image of God. God is the ideal in Whom all created things have their subsistence. "There is an eternal humanity in God and eternal divinity in man." Like his teacher Soloviev, who later in life joined the Roman Church, Bulgakov shows a keen interest in a real unity of a divided Christendom. Of his writings available in English we mention *The Orthodox Church* (1936) and *The Wisdom of God* (1937).[5]

---

[5] Compare in Horton, *op. cit.*, Chaps. 1 and 2; also see W. A. Visser 't Hooft, *Anglo-Catholicism and Orthodoxy*, 1933; E. E. Aubrey, *Present Theological Tendencies*, 1936, pp. 113 ff.; J. Maritain, editor, *Religion and the Modern World*, 1941, pp. 27 ff.

SECTION TWO

Theological Thought in Great Britain

Chapter One

INTRODUCTORY REMARKS

Literature: JOHN HUNT, *Religious Thought in England,* III (1896); JOHN TULLOCH, *Movements of Religious Thought in Britain during the Nineteenth Century,* 1901; A. W. BENN, *The History of English Rationalism in the Nineteenth Century,* 2 vols., 1906; V. F. STORR, *Theological Development in Great Britain 1800-1860,* 1913; OTTO PFLEIDERER, *Development of Theology in Germany since Kant and its Progress in Great Britain since 1825,* 3rd English edition, 1909; EDWARD C. MOORE, *History of Christian Thought Since Kant,* 1912; S. C. CARPENTER, *Church and People 1789- 1889,* 1933; A. H. NEWMAN, "Englische Theologie des 19 Jahrhunderts," in *Realenzyklopaedie fuer protestantische Theologie und Kirche,* XXIII (1913), 401 ff.; W. DIBELIUS, *England,* II, 1923; W. VOLLRATH, *Theologie der Gegenwart in Grossbritanien,* 1932; C. C. J. WEBB, *A Study of Religious Thought in England from 1850,* 1933. I want to express my special acknowledgment to the Reverend J. SHELLHAAS whose thesis for the degree of Master of Sacred Theology on *English Theology since the Age of Deism,* 1931, deposited in the library of Hamma Divinity School, Springfield, Ohio, has been a very helpful survey of the field.

1. In the eighteenth century theological leadership had passed from Germany to the countries of Western Europe. Holland and England took the lead during the period of enlightenment. It was not till the end of the eighteenth century that Germany, through the work of Kant and Schleiermacher, regained the position which she had held during the time of the Reformation. Since Kant the English mind has always, during the greater part of the nineteenth century, been a few decades behind the German mind in theological reconstruction. But if German theology has come to fruition more rapidly than English theology, it often has tended toward the extreme in radical criticism and humanism. The wholesome conservatism of the English mind ultimately led to the triumph of a *mediating theology* in England. The genius of English theology is that it is liberal but not modernistic. "Adaptive traditionalism," as W. M. Horton[1] fittingly remarks, is the chief characteristic of the English mind. English theologians are allowing progress in theological thinking while maintaining the continuity of thought. They are liberal conservatives. Even the so-called Modernists are not modernists in the sense of German or American Modernism. Though the dogmatic formulation of the past may be questioned, English theologians try to preserve the great Christian truths.[2]

Another characteristic of English theology is its *emphasis on the Church.* The Anglicans view the Church largely as a unifying force in society. The Apostolic succession, for example, is the force which unites the past and present generations. In Germany since the days of Schleiermacher German theology tends toward individualism and

---

[1] *Contemporary English Theology,* 1936, p. 3.

[2] On the respective merits and demerits of the English and German mind, compare, for example, H. R. Mackintosh, *Types of Modern Theology,* 1937. pp. 2 ff.

197

the break-up of the corporate consciousness of the Christian religion (although such men of the nineteenth century as Stahl, Kliefoth, Loehe, and Vilmar were hardly less emphatic on the corporate nature of the Church than the English theologians). Pietism in Germany struck directly at the Church. It was not so in England. Even the pietistic the evangelical, or Low Church man has an appreciation of the Church.

The third characteristic feature of English theology is its *apologetic element*. The irrationality of faith is thought of lightly while it is held that it is precisely the "business of theology" to show that the Gospel is a reasonable thing.[3]

A fourth trait of English theology is its contradictory or compromising element.[4] This trait appears among the English theologians who hold the highest views of the Church and the sacraments and at the same time accept all the critical knowledge of Biblical scholarship. Take, for instance, the case of the late Charles Gore who tried to bring the sacramentalism of the High Church party into harmony with the radical results of Biblical criticism. This apparent inconsistency, however, is easily understood, if we keep in mind the influence of Hegel in modern English thought.

2. A word ought to be said about the *center of English theology*. In German theology the atonement is the foremost problem. Lutheran theology considers the Cross the center of its system. While the theology of the Non-Conformists bears, in this respect, a resemblance to Lutheran theology, Anglican theology looks to the incarnation as its main problem. From this point it discusses the inspiration of the Scriptures, the atonement, miracles, sacraments, and the Church. The incarnation, sacraments, and tradition, these are the three great problems of Anglican theology. The theology of the Non-Conformists, on the other hand, revolves about such conceptions as the atonement, faith, and experience.[5]

3. Following the disintegration of the eighteenth century Deism, through the influence of Hume and Butler, there are *three great movements* that can be traced in their working through a great part of the nineteenth century the fruits of which extend right up to our day: *the Evangelical movement,* the Liberal movement sometimes called the *Broad Church movement,* and the *High Church movement.* Of these the first was most influential early in the century; the other two may be regarded as more or less synchronous, though the period of the greatest activity of the second precedes that of the third. Of course, there are other movements that cannot be brought under any of the three, nor did any of the three act in isolation. We see action, reaction, and interaction under different various circumstances, resulting in the complexity of the religious condition in which we find England today.

4. With respect to *Scottish theology* it may be said that theology in Scotland moved still slower than in England proper. Calvinism remained the common creed of the country. However, the critical tendencies of the age were also strongly felt there, greatly disturbing the tranquility of Scottish Presbyterianism. W. R. Smith, the interpreter of Wellhausen in England, for instance, had to yield his position in the Free Church to his orthodox opponents. Naturally still stronger inroads of modern ideas are found among the divers groups of the Non-Conformists who had always been wavering between a

---

[3] Cf. E. G. Selwyn, *The Approach to Christianity,* 1925; also L. Hodgson, *The Place of Reason in Christian Apologetic,* 1925.

[4] Cf. W. Vollrath's remarks on the German and English mind. *Op. cit.,* pp. 24 ff.

[5] Cf. *op. cit.,* pp. 259 ff.

legalistic pietism and critical rationalism, proceeding from a religious subjectivism.

5. *The intellectual record of the nineteenth century* presents a growing conviction that history offers a key to the right understanding of life. This century is above all historically minded. The *historical method* comes to its own. The sciences of history of religion and comparative religion were born, opening a wide field for historical investigation. The historical method is genetic and organic. Scientifically speaking, it has no place for the supernatural. No event takes place in isolation. There are antecedents that make possible the flow of history. Thus there is a growing tendency toward naturalism and away from a supernatural interpretation of history. Lessing and Herder in Germany and Montesquieu in France were the fathers of the historical method. But in England it was not before the latter part of the nineteenth century that this method came to be recognized.

But in spite of the triumph of the historical method in the nineteenth century, the leading theologians are unhistorical to the core (Schleiermacher and Ritschl in Germany, Coleridge and the large train of his followers in England). Nineteenth-century theology is above all established on the search for an interpretation of the divine idea, the principle, and spiritual truth. Even Ritschl remained in line with this tradition interpreting Biblical history by a pre-conceived notion, i.e., the Kantian secularized conception of the Kingdom of God. The three great religious postulates of the Enlightenment theology, God, virtue, and immortality, we see firmly rehabilitated at the close of the nineteenth century in the modern garb of the fatherhood of God, the brotherhood of mankind, and the supreme value of the human soul.[6]

6. Another spiritual force of the nineteenth century was *Romanticism* as a protest against the over-intellectualization of the preceding century. This movement gave to England such geniuses as Burns, Shelley, Coleridge, Byron, Browning, and Tennyson. It has formed the spiritual background of the Oxford movement. Newman in the *Apologia,* when describing the sources of the Oxford movement, speaks of a "spirit afloat" as the background of the religious revival.

7. The influence of the Romantic movement was counteracted by a growing interest in the *physical sciences* in England which began to apply the principle of historical development in explaining the genetic growth of physical specimens in the natural world. In 1830 the first British association of scientists was founded. This force came to the front in Charles Darwin who more than any other man in England changed its thinking. All readers are familiar with the part science played from his time on through his two great disciples, Huxley and Spencer. Of all the new movements, the Darwinian theory of evolution is the one which materialism appropriated most readily, and to which it is most indebted.

8. The nineteenth century was furthermore noted for a *philosophical idealism* which in Germany was closely allied with the Romantic movement in the earlier part of this period. In England, theology as a whole did not feel the influence of German philosophy until after 1860. Nowhere has English insularity been more marked than in the philosophical outlook of the first half of the nineteenth century. The last fifty years, however, have witnessed German idealism taking hold of British thinking. Kant and Hegel are studied in earnest and some of the very best interpreters of the two great

[6] Cf. G. Aulén, *Das Christliche Gottesbild,* 1930, pp. 285 f., 291, 323 ff.

philosophers are found in the British field of philosophy: Thomas Hill Green, John Caird and his younger brother Edward Caird.

9. During the whole period under discussion the *social problem* has played an important part in English life. England was the first country to experience the sweeping changes of the so-called industrial revolution. Soon after 1800 English society witnessed the rise of a proletariat that was in utter want and despair. Among the novelists Dickens is probably best known as the champion of the underprivileged. In the churches it was the Broad Church movement that supplied England with men far-sighted and able to arouse the English Christians to their social responsibility. F. D. Maurice became the leader of the Christian Socialists. In 1854 he founded a Working Men's College in London for the education of his neglected brethren. His ideas and endeavors were shared, among many others, by C. Kingsley (*Sermons on National Subjects,* 1852 and 1854; *Sermons for the Times,* 1855; also two of his novels, *Yeast,* 1848, and *Alton Locke,* 1849). After 1889 the increasing social responsibility led to the formation of "Associations for Christian Social Service" in all the denominations of the country. All these various Associations met for the first time in 1924 at Birmingham to form a "Conference for Christian Politics, Economics, and Civics" (Copec). Through this joint effort of the Established Church and the Non-Conformists the English churches have succeeded in taking the antireligious sting out of the labor movement in England, while the Socialists of the Continent are much more pronounced in their opposition not only to the established churches but to religion and Christianity as such.

Chapter Two

THE EARLY EVANGELICAL AND THE EARLY ORTHODOX PARTIES

1. We must not look for any worth-while theological developments among the Evangelicals during the first half of the nineteenth century. The field of this party rather lay in the great service it rendered to practical religion. Always in the minority, these Evangelicals were never popular. But gradually they crept into the ranks of the episcopacy: B. Porteus, Bishop of London; H. Ryder of Gloucester, J. B. Sumner of Chester and Canterbury, and C. Sumner of Llandaff, were Evangelicals.

The great centers of Evangelical influence were Claphan, London, and Cambridge. Cambridge produced the following men of influence: C. Simeon, I. Milner, W. Farish, J. Scholefield, W. Dealtry. The "Claphan Sect" had W. Wilberforce as its leader and gave to the Evangelical party such men as H. Thornton, Lord Teignmouth, G. Sharp, Z. Macaulay, J. Stephen, and J. Venn. The London group presented the following great men: R. Cecil, T. H. Horne, T. Scott, J. Pratt, B. Wood, and H. Blunt. In addition three other men should be mentioned: H. More, L. Richmond, and T. Gisborne. This party had no real foothold in Oxford. The literary organ of the party was *The Christian Observer*, first published in 1802.[1]

Before inquiring about the theology of this group in general, it might be well to consider *some of the individual leaders*. In 1798 Archdeacon DAUBENY published a dissertation called a *Guide to the Church*. It was a warning to all Evangelicals. Daubeny contended that the Church was the foundation of doctrine. Its constitution was a hierarchy of bishops, with priests and deacons. The priesthood has the power to remit sins. The Methodists are deceiving the people, the increase of the Methodist movement is a sign that the last perilous days have come.

RICHARD HILL answered Daubeny in a series of letters called *An Apology for Brotherly Love*. He avowed himself a devoted churchman, but never did believe that outside of the Church of England there was no salvation. Bishops were not necessary. Doctrine was more important than ecclesiastical polity.

Daubeny replied in his *Appendix to the Guide* saying that doctrine and polity are equally divine.

CHARLES SIMEON (1759-1836) was a great spiritual power in Cambridge. His great theme was "Christ and Him crucified." Simeon was a strict churchman for he clearly followed the service of the Prayer Book and adhered tenaciously to the Articles of Faith. His theology bears a Calvinistic stamp. ISAAC and JOSEPH MILNER were prominent members of the Evangelical party. They had been influenced by Wilberforce, and mainly adopted his religious opinions. Isaac argued that repentance and faith were necessary to those who were to be baptized; baptism in Apostolic days was administered only to adults. The Liturgy should be measured by the Scriptures. His brother Joseph

---

[1] Cf. Storr. *op. cit.*, p. 63 f.

wrote *A History of the Church from the Earliest Times,* in which he presents a religiou evangelical interpretation of ecclesiastical history. LEGH RICHMOND (1772-1827) w known by his popular religious tracts.

The chief lay pillars of the Evangelical party were W. WILBERFORCE (1759-1833 and H. MORE (1745-1833). To help the underprivileged in their spiritual and mor struggle, More published for three years the *Cheap Repository Tracts* which led to tl founding of the Religious Tract Society in 1799. The most influential book produce by the early Evangelicals is Wilberforce's *Practical View.*[2] This book presents a fa cross-section of doctrines confessed by the party. The Evangelicals were not chief interested in problems of church polity and tended towards individualism. The Eva gelicals therefore often showed a pronounced preference for co-operation with tl various Non-Conformist groups in England. In general, their theology was Calvinist modified by the trends of revivalism which had swept over England in the eighteent century. Their view of the arts and sciences was rather Puritanic. Their passion w for saving souls, and for large schemes of religious and philanthropic enterprises. F the attainment of divine truth nothing seemed to be necessary except an open Bib and a devoted spirit individually enlightened by divine grace. The doctrinal syste had as its center soteriology, i.e., as a basis of redemption, stress was laid on the depravi of human nature showing the Augustinian trend of thought. Redemption for mankin is wrought by Christ on the Cross. Justification was a watchword of the party. Emphas was also laid upon the Holy Spirit working in the life of man. In Biblical interpretatio they were literalistic, continuing the belief of the pre-enlightenment orthodoxy in verb inspiration without the historical approach. In short, the Evangelical party represen eighteenth century revivalism with most of its strong and weak points within tl Established Church.

In conclusion we might mention four great works which were written against tl Evangelical party: *Religious Enthusiasm* by G. F. Nott (the Bampton Lectures, 1802) *On the Question of the Calvinism of the Thirty-Nine Articles* by R. Lawrence (Bampto Lectures, 1804); *An Appeal to the Gospel* by R. Mant (Bampton Lectures, 1812); an *A Refutation of Calvinism* by G. Tomline (1811).

2. Side by side with the Early Evangelical party in the first quarter of the nin teenth century was the *Early Orthodox party.* This party deserves the name "Orthodox not so much with respect to its position on questions of Biblical criticism but rather i regard to its highly conservative appreciation of the Church and of ecclesiastical trad tion. As the Evangelical party included the Latitudinarians which later became know as the Broad Church party, so the Early Orthodox party was likewise composed of tw elements: the "Church and State Group" and the "Spiritual High Churchmen," wh were the lineal ancestors of the Tractarians.

We shall note first a few of their leaders and their theological position. The fath of this party was WILLIAM PALEY (1743-1805), who, in spite of his strong leanin toward a naturalistic conception of religion, held fast to a supernatural revelation in th Scriptures and the validity of the Thirty-Nine Articles. He wrote *Principles of Mor and Political Philosophy* (1785), *Horae Paulinae* (1790), *View of Evidences of Chri tianity* (1794), *Natural Theology or Evidences of the Existence and Attributes of th*

---

[2] See R. I. and S. Wilberforce, *Life of William Wilberforce,* 5 vols., 1838; *Correspondence of Willia Wilberforce,* 2 vols., 1840.

Deity Collected from the Appearances of Nature (1802). Next to him, SAMUEL HORSLEY (1733-1806) must be mentioned who with much fire and fury contended equally against Unitarians and Methodists, the Rationalists and the Pietists of his days. HERBERT MARSH (1758-1838), bishop of Llandaff and later of Peterborough, had spent some years at Goettingen, and knew German, a rare accomplishment for an Englishman of that time. While Margaret Professor of Divinity in Cambridge, he translated Michaelis' *Introduction to the New Testament*, adding a *Dissertation* of his own on the origin of the synoptic Gospels. This is probably the first attempt to introduce German higher criticism into England. But it did not take root. Its publication caused a panic in orthodox circles which held to the infallible inspiration of Scripture. J. RANDOLPH, Regius Professor at Oxford, wrote, anonymously, *Remarks on Marsh's Hypothesis*, accusing Marsh of making the Evangelists "copiers of copiests." Marsh repudiated this accusation but defended the critical position of Michaelis. As a bishop Marsh was radical and resolved to drive from the Church the Evangelical party.

EDWARD MALTBY, bishop of Durham, was a great Greek scholar and a theologian after the manner of Paley. GEORGE S. FABER (1773-1854) deserves special mention as one of the first writers on comparative mythology. In his theology he was anti-Calvinistic, holding that there was no predestinarian theology among the Fathers. His work on prophecy, *A Dissertation on the Prophecies that have been fulfilled, are now fulfilling, or will hereafter be fulfilled relative to the Great Period of 1620, the Papal and Mohammedan Apostasies and the Tyrannical Reign of the Antichrist or the Infidel Rome and the Restoration of the Jews* (1814), shows the strictest orthodox view on inspiration, and is an index to the state of the doctrine of inspiration in England in the beginning of the nineteenth century. His anti-Calvinistic feelings were fully shared by G. PRETYMAN, bishop of Lincoln and Winchester. To these may be added Archdeacon Daubeny, T. Sikes, T. Rennell, A. Knox, and W. Cleaver who hated the evangelical theology and attributed to the efficacy of the sacraments "every virtue under heaven, not only regeneration but justification and sanctification."

The theologians of this Orthodox party were the learned and cultured men of the early part of the nineteenth century. Unlike the Evangelicals, this group was genuinely theological. They had inherited a great creed, and they rationally defended the creed, though their theology was still shackled by eighteenth century methods. Paley was their ideal. The following tenets were held by this party: (1) The doctrine of the catholicity of the Church and of the Apostolic Succession; (2) the sacramental conception of Christianity; (3) the stress on the unity of the Church. This party hated schism and non-conformity. (4) Private judgment, they held, has no place in religion. Bishop HORSLEY condemned the irregularity of the ministry of the Methodists. T. SIKES laid emphasis upon the Creed as the center of the one church. (5) This party was on the whole anti-Calvinistic, though there were some Calvinists or at least moderate Calvinists among them.

By way of criticism we must admit that this party lacked appreciation of things outside their Church. Their theology was isolated from outside influences. It lacked the critical spirit. On the whole, this party stood for the same principles in the Church of England for which the exponents of the "theology of Repristination" stood in the Lutheran churches of the Continent, while the Early Evangelicals can claim the Pietists in the Prussian Union and the men of the Inner Missions as their brethren.

Chapter Three

COLERIDGE: THE EARLY ORIEL SCHOOL

Literature on Coleridge: J. H. GREEN, *Spiritual Philosophy, founded on the Teachings o*
the late Samuel Taylor Coleridge, 1865; J. T. WISE, *Bibliography of the Writings of Coleridge*
1913. Of recent biographies we want to mention the one by J. D. CAMPBELL, 1894, and b
J. AYNARD, 1907. For further literature we refer to STORR, *op. cit.*, pp. 318 ff.

1. *Modern theology in England has its beginning* with SAMUEL TAYLO
COLERIDGE (1772-1834), poet, lecturer, political and literary critic, philosopher and
theologian. His work must be judged along philosophical and spiritual lines. Hi
interest was not centered in the Church's conception of a special revelation; on the con
trary, he laid stress on the religious *a priori* in man. In many respects his work is com
parable to that of Schleiermacher in Germany. He led away from the religion of the
Reformation, from the theocentric thought to the anthropocentric. His interest moved
along three main lines: (1) the principles of religion, (2) Biblical criticism, (3) the
Church.

His work was directed against the materialistic negation of his age, on the one
hand and, on the other, against the position of the Evangelicals. Lockean philosoph
had eventuated in a materialism which denied the freedom of the will. The Evangelicals
in his eyes, had separated religion from life and made it a special compartment. Now
Coleridge hated the materialism of the Lockean school and he sought to show tha
religion is not an isolated purely supernatural matter but that it is written in the very
heart of man and is therefore regulative in human life. Religion, he emphasized, is a
home in the soul of man, it is native to his constitution. Coleridge postulated three
assumptions: first, he held that there is a universal law of conscience; second, man ha
freedom of will; third, religion is native to man because he is made in the image o
his Maker.

Coleridge, like Kant, distinguished between reason and understanding. The latte
has to do with outward facts that are conditional, while the former has to do with the
necessary truths of life. The understanding is dependent upon the sense experience o
life and follows the mechanical law of nature. Not so with reason. It possesses freedom
of will, orders its own world and does not follow necessitarian lines. "The Will," he
says, "is ultimately self-determined, or it is no longer a Will under the law of perfec
Freedom, but a Nature under the mechanism of Cause and Effect." [1] And by this last
fact man comes to the great spiritual truths of life. It is a sort of intuition. He asserts
that experience is the criterion for the truthfulness of religion, thus shifting the question
of religious authority from an objective basis to a subjective basis. So much does he do
this that he has been accused by some of being a pantheist. He is the founder, or perhaps
we should say, the precursor, of the school of empiricism in religion that considers
experience to be the basis of religion and consequently the basis of theology. Christian
truth also is self-evidencing. "In all our creed," he says, "there can be nothing against

---

[1] *Aids to Reflection*, new edition of 1873, p. 250.

eason. If Reason justly contradicts an article, it is not of the household of Faith." [2] In No Case Can True Reason and a Right Faith Oppose Each Other." [3]

With respect to the question of Biblical criticism, Coleridge anticipated in English heology the modern conception of the Bible that is both spiritual and rational. The Bible is divine, it is inspired because the deepest in the human heart finds itself expressed n the Bible. The Bible finds the human spirit. "In the Bible there is more that finds he than I have experienced in all other books put together. The words of the Bible nd me at greater depth of my being; and whatever finds me brings with it an irresistible vidence of its having proceeded from the Holy Spirit." [4] Its divinity, therefore, does ot reside in a literally infallible text. Historical criticism is not to be rejected, Coleridge olds; rather it has exactly the same task with respect to the Bible as to any other book f antiquity. Its right interpretation also "must be determined by the industry and nderstanding of fallible, and alas! more or less prejudiced theologians." [5]

The Catholic emancipation movement prompted Coleridge to express his views on he nature of the Church.[6] Proceeding from the assumption that Church and state are ot identical, he follows the Laudian and Non-Juror tradition in Anglican theology. He distinguishes between the Christian Church as such and any national church. The former s spiritual and universal, identical "with the spiritual and invisible church known only o the Father of Spirits." [7] It is the Divine and Christian represented in "every true church." A national church, on the other hand, is the embodiment of all learning and ulture in a country. Every nation, for the true well-being of its citizens, requires not only an agricultural, industrial, and commercial class but also an educative class embracing all the spiritual forces of the nation and communicating to the citizenry a clear conception of its right and duties. The knowledge which this class, the "Clericy," has o cultivate and to diffuse is not only theology but "all the so-called liberal arts and sciences, the possession and application of which constitute the civilization of a country." [8]

The student will note how much Coleridge is in line with the Kant-Schleiermacher-Hegelian movement in Germany where he had visited in 1798-1799. His theology is really the apotheosis of man. As with Schleiermacher, the heterogeneous elements in his system were capable of development into a conservative and also a liberal school. His conception of the Church helped to promote the cause of the Oxford movement, while his purely religious subjectivism became the starting point for a liberal school in English theology.

Of the more direct followers of Coleridge we shall mention only J. C. HARE (1795-1855). Like his master, he was an ardent student of German philosophy and theology (Schleiermacher, Neander, Tholuck). Of his works we would name at least two: *Contest Against Rome,* published in 1842 against Cardinal Newman, and *Vindication of Luther* (1885), written against Sir William Hamilton, an exponent of the Scottish "Common Sense" philosophy.

---

[2] *Op. cit.,* Aphorism CXIX.
[3] *Op. cit., Aphorism CXXI.*
[4] *Confessions of an Inquiring Spirit,* 3rd edition, 1853, p. 47.
[5] *Op. cit.,* p. 81.
[6] *On the Constitution of Church and State,* 1830.
[7] *Ibid.,* edition of 1868, p. 107.
[8] *Ibid.,* p. 53.

2. *From the year 1815 to the middle of the nineteenth century* Oxford was th center of two great theological movements. There was the Earlier Oriel School and th Later Oriel school. The first was a liberal movement, and the second was the grea Tractarian movement. Let us first consider the *Early Oriel School.* We regard EDWAR COPLESTON, Provost of Oriel (1814-1848) and afterwards bishop of Llandaff, as th father of this group. It is true that Eveleigh, his predecessor, introduced into the un versity reforms which removed sloth and haphazard scholarship. But it was Coplesto who carried on this work and developed it. A brilliant group of scholars came unde his direction and influence. We need only mention Whately, Hampden, and Bade Powell, to show that he was a magnetic teacher. In regard to the Church, Coplesto "may be placed in the more liberal wing of the old High Church or Orthodox party" for he denied the necessity of the episcopacy and the sacramental character of the Apos tolic succession.

EDWARD HAWKINS (1789-1882) followed Copleston as Provost at Oriel. He wa an enemy of the Tractarians, having dismissed Newman and Froude from Oriel. He di not, however, always hold to the Noetics, as this group was called. He had a higher vie of the Church holding that doctrines were not derived from Scripture but from th Church, while he viewed the Bible only as a witness to verify the teaching of the Churcl

RICHARD WHATELY (1787-1863) held an intermediate position between the hig dogmatic school and the school of religious subjectivism. If it was the aim of Coleridg to bring the doctrines of the Church to the test of spiritual experience, Whately aime to bring the doctrines of the Church to the test of historical criticism. He assaile "errors" on both sides, those of the Puritans as well as those of the Sacramentarians. I is noteworthy that he rejected the Calvinists' teaching on predestination as non-Paulin He based justification on the moral renewal of man, rejecting, as he did, the idea tha the merits of Christ are imputed to the sinner. Apostolic succession, he held, cannot b proved from Scripture. The Lord's day is not to be based on the legal command of the Old Testament.[10]

R. D. HAMPDEN (1793-1868) deserves special mention among the scholars of thi school. His article on Thomas Aquinas and the Scholastic Philosophy, written for th *Encyclopedia Metropolitana,* was an attack on the "excessive" development of dogma an an attempt to evaluate the dogmatic principle in the light of history. He insists upoi the difference between the Christian faith and its mode of expression. Religious experi ence comes first and that alone is divine; theological terms are but symbols. Hampden' motto is "Back to the Scriptures; Scripture, not Tradition." "The difference between th New Testament and technical theology is that in the one you have divine truth, guar anteed by inspiration, in the other the human rendering of divine truth." [11] What i the justification for dogmatic theology? (1) It is to guard the original deposit o Biblical revelation and see to it that in theological development this revelation is no eviscerated; (2) it seems to keep together the religious community, it is a social bond When we see Hampden heralding the cry: "Back to Scriptures," we should, however keep in mind that he did not do this in the interest of a pietistic Evangelicalism

[9] Storr, *op. cit.,* p. 95. By permission of Longman's, Green & Company, publishers.

[10] E. J. Whately, *Life of Richard Whately,* 2 vols., 1866; Fitzpatrick, *Memoirs of Richard Whately,* 2 vols. 1864; F. Arnold, *Our Bishops and Our Clergy,* I, 168 ff. (1875); A. Martineau, *Biographical Sketches,* 1876 pp. 175 ff.

[11] Storr, *op. cit.,* p. 102. By permissions of Longman's, Green & Company, publishers.

intended thereby, more or less, to discredit the development of dogma like that of arnack and other liberal men in Germany. Of his works we mention *Essay on the Philosophical Evidence of Christianity* (1827), and *Scholastic Philosophy Considered in Relation to Christian Theology* (1833).

THOMAS ARNOLD (1795-1842) was a follower of Whately. Christianity was to m ethics. His idea of the Church pleased neither Liberals nor Orthodox. He reproduced Hooker's theory of the identity of Church and State in a Christian commonwealth, but repudiated the idea of a priesthood and of Apostolic succession.

There are two other men who are not of the Oriel group but partake of the Noetic spirit. We refer to Bishop THIRLWALL (died 1875) and HENRY HART MILMAN (died 1868). In these two men the historical spirit reached its height. Thirlwall knew the German language and also German theology, and he breathes its critical spirit. Milman in his work *History of the Jews* (1829) took the historical view of the Old Testament and dared to interpret sacred history on the same basis as profane history.

Another man who deserves consideration is ROBERT FELLOWES (1771-1847), known as a theological free-lance. He wrote two important books, *Religion Without Cant* (1811), and *The Religion of the Universe* (1836). The first work was an attempt to defend the tenets of the Church of England against the misinterpretations of the Dissenters. He denies original sin and the doctrine of the Trinity. In his second work he is in open revolt against the traditions of the Church. He accepts an evolutionary creed and contends that religion is a matter of intellectual culture.

Chapter Four

THE OXFORD MOVEMENT

Literature: R. W. CHURCH, *The Oxford Movement, Twelve Years, 1833-1845*, 1891; S. OLLARD, *A Short History of the Oxford Movement*, 1915; THUREAU-DANGIN, *La Renaissance Catholique en Angleterre, au* XIX Siècle, 3 vols., 1899-1906; S. LESLIE, *The Oxford Movement 1833-1933*, 1935; Y. BRILIOTH, *The Anglican Revival*, 1925. This valuable study of the movement by a Swedish Lutheran is replete with references to older literature. It contains a systematic review of the bibliography on the movement published in English, French, German, and Scandinavian (pp. 334-342). All quotations from Brilioth refer to this study. He has also published another little volume, *The Oxford Movement and Evangelicalism*, 1934. S. L. OLLARD has compiled an excellent bibliography of the Oxford Movement in the *Cambridge History of English Literature*, vol. 12.

1. As the English Reformation of the sixteenth and the seventeenth centuries was rooted more in a *national protest against Rome* than in a genuine religious appreciation of the continental Reformation, so the political situation at the beginning of the nineteenth century is in a high degree responsible for the inception of the Oxford Movement. France had gone through a bloody revolution and had failed, and democracy was obnoxious to the more aristocratic intellectuals. The political events, the rise of liberalism in politics and religion, and the reaction against the French revolution served as fertile soil from which could grow a movement aristocratic and conservative. Then too the Romanticism of Walter Scott, which looked to the past, would easily take root in church with a rich past. On two previous occasions Oxford had been the center of religious life in England. The university had produced Wyclif in the fifteenth century and the Wesleys in the eighteenth. Now again in the nineteenth century it gave birth to a new religious movement which thoroughly changed the structure of the Established Church. The Anglican Church which had been preponderantly evangelical and Protestant at the beginning of the nineteenth century, was dominantly ritualistic and disposed to minimize its relation to the Reformation when the nineteenth century closed.

The Oxford Movement was an ecclesiastical rather than a theological movement. Theology was of secondary consideration. Inspired by the religious zeal of the Evangelicals, the Oxford men gave a new and lofty application of the ecclesiasticism of the old High Church Party to the practical needs of the time. Also Coleridge, by way of his conception of the Church, exerted a considerable influence on the movement.

2. In speaking of the *leaders of the Oxford Movement* we must first mention HUGH JAMES ROSE of Cambridge (1796-1838). Although he is more properly classified with the old High Church party, he, in some degree, prepared the way for the new movement. In 1825 he delivered a series of lectures on *The State of Religion in Germany* in which he drew, on the basis of incomplete knowledge, a very dark picture of the admittedly ravaging influence of Rationalism in that country. His action evoked a sharp reply from the pen of Pusey, who, at that time, was suspected of liberal tendencies, *Historical Inquiry into the Probable Causes of the Rationalist Character Lately Pre-*

---

[1] Cf. Moore, *op. cit.*, p. 221.

dominant in the Theology of Germany (1828). *The British Magazine,* founded by Rose in 1832, soon became the chief literary mouthpiece of the Movement.

The real forerunner of the Oxford Movement was the Irish lay theologian ALEXANDER KNOX (1757-1831) and his friend and pupil JOHN JEBB, bishop of Limerick. In Knox a fusion had taken place between the "enthusiasm" of the Evangelicals (after 1776 he had entertained a lively correspondence with John Wesley) and the ecclesiastical principles of the old High Church party. He anticipated in his teaching all that which later became typical of the Oxford men: Anglicanism as a *via media,* Apostolic succession, and the Anglican liturgy as the basic principle by which the catholicity and continuity of the Church is safeguarded.[2]

The foremost leaders of the movement proper were Newman, Pusey, Keble, Froude, William Palmer, Perceval and Ward. The most important men in this group were Newman and Pusey.

JOHN HENRY NEWMAN (1801-1890) was brought up on the Calvinistic theology of William Romain, John Newton, and Thomas Scott. At the age of fifteen he underwent a religious crisis which he always regarded as his real conversion. From John Newton's *On the Prophecies* he learned to look to Rome as the seat of Antichrist. Likewise, the Romanticism of Walter Scott charmed his highly imaginative soul. In 1833 he became fellow at Oriel College. Here he came, for a time, under the more liberal influence of the Noetics. Through his Oriel friends, Keble and Froude, his interest centered in patristic studies and the High Churchmanship of Rose and his party. As the chief editor of the *Tracts* and through his *Parochial and Plain Sermons* (8 vols., 1837-1843) he soon became the recognized leader of the Movement. As early as 1837 he began to express his outspoken dislike for Wesley.[3] Still more repugnant to him than Wesley was Luther.[4] Ignorance of Luther's language has, very likely, helped to obscure his historical vision of the ancient and medieval Church. As Dean Stanley once remarked, "How different the fortunes of England might have been if Newman had been able to read German." [5] Newman ranks foremost as a Christian preacher. As a poet (in *Lyra Apostolica*) and prose writer he commands the respect of the student of English literature. As a Catholic apologete he is an anti-intellectual voluntarist.[6]

EDWARD PUSEY (1800-1882) was, next to Newman, the most influential man of the Oxford Movement. His theology is centered around a mystic-sacramental conception of the incarnation and the cross. He was the editor of the *Library of the Fathers of the Holy Catholic Church* (since 1836). When Newman went over to Rome, Pusey gathered the forces of the Anglo-Catholics together and continued to be the leader to the end of his long life in 1882.

JOHN KEBLE (1792-1866), poet and theologian, has provided the Anglican Church with one of its most widely circulated devotional books, *The Christian Year* (1827). In these hymns, written in praise of the church of his fathers, the author has given a Christian sacramental interpretation to the nature symbolism of the Romantic school.

---

[2] *Remains of Alexander Knox, Esq.,* posthumously edited, vols. 1 and 2 in 1834, vols. 3 and 4 in 1837; *Thirty Years' Correspondence between John Jebb, D.D., F.R.S., Bishop of Limerick, Ardfert and Aghadoe, and Alexander Knox, Esq., M.R.I.A.,* edited by Ch. Forster, 2 vols., London, 1834.

[3] *Letters and Correspondence,* II, 200 (1903).

[4] *Essays, Critical and Historical,* I, 387.

[5] Quoted by Fisher, *op. cit.,* p. 462 from the *Memories of Mark Pattison,* p. 210.

[6] *University Sermons,* 1843; *Grammar of Assent,* 1870; *Apologia pro Vita Sua,* 1864; cf. Metz, *A Hundred Years of English Philosophy,* 1938, pp. 185 ff.

It was RICHARD HURRELL FROUDE, a pupil of Keble, who brought Newman and Keble together. This youthful spirit who died at the age of thirty-three (1836), hated with equal passion the "rationalist spirit which the Reformers set afloat" [7] and the "idolatrous Romanists." [8] Very likely it was Froude as the first of the Oriel friends who conceived the idea of an Anglican *via media* which Newman was later to develop.

A. P. PERCEVAL, divine counselor to George IV, William IV, and Victoria, was the spokesman of the Movement at the royal court. WILLIAM GEORGE WARD became the leader of the radical faction of the Movement. Possessed of an inconsistency of temper and devoid of any particular love for the Church of England, he was predisposed to Rome and the Jesuit teaching long before Newman could ever swallow the *doctrina Romanensium*, i.e., the particular Romish Jesuitic tenets in Roman Catholicism (*Tract 90*).

3. *In 1833 a Whig government was formed,* and the new prime minister, Lord Grey, warned the bishops "to set their house in order." He very likely meant only that the bishops should remedy the gross abuses of nepotism, sinecures, pluralities and non-residence which then were widely practiced in the Church of England.[9] Others, however, took the words of the Premier as a quotation from Isaiah's death message to King Hezekiah, "For thou shalt die, and not live." (II Kings 20:1.) The Erastian spirit of the government aroused the apprehension of the Oriel friends, and they were resolved to act. The inception of the Oxford Movement begins, in the eyes of its adherents, with Keble's sermon on Sunday, July 14, 1833, on *National Apostasy*. This was followed by a meeting at the Hadleigh rectory where Rose met with Froude, Perceval, and Palmer (July 25-29). The Oxford Movement proper may be divided into three periods: (1) 1833-1835; (2) 1835-1839; (3) 1839-1846. During the first period the conservative and static element dominated. The main issue was the defense of the spiritual nature and independence of the Church. In the second period the specific characteristics of the Movement became progressively more pronounced. Emphasis was laid on the awfulness of religion, the incarnation, mystic sacramentalism, and an ethical asceticism. This period was very prolific in producing new literature. The *Tracts,* which at first were rather brief, now became real dissertations. The Greek Fathers were translated and presented to the English speaking public. As time went on, in the third period, the progressive ideal of the Church received a wider recognition. The ascetic ideals became more pronounced. Both these factors help to open the way for a deeper appreciation of Roman Catholicism. The crisis came when Newman, in *Tract 90*, undertook to prove the harmony between the Thirty-nine Articles and Tridentine Romanism. Newman went over to Rome in October, 1845, followed by a group of the radical element.

4. In order to arrive at a clearer conception of the *importance of this Movement,* we shall attempt to set forth systematically the teachings of the Oxford men on some of the vital Christian doctrines such as the Church, Sacraments, Justification, and practical piety.

(a) As stated above, the Oxford men were inspired by the desire to uphold the spiritual and independent character of the Church. In order to achieve this end, the doctrine of Apostolic Succession was made the cornerstone of the whole structure. This

---

[7] *Remains,* I, 387.
[8] *Ibid.* I, xiii.
[9] Cf. Ollard, *op. cit.,* p. 16 ff

idea is clearly brought out in *Tract 1* written by Newman, *Thoughts on the Ministerial Commission*. Succession, as a historical fact, Newman tries to prove in *Tract 7, The Episcopal Church Apostolical*, while the proof from the Scriptures is advanced by B. Harrison in *Tract 24, The Scripture View of the Apostolic Commission*. As to the standard by which all doctrine should be judged, the maxim of Vincent of Lerins, *quod semper, quod ubique, quod ab omnibus*, was given a new and vital application. The purest form of the Church was believed to be found in an earlier phase of the Anglican Church and in the primitive Church of the Greek Fathers. Consequently, the Oxford men were borb anti-Roman and anti-Protestant (*Tracts 15* and *20*). Their ideal was the *via media* which will steer the ship of the Church safely through the Scylla of Roman ecclesiastical infallibility and the Charybdis of Protestant individualism. While they were unanimous at this time in rejecting the claims of Rome, they varied considerably in their estimation of the Reformation. Most outspoken in his criticism was Froude, who says of himself that he hated the Reformation, "The Reformation was a limb badly set; it must be broken again to be righted."[10] "The faith once delivered to the saints" is none other than the Apostolic and Nicene Creeds, in comparison with which the other creeds have but a secondary importance. The chief exponents of this static view of the Church, which rejects every development in doctrine, are Rose and Palmer, and later Pusey when it fell to him to gather the forces of the wrecked movement.

Alongside of this static view goes the progressive view of the Church in which Newman took the lead. Newman, in speaking of the prophetical tradition, maintains that "Almighty God has placed in the Church first Apostles, secondarily Prophets. Apostles rule and preach, Prophets expound. Prophets or Doctors are the interpreters of the Revelation. Their teaching is a vast system pervading the Church." Besides, it is this prophetical tradition that imparts doctrine, while in Scripture we have only the proof of it.[11]

It is evident that we are here confronted with a view of the Church which is capable of leading its exponent over into the fold of the Roman Church. In 1844 Newman published his *Essay on the Development of Christian Doctrine*. In addition his genuine passion for an ascetic ideal of life based on obedience to authority served as a further incentive to accept finally the Church of Rome as the ideal of his life.

(b) The statements on the sacraments in the Thirty-nine Articles plainly reflect that a compromise was sought to harmonize the Lutheran view with Calvin's. In general, the Tractarians came nearer to the historical meaning of these statements than their opponents, the Evangelicals, who had yielded to a Zwinglian conception of the sacraments. Baptism was pronounced unreservedly as the means of regeneration by Pusey (*Tracts 67, 68, 69*). Post-baptismal sins are effaced by repentance and penance as a "plank after shipwreck."[12] As to the Eucharist, the Tractarians rejected the Roman teaching of transubstantiation as well as Luther's view of the presence of Christ's body under the bread. The Oxford men taught the virtual presence of Christ. In this they remained true to the Anglican tradition. However, they departed from it when Pusey, Palmer, and others taught the *manducatio indignorum*. One other trend in their think-

---

[10] *Remains*, I, 433 f.

[11] Cf. *Apologia*, edition of 1921, pp. 108 ff.; also in Brilioth, *op. cit.*, pp. 180 ff., 260 ff.

[12] Brilioth, *op. cit.*, p. 312, calls attention to the fact that Luther was bitterly opposed to the idea that sin should have the ability to suspend the power of baptism, Weim. ed., 7, 529.

ing is important: the efficacy of the sacraments does not rest, as with Luther, in the promise of Christ, but in the priestly character of the ministrant imparted to him by the rite of ordination.[13]

(c) According to Lutheran thinking the doctrine of justification is the touchstone of a man's theology. The Church has produced three types of this doctrine: the prophetic or forensic, the mystic or sacramental, and the ethical conceptions. Within Anglican theology both the forensic and sacramental views have an equal right to run along side by side. In the nineteenth century Joseph Milner, the Church historian, was an ardent defender of the Lutheran forensic view, while Alexander Knox was opposed to it and saw in justification "the acquisition of a condition of inward not merely outward and formal righteousness, a moral change." [14] The Lutheran view was so detestable to W. G. Ward that Lutheranism was to him "an abstract doctrine, which cannot, we verily believe, be held consistently even by the devils . . ." which is "more fundamentally at variance with our higher and better nature than Atheism itself." [15] Newman in his *Lectures on Justification* (1838) again extolled the Anglican view as a *via media* between the Lutheran conception which, in his eyes, is false and the Roman idea which, as he claims, is incomplete, but which is complete in the teaching of Augustine. He argues for the idea of justification through baptism, not by faith as the "primary instrument" (Lutheran) without the exercise or even presence of love; nor by obedient works (Rome) alone, but by an acquittal of the sinner which results in actual holiness of life. According to Newman, justification becomes a quality, substance, which changes man. It is the *Christus in nobis* who justifies. This indwelling of Christ is effected by the sacraments, first by baptism, then by the Eucharist for "as Holy Communion conveys a more awful presence of God than Holy Baptism, so it must be the instrument of a higher justification" (p. 169). Man in an ever-increasing measure appropriates the nature of God. The Incarnation of the Logos is perpetuated through the sacraments in all believers. In this inner mystic union Newman sees a bulwark not only against the Protestant conception of an outward imputation of divine righteousness but also against the Roman teaching of a human merit. Like all advocates of the mystic sacramental conception of justification, Newman emphatically rejected the doctrine of "assurance." [16]

(d) To the Oxford men the realities of Faith form a *mysterium tremendum.* "Awfulness," as the vivid feeling of the presence and majesty of God, is a catchword of their religion. The doctrines of the Trinity and Incarnation, therefore, are specially dear to them. An earnest desire to strive daily after holiness of heart and life marks the piety of these men. Right belief must result in right action. Action is the criterion of faith.[17] Religious discipline is highly praised, and the fast days as prescribed in the Prayer Book, were early made a central point in the Oxford Movement.[18] Through Pusey whom Brilioth calls "the *doctor mysticus* in earlier Neo-Anglicanism" (p. 296),

[13] *Tracts 25-28, 81;* Pusey's sermon, *The Holy Eucharist a Comfort to the Penitent,* 1843. *"The Christian Life in Christ"; "Heaven the Christian's Home,"* in *Sermons during the Seasons from Advent to Whitsuntide* (2 vols., 1848-53). For a complete orientation of the Anglican doctrine of the Eucharist see Darwell Stone, *A History of the Doctrine of the Holy Eucharist,* 1909, II, 107 ff.; also *Doctrine in the Church of England,* 1938, pp. 120 ff.

[14] Brilioth, *op. cit.,* p. 279.

[15] *Ideal of a Christian Church,* 1844, p. 305.

[16] *Parochial and Plain Sermons,* IV, 127; on the whole subject of Brilioth, *op. cit.,* pp. 274 ff.

[17] Froude, *Remains,* I, part 2, 76.

[18] Pusey, *Tract 18.*

the mystic contemplation of the Cross was introduced into Tractarian piety. On the other hand, a piety with so strong an emphasis on the ascetic ideals may easily lead to Pelagian tendencies. Froude, for instance, was actually in danger of reducing divine grace to a minimum in the process of sanctification.[19]

5. *And now a brief word of criticism will be expected.* The importance of the Oxford Movement is in the realm of practical religion. In contrast to the older State-Church conception of Hooker, this Movement has made the Church of England conscious of its spiritual foundation and commission. It further has made the Church mindful of its Catholic heritage. It has given new weight to the idea of a united Christian Church on the basis of the *consensus quinquesaecularis.*[20] The World Conference on Faith and Order is a legitimate child of the Oxford Movement. Through the interest of the Oxford men in the early Church, the Greek Fathers became living realities to the English public and through the study of the Greek Fathers, in turn, English theology became orientated on the incarnation as the center of Christian doctrine. As to the scientific methods, the Movement was scholastic, pre-critical and pre-scientific. It revived a sense of worship, which has borne rich fruit in English pre-Raphaelite art. One of its finest features is the social passion which it infused into the life of the Established Church.

Last—but not least—the question is in order: were the Oxford men still Protestants? If the doctrine of justification is made the touchstone of all theology, it cannot be denied that these men definitely crossed the line from Protestantism into Catholicism. A theology which considers justification a process by which man is made whole by virtue of an infusion of a divine substance, and which makes the sacraments the main channels by which this divine medicine is infused and which, furthermore, sees in the ordination of the ministrant the guarantee of the efficacy of the sacraments, has surrendered the historical meaning of the Thirty-nine Articles as well as the very principles of the Reformation.

The Ritualistic Movement of the later decades was not started by the early Oxford leaders. Although it received its impetus from the Movement, it was born outside the university.

---

[19] *Remains,* I, part 2, 152 ff.
[20] See J. L. Neve in this Volume. Chap. I, 2 (on Calixtus).

Chapter Five

PHILOSOPHY AND THE NEGATIVE MOVEMENT

Literature: W. R. SORLEY, *A History of English Philosophy*, 1921; RUDOLF METZ, *A Hundred Years of English Philosophy*, 1938.

1. In Chapter Three we have touched upon *the critical and idealistic tenets* in the system of Coleridge. The same ideas lie at the basis of Carlyle's world of thought. The idealism of these two thinkers was then met by the nineteenth century representatives of Lockean empiricism, the critical philosophy of Hamilton, and the agnostic movement in its various forms. There followed then the positivistic and evolutionary philosophy of Herbert Spencer and the idealistic-evolutionary philosophy of the Neo-Hegelians. In this Chapter we shall briefly discuss a few of the philosophers and intellectual notables connected with these movements, save the Neo-Hegelians. We shall reserve for Chapter Ten the critical discussion of those thinkers.

The sole purpose of this Chapter as well as of Chapter Ten is to provide the student with a bird's-eye view of philosophical thought in Great Britain. No claim of original investigation is made by this writer as to most of the characters discussed in these chapters.

2. THOMAS CARLYLE (1795-1881) was the eldest son of a Scotch mason and was of puritanic heritage. These *early puritanic influences* touched his life even after he had given up the dogmas of Calvinism. While he was a student in Edinburgh, the study of Gibbon and Hume made him a confirmed skeptic. He was unhappy in this negative philosophy, and while rejecting the traditional faith, his soul found freedom in a religion that put a soul in the universe. His moral consciousness stood out and became the dynamic which led him to deliver great blows against the mechanical interpretation of the materialists. Pfleiderer says of him (p. 313): "It is not any want of religion, not frivolous skepticism, but rather a good piece of old Scotch Puritanism, combined with modern critical idealism, which makes him ruthlessly indignant at every form of religious cant, at all ecclesiasticism that has become external form and convention. Yet, what is almost more repulsive and hateful to him than the latter are the empty and windy negations of frivolous skepticism, atheism, and materialism." These men who were trying to bottle up the universe in their scientific test tubes were as obnoxious to him as the men who were trying to limit religion to a particular interpretation of a creed. Creeds, whether religious or scientific, received his blows. His is an ethical idealism after the manner of Fichte, Herder, and Goethe. To feel God in one's own soul and to keep in mind that God is not Out There, but in the soul, was the deep religious incentive of Carlyle. He is not a theologian nor a churchman, but a religious thinker who conceives of the Divine in a broad general religious concept. God was to him not a personal Being, "and still less a Father in Heaven." [1] His idea of God, then, is pantheistic. He speaks of God as of Eternities, Immensities, and Veracities. Coupled with this Spinozistic pantheism we note in him the remnants of the puritanic

---

[1] Tulloch, p. 204.

Calvinism of his childhood. Force, law, duty, and order are great ideas with him. These puritanic virtues received new vitality in him through his intimate knowledge of and great love for German philosophy and literature. "Carlyle, for the first time, made us alive to the power, beauty and genuine depth of the meaning there was in the great German poets and writers, their freer and richer views of life, and their higher and more comprehensive canons of criticism." [2] His philosophy is contained mainly in *Sartor Resartus* (1834), *Heroes and Hero Worship* (1841), and *Past and Present* (1843). This influence of Carlyle meant, of course, admitting into the religious expression of British thought and literature much of the language of the world, which was characteristic of German Idealism as a movement in that age of German classicism.[3]

3. *The Lockean philosophy of the eighteenth century was handed on* by Bentham and attained new significance by the two Mills, father and son.

According to JEREMY BENTHAM (1748-1832) man, in all his actions, is moved by an innate desire for happiness. Happiness is the ultimate aim of all human actions and the ultimate standard of morality. "The greatest possible happiness for the greatest possible number." [4]

JAMES MILL (1773-1836) conceived of God after the fashion of the eighteenth century Deists according to whom God stands in a purely external relation to the world. Religion is, in his eyes, an outgrowth of the wickedness of the human mind. The most perfect conception of wickedness, according to his view, was called by all ages and nations "God." No wonder that a man who held such misconceived notions about God provided for his son a strictly non-religious education. As to his ideal of education, his son, John Stuart, says of him, "His fundamental doctrine was the formation of all human character by circumstances, through the universal principle of association and the consequent unlimited possibility of improving the moral and intellectual condition of mankind." [5]

JOHN STUART MILL (1806-1873) became a still greater champion of the experience-philosophy of the nineteenth century. All knowledge, according to him, is derived from observation and a generalized experience of sense. The law of scientific induction is universal and unalterable. There is, in his system, no place for metaphysics and the idea of "innate objects" of the mind. His *System of Deductive and Inductive Logic* (1843) became the standard guide in the field of methodology of natural science. As a political economist John Stuart Mill holds that protection of possessions and earning of the individual is the ultimate aim of government. While the conditions of production are controlled by physical laws, the way of distribution is dependent on human arrangement and customs which are changeable. Mill is a thoroughgoing utilitarian and helped much to liberalize the political institutions of England. (*Principles of Political Economy*, 1848). The *Utility of Religion* (posthumously edited in 1874) is a work in which Mill contends for the thesis that in its early days religion was a good thing to add sanction to law. Since we, however, have outgrown these earlier days, religion persists like poetry, answering to the higher cravings of man. Religion has utility, but we cannot be sure that it is the expression of what *is*. In his essay on *Theism* (also posthumously edited

---

[2] Tulloch, *op. cit.,* p. 194.
[3] For a fuller view of this situation we refer the reader to J. L. Neve, in this volume, on "German Idealism," pp. 98 ff.
[4] Cf. Sorley, *op. cit.,* pp. 206 ff.
[5] *Autobiography*, 1874, p. 108.

in 1874) his inquiry is not simply with regard to the utility of religion but concerning the truth of religious teachings. Though still being far removed from orthodox Christianity, it led him to the acceptance of the probability of some fundamental suppositions of faith such, for instance, as the creation by an Intelligent Mind. The problem of harmonizing the suffering of man with divine providence, he tried to solve by professing belief in a "finite God" who is love but not almighty.[6]

4. In SIR WILLIAM HAMILTON'S (1788-1856) system we discern *Kantian criticism* grafted upon Thomas Reed's "common sense philosophy." In the eighteenth century, in opposition to Hume, Locke, and Berkeley, Reed had held to the conception of innate principles, metaphysical and moral. According to him, sight and touch are only the occasion, not the material of human perception. Hence the belief in a metaphysical world is with him an original datum of "common sense." This term does not mean to him "vulgar opinion," but a belief "common to rational beings." Also the moral principles, such as freedom of will and deliverance of conscience, are "first principles" laid down in the constitution of man.

Upon this background Hamilton contended against Kant's belief that practical reason can establish the veracity of God, freedom and immortality. The Unconditional is neither conceivable nor knowable. Kant has stopped too short in his criticism. The philosopher must either rest in agnosticism or call on supernatural revelation. This conception is essentially the position of the German philosopher Jacobi, who claimed to be at heart a Christian but with his reason a heathen.[7]

These ideas became the basis of a dogmatic supernaturalism in the system of HENRY MANSEL (1820-1871), a disciple of Hamilton. Notwithstanding the fact that man cannot know the Infinite, it does not mean that the Infinite does not exist. If by thought and inquiry we cannot reach it, we are to accept the Bible and its revelation as authority. If reason is incapable of solving the philosophical problems, it is not justified in rejecting the religious beliefs or revelation because they are inconceivable.[8]

5. *But this philosophical agnosticism proved to be a dangerous two-edged sword* aiding the cause of the negative movement. First, upon this agnosticism, in the course of the next decade, MATTHEW ARNOLD (1822-1888) based his ethical idealism. In our age of scientific investigation, Arnold claims, nothing will stand which cannot be proved by experience. The old authoritarian belief in the supernatural elements of Christianity is no longer tenable. Yet the true spirit of religion has nothing to do with supernatural dogma. Religion is a matter not of belief but of conduct; it is "morality touched with emotion." For the Christian conception of a personal God, Arnold substituted the impersonal ethical idea of "the eternal power, not ourselves which makes for righteousness."[9]

This purely ethical conception of religion, however, did not satisfy SIR JOHN ROBERT SEELEY (1834-1895). He therefore developed the ethical idealism of Arnold into the broader view of esthetical idealism. Whatever is beautiful, good, and true in nature and man should be, according to him, the object of religious worship.[10]

[6] On Bentham and the Utilitarians see W. R. Sorley, *op. cit.*, pp. 206 ff.

[7] *Discussions on Philosophy and Literature*, 1852; *Lectures on Logic and Metaphysics*, 4 vols., posthumously edited by Mansel and Veitch, 1859 ff.

[8] *The Limits of Religious Thought*, 1852, and subsequent editions.

[9] *Saint Paul and Protestantism*, 1870; *Literature and Dogma*, 1873; *God and the Bible*, 1875; *Last Essays in Church and Religion*, 1877.

[10] *Ecce Homo*, 1865; *Natural Religion*, 1882.

The chief representative of philosophical agnosticism was HERBERT SPENCER 1820-1903). His significance lies in the fact that he made the idea of evolution the ominant view of philosophy. Evolution and Dissolution, working jointly, consti-ate, according to him, the entire process through which things pass.[11] He is agreed ith Hamilton "that the reality existing behind all appearances is and must ever be, nknown" (p. 57). The truth which the various religions claim to represent, is but ne; therefore, he argues, that truth must be looked for not in those points in which ae various religions disagree but in that element which they hold in common with each ther. Furthermore, since there are not two truths, the one religious and the other cientific, "our aim must be," he states, "to co-ordinate the seemingly opposed convictions hich Religion and Science embody" (p. 17 f.). The natural sciences have revealed he Persistence of Force" to be the abiding element in all phenomena. While these, in hich Force manifests itself, may change, Force itself always remains unchanged. "The ersistence of Force," then, is the philosophical and universal truth (p. 231), not a efinite conception of the Infinite, the Absolute, or the First Cause.

6. *Other critical writers of this age* who sought to combine religion and morality ith the severest criticism of orthodox Christianity were C. G. Hennell, who wrote *In Inquiry Concerning the Origin of Christianity* (1838), Ch. Bray, author of *The hilosophy of Necessity* (1841), J. A. Froude, Francis Newman, brother of J. H. New-aan, George Eliot (Mary Ann Evans) who translated Strauss's *Life of Jesus* and Feuer-ach's *Essence of Christianity* into English.

---

[11] *First Principles,* American edition, p. **457**.

Chapter Six

THE CONSOLIDATION OF LIBERAL FORCES

1. Nineteenth century Latitudinarianism is usually comprehended under the rath
vague term *"Broad Church."* The name "Broad Church" was first used by Arthur
Stanley, Dean of Westminster, in an article in the *Edinburgh Review* in July, 1850, c
the Gorham controversy. Gorham, a divine of the Established Church, who had deni
the doctrine of baptismal regeneration, was refused installation in a parish of the Exet
diocese. The decision of the Bishop, however, was reversed by the Judicial Commissic
of the Privy Council. As a result the Archdeacons Manning and R. I. Wilberforce, ar
other divines and laymen seceded from the Anglican Church and went over to Rom
In this article of the *Edinburgh Review* Stanley pleaded for a liberal church polity, fi
the Church of England was, as he said, "by the very condition of its being neither Hig
nor Low, but Broad." The term then was used by him not in any party sense, but in
characterization of the nature of the Church of England. A few years later, howeve
there was published an article in the same periodical by J. J. Conybeare and "here th
name was distinctly applied in a party sense as denoting a succession of liberal no le
than Anglo-Catholic and Evangelical teachers, which have always prevailed in th
Church." [1]

2. The Broad Church really began with Coleridge. It was given impetus by th
Liberal School at Oriel. This party sought to preserve the ethical postulates of Chri
tianity and to give room for broad thinking. It is due to this school that the soci
implications of Christianity were brought to the front.

As regards its ecclesiastical polity, A. M. Fairbairn says that the Broad Church w;
as "civil" in its basis as the old High Church party. And in comparing its polity wit
that of the Oxford men, he makes this fitting remark: "The modern Broad Church is
theory as to how the old connection of the civil and ecclesiastical states may be mair
tained under a democracy; the modern High Church is a theory as to how the Churc
may, while living within and under a democracy, yet be independent of it. What occa
sioned the rise of the two were the same events differently regarded; love of the libera
ism which had gained the ascendency in the State made the Broad Church, fear of :
created the High. [2]

3. The first man to whom our attention is called is FREDERICK DENISON MAURIC
(1805-1872). He was first a Unitarian. He was a friend of J. Sterling and an admirin
student of Coleridge. Add to the Coleridgian and Unitarian influences a third, Erskine
writing (see Chapter Seven) and you have the three influences that made Maurice. H
says, "I was led to ask myself what a gospel to mankind must be; whether it must nc
have some other ground than the fall of Adam, and the sinful nature of man. I wa
helped much in finding an answer to the question by Mr. Erskine's books . . . and by th
sermons of Mr. Campbell. The English Church I thought was the witness for tha

---

[1] Tulloch, *op. cit.*, p. 261.
[2] *The Place of Christ in Modern Theology*, 1916, pp. 177 f. By permission of Scribner's, publishers.

iversal redemption which the Scotch Presbyterians had declared incompatible with
eir confessions." [3] Three years later, in January, 1834, he became a minister of the
urch of England.

The thought of Maurice is based on two fundamental principles: The first is that
ery man is in Christ. Maurice begins with the divine capacity of man, and not with
e Fall. Man, as a creature of God through Christ, is a child of God. He does not
ed to become a child of God, either by baptism (High Church) or by conversion
Evangelicals). [4]

The second great principle for which Maurice contended is the idea of Christian
ity. Like him, his mother and his three sisters had left the Unitarians and embraced
e theology of the Anglican and Baptist churches. What kept the family apart? Not
e affirmatives of their religion, as he argued. If men could only forget their negatives
d quit quarreling about things divisive, there are left the essentials around which men
uld unite. This desire for unity Maurice shared with Newman and the other leaders
the Oxford Movement. But unlike them, he did not seek this unity in dogma and
urch ritual, rather in the fundamental positive principles which underlie the Christian
ith. This note runs through both of his notable works, *The Religions of the World*
1847), and *Moral and Metaphysical Philosophy* (1861). As to the doctrine of the
tonement, he denied the idea of an "artificial substitution." "Christ satisfied the Father
presenting the image of His own holiness and love." "He bore the sins of the world
the sense that He felt them with that anguish with which only a perfectly pure and
oly being, which is also a perfectly sympathizing and gracious being, can feel the sins
others." [5] The reader will note how much this view is in harmony with the "moral
onception" of the Atonement of the Abelard tradition. In 1853 Maurice was expelled
om his professorship in King's College at London, in a dispute on eternal condemna-
on. Following Erskine, he interpreted the Greek word *aionios* (eternal) as denoting
ality not duration. It is, according to Maurice, applied to God and to things extra
mporal. [6]

The characteristic traits in Maurice's teaching must be understood in the light of
e idealistic philosophy of Plato. All "reality," according to this view, is recapitulated
nder one head: Christ who is the divine idea of humanity. By His incarnation He
ecame the historical Saviour Jesus. Apart from Him, no one has independent existence.
he difference between a believer and unbeliever is that the latter does not know or
cknowledge the truth. Consequently, the Atonement cannot involve the idea of substi-
ation, for Christ and humanity are one. Christ only helps man to overcome his separa-
on from God by revealing the love of the Father. [7]

It was Maurice's *Kingdom of Christ* (1838) that brought him and CHARLES
INGSLEY (1810-1875) together, and it was the social note of the Gospel that cemented
e friendship of these two men. In his historical novel *Hypatia*, Kingsley implies a
eiled warning against the fanaticism and intolerance of the Oxford men. His repeated

---

[3] *Life of F. D. Maurice* by his son F. Maurice, 1884.
[4] In a letter to his mother, *Life*, I, 155 f.
[5] *Theological Essays*, 1853; *The Doctrine of Sacrifice*, 1854.
[6] *The Word "Eternal,"* 1863.
[7] Cf. Pfleiderer, *op. cit.*, pp. 373 ff.; and the German theologian Dorner, in the present volume, pp. 143 f.
f. also R. S. Franks, *A History of the Doctrine of the Work of Christ*, vol. II, 387 ff., and the recent study by
harles Jenkins, *Frederick Denison Maurice and the New Reformation*, 1938.

attacks upon the insincerity of Roman Catholic writers in general, and on Newman i particular,[8] prompted Newman to publish his *Apologia* (1864).

When we come to F. W. ROBERTSON (1819-1875) we have a man who wa keenly alive to the needs of his days. Robertson was the greatest preacher England eve produced, and in his sermons we have a very penetrating analysis of the meaning of th Gospel as he saw it.[9] Robertson did not reject the dogma and creeds of the Churc However, he was not concerned with the historical meaning of their formulas but trie to reach at the "underlying truth" which they express. For, in his view, the whole divin verity, no dogma can express adequately. As to content his theology clearly bears humanistic stamp. God is Father because He is the Creator! Neither baptism nor fait make God our Father, he says. The paternity of God is authoritatively declared b baptism and personally apprehended by faith.

Among other theologians who were "broad" in their thinking there should b mentioned Dean STANLEY (1815-1888), who was in full sympathy with Thoma Arnold's view of the identity of Church and State, and Bishop ALEXANDER EWING, t whom the "free air" of history and life was truly congenial.[10]

4. Looking back over our period *we see five forces at work:* the Evangelica party, the early Orthodox party, Liberalism and Latitudinarianism which were converg ing into a Broad Church party, the Tractarian movement, and a Naturalistic movemer which had its basis in an empirical philosophy. We can understand the climax of a these forces in the *Essays and Reviews.* Pfleiderer (p. 387) likens the year 1860 i which the *Essays and Reviews* appeared to the year 1835 in German theology. He com pares the storm which this collection of theological essays evoked in England with th indignation in Germany over Strauss' *Leben Jesu.* The promoter and planner of th' series of essays was Henry Briston Wilson. He was Bampton Lecturer in 1851, *Th Communion of Saints.* The seven authors, however, wrote independently of one anothe The book was purposed, according to its Preface, by the desire of attempting "to illus trate the advantage derivable to the cause of moral and religious truth, from a fre handling, in a becoming spirit, of subjects peculiarly liable to suffer by the repetition c conventional language, and from traditional methods of treatment." This publicatio was a milestone in the ascendency of theological liberalism in England.

The collection opens with the essay of Frederick Temple on "The Education of th World." Following Lessing, Temple maintains that there are to be distinguished thre stages in the development of the human race, corresponding to childhood, youth, an maturity. The education during these different stages is met by rules (the Law), exampl (the Son of Man), and principle (the Spirit). We today must study the Bible not a children but as men. A certain ambiguity prevails in the terminology as to the historicit of the miracles and the implication of Scripture authority.

The second essay by Rowland Williams on "Bunsen's Biblical Research" is mor aggressive. Baron von Bunsen, a sincere Christian and lay theologian, had been Prussia minister at the Vatican and London (1841-1854). He had welcomed the results of th Biblical criticism of Ewald at Goettingen without relinquishing the essentials of th Christian faith. In this essay the distinction between a natural and revealed religion i

---

[8] *What Then Does Dr. Newman Mean?*
[9] *Sermons,* 4 vols., 1861.
[10] Cf. Tulloch, *op. cit.,* p. 322.

bscured. On the whole, the author adopts the results of so-called "higher criticism"; he Pentateuch is a gradual growth, not the work of one man; Isaiah, chapters 41-66 are ot Isaiah's work; the narrative of Jonah "contains late legend founded on misconcepion"; the book of Daniel was written in the second century B.C.; the Letter to the Iebrews is not Pauline, but was very likely written by Apollos; and the Second Letter f Peter is unauthentic.

Next comes Baden Powell's essay on "The Study of Evidences of Christianity." The uthor was Savilian Professor of Astronomy at Oxford, and believed whole-heartedly in volution. He hailed Darwin's book on *The Origin of Species* as the dawn of a new lay in the study of the development of mankind. As to the problem of the supernatural n history, this essay was the most destructive of all.

The fourth essay on "The National Church" by Wilson himself, pleads for a liberalzation of doctrine and discipline in the Church of England. Subscription to the Thirtynine Articles should be abolished. His reference to "the dark patches of human passion nd error which form a partial crust upon it (the Bible), and the bright center of piritual truth within" (p. 177), caused much resentment.

C. W. Goodwin, a layman, wrote on "The Mosaic Cosmogony," contending that he scientific conceptions of the author of Genesis cannot be reconciled with scientific acts.

Mark Pattison, Rector of Lincoln College, Oxford, contributed the sixth essay on 'Tendencies of Religious Thought in England, 1688-1750." He pointed out the continuty of religious thought and the need for revision of former beliefs.

The last essay is written by Benjamin Jowett on "The Interpretation of Scripture." Contrary to the custom of the past, he says, the Bible should be interpreted like any other book. The actual nature of the Bible, which is not inerrant with respect to historcal and scientific facts, should determine our conception of inspiration. Historical ympathy is required of the interpreter; but he must be cautious not to make the dogmatic development in the Church the measure by which the Bible should be judged. Though interpreted like any other book, Jowett believed that the Bible "will still remain unlike any other book" (p. 375).

The volume created no small sensation in England. Low Church and High Church men alike united in a common attack upon its writers. After a lengthy trial the book was condemned by both Houses of Convocation. Its opponents contended that the critical spirit of *Essays and Reviews* was subversive to the very essence of faith. It may be true that some of the facts stated in the volume have now become a commonplace with theologians. Yet the conservatives were right when they felt that the tenor of the book was not constructive, but rather destructive in its criticism.

Chapter Seven

SCOTTISH THEOLOGY

1. *Scottish theology has been always slower moving than English theology.* Whil Scotland contends assiduously for "the faith once delivered to the saints," she has als produced naturalists whose philosophical implications are defiant of religion. Tulloch who was Scottish himself, calls it a superficial judgment to suppose that the Calvinisti creed of the country has remained unshaken under all its mental progress. "There ha always, from the days of Hume, survived in Scotland a vein of naturalistic speculation (p. 126 f.). Sir John Leslie and Thomas Brown might be pointed out as naturalists i the earlier part of the nineteenth century. The writers in the *Edinburgh Review* wer naturalistically inclined. In the early nineteenth century no one represented thi type of thought so ably as did George Combe. In 1825 appeared his *System o Phrenology* and in 1828 *The Constitution of Man.* In line with him were William an Robert Chambers. Combe was attempting to combine a theism with views that woul lead to materialism. The circulation of his *Phrenology* in England caused great unre among the Evangelicals. Those early days are spoken of in the *Christian Instructo* the literary organ of Scottish orthodoxy, as an age of "modern heresies." The mos conspicuous leaders of those "heresies" were Erskine and Campbell.

2. THOMAS ERSKINE (1788-1880) *was not a professional theologian,* but a juris His theological thought revolves around two main conceptions: (1) He is concerne almost exclusively with the internal aspect of religion. Christianity is not a matter o mere conventional or historical forms, not a matter of creeds, dogma, and history. Th question concerning the historical veracity of the Gospel narrative is altogether o minor importance in comparison with man's inward spiritual experience of God. (2 Salvation, according to him, is universal. As forgiveness is already obtained for ever sinner in the mission and death of Christ, so the love of God will not rest until the los are found, and till He has gathered together in one all things in Christ. Christ came he says, as the head of a new humanity. His sufferings manifested the character of Go and the character of man's rebellion. The Cross is an open vindication of the holines and truth of God, "against which the Fall was an offence." Therefore God was please with the sufferings of Christ. But He was also pleased because they exhibited th triumph over the powers of evil. The Gospel now is the declaration of the truth tha the human race is pardoned in Christ.

Erskine's main writings are *Internal Evidence of the Truth of Revealed Religio* (1820), *The Unconditional Freeness of the Gospel* (1828), and *The Brazen Serpen* (1831).

The influence of Erskine and Coleridge became very pronounced in JOHN McLEO CAMPBELL (1800-1872). In 1831 he was removed from office in the Church of Scot land for his heretical conception of the Atonement. Although Campbell went beyon the so-called "moral view," he regarded the suffering and death of Christ only a conditio by which God became mindful of Christ's expiatory confession of the sins of the world is confession was, in his own words, "a perfect Amen in humanity to the judgment God on the sin of man." [1] This is what he calls the "retrospective" aspect of the onement. Next, he lays great stress on the "prospective" aspect of the work of Christ. Christ is the "revealer of the Father," He also is the "revealer of man," disclosing the estimable preciousness which was hidden in humanity (p. 160) and imparting to it at same atttitude to the holiness and love of God which was realized in His own rifice.

In its "prospective" aspect the fundamental agreement of Campbell's view with e theories of Schleiermacher and Ritschl is very obvious, while in its "retrospective" pect it offers a point of contact with Jonathan Edwards, who had advanced the thought at a *perfect repentance* on man's part would have sufficed to satisfy for sin. Christ's rk is that of *vicarious penitence,* not of vicarious punishment. Later this line of ought was further developed by R. C. Moberly. See on him p. 251. In the Lutheran mp we may refer to Thomasius of Erlangen, who likewise compares, though in a odified sense, Christ's expiation of sin to an act of penitence.[2]

The General Assembly of 1831 not only deposed Campbell but also took action ainst the eschatological fancies of E. IRVING (1792-1834). Irving never was a real inker, but as the founder and as one of the "angels" of the Catholic-Apostolic Church will be remembered in the history of the nineteenth century.

3. *At the time of the liberal movement,* a fresh accession of evangelical life gan to pour into the Church of Scotland. First there is THOMAS CHALMERS (1780-847). He was a great churchman and did his work along ecclesiastical lines rather an theological lines. He was a great orator of the Evangelical school. A friend of skine, he shared many of his views. Chalmers helped gain back to the evangelical ing the power of leadership and prestige which had been lost to the power of the moderate wing" led by F. W. Robertson and Principal Hill. In 1810 Chalmers blished his well-known paper on Christianity in the *Edinburgh Encyclopedia.* In this per he denounced the ability of natural reason to judge the revelation given in Chris-nity. Reason might have a say about external evidences but of the internal evidences Christianity reason has nothing to say. The article met the severe criticism of Duncan earns of Aberdeen. Mearns replied that religion must meet the rational needs of man fore it can be accepted as divine.[3]

The true interpreter of the mind of Scotland as well as of the differences between e new and the old theology was ANDREW THOMPSON (1779-1831). He was inferior Chalmers but was the most zealous defender of the works of the traditional orthodoxy the Scottish Church.

Besides the works of Erskine and Campbell, there was another book that brought rest into the staunch orthodoxy of Scottish Calvinism. We refer to the work called he *True Plan of a Living Temple* published in 1830. It was anti-Calvinistic and ressed the inherent goodness in the world and the individual. It criticized Calvin, unyan, and Wesley. When T. Wright (1785-1855) became known as its writer, was removed from his country parish at Berthwick.

---

[1] *Nature of the Atonement,* 2nd. edition, 1867, pp. 135, 160.
[2] *Christi Person und Werk,* Vol. II (1888), p. 54. On Maurice and Campbell, compare Franks, *op. cit.,* 387 ff.
[3] Cf. Tulloch, *op. cit.,* p. 134 f.

4. *As we enter the next decade, 1840-1850,* we find it a momentous age for Scotti Presbyterianism. The opposition to the legal exercise of patronage led to the withdraw of 541 ministers from the Establishment and to the organization of the Free Church Scotland in 1843. In May, 1841, the United Presbyterian Church was formed. Th church body originated in a merger between the United Secession Church of 1733 a the Relief Church of 1752. During this age Carlyle was at the zenith of his influen and in this same decade we have the influence of John Stuart Mill.

The *Burnett Lectures* of Thompson and Tulloch on *Theism* appeared in 1855. It interesting to note how in Thompson's lectures the compatibility of a progressive theo of creation, from the scientific standpoint, with theism is put forth, in connection wi the then famous work on *The Vestiges of Creation* (1844) by Robert Chambe Thompson thought that much remained to be done before it could be said that a theo of development could be "applied to living beings." He little thought that Darwi *Origin of Species* would appear in 1859.

5. *Around 1860, in Scottish theology,* we are in the midst of the time when ROBE LEE exercised a widening influence on men's mind in things liturgical and hymnologic as NORMAN MACLEOD did in matters of a more rational Sunday observance. In 18 R. S. CANDLISH delivered the first series of the Cunningham Lectures on the *Fatherho of God,* in which he maintained a particular and adoptive theory. This was opposed I THOMAS J. CRAWFORD, to whom the Fatherhood was universal. George Smeato *Doctrine of the Atonement* began to appear in 1868 (second volume in 1870). It w followed by Crawford's *Doctrine of the Holy Scriptures* respecting the Atonement 1871.

WILLIAM ROBERTSON SMITH published his article on the Bible in the *Encyclopea Britannica* in 1876. Smith contended for the position of the Wellhausen school, wi the result that he was removed from his professorship in the Free Church College Aberdeen (1881). The attempt of Smith to introduce Wellhausen to the English spea ing world, prompted statesmen, bishops, professors, and moderators to contend agair him.[4] The deposition of David Macrae from the ministry of the United Presbyteri Church took place in 1897 in consequence of divergence from the confessional teachi on matters of retribution.

The greatest apologist of the times was ALEXANDER B. BRUCE (1831-1899). 1874 this great Glasgow theologian wrote *The Humiliation of Christ in Its Physic Ethical, and Soteriological Aspects.* Bruce in this book follows the view of the Erlang theologian Hofmann that Christ entered into the condition of the human race whi lay under the wrath of God so that He felt in Himself the effects of the divi wrath though He, in His relation to God, was not the object of it. The value of tl sacrifice of Christ was equal to His divine dignity, multiplied by His perfect obedien boundless love, and His sufferings. Later Bruce wrote his great work *Apologeti* (1902). Also *The Training of the Twelve* (1871) is significant and has gone throu several editions.

6. *At the close of the nineteenth century* JOHN TULLOCH (1823-1886), JOH CUNNINGHAM (1819-1893), GEORGE MATHESON (1842-1906), and ROBERT FLII (1838-1910) held the leadership of thought in the Established Church of Scotland,

---

[4] Cf. Vollrath, *op. cit.,* p. 48 ff.

ontributing to a liberalization of Scottish Calvinism. The principal work of Tulloch
; *Rational Theology and Christian Philosophy in England in the Seventeenth Century*
2 vols. 1872). Matheson wrote *Studies on the Portrait of Christ* (2 vols. 1899 f.), of
vhich 11,000 copies were sold within the time of one year. Flint, who wrote *Theism
nd Antitheistic Theories* (1877) and *Agnosticism* (1903), opposed the prevailing
gnostic interpretation of Kant, holding that agnosticism is not a corollary of Kantian
riticism.

7. In 1894 Otto Pfleiderer, the *liberal Hegelian* and persistent opponent of the
nti-metaphysical tenets in Ritschlianism, delivered the Gifford Lectures on *Philosophy
nd Development of Religion* in which he eliminated the supernatural from Christianity.
`hese lectures met with the protest of three of the Free Church theologians: ROBERT
LAINY, JAMES ORR, and MARCUS DODS.[5] Orr also declared the Ritschlian theology to
e "radically unsound." [6]

8. *Some independent theological influence* developed outside the three great Pres-
yterian bodies, notably the Arminian Evangelical Union since 1843 under the leader-
hip of J. MORISON. Scottish Congregationalism was ably presented by such men as
V. L. ALEXANDER, and, still earlier, by R. WARDLAW.

---

[5] *The Supernatural in Religion*, 1894.
[6] *Ritschlianism*, 1903, p. VII; and earlier *The Ritschlian Theology and the Evangelical Faith*, 1898.

Chapter Eight

NON-CONFORMIST THEOLOGY

1. In our discussion of Non-Conformist theology we begin with the *Congregational theology* of the nineteenth century. It is characteristic of the theologians of this type that they have not been "cloistered academics, but, generally speaking, men with pastoral experience and a wide knowledge of human nature." [1] With their emphasis on subjective experience, they were more open to the new learning than either Anglican or Presbyterians. (This is equally true of the other Non-Conformist groups.)

2. *The first Congregational theologian* who taught a purely governmental view of the Atonement was EDWARD WILLIAMS (1750-1813). He was minister of Carr's Lane Church, Birmingham, and afterwards tutor at Rotherham College. His work on *The Cross of Christ,* published in 1792, was the first attempt to reconcile the Calvinistic doctrine of the absoluteness of the divine decrees with divine justice. He also made it plain that God does not will evil in that He decrees any man to reprobation.

The rigid Calvinism of the Scottish Church prompted RALPH WARDLAW (1779-1853) to join the Congregational Church, and he influenced thought on both sides, in Scotland as well as England. His work *The Extent of the Atonement and Universal Pardon* (1830) was along the same lines as E. Williams'. His view also was governmental, and he likewise retained the view of election to reprobation and the decree of God.

The first outspoken voice against Calvinism in Scotland was that of JOHN KIRK Congregational minister of Hamilton. In 1842 he published *The Way of Life Made Plain,* in which he maintained the thesis that Jesus Christ died for every man, and that the Spirit of God is inclusive not exclusive. The saved are those that yield to God, and the unsaved are those that do not yield. This caused much trouble, and a number of ministers were expelled from the Congregational Union and united, under the leadership of James Morison, to form the Evangelical Union.

One more name deserves mention in the early years of the nineteenth century that of JOHN PYE SMITH (1774-1851), tutor at Homerton College. He published in 1818 *The Scripture Testimony to the Messiah* (4 vols.) in which he undertook to defend the divinity of Jesus against the English Unitarians as well as the German Rationalists. He had a good knowledge of natural science. In 1839 he gave the "Congregational Lectures" (reprinted in *On the Relation between Holy Scripture and Some Parts of Geological Science,* 5th edition 1852). Here he attempts to arrive at a compromise between the Scriptures and science.

3. *Among the older generation of English Congregationalists,* in whom the Latitudinarian tendencies were more manifest, were such men as G. PAYNE, H. ROGERS a friend of Whately, who was equally opposed to the Tractarians as well as to the rising tide of skepticism (*Eclipse of Faith,* 1852), and JAMES B. BROWN. More outspoken in his liberal views was SAMUEL DAVIDSON (1807-1898). His views on the inspiration

---

[1] W. B. Selbie, *Congregationalism,* 1927, p. 164.

ost him his position in Lancashire College. The greatest figure among Congregational
reachers at that time was ROBERT WILLIAM DALE (1829-1895). His special contri-
ution to theology is his volume on *The Atonement* (1875) This book too is anti-
Calvinistic. He was not satisfied with the moral view of the Atonement, but stopped
hort of penal substitution. What we find in it, says his critic, "is rather in essence the
Grotian idea of penal example." Yet Dale went beyond Grotius in that, according to
im, it is God Himself who suffered in the sufferings of Christ.[2]

4. *The outstanding Congregational scholar in the nineteenth century* was ANDREW
MARTIN FAIRBAIRN (1838-1912). He was Scottish but joined the Evangelical Union
nd "became the greatest of its sons." He was schooled at Edinburgh under Morison,
ut later studied in Germany and found here the scholars that fitted his mind, following
specially the mediating school of the Dorner type. He was the first principal of Manchester College, Oxford, 1886-1909. His most important books include *Studies in the
Philosophy of Religion and History* (1876), *The Place of Christ in Modern Theology*
1893), and *The Philosophy of the Christian Religion* (1910). For a sympathetic
eview of his life and work consult W. B. Selbie, *The Life of A. M. Fairbairn* (1914).

Fairbairn's position is essentially Christo-centric. At a time when the interest of
German theology was almost absorbed by the "quest of the historical Jesus," Fairbairn
nd other English scholars[3] revealed a keen interest in restating the Christological
dogma. Like most of his contemporaries, both in England and in Germany, Fairbairn
held to the kenotic position. He also combined the speculative and ethical in a very
novel manner. The best illustration of this combination comes out in his doctrine of
he Trinity. He distinguishes between God and the Godhead in the following manner:
God is the Godhead in action," in His relation to the universe; but "the Godhead is
God in the region of transcendental existence." God is love; He therefore must be by
nature social; "for if He were an infinite simplicity, then emotion with all its complex
elations and many-fold interactions, would be to Him unknown." [4] Likewise God is
eason; but reason is communicative and must have an object to communicate with.
f this object were not in God, He were not perfect in Himself. In these terms Fairbairn finds the justification for the Trinitarian dogma which represents the highest
chievement of speculative intuition. The Deity as God is an object of natural knowledge; the Deity as the Godhead is the subject of supernatural revelation.

5. We now pass to the *English Unitarians* of the nineteenth century. These differed
considerably from their American brethren, especially from those of modern times.
They were less radical. The Biblical tenets of Socinianism were still very pronounced.
The founder of the Unitarian Society (1791) was THOMAS BELSHAM (died 1829).
n his view of Jesus, he had moved from Arianism to Socinianism. The *Inquirer* was the
iterary organ of this Society. The early years when the Society was under the influence
of JOSEPH PRIESTLY (died 1804) and Belsham represent the first stage of Unitarian
heology. Its fundamental tenets were: belief in the unipersonality of God, human
determinism, utilitarian ethics, and in the religious authority of the Bible. These older
Unitarians meant to teach the doctrine of the New Testament. They would have been
Trinitarians if they could have found any Trinitarian doctrine in the New Testament.

---

[2] Cf. Franks, *op. cit.*, pp. 414 ff.
[3] Cf. Vollrath, *op. cit.*, pp. 284 ff.
[4] *Christ in Modern Theology*, edition of 1916, p. 394. By permission of Scribner's, publishers.

They believed in the inspiration of the Scriptures, miracles, and the resurrection of Jesus. This period was the epoch of intellectualism in religion. The second stage was that of the influence of Channing, when human freedom was proclaimed with the insistence of a zeal of the Evangelicals. In this stage Unitarian theologians stressed the ethical side of religion rather than the iron necessities of nature. The third stage was ushered in by the greatest of all Unitarian scholars, Martineau, and on this stage we have the religion of the human spirit.

JAMES MARTINEAU'S (1805-1900) thinking on life was ruled by Locke, Hartley Collins, Edwards, Priestly, Bentham, and Mill. Under this empirical and necessarian philosophy he staggered on till 1834. A change is seen in his review of Bentham' *Deontology*. Here he clashed with Utilitarianism and began to emphasize the importance of motive rather than consequences. This was brought about not by any reading, but by reflection on his own inner experience. He became a believer in the freedom of the will and the intuitive faculties of the soul. Like Kant he found in conscience the significance of the religious life, and Duty was a divine conception for him. Will rather than intellect became the basic element of his theology.

Rejecting the agnostic, materialistic, and pantheistic tendencies of his age, he taught a philosophical theism. God is eternal will, and the sole cause of the universe In Christology, he drifted from Arianism to complete humanitarianism. Jesus is but one of the many explorers of religious truth. There is no supernatural divine revelation Revelation is from within and not from without. As to the canon, he accepted, on the whole, the critical conclusions of the Tuebingen school. Man is a rational, moral, and spiritual being, and free to choose the good. His main works are, *A Study of Spinoza* (1882), *Types of Ethical Theory* (1885), *Study of Religion* (1888), *Seat of Authority in Religion* (1890), and *Essays, Reviews, and Addresses* (1890 f.).

Moore (p. 235) calls attention to a striking parallel between Martineau and New man. Both busied themselves with the question of religious authority, and since criticism was fatal to both concerning the view of the Scriptures, Newman turned to find that authority in an infallible church, while Martineau embraced the principle of an inward authority of the religious personality.

6. The *Methodist theologians* remained true to their Semi-Augustinian heritage during the greater part of the nineteenth century. The first great scholar of this period was RICHARD WATSON (1781-1833). He edited *The Liverpool Courier* (1808), and wrote *Remarks on the Eternal Sonship of Christ* (1818) against Adam Clarke. He wrote his theological masterpiece *Theological Institutes* in 1823 f. This was for many year the standard work in Wesleyan divinity. Watson was an exponent of a strictly super natural rationalism. He made a distinction between external and internal evidence The first is primary in his thinking as he appealed to miracles and prophecy for an absolute evidence of a divine revelation. Internal evidence is a mere impression of truth and therefore cannot be distinguished from any other discovery of the human intellect. It could have no authority.

WILLIAM BURT POPE (1822-1903) was the first to write from the standpoint of modern theological science. In 1867 he became professor of systematic theology at Didsbury College, Manchester. He gave the "Fernley Lectures" on *The Person of Christ* in 1875, and published his *Christian Theology* (3 vols., 2nd edition, 1877 ff.). This last mentioned work is a scholarly exposition of Christian doctrine from the Methodist

oint of view. Though he gave a larger place to the self-evidencing power of experience
an Watson his viewpoint also was essentially rational.

Other names of renown are those of THOMAS COKE, HENRY MOORE, JOSEPH
ENSON, ROBERT NEWTON, WILLIAM ARTHUR, JOHN TELFORD, JOHN SHAW BARKS,
 al.[5]

7. The *Baptist theology* in the nineteenth century was represented by JOHN
OSTER (1770-1843). Although a predestinarian at heart, he contended against the
aching of eternal punishment. In his Christology the Arminian tendencies are notice-
ble. Coleridgian tenets are likewise manifest. JOHN HOWARD HINTON (died 1863)
vas a true Evangelical but open to Broad Church influences. He wrote *Harmony of
Religious Truth and Human Reason* and published other works. Under JOHN CLIFFORD
1836-1923) doctrinal tolerance gained a footing in the Baptist Union. When he
ucceeded in keeping the Union from commitment on such doctrines as the infallibility
f inspiration, vicarious atonement, and eternal punishment for the unconverted, Spur-
eon with his followers withdrew from the Union. From his pen we have *The Inspira-
ion and Authority of the Bible* (1892); *Ultimate Problems of Christianity* (1906),
nd *Gospel of Gladness* (1912). Outstanding among the leaders of the liberal wing
vere THOMAS W. DAVIES, JOHN T. MARSHALL (commentaries on Job and Ecclesi-
stes), NEWTON H. MARSHALL, and others.

---

[5] We refer to the orientating article on Methodist theology by Dean Kundson of Boston School of Theology
n the *Methodist Review*, March, 1925.

Chapter Nine

THEOLOGICAL DEVELOPMENT IN THE ANGLICAN CHURCH (1860-1900)

1. In Chapter Four we discussed *the beginning of Neo-Anglican theology.* We left the Oxford Movement when Newman went over to Rome. We now shall resume this discussion by giving a brief review of the theological movements and tendencies in the Established Church during the last half of the nineteenth century.

2. After 1860 the Oxford Movement went under the name of *Ritualism.* Although the ritualistic movement was not planned by the early Oxford men — Pusey, in fact the outstanding theological force at this time, never was in favor of it — it grew out of the teachings of the Oxford Movement almost inevitably. Samuel Wilberforce stressed the sacrificial aspect of the Eucharist, and Keble defended the adoration of Christ in the sacramental elements.[1] Pusey taught sacramental confession (*The Entire Absolution of the Penitent,* a sermon preached February 1, 1846), and others followed him as is witnessed by the book *The Priest in Absolution,* anonymously published in 1877. Wherever sacramentalism becomes the center of gravity, ceremonialism will follow inevitably. The tragic story of the ritualistic movement does not concern us here. It belongs to church history. Suffice it to say that much of the passion and hatred which it displayed is strange to a Lutheran. Luther's evangelical attitude toward the prohibition of image worship in the Decalogue would make such a conflict impossible. The use of crucifixes, crosses, and candles as an aid to worship has always survived in the Lutheran churches of the European continent, but it is without abuse.

The leading men of the party at this time were PUSEY, MOZLEY, CHURCH, and LIDDON. (On Pusey see Chapter Four.) JAMES B. MOZLEY (1813-1878) agreed with the predestinarianism of Augustine, and was at odds with his party as regards the doctrine of baptismal regeneration which he did not hold. He wrote *Augustinian Doctrine of Predestination* (1855) and *Essays Historical and Theological* (1859). RICHARD WILLIAM CHURCH (1815-1890) is the classical historian of the Oxford Movement (see our Literature for Chapter Four). HENRY PERRY LIDDON'S (1829-1890) influence was due to his oratory and pulpit eloquence. His conservatism became evident in his defense of the continued use of the Athanasian creed.

3. *Apart from these Oxford men* there was another group of scholars who, though they were loyal to the Anglican Church, showed little interest in the characteristic traits of the Oxford theology. The Biblical scholars such as F. B. WESTCOTT (1825-1901), T. B. LIGHTFOOT (1828-1889), and F. J. R. HORT (1828-1892) belonged to them. All three served on the committee for the revision of the King James Version. Hort and Lightfoot in conjunction with I. E. B. Major founded the *Journal of Classical and Sacred Philology* in 1854. Lightfoot's commentaries rank foremost in the field of New Testament interpretation (*Galatians,* 1865; *Philippians,* 1868; *Colossians,* 1875).

---

[1] *On Eucharistical Adoration,* 1857.

Westcott and Hort gained international recognition for their edition of the *Greek New Testament* (first edition 1881).

4. In 1889 *Lux Mundi* was published. This volume is a landmark in Anglican theology. It was a sober attempt at reconciling the conservative element that came from Newman through Church and the liberal stream that came from Coleridge and Maurice through Westcott and Hort. The twelve essays of the volume move somewhat along the line of the older Erlangen school, i.e., they aim at teaching the old truth in a new garb, harmonizing the new learning with the faith of the fathers. Unlike the authors of *Essays and Reviews,* these writers have a dogmatic basis and display a genuine appreciation of the historic creeds of the Church. From *Lux Mundi* there flowed a living stream of theological thought which has more or less affected every Anglican treatise written since 1889. When the book appeared it caused even more comment than *Essays and Reviews* for it was written from the very center where Froude, Newman, and Pusey had reigned.

The essay that startled the Anglican world most was the one written by the editor, Charles Gore, "The Holy Spirit and Inspiration." The writer makes revelation a historical process. The Biblical records, though they are broadly correct, lack historical preciseness in detail, he insists. The Pentateuch, for example, contains much material, which is post-Mosaic. The books of Jonah and Daniel are "dramatic compositions worked up on a basis of history." Our Lord's reference to Jonah and His apparent assumption of the Davidic authorship of Psalm 110 should not be regarded as a scientific solution of the literary problem. For due to the kenotic understanding of the Incarnation, the historical Jesus was, in the opinion of Gore, not omniscient in things temporal. To draw the line between the human and the divine in the Bible, the author distinguishes that what God "revealed" from that what He "used." "He (Jesus) revealed God, His mind, His character, His claim, and within certain limits His Threefold Being. He revealed man, his sinfulness, his need, his capacity. He revealed His purpose of redemption and founded His Church as a home in which man was to be through all ages reconciled to God in knowledge and love. All this He revealed, but through and under conditions of a true human nature. Thus He used human nature, its relation to God, its condition of experience, its growth in knowledge, its limitation of knowledge." [2]

5. We shall now trace the development of the *Broad Church Party* to the twentieth century. In the field of Biblical criticism BENJAMIN JOWETT (1817-1893) took the lead in Great Britain. In 1855 he published *The Epistles of St. Paul to the Thessalonians, Galatians, and Romans, with Critical Notes and Dissertations*. In this publication Jowett introduced to the English reading public the critical view of Baur. Jowett took a mediating position. While Baur had seen a complete disharmony between Paul and the older church, Jowett found "there was not complete harmony, but neither was there absolute antagonism" between the two.

Among leading scholars there were SAMUEL R. DRIVER (1846-1914),THOMAS K. CHEYNE (1841-1915) in the field of the Old Testament, WILLIAM SANDAY (1843-1920), and FREDERICK C. CONYBEARE (1856-1924) for New Testament literature and criticism. Cheyne gained renown as editor of Armenian texts. Special mention deserve the two theologians EDWIN HATCH (1835-1889) and HENRY A. REDPATCH (1848-

² *Lux Mundi*, American edition, undated, pp. 300 ff.

1908) who are the authors of the famous *Concordance to the Septuagint* (1891 ff.)
It is due to the inspiration and initiative of this group of scholars that *The Internationa*
Critical Commentary was started.

6. That *Biblical criticism was coming to its own* in the English Church is shown
in the case of JOHN W. COLENSO (1814-1883), bishop of Natal. In his missionary
endeavors he had found time to study the problems of the Pentateuch. In his book
entitled *The Pentateuch and the Book of Joshua Critically Examined* (1862), Colenso
bringing out the composite character of these writings, called in question the historical
and scientific accuracy of the Biblical narrative and the Mosaic authorship of the
Pentateuch. The Bishop was condemned by both Houses of Convocation of the Province
of Canterbury. The sentence, however, was declared null and void in 1865 by action of
the secular court, the Privy Council.

7. In 1874 appeared *Supernatural Religion* (3 vols.), a book against the supernatural and miraculous in Christianity. Miracle is explained on psychological grounds
and the unreliability of human testimony. The canonical gospels are said not to be
apostolic. Acts is declared to be a legendary composition of a late date. In short, this
book is a historical criticism of Christianity followed by an attempt to prove that it has
no better foundation than any other religion. "Never before had such a systematic
attack, based upon solid learning, been made in English upon the external evidences of
the Christian religion, which still continue to hold a foremost place, not merely in the
popular, but also in the theological apologetics of England (Mansel, Newman,
Mozley)." [3]

8. *Another outstanding force in the theological world* in the last quarter of the
nineteenth century was FREDERICK WILLIAM FARRAR (1831-1903). Through the
influence of Maurice he was led to study Coleridge, whose writings had a profound
influence upon his faith and opinions. As a theologian he occupied a mediating position
between the Broad Church party and the Evangelical party. He gained his place in the
theological world through two volumes *Eternal Hope* (1878) and *Mercy and Judgment*
(1881), in which he defended the doctrine that, though there may be an endless hell
for some because they resist the grace of God beyond the grave, there is no hell of
material fire, and for the great majority, through God's mercy and Christ's sacrifice, a
complete purification and salvation will be obtained.

9. Concerning tne *Evangelical Party* we can say that it made no great theological
contribution save in the work of HANDLEY C. G. MOULE (1841-1921), professor of
divinity at Cambridge and bishop of Durham. He was a real theologian of the Evangelical type. His devotional and expository writings reflect the position of the Evangelical party of this period: *The Epistle of Paul to the Romans* (1894), *Ephesian
Studies* (1900), *Christus Consolator* (1915), and many others.

---

[3] Pfleiderer, *op. cit.*, p. 397.

Chapter Ten

BRITISH PHILOSOPHY FROM 1860
TO THE PRESENT

Literature: J. H. MUIRHEAD, editor, *Contemporary British Philosophy*, 1924 f.; A. G. WIDGERY, *Contemporary Thought of Great Britain*, 1927; R. METZ, *Op. cit.*, pp. 286 ff. As to the intention of this chapter compare the remark in the introduction of Chapter Five.

1. In a former chapter (Five) we brought English philosophy *up to the time of the Cairds.* In this chapter we shall begin with them and follow the various philosophical movements to the present time.

2. At a time when speculative philosophy was discredited in Germany, Hegelianism was in the ascendency in England. The *British Idealism* in the latter part of the nineteenth century flourished in opposition to the agnosticism of Spencer and the scientific materialism of the day, while in Germany these negative tendencies arose in opposition to the speculative forces in the Hegelian philosophy.

JOHN CAIRD (1820-1898) of Glasgow took the lead. In 1880 he published his volume on *Introduction to Philosophy of Religion* in which he gives a very trenchant criticism of Spencer's agnosticism. He defends the idealistic form of philosophy. Like Hegel he bases his belief in God on the ontological argument, the essence of which is "that the correlation of thought and being in our consciousness involves as its necessary presupposition the absolute unity of both in the divine consciousness." [1] Although Caird's view of religion follows along Hegelian lines, it also has a close affinity to Fichte because of its emphasis upon the ethical.

The Hegelian philosophy was fully introduced to the English world by EDWARD CAIRD (1835-1908), brother of John Caird,[2] HUTCHISON STIRLING, and THOMAS H. GREEN. It was through the Cairds that Glasgow and Oxford became the strongholds of English Idealism, while Cambridge espoused the cause of scientific empiricism. E. Caird and Stirling contended against the agnosticism of the German Neo-Kantians and tried to prove that Kant is the father of the speculation which found its climax in the great thought-system of Hegel.

Green came to his fame in striking deadly blows at the Lockean philosophy.[3] The basis for belief in God, Green finds in the moral and intellectual nature of man. The "Eternal Ought" in man is the light shining from God to man. The human mind is in principle one with the divine mind and is the presence of the Divine under finite conditions. However, for the supernatural, as Christianity understands it, Green has no place. There can be no miracle in the sense in which historical traditions have held it.

ANDREW SETH'S book *Hegelianism and Personality* appeared in 1887 and is a criticism of Green. The fundamental error of Hegelianism, according to Seth, is that it

---

[1] Pfleiderer, *op. cit.*, p. 342.
[2] *A Critical Account of the Philosophy of Kant*, 1877; *The Evolution of Religion*, 1893, *et al.*
[3] *Introduction to Hume's Treatise on Human Nature*, 1874; *Prolegomena to Ethics* 1883.

identifies the human and the divine self-consciousness. To identify the two is not only to destroy the human but also the divine side.

British Idealism reached its full force in FRANCIS HERBERT BRADLEY (1846-1924) The underlying principle of Bradley's philosophy of Absolute Idealism is the conception of a "perfect experience." [4] Only absolute experience can know absolute truth. Finite experience is partially false. As to the idea of God, Bradley frankly confessed that the Absolute is not God because it has no relations, while it is the nature of the god of religion that he has relation with the worshiper. The god of religion is something less than the Absolute. The central truth for religion is "the real presence of God's will in mine, our actual and literal satisfaction in common." This rather than the personality of God is the determining factor in religion.[5]

Akin to Bradley's is the philosophy of BERNARD BOSANQUET (1848-1923). According to him, thought and being are identical. All experience has a metaphysical implication. The perfect whole is the only true Real, and we partake of the infinite because we are essential to the whole.[6]

CLEMENT CHARLES JULIAN WEBB is another representative of Absolute Idealism but with a theological approach to his problems. We have seen that Bradley would not identify God and the Absolute, but Webb identifies the two. God must contain everything, even sin and error (Schelling).[7]

Idealism in Great Britain developed in two directions. The one inspired by moral enthusiasm was presented by Sir HENRY JONES (1852-1922) who wrote: Idealism as a Practical Creed (1909), The Working Faith of the Social Reformer (1910), and A Faith That Inquires (1922). His teaching is continued by his disciples, John Henry Muirhead and John Stuart Mackenzie. The other tendency is logical and metaphysical and has been carried on by Harold H. Joachim, Norman Kemp Smith, and John Alexander Smith.[8] With the decline of this metaphysical idealism the ground of Idealism is found in the different aspects of human nature. This is seen in the works of Richard Burton Haldane who wrote The Pathway to Reality (1904 f.), and The Philosophy of Humanism and of Other Subjects (1922). This shift from idealism in its absolutist form to experience also is manifest in JAMES BLACK BAILLIE.[9]

During the period which we are considering there was only one outstanding philosopher at Cambridge who expounded an idealism which had close affinity with Absolute Idealism. We refer to JOHN M. E. MACTAGGART. He calls his philosophy "Ontological Idealism." [10]

It is a question whether we should consider ANDREW SETH PRINGLE-PATTISON here under the heading of Absolute Idealism or leave him for our discussion of Theism.[11] His view lies between Absolute Idealism and Theism, partaking of both in a way that makes his philosophical position unique in British thought.[12]

---

[4] Cf. Widgery, op. cit., p. 85.

[5] Ethical Studies, 1876; Appearance and Reality, 1893; Essays on Truth and Reality, 1914, et al.

[6] What is Religion?, 1920; The Meeting of Extremes in Contemporary Philosophy, 1923, et al.

[7] Studies in the History of Natural Theology, 1915; Problems in the Relation of God and Man, 1911; God and Personality, 1919; Divine Personality and Human Life, 1920.

[8] Widgery, op. cit., p. 101 f.

[9] The Idealist Construction of Experience, 1906; Studies in Human Nature, 1921.

[10] Some Dogmas of Religion, 1906; The Nature of Existence, 1920.

[11] Cf. Widgery, op. cit., pp. 110 ff.

[12] Hegelianism and Personality, 1887; The Idea of God in the Light of Recent Philosophy, 1917; The Idea of Immortality, 1922, et al.

3. We now pass to consider *Pragmatism.* Several factors helped to produce pragmatism. In the realm of psychology the work of JAMES WARD (1843-1925) and his pupil GEORGE FREDERICK STOUT, had shown that the mind is essentially conative and volitional. WILLIAM JAMES (1842-1910) added prestige to the movement; his work has been used quite extensively in English schools. Add to these forces the work of the eminent German psychologist Wilhelm Wundt (1832-1920), the father of modern experimental psychology, and you have the significant causes that produced a pragmatistic humanism.

The first real revolt against Absolute Idealism in England arose at Oxford with the publication in 1902 of a volume called *Personal Idealism* written by eight members of the University faculty. This book simply was a call to viewing human life in its various aspects as against the emphasis of the absolutist on the intellectual only. In British thinking, however, there is only one great scholar who has insisted upon a thorough pragmatist attitude, and that is FERDINAND C. S. SCHILLER (1864-1937), and he calls his view "Humanism" rather than "Pragmatism." His works include the following volumes: *Riddles of the Sphinx* (1891), *Humanism* (1903), *Studies in Humanism* (1907), *Formal Logic* (1912), and *Tantalus, or the Future of Man* (1924). According to Schiller a truth is a proposition of value and therefore no thesis is necessarily final and eternal. It is true only as long as it has value. "All truth works," but that does not imply the conclusion that "all that works is true." Schiller was a pluralist and agrees with William James that there is no point of view from which the world is really one. He conceived of God as a personality, being good and holy. But unable to deny the reality of evil, Schiller makes God finite. Another philosopher who accepts this pluralistic interpretation is HERBERT W. CARR.[13]

4. We now take up *Realism.* For the Realist the particular rather than the universal is the point of emphasis in his system. Realism insists upon the existence of physical objects and finite selves. The Realist revolt against idealism was born in an article by GEORGE E. MOORE, published in *Mind* in 1903. He rejected the idealistic idol *esse est percipi,* i.e., to be and to be known are one and the same thing. Over against this identification of thought and being, the realists seek to maintain the view that objects have their existence independent from their being known. Neo-realism, therefore, is a healthy reaction against the one-sided overemphasis on the epistemological problem in post-Kantian philosophy.

One of the keenest British realists is BERTRAND RUSSELL. The output of his books is amazing: *Philosophical Essays* (1910), *The Problems of Philosophy* (1912), *Our Knowledge of the Eternal World as a Field for Scientific Method in Philosophy* (1914), *The Analysis of Mind* (1924), *Icarus, or the Future of Science* (1924), and *What I Believe* (1925) form quite an able defense of British realism. He criticizes pragmatism and shows that in essence it leads to skepticism. He styles his own philosophy as "Logical Atomism." Man is but "the outcome of accidental collections of atoms" and "the whole temple of man's achievement must inevitably be buried beneath the debris of a universe in ruins."

Of other recent studies in Realism there may be mentioned such publications as *Space, Time and Deity* (1920) by SAMUEL ALEXANDER, *Problems of the Self* (1917) and *A Study of Realism* (1920) by JOHN LAIRD.

---

[13] *Outlines of the Philosophy of the Principle of Relativity,* 1922, *et al.*

Related to Realism but more independent is the position of CHARLES D. BROAD,[14] and that of ALFRED N. WHITEHEAD, whose philosophy tends towards the Platonic view of reality.[15]

5. We now turn to the contemporary *Naturalists*. The shallow materialism of the nineteenth century was soon tempered by an increasing awareness of the nature of scientific problems themselves. CHARLES ROBERT DARWIN (1809-1882) and THOMAS HENRY HUXLEY (1825-1895) were too penetrating and too broad-minded to be satisfied with a materialistic conception of life. In the history of religion they are more properly classified with the Agnostics as Huxley styled himself, i.e., the metaphysical remains an open question. GEORGE JOHN ROMANES in a posthumous volume, *Thoughts on Religion* (1904), and ALFRED R. WALLACE both felt disposed to admit the unsatisfactory position of a thoroughgoing materialism. Sir OLIVER J. LODGE, who wrote *Life and Matter* (1906), *The Substance of Faith Allied with Belief* (1907), *Man and Universe* (5th edition, 1909), *Immortality of the Soul* (1908), and other works, is noted for his attempt to join a strictly scientific method to an earnest faith in religion. He holds that man has evolved under divine guidance from the lower forms of life. Sin is the relapse to a lower level of evolution, choosing a course of action of a type already transcended. Jesus is to him divine in the same sense as other noble and saintly souls are manifestations of the Divine. To believe in the Virgin Birth is "materialism rampant." To link the Christian faith "inextricably with an anatomical statement about flesh and bones is rash." This shows that Sir Oliver is far from accepting the orthodox creed of the Church.

While some of the leading scientists of the day such as John Arthur Thompson, Ernest William Hobson, William Bateson, Charles S. Sherrington, and Frederick Soddy are very pronounced in denying that materialism is able to solve all the enigmas of life, two great British scientists still hold to a pure naturalism: LLOYD MORGAN (died 1936),[16] the most distinguished pupil of Huxley, and JULIAN HUXLEY (born 1887), the grandson of Henry Huxley.[17]

In this section on Naturalism we have one more name to present and that is the great scholar JAMES Y. SIMPSON (1873-1934), late Professor of Natural Sciences in New College, Edinburgh. Simpson accepted the spiritual implications of the universe. No scholar has been striving more earnestly for a reconciliation of science and religion than this professor of Edinburgh. His philosophy is laid down in such volumes as *Nature: Cosmic, Human, and Divine* (1929) and *Garments of the Living God* (1934). He also wrote *Landmarks of the Struggle between Science and Religion* (1925), and *World Politics and the Kingdom of God* (1933).

6. There remains another group of thinkers whose world view is best understood under the comprehensive term of *Theism*. Here we must mention first the late English statesman ARTHUR JAMES BALFOUR (1848-1930). In his famous volume *The Foundations of Belief* (first edition, 1895), Balfour contends against a narrow type of Rationalism and holds to the view that all beliefs are based on Authority. All knowledge and practical conduct are based on self-evident axioms. And these axioms are accepted

---

[14] *Scientific Thought*, 1923; *The Mind and Its Place in Nature*, 1925.
[15] *Religion in the Making*, 1926, et al.
[16] *Life, Mind, and Spirit*, 1929, et al.
[17] *Religion without Revelation*, 1927; *What Dare I Think?*, 1931; et al.

olidly by man, on some other basis than a rational one. It is authority rather than reason which lays deep the foundation of social life. Science as well as theology is compelled to postulate a "Rational Ground or Cause of the World who made it intelligible and us in some faint degree able to understand it." [18]

It is JAMES WARD (1843-1925), the eminent English psychologist, who disposed of the case of Dualism and of Absolute Idealism as leading either to materialism or an unreal idealism. In his own teaching he insists upon "the unity and correlativity of subject and object." Following the inductive method, Ward starts from the admission of the plurality in experience. But Ward does not stop with Pluralism. The apparent Unity found in nature and history will not allow us to rest in Pluralism. And the ground of this unity Ward finds in God who transcends the individuals. Of his works we may mention *The Realm of Ends; or Pluralism and Theism* (1911), and *A Study of Kant* (1922). A complete list of his writings was published by the *Monist* (Chicago, 1926).

Theism was philosophically also defended by the philosopher and theologian HASTINGS RASHDALL (1858-1924), who exerted a great influence on the Broad Church-men within the Anglican communion. Rashdall was a modern representative of Berkeleyanism.[19] He accepted the unscriptural idea of a "finite God" on the basis that the reality of evil leads man to face the alternative that either God wished to create all good and He could not, or he could and would not. Rashdall chose the former alternative and insisted, on metaphysical grounds, that there is no real meaning in the term "infinite power." [20] His principal works are *The Universities of Europe in the Middle Ages* (1895), *The Theory of Good and Evil* (1907), *Conscience and Christ* (1916), *The Idea of Atonement in Christian Theology* (1919).

And this brings us to WILLIAM RITCHIE SORLEY (1855-1935), who developed a theistic philosophy with reference to the implications of moral values and the moral life. His Gifford Lectures on *Moral Values and the Idea of God* (1918), H. R. Mackintosh judges to be among the best of those Lectures.[21] He also wrote *The Moral Life* (4th edition, 1930).

In the University of Edinburgh we find ALFRED EDWARD TAYLOR defending the theistic interpretation of life. His Essay on "The Vindication of Religion" in *Essays Catholic and Critical* is said to be the best contribution to that volume and is an able defense of the theistic world view on a rational basis. Theism, in his words, is "the doctrine that the ultimate ground of things is a single supreme reality which is the source of everything other than itself, and has the character of being (a) intrinsically complete or perfect; and (b) as a consequence an adequate object of unqualified adoration or worship."

7. In concluding this chapter *we shall note five other thinkers* who have influenced English thought: Hardy, Shaw, Chesterton, Wells, and Murry.

THOMAS HARDY'S (1840-1928)) masterpiece is *The Dynasts* (1904 ff.), a chronicle play of England's struggle against Napoleon. In this epic-drama he contends for a monistic theory of the universe. He holds that Will is the ultimate reality of the

---

[18] Widgery, *op. cit.*, p. 192.
[19] Cf. *Ibid.*, p. 206.
[20] See in this Volume p. 257.
[21] *RGG*, V. 615

universe, and applies an "Ever-unconscious" to this Will. Nature and man are the outcome of Will and devoid of freedom.

GEORGE BERNARD SHAW, who resembles Hardy in many ways, differs from him in that at the basis of his teaching is an optimistic belief. In place of Hardy's "Unconscious Will" we have "Life-Force." The "Life-Force" is blind but is gradually coming to greater light and consciousness. Shaw believes in an imperfect God, for the existence of certain horrors in the universe is, as Shaw claims, inconsistent with a perfect God. All the time God is busy in His experiments with the other beings through which He is trying to perfect Himself. If these fail, they will be wiped out. This judgment of God explains, according to Shaw, the tragic destruction of the mammoth beasts. And if mankind fail, it also will be scrapped by God.

GILBERT KEITH CHESTERTON offers a trenchant criticism of the religious and moral weakness of our time. Materialism is, in his judgment, more dogmatic than religion. Christian dogmas and institutions transmit valuable experiences. Man must change the world and not adapt himself to it, and to change this world there must be an ideal toward which it can go, and that ideal he finds in Christianity. In 1922 Chesterton was received into the Roman communion. He died in 1936. We have from his pen Heretics (1905), Orthodoxy (1908), What's Wrong With the World? (1910), St. Francis of Assisi (1925), Catholic Essays (1929).

We need say only a few words about HERBERT GEORGE WELLS (born 1866). His strong appeal to the general reading public is reflected in the sale of his books, particularly Outline of History (1920). The key to all his thinking is biological evolution and the naturalistic aspects of human sociology. His god is a finite god, but a person who suffers with the human race. Religion is the attitude of universal brotherhood and self-sacrifice.

The emphasis on mysticism becomes apparent in the writings of JOHN MIDDLETON MURRY (born 1889). He finds that the world is, as he says, "often painful, often beautiful, always mysterious." He looks upon Jesus as a mystic genius. The mystic experience of a "rebirth" was, according to Murry, the secret of His life and the sum total of His teaching. The miraculous in the Gospel is to him "stupid" and "utterly meaningless." The Soul is "consubstantial with God." Among his religious writings are Jesus — Man of Genius (1926), God (1929), To the Unknown God (1930), and Life of Jesus (1934).

Chapter Eleven

THEOLOGICAL MOVEMENTS IN THE TWEN-
TIETH CENTURY: THE LIBERAL, PROTESTANT,
AND CATHOLIC TRADITIONS

Literature: WALTER M. HORTON, *Contemporary English Theology*, 1936; H. D. A. MAJOR, *English Modernism*, 1927; CHARLES GORE, *The Anglo-Catholic Movement Today*, 1925.

With the beginning of the twentieth century we notice in Great Britain, as in Germany, a gradual dissolution of theological schools and parties. The scholars of the conservative wing have learned to respect and utilize many of the historico-critical tenets of the liberal schools, and—due to the disastrous results of the first World War—many of the liberal theologians, turning against the naive and optimistic evolutionism and immanentism of pre-war theology, have recaptured a deeper appreciation of the religious values of Biblical Christianity.

In our discussion in this chapter it is better to disregard completely the old party labels such as High, Low, and Broad, for a twentieth-century High Churchman may be a Liberal as regards his method and his views of inspiration and the beginnings of Christianity, while in turn a Liberal may have a genuine understanding of the sinfulness of man and his need of redemption. Besides, the liberal Broad Churchmen never formed a real party. Theological liberalism in England never crystallized in a real party or a denomination, save the Unitarians. The Liberals had all along been theological free lances, tilting their shafts against each other as much as against their High or Low Church opponents. We shall arrive at a much clearer conception of the actual present-day situation in England, by simply tracing the respective theological traditions which are typical in English theology: the Catholic, Protestant, and Liberal traditions.

In this process of rethinking and restating religion and theology, the moderation of the English mind again stands out in quite a contrast to the radicalism of German and also of American theology. English Liberalism is less radical than the naturalistic theology of Germany (and America), and the post-war reaction against Liberalism likewise is less radical than Continental Barthianism. The old Socinian emphasis on the historical in Christianity exercised a check even on some of the Modernists proper. Such radicals as Major and Cadoux (see paragraph 11 f.) have a higher regard for the person of Jesus than Troeltsch and his school on the Continent.

Whatever is true of England proper, also applies to the situation in Scotland. Traditionalism and Liberalism both have contributed to mold the thought of the younger theologians in the Presbyterian Church which, not counting a small dissenting minority, became reunited in 1929.

I. ENGLISH LIBERALISM

1. We shall begin our review with a brief discussion of *theological Liberalism*. Liberalism in England on the one hand, grew out of the eighteenth century Deism and

Moralism crystallizing in Unitarianism and, on the other hand, it is an offshoot of that Broad or Liberal church group beginning with Coleridge and the authors of *Essays and Reviews*. The difference between the Broad Church basis and the present movement is admirably expressed by Major in his book on *English Modernism* in these words: "The tendency of the older English Broad Churchmanship or Liberalism was to be rationalistic and *a priori*, individualistic and negative, unemotional and undevotional, unsacramental and anti-ecclesiastical, Erastian and academic. It regarded Christianity as a religion of illumination and good conduct. Its approach to Christianity was philosophical or ethical rather than religious and mystical. The tendency of Modernism is scientific and historical; its ideal of religion is mystical and social" (p. 37).[1] The last two adjectives aptly indicate the point in which English Modernism differs from Modernism in Germany. German Modernism is—or better—was (for most of its former followers are now to be found in the German Christian Movement) academic, intellectual and individualistic, for such men as Naumann, Geyer, and Rittelmyer, were theological outsiders. With Horton (p. 30) we may discern two cycles in this movement of thought: "The pre-war cycle, revolving about the Modernist controversy and issuing in a reaffirmation of the transcendence of God; (2) the post-war cycle, revolving about the problem of evil and issuing in a fresh emphasis upon the suffering love of God."

2. *At the beginning of our century* six Oxford scholars jointly produced the volume known as *Contentio Veritatis* (1902). In this volume we find again a Broad or Liberal Church theology at home in Oxford. Outstanding among the various contributions are the two essays by DEAN INGE on the Person of Christ (pp. 59 ff.) and on the Sacraments (pp. 270 ff.). The enthusiastic liberals of the Harnack-Troeltsch school of thought would have profited much if they had taken to heart such a keen remark: "If we reject Christ's testimony to Himself as recorded in the New Testament, we must regard His moral perfection as a hypothesis which is supported by no sufficient evidence, and which is in itself extremely improbable" (pp. 96 f.).

Cambridge followed suit. In 1905 H. B. SWETE published a volume containing fourteen essays entitled *Cambridge Theological Essays*. Swete says, "The purpose of the book will have been gained if, taken as a whole, it is judged to have set forward what is perhaps the most important work that lies before the theology of the twentieth century; if it has helped to assimilate the new views of truth suggested by modern knowledge without sacrificing any part of the primitive message, and to state in terms adapted to the needs of a new century the truths which the Ancient Church expressed in those which were appropriate for its own times" (Preface p. x).[2] The tenor of the book reveals a mediating theology. In the list of contributors we find such names of renown as F. R. TENNANT, who writes on "The Being of God in the Light of Physical Science" (pp. 55 ff.) and F. J. FOAKES-JACKSON, whose essay on "Christ in the Church: The Testimony of History" repudiates the narrow Christo-centric and antimetaphysical theology of Ritschl and Harnack (pp. 469 ff.).

In line with these Cambridge Theological Essays are the *London Theological Studies* (1911). In this venture each of the six theological schools of the University of London is represented and each of the principal parts of theological curriculum has some share of attention.

---

[1] By permission of Harvard University Press, publishers.
[2] By permission of The Macmillan Company, publishers.

Outstanding among the essays are the discussions of the Christological problem by
I. T. ANDREWS ("The Significance of the Eschatological Utterances of Jesus," pp.
55 ff.) and P. T. FORSYTH ("Christ and the Christian Principle," pp. 133 ff.). The latter
boldly states in opposition to the Ritschlian tendencies of that age, that "we do not
continue to get the Christian ethic or the Christian philanthropy without the Christian
creed" (p. 137). Andrews tries to distinguish between the transitory and the permanent
in the eschatological sayings of Jesus. The Lord, due to the kenotic implications of the
incarnation, "did not possess the necessary historical perspective to predict a continuous
event, spread over many centuries, in the history of the Church" (p. 87). "No Parousia
happened or will happen in the manner in which Jesus foretold it" (p. 91). Yet, says
he, the Parousia utterances retain their significance for the modern mind. "They illustrate the indestructibility of the Christian hope . . . They imply a transcendental conception of the Person of Christ by portraying Him as Lord of the future, seated at the
right hand of God and swaying the destinies of the human race. And finally, they teach
us that the Kingdom of God must come from God and cannot be evolved from man"
(pp. 94 f.).

All three composite volumes, as it may be seen from these quotations, are, strictly
speaking, critical rather than liberal. The uniqueness of the Christian message remains,
on the whole, unabated; all writers hold to a theistic or supernatural interpretation of
Christianity. The dissensus of opinion from the older theology is pronounced chiefly
in the field of Biblical criticism and in those conceptions which have a bearing on the
origin and evolution of man.

3. *The liberal tendency of the early years of our century* found its climax in the
Modernist Controversy, which stirred the mind of Protestant and Roman Catholic
theologians alike. Its most significant Protestant exponent was the then Congregational
theologian R. J. CAMPBELL. At that time Campbell held to the view of Absolute Idealism and extreme immanentism. Evil was to him a "non-being," the devil a "vacuum,"
sin only a mistake which is in itself "a quest for God," though a blundering quest
(*A Faith for Today, and The New Theology,* 1907). In 1907 he was excluded from the
National Free Church Council. As time went on, Campbell passed through a thorough
spiritual transformation. His optimistic belief in immanence and progress received a
severe shock especially from the extreme and radical position as revealed in the Christological controversy over Tyrell's posthumous work, *Christianity at the Cross Roads*
(1910). Influenced by von Huegel's strong vein of transcendentalism and the sympathetic attitude of Bishop Gore as expressed in his *The New Theology and the Old
Religion* (1907), Campbell was prompted to join the Church of England and was
reordained to the Anglican priesthood in 1916. Among his recent writings are *Christian
Faith in Modern Light* (1932), *The Call of Christ* (1933), *Grace Abounding* (1934),
The Story of Christmas (1935), *The Peace of God* (1936).

The *Modernist Movement in the Roman Church* was of international importance
with a galaxy of French theologians taking the lead. (Ollé-Laprune, Blondel, Fonse-
grive, Laberthonnière, Loisy, Lagrange, and others.) Its most conspicuous representative in Great Britain was G. TYRELL (1861-1909). Pope Pius X condemned the whole
movement in the encyclical *Pascendi* published in September, 1907. In October Father
Tyrell was excommunicated from the Church of Rome which he, born as an Anglican,
had joined in 1879.

The program of the Catholic Modernists included three principal objectives: (1) They accepted the most liberal results of New Testament criticism and applied them to a radical reconstruction of the Jesus of History. (2) Contending against the scholastic intellectualism in Catholic theology, they held to a dynamic conception of reality: God is a supreme life and immanent action, not an abstract being. They, therefore, considered it to be wrong to isolate one moment in the divine process as possessing a unique significance for religion. The question as to the historicity of Jesus, His birth and resurrection, and the institution of the sacraments by Him, was, in their eyes, meaningless in comparison with the religious *stimuli* couched in these concepts. (3) They advocated a measurable amount of practical reform within the Roman communion.

For English literature on Catholic Modernism we refer to A. L. Lilly, *Modernism* (1908), M. D. Petre, *Modernism, Its Failure and Its Fruits* (1919), A. R. Vilder, *The Modernist Movement in the Catholic Church* (1934). See also the article on Modernism in Hastings, *Encyclopedia*, VIII, 763 ff.

4. The years of the first World War are the landmark which separate us from the nineteenth century. The conflict over such problems as immanentism and evolution is really a nineteenth century problem. The war actually shattered the optimism of most thinking men. A question often asked at that time was, How may the horrors and injustice of the war be reconciled with the idea of human progress and of an all-loving and almighty God? The religious interest, therefore, in the post-war period centers around the problems of evil and the suffering love of God.

The most outspoken champion of this school of thought was the late G. A. STUDDERT-KENNEDY (1877-1929), who was known as "Woodbine Willy" to the soldiers in the trenches of the first World War. His message is couched in an unconventional language. Evil, he held, is the most insoluble problem; it is "not rational and cannot be explained. God did not will it, that we are certain of, and our business is not to explain it but to destroy it." [3] He was utterly at odds with a conception of God as an oriental despot "upon a throne, calm, serene, and passionless, ruling the world with a wave of the hand." [4] Such a God was to him the devil in disguise, an "Almighty Cat." "Almighty Cat, it sits on the throne of the world,

> With paw outstretched, grinning at us, the mice
> Who play our trivial games of virtue and vice
>   and pray—to that which sits on the throne
>   of the world." [5]

Over against this god, Kennedy, under the trials of life, took refuge in the thought that upon the Cross there is revealed the "suffering" of God, not only His "sympathies." [6] It was the mission of Jesus, in his view, to blend into the unity of a new creation the agelong creative discord of the universe, the warrior and the woman, brutal force and tenderly sacrificial love, revealing, as He did, "a perpetually creative God travailing to bring to birth a new heaven and a new earth." [7] Thus the eternal God became the

---

[3] *The New Man in Christ,* posthumously edited, undated, p. 72.
[4] *The Hardest Part,* 1919, p. 149.
[5] *The Warrior, the Woman, and the Christ,* 1929, p. 194.
[6] Cf. *The Sorrows of God, and Other Poems,* 1924.
[7] *The Warrior, etc.,* pp. 124, 194.

"comrade God" and Kennedy, amidst the great agony of life, became a "rebel for God," and not, like others, one against God.[8]

5. "Next to the World War, *von Huegel's influence is*," in the words of Horton (p. 44), "the greatest single cause to which the decline of pre-war immanentism can be ascribed." [9] FRIEDRICH VON HUEGEL (1852-1925), a German baron who spent most of his life in England, was perhaps the most prominent Roman lay theologian of recent times. As a student of W. G. Ward and J. H. Newman, and of the critical scholars Bickell and Holtzmann, von Huegel exercised a great influence not only on the Catholic Modernists in England and France, but also on such men as Soederblom, Troeltsch, and Heiler. Heiler calls von Huegel's theology a "classical example of Catholic universality, synthesis and balance." [10] Von Huegel's thought revolves around three main ideas: The transcendentality of God, the insufficiency of all dogmatic formulas to define the Absolute, and the Incarnation as the process in which the Eternal and Infinite condescends into the finite space and time of history, of the institutional and sacramental. His works include *Eternal Life* (1912), *Essays and Addresses on the Philosophy of Religion* (2 vols., 1921, 1926) and other publications.[11]

6. *Next we may speak of* WILLIAM RALPH INGE, the "gloomy Dean." His greatness lies in his dauntless boldness under all circumstances "to tell the truth and shame the devil." As a theologian Inge is often classified as belonging to the right wing of theological liberalism, though he himself prefers to be called a "Christian Platonist." His chief contribution lies in the fact that he has shown Englishmen the significance of Mysticism. His works include: *Christian Mysticism* (1892), *Science and Ultimate Truth* (1916), *Outspoken Essays* (1919 and 1922), *Personal Religion and the Life of Devotion* (1924), *The Platonic Tradition* (1926), *The Church in the World* (1927), *Christian Ethics and Modern Problems* (1930), *A Rustic Moralist* (1939), and other volumes.[12]

7. *On the background of a scientific empiricism* FREDERICK ROBERT TENNANT has wrestled with the problem of evil and sin. His presentation is biological and moral. He regards original sin as a survival of animal tendencies in man, and the divided self (the sense of sin) is due, he says, to the attempt of man in moralizing these animal tendencies.[13] The view that sin is "empirically inevitable" met with much criticism. Tennant replied to his opponents in a later volume, *The Concept of Sin* (1912) in which he rejected any such implications of his view. "Characters are not made evil, in the strictly moral sense, by environment or by disposition." Man is accountable "for the response to his environment such as it is, and for usage of such disposition as he is endowed with" (p. 234).[14]

Tennant likewise has done some important thinking on other subjects such as

---

[8] Cf. also *I Believe: Sermons on the Apostles' Creed*, 1921, and *The Wicket Gate: Sermons on the Lord's Prayer*, 1923.

[9] By permission of Harper & Brothers, publishers.

[10] *RGG*, II, 2034.

[11] See A. H. Dakin, *Von Huegel and the Supernatural*, 1934; M. Nedoncelle, *Baron Friedrich von Huegel: a Study of His Life and Thought*, French edition, 1935; English, 1937.

[12] In this connection we call attention to the work of Evelyn Underhill (1875-1941), the Anglican mystic writer *par excellence*. Her book entitled *Mysticism, A Study in the Nature and Development of Man's Spiritual Consciousness* (1911), went through many editions. Also *The Mystic Way, A Psychological Study in Christian Origins* (first edition, 1913), is remarkable.

[13] *The Origin and Propagation of Sin*. 1902; *The Sources of the Doctrines of the Fall and Original Sin*, 1903.

[14] By permission of The Macmillan Company, publishers.

miracles[15] and the Trinity.[16] His theory of knowledge is worked out in the first volume of his *magnum opus, Philosophical Theology,* entitled, *The Soul, Its Faculties* (1935). Horton (p. 87) fittingly calls this "a kind of modernized version of Locke's *Essay on Human Understanding,* influenced, of course, by the skepticism of Hume and the criticism of Kant, and deeply indebted to the Psychological Principles of the late Professor J. Ward." [17] In the second volume, entitled, *The World, the Soul, and God* (1937), Tennant enters upon a discussion of the conclusions which emerge from his principles. He conceives of God as "non-infinite" both as regards His being and attributes. For God as a personal spirit is not "the Absolute in the sense of the All, since the created World is not Himself, nor His modes, but His utterance or deed." His power and love, Tennant says, is limited by the human freedom and evil (p. 173). Divine immanence he holds to be an "active" not a "contemplative" relation of God to the world (p. 211). Christ is regarded "as a manifestation of God in the flesh, and as the unique revealer of God" (p. 240).[18]

8. *An able and versatile writer of the present generation is* BURNETT HILLMAN STREETER at Oxford. Streeter is a specialist in the field of the New Testament. *The Four Gospels* (1924) probably is the most outstanding publication in English on the Synoptic problem. Streeter holds the view that the priority of Mark is established beyond peradventure (?). The Gospel of John, in his eyes, is not a biography but a mediation. "It is a mystic's interpretation of the essence of Christianity cast in dramatic form."

In 1912 Streeter published, in co-operation with six other Oxford scholars (R. Brook, W. H. Moberly, R. G. Parsons, A. E. J. Rawlison, N. S. Talbot, and W. Temple) the volume, *Foundations: a Statement of Christian Belief in Terms of Modern Thought.* The position of this book is a mediating theology. The writers are dominated by the psychological approach. Dismissing as untenable the idea both of an infallible book and of an infallible church, they base religious authority on the corporate experience of the Church. In his volume, *Reality* (1926), Streeter recants Absolute Idealism, conceiving of God as a personal Life-Force. Other stimulating publications of his include *Concerning Prayer* (1916), *Immortality* (1917), *The Spirit* (1919), and *The Buddha and the Christ* (1932). His interest in the Oxford Group Movement is reflected in his later volume, *The God Who Speaks* (1936). Here he argues that "provided certain conditions are fulfilled, the voice within ought to be regarded as an authentic communication from God." Streeter died in 1937.

9. *Two other scholars should be mentioned here,* CHARLES E. RAVEN and JOHN MACMURRAY. Raven, as a theologian and trained scientist, is a monist. He contends, pantheistically, that God is revealed as much in creation and the secular realm of life— in the devotion of man to his family and country, and in the social passion of "atheistic" communism—as in the "rigid structure of dogma and ritual of the Established Church." He holds with F. D. Maurice that Christ is the Head of Humanity, not only of the Church. Among his works are *Our Salvation* (1929), *Jesus and the Gospel of Love* (1931), *The Life and Teaching of Jesus Christ* (1933), *Christian Socialism* (1936),

---

[15] *Miracle and its Philosophical Presupposition,* 1925.
[16] *Congregational Quarterly,* January, 1925, pp. 8 ff.
[17] *Op. cit.,* p. 87. By permission of Harper & Brothers, publishers.
[18] *Philosophical Theology,* II, pp. 173, 211, 240. By permission of The Macmillan Company, publishers.

and *The Gospel and the Church* (1940). Macmurray is an authority on Karl Marx. He claims, like Raven, that the reconciliation between Christianity and communism is the most urgent issue of our time. A passionate Communism is, in his eyes, closer to God than an indolent Church. He has published or contributed to a number of volumes such as *Philosophy of Communism* (1933), *Marxism* (1934), *Creative Society* (1936), *The Boundaries of Science* (1939) *et al.*

10. *Unitarian liberalism* is well represented by LAWRENCE P. JACKS, the editor of the *Hibbert Journal*. His liberalism is rather mild when compared with American Unitarianism. He is not a systematic theologian; his writings are "journalistic in style." [19] He is a religious pragmatist with a neo-Kantian background. Religion, according to him, springs from the spiritual depth of the human soul. Consequently, the Church is to him not a supernatural institution but rather, as he said in a sermon preached in Liverpool cathedral, June 11, 1933, "the Spiritual University of the Human Race." [20] Of his numerous writings we may mention, beside the one referred to, *Religious Perplexities* (1923), *The Inner Sentinel* (1930), *The Education of the Whole Man* (1931), and *A Living Universe* (1933).

11. *In concluding our discussion of English Liberalism and Modernism* a number of questions are in order concerning the Modernists' attitude toward the fundamental beliefs of conservative Christianity.

What about the English Modernist's attitude toward dogma? Differing from most American Modernists, he sees the need of dogma; but he holds that dogma is developing. Experience comes first and doctrinal formulation next, and formulation must change its method of expression as new categories of thinking emerge. Spiritual dogmas such as, "God is Love, Light, Truth, Spirit, that Jesus is in His character the reflection of the invisible Father—The Very Word of God in human history"—"these dogmas are," in the words of Major, our spokesman for English Modernism, "of supreme importance" (p. 83).

Then Major goes on to speak of the historical dogmas and says, "Such dogmas as that Jesus was born of the Virgin Mary, was crucified, dead, and buried, etc., that He rose from the dead on the third day, these dogmas are of less importance to the Christian Religion than the first class of dogmas. The Christian Religion may survive without them" (p. 85).

In general, What does the English Modernist propose in his theological thinking? (1) As to the idea of God, he combines the idea of Immanence with Transcendence, and the doctrine of the Trinity, though it "is liable to be perverted into Tritheism," is, in the words of Major, "preferable to the old Unitarian doctrine" (p. 105). (2) His attitude toward original sin is negative. Children are to be baptized because they belong to God and have no original sin. (3) The idea of propitiatory sacrifice is thrown aside as a pagan doctrine. The English Modernist accepts the moral theory of the Atonement. (4) Belief in miracles is dismissed as a survival of a pre-scientific age. (5) As to eschatology, the Second Coming is rejected with all the catastrophic elements of Biblical eschatology. (6) As to everlasting punishment, the English Modernist does not believe in it. (7) Then, too, he rejects the infallibility of the Bible. Its truth is dependent on whether it meets the need of the human soul. (8) Revelation is not supernatural in

---

[19] Horton, *op. cit.*, p. 63.
[20] Printed in *Elemental Religion*, 1934. p. 122.

the sense that it is extraordinary; but revelation comes because man's mind is naturally religious (pp. 106 ff.).

What about Jesus? English Modernism lays down the following axioms: (1) Christianity is Jesuanity. (2) The Virgin Birth is not necessary to the Incarnation. (3) The Incarnation is a higher form of divine Immanence. (4) The Incarnation and indwelling of the divine Logos in Jesus Christ and in us is a difference not of kind but of degree (p. 139 ff.).

On the sacraments the English Modernist places high valuation. "He interprets them both dramatically and mystically. Their reverent use in his experience unites him with past generations of fellow Churchmen, and also provides him with an ideal means of communion with the spiritual world" (pp. 35 f.).[21]

The position of Major is, in all the essentials, shared by Cecil John Cadoux, as expressed in his recent study, *The Case for Evangelical Modernism* (1939). The author, of course, is fully aware of the disfavor into which theological liberalism has fallen during the last decade. He emphatically renounces all allegiance to any kind of a rational humanism. Liberal Modernism means to him "that attitude to Christian doctrine which, taking due account of the occasional conflict between truth and tradition, rejects the customary identification of tradition and orthodoxy and sees the real test of orthodoxy (i.e., right belief) in truth" (p. 10). "Whatever validity the traditional Christian doctrines possess they owe ultimately, not to their antiquity, nor to their ubiquity, nor even to their scripturality, but to their capacity to vindicate themselves to Christian hearts and minds as true" (pp. 16 f.). In other words, Cadoux looks to reason and experience as the final test of religious truth. Over against a non-Christocentric humanism, Barthianism, and traditionalism—which he denotes as the "three blind alleys" in contemporary theological thought—Cadoux believes that we may draw nearer to the truth by keeping close to the gospel of the "historical Jesus."

A modern historical picture of the Lord would, "in all probability," he says, be as follows: Jesus was the legally born son of Joseph and Mary, born at Nazareth, not at Bethlehem. He was not conscious of His being pre-existent with the Father, nor was he, as regards moral perfection, exempted from "unintentional imperfections" (p. 145). He was not omniscient, nor did He "claim to forgive sins in His own right." The alleged nature miracles are ill attested, they are "probably" unhistorical. His physical body did not leave the grave, "nor can we think of it as having ascended into the sky" (p. 154). On the other hand, of what we can be "historically sure," he claims, is "that Jesus lived a life of unbroken, growing and intimate fellowship with God and of unstinted love for man. His ministry was shaped primarily with an eye to the moral and spiritual needs of Israel and the world at the particular junction in human history; but in being so perfectly adapted to them, it displayed then, and for all time will display, the universal sweep of God's love and the eternal meaning of His will" (pp. 156 f.). Jesus' divinity, he says, is to be explained by belief in "the divinity of the human race, as proclaimed by Him and in which He shared, by virtue of his moral excellence, in a unique way." Can such a Jesus still be the object of our worship? Cadoux answers, Yes. For worship is nothing else but reverence for worth, he explains. "All that is worthy of our reverence, our adoration, our obedience, either is, or in some way embodies and

---

[21] *English Modernism.* Quotations by permission of Harvard University Press, publishers.

represents, God" (p. 161). To this picture of Jesus he adds the defiant statement: "And if anyone shall have said that to rest content with such a formula as this is virtually to deny our Lord's divinity and to abandon the Christian gospel, let him be anathema!" (p. 167).

12. *From this review the three main ideas current in English Modernism* are very perspicuous: the metaphysical, critical, and social. English Modernism is, in short, a twentieth century expression of the left wing of Hegelianism. The English Modernists, like the German theologians under the influence of Hegel (cf. pp. 119 ff.), are a lesson of history that *an alliance between philosophical idealism and Christianity will bring disaster upon the Biblical religion of redemption.* Under idealistic influence Christianity must of necessity lose its identity and disappear in a general ethical humanism.

It is only the cautious and moderate attitude of the English mind which does not permit realization of the impending danger as clearly as in the case of German and American radicalism.

II. Protestant Theology

1. We now come to a consideration of the *Protestant tradition* in contemporary English theology. The Keswick Movement as well as a company of able Non-Conformist and Scottish theologians proves that the Protestant tradition not only is still alive but that it occupies a dominant position in the life of the churches. Contemporary English Protestantism is a blend of the Evangelical and Non-Conformist tradition. It is represented today both by the men of the Low Church tradition and the Council of the Free Churches and by the Presbyterian theologians of Scotland. While the orthodox Evangelicals in the nineteenth century contributed little to theological thought in England, there is evident in our century a kind of liberal Evangelicalism displaying a keen interest in theology as a science. Liberalism also has encroached more and more upon the theology of the Dissenters. Presbyterians or Congregationalists who still hold fast to the "Five Points of Calvinism" without qualification are rather exceptional. Among the Dissenters the former gulf between Calvinism and Arminianism has been closing. All Protestant forces have been drawn together in their common defense both against the irreligious sentiment of our age and the bold inventions of the Anglo-Catholics.

2. Among the prominent leaders of the Evangelical group in the *Anglican communion* are such theologians as V. F. Storr and W. R. Matthews, the successor of Inge as Dean of St. Paul's, who, in co-operation with the Baptist scholar H. Wheeler Robinson, is the editor of a series of theological monographs, *The Library of Constructive Theology.* The literary productivity of this group has been commendable. The list of contributors shows such names as C. H. Dodd, O. C. Quick, H. R. Mackintosh, H. H. Farmer, Evelyn Underhill. Anyone who wants to know how a theologian who is "low" as a churchman, "critical" in the study of the Bible, and "liberal" as to the metaphysical in Christianity approaches the problem of the sacramental in religion, will profit much from reading O. C. Quick's *The Christian Sacraments* (1927). Of particular interest is his conception of the Real Presence which he sees to be constituted by the efficacious relation of the Glorified Lord to the sacramental elements. For "whatever is the organ of Christ's activity is, so far, His body" (p. 209). Quick even is willing to "accept the statement that the bread and wine are changed so as to become the Body and Blood of Christ, if it be understood that the terms body and blood denote, not

material things as such, but outward things as they are in relation to a spiritual activity which operates and expresses itself through them" (p. 226).[22]

To W. R. MATTHEWS religion is "one of the ways of 'coming to terms' with the Other by means of a special mode of interpretation." [23] "The main function of theology is to act as an intermediary between philosophy and religion" (p. 97). The Christian doctrine of the Trinity, according to his opinion, "springs from the Christian experience of God" (p. 184). As to the person of Christ, there can be no doubt, he says, that for Paul "Christ has 'the value' of God" (*ibid.*). In Christian experience, according to his view, man lays hold of metaphysical Reality (p. 190).[24]

3. In 1923 some twelve Anglican scholars issued *Liberal Evangelicalism* as a kind of a theological manifesto of the younger Evangelicals. In the Preface to the volume they declare that the Bible "still stands in its unique position." But, they add, "it is the mind of Christ, not the letter of Holy Scripture, which is authoritative" (vi). The Bible is for them, "the record of God's self-revelation to mankind" (p. 80).[25] As regards the central doctrine of the Protestant tradition, that of the Atonement, R. T. Howard's exposition of "The Work of Christ" (pp. 121 ff.) bears a decidedly Ritschlian stamp. The Cross was necessary, he says, "because nothing short of the Cross could make man sure that God was of such a nature," i.e., to be loving and ready to forgive. In Jesus God "identified Himself completely with man in order that by the power of His personal influence He might bring him back to Himself" (p. 129). As Evangelicals these writers are proud to be called heirs of the Reformation (p. 291). They are not sympathetic with the trend of Medievalism in the Anglican Church. "We need," says E. W. Barnes, "at the present time not a modified but a new Catholicism, a true synthesis of the Gospel and modern knowledge" (p. 293).

4. We now turn to *Congregational theology.* P. T. FORSYTH'S great work *The Person and Place of Christ* (1911), next to Fairbairn's *Philosophy of the Christian Religion,* is the one outstanding contribution of the Congregationalists during the first quarter of the twentieth century. FORSYTH (1842-1921) was a Scot, partly trained in Germany. He was considerably influenced by the practical emphasis of the Ritschlian theologians. His *magnum opus* has as motto Butler's saying, "Morality is the Nature of Things." Christianity is to him not a philosophy of the Absolute. Evangelical faith is personal and predominantly ethical. Forsyth also applies the ethical approach to his discussion of the Christological dogma. "It is the work of Christ that gives us the key to the nature of Christ" (p. 346). Jesus is not a genius. "Geniuses are repeated, but Christ never, the Son never" (p. 285). As to the mode of the Incarnation, he follows the kenotic theory discarding, however, the view that Christ renounced some of His attributes; He retained them all, yet in a new mode of being. The possibility of the *kenosis* is found in the divine infinitude. "If the infinite God was so constituted that He could not live also as a finite man then He was not infinite" (p. 315). Implicit in the *kenosis* is the *plerosis,* the self-fulfillment of Christ, i.e., in Christ's historic person God offered Himself in His saving fullness as He identified Himself with humanity. Later, Forsyth seems to have accepted the favorite Christological formula of Seeberg when he

---

[22] Quotations by permission of Harper & Brothers, publishers.
[23] *God in Christian Experience,* 1930, p. 11. Quotations by permission of Harper & Brothers, publisher.
[24] *Ibid.,* p. 190.
[25] Cf. in *Library of Constructive Theology,* the volume by C. H. Dood, *The Authority of the Bible,* 1929.

ays that Christ's "person came back to be the Holy Spirit of all He had done." [26] As egards the teaching of the Atonement, he preserved the penal idea in the doctrine, yet ie insisted strongly on the initiative of God's love.[27] Over against the critical tendencies of our age, Forsyth contended, like Kaehler, that the whole Biblical Christ is truly and leeply the historic Christ.

5. *Another Congregational theologian of repute is* ALFRED ERNEST GARVIE. Born n Russian Poland (1861), educated at Edinburgh, Glasgow, and Mansfield College of Oxford, he became prominent as a leader of the Congregational Churches of Great 3ritain. At heart he is a liberal Evangelical, with a pronounced interest in the social mplications of the Gospel.[28] Though not a Ritschlian himself, he says, he has con- ributed much to interpret Ritschl to Anglo-Saxon scholars.[29] Ritschl's reduction of Christ's deity to a mere judgment of value, he regards as unsatisfactory; nevertheless, ie is agreed with him as to the place which experience holds in religion, and with Herrmann concerning the importance of the "inner life of Jesus" as a means to com- nunion with God.[30] In keeping with this we have a Christocentric theology with its emphasis on the person of Jesus as the manifestation of God.[31]

Note: Other important discussions of the Christological dogma include those by Ch. Gore, *The ncarnation of the Son of God* (1891); R. L. Ottley, *The Doctrine of the Incarnation* (1896, ith edition, 1911); D. W. Forrest, *The Authority of Christ* (1906); H. R. Mackintosh, *The Doctrine of the Person of Jesus Christ* (1912; 2nd edition, 1913); W. Temple, *Christus Veritas* (1924); S. F. Davenport, *Immanence and Incarnation* (1925); H. N. Relton, *A Study in Chris- ology* (1917); *The Christian Conception of the Incarnation* (1926) by the same author. The general tenor of these writers is mediating-conservative. The Incarnation is held to bridge the gulf between the divine transcendence and immanence. The relation of the divine and human in Christ is interpreted in the terms of the Leontian teaching of the "enhypostasy," Christ's Sonship n the terms of will rather than of substance. As to the mode of the Incarnation, the kenotic view prevails though mostly in a modified form. As regards the earthly beginnings of Jesus, it is felt that the article of the Virgin Birth "cannot be lightly swept away," [32] although this doctrine, in he eyes of some, is not a necessary implication of the Incarnation.

6. In recent times the Protestant theological leadership has descended on a *Presby- terian,* JOHN WARD OMAN (1860-1939). His volume on *Grace and Personality* (1918) is a theological classic. With his Calvinistic background and German training (Kant, Schleiermacher, Ritschl) Oman has revived for English theology Augustine and Calvin by making one important alteration in their teaching; he substituted "persuasive" grace for "irresistible" grace. While the *sola gratia* of Paul and Augustine remains uncurtailed, the old antinomy of religion and morality, grace and works, finds its solu- tion in the higher synthesis of God and human personality. Absolute moral inde- pendence and absolute religious dependence are thus not opposites "but necessarily one and indivisible" (p. 22). "Grace has always a convex side towards God, and a concave side towards man. Taken separately, they are contradictory and opposite, but, united,

---

[26] *This Life and the Next,* 1918, p. 108.
[27] *The Work of Christ,* 1911.
[28] *The Christian Ideal for Human Society,* 1930; *Can Christ Save Society?* 1933; *Christian Moral Conduct,* 1938.
[29] *The Ritschlian Theology,* 1899.
[30] *Studies in the Inner Life of Jesus,* 1907.
[31] *The Christian Doctrine of the Godhead,* 1925; *The Christian Belief in God,* 1935; *Revelation through History and Experience,* 1935; *The Christian Faith,* 1936; also his *Memories and Meanings of My Life,* 1938.
[32] E. J. Bicknell, *A Theological Introduction to the Thirty-nine Articles of the Church of England,* 2nd edition, 1925, p. 97.

they are perfectly one as the convex and concave sides in one line" (p. 182).[33] The same problem he had treated earlier from the historical point of view in his volume, *The Problem of Faith and Freedom in the Last Two Centuries* (1907).

We must add a few remarks on the later volume, *The Natural and Supernatural* (1931). Though following in time *Grace and Personality*, it logically precedes it. Oman denies that there is no other way to reality save that of natural sciences. The total richness of life, he holds, is not discovered by scientific empiricism; it discloses itself only to the intuitive faculties of man. All monistic conceptions of religion (pantheism) and of piety (mysticism) are rejected. Only in monotheistic religion, he asserts, the natural world remains real, and man is inspired with zeal and hope to conquer the evil inherent in the natural order. His book *Honest Religion* (published posthumously in 1941) represents a type of matured Ritschlianism. As may be expected in such a book, the author remains somewhat vague as to the doctrinal content of the Christian faith.[34]

7. A brief remark on theological scholarship among the *Methodists* and *Baptists* should find its place here. Representing the experimental type of Christianity, we find the two Methodist scholars LESLIE WEATHERHEAD and ERIC S. WATERHOUSE engaged in relating the Christian dogma and ethics to the new science of psychology. Both men are prolific writers. Among the books of Weatherhead are *Psychology in the Service of the Soul* (1930), *The Mastery of Sex through Psychology and Religion* (1932), *How Can I Find God?* (1934), *Psychology and Life* (1935), *After Death* (1937), and *This Is the Victory* (1941). Waterhouse wrote *What Is Salvation?* (1933), *Psychology and Pastoral Work* (1940), etc.

The most eminent scholar among the *Baptists* is H. WHEELER ROBINSON, whom we had occasion to mention above in connection with Dean W. R. Matthews. As in the case of the Methodist theologians, the emphasis on experience is predominant in his writings. Though critical of the traditional terminology, he is anxious to retain the "religious values" which are embodied in the *termini* of the past and which, as he says, are vital to Christian experience. In *The Christian Doctrine of Man* (first edition, 1911) he lays stress on the religious and moral concept of man over against the rational and esthetic view of man inherent in Greek thought. He also wrote *The Christian Experience of the Holy Spirit* (1928). While critical of the doctrine in its conservative form, he nevertheless rejects emphatically the purely immanental aspect of the Spirit as taught by Schleiermacher and Ritschl. His recent book, *Redemption and Revelation in the Actuality of History* (1942), is a "representation of the doctrine of redemption, based upon the actuality of history as interpreted by criticism, psychology, and philosophy." As to doctrine, the book likewise is mediating. He also wrote on the problem of theodicy, *Suffering Human and Divine* (1939), and published *The Old Testament, Its Making and Meaning* (1937), and a *History of Israel* (1938).

8. When we turn to consider the *Scottish theology* of the twentieth century, we find a great array of notable scholars and theologians.[35] Standing at the head of this list is JAMES DENNEY (1856-1917). Being at first critical about Ritschlian theology,[36]

---

[33] By permission of The Macmillan Company, publishers. Cf. P. Tillich's "theonomous" conception of man. p. 192.

[34] For a more detailed discussion of Oman see Horton, *op. cit.*, pp. 126 ff.

[35] For a fine summary of Scottish theology compare *The Christian Century*, December 22, 1927.

[36] *Studies in Theology*, 1894.

Denney himself became later known as a semi-Ritschlian. In his theology he also shows peculiarities that connect him with A. Schlatter. His method is modern and progressive. All religious knowledge is based on experience. This experience, however, is found only in the historical revelation of God in Christ. The Scriptures, recording the experience of the early Church, are the records of that divine revelation. In *Jesus and the Gospel* (1918) Denney argued that there are not two gospels in the New Testament, but one, and that the Church at all times has rightly regarded Christ as an object of faith. Christianity is a mediatorial religion, the blessings of which are dependent on the work of Christ. He insists that there enters into the substance of Christianity not merely an experience of forgiveness that comes to us through Christ, but a doctrine of an objective Atonement. Christ accomplished not merely a subjective influence over the minds of men, but He did a work "which tells upon God as well as upon the sinful." [37] Man's reconciliation, his return to God and acceptance with Him, is based on the Atonement wrought by Christ. "Even if no man should ever say, Thou, O Christ, art all I want, more than all in Thee I find, God says it. Christ and His work have this absolute value for the Father whatever this or that individual may think of them" (p. 235). In his laborious search for a satisfactory theory of the *modus operandi* of Christ's sacrifice, he ended by proclaiming that no theory showed so deep spiritual insight as that of MacLeod Campbell.

NOTE: Related to Denney's view of the Atonement is the theory set forth by R. C. Moberly (1845-1903), *Atonement and Personality* (1901): Christ is the Perfect Penitent; His Suffering is the expiation for the corporate guilt of humanity.[38] Also J. K. Mozley's *The Heart of the Gospel* (1926) belongs to this class of theological literature. On the other hand, the purely moral view is quite pronounced in such scholars as, for example, V. F. Storr (Anglican), *The Problem of the Cross* (1919); W. F. Halliday (Presbyterian), *Reconciliation and Reality* (1917); C. J. Cadoux (Congregationalist), *The Message About the Cross* (1924); and his brother, A. T. Cadoux, *The Gospel that Jesus Preached* (1925); H. Maldwyn Hughes (Wesleyan), *What is the Atonement?* (1925); William E. Wilson (Quaker), *Atonement and Non-Resistance* (2nd edition, 1923). This sentiment is also very outspoken in Hastings Rashdall (Anglican), *The Idea of the Atonement in Christian Theology* (1919). The Atonement has, in his eyes, no place in the gospel of Jesus; it is a product of the mind of Paul. The Reformation theology is said to be a one-sided and exaggerated version of St. Augustine.

9. *Another of the outstanding theologians of Scotland was* HUGH ROSS MACKINTOSH (1870-1936), who, among other volumes, published the following remarkable books: *The Doctrine of the Person of Jesus Christ* (1912), *Christianity and Sin* (1913), *Immortality and the Future* (1917), *The Originality of the Christian Message* (1920), and *The Christian Experience of Forgiveness* (1927). By translating from Schleiermacher and Ritschl, Mackintosh helped materially to acquaint the English theologians with masterpieces of German scholarship. He also contributed a number of biographical sketches to *Religion in Geschichte und Gegenwart*.

As a theologian Mackintosh held a mediating position. Through him, Ritschl, whose anti-metaphysical tenets held little appeal for the English world which was saturated with philosophical idealism, was given a fair trial in Scotland. But Mackintosh was far from being a full-fledged Ritschlian. That which appealed most to him was not the pragmatism and moralism in Ritschl but the quite un-Ritschlian, Tholuckian trend in Herrmann, i.e., the emphasis on the mystical experience of the forgiveness of sin medi-

---

[37] *The Christian Doctrine of Reconciliation*, 1918, p. 234.
[38] Cf. Franks, *History of the Doctrine of the Work of Christ*, II, 428 ff.

ated through the person of Jesus.[39] Mackintosh was untiring in emphasizing the "essential" Deity of Christ, remaining close to the Erlangen conception of the Incarnation. He followed Thomasius in accepting the kenotic view, rejecting, however, the theory that Christ had relinquished in the act of His Incarnation the external divine attributes. With Forsyth, Mackintosh preferred to speak of a "transposition of attributes." The historic Christ was very dear to him. And it is here where we may discern the influence of Ritschl on his thought. He disowned a speculative rationalism in deference to the concrete and historical in Christianity.

10. Whereas English theologians usually had been slow in acquainting themselves with new movements in Continental theology, the *Barthian movement* became known in the British Isles almost at its inception. Since 1924 there have appeared a number of articles on Karl Barth in the *Expositor* (by Adolf Keller), in the *Hibbert Journal* (1927, by J. McConnachie), in the *Expository Times* (1928, by H. R. Mackintosh), in the *Times Literary Supplement* (1929, "The New Theologians from Harnack to Barth"), and in the *Review of Churches* (1929, by J. K. Mozley). The first comprehensive study of the teaching of Karl Barth was made by R. Birch Hoyle, *The Teaching of Karl Barth* (1930). This critical volume was followed by John McConnachie, who wrote as a thankful pupil of Barth, *The Significance of Karl Barth* (1931), and *The Barthian Theology and the Man of Today* (1933). In 1936 Karl Barth was called to deliver the Gifford Lectures (see p. 177). An excellent proof of his influence on Scottish theology is found in George S. Hendry's little book, *God the Creator* (1937), containing the Hastie Lectures of 1935. The book voices an ardent plea to Scottish theologians to turn from the current theology of England and America, engaged with rationalizing religion by the empirical method of science, and to go back to Luther for theological food. (For translations of Barth's writings compare p. 179.)

III. The Catholic Tradition

1. The *Catholic tradition* received a fresh and strong inspiration from the Oxford movement. This has been shown in our Chapter Four. In *Lux Mundi* we saw a critical theology at home in Oxford. Modern Anglo-Catholicism is characterized by this blend of High Church principles and a critical approach to the Scriptures.

2. *As an illustration of the critical element* we may point to CHARLES GORE (1835-1932). It was his article in *Lux Mundi* on "The Holy Spirit and Inspiration" that caused more tumult than any other article in that remarkable volume. In the field of Old Testament criticism Gore held, in general, the views of modern critical scholarship, while his views on the New Testament were more conservative.[40] But in spite of these critical tenets, he proved to be a staunch defender of a supernatural and sacramentarian theology. He accepted wholeheartedly the Biblical conception of the Virgin Birth and bodily resurrection of Jesus. He defended the theological language of the ancient councils and was suspicious about the motives of their modern critics. Gore also showed an intense interest in the social problems of his country. Among his books we may mention *The Body of Christ* (1901), which contains a constructive discussion of the doctrine of the Eucharist, *The New Theology and the New Religion* (1907),

---

[39] See his note on "The Theology of Herrmann," in *The Christian Experience of Forgiveness,* pp. 44 ff. Cf. in this connection the striking remark of the Congregational theologian Robert Mackintosh: *"Ritschlio non crederem nisi me Hermani commoveret auctoritas." Albrecht Ritschl and His School*, 1915, p. 21.

[40] See *The Doctrine of the Infallible Book,* undated.

Work and the Church (1916), *Belief in God* (1922), *Belief in Christ* (1923), and *The Holy Spirit and the Church* (1924). Gore called these last three books his "Reconstruction of Belief."

3. The literary manifesto of modern Anglo-Catholicism is found in the volume entitled *Essays Catholic and Critical* (1926). Both a very intense supernaturalism and the highest criticism are represented in this book. OLIVER E. JAMES wrote the first essay on "The Emergence of Religion." He attempts to make the Incarnation a climax of the evolution of all primitive faiths. The second essay is on "The Vindication of Religion." It is by that noted metaphysician A. E. TAYLOR. Its summit is the upholding of religious experience as the source of evidence. The next essay is on "Authority." The first part deals with Authority as a ground of belief written by A. E. J. RAWLINSON, while the second part, the Authority of the Church, is written by WILFRED L. KNOX. Authority here is held not to be vested in an infallible Bible nor in individual experience, but in the corporate experience of the Church. The authority of the Church, however, is held to be neither "oracular nor infallible," but must at all times, it is said, vindicate its claims "at the threefold bar of history, reason, and spiritual experience" (p. 95). The following essay on "The Christ of the Synoptic Gospels," by the late SIR EDWYN CLEMENT HOSKYNS, is a masterpiece of constructive Biblical criticism. He rejects as historically unsound the prevalent liberal theory that the Christ of the Church was the product of "the gradual apotheosis of a Jewish prophet under the influence of Greek-Christian belief and worship" (p. 157). "The contrast," he continues to argue, "is not between the Jesus of history and the Christ returning to glory; the two being held together by the title Son of Man, which suggests both" (pp. 176 f.). The second series includes discussion on God, Christ, Man, Salvation, and Eschatology. In the last four essays the authors set forth the Catholic interpretation of such disputed doctrines as Ecclesiology, The Spirit and the Church in History, The Reformation, The Origins of the Sacraments, and The Eucharist. The appraisement of the Reformation naturally is not too liberal. The number of the sacraments is fixed at four. "It is, however, possible," says the writer, N. P. WILLIAMS, "to simplify the subject-matter . . . for Penitence, Baptism, and Confirmation are in primitive Catholicism not three distinct sacraments, but rather parts of, or moments in, one great cleansing, regenerating, and Spirit-imparting rite . . . This single original rite of entrance to Christianity we will designate by the word 'Initiation' "(p. 376). The Last Supper he considers to be "but a 'shadow' Eucharist—a typical object-lesson, not the mystic and glorious reality which could only be consummated in the 'Kingdom of God' (i.e., the new Christian dispensation) which His death was to inaugurate" (p. 423). On the question of the Eucharistic sacrifice the last writer, W. SPENS, remarks that "the Last Supper and the Eucharist are not separate sacrifices from that of Calvary, but supply a necessary element in the sacrifice of Calvary, by expressly investing our Lord's death before God and man with its sacrificial significance" (p. 436). "The immolation once made can never be repeated. But equally necessary in its bearing upon the salvation of the world is the rite by which down the long succession of ages our Lord makes His death to be our sacrifice and enables us to appropriate the blessings thus secured" (p. 439).[41]

4. *The Roman influence in the Anglo-Catholic group* was very pronounced during the time of the "Conversations of Malines" (1921-26). These conversations were car-

---

[41] Quotations by permission of The Macmillan Company, publishers.

ried on between representatives of the Anglo-Catholics and Cardinal Mercier, Primate of Belgium, with a view to a possible reunion of the Church of England with Rome. The publication of these proceedings, however, was received with much indignation in England. When the Pope also made it known that union meant subjection to Rome, the majority of the Anglo-Catholics turned to tread again the *via media* of their fathers. During the next two years the English Parliament gave a forceful expression of the Protestant sentiment of the country when the Lower House rejected the Romanized revised edition of the Common Prayer Book. (While the Evangelicals lean on the theology of the Thirty-nine Articles, the Catholic group shows a decided preference for the Prayer Book.) All these things helped in bringing to prominence a so-called "Central Party." Under the leadership of this party the Established Church has succeeded in making Canterbury a Western patriarchate equal in rank with and superior in influence to the ancient sees of the East. Full communion has been extended, and partially established, both with the Eastern Orthodox churches and the Lutherans of the Baltic region who have preserved the historic episcopate. The Anglican Church even approached the Dissenters in England, and its appeal has met with a very cordial response from that group.

5. The "Catholic" tendencies of the Anglicans crystallized in the so-called *World Conference on Faith and Order*. The movement itself goes back to the initiative of Charles Brent, bishop of the Protestant Episcopal Church of America. It has met in two important international conferences, at Lausanne (1927) and Edinburgh (1937). That the Church of England has approached the problem of church unity from the standpoint of the Central Party and that of a mediating theology is evident from the Report of the Commission on Christian Doctrine published under the title *Doctrine in the Church of England* (1938). In the introduction it is stated that the Anglican Churches "are heirs of the Reformation as well as of Catholic tradition" (p. 25). The claim of catholicity, in the eyes of the Commission, "does not depend on mere numbers or on the extension of a belief at any one time, but on continuance through the ages and the extent to which the consensus is genuinely free" (p. 35), i.e., the Commission has upheld only the first part of the Vincentian maxim that that is Catholic which is accepted *semper, ubique, et ab omnibus.* Though all hierarchical claims are denied, the Report stresses the Episcopate, *iure divino,* as a guarantee of continuity and an identity of teaching (p. 115). The Church is defined not as a communion of believers, but as "the whole company of those who share in the regenerate life" (p. 106). The Scriptures are viewed as the first but not as the sole seat of authority, for "Scripture and the Church alike bear witness" to the revelation of God in history (p. 27). The tradition of the inerrancy of the Bible, it is said, "cannot be maintained in the light of the knowledge now at our disposal" (p. 29). The actual teaching of Jesus was "called forth by particular occasions and was conditioned by the thought-forms and circumstances of the time," and its record in the Gospels "cannot be accepted as always reproducing the *ipsissima verba* of our Lord" (p. 32). In keeping with this view of the Bible is the Commission's attitude toward the Anglican Formularies. Their language is not final but subject to modifications in accordance with fresh knowledge or fresh conceptions (p. 37). God is defined as "the perfect Truth or ultimate Existence," and the causal

ound of the world (p. 41).[42] The Commission's conception of sin is bordering on
elagianism (pp. 56 ff.). In its view of grace it has remained close to the theology of
ıe East by defining it as *favor Dei* and *gratia infusa* (p. 52). As to the earthly begin-
ings of Jesus, it is stated that some members of the Commission believe that the
ıcarnation is "integrally bound up with belief in the Virgin Birth," while others hold
ıat "a full belief in the historical Incarnation is more consistent with the supposition
ıat our Lord's birth took place under the normal conditions of human generation"
p. 82). These critical scholars are likewise inclined to the belief that "the connection
ıade in the New Testament between the emptiness of a tomb and the appearances of
ıe Risen Lord belongs rather to the sphere of religious symbolism than to that of
istorical fact" (p. 86).

6. *This type of a Central theology* also is quite pronounced in the later writings
f Archbishop WILLIAM TEMPLE. In fact, Temple was a member of the Commission
om ıts inception in 1922, and served as chairman after the death of Bishop Burge in
925. He sees the solution of our problems in a return to the healthy objectivism of
ıe medieval mind, combined with the sincerity of the modern mind. His argument
roceeds from a scientific materialism to an immanent theism and from thence to a
ıpernatural, divine personality who in turn descends into this world. Temple is very
mphatic in maintaining the reality of general revelation in nature and history. As God
the ground of all, so all existence is a revelation of God. Only upon this basis the
xpectation of particular revelation is well grounded. The nature of special revelation,
ccording to Temple, is not to be seen in dictated words or sacred books, nor in an
ırganized society." [43] "It is the faith of Christendom," he says, "that in the Gospel
ıere is given an unalterable revelation of the eternal God, not in the form of doctrinal
ropositions which once and for all have been drawn up for the acceptance of men of
very age, but in the form of a Person and a human Life to which all the doctrinal
ırmulations point" (p. 35). The Gospel is unchanging, he told his American audience,
ıough the world in which it appeared is changing. Therefore, theology must always
e changing (p. 34 f.). The possibility of miracles is not altogether denied by him.
'hey are, he writes, "if they occur, a manifestation of the God immanent in the same
ıay as in the ordinary process of nature," [44] for God has not left, he said in his lectures
t Harvard, "nature as a closed system into which he periodically intervenes from out-
ıde" (p. 46). His conception of the sacraments has all the earmarks of philosophical
dealism.[45] The fundamental sacrament "extensively," he says, is the universe. But it
ecame this only, so runs the argument, by virtue of the Incarnation "which is the perfect
ıcrament intensively," because the Incarnation is a momentary perfect expression of
ıe Will of God. Resulting from the Incarnation we find the Church, which is the
Spirit-bearing Body." The sacramental nature of the Church, however, remains incom-
ılete, he holds, as long as its members "are not utterly surrendered to the spirit within
:." Thus sacred rites of the Church, commonly called "sacraments," are then nothing

---

[42] This definition reminds one of Charles S. Macfarland's fitting remark in his criticism of T. H. Hughes'
ınception of God as "Ultimate Reality." Says he: "One can almost see Karl Barth's cynical smile at this," *The
hristian Faith in a Day of Crisis*, p. 138. By permission of Fleming H. Revell Company, publishers.

[43] *The Church and Its Teaching Today*, 1936. (The Noble Lectures delivered at Harvard, 1935.) Quotations
y permission of The Macmillan Company, publishers.

[44] *Nature, Man, and God*, 1933, p. 295. By permission of The Macmillan Company, publishers.

[45] Temple started out as an adherent of the idealistic tradition as demonstrated by his earlier publications
The Nature of Personality, 1911; *Men's Creatrix*, 1917). He once held a philosophical lectureship at Oxford.

but a part of this Body of Christ.[46] We ought not to think of the Real Presence, Templ holds, in the term of transubstantiation, i.e., as a change of matter, but should conceiv of it as a "transvaluation" or "convaluation" of the blessed element (p. 295); and valu ation, he holds, is foundational of Reality. "Everything exists as far as it is good (p. 16).[47] The "thing signified" is neither the human Body of Christ in its physico chemical substance, nor the risen and glorified Body, Temple says. In addition to th use of the term "body" in the New Testament signifying the fleshly Body of the Lor as well as the Church, there is, in his views, a third use of the term: the Eucharisti Body. "That Bread is not itself the Glorified Body of the Lord, but it is the Body o the Glorified Lord—the Body of Christ who is known to us as crucified, risen, ascended glorified" (p. 299). As His Body, the Bread is the "instrument" by which the Lor gives Himself to us (p. 285). It is the means by which He is "accessible"; but, h continues, "the accessibility is spiritual, not material or local, and Christ is only actuall present to the soul of those who make right use of the means of access afforded (p. 287).

As to the Kingdom, Temple holds that it is not to be equated with any economi order. It is in the world, but its consummation is not conceivable in the conditions o this mortal life.[48]

7. Just a passing remark on *Roman Catholicism in England.* Since the death o Friedrich von Huegel no single outstanding figure has arisen to take his place. Amon professional theologians WILLIAM E. ORCHARD, a Congregational convert, ranks high In *From Truth to Truth* (1933) he has analyzed the different movements of though through which he has passed. A liberal in 1907, he joined the Church of Rome in 1932 He was ordained a Roman Priest in 1935. Orchard is Thomistic in his theology an Catholic to the core. In his *Foundations of Faith* (4 vols., 1924 ff.) we have the com bination of Scholasticism with the modern approach of experience. For those who ar making experience the norm of theology, he would correct their individualism by stress ing the experience of the past. Thus the Catholic testimony of the experience of th past finds complete sway in Orchard.[49]

A leading figure among the laity is CHRISTOPHER DAWSON, historian and socia philosopher. He wrote, among other volumes, *Progress and Religion* (1929).

IV. CONCLUDING OBSERVATIONS

1. In *concluding our discussion* of contemporary theological thought in Grea Britain, the question is in order, How successful have English theologians been i presenting to our age the fundamentals of our Christian religion? When we compar the development in England during the last fifty years with the trend of Continenta thought, it seems, at first glance, that English theology, moving with greater caution has less radically surrendered to the intellectual fads of our times. English theologians especially the Anglo-Catholics, are, in spite of their critical tenets, very emphatic i stressing the metaphysical aspect of religion. Thus it seems that the healthy moderatio

---

[46] *Christ the Truth,* 1924, p. 279. Quotations by permission of The Macmillan Company, publishers.

[47] In this connection we want to call attention to Temple's criticism of Ritschl: "This Ritschlianism is (i our view) right in so far as it contends that all religious doctrines are value-judgments, but is wrong, and eve hopelessly wrong, in so far as it regards these as other than metaphysical and ontological judgments" (p. 17).

[48] *The Church and Its Teaching Today,* pp. 21 f. By permission of The Macmillan Company, publishers.

[49] Cf. *The Necessity for the Church,* 1940.

of the English mind has rendered a better service to the Church than the critical genius of the Continent. But if the question is asked, whether this metaphysical trend in English theology is genuinely Scriptural or Hegelian, the answer is clear. The English are still, a hundred years after Hegel, Hegelian to the core. The Hegelian background is the common possession of the English Modernists and Anglo-Catholics. And Hegelianism implies immanentism (sacramentarianism and religious socialism), mysticism, subjectivism, and experience. Consequently, a Biblical truth as the Incarnation is for the Modernists only a higher form of divine immanence,[50] and the modern High Churchmen's conception of the Church and sacraments rests essentially on the Hegelian idea of divine Reality. The distance between God and man is being obliterated. Revelation becomes religious self-consciousness, and justification a mere change of man's disposition. The "idea" of God is a phrase very current in English theology. The word "idea," however, has a common etymological root with "idols." "Ideas of God," therefore, are idols, mental idols, the fabrication of which Christian theology should leave to philosophy.[51] English theology still is busy with adjustment, with harmonizing the Bible and the modern mind. This is essentially the approach of Schleiermacher and Hegel and of all their followers in the nineteenth century.

Note: In this connection we may call attention to the concept of a "suffering God" which has considerable vogue in English thought. The late Studdert-Kennedy, Dean Inge, and Archbishop Temple are quite conspicuous in this respect. The theory may be regarded as a dualistic reaction against the monistic tendencies in the theology of Schleiermacher and his followers to whom the Greek concept of *apatheia* expressed the highest perfection of God. It is, nevertheless, in keeping with the Idealistic tradition to regard the Divine Being Himself as growing and struggling. (That the theory, however, is not limited to Idealistic theologians is proved by the fact that such a Neo-Kantian scholar as the late Soederblom has—though rather timidly—expressed the same idea. Cf. G. Aulen, *Das christliche Gottesbild*, p. 369. See also the book by Archbishop Eidem, as quoted in this volume, p. 163.)

Other thinkers outside the Church, especially H. G. Wells, have carried the idea a step further when they speak of the Divine Being as of a "finite God." Regarding evil as eternal, they teach, like the Manicheans, a thoroughgoing metaphysical dualism. The "good God" is a "finite God," ever struggling on, whose sole concern is to disentangle Himself from the opposing evil powers. A more subtle form of Manichean dualism is that which conceives of the power of God as limited not by some external principle or substance, but a resisting element within His own self. While it regards God as a unitary being, it holds that His divine will is limited by His own imperfect nature. Hence the world which He created is, in some way a disappointment to the Creator Himself. The most ardent champion of this Neo-Manicheanism in America is E. S. Brightman of Boston University (cf. p. 315 f.).

It is self-evident that the Church must reject this type of metaphysical dualism as contrary to the Biblical concept of divine sovereignty. Likewise, a theologian should be on his guard when speaking of God as "suffering" lest he may fall into the error of the Patripassian Modalists of the Ancient Church (see Vol. I, 110 ff.) and obscure the hypostatic distinctions in the Holy Trinity.

The most comprehensive study of the subject under discussion is the book by J. K. Mozley, *The Impassibility of God* (1926). The reader will find the subject also discussed by A. C. Knudsen, *Doctrine of God* (pp. 245 ff.), *Doctrine of Redemption* (pp. 200 ff.). Aulén also has some fitting remarks on the problem in the volume quoted (pp. 363 ff.).

2. While the Church of England is neither Roman nor Protestant but "Broad," Scotland in the sixteenth and seventeenth centuries established itself firmly on the principle of the Calvinistic Reformation. The Scots, therefore, were better qualified to appreciate Ritschl's protest against the philosophizing tendencies in theology and religion. And they are now, since Continental theology has learned to disencumber

---

[50] Cf. Major, *op. cit.*, pp. 163, 166.

[51] G. Kittel, *Theologisches Woerterbuch zum Neuen Testament*, IV, 5, Beilage, p. 3.

itself from Ritschl's attempt to reduce Christianity to a system of ethics, seemingly more appreciative of the renascent voice of the Reformation.

3. *The section on Great Britain* was practically finished when the outbreak of the new World War caught the writer while traveling on the Continent. As the manuscript is put in its final form, the war is still raging. It would be presumptuous at such times of high nervous tension to predict anything as regards the future of theology. In a Postscript to page sixty-one, dated 1940, W. M. Horton quotes from W. Temple's article on "Theology Today" in the November, 1939, number of *Theology*. This statement is the words of the Primate of the Church of England: "Theologians of today are more concerned than we were in 1910 or 1920 about the theological status of the Church. The Church is part of its own Creed. To be in Christ is to be in the Church—and vice-versa." Dr. Temple, according to the Postscript, concludes with the remark that the present task of theology is not to embrace all experience in a coherent and comprehensive scheme, but to declare salvation to them that believe. It is to light beacons in the darkness rather than to illuminate the world. "These words," Horton adds, "sound more 'Continental' and less 'Anglo-Saxon' than anything he has hitherto said." [52] May God grant to theologians everywhere an humble heart that they will listen when God speaks.

---

[52] *Op. cit.* By permission of Harper & Brothers, publishers.

SECTION THREE

Theological Thought in America

Chapter One

FACTS AND FORCES IN AMERICAN THEOLOGY

Literature: CHARLES L. THOMPSON, *The Religious Foundations of America*, 1917; WILLIAM A. BROWN, *The Church in America*, 1922; EDWARD F. HUMPHRY, *Nationalism and Religion in America*, 1774-1789, 1924; HENRY K. ROWE, *The History of Religion in the United States*, 1924; THOMAS C. HALL, *The Religious Background of American Culture*, 1930; H. RICHARD NIEBUHR, *The Kingdom of God in America*, 1937; WILLIAM W. SWEET, *The Story of Religion in America*, 1939; KENNETH S. LATOURETTE, *The Great Century A.D. 1800- A.D. 1914*, 1941, pp. 175-456. EVARTS B. GREENE, *Religion and the State in America*, 1942. WILLIAM W. SWEET, *Religion in Colonial America*, 1942.

1. *Calvinism* was the creed of the New England progenitors. The *Pilgrims at Plymouth* were radical Separatists. As such they rejected a static conception of the Reformation. In his farewell address, John Robinson remarked, "Luther and Calvin were great and shining lights in their times, yet they penetrated not into the whole counsel of God. I beseech you, remember this—'tis an article of your church covenant— that you be ready to receive whatever truth shall be made known to you from the written word of God." In the new world the Pilgrims established themselves on their separatistic principles, i.e., membership in the church, they held, should be restricted to the "saints," and the local church was to be considered autonomous. Besides, joining the church did not involve subscription to a creed, it simply meant to join a covenant. As Dissenters they were more interested in conduct than in dogma. Thus the original Calvinism underwent a strong modification in their teaching.[1]

In comparison with these Pilgrims, the *Puritans who later settled at and around Boston* were potential Presbyterians and no friends of the Separation. But the two factions soon became amalgamated into one harmonious group. In 1629 the Puritans accepted the Plymouth model of church administration while the whole body of Congregational churches expressed belief in the very principles of the Westminster Confession, first, by adopting the *Cambridge Platform* in 1648 and, later, the *Savoy Confession* in 1680. Since, furthermore, religious liberty was restricted to the Congregational churches and the holding of civil offices was made dependent on church membership, the New England churches came close to the point of abandoning their Dissenter church

---

[1] Thomas C. Hall, in his book, cited above, declined the view that Calvinism had a hold over the English Dissenters. Dissent, he says, was not a product of Calvinism, but had its beginning with Wyclif and Lollards in the Middle Ages. Undoubtedly, he has worked out this thesis with keen logical acumen. Yet, when all is said, it seems that he underrates the spiritualistic and puritanic element in Calvinism. For example, he says repeatedly that Calvin was agreed with Luther in the conception of the "grace-imparting" nature of the sacraments while such a thought was utterly strange to the English Dissenters. A student of the Reformation should know that such a statement is untenable. Hall also seems to underrate the actual part which Calvinism played in the establishment of the new ecclesiastical order in England during the sixteenth and seventeenth centuries.

conception for a new Establishment. This is the more conspicuous when we take into consideration the idea of a Half-Way covenant, as the arrangement was called, whereby limited religious rights were granted to the still "unconverted" though baptized people in the community. Thus Thomas Shepard was right when he defined New England Congregationalism as a *via media* between English Brownism and Presbyterianism.

2. In the eighteenth century the modified Calvinism of the Puritans underwent a further modification through the influx of Anabaptistic, Spiritualistic, Socinian, and Arminian tendencies. When the Puritanic Calvinism clashed with the Anabaptists and Quakers, these radicals were banished, tortured, or put to death by the civil magistrates. In all fairness to the Puritans it must be said that the behavior of some of these radicals would even today, in many instances, incur the action of our civil authorities. The opposition, however, was short-lived. Gradually the Calvinism of New England was drifting into eighteenth-century Deism. New England even proved to be a more fertile soil for the Deistic optimism than Old England because of its unlimited natural resources and greater freedom from conventional and social forms of the past.

The clash between Arminian and Predestinarian ideas, on the other hand, gave rise to a long and trenchant literary controversy crystallizing into a new and modified conception of Predestination and man's moral ability in the New England Theology of Jonathan Edwards and his school.

3. In the course of time the free church principle of the Puritans proved to be a strong factor for *religious individualism and toleration.* Especially Rhode Island and Pennsylvania became the haven for religious radicals from New England and Europe. This trend towards individualism and toleration was strengthened in the eighteenth century by the prevailing political theories of French philosophy. The National Constitution declared Church and state mutually independent (Article VI, 3, Amendment 1). The states followed suit. Shortly after the adoption of the National Constitution the Anglican Establishment in the southern colonies was repealed. The New England states were slower in moving. It was not till the first decades of the nineteenth century, 1816 in Connecticut and 1833 in Massachusetts, that the special privileges of the Congregational churches were discontinued. We thus observe in the period of one century a change of the whole structure of American society which has no parallel elsewhere: in politics a complete change from a state supported church to complete religious toleration; in philosophy a turning from the supernatural to scientific empiricism, and in religion from revelation to reason. This change is marked by the life and work of three men: the political by Thomas Jefferson, the philosophical by Benjamin Franklin, and the religious by Ethan Allen.

4. The condition in the New World forced the churches to adopt *new methods of work.* In European countries where state churches existed, church membership was general. In the New World the actual membership of churches was comparatively small. Even in New England a comparatively small number of the total population belonged to the Church. Thus there happened to be a greater number of unchurched people in New England than in any country of Europe. It was this situation that gave impetus to the development of a new technique to win the unchurched. This new method peculiar to our country was revivalism. The Awakening in 1735 and 1740 was only the beginning of other revival movements that are characteristic of American Christianity. The

religious camp-meetings and the Methodist circuit riders are genuine products of American frontier life.[2]

The missionary character of the American churches has also put the stamp of adaptability and practicability in the church life and theology of our country. There is no such thing as a rift between theology as a science and the church. American theology is preachable. The really great theologians have been, at the same time, the great preachers of their day (Edwards, Channing, Finney, Parker, Walther, etc.), and some of the great sermons have carried the weight of important theological manifestoes as, for instance, Channing's Baltimore sermon on *Unitarian Christianity*. This feature of American theology, though it may have its parallel in England, is quite different from conditions as they existed in Germany. The style of German theological books used to be ponderous, written with an eye only on the expert. Ordination was no requirement for holding a theological professorship, and consequently some of the German professors would never officiate in the services of the church. In all fairness, however, it must also be said that the German preacher is more strictly devotional in his message and more practical in his delivery than many of his American brethren. The reading of a semi-theological lecture to a congregation assembled for worship is a thing altogether unknown in German churches.

5. Another feature of American Christianity is its *schismatic character*. New schisms in American churches were due mainly to two causes. The first cause is religious. On the one hand, the radical application of the dogmatic and confessional principle has caused endless friction in American Christianity. This trend was not without precedence in the Calvinistic countries of Europe, for the literalism, legalistic, and spiritualistic tendencies in Calvinism breed the germ of dissent. Even the Lutheran Church became subject to this development in America when a specific theological interpretation of the Lutheran confessions was made the prerequisite of altar and pulpit fellowship. On the other hand, the number of denominations was unduly multiplied by immature attempts at church union as represented, for example, by the Disciples and the "Federated Churches."[3]

The other cause is political and economic. The problems of slavery and the Civil War have seriously hampered the unity of the churches. The disruption in the Lutheran Church caused by the Civil War was not healed before 1918, the Methodists became reunited as late as 1939, while some of the other denominations are still divided into Northern and Southern groups. Today, however, dogmatic problems have also entered in to perpetuate these schisms. The Southern Baptists, for instance, are far more conservative than the Northern Baptists.

It is often claimed that likewise the divers nationalities have added to the confusion of American church life. This, however, is true only with respect to church organization and administration. The real cause of friction in the Lutheran Church, for instance, was not racial and linguistic but theological. Besides, the rapid decline of the "foreign" speaking or bilingual congregation will soon have removed the chief reasons for racial diversities and aloofness.

6. America was called by Israel Zangwill a "melting pot"; others, more correctly,

---

[2] Cf. Sweet, *Story of Religion in America*, pp. 7 f.
[3] Cf. Neve, *Churches and Sects of Christendom*, 1940, pp. 464 ff.

have said "mixing pot."[4] Consequently, since many nationalities have contributed to the making of America, it is somewhat presumptuous to speak of an American Church or of American Theology. We never have formed a church, we rather have churches with a various background and theology. A discussion of American theology, therefore, should not be limited to the English tradition in American life. Continental Lutheranism and Calvinism, even Roman Catholicism, can claim a just share in building the spiritual forces of our country.

7. Since the American population, its culture and civilization, are but a scion of European peoples, it cannot be expected that American theology is altogether something peculiar. The general trend of thought and religion in Europe has inevitably been felt on this side of the Atlantic. As English, French, and German philosophy has found a response in America, so the development in European Calvinism and Lutheranism has acted and re-acted on American theology. On the other hand, the frequent assumption that American thought is but a mere reflection of Europe, is equally not true. America has produced original thinkers and the American churches have developed a church life and theology of their own. As in the case of the Lutheran Church, the combination of a theological background from Germany and Scandinavia with a cultural background of English life and thought has produced in America a type of Lutheranism distinctly of its own.

8. The Civil War is a landmark in American history. Up to 1870 America was an agricultural country and traditional Christianity held its sway in public life. After the Civil War the industrialization of our country made headway rapidly. Consequently, the evils of such a process, e.g., the disintegration of family life and the proletarization of the individual have become an ever greater problem to the Christian character of America. This de-Christianizing process was greatly abetted by the naturalistic philosophy which has made its inroads into our public school system since 1890. The clash between traditional Christianity and the new learning has created a great unrest in most churches. The conflict between the Fundamentalists and Modernists was especially bitter in the decade after the first World War.

9. Viewed from the broader aspect of European-American solidarity, there are discernible *five main currents* that have contributed to theological thought in America: (1) the seventeenth century orthodoxy; (2) the eighteenth century theology of the inner light and of reason; (3) the spiritual tenets of German idealism (Kant, Schleiermacher, Hegel, and Ritschl); (4) the revival of Lutheran confessionalism in the nineteenth century; (5) the rise of modern sciences. We thus have at present in our country a powerful radical liberalism side by side with an influential pre-scientific view of religion. American theology is tending to the extreme both of liberalism and conservatism. The modern spiritual crisis, which is in fact universal, is in America accentuated by our unhistorical and rational mind according to which historical tradition counts little but usefulness almost every thing.[5] American theology therefore is dogmatic, or speculative and critical. We have produced dogmatic treatises with a mark of originality. But American theology too often lacks a Biblical and historical basis. American conservatives and fundamentalists are traditionalists. Their weakness lies in that

---

[4] *Literary Digest*, October 13, 1926.

[5] Cf. on this the stimulating article by Ch. C. Morrison, "Oxford, Edinburgh, and the American Mind," *Christendom*, Autumn, 1937, pp. 582 ff. Says Dr. Morrison, "The American mind is an empirical mind. It is less conscious of dependence upon the past than any other type of mind in Christendom."

they have been neglecting a fresh analysis of faith in the light of advanced linguistic and historical studies of the Scriptures. The modernists are equally superficial as regards the Biblical foundation of their position. They are really more a kind of religious philosophers than Christian theologians. There is shown very little interest in Luther and the Reformation. Even the Lutheran church bodies are more orientated to the post-Reformation theology than to Luther himself.

Chapter Two

PHILOSOPHICAL THOUGHT IN AMERICA

Literature: W. RILEY, *American Thought from Puritanism to Pragmatism,* 1915; ARTHUR K. ROGERS, *English and American Philosophy Since 1800,* 1922; RALPH B. PEERY, *Philosophy of the Recent Past,* 1926; VERNON L. PARRINGTON, *Main Currents in American Thought,* 3 vols., 1927 ff. These volumes contain a very extensive bibliography both as to original sources and studies of the various movements. G. P. ADAMS and W. P. MONTAGUE, editors, *Contemporary American Philosophy,* 2 vols., 1930; HARVEY G. TOWNSEND, *Philosophical Ideas in the United States,* 1934.

1. In Chapter One we have briefly touched upon the religious inheritance of the New World. In this chapter we are purposed to give a very brief résumé of philosophical thoughts which have contributed to the intellectual development of America.

2. Indigenous philosophical thought in the New World began with JONATHAN EDWARDS. Edwards was an exponent of Platonic Idealism. In his essay on *Being* he opposes the current notion that material things are the most substantial. Edwards held to the view that only spirits are properly real. Over against the nominalistic trend in Protestant thought, he stands out as one of the principal champions of metaphysical realism.[1] He also is a fine example of a mystic intuitionist and ascetic idealist bent to cultivate the inner self. In his conception of the mind as active in sentiment, choice, etc., and as guided by certain principles (being, cause, finality, etc.) he anticipated several features of the critical philosophy of Kant.[2]

Another exponent of the early idealism was SAMUEL JOHNSON of Connecticut. He became attracted to the "New Principle" when in 1727 Berkeley came to America to take up his residence in Newport, Rhode Island.

Viewed from a philosophical point of view, *Quakerism* also belongs to the school of the idealists. In principle it is intuitive and spiritualistic. Its theology of the inner light struck at the very basis of orthodox faith, i.e., the sole authority of the written Word.

3. Mystic idealism, however, was only a side-issue in the eighteenth century. The main current of this age is to be seen in *English Deism* and *French Materialism,*[3] and ever since that time, both schools of thought have exercised a strong influence on the mind of the American intelligentsia. The chief concern of the Deists was the search for a natural and universal religion, "a platform of belief on which all good men could unite." The Deists also were free-thinkers, i.e., they stood for the principle of free scientific investigation untrammeled by the authority of either the Bible or the Church. Thus as time went on, reason supplanted revelation, the supernatural in Christianity was being eliminated, and miracles relegated to mere myths. The Deists exchanged the pessimism and determinism of the Calvinistic Puritans for the optimism of the Deistic creed. The colonial college became the vehicle of transmitting this new world view.

---

[1] Cf. O. Piper, *God in History,* 1939, pp. 53 ff.

[2] Cf. M. M. Curtis, *Kantian Elements in Edwards,* 1906; also the instructive chapter on Edwards in Townsend, pp. 35 ff.

[3] *Ibid.,* pp. 50 ff.; 67 ff.

At Harvard the Dudleian lectureship was founded for "the proving, explaining, and proper use and improvement of the principles of natural religion." President Charles Chauncy, the keen critic of revivalism,[4] and Edward Holyoke, Ezra Stiles of Yale, and Samuel Johnson, first president of King's College at New York, took a leading part in promulgating the new creed of Deism.

4. Epoch-making in changing the trend of thought in America was the work of ETHAN ALLEN, who, in his book, *Reason, the Only Oracle of Man* (1784), denounced with rustic wit and in a coarse language the prevailing Calvinism of his day. Still more significant were the life works of BENJAMIN FRANKLIN, THOMAS JEFFERSON, and THOMAS PAINE. FRANKLIN'S peculiar creed is expressed in his *First Principles*. Here he states that he believes that "there is one supreme, most perfect Being, Author and Father of the Gods themselves." Man endowed with reason is inclined to pay "Divine Regards to Something." God "delights in the happiness of those He has created; and since without virtue man can have no happiness in this world, I firmly believe," Franklin says, "He delights to see me virtuous, because He is pleased when He sees me happy." The *First Principles* are a unique document, for they teach, as Riley points out (p. 72), a veritable polytheism in a land monotonously monotheistic." Riley, very likely, is correct when he wants to trace this peculiar notion of Franklin back to Platonic influences (p. 73).

Though charges of atheism were brought against THOMAS JEFFERSON when he occupied the White House, he is more properly classified with the Deists. He was, properly speaking, an Eclecticist. Deistic and naturalistic tenets may be discerned in his world of thought. The spirit of New England was thoroughly unsympathetic to this Virginian gentleman. As Franklin eliminated all religious tests from his intellectual child, the University of Pennsylvania, Jefferson proposed the establishment of the University of Virginia against "the pious young monks from Harvard and Yale." His religious views are reflected in the—fragmentary— *Syllabus of an Estimate of the Merit of the Doctrines of Jesus, Compared with Those of Others,* and in the so-called *Jeffersonian Bible* which is a compilation of the ethical sayings of Jesus from the four Gospels.

The most popular book and the best seller of all Deistic literature was THOMAS PAINE'S *Age of Reason* (1794 ff.). The first edition was printed in France but the author had it dedicated to his fellow citizens in the United States of America. The book is a rather crude attack not only on the faith but also on the ethical teachings of the Bible[5]

Since Jefferson was a great admirer of French culture, he tried hard to give French philosophy a chance in the South which was quite well prepared for its reception through the Arminian teachings of its Episcopal clergy. Likewise, the coming of John Priestly to America in 1794 considerably aided the cause of materialism.[6] Priestly's philosophy was carried to the South by his son-in-law, the great chemist, Thomas Cooper. To the influence of Priestly we must add the teachings of Benjamin Rush (1745-1813), the most distinguished American medical materialist of the earlier days of our country. In

---

[4] *Thoughts of the State of Religion in New England*, 1743.

[5] "The Bible (i.e., the Old Testament) and the New Testament," he says, "are impositions upon the world." The only Word of God, in his eyes, is the "creation which we behold." Though he calls Jesus "a virtuous and an amiable man," he denounces Paul as "a manufacturer of squibbles." Rejecting all historical creeds, he sums up his faith as belief in one God, virtue, and immortality. The book of Ruth is to him "an idle, bungling story," etc.

[6] *Disquisitions Relating to Matter and Spirit*, 1777.

several ways Rush anticipated modern thought. He is credited with being a forerunner of the present-day studies in psychiatry.[7]

5. A third formative force in philosophical thought was natural realism, the so-called *Scottish Common Sense Philosophy* (for a discussion of this system compare p. 216). Natural realism was very welcome in America as an orthodox antidote against the idealism of New England and the materialism of the South. Its cause was promoted by the denominational colleges, Princeton College being its stronghold. The teaching of Princeton realism was thoroughly dualistic; God and nature, body and soul were carefully kept separate.

6. While all the philosophical forces discussed so far are of the type of immigrant philosophy, there now sprang up a new teaching which was a genuinely native plant of the virgin soil of America, *New England Transcendentalism*. It was the reaction of Unitarian divines against what one of them called "the meager and uninteresting system of Unitarian theology" which had "disenthralled the minds of men." It was a return to nature proclaiming individual liberty. In time it coincided with the Romantic movement in Europe with which it had much in common.[8]

The creed of transcendentalism included four fundamental beliefs: (1) It was monistic; the world is a unity with God and God is immanent in the world. Nature is an expositor of the Divine Mind, and man is the soul of the Eternal One. (2) A second principle is that of microcosm. Every part of the world contains within itself all the laws and meaning of the universe. There is a universal soul in man supplying him with the faculties of intellectual apprehension and psychic penetration of the Whole. (3) Man also is a macrocosm. The individual soul is identical with the world soul, it is the mirror of the universe. (4) A fourth belief is that of symbolism. Nature is considered to be the embodiment of the spirit. It is a great book to be read and studied, for it reveals everywhere the divine verities.[9] The greatest representative of this type of transcendentalism was R. W. Emerson, whose influence in changing the thought of his contemporaries we shall discuss in Chapter Four. For the proper background of American transcendentalism we must look to English sources, to the Cambridge Platonists of the seventeenth century.[10] German influences were but secondary. In fact, the knowledge of German was so scanty in New England that George Ticknor, the Harvard historian, before sailing to Goettingen in 1815, had to send to New Hampshire "where he learned there was a German dictionary." Emerson's knowledge of Kant and Fichte was only slight and secondary. It was through Coleridge whose *Aids to Reflection* were published in New England in 1829, by James Marsh, president of the University of Vermont, that German thought became known to America and later through Carlyle that Emerson "contrived to read almost every volume of Goethe."

7. As in Europe so in America, the greatest change of theological thought in our country was effected by Darwin's book *Origin of Species,* which was published in 1859. Darwin had his forerunners in America. As early as in 1787 the Princeton ethnologist STANHOPE SMITH, in his *Essay on the Causes of the Variety of Complexion and Figure*

---

[7] *Medical Inquiries and Observations Upon the Diseases of the Mind,* 1812.
[8] Cf. Townsend, *op. cit.,* pp. 253 ff.; O. B. Frothingham, *Transcendentalism in New England,* 1876; H. C. Goddard, *Studies in New England Transcendentalism,* 1908; C. Gohdes, *The Periodicals of American Transcendentalism,* 1931.
[9] Cf. Riley, *op. cit.,* pp. 142 f.
[10] *Ibid.,* p. 64.

n the Human Species "had virtually accepted the Lamarckian principle of the origin of ariations from the factors of use and disuse, food, climate, or the effort of the individual." [11] The doctrine of the mutability and adaptability was further developed by WILLIAM CHARLES WELLS (1757-1817), SAMUEL GEORGE MORTON of Philadelphia 1799-1851), SAMUEL STEHMAN HALDEMAN (1812-1880), and the naturalist JOSEPH LEIDY (1823-1891). There were also the scholars in America who wrote books on econciling Genesis with natural sciences. Of these we may mention EDWARD HITCH-OCK, president of Amherst College, who wrote *Religion and Geology and Its Con-ected Sciences* (1851) and the Swiss-American scholar ARNOLD GUYOT, who had come o Princeton in 1848. The greatest asset to the conservative forces was the coming of nother Swiss to America, the naturalist JEAN LOUIS AGASSIZ (1807-1870). Agassiz emained a consistent defender of the principle of special creation.[12]

Evolution was fully accepted in America by ASA GRAY of Harvard. Gray was a otanist of the first magnitude. As to his religious views, he was a theistic evolutionist *Natural Science and Religion,* 1880). The reception given to evolution at Yale was ather lukewarm. It was only with reluctance that JAMES DWIGHT DANA (1813-1895) ccepted the new principle. The same is true of Princeton. The attitude of its new ead, the Scotch divine, JAMES MCCOSH, was that of a compromise (*Typical Forms and pecial Ends in Creation,* 1855).[13] Equally compromising was the position taken by CHARLES WOODRUFF SHIELDS (*Religion and Science in Relation to Philosophy,* 1875). n contradistinction to these Princeton apologists, we find at Philadelphia a man who ubscribed to the evolutionary creed wholeheartedly, the eminent American zoologist nd palaeologist, EDWARD DRINKER COPE (1840-1897). Two other scholars should be nentioned here: the historian and philosopher JOHN FISKE, who proved to be a very nergetic defender of Darwinism before the eyes of the public (*Excursions of an Evolu-ionist,* 1883; *Darwinism and Other Essays,* 1897), and the psychologist and philosopher AMES MARK BALDWIN, who supplanted the older theory of "conscious accommodation" y his new principle of "organic selection." [14]

8. The next great spiritual force in American life was *German Idealism.* Riley p. 229) contends that "it may safely be said that the German influences on American hought have been the most significant and the most weighty of all the foreign forces." The earliest discovered reference to Kant, according to him (p. 232), is to be found in he *Philadelphia Monthly Magazine* of 1798 containing a sympathetic review of Kant's *Critique of Pure Reason.* But German scholars in this country had their limitations. uch men as SAMUEL SCHMUCKER at Gettysburg Seminary (*Elements of Mental Philosophy,* 1842), and FREDERICK A. RAUCH at Marshall College, whose book *Psy-hology or a View of the Human Soul, Including Anthropology* (1840) was a first ttempt at uniting American and German thought, were little known outside of the Lutheran and Reformed churches.[15]

The honor of making German philosophical thought a vital energy in American

---

[11] Riley, *op. cit.,* p. 179.

[12] Cf. Mabel L. Robinson, *Runner of the Mountain Tops: The Life of Louis Agassiz,* 1939.

[13] For a fine appraisement of this exponent of the Scottish Common Sense Philosophy in American thought ee Townsend, *op. cit.,* pp. 102-108.

[14] Cf. F. H. Foster, *The Modern Movement in American Theology,* 1939, pp. 38 ff.

[15] When Riley (p. 234) says that both Schmucker and Rauch were "not much known outside of their local utheran circles," he obviously is mistaken as to the church affiliation of Rauch. Rauch was not a Lutheran but Reformed theologian, and through his presidency at Marshall College he became one of the chief exponents of he conservative Reformed "Mercersburg theology" (see Chapter Five).

life belongs to the West. It was at St. Louis with such scholars at the head as William
Thomas Harris, Henry C. Brockmeyer, and Denton J. Snider, that Kant,[16] Fichte
Schelling, and Hegel were studied systematically. This St. Louis school also has the
distinction of having founded the first metaphysical journal in America, *The Journal
of Speculative Philosophy*. Here under the influence of German philosophy arose the
aim of "thought for thought's sake." [17]

The most influential expounders of Hegelian monism in America were JOSIAH
ROYCE (1855-1916) at Harvard, and GEORGE TRUMBALL LADD (1843-1921) at Yale
While Royce was a romanticist with a high poetic imagination, Ladd was interpreter
and systematizer of philosophical thought. Both have exercised a profound influence on
modern New England theology. Of Royce's works we wish to mention *The Conception
of God* (1897), *The Conception of Immortality* (1900), and *The Problem of Chris
tianity* (2 vols., 1913). Ladd, who had been a Congregational minister, wrote among
other books, *The Doctrine of Sacred Scripture* (1884), *What Is the Bible?* (1888)
and *What Should I Believe?* (1914 f.). His monistic idealism verges on personalism
He also introduced from Germany (Wundt) the study of psychology. The fruit of
such studies he laid down in *Elements of Physiological Psychology* (1887).

9. At the beginning of the twentieth century abstract idealism received a strong
competitor in the doctrine of *Personalism*. Personalism is a system of philosophy "which
views personality as the active ground of the world." [18] It has linked itself with volun
tarism and metaphysical individualism. It therefore is theistic; but "the divine being
exists in, and not apart from, his activity" (*ibid.*) It combines Kant's emphasis on the
personal self with Hegelian metaphysics in a very novel manner. It is quantitatively a
pluralism. The universe is a society of personal selves. But qualitatively it is monistic
The Supreme Self is immanent in the human self. Six marks are said to be character
istic of it: (1) it is metaphysical, (2) ethical, (3) as a social philosophy it stresse
"the free co-operation of different distinct individual persons in a common purpose,"
(4) it is rational, (5) mystical, and (6) it infers the immortality of the human person.[19]
With its stress on the personality of God and sacredness of human life, it regards itself
as the Christian philosophy of today, *par excellence*. In its American version it shows
a close affinity to the philosophy of H. Lotze. It had its beginning in America with
GEORGE HOWISON and, especially, with BORDEN P. BOWNE.[20]

10. We now must speak of *Pragmatism*, the philosophy of practicality, the "bread
and butter view of life." The Pragmatism of the Chicago School is materialism rampant
But it also includes a note of personalism. To be successful means to possess personal
qualities of aggressiveness. Pragmatism has passed through three stages of development
In its primitive stage it was logical. As a logical method it was used in 1878 by
CHARLES S. PEIRCE in a paper entitled "How to Make Our Ideas Clear." [21] In this paper
Peirce said that in deciding on the rival theories of free will and fatalism, man should

---

[16] The first biography of Kant in English was written by the Lutheran scholar, J. H. Stuckenberg, *The
Life of Kant*, 1882. See below, p. 302.

[17] Cf. D. J. Snider, *The St. Louis Movement in Philosophy*, 1920; Ch. M. Peery, *The St. Louis Movement in
Philosophy, Some Source Material*, 1930.

[18] R. T. Flewelling in Hastings, *Encyclopedia* IX, 771-773.

[19] Cf. Wieman-Meland, *American Philosophies of Religion*, 1936, pp. 139 ff.

[20] See his volume, *Personalism*, 1908., also A. C. Knudson, *The Philosophy of Personalism*, 1927, and
F. J. McConnell, *Borden Parker Bowne: His Life and Philosophy*, 1929.

[21] *Popular Science Monthly*, 1878, p. 293; reprinted in *Collected Papers* (1931 ff.) V, 402.

consider "what effects, that might conceivably have practical bearings, we conceive the object of our conception to have. Then our conception of these effects is the whole of our conception of the object." Viewed from the standpoint of the philosopher, this principle is a maxim of clearing up metaphysics; but if interpreted wrongly, as it has often been, it implies nothing but a rule of action.[22]

The thought of Peirce was taken up and developed by JOHN DEWEY and the Chicago School. Dewey is anti-metaphysical and anti-religious. His creed is impersonal and biological. For him pragmatism is a useful tool of action. As such it allied itself under him with the method of modern sciences. Dewey's teaching also is genetic and evolutionary. Values are not fixed but vary with the varying functions to which they belong. His system furthermore is social. A catchword of his is "adaptation to environment." Thus the Chicago pragmatist became associated with the Humanist movement. For a very readable presentation of his religious views we call attention to his little book, A Common Faith (1934).[23]

In its third stage, as represented by WILLIAM JAMES (1842-1910), pragmatism is transcendental and temperamental. James maintained the superiority of spirit to matter. As to the theory of knowledge, he wanted to mediate between the a priori conception of reality and empirical materialism. Truths emerge from facts, they are not ready-made from all eternity but man-made. While he gave up the conception of "objective certainty," he did not decline the quest or hope of truth itself. He thus took his stand in between the absolute idealists and the materialists of the Dewey type. His pragmatism is temperamental, i.e., it purposes to meet the needs of the individual whose liberty over matter he upheld. From the limited experiences of man and his temperamental preferences, James proceeded to defend a pluralistic interpretation of the universe. Only a pluralistic world, he said, is truly democratic, while absolutism is unable to grant life, liberty, and the pursuit of happiness to all individuals.[24]

11. The opening of the new century witnessed the rise of a new approach to the study of religion: the psychological investigation of religion along empirical and scientific lines. American scholars can rightly claim the honor of having been the real pioneers of psychology of religion. Both English and German scholars are ready to admit that the Americans have accomplished more than the others.[25] To the early American contributors belong William James with his book, The Varieties of Religious Experience (1902), and George Stanley Hall, who established in 1904 the pioneering journal entitled, American Journal of Religious Psychology and Education. It continued till 1911, when its name was changed to Journal of Religious Psychology, Including Its Anthropological and Sociological Aspects. Of other scholars who have pioneered in this field of investigation we may refer to Rufus Jones, who wrote Studies in Mystical Religion (1909), and G. A. Coe who is the author of The Psychology of Religion (1916).[26]

---

[22] Cf. Justus Buchler, Charles Peirce's Empiricism, 1939.

[23] Cf. W. T. Feldman, The Philosophy of John Dewey, 1934; also Paul A. Schlipp, The Philosophy of John Dewey, 1939; and the collection of essays in honor of Dewey's eightieth birthday, The Philosopher of the Common Man, 1940. The purpose of humanism within the general field of theology the student will find discussed by A. J. F. Auer in Humanism States Its Case, 1933.

[24] Principles of Psychology, 1890, The Will to Believe, 1890; Pragmatism, 1907; A Pluralistic Universe, 1909. Cf. R. B. Peery, The Thought and Character of William James, 2 vols., 1935.

[25] W. B. Selbie, Psychology of Religion, 1923, p. 4; Karl Girgensohn, Der seelische Aufbau des religioesen Lebens, 1921, p. 17.

[26] On the whole subject compare Edward L. Schaub, "The Psychology of Religion in America" in Gerald B. Smith, Religious Thought in the Last Quarter Century, 1927, pp. 116 ff.

12. In concluding our discussion of this chapter we may add a passing remark o Neo-Realism in America (cf. pp. 235 f.). American realists may conveniently be classifie either as "neo-realists" or as "critical realists." They are all agreed, however, that "the min somehow apprehends reality rather than constitutes it." The former group has publishe a co-operative volume entitled *The New Realism* (1912) by E. B. Holt, W. T. Marvi W. P. Montague, R. B. Perry, W. B. Pitkin, and E. G. Spaulding; the latter group fol lowed in 1920 by publishing a similar volume, *Essays in Critical Realism* by D. Drak A. O. Lovejoy, J. B. Pratt, A. K. Rogers, G. Santayana, R. W. Sellars, and C. A. Stron The significance of Neo-Realism is to be seen in this that it stresses the view that th religious object exists independently of our consciousness thereof.[27]

From the ethico-religious point of view many of these philosophers have lon been recognized as leaders of the *Humanist Movement.* American humanism was revolt against the "otherworldliness" implied in Biblical Christianity. The humanist substituted belief in man for the Christian belief in God. They exercised a very stron effect on the educational system and ideals of the public schools in our country. Thei influence in the intellectual world seems to be abating. Charles Hartshorne of th University of Chicago, in his volume *Beyond Humanism* (1937) argues that philosoph must go "beyond humanism" and search for a synthesis which embraces not merel human values but the wheel of nature. He describes his new philosophy as "theisti naturalism" or "naturalistic theism," though God is to him little more than the sur total of nature.[28]

---

[27] Cf. the volume by D. C. Macintosh, editor, *Religious Realism,* 1931.

[28] Cf. Charles S. Macfarland, *The Christian Faith in a Day of Crisis,* 1939, pp. 120 ff. 207; also the pen(trating criticism of Humanism by A. H. Dakin, *Man the Measure,* 1939.

Chapter Three

THE NEW ENGLAND THEOLOGY: JONATHAN EDWARDS AND HIS SCHOOL

Literature: GEORGE P. FISHER, *History of Christian Doctrine*, 1906, pp. 394 ff.; GEORGE L. WALKER, *Some Aspects of the Religious Life of New England*, 1897; GEORGE N. BOARDMAN, *History of New England Theology*, 1899; FRANK H. FOSTER, *A Genetic History of the New England Theology*, 1907; JOSEPH HAROUTUNIAN, *Piety Versus Moralism*, 1932; EZRA H. BYINGTON, *The Puritan as a Colonist and Reformer*, 1899; HERBERT W. SCHNEIDER, *The Puritan Mind*, 1930: The life of Edwards has been told by SAMUEL HOPKINS (1765), SERENO E. DWIGHT (1829), ALEXANDER V. G. ALLEN (1889), ISAAC CROOK (1903), PAUL E. MORE (*in Cambridge History of American Literature*, 1917, I, 57 ff.), HENRY B. PARKES (1930), ARTHUR C. McGIFFERT (1932), and OLA E. WINSLOW (1940).

1. Before entering upon the discussion of the New England Theology, we shall give a brief sketch of *the original faith of the Pilgrims and Puritans.* Their religion, as stated in Chapter One, was the modified Calvinism of the English dissenters. To them the Scriptures were all-sufficient and the final authority in all matters of faith and life. Upon this position they argued that the Bible was a law-book, not only of religion but also of civil affairs. A quotation from the Bible — irrespective of its historical content and meaning — carried weight to settle any question. God was looked upon as the sovereign Ruler of the universe. His will was supreme, His decrees unchangeable. Along with this idea of God went the conception of man's utter inability to contribute anything to his salvation. Thomas Shepard said, "Oh thou mayest wish and desire to come out sometime, but canst not put strength to thy desire, nor *indure* to do it. Thou mayest hang down thy head like a Bulrush for sin, but thou canst not repent of sin." [1] Having turned against the formalism of the Roman and Anglican form of worship, their religious life was marked by the most minute and rigorous self-introspection. A hundred years before Hopkins, Thomas Hooker promulgated the doctrine of "unconditional resignation" and willingness to be rejected eternally if the will of God require it. Theirs also was a very vivid feeling of the machinations of the devil. His trails and footprints were believed to infest all the narrow roads through the primeval forests of New England. In 1648 a woman was executed in Hartford for alleged communion with the devil. And in the years 1692 and 1693 more than a hundred women were arrested on that same charge, and twenty of them died from torture and execution. In short, the religious life of New England was marked by that awfulness in religion which leaves the sinner alone in the very presence of Almighty God.

This Calvinistic theology was preached in New England by such men as Thomas Shepard, the radical Thomas Hooker (died 1647), the learned John Cotton, who wrote *The Keys of the Kingdom of Heaven* (1644), and a Catechism: *Milk for Babes* (1646), the members of the noble Mather dynasty: Richard (1596-1669), who advocated the establishment of the Half-Way Covenant, Increase (1639-1723), Cotton (1662/63-1727/28), and Samuel (1700-1785), and many others.

---

[1] *Sincere Convert*, 1646, p. 71, quoted from Walker, *op. cit.*, p. 23.

2. *The proper background of the New England Theology* is to be seen in th general decline of religion and morals which began with the second generation of th Pilgrims. The great emphasis which was laid by the New England clergy on the divin sovereignty and man's moral inability led to the result that this type of preachin reduced the number of conversions and depleted the churches of members. In ord to overcome the difficulties, the New England divines resorted to the method of th Half-Way Covenant. This new arrangement recognized in principle the method of th Anglican and Presbyterian Establishment of Old England from which "corrupt pra tices," in the words of John Higgison, the Puritans had fled. They thus came close a new Establishment, especially if we remember that, for instance, in Massachusett full civic rights depended on church membership. The full scope of change was n realized till in 1707 Solomon Stoddard of Northampton, Massachusetts, made an ope appeal to admit the "unregenerated" to the Lord's Supper.[2] This decline of Puritan pie was increased by the spread of Arminian literature in New England. Tillotson, Whitb Taylor, and Clarke, and subsequently the Socinian writings of Thomas Emlyn wer widely studied.[3] The change to the better came with a succession of revival movemen (December, 1735, and later the Great Awakening in 1740). The revival took its incep tion from a series of sermons preached by Jonathan Edwards, pastor at Northampto Massachusetts.

3. JONATHAN EDWARDS was born in 1703. Taking his degree at Yale in 1720, h was installed at Northampton in 1727 as the colleague of his grandfather, Solomo Stoddard. The attempt to revert to the stricter disciplinary principles of the earlie period led to his dismissal by the congregation in 1750. For a number of years he wa active in missionary work among the Indians. In 1758 he was called as president o Princeton College but he died in the same year. Among his writings we mention th following: *The Distinguishing Marks of a Work of the Spirit of God* (1741), *Though on the Revival* (1742), *Religious Affections* (1746), *Qualifications for Full Communio* (1749), *Freedom of the Will* (1754), and *Original Sin* (1758). Of posthumou editions we refer to *History of Redemption* (1774), *Nature of Virtue* (1788), *God Last End in Creation* (1788), and *Essay on the Trinity* (1903). There is no complet edition of his works. The most inclusive is the one by S. E. Dwight in ten larg volumes (1829 f.).

4. Jonathan Edwards, in the words of Foster (p. 50) was "profoundly attached t the Calvinistic system, and his first instinct was to restore it to its high place of influ ence." But the great originality of his mind and the wide range of his studies did n permit him "to remain where his fathers had been" (*ibid.*).[4] While a sophomore a Yale he read Locke's *Essay on Human Understanding*. The book made a profoun impression on his mind. He put the Calvinistic theology which he had inherited from

---

[2] *The Inexcusableness of Neglecting the Worship of God Under the Pretense of Being in an Unconverte Condition.*

[3] *An Humble Inquiry into the Scripture Account of Jesus Christ, or a Short Argument Concerning His Deit and Glory, According to the Gospel.*

[4] By permission of the Chicago University Press, publishers. Once more attention should be called to th statement of Hall in *The Religious Background of American Culture*, "In truth Jonathan Edwards moved in quit another world of thought from that of Calvin. . . . He can only be really understood in connection with h background of congregationalistic Protestantism" (p. 149. By permission of Little, Brown & Company, pub lishers.) So far so good. New England was neither Scotland nor Geneva; but neither was it an outrigh Separatistic commonwealth. It must be kept in mind that Edwards began his ministry in a Presbyterian congrega tion; that he wholeheartedly believed in the Calvinistic scheme of salvation; that he, after his forced retiremen from the church in Northampton, gave some thought to accepting a call from the Presbyterian Church in Scot land, and that he ended his career as president of a Presbyterian college.

his progenitors on the new basis of an empirical piety. But he was far from accepting Locke's view of the mind as a white sheet of paper prepared to be written upon by experience. He combined with Lockean empiricism a thoroughgoing metaphysical realism. With him "God and real existence are the same." Created spirits are "immanations" and "communications" of God's being.

There was a double soul in Edwards. On the one hand, he spoke of the excellency of God in the glowing language of an ardent mystic. When he read the First Epistle of Paul to Timothy, there came upon him, according to his own narrative, "a sweet delight in God and divine things." From then on he often experienced, when "sweetly conversing with Christ," to be "wrapt and swallowed up in God." [5] Edwards was never satisfied with a moralistic conception of piety. Religion was to him not morality but "affection," emotion, a gracious experience of the reality of God, and a feeling of divine joy and happiness. On the other hand, God was to him, in a truly Calvinistic fashion, the sovereign Lord possessed of awful wrath who holds the unconverted sinner over the pit of hell, "much as we hold a spider, or some loathsome insect over the fire." [6] In keeping with this is the stress which Edwards at times placed on man's complete dependence "on God's arbitrary and sovereign good pleasure,"[7] and at other times on the principle of mystical illumination by the Supernatural.[8]

5. Foster, in his great work on the New England theology, has presented the teachings of Edwards in their relation to *his psychology of the will*, and criticized them as they do or do not measure up to the psychology of Foster himself. "This is unfortunate," as Haroutunian correctly remarks (p. xxiii), "because the chief aim of the Edwardian theology was not to formulate a theory of the will; it was inspired by a piety which sought to glorify God and His sovereignty over man. On the other hand, it asserted human responsibility, and sought to reconcile it with its theocentric piety." [9] In other words, Edwards' chief concern was to harmonize Calvinistic predestinarianism with a proper emphasis on man's moral responsibility. Over against Arminianism he held to the necessarian view. His conception of freedom he worked out in the famous treatise on the *Freedom of Will*.[10] He divides the "mind" into the "faculties" of "understanding" and "will." Following John Locke, he defines the latter as "that by which the mind chooses anything" (p. 16). The mind perceives. That which it perceives is a "motive." When confronted with several alternatives, the mind will follow that "which, as it stands in view of the mind, is the strongest." This is the determining factor over the will (p. 19). As to the "abilities" of man, Edwards distinguishes between "natural ability" or "inability," i.e., "whatever a nature does or does not allow of," and "moral inability" which consists, as he says, "in the opposition or want of inclination" (p. 35). A man has the natural ability "to hold his hand from striking," or "to show his neighbor kindness," or "to keep the cup (of intoxicating liquor) from his mouth" (p. 37). Inasmuch as man is under no physical impediment to do or not to do these things, he is said to be free. Such is the only liberty there is. That which man is lacking is "moral ability." But "moral inability," "which consists in disinclination," Edwards says, "never

---

[5] S. Hopkins, *Life and Character of J. Edwards*, p. 26.
[6] See the sermon "Sinners in the Hands of an Angry God," Dwight, VII, 163 ff.
[7] See the sermon "God Glorified in Man's Dependence," Dwight, VII, 149 ff.
[8] See his sermon "The Reality of Spiritual Light," Dwight, VI, 171 ff.
[9] By permission of Henry Holt & Company, publishers.
[10] Dwight, II, 9 ff.

can excuse any person in disobedience, or want of conformity to a command" (p. 163).

6. Although Edwards was an ardent supporter and defender of the revival, he proved to be very sober and circumspect as to the development of the movement. He was *no friend of the "enthusiasts,"* for he did not look to personal experience or immediate inspiration as the authority of religion. He includes among the "erroneous principles" the notion "that it is God's manner in these days, to guide His saints, at least some that are more imminent, by inspiration, or immediate revelation." "By such a notion," he says, "the devil has a great door opened for him." [11] The Bible is, in his opinion, the only infallible guide both of doctrine and conduct. He made a careful distinction between inspiration and illumination. While he defined inspiration as "suggesting of new truths or doctrines to the mind, independent of any antecedent revelations . . . either in word or writing," "illumination," he says, "reveals no new doctrine, . . . but only gives a due apprehension of those things that are taught in the word of God." [12] Nevertheless, Edwards was at heart a Calvinist when, in the sermon referred to, he stresses the Reformed conception that the divine light is given *immediately* and that "the word of God is no proper cause of this effect."

In keeping with this is his *view on the ministry* which is rather "high." He looked askance at itinerant ministers who would break over established parochial limits. The ordaining of a person, spiritually qualified for the ministry but lacking a proper education at college, he considered in its consequences to be "a greater calamity than the missing such persons in the work of the ministry." The admission of unlearned men to the ministry, he held, might easily lead to "impulses, vain imaginations, superstitions, indiscreet zeal, and such like extremes." Lay exhorters, he says, "ought not to clothe themselves with the like authority with that which is proper for ministers"; if they do, "they invade the office of a minister." [13]

7. Edwards, like Zwingli, viewed Baptism as a "sign" and "sacred badge" of Christian people. He upheld the practice of pedobaptism but wanted to extend its right only to such parents as are themselves in a state of sanctifying grace. Likewise, church membership, in his eyes, should be restricted to those that are "visibly gracious Christian," and open professors of godliness, while those who are merely "visibly moral livers, and only confess common virtures," should be excluded from the visible church. In other words, Edwards sought to restore the original church ideal of the Pilgrims, advocating as he did, the abrogation of the Half-Way Covenant.

The *Church* was to him the communion of "visible saints," i.e., of Christians professing "a saving grace," not merely "religion and virtue that is the result of common grace, or moral sincerity." This, as the student of history will note, is the same view as held by the Donatists in North Africa. In New England it helped to widen the gap between church and state and to prepare the Congregational churches for the new principle of separation after the Declaration of Independence. After Edwards the old Calvinistic antithesis of "elect" and "non-elect" lost its significance in New England being replaced by the spiritualistic alternative of "converted" and "unconverted."

In keeping with this view of the Church was his conception of the *Lord's Supper.* He regarded it not as a "converting ordinance," but as a "confessing ordinance." "There

---

[11] Dwight, IV, 198.
[12] *The Reality of Spiritual Light.*
[13] See his *Thoughts on the Revival*, Dwight, IV, 77 ff.

is in the Lord's Supper a mutual solemn profession of the two parties transacting the covenant of grace, and visibly united in that covenant; the Lord Christ by His minister, on the one hand, and the communicants (who are professing believers), on the other." For who else but a person who is in the state of sanctifying grace, he asks, is qualified, while he takes, eats and drinks those things "which represent Christ," to profess: "I take this crucified Jesus as my Saviour, my sweetest food, my chief portion, and the life of my soul . . . ?" [14]

8. As to the problem of the *origin of evil,* Edwards adhered to the supralapsarian view though he had no liking for the saying that God willed the fall of man.

He also introduced a new element into the discussion of Original Sin.[15] By divine disposition, he says, the human race is one person and is guilty in this way of the transgression of Adam. God "dealt with Adam as a *public* person — as the head of the human species — and had respect to his posterity, as included in him" (p. 438). The imputation of the first transgression, therefore, is mediate, not immediate. It has a justifying reason in the actual corruption of every human being. This conception, again, reflects the metaphysical realism of Edwards. But original sin, in his teachings, is no positive taint. When God made man, he says, "He implanted in him two kinds of principles. There was an *inferior* kind, which may be called the *natural,* being the principles of mere human nature," and the *"superior* principles, the spiritual, holy, and divine," which may be called, as he adds, the *supernatural.* Though in a footnote (p. 536) Edwards desires the reader to observe that the words "natural and supernatural" are not used here "as epithets of distinction between that which is concreated or connate, and that which is extraordinarily introduced afterwards . . . but as distinguishing between what belongs *to,* or flows *from,* that nature which man has, merely as man, and those things which are above this," . . . which is not "essential to the constitution" of nature, he comes very close to the Semi-Pelagian conception of man when he defines the effect of the Fall as a withdrawal of those supernatural gifts.[16]

9. In his view of the *order of salvation* he sided with the spiritualistic trend in Calvinism, when he lays stress on the Spirit's immediate operation on the soul. There is with him no such thing as a gradual, quiet growth into the Kingdom. "Conversion," he says, "is a great and glorious work of God's power, *at once* (italics are ours) changing the heart, and infusing life into the dead soul." Yet is he ready to admit that as to fixing the precise time of conversion, "there is a great deal of difference in different persons."[17]

As to the teaching of justification, Edwards says that "justification is manifestly a forensic term." [18] This forensic conception, however, underwent a vital modification in him because he saw in faith a spiritual qualification which renders man, if not deserving, yet "fit" and "meet" to be justified. "God justifies a believer . . . because He sees something in this qualification that . . . renders it a fit thing that such should be justified" (p. 358). In the act of justification God and man are almost placed on the same level when Edwards says, "God sees it fit, that in order to a union being established between two intelligent active beings or persons, so as they should be looked upon as one, there

---

[14] See his *Qualifications for Communion,* Dwight, *op. cit.,* IV, 281 ff.
[15] *Ibid.,* II, 301 ff.
[16] Cf. Allen, *op. cit.,* pp. 65 f., on Edwards' distinction between the "natural and supernatural."
[17] *A Faithful Narrative of Surprising Conversions,* Dwight, *op. cit.,* IV, 3 ff.
[18] *Justification by Faith Alone,* Dwight, *ibid.,* V, 351 ff.

should be the mutual act of both, that each should receive the other, as actively joining themselves one to another. . . . And if there be any *act* or qualification in believers of that uniting nature, that it is meet on that account the judge should look upon them and accept them as one, no wonder that upon the account of the same act or qualification, he should accept the satisfaction and merits of the one for the other, as if these were their own satisfaction and merits" (p. 364). Evidently, Edwards shared the common error of Pietism which looks upon faith as a virtuous quality in man. Such a thought must of necessity lead to a synergistic and moralistic conception of salvation; and while this remained latent in Edwards, it became an open fact in the theology of his successors.[19]

10. *Virtue,* according to Edwards, is beauty, the highest spiritual beauty. Its nature is benevolence. It is love to the entire society of intelligent beings in proportion to the amount of "being" which they possess. Virtue, then, is absolute love to God and limited love to the other beings, for he who "has the greatest share of universal existence, has proportionately the greatest share of virtuous benevolence."[20] In contradistinction to this, sin is defined as selfishness.

11. *Man* was created for an ever-increasing union and nearness with God. The creation of the world has its cause in a "disposition in God . . . to an emanation of His own fullness." He makes Himself His end. From this it is evident that Edwards was, philosophically, a monist. All reality is subsumed in God.[21]

12. *Jonathan Edwards had coadjutors and followers* able to confute Arminianism and to rouse the old school of Calvinism out of its lethargy. Yet gradually the initial emphasis of Edwards on the glory of God as the last end in creation gave way to a utilitarian aspect of religion. While in the opinion of Calvin and Edwards man lives to worship God, in the theology of Edwards' successors God lives to serve human happiness.[22]

First we must mention JOSEPH BELLAMY (1719-1790). He forcefully contended against the Half-Way Covenant. He was agreed with Edwards that man has the ability to repent, and that every minister is under solemn obligation to call his hearers to repentance. God is to him not a capricious being but a being of infinite benevolence. The eternal decrees, therefore, rest in the love of God. The origin of sin is limited to divine permission. On the basis of Leibnitzian optimism he declared that sin is the necessary means of the greatest good. In the act of conversion he laid emphasis on the use of the "means of grace."[23]

13. In SAMUEL HOPKINS' teaching (1721-1803) *the theology of Edwards underwent a further degradation.* He also based the divine eternal decrees on the love of God. He took great pains to uphold the optimistic belief in the loving government of God. As to the question of evil and human freedom, he said that the divine decrees include freedom for man, for God saves man through his volition and sin is for him, as

---

[19] Cf. the thorough investigation of this problem by H W Heidland. *Die Anrechnung des Glaubens zur Gerechtigkeit,* 1936.

[20] *The Nature of True Virtue,* Dwight, *op. cit.,* III. 93 ff

[21] *God's Last End in Creation, ibid.,* III, 5 ff.

[22] Cf. Haroutunian, *op. cit.,* p. 145.

[23] *Wisdom of God in the Permission of Sin,* 1758, in *Complete Works,* 1850, Vol. II. We want to call the attention of the reader to a difference that exists between Reformed and Lutheran theologians in the definition of the term "means of grace." According to the standards of Reformed theology there are three distinct means of grace: the Word, sacraments, and prayer, whereas Lutherans do not conceive of prayer as a means of grace. They apply the term only to those means by which God reaches out for man.

with Bellamy, the necessary means of the greatest good. Thus all is included in the divine decrees and nothing is done by man in distinction to God.

The conception of sin is still more Pelagianized in his system. Sin, he held, is a free act. All sin is, strictly speaking, voluntary sin. There is no imputation of the first transgression. "If the sinfulness of all the posterity of Adam was certainly connected with his sinning, this does not make them sinners, before they actually are sinners. . . . The children of Adam are not answerable for his sin." [24] Man has not lost any of his natural powers, he only has lost his inclination to serve and obey God (p. 233). This is the meaning of his teaching of "divine efficiency" even in the sinful choices of man. Since Hopkins, as Fisher remarks (p. 412) "imputation is discarded from the New England theology."

Regeneration is an act of God. It consists in illumination (pp. 399 ff.). Man reacts to the regenerative work of God by conversion. As a supporter of revivalism Hopkins says that regeneration is "instantaneous, wrought not gradually, but at once" (p. 368). Hopkins conceives of justification as a "moral union" which takes place between the sinner and the Saviour (p. 463). God treats the sinner, he says, for Christ's sake "as if he had never sinned" (p. 458). *Expressis verbis* he rejects the idea of imputation of Christ's righteousness (p. 477). The effect of the Atonement is universal. The essence of sin is self-love. Virtue is disinterested benevolence. Man should love himself not as a self but only as a part of universal Being. If God requires it, man should unconditionally consent to be cast off eternally.[25] Through his book *System of Doctrines,* published in 1793, Hopkins had a great influence on the founders of Andover Theological Seminary. His works were published by Edwards A. Park in three volumes in 1852.

14. Substantially in agreement with Hopkins were JONATHAN EDWARDS, JR. (1745-1801), and NATHANAEL EMMONS (1745-1840). Edwards made his principal contribution to theological thought in his discussion of the Atonement (see page 279). Emmons further atomized the conception of sin. Sin is no natural state. Sin, like holiness, consists in "free voluntary affections and exercises." Man is not merely passive but active in regeneration. Justification he defines as the pardoning act of God. His sins forgiven, man may live a godly life and by his good works win a reward, the blessed life of heaven. *The Works of Nathanael Emmons with a Memoir of His Life by E. A. Park* were edited by J. Ide, in six volumes, 1861 ff.

15. The influence of Hopkinsianism in New England Theology was perpetuated at the Andover Seminary through the teaching of LEONARD WOODS (1774-1854), while TIMOTHY DWIGHT (1752-1817), president of Yale and grandson of Jonathan Edwards, Sr., was the most distinguished representative of that school of Edwardians that was opposed to the Hopkinsian peculiarities. Dwight was a moderate Calvinist. Divine foreknowledge and the decrees to him are "coetaneous." Sin is based on divine permission. Its essence is selfishness. "Virtue is founded in Utility," for it tends, in his view, to promote the happiness of the universe.[26]

16. The chief exponent of the New Haven Theology was NATHANIEL W. TAYLOR (1786-1858). In his teaching he attempted to modify the older New England doctrines

---

[24] *Works* I, 233, 235.
[25] Cf. *Ibid.*, p. 389. Cf. Also Hopkins, *Works,* I, pp. 368-477.
[26] *Theology Explained and Defended,* posthumously edited in 5 vols., 1818 f. Cf. Ch. E. Cunningham, *Timothy Dwight: A Biography,* 1942.

of man's depravity and responsibility, the divine permission of sin and regeneration. Like Hopkins he denied original sin. The universality of sin, he teaches, is due to the present condition of man and the circumstance of his life. But he rejects the Hopkinsian doctrine which reduces sin into individual acts of the will. Sin, he says, is a permanent state of the will. He also is opposed to the doctrine that sin is the necessary means to the greatest good. To avoid the least resemblance of fatalism, Taylor introduced into the discussion of human ability "the power of contrary choice." The Pelagian implication of this conception he met with the assertion of the prior certainty of all moral choices. There is the certainty, he held, that all men will persist in sinning until, under the power of divine grace, they are converted. He distinguishes between selfishness and self-love, the natural desire for happiness. Self-love is a neutral state of the soul which is neither good or evil. In this state, irrespective of grace, man is capable of obeying the gospel call.[27]

Taylor had able defenders of his teachings in CHAUNCY A. GOODRICH (1790-1860) and ELEAZAR T. FITCH (1791-1871). His most prominent opponents were Joseph Harvey, Leonard Woods, and Bennet Tyler. The opposition to Taylorism was so pronounced in Connecticut that it led to the establishment of a new theological institution, which was first located at East Windsor but later removed to Hartford.

17. *The Pelagian tendencies in the New Divinity* are likewise manifest in the revivalistic *theology of Oberlin College.* The two most prominent leaders of the Oberlin Theology were CHARLES G. FINNEY (1792-1875) and ASA MAHAN (1799-1889). Their theology centers in the preaching of entire consecration, and sinless perfection, that is, a life free from transgression of the divine law. Finney rejects the Edwardian distinction between "natural ability" and "moral ability." His view of the will is wholly Pelagian. Man is free to choose. To the doctrine of "natural ability" the Oberlin theologians added that of the "simplicity of moral action." This doctrine was first proclaimed by William Cochran, a member of the graduating class of 1839. Since a moral action is not of a mixed character and the will is competent to make but one choice at a time, whenever a man makes a right choice he is perfect at that moment and continues in this state as long as the succession of right choices prevails. Finney identifies regeneration and conversion. Regeneration is a turning to God, it is "nothing else than the will being duly influenced by the truth." The preacher should use the force of persuasion to convert the sinner. Perfect sanctification is to be attained by the baptism of the Holy Ghost, who is indispensable to the "appropriate happiness and befitting characteristics of the children of God." [28]

Note: The teaching of these Oberlin men left a permanent mark on American church life in that it gave impetus to the establishment of Holiness and Pentecostal churches. Prominently identified with this movement are W. E. Boardman (1810-1886), A. B. Simpson (1843-1919), and A. M. Hills (1848-1935). Though differing on many points of doctrine and practice (baptism with the Holy Ghost, gift of tongues, divine healing, feet washing, etc.), they are all agreed, on the basis of an Arminian view of man, in the Wesleyan teaching of "entire sanctification." [29]

18. *The last outstanding representatives of the New England Theology* were Fairchild and Park. JAMES HARRIS FAIRCHILD (1817-1902), the successor of Finney at

---

[27] Cf. Fisher, *op. cit.,* pp. 414 ff.

[28] Cf. Foster, *op. cit.,* p. 453 ff.

[29] See Neve, *Churches and Sects of Christendom,* pp. 441 ff.; also *Popular Symbolics,* St. Louis, Mo., 1934. pp. 334 ff.

Oberlin, represents in his teaching the same fundamental principles which Finney had taught.[30] EDWARDS AMASA PARK (1808-1900), at Andover Seminary, was a pupil of Woods and even more so of Taylor. At one time he was considered to be the greatest dogmatic genius of America. In general, Park holds to the modified Calvinism of Edwards and Taylor. God is all-co-operative, but His decrees are based on His love. Park uses the scholastic method: to prove the Biblical truth on rational grounds. He was one of the founders and the first editor of the *Bibliotheca Sacra*. *The Theology of the Intellect and That of the Feelings* (1850) is the result of his violent controversy with Charles Hodge.

19. Finally, a passing word is in order on the teaching of the New Divinity concerning the *doctrine of the Atonement*. As early as 1650 a book had been published by William Pynchon, who had come to America in 1630, on *The Meritorious Price of Our Redemption*. Though Pynchon held to the idea of a limited Atonement, he protested against the current representations of the doctrine which teaches that Christ upon the Cross suffered the pains of hell of the condemned and against the theory of the imputation of the Saviour's righteousness. His theory was that Christ through His obedience satisfied the wrath of God and wrought the pardon of the elect. The book was ordered to be burned and refuted by order of the Massachusetts General Court and John Norton of Ipswich was requested to prepare a refutation: *The Orthodox Evangelist* (1654). Pynchon returned to England where he died in 1662.

The discussion of the Atonement had attracted much interest in the New Divinity, but it came not into prominence before the opposition of the Liberal movement had not singled out this doctrine for attack. The New England theologians tried to define their teaching so as to reject the older conception of a limited Atonement as well as to give greater emphasis to the grace and mercy of God in the conversion of the sinner. Their doctrine, commonly called the "Governmental," or less fittingly, the "Benevolence" theory, united certain tenets of the Grotian and Arminian conception of the Atonement with the Calvinistic doctrine of Divine sovereignty. The chief contributors are Bellamy[31] and Jonathan Edwards, Jr.[32] According to the new theory, the atoning work of Christ removed a bar to the forgiveness of sin. God made His own Son suffer on the Cross in order to demonstrate that His law had not changed. The heinousness of sin committed by man demanded God's reaction. The sufferings of Christ, however, are no punishment, for the Law had no claim on Him: they are an adequate exhibition of God's wrath against sin. Thus the moral government is maintained, and God will forgive him who turns from evil to good. The work of Christ has not changed God's attitude to man, but it purposes to effect a change in man's disposition to God.[33]

20. From our discussion it will be sufficiently clear that *the New Divinity sought a happy medium* to bridge the chasm between stark Calvinism and Pelagian Arminianism. The New England theological controversy was, like the Arminian dispute, a Protestant counterpart to the Semi-Pelagian controversy in the ancient Church of the West. While, however, the Arminians placed emphasis on the human side in the work of salvation, the New Divinity kept itself closer to the divine. The exalted place which

---

[30] *Elements of Theology*, 1892.
[31] *The True Religion Delineated*, 1750, *Complete Works*, Vol. I.
[32] *Three Sermons on the Atonement*, 1785.
[33] Cf. Boardman, *op. cit.*, pp. 221 ff.

reason had in the Arminian system found no favor with Edwards. He was a mystic. Illumination comes upon man as a divine gift. Edwardian theology is Semi-Calvinism shading off, in Hopkins and Taylor, into Semi-Pelagianism. Trained in a religion that was marked by rigid self-introspection, the New England theologians ventured upon a minute analysis of the psychological faculties of man. Stephen West's *Essay on Moral Agency* (1772), and Asa Burton's *Essays on Some of the First Principles of Metaphysics, Ethics, and Theology* (1824) are, along with the contributions of the leading figures of the movement, classics of the New Divinity.[34] In these minute psychological studies on the background of Calvinistic determinism lies the unique contribution of the New England theology to the development of theological thought. For this reason the New Divinity is a world phenomenon. Nevertheless, it was doomed to collapse. As a *via media* between Puritan Calvinism and eighteenth century Arminianism it aroused the antagonism of the genuine Calvinists and lost the support of the progressives when the latter attempted to reconstruct theological thought in the light of natural sciences. To the progressives it proved too narrow and supernaturalistic; while it conceded too much to human ability to satisfy the genuine Calvinists. These rightly felt that the Calvinism of the New Divinity was nothing but "the faith of the fathers ruined by the faith of their children"[35] because with the leaders theological interest was focused in man, in his ability, and happiness. The grand conception of Edwards, "affection for being in general," was lowered into love for all intelligent beings. In short, Christianity stripped of its metaphysical and supernatural had become a humanitarian creed. "And thus New England theology perished from the earth."[36]

21. *The opposition to the New Divinity* branched off into two directions: the Liberal Movement which struck at the supernatural element retained in the system of the Edwardians, and the conservative reaction which attempted to restore Calvinism to its proper propensities. With these two movements we shall deal in our subsequent Chapters.

[34] Cf., the chapter on The Theory of Will in Foster, *op. cit.*, pp. 224 ff.
[35] Haroutunian, *op. cit.*, p. 281. By permission of Henry Holt & Company, publishers.
[36] Foster, *op. cit.*, p. 552.

Chapter Four

THE LIBERAL MOVEMENT IN AMERICAN THEOLOGY

Literature: G. P. FISHER, *History of Christian Doctrine*, 1906, pp. 418 ff.; FRANK H. FOSTER, *A Genetic History of the New England Theology*, 1907, pp. 273 ff.; *The Modern Movement in American Theology*, posthumously edited in 1939; JOHN W. BUCKHAM, *Progressive Religious Thought in America*, 1919. As the manuscript is completed we receive the latest book dealing with this particular phase of theological thought in America: DANIEL D. WILLIAMS, *The Andover Liberals*, 1941. For special literature on the UNIVERSALISTS we refer to RICHARD EDDY, *Universalists in America* 1884 ff.; *History of the Universalists in the United States*, 1894; on the UNITARIANS: J. H. ALLEN, *The Unitarians*, 1894; I. E. MANNING, *The Religion and Theology of the Unitarians*, 1906; A. S. ELIOT, *Heralds of the Liberal Faith*, 3 vols., 1910; G. W. COOKE, *Unitarians in America*, 1910; E. EMERTON, *Unitarian Thought*, 1920; E. M. WILBUR, *Our Unitarian Heritage*, 1925; *The First Century of the Liberal Movement in American Religion*, 1933; C. W. CASSELL, *History and Characteristics of Unitarianism*, 1926, a typewritten manuscript in the library of Hamma Divinity School, Springfield, Ohio.

1. In America the *rise of Rationalism and Liberalism* grew as a reaction to the Calvinistic way of using the Bible as a book of rules, laws, and settlement of matters of nature. The Liberal Movement had its root in English Arminianism, Latitudinarianism, Socinianism, and Unitarianism. The theological unrest was still more intensified by the spread of French infidelity, "the legacy of French co-operation in the War of the Revolution." [1] Likewise, the religious individualism inherent in Puritanism and its conception of Christianity as a "way of life" (covenant) proved in time to be a strong factor in liberalizing the substance of faith. Before two hundred years of Congregational church history had elapsed, Calvinism had lost the famous Puritan pulpits in Boston and vicinity to Unitarianism. In this restricted sense there is some truth in the saying that "the seeds of American Unitarianism were brought to this country in the Mayflower and planted here by the Pilgrims." [2]

In 1692 the change of the colonial charters had served as another stimulus to a growing liberalism in America. As a result, liberal books and other literature were brought into the Colonies from England. During the eighteenth century the growth of liberalism became progressively more apparent. Among those who exercised a great influence on the liberal side of Puritanism was Ebenezer Gay of Hingham, Massachusetts (1696-1787), who has been called the "Father of American Unitarianism," and John Wise (1652-1725) of Ipswich, Massachusetts, called the "Father of American democracy," whose book on the *Vindication of the New England Churches* (1717) is a remarkable exposition of the principles of civil government. Liberalism in America was primarily a humanitarian movement with emphasis on the ethical and social aspect of Christianity. The controversy over the Atonement was rooted in the humanitarian protest against the gruesome outlook of Calvinism for the majority of men; and the dispute over the Trinity, which became the dividing issue between the Unitarians and the Athanasians, "merely crystallized the growing estrangement between Calvinism and

---

[1] Foster, *op. cit., Genetic History*, p. 273.
[2] Cassell, *op. cit.*, p. 100.

the spirit of the new age, and brought it to a head."[3] The difference between the Unitarians and the Universalists was a difference in degree only. With the Universalists the main stress was placed on the conception of a General Atonement, with the Unitarian on the unity of God. In the view of the former God is too good to damn man, in the eyes of the latter man is too good to be damned.

2. As early as in 1650 there appeared in the Colonies *the first attack* upon the Calvinistic doctrine of the Atonement (compare the preceding chapter). But the time was not yet come that a man in New England could openly deny a fundamental principle of Calvinism. As stated above, Pynchon's book was ordered to be burned and the author returned, a few years later, to Old England.[4]

3. *Universalism* was introduced into America by JOHN MURRAY, who arrived in New Jersey in 1770.[5] He had been brought up a strict Calvinist and had been co-worker of John Wesley and Whitefield till he became attracted to the teaching of James Relly who had expounded in England the Universalist doctrine in its grosses form.[6] Relly taught that the human race was so united to Christ that this union "render His condition theirs in every state which He passes through."[7] The next great leader of the movement was ELHANAN WINCHESTER (1751-1797). He was a Trinitarian. As to the eschatological consequences of a general Atonement, he taught the "restoration of all," contending that there must be "adequate" punishment, but "adequate" not eternal. His influence was soon superseded by that of HOSEA BALLOU (1771-1852) who became the recognized leader of the movement. Ballou effected the transfer of the Universalists from the Trinitarian to the Unitarian basis. He was a determinist, for according to him, if the will of God to save all shall be carried out, the will of man must be denied the power of resistance. The effect of the Atonement is universal, it purpose is universal holiness, i.e., the happiness of mankind. The human race which originated in God must finally be united with the fountain from which it sprang. On the principle of sympathy, it is argued, that everlasting punishment for some of it members would interfere with the happiness of the whole race.[9]

Ballou's neglect to give a Scriptural basis to his doctrine was corrected by Walter Balfour in his book, published a decade later, *An Inquiry Into the Scriptural Import of the Words Sheol, Hades, Tartarus, and Gehenna, All Translated Hell in the Common English Version* (1824). In this treatise, as the title indicates, Balfour presents an analysis of the Scriptural teaching of eternal condemnation. He reaches the conclusion that since none of the words under investigation designates an eternal condition, there is, in his opinion, no such thing in the Bible as eternal punishment.

4. *The most formidable opponent of Universalism* arose in the person of MOSES STUART, professor at Andover. He tried to refute Balfour in his book entitled *Exegetical Essays on Several Words Relating to the Future Punishment* (1830). Stuart upheld the orthodox view of eternal punishment. Also Thomas Whittenmore, himself a Universalist, opposed the peculiar tenets of Balfour's exegesis in his book *Plain Guide to*

---

[3] Haroutunian, *op. cit.*, p. 180.
[4] Cf. Boardman, *op. cit.*, pp. 221 ff.
[5] Cf. C. R. Skinner-A. L. Cole, *Hell's Ramparts Fell. The Biography of John Murray*, 1941.
[6] *Union; or a Treatise of the Consanguinity and Affinity between Christ and His Church.*
[7] Cf. Foster, *Genetic History*, p. 190.
[8] *The Divinity of Christ Proved from the Scriptures*, undated.
[9] *A Treatise on the Atonement*, 1804, 4th edition, 1882.

niversalism (1839). The Universalist denomination today is Unitarian but holds that the sinner cannot escape punishment which, however, "is remedial and is meant to indicate the inflexible righteousness of God and to induce repentance and reformation in His wayward children." [10]

5. Of far greater significance than the Universalist movement is the rise of *Unitarianism in America*. The momentous event in the early history of American Unitarianism was the action taken by James Freeman and his congregation at King's Chapel, Boston, whereby that first Episcopal Church in New England became the first church openly acknowledging Unitarianism. Soon Harvard became a hotbed of Unitarianism. In 1805 Henry Ware (1764-1845), an outspoken liberal, was elected to the Hollis chair of divinity at Harvard. The intellectual and liberal theology was cultivated through the Anthology Club, through *The Monthly Anthology, The Christian Monitor* (after 1806) and the aggressive *General Repository and Review* (after 1812). New England Congregationalism began to split into a conservative and liberal wing. The former founded Andover Seminary in 1808 for the purpose of training a clergy who would be free from the "taint of the Unitarian heresy." The formation of a new denomination out of the liberal wing, however, was a very slow and gradual progress. The separation of the two wings was not complete before 1833, by which time the Liberal movement had passed through its first radical transformation.[11] But whatever headway the movement had made in America at the beginning of the nineteenth century, it remained for Channing, Emerson, and Parker to crystallize the Unitarian principles.

6. WILLIAM ELLERY CHANNING was born at Newport, Rhode Island in 1780, of stern Calvinistic parents. At Harvard he became a pupil of Samuel Hopkins. In 1803 he became pastor of Brattle Street Church at Boston, which position he held till his death in 1842. In 1819 he delivered his famous epoch-making *Baltimore Sermon* at the installation of Jared Sparks on "Unitarian Christianity." In the introduction of this sermon Channing exalts reason as being capable of perceiving revelation and expounding the Scriptures. The speaker then goes on to reject the Trinitarian doctrine, the Church's doctrine of Christ's twofold nature, and the orthodox view of the Atonement. Salvation is to be obtained by the exercise of the moral faculties of man. The sermon furnished the Unitarians, which hitherto "had disagreed among themselves as to every doctrine save the Trinity," with something which they could regard as a platform.[12] In the later years of his life Channing became a champion of the Abolitionist movement.

The keynote of Channing's theology is his supreme faith in man. Reason is the ultimate source of authority. Man is endowed with a knowledge of right and with the ability to materialize it. To deny him the exercise of a free will, would make the sentiment of duty illusory. God is the Infinite Being, the Parent Mind, the Universal Father, and the Father of our spirits. He is substantially immanent. Man experiences the fact of revelation in his own conscience. A special revelation can be merely supplementary to the laws of nature, not contradictory. Of Jesus he says in his *Baltimore Sermon,* "We believe that Jesus is one mind, one soul, one being, as truly one as we are, and equally distinct from the one God." At another place (*Imitableness of Christ's Character*) he says of Jesus, "I believe Him to be a more than human being" continuing, however,

---

[10] E. O. Watson, *Yearbook of the Churches,* 1921 f., p. 242; cf. also Foster, *Genetic History,* pp. 189 ff., 16 ff.

[11] Wilbur, *First Century of the Liberal Movement,* p. 10.

[12] *Ibid.,* p. 9.

a little later, "For though so far above us, He is still one of us, and is only an illustration of the capacities which we all possess. . . . All minds are of one family." According to his peculiar conception, Christ is a pre-existent rational creature of God. This notion is with him a crude and unphilosophical sort of Arianism "which strikingly indicates," in the words of Fisher (p. 431), "the transitorial character of Channing's type of theology." God's justice is, according to Channing, in perfect harmony with His mercy God "desires strongly the happiness of the guilty; but only through their penitence." There is no place in Channing's theology for the doctrine of the vicarious atonement of Christ. Christ's mission is "the recovery of man to virtue." "We regard Him a Saviour chiefly as He is the light, physician, and guide of the dark, diseased and wandering mind" (*Baltimore Sermon*).

In his controversial argument against the doctrines of the Trinity and the double nature of Christ, Channing revived the old Socinian arguments. His attitude toward the older Unitarians, such as Priestly and Belsham, was only lukewarm. His piety was of a high emotional and spiritual quality thus refuting the current conception among his contemporaries that a liberal theology is of necessity cold and dull. Channing was not interested in denominational lines; he even disliked to be called a Unitarian. His Works have been collected into three volumes and edited by the Unitarian Association (1848 and subsequent editions).

7. *Next to Channing,* RALPH WALDO EMERSON'S magnetic personality stands out as one of the greatest leaders of the Liberal movement. Emerson was born in 1803 at Boston. Educated at Harvard, he was ordained to the Congregational ministry in 1829. After three years of service at the Second Church, Boston, he resigned his charge because the congregation was unwilling to discontinue, or, at least, radically change the communion service. Upon his resignation he continued to speak to an ever-growing audience as philosopher and poet, till his death in 1882.

Emerson is generally considered as one of the truly great sons of America. In his world of thought three different currents meet: the skeptical or empirical, the ethical and the mystical. While the skeptical vein in Emerson is regarded as merely methodological, the ethical is the basis, and the mystical the subcurrent, of all his thought. His view of God borders upon pantheism. Consequently, evil is denied ontological reality. While he does not deny the immortality of the individual, his emphasis is on the ethical import of it. As in Jesus, God incarnates Himself in every man. Under the impact of the Church's theology, Christianity became a mythus, and Jesus, the friend of man, was made the injurer of man. The word Miracle, as pronounced by the churches, is a monster. Revelation is progressive, it comes from within. If a man leaves his own knowledge of God and takes secondary knowledge, as St. Paul's or George Fox's or Swedenborg's, "you get wide from God with every year this secondary form lasts." [13] While the older Unitarians wanted to uphold the truth of the Scriptures against the historical creeds of the Church, Emerson's theology is just as un-Scriptural as uncreedal. To him the ultimate authority of religion rests in the law of reason and of right as it stands revealed in the mental and moral constitution of man. "In the soul let redemption be sought." Thus Emerson became the foremost exponent of American Transcen-

---

[13] *The Divinity School Address of July 15, 1838.* Printed by the American Unitarian Association as Tract C, 1935, p. 18.

dentalism which sought to comprehend the transcendental verities by the intuition of the soul.[14]

8. *There is manifest in Emerson* an important change in the thinking of American scholars. His theology struck not only at the fundamentals of Congregationalism but also at the foundation of Unitarianism of the Channing type. The Emersonian teaching made the question as to the place of the supernatural and the concept of God a pointed issue. The age of Emerson was the time when German philosophical and theological thought was first introduced into the English-speaking world by Coleridge, Carlyle, and others. The wealth of German thought began to open new vistas before the eyes of the Anglo-Saxons. American students crossed the ocean in great numbers to study at German universities. A question then much discussed by German scholars was the question of miracles. German theology was just coming out of Rationalism and was now under the influence of thought emanating from Kant, Schleiermacher, and Hegel. This new thought completed the critical work of eighteenth-century English Deism and French Naturalism. The supernatural and miraculous foundation of Christianity was being discarded. The Rationalist had given a rational interpretation of the miracles related in the Bible; the new school interpreted them mythologically or symbolically.

Equally harassing was the new concept of God. With Spinoza it was substance, with Hegel it was thought. For Kant religion was an ethic, for Schleiermacher feeling, and for Hegel it was thinking. Emerson's *Divinity Address* clearly reflects this new trend in religious thinking. The beginning of Unitarianism goes back to Socinianism resembling the Dynamic Monarchianism of the Ancient Church: the one personal God. This still was the view of Channing. In Emerson we see the Spinozian concept, which was soon replaced by Hegelian pantheism, beginning to take hold of the mind of the liberal thinkers.

9. *The transcendental principle expressed by Emerson* was given a more concrete application by THEODORE PARKER (1810-1860). While a student at Harvard, Parker had acquainted himself with the writings of the German Rationalists such as de Wette, Eichhorn, Ammon, Paulus, and Wegscheider. He also studied Spinoza, Descartes, Leibnitz, Lessing, and Herder. In 1843, while on a visit to Europe, he came into personal contact with Schelling, Vatke, Tholuck, Ewald, Bauer, and de Wette. In 1836 he had translated de Wette's *Introduction to the Old Testament* into English. Parker's sermon on *The Transient and Permanent in Christianity*, preached at South Boston in 1841, is a landmark in the development of American Unitarianism. Here Parker takes the stand that Christianity is nothing but "absolute pure morality, absolute pure religion — the love of man; the love of God acting without let or hindrance." [15] The authority of Jesus does not rest on His divine nature but on the truth of His words. These in turn need no miraculous confirmation. Even "if it could be proved — as it cannot — . . . that the Gospels were the fabrication of designing and artful men, that Jesus of Nazareth had never lived, still Christianity would stand firm, and fear no evil" (p. 20). Likewise, the "idolatry of the Old Testament" must cease in the Church (pp. 12 ff.). As with the eighteenth-century Rationalists, the idea of God, the moral law, and the immortality of the soul are the great axioms of Parker's theology. In his view about God he wavers between the concept of theism and pantheism. Special revelation has no place in

---

[14] Centenary edition of his *Works* in 12 vols., 1903.
[15] Published by the American Unitarian Association as *Tract D*, 1935, pp. 12 ff., 20, 27.

his system. Christianity is a purely natural product. Miracles are pronounced to be a myth. The fall of man is as inevitable as the fall of a child who learns to walk. By stumbling the child learns to walk. Each fall is a fall upward. The *Works* of Parker were edited by F. T. Cobbe, London, 1863.

10. *Parker's innovations in theology* caused no little concern to the more conservative Unitarians. The chief antagonist of Parker was Andrews Norton, professor at Harvard (1786-1853). Unitarian scholars friendly with Channing were Orville Dewey (1794-1882) and Ezra Stiles Gannett (1801-1872). For half a century the Unitarians were divided into two warring factions. In order to check the growing radicalism, the conservatives were constantly struggling for a creedal statement in the constitution of the Unitarian denomination; but they never succeeded. By the end of the Civil War the issue of miracles had lost interest. The question as to "whether a religious organization is primarily to be formed about a belief or about a purpose, a common point of view or a common end of action" was decided in 1894 in favor of the latter interpretation. [16] Unitarianism today is religious pragmatism.

During the latter decades of the nineteenth century the radical wing was represented by such able scholars as Octavius Brooks Frothingham (1882-1895), author of *Life of Theodore Parker* (1874), James Freeman Clarke (1810-1888), who wrote *Ten Great Religions* (1873-1883), and *Essentials and Non-Essentials in Religion* (1878); and Joseph Henry Allen (1820-1898), the historian of the Unitarian Movement, *Our Liberal Movement in Theology*, 1882, *Historical Sketch of the Unitarian Movement Since the Reformation* (1894), et al.

11. *By the middle of the nineteenth century* the liberalizing influence of German thought was also beginning to influence the Congregational theologians. The anthropological problems which had been discussed by the Edwardians were receding into the background. Naturalism and supernaturalism, the question of Scriptural authority, of the person of Christ, and of the Atonement were the topics that were attracting the interest of the younger generation. The "Later New Haven Theology" is best exemplified in the life and work of HORACE BUSHNELL (1802-1876). Bushnell was preeminently a preacher not a technical scholar. He was the example of a conscientious theologian, leaving a mark upon the Congregational theology of the last century. In his two volumes entitled *God in Christ* (1849) and *Christ in Theology* (1851), Bushnell undertook to solve the doctrine of the Trinity on the Sabellian hypothesis. Father, Son, and Holy Spirit are three different modes through which the Ineffable One disclosed Himself to man. The Trinity was to him a "Trinity of revelation," an "instrumental Trinity," as he called it. The language of the historical creeds of Christianity should not be pressed to the letter "for the very sufficient reason that the letter is never true. They can never be regarded as *proximate* representations, and should therefore be accepted not as *laws over belief* or opinion, but more as badges of consent and good understanding." [17] But his aversion against the creeds at this time was largely due to a lack of proper historical studies, for he later admitted that upon a new and more thorough investigation of the Nicene Creed, its language then appealed much more to him. In an article, "The Christian Trinity a Practical Truth," published in the *New Englander* (Nov., 1854) he made some striking advance toward the Athanasian theology. "He (God) is

---

[16] Wilbur, *op. cit.*, p. 23.
[17] *God in Christ*, p. 81.

ernally threeing himself, or generating three persons," he wrote. "By a certain inward necessity (God) is being accommodated in His action to the categories of finite apprehension." "Here is a certain real immanence of the Trinity," as Fisher rightly remarks (p. 441), but it is an immanence "conditioned on relativity" (*ibid.*). According to Athanasian theology, God is triune, independent of His relation to the world. In his reconstruction of the Christological doctrine, Bushnell stressed the divine in Christ. The human element in Christ he held practically of little or no account. Though he did not exactly deny the human soul of Christ as Apollinarius did, yet over against the Nestorianizing form of the Christological dogma common to Reformed theology, he denied what he called the "*distinct* subsistence (of the soul) so as to live, think, learn, worship, suffer by itself." [18] In his view on the Atonement, Bushnell anticipated Ritschl, whom he, very likely, did not know. Christ came into this world, he held, to renovate the character of man. He did this by demonstrating in His life and death the pity, forbearance, and yearning love of God (*Vicarious Sacrifice,* 1865). As in his studies on the Trinity, Bushnell, in a later treatise on the Atonement entitled *Forgiveness and Law* (1874) expressed himself more favorably to the traditional orthodox view. He then admitted that in the atoning work of Christ God entered upon a self-sacrifice and self-propitiation. By the agony on the Cross God appeased His own sentiment justly indignant over the sin of mankind.[19] Bushnell also dealt a heavy blow at the revival method of the New England theologians. The spasmodic excitement and sporadic conversions, he pleaded, should give way to a systematic method of Christian nurture in the home. (*Christian Nurture,* 1846.) In this way he became instrumental in inaugurating the modern era of religious education. When Bushnell's view became known, the criticism was made that he was discounting the special agency of the Holy Spirit in man's salvation by an appeal to the congenital origin and progressive growth of character by the law of heredity on the plane of naturalism. Essentially the same note he struck in a later volume entitled *Nature and the Supernatural* (1858). Both the natural and the spiritual, reason and revelation, he says here, are "parts of one system." Bushnell thus arrived at a conception of religious authority which he held, like the mystics, to be innate in human reason.[20]

Another scholar of this school of thought was SAMUEL HARRIS (1814-1899). He holds a transitional position in the New England theology. Kant has an established place in his system and with Hegel he conceived of God as absolute Reason progressively revealing Himself. His principal works are *Philosophical Basis of Theism* (1883), *The Self-Revelation of God* (1887), and *God, the Creator and Lord of All* (1896).

12. *The greatest stumblingblock to the liberals* was the Calvinist doctrine of the eternal decrees, the conception of a limited atonement, and eternal punishment for the reprobate. With the teaching of evolution in the ascendency, the liberals attempted to interpret Christianity in terms of Hegel's conception of divine immanence and of progressive unfolding of divine truth. Hegelian idealism was just then being fully introduced into the English-speaking countries by the Cairds in England and by Royce in America. In addition, Otto Pfleiderer, whose lecture room in the Berlin University

---

[18] *God in Christ,* p. 154.

[19] According to A. H. Strong, *Systematic Theology,* 1907, pp. 739 f., Bushnell recanted on the deathbed this moral influence theory of the Atonement. As to a similar incident in the life of Ritschl, see above, p. 152.

[20] T. T. Munger, *Horace Bushnell,* 1899; G. B. Stevens, "Horace Bushnell and Albrecht Ritschl," in *American Journal of Theology* (1902), VI, 36-56; cf. also Foster, *Genetic History,* pp. 401 ff.

was much frequented by students from both countries, aided greatly the cause of Hegel ianism in the Anglo-Saxon world. Under the influence of Hegel's conception of God as the ever immanent power and the organizing and rationalizing principle of the universe, the supernatural and miraculous revelation of God in Christ and the Scripture was in danger of being eliminated from Christianity. The seat of religious authority was being transferred from the Bible or the Church to human experience in which according to Hegel, the Infinite becomes self-conscious.

13. *Though Darwinism was branded* by Charles Hodge of Princeton as atheism (*What Is Darwinism?* 1874), Henry Ward Beecher (*Evolution and Religion,* 1885) and Lyman Abbott (*Theology of An Evolutionist,* 1897) decidedly cast the lot of Con gregational theology with evolution. The Bushnellian interpretation of the Trinity was given further thought by James M. Whiton (*Gloria Patri,* 1892). The Sonship of Jesus he conceived of as a divinity of moral attributes. Lyman Abbott's volume, *The Evolution of Christianity,* published in the same year, strikes essentially the same note, and from 1892 liberal theology was largely Unitarian. Eschatological questions received special attention at Andover where Egbert Smyth, co-editor of *Progressive Orthodoxy* (1885) shared with others of his colleagues the view of a continued probation after death for those who had not known God in Christ during their earthly life. Strange as it seems to us today, this view created much resentment among the rank and file of the conserva tives in those days. Theodore T. Munger, who wrote *Freedom of Faith* (1883), *Appeal to Life* (1887), *Essays for the Day* (1904), *et al.,* wanted to reconstruct Christianity on the basis of its "entire reasonableness." He transferred unreservedly the seat of religious authority from the Bible to individual experience. To George A. Gordon divine revela tion and human discovery were reciprocal, and the distinction between natural and revealed religion was an "unholy distinction." [21] The doctrine of the Trinity he inter preted socially. As man is a social being, so there is in the Godhead a social proto type of man's social personality (*Who Wrote the Bible?* 1891; *Ultimate Conceptions of Faith,* 1903, *et al.*). Epoch-making was the work of Newman Smyth, who as one of the first caught the significance of biology to the spiritual order and who conducted his theological research in scientific laboratories. The result of such an investigation is evidenced in three volumes: *The Place of Death in Evolution* (1897), *Through Science to Faith* (1902), and *Constructive Natural Theology* (1913). A still more consistent liberalism is manifest in the work of Levi L. Paine (*The Evolution of Trinitarianism,* 1901, and *The Ethnic Trinities,* 1902), and of Frank Hugh Foster during the later part of his life. When the nineteenth century was drawing to its close, theological liberalism in the Congregational Church had, roughly speaking, arrived at the following position (1) the principle of evolution was generally accepted and being applied to the field of historical investigation; (2) Biblical criticism was recognized in principle and in some of its results; (3) the doctrinal position of the Church had undergone various modifications, e.g., the belief in a metaphysical Trinity and Christology was widely shaken, the nature of the Atonement was generally conceived of in agreement with Bushnell, eternal condemnation was rejected, and such topics as predestination and original sin were eliminated from a serious consideration in theology.

14. *The liberalizing and humanizing process in theology* naturally did not confin

---

[21] *Harvard Theological Review,* I, 2, p. 145

tself to the Congregational Church. However, while in the latter denomination it was
slowly evolving movement, it proceeded with revolutionary force in the more strictly
organized *Episcopal and Presbyterian churches*. Evidences of a "broad" theology in the
Episcopal church are the lives and works of such as Frederick D. Huntingdon (1819-
904), William R. Huntingdon (1838-1910), author of *The Peace of the Church*
1891), Alexander M. G. Allen, from whose pen we have *Continuity of Christian
Thought* (1884), *Life of Jonathan Edwards* (1889), and *Life and Letters of Phillips
Brooks* (1900), Charles C. Tiffany, the historian of the Episcopal church in America,
Phillips Brooks (1835-1895), Richard H. Newton, who wrote *Right and Wrong Uses
of the Bible* (1883), *The Book of the Beginnings* (1884), and *Church and Creed*
(1891), and other able writers.

Outstanding among the liberal scholars of the Presbyterian church were such men
as Charles W. Shields, who wrote *Religion and Science in Their Relation to Philosophy*
(1875), and Henry M. Baird, who was an authority on the Huguenot movement in
France. Other prominent theologians of this type were Willis J. Beecher, James F.
McCurdy, Robert E. Thompson, Francis Brown, *et al.*

Latitudinarian Theology among the *Methodists* was represented by William F.
Warren, who wrote *Systematic Theology* (1895), and *Religions of the World* and *The
World Religion* (1911), Milton S. Terry, who is the author of a number of Old Testa-
ment commentaries; John F. Hurst, editor, in co-operation with Faulkner and Richell, of
History of the Christian Church (1897-1900); Henry C. Sheldon, author of *History of
Christian Doctrine* (1886), Robert W. Rogers, Wilbur F. Tillett, John J. Tigert, Gross
Alexander, Hinkley G. Mitchell, Olin A. Curtis, *et al.*

Though the *Baptists* were at first rather slow in accepting the new learning, an
extreme type of radicalism made great headway among them. One of their first liberal
thinkers was Ezekiel G. Robinson (1815-1894). In 1879 Crawford H. Toy was suspended for his liberal views at the Southern Baptist Seminary. Under the presidency
of William Rainy Harper (1856-1906) Chicago University became a center of liberal
learning. One of the most radical Baptist scholars was George B. Foster (1858-1918),
of the University of Chicago. He was a student of Ritschl and Harnack. In many
respects his development was similar to that of E. Troeltsch. He finally discarded the
name of a Christian altogether calling himself an "Ethical Culturist." In 1909 his name
was removed from the Baptist Ministers' Conference of Chicago. His main writings are
The Finality of the Christian Religion (1906), *The Function of Religion in Man's
Struggle for Existence* (1909).[22]

Finally we want to include in our review the names of George Washington
Northup and Augustus H. Strong (1836-1921), president of the Rochester Theological
Seminary, 1872-1912.

15. Along with these rational and critical tenets in theology there is in American
thought a current of philosophical and religious idealism which is fundamentally at
variance with the orthodox belief in the Bible as the sole authority of faith. Our reference is to such organizations as the Quakers, the Mormons, Christian Science, and Theosophical societies. Notwithstanding the great difference among these groups as to the
positive tenets of their faith, all of them are religious intuitionists. The theology of

[22] Cf. D. C. Macintosh, *The Problem of Religious Knowledge*, 1940. pp. 97 ff.

the inner light and new revelations, as claimed by their members, are strongly counteracting the authority of the Written Word. Upon the background of philosophical idealism, matter counts little with them. The true reality is metaphysical, man is a spiritual intelligence. The doctrines of pre-existence and reincarnation are cherished ideas. Christ is pre-eminently the teacher, not the Saviour.

Chapter Five

CONSERVATIVE FORCES IN AMERICAN CALVINISM DURING THE NINETEENTH CENTURY

1. While English Puritanism controlled theological thought in the eastern states, Scottish-English Calvinism gained a strong foothold in the central states. As both schools of thought had in common the Calvinism of Geneva and Dort, both were likewise divided into a conservative and a progressive wing. While, however, in the New England theology the liberals far outnumbered the conservatives during the second half of the last century, the doctrinal grounding of Presbyterianism exerted a much stronger check on the rise of a liberal party in the Presbyterian church. For more than a century Princeton remained a stronghold of a sound conservative theology.

As the story of liberal theology is, to a large extent, the story of Congregational theology, the story of conservative theology is predominantly the story of Presbyterian theology. While, however, the modernization of theological thought was an evolutionary process among the Congregational churches, it proceeded with the force of a revolution in the more strictly organized Presbyterian denomination.

2. The first notable theologian of the American Presbyterian church was JONATHAN DICKINSON (1688-1747). He was the first incumbent in the presidency of the College of New Jersey. In his chief work, *The Scripture Doctrine Concerning Some Important Points of Christian Faith* (1741), and many subsequent editions, he undertook to defend the five knotty points of Calvinism: supralapsarian predestination, limited atonement, total depravity, irresistible grace, and perseverance of saints. These five points he regarded as a "golden chain which extends from everlasting to everlasting and connects a past and future eternity, which takes its rise in God's foreknowledge and eternal purpose of grace to the elect and reaches through their vocation and justification on earth into their eternal glorification in heaven." [1]

3. The founding of the Princeton Seminary in 1812 ushered in a new epoch in the history of Presbyterianism. This seminary through its illustrious teachers exercised for a long time a strong influence not only on the Presbyterians but on American Protestantism as a whole.

The first professor in the chair of systematic theology was ARCHIBALD ALEXANDER (1772-1851). He was the father of what was called after 1832 "the Princeton theology." The Reformed theologian Philip Schaff defines the Princeton theology as a "scholarly, logical, luminous and warmhearted reproduction of the Calvinism of the seventeenth century as laid down in the Westminster standards of 1647, and revised in America, 1788." [2] As the chief exponent of the Princeton school we have to consider CHARLES HODGE (1797-1878). Upon his election to the professorship he spent two years at

---

[1] It is significant that later, during the nineteenth century, no leading Presbyterian has subscribed to these points unqualifiedly. On the contrary the teaching of double predestination was openly repudiated by the leaders of the Princeton and Mercersburg schools.

[2] *Theological Propeduetic*, 2nd edition, 1894, p. 390.

the University of Halle, where he became intimately acquainted with Tholuck. He wa:
the founder and first editor of the *Princeton Theological Review*. He wrote commen
taries on Paul's letters to the Romans (1835), Ephesians (1856), and Corinthian:
(1857-59), also a *History of the Presbyterian Church* (2 vols., 1839). The ripes
product of his pen, however, is his *Systematic Theology* in three elaborate volume
(1874). He followed Francois Turretin of Geneva (1623-1687) and the *Helveti*
Consensus Formula (1675) in his teaching of "immediate imputation" and of verba
inspiration. Hodge, likewise, made the "federal system" of Coccejus a consistent par
of his theology. According to this theology, God entered into a covenant with Adam
as the head and representative of the whole race. Consequently, everything promise
or granted to Adam, or threatened against him, has a bearing upon the whole race
(II, 117 ff.). The soul of each child is created by the immediate agency of God (II
170), and the sin of Adam is immediately imputed to all (II, 192 ff.). Equally the
plan of salvation is conceived of as a covenant. Hodge distinguishes between a "cove
nant of grace" and a "covenant of redemption." The former between God and hi:
people is universal, for "God offers to all men eternal life on condition of faith in
Jesus Christ" (II, 363). Since this covenant of grace, however, is being founded on
the covenant of redemption between the Father and the Son, the grace becomes effi
cacious only in the elect who are given by the Father to the Son. In unmistakable
terms Hodge rejects all the special tenets of the New England theology. In some
important doctrinal matters, Hodge's theology marks a real advance over the older
Calvinism: (a) He allows more room for the human agency in the composition of the
asserts to be true," including "incidental circumstances, or facts of apparently minor
Bible. True, he teaches plenary inspiration and holds that all the books of the Bible are
equally inspired. "Inspiration," he says, "extends to everything which any sacred write:
importance, as e.g., that Satan tempted our first parents in the form of a serpent'
(I, 163). But he wants the theologian to distinguish "between what the sacred writers
themselves thought or believed, and what they teach. They may have believed that the
sun moves around the earth, but they do not so teach" (I, 170). (b) His theology is
less polemical. He freely gives credit to the Roman Catholic church on whatever point
she has preserved the truth of Scripture. He opposed the Old School General Assembly
when in 1845 it declared Catholic baptism to be invalid. (c) As to the doctrine of
predestination, he taught infralapsarianism. God *permitted* the fall of man, He is not
the cause of it (II, 313). (d) Most significant is the fact that Hodge holds a more
liberal view as regards the number of the saved. Siding with the humanistic trend in
Calvinism, he teaches that all are saved who die in infancy (I, 26 f.). And in the closing
paragraph of the whole work he has the remarkable sentence, "We have reason to
believe . . . that the number of the finally lost in comparison with the whole number of
the saved will be very inconsiderable" (III, 879 f.).

   Essentially the same position was held by his son, ARCHIBALD ALEXANDER HODGE
(1823-1886), who wrote *Outlines of Theology* (1860), and *The Atonement* (1868).

   WILLIAM G. T. SHEDD (1820-1894), professor at Andover and later at Union
Theological Seminary, elaborated a similar system of Calvinism. Of his many writings
we refer to *A History of Christian Doctrine*, (1865), and *Dogmatic Theology* (2 vols.,
1889 ff.). In matters of anthropology, however, there is real difference between Shedd

nd Ch. Hodge. While the latter held to the view of philosophical nominalism, Shedd istinguished, on the basis of philosophical realism, between the generic human nature nd the individual. According to him, humanity is numerically one and the same sub-tance in Adam and in all his posterity. Adam's sin was, therefore, the sin of all man-:ind. Imputation is mediate, not immediate, and traducianism is the only logical view f propagation.

Other prominent Old School theologians in the nineteenth century were Ashbel Green, Robert J. Breckenridge, Robert L. Dabney, Francis L. Patton, Benjamin B. War-ield. WARFIELD (1851-1921), successor to A. A. Hodge at Princeton, firmly held o the doctrine of plenary inspiration and of original sin. However, he confined criptural inerrancy to the — non-existing — autographs.[3]

4. *The New School Theology* held a mediating view between the Princeton the-ology and New England Congregationalism. A number of its distinguished leaders, such us for example, Lyman Beecher and H. B. Smith, were New Englanders. There always had been a frequent intermingling between Presbyterians and Congregationalists. In 1836 both denominations combined their efforts in establishing Union Theological Seminary. The New School theology purposed to unite the progressive thought of the New England theology with the teachings of the Westminster Confession. The fac-ional spirit in the Presbyterian church led to a schism in 1838 (until 1869). The points of controversy were at first such as were raised in the New England theology, mediate or immediate imputation and the extent of the Atonement. Other problems of a more practical nature entered in, i.e., conflicting views as to the authority of the General Assembly, the Plan of Union with the Congregationalists, the slavery question, and moral reforms.[4] In the second part of the nineteenth century the controversy centered about the question of Biblical infallibility and eschatology.

The older generation of the New School theology was represented by James Richards (1767-1843), who presided over the Auburn Convention in 1837; Baxter Dickinson (1794-1876), author of the Auburn Declaration; Lyman Beecher 1775-1863), the famous antagonist of Unitarianism (*Views of Theology,* 1853); Albert Barnes (1798-1876), author of a number of commentaries on the Bible, *The Atone-ment in Its Relation to Law and Moral Government* (1859), and *The Way of Salvation* (1863), and Thomas H. Skinner (1791-1871). The most outstanding theologian of this school was HENRY B. SMITH (1815-1876). He was a pupil of L. Woods at Andover and of E. Pond at Bangor. While in Europe he came into contact with Tholuck, Fichte, and Hegel. His German studies, however, did not essentially modify his thought. He remained a New Englander holding, in general, to the doctrine of mediate imputa-tion and the governmental theory of the Atonement. His chief contribution to theology lies in his systematic effort to "make Christ the central point of all important religious truth and doctrine."[5] His *System of Christian Theology* was posthumously edited in 1884.

The Christocentric principle was carried out with still greater consistency by

---

[3] *An Introduction to the Textual Criticism of the New Testament,* 1886; *The Gospel of the Incarnation,* 1893; *The Lord of Glory,* 1907; *Calvin and Calvinism,* 1931; *Perfectionism,* 2 vols., 1931 f. The distinction between "inerrant autographs" and "errant copies," set forth in the seventeenth century by the Catholic scholar Richard Simon, plays at present an important part in the discussion of Lutheran theologians. The American Lutheran Church has officially committed herself to this theory in her constitution of 1930.

[4] Schaff, *Propedeutic,* p. 396.

[5] Quoted from a letter by Schaff, *ibid.,* p. 398.

LEWIS E. STEARNS (*Present Day Theology,* 1893). His training under Hodge, Smith, Dorner, Kahnis, and Luthardt reflects the breadth of his theology. In Christology, he held to the view of the kenotic theory and progressive incarnation. His main concern was to formulate a consistent doctrine of predestination which "shall be Calvinistic in its assertion of the divine sovereignty and yet do justice to real truth to which Arminianism bears witness," i.e., human responsibility (p. 431). Stearns, likewise, became the interpreter of the Erlangen theology to American scholars. With Frank he believed in the apologetic value of Christian experience for the defense of the fundamental doctrines of Christianity (*Evidence of Christian Experience,* 1890).

5. Synchronously with the Old and New School theology in the Presbyterian Church, there developed another school of thought in the German Reformed synod, the *Mercersburg Theology.* As its name indicates, it took its inception at the Mercersburg institutions of the German Reformed Church, Marshall College and the theological seminary. The outstanding leaders of the movement were F. A. Rauch, J. N. Nevin, and Ph. Schaff.

FREDERICK A. RAUCH'S labor was frustrated by his premature death in 1841. JOHN W. NEVIN (1803-1886) held the chair of theology in the theological seminary. His chief contribution to the Mercersburg theology lies in his discussions concerning the nature of the Church and the sacraments (*The Mystical Presence a Vindication of the Reformed or Calvinistic Doctrine of the Holy Eucharist,* 1846). The greatest genius of this school was PHILIP SCHAFF. He was born in Switzerland in 1819. Receiving his theological education at Tuebingen, Halle, and Berlin, he came in close contact with such theologians as Ferdinand Christian Baur, A. Tholuck, and A. Neander. He emigated to the United States in 1843, and for twenty years he held a professorship at Mercersburg. In 1870 he was made professor at Union Theological Seminary, which position he held till his death in 1893. Through his connection with the Presbyterian Church, he became a powerful leader among the English branch of the Reformed Church, and the New School theology may claim him just as well as earlier the Mercersburg School. In fact, his influence far transcended both his own denomination and his adopted country. As a co-founder of the Evangelical Alliance, he was president of its American branch. He also was president of the American committee of Bible Revision. He joined in the formation of the Alliance of the Reformed Churches and delivered the opening address of its first council held in Edinburgh, 1877. In his teaching career he was obligated to teach all the various theological disciplines, though his chief interest was in the field of church history. By his background and position he was eminently fit to act as a mediator between American and European thought. Schaff was a voluminous writer. His most important books are *The Principle of Protestantism as Related to the Present State of the Church* (1845), *History of the Christian Church* (3 vols., 1858 ff.; in the 5th edition revised and enlarged to 5 vols., 1884 ff.), *The Creeds of Christendom* (3 vols., 1877), and *Theological Propedeutic,* (1894). He edited the first seven volumes of *Nicene and Post-Nicene Fathers* (1886 ff.) and the first edition of the *Schaff-Herzog Encyclopedia of Religious Knowledge* (3 vols., 1884). He also arranged for the authorship and publication of the *American Church History Series* (13 vols., 1893 ff.), while Lange's *Bibelwerk,* translated, edited, and enlarged under his direction (*A Commentary on the Holy Scriptures,* 25 vols., 1865 ff.), and the *International Illus-*

trated Commentary of the New Testament (4 vols., 1882 ff.) bear testimony to his attainment in the field of Biblical scholarship.

The Mercersburg theology received its characteristics from a contact of German Evangelical thought with Anglo-American church life. It purposed to combine personal Evangelical piety with a Catholic outlook on the Church. It was opposed both to the teaching of a double predestination and the Arminian emphasis on the free will. It was strictly Christocentric. In fact, it produced the first thoroughgoing Christocentric system in American Calvinism. It conceived of Jesus Christ, the incarnate Son of God, as the federal head of the human race. All believers, born by the Spirit, are Christ's members, constituting a mystical body with Him. This is the holy, Catholic, and Apostolic Church which is one through all the ages and is never changing though the form of her life and doctrine may change. Hence no doctrinal statement formulated must needs be final. The Church may modify her teachings according to her progress in Christian knowledge. Christ perpetuates his mediatorial work through the order of chosen men who, by the rite of ordination, are duly invested with divine authority to preach the word, to administer the sacraments, and to rule over Christ's flock. The sacraments are not empty symbols, they are regarded to be significant signs and seals of God's covenant with men. The Mercersburg theologians also advocated a return to sound liturgical principles of the past. Since their views on the ministry, the sacraments, and the liturgy were a novelty among their own constituency, the Mercersburg teachers were subject to three heresy trials in 1845 and subsequent years. But in each case they were acquitted almost unanimously. Their opponents charged them with Romanizing tendencies intending to substitute for the doctrine of salvation by faith in the Atonement, the teaching of redemption through a substantial conveyance of a regenerated humanity, in and by the incarnation of Christ, through outward channels such as the Church and the sacraments.[6]

The rise of the Mercersburg school was a highly significant fact constituting, as it did, a Reformed counterpart to the Oxford Movement in England and the nineteenth-century Neo-Lutheranism in Germany. Under the impact of philosophical transcendentalism all three movements were bent to develop the sentiment of high churchism and of a mystical sacramentarianism.[7]

6. In the *Episcopal church* the influence of the Oxford Movement began to exert a considerable influence about 1850. The outstanding representative of the Old High Church party was Bishop SEABURY (died 1796), and later JOHN H. HOBART, author of *Apology for Apostolic Order* (1807). Of other prominent high church men we may mention such as George Washington Doane, editor of the first American edition of Keble's *Christian Year* (1834), Morgan Dix (*Lectures on the Authority of the Church,* 1891; *Three Guardians of Supernatural Religion,* 1891, *et al.*), Samuel H. Turner, William H. Odenheimer, and Arthur C. Coxe, editor of the American reprint of *Ante-Nicene Fathers* (1885 f.).[8]

The father of the Evangelical party was Bishop WILLIAM WHITE (died 1836). Next to him we must mention Stephen H. Tyng, William Meade, Alexander V. Griswold (*The Reformation a Brief Exposition of Some of the Errors and Corruptions of*

---

[6] Cf. B. S. Schneck, *Mercersburg Theology Inconsistent with Protestant and Reformed Doctrine,* 1874.
[7] Cf. the article on the "Mercersburg Theology" in *NSH,* VII, 311 ff.
[8] Cf. G. E. DeMille, *The Catholic Movement in the American Episcopal Church,* 1941

the Church of Rome, 1843). A theologian of no ordinary ability was WILLIAM AUGUSTUS MUHLENBERG (1796-1877), a grandson of Henry Melchior Muhlenberg, patriarch of the Lutheran Church in America. He combined a great love for the Episcopal form of the Church with a deep mysticism and a genuine social passion. An eminent writer also was Charles P. McIlvaine, author of *Oxford Divinity Compared With That of the Romish and Anglican Churches* (1841), and *The Holy Catholic Church* (1844). As in the Lutheran Church, the discussion of denominational principles occupied much of the time and energy of conservative Episcopalians. This fact explains a kind of isolation of Episcopal theology.

7. Conservative theology among the *Methodists* was represented by NATHAN BANGS (*Errors of Hopkinsianism,* 1815; *Predestination Examined,* 1817; *Reformer Reformed,* 1818), DANIEL D. WHEDON, who, as an ardent defender of Wesleyan Arminianism, wrote *The Freedom of the Will* (1864); G. R. CROOKS, who wrote an elaborate introduction to the American edition of the Gospel according to St. Matthew in Meyer's *Commentary* and who, likewise, on the basis of Hagenbach's work, wrote an *Encyclopedia and Methodology* (1884). Space permits us just to mention a few other names such as Daniel Steele, Matthew Simpson, Daniel Dorchester, John McClintock, *et al.*

8. Conservative *Baptist theologians* have made a real contribution to Biblical studies: Horatio B. Hackett, John A. Broadus, Asahel Kendrick, and Howard Osgood, all were great linguists and Biblical scholars. Other noteworthy writers were William C. Wilkinson, Elijah H. Johnson, Alvah Novey, Thomas Jefferson Conaut, Henry C. Vedder, Calvin Goodspeed, Edgar Y. Mullins, Edwin Ch. Dargan, *et al.*

9. In concluding this chapter another force in Calvinism may briefly be touched upon, the theology of the *Disciples of Christ.* This denomination originated with THOMAS CAMPBELL (1763-1854) and his son ALEXANDER (1788-1866). It established itself on a Puritanic Biblicism and thoroughgoing unionism. No creeds, but Christ! The theology of the Disciples was more a type of a simple lay theology than a scientific exposition of Christianity. The present disruption in this group, caused by the inroad of theological liberalism, is a striking example of the fact that a vague appeal to the Bible and Christian experience is no safeguard against theological modernism.[9]

---

[9] Cf. Neve, *Churches and Sects,* pp. 469 ff.

Chapter Six

LUTHERAN THEOLOGY

Literature: V. FERM, *The Crisis in American Lutheran Theology,* 1927; by the same author, *What is Lutheranism?* (A Symposium) 1930; M. REU, *"Die Eigenart der amerikanisch-lutherischen Kirche,"* in *Kirchliche Zeitschrift,* August, 1926, pp. 690-708; W. H. GREEVER, "The Place of Lutheranism in American Protestantism," in *The Lutheran Church Quarterly,* July, 1937, pp. 213-236. Helpful for consultation on the doctrinal controversies are especially the Church Histories by NEVE-ALLBECK, *History of the Lutheran Church in America,* 1934, and by J. M. ROHNE, *Norwegian American Lutheranism,* 1926. Compare also *The Lutheran Cyclopedia* by JACOBS-HAAS, 1899 ff.; and *The Concordia Cyclopedia,* 1927 ff.

1. *Lutheran theology holds a unique position in American thought.* In spite of the numerical strength of the Lutheran church — she ranks third among the Protestant denominations — she is little known to the public, and her great epoch-making writings are often ignored in theological discussions. Compared with the other Protestant churches, the Lutheran Church in America has suffered from peculiar disadvantages. The great majority of her people, when they migrated to America, belonged to the underprivileged classes of Europe. The Lutherans in America, therefore, lacked unified theological leadership, "they were scattered abroad, as sheep having no shepherd." The state churches of Germany were too provincial, they took no interest in their people who had settled beyond their territory. The Fatherland found itself in a struggle with Rationalism, and the great conservative theologians of the nineteenth century had only gradually succeeded in the gigantic reconstruction of a positive Lutheran theology after the breakdown of Rationalism. Besides, there were in Germany the adherents of the Union of 1817, on the one hand (Prussia and states toward the South and West), and the Lutherans, on the other (Hanover, Saxony, Bavaria, Wuerttemberg, Mecklenburg, and others). In addition, the language question created a special handicap for the Lutherans in America. All of them came from non-English-speaking countries. And difference in language is a barrier for the exchange of thought. For this reason eminent Lutheran theologians, writing in the German or Scandinavian languages, remained unknown to their English-speaking contemporaries. In addition, when the children of the immigrants had become Anglicized, the church was unable to minister to them because of dearth of Lutheran literature in English. Thus the second generation was at once excluded from the rich treasures of Lutheran devotional and hymnological productions. The early American Lutherans were also seriously handicapped in the training of a native ministry. Students at first had to be tutored privately or to be sent to seminaries of the Reformed denominations. With the use of English, therefore, the church did not only undergo a linguistic change. Americanization, in many instances, meant Puritanization, and loss of the confessional heritage from the land of Luther. It took more than a century till the church had recovered from this process of theological disintegration which had followed.

Connected with it all there was an intense struggle for the preservation of her historic faith. This also explains the apparent backwardness of Lutheran theology. If measured by the standards of Congregational theology, Lutheran theologians in America have contributed little to the solution of the theological issues of the nineteenth century. At most, it has been apologetic, and this frequently on the basis of a Protestant scholasticism which had been overcome in Germany and Scandinavia. However, the modern issues such as evolution and higher criticism were, strictly speaking, not problems of the Lutheran Church. The real issue whether to live or not to live was the problem of confessional self-preservation. So it came that the above-mentioned conflict in Germany between conservative Lutheranism and the Union offered itself as a chief occasion for theological discussion in America. This was particularly an American issue. It had something to do with the establishment of a Lutheran Church in a new world. All this does not mean that there were not Lutherans in America who kept themselves abreast in all other theological issues of the European continent. Read the issues of the *Evangelical Review* during the editorship of Philip Krauth and similar articles in *Lehre und Wehre, Theologische Zeitblaetter, Kirchliche Zeitschrift* and the journals of the Scandinavian synods. But the American Lutherans were not leaders in these conflicts.

2. Since we are not concerned here with writing a history of the Lutheran Church, we can be brief as to the beginnings of American Lutheranism.[1] The achievement of the pioneering pastors lay in the field of practical work. Their contribution to American theological thought was insignificant, save for the confessional principle on which they established the Lutheran Church in America. HENRY MELCHIOR MUHLENBERG (1711-1787) was a loyal son of the Lutheran reformation. The pietism of the Halle University had given a certain color to his Lutheranism but had not displaced it. In the Liturgy prepared by him and his co-laborers, Muhlenberg retained the strict orthodox formula of the words of distribution at the Lord's Supper, "This is the true body," etc. "This is the true blood," etc. In the ritual of Baptism, also, the child is asked, as in the older liturgies of the Reformation and post-Reformation period, "Dost thou renounce the devil?" etc.[2] The doctrines of Baptismal regeneration and of the Real Presence were also expressed in the revised edition of the Liturgy of 1786. Luther's Small Catechism was the textbook of religious instruction and the constitution both of the Ministerium of Pennsylvania and of New York obligated the ministry to confessional loyalty in unequivocal terms.

3. With the departure of the Patriarch the Lutheran Church passed into a *period marked by a deterioration of her confessional life.* Unionism and Socinianism threatened to undermine her very existence. In 1792 the Pennsylvania Ministerium removed from its constitution all references to the Symbolical Books. The New York Ministerium considered a union with the Episcopal church, and the Ministerium of Pennsylvania contemplated a union with the German Reformed synod. Many union churches were built to be used by both churches. Both churches engaged in co-operative educational work (Franklin College at Lancaster, Pa.), a union hymnbook with frank concessions to Socinianism was published in 1817, and the *Evangelisches Magazine,* established by the Ministerium of Pennsylvania in 1811, was frequently circulated also among the Reformed and the Moravian Brethren. In 1807 F. H. QUITMANN, a pupil of Semler at Halle and Doctor of Divinity of Harvard, was elected to the presidency of the Ministerium of New York, which position he held successively for twenty-one years. He published in 1814 an *Evangelical Catechism,* in which he openly denied the

---

[1] Cf. Lars P. Qualben, *The Lutheran Church in Colonial America,* 1940.
[2] W. J. Mann, *Life and Times of Henry Melchior Muhlenberg,* 1887, pp. 184 ff.

supernatural teachings of the Lutheran Confessions. A similar rationalistic catechism had been prepared as early as 1787 by J. C. VELTHUSEN, *The North Carolina Catechism*. The year 1818 marked the appearance of a little book bearing the title *The History, Doctrine and Discipline of the Evangelical Lutheran Church* by G. LOCHMAN. The translation of the Augsburg Confession was significant for its numerous omissions, especially of the strong condemnatory clauses, and of the Articles XXII and XXVIII. Rationality was made the test of the doctrine of the Trinity. Lochman had no liking for the teaching of the imputation of original sin. The doctrines of Baptismal regeneration and of the Real Presence were eliminated. The Formula of Concord particularly was in disfavor because of its anti-Calvinistic attitude and because of its decisively Lutheran way in settling the conflicts which had threatened the existence of the Lutheran Church in the post-Reformation period. Four years later Lochman expressed that same anti-confessional sentiment in a *Catechism* prepared by him. The knowledge of Luther's theology at this time was very faulty. His works were not easily obtained, and when he was actually studied, the theologians did not hesitate to interpret him according to their own preconceived ideas.

It was upon this background of confessional laxity that the first general Lutheran church body was established in 1820, the General Synod, with a constitution containing no reference to the Lutheran Confessions. The theology of the leading men in the General Synod was a Lutheranism modified by Puritanism and Revivalism. It was a religion more of the anxious bench than that of a piety founded upon Lutheran theology (justification by faith). Pelagian tendencies also were quite obvious. Article II of the Augsburg Confession on Original Sin created bitter resentment, for natural depravity prior to moral action was considered not to be condemnatory. In the eyes of its leaders, however, this "American Lutheranism" was a legitimate modification of "Old Lutheranism" justified by the theological development of the eighteenth century and by the new American environment.

4. A brief review of a few of the leading theologians may here be of service. ERNEST L. HAZELIUS, of Moravian descent and education, and professor first at Hartwick (1815), later in Gettysburg (1830), and from 1834 till his death (1853) in the seminary of the Synod of South Carolina, followed the general tenor which prevailed in his synod. Both the historical Lutheran conception of the Eucharist and of Baptism were untenable to him. Our reference is to *Discipline, Articles of Faith and Synodical Constitution, as Adopted by the Evangelical Lutheran Synod of South Carolina and Adjacent States, in Synod Assembled* (1841). As publications he left *A History of the Christian Church from the Earliest Ages to the Present Times* (4 vols.), and a *History of American Lutheran Church* (1846).

BENJAMIN KURTZ (1795-1865) was editor of the *Lutheran Observer*. In a series of articles in his paper he discussed the question, "Why are you a Lutheran?" [3] According to him, the great fundamental principle of the Lutheran church is belief in the sole authority of the Bible "without note or comment." His teaching on the Eucharist had the language of the Reformed churches. In an elaborate treatise on Baptism, he makes no mention of the Lutheran position. See his *Arguments Derived from Sacred Scripture and Sound Reason, Exhibiting the Necessity and Advantages of Infant Baptism, and*

---

[3] Reprinted in 1843.

Proving Sprinkling or Affusion to be the Most Scriptural and Appropriate Mode of Administering It: Together with a Number of Essays Connected with Baptism (1840).

The most dominant figure in the General Synod at that time was SAMUEL SIMON SCHMUCKER (1799-1873). He had received his theological training at Princeton. Upon the establishment of the Lutheran Seminary at Gettysburg, he became the first professor in this institution.[4] When still a student at Princeton, he envisaged a return to the Augsburg Confession, and with his election to the professorship at Gettysburg, we observe the first reference to the Lutheran symbols officially made in any declaration of the General Synod. However, Schmucker was a true son of his age. His subscription to the Augsburg Confession was conditional. In his devotional life he was essentially puritanic. He disliked the liturgical element in the Lutheran services. By training and disposition Schmucker was a man of the Evangelical Alliance in the formation of which he took a leading part. The rise of a new confessionalism in Europe and among the new type of immigrants he viewed with deep distrust. In a paper read before the Synod of Western Pennsylvania in October, 1840, "Portraiture of Lutheranism," [5] the author pointed out six features of the Lutheran Church which needed improvement: (1) the church should commit herself to the Bible, to the whole Bible, and nothing but the Bible; (2) the teaching of the presence of the glorified human body of Christ in the Eucharist has become obsolete, "bread and wine are merely symbolic representations of the Saviour's absent body"; (3) the Lutheran practice of confession in the preparation for holy communion should be relinquished; (4) a new systematic adjustment of the doctrines of the Lutheran Church is needed; (5) the merely advisory power of the General Synod should be changed in favor of a more rigid system of church government; (6) as to the confessional subscription of the ministers, all that should be required is a subscription to "the Bible and the belief that the fundamental doctrines of the Bible are taught in a manner substantially correct in the Augsburg Confession."

In 1855 Schmucker determined to deal a decisive blow against the "New Measures" of the "Symbolists." Anonymously, with the co-operation of Kurtz and Sprecher, he had printed and distributed by mail a pamphlet entitled *Definite Synodical Platform*. The pamphlet was meant to offer to the General Synod a new doctrinal basis on which she should establish herself in order to safeguard the deposits of "American Lutheranism." The chief importance of the document lies in its attitude toward the Augsburg Confession. While the remaining Lutheran symbols are flatly rejected, the Augsburg Confession is presented in a new abridged recension in which the author omitted Articles XI, XXII, and XXVIII, nearly all the condemnatory clauses and such references as are discarded as "errors." In five points, the author claims, the teachings of the Augsburg Confession are to be rejected: (1) the sanction of the ceremonies of the "mass," i.e., the communion service as drafted by Luther (Art. XXIV); (2) the commendation of private confession (Art. XI); (3) the denial of the divine obligation of the Sabbath (Art. XXVIII); (4) the doctrine of Baptismal regeneration (Art. II);[6]

---

[4] P. Anstadt, *The Life and Times of Dr. Schmucker.* 1896; A. R. Wentz, *History of the Gettysburg Theological Seminary*, 1926.

[5] Published in *The American Lutheran Church, Historically, Doctrinally, and Practically Delineated, in Several Occasional Discourses*, 5th edition, 1852, pp. 41-89.

[6] Article IX is changed to read: Concerning Baptism, our churches teach, that it is a "necessary ordinance," that it is a means of grace and ought to be administered also to children, who are thereby dedicated to God, and received into His favor.

(5) the doctrine of the Real Presence.[7] In Article VIII the phrase is removed that "it s lawful to use the Sacraments administered by evil men." [8]

The intended result, the general assent of the Church, failed to materialize. The axe which Schmucker had raised against the Confession was turned against himself. The publication of the *Definite Synodical* form marked a turning-point in the development towards a better appreciation of the confessional inheritance of the Lutheran Church. The tragic end of Schmucker, however, should not belittle the historian's esteem of him. He was a warm-hearted Christian, a great scholar, and a prolific writer. His career, however, is a warning to the whole Lutheran Church that she cannot repudiate the Book of Concord without serious injury to Lutheranism.[9]

The same tragedy marked the life of Schmucker's brother-in-law, SAMUEL SPRECHER, from 1849 to 1884 president of Wittenberg College, Springfield, Ohio. He died in 1906 at the advanced age of ninety-six years, having lived long enough to witness the complete collapse of the cause for which he had labored. But he had the courage of a Christian gentleman to revoke, to a large extent, his former position.[10] His greatest contribution to theology is *The Groundwork of a System of Evangelical Lutheran Theology* (1879). The central idea in this *System* is the personal assurance of salvation, the Christian certainty and decision which, as the author holds, are indispensable to the purity of the Church.

5. *The ambiguity of the doctrinal position of the General Synod* continued to make it a hotbed of theological unrest. The secession in 1866, which led to the formation of the General Council, was by no means a clear cleavage between the confessional and non-confessional theologians. A mediating party dominated with the motto, "The Augsburg Confession, nothing more, nothing less." [11] The Gettysburg Seminary was the chief theological school of this Neo-Melanchthonian theology. Prominent among its exponents was M. VALENTINE (1825-1906), an original thinker on philosophical foundations, author of *Christian Theology* (2 vols., posthumously edited in 1906), and J. W. RICHARD (1843-1909), who wrote as his *magnum opus The Confessional History of the Lutheran Church* (2 vols., 1909). These are two very ably written works with much truth in many points of their emphasis. But both theologians aimed at perpetuating the unsettled confessional position of the General Synod by accommodations to the Melanchthonian point of view. According to Valentine, Scriptures are a supernatural revelation from God presenting "themselves before us as rationally capacitated to discern their credentials and meet our responsibility in relation to them" (I, 60). As to the sacraments, he held a mediating view. In Baptism "regeneration is fully provided for," he says, "but the actuality can come only in the time and order of the ongoing process" (II, 330). The Eucharist is said to be a means by which Christ

---

[7] Article X reads, In regard to the Lord's Supper they teach that Christ is present with the communicants in the Supper, "under the emblems of bread and wine."

[8] The text of Schmucker's recension is reprinted by V. Ferm. *The Crisis in American Lutheran Theology,* pp. 351 ff.

[9] To this the objection should not be made that Norway and Denmark did not accept the Formula of Concord. This was a measure merely for the days of its publication when it was not wise to introduce that document into countries which at that time did not want to become involved in the German conflicts. At the Eisenach World Convention (1923) Dr. Juergensen of Copenhagen declared publicly that the Scandinavian churches work with the whole Book of Concord. And all the Lutheran churches of Scandinavian descent in America are now united in the American Lutheran Conference which has taken its position on the whole Book of Concord.

[10] Cf. Neve-Allbeck, p. 118.

[11] Cf. *op. cit.,* pp. 122 ff.

"through a real, special, definitive Presence . . . gives Himself to believers as the ever-living Saviour" (II, 358). With Bucer he rejected the Lutheran teaching of the oral receiving of the body of Christ by the worthy and unworthy communicants alike.

6. JOHN H. W. STUCKENBERG (1835-1903) should not be passed by. He was a scholar of no ordinary ability, pastor of the interdenominational American Church in Berlin, Germany, where he distinguished himself as author of widely read articles on European thought and as a pioneer in the field of sociological studies for both America and England.[12] Among the many writings of Stuckenberg, besides the numerous articles he wrote for the *Homeletic Review*,[13] there is a *History of the Augsburg Confession, from Its Origin till the Adoption of the Formula of Concord* (1869, with a revised edition in 1897). He also wrote a book on *The Life of Kant*,[14] an *Introduction to the Study of Philosophy*, 1888, and three volumes on Sociology (1897-1903). He was a man of the Evangelical Alliance and was naturally in fullest sympathy with the genius of the General Synod. He looked upon the growing friendliness of the General Synod with the General Council and its approach to conservative standards as a deplorable innovation, and he communicated his reaction to the conservative developments in America through pamphlets and articles. In 1892 he published *Greetings from the Fatherland,* and in another pamphlet which was reprinted from articles in *The Lutheran Observer* (1892-1893) he wrote on *Orthodox Lutheranism in Germany and the Confessional Position of the General Synod of the Evangelical Lutheran Church in the United States; Testimony of Leaders, An End of Controversy.*

7. The issue of *Pietism versus Confessionalism* also caused considerable division among the *Norwegian Lutherans in America.* Norway has given to America a larger proportion of her sons and daughters than any other country save Ireland. In the nineteenth century they began to come in a steady stream from 1825 on. Norway had then been under a cloud of Rationalism for a century, from which it was awakening through the revival efforts of H. N. HAUGE, a layman, the Wesley of Norway. One of his ablest followers, ELLING EIELSEN (1804-1883) came to America in 1839 and straightway began to preach to his countrymen scattered in small settlements throughout the midwest. Like Hauge, Eielsen had been persecuted and imprisoned for having preached without ordination, and even after his ordination in 1843, Eielsen distrusted the university-trained pastors who were coming over, and he always feared the formalism and Rationalism of the state church.

In 1846 he and his friends organized the "Evangelical Lutheran Church of America," the Eielsen Synod. A constitution was drawn up and put into final form in 1850. This so-called "Old Constitution" recognized as the rule of church order "God's Word in the Holy Scriptures in conjunction with the Apostolic and Augsburg Articles of Faith." According to paragraph two, no one was to be accepted as a member of synod except the converted or nearly converted. In paragraph six the Constitution rejected "popish authority and also the common ministerial garb" of the Norwegian clergy. Likewise, the Lutheran practice of Absolution is rejected in several pronouncements. Though Eielsen stood in a sharp opposition to the theology of Grundtvig, his opponents were right when they assailed the Constitution as Grundtvigian in character because in paragraph one

---

[12] Cf. J. O. Evjen, *The Life of J. H. W. Stuckenberg,* 1938.

[13] *Ibid.,* p. 535.

[14] See above, p. 268.

the Apostles' Creed is virtually put on the same level with the Scriptures. They likewise were right when they objected to the view of the Church, set forth in paragraph two, as Donatistic in character.[15] Prominently identified with Eielsen was P. A. RASMUSSEN (1829-1898). He made it his task to defend the peculiarities of Eielsen against the attacks of the orthodox pastors of the Norwegian Synod (founded in 1853). In later years, however, he retracted his Donatistic view of the Church and joined with the Norwegian Synod.

A comparison between Eielsen and Schmucker offers some interesting observations. Though there was no direct personal contact between these two men, both aimed to perpetuate in the New World the name Lutheran while renouncing the very essentials of Lutheranism in favor of a revivalistic and puritanic conception of Christianity.

The most distinguished leader of a pietistic Lutheranism among the Norwegians was GEORGE SVERDRUP, a theologian and linguist of first importance. He was born in Norway in 1848. He studied theology and Semitic languages in the universities of Oslo, Erlangen, and Paris. In 1874 he was called to Augsburg Seminary at Minneapolis, Minnesota, where he taught theology for thirty-four years, till his death in 1907. In his view of the Church he held a mediating view between the men of the Eielsen Synod who conceived of the Church as an unorganized federation of separate societies to be edified by lay preachers, and the pastors of the Norwegian Synod who laid stress on the unity of organization and in doctrine. He stressed the autonomy of the local congregation. He wished, as his biographer says, "that the separate congregation should take seriously its tasks of representing the 'Body of Christ.'" [16] His view on the origin and history of Christianity was conservative although he did not hold to the teaching of plenary inspiration. In his conception of the Christian life he laid stress on a personal religious experience. He opposed the teaching of predestination, the Lutheran practice of Absolution, and the distinctive Lutheran elements in Baptism and the Supper. The dogmatic exclusiveness, as it developed among the "Confessionalists," was rather repugnant to him. When the majority of the Norwegian-Danish Conference merged with other two bodies to form the (Norwegian) United Church in 1890, he and his friends withdrew and founded in 1897 the (Norwegian) Lutheran Free Church to perpetuate a pietistic Lutheranism.[17]

As a writer Sverdrup was chiefly concerned with the question of church polity. His works, all written in Norwegian, include: *Fri menighet i fri Kirke* (Free Congregations in a Free Church, 1882); *Det frie Kirkesamfund* (The Free Church Organization, 1897), and *Veileding i den Luterske Frikirkes Principer* (Guide in the Lutheran Free Church Principles, 1904). He also was editor of several Norwegian church papers.

Note: For readers outside of the Lutheran Church in America it may be difficult to understand why so much emphasis is placed in the history of the Lutheran Church of America on the adherence to its historic confessions of faith and why from this viewpoint we should measure success and failure. But this needs to be remembered: In America the Lutheran Church, much like the Presbyterian, is a doctrinal church. She cannot sacrifice her system of fundamentals without losing her very life, her heritage, her mission, the justification for her existence. The danger of losing all this is far greater in America where she is, and always will be, surrounded by many denominations which bear the Reformed stamp than, as for instance, in the Scandinavian countries

---

[15] The text of the Constitution is printed in an English translation by J. M. Rohne, pp. 107 ff.

[16] John O. Evjen in *Augsburg Seminary and the Lutheran Free Church*, edited by L. Lillehei, 1928, p. 7.

[17] A like spirit is characteristic of the very small group of the (Norwegian) Lutheran Brethren and of the (Finnish) Apostolic Lutherans.

and in Finland. We purposely do not include Germany because there the established Union has functioned, and still is functioning, as a disintegrating factor.

8. *The pietistic and unionistic modification of Lutheranism,* which the majority of Lutheran church bodies in America succeeded in rejecting, was offered a more organized home in American thought through the theology and church polity of the former *German Evangelical Synod of North America,* organized about 1840, now united with the Reformed Church of German origin. ANDREW IRION (1823-1870) and CARL EMIL OTTO (1837-1916) were outstanding leaders during the first generation. While Irion represented the genuine pietistic theology of his synod, Otto was a more critical scholar. His allegorical interpretation of Genesis 3 cost him his position as professor of Eden Seminary at St. Louis, Missouri. On the theology of this church body compare the *Histories* by A. Schory (1889), A. Muecke (1915), H. Kamphausen (1924), and C. Schneider (1939). Compare also Neve, *The Lutherans in the Movement for Church Union* (1921, pp. 138 ff.).

9. *The new confessional theology*[18] which arose as a consequence of the revival of confessionalism in Germany and the Scandinavian countries had two distinctive centers in America. In the East it was sponsored by a confessional party in the old Muhlenberg synods, and in the West by the new immigration of Germans and Scandinavians. The leader in the East was CHARLES PORTERFIELD KRAUTH (1823-1883). Prominent in the General Council, which in 1867 was founded against the General Synod, his most noteworthy contribution is the book entitled *The Conservative Reformation and Its Theology* (1871). Other scholars of distinction were B. M. SCHMUCKER, who became one of the finest liturgical scholars of the Lutheran Church; W. J. MANN, author of *A Plea for the Augsburg Confession* (1856); G. F. KROTEL, A. SPAETH, R. F. WEIDNER, and J. A. SEISS, who wrote *The Last Times; Lectures on the Apocalypse* (3 vols., 8th edition 1901).

10. *Among the conservatives of the General Synod* there were E. J. WOLF of Gettysburg and the faculty of Hamma Divinity School (S. A. ORT, L. A. GOTWALD, S. F. BRECKENRIDGE), in connection with Wittenberg College in Springfield, Ohio, who combined their influence with the theologians of the General Council. It was especially E. J. WOLF (died 1905), colleague of Valentine and Richard, with studies in German universities, with a great influence upon his students and upon many influential men throughout the whole Church, who contributed much to turning the tide in the old General Synod from Melanchthonianism to Lutheranism. Soon there was co-operation between the theologians of the General Synod and those of the General Council and of the United Synod of the South, especially for a standing committee for the creation of a common liturgy (the "Common Service") and of common forms for ministerial acts, etc. Wolf published a volume on *The Lutherans in America* (1889) and translated two volumes of Neve's *Sermons on the Pericopes* into a condensed English edition. His *Exposition of the Gospels of the Church Year* (1900) is especially much used. The details of the great movement which matured the Eastern synods for the soon-to-come union in the United Lutheran Church must be read in the above-mentioned *History of the Lutheran Church in America* by Neve-Allbeck, pp. 95 ff., 342 ff.

11. *In the Western synods* CARL FERDINAND WILHELM WALTHER (1811-1887)

---

[18] Cf., above, pp. 128 ff.

became the unrivaled leader of the Missouri Lutherans. With him as co-laborers F. C. D. WYNEKEN, W. SIHLER and quite a number of other university trained pastors from Germany helped to shape the theology of the Missouri Synod. The brothers GOTTFRIED (died 1899) and SIEGMUND FRITSCHEL (died 1900), together with JOHN DEINDOERFER distinguished themselves as leaders of the Iowa Synod. The Ohio Synod after its rupture from the Missouri Synod was led by MATTHIAS LOY (1820-1915) and F. W. STELLHORN (1841-1919).

The pioneering theologian among the Swedes was L. P. ESBJORN (1808-1870), who did valuable work both as pastor and professor. From the beginning of his teaching in Springfield, Illinois, he stressed the confessional basis of Lutheranism. It is not without meaning that both the Synod and the Seminary established in 1860, at Chicago, bore the name of the Augsburg Confession, in a Latinized form. In the developing years the strict orthodoxy was represented by ERIC NORELIUS (1833-1916). He was a prolific writer. His greatest contribution is his *De Svenska Lutherska Foersamlingarnas och Svenskarnas Historia in America* (2 vols., 1890 and 1916). The schoolman of the first half of the Augustana Synod's history was T. N. HASSELQUIST (1816-1891). He was very efficient as an expositor of the Bible.

The leaders of the Norwegian Synod were at first handicapped by the division which Grundtvigianism caused among their own ranks. J. W. C. DIETRICHSON (1815-1883), for example, was thoroughly committed to the teachings of this great Danish theologian. Like tendencies are traceable also in C. L. CLAUSEN (1820-1892), and H. A. STUB (1822-1907). The ascending tide of anti-Grundtvigianism, on the other hand, was represented by H. A. PREUS (1825-1894), N. O. BRANDT (1824-1921), and G. F. DIETRICHSON (1813-1886), students of G. Johnson of Oslo University.

It was in these synods that a peculiar confessional Lutheran theology was developed which was strictly supernatural. In spite of the fact that all synods subscribed unreservedly to the whole Book of Concord, they, nevertheless, became involved in a number of trenchant controversies. The dominating figure throughout the whole period was CARL FERDINAND WILHELM WALTHER, professor at the Concordia Seminary in St. Louis, Mo. His theological labors were marked by a persistent attempt at purging American Lutheranism of all alien principles and at restoring the theology of the Reformation and post-Reformation period in its full propensities. The theological controversies centered mainly about the following five problems: (a) the doctrine of the Church and the ministry; (b) open questions; (c) eschatology; (d) Sunday observance; (e) predestination.

(a) J. GRABAU, a leader of the band of Lutherans who had left Prussia in protest against the establishment of the Union in 1817 and who had settled in and near Buffalo, N. Y., and Milwaukee, Wisconsin, expressed in a pastoral letter in December, 1840, *a high view of the Church and the ministry*. This letter gave offense to the Lutherans of the Missouri Synod. Walther, insisting that the Church is essentially invisible, developed what has become known as the "transference" theory: Since every Christian is a priest of God, he would have the right of functioning as a minister. But in the interest of order, by divine command, the many Christian priests choose one among them as pastor who, as the representative of the congregation, performs the ministerial rites. The ministerial office is, therefore, the spiritual priesthood of all believers transferred to an individual. This transfer takes place in the call of the congregation, while the act of ordination is merely an ecclesiastical usage. Walther's view is mainly contained in three publications of his, *Die Stimme der Kirche in der Frage von Kirche und Amt* (1852) and *Die rechte Gestalt einer vom Staat unabhaengig evangelisch-lutherischen Ortsgemeinde* (1863), and *Die evangelisch lutherische Kirche die wahre Kirche Gottes auf Erden.*[19]

This conflict also involved the theologians of the Iowa Synod. Loehe, the spiritual father of this synod, rejected like Walther any hierarchical claims of the ministry, but he held to the view that the ministerial office has been committed to the Church as a whole. The individual Christian cannot, therefore, transfer his personal share, but the Church as an entity transmits, in the rite of ordination, the office to the pastor.

(b) The Iowa theologians, under the influence of the historically progressive Erlangen theology, considered certain tenets of *pre-Millennialism* as matters on which Lutheran theologians should be given freedom of interpretation, provided that their teaching be held in harmony with the "analogy of faith" (Rom. 12:7). Into this class belonged the expectation of a personal Antichrist, to be revealed in the future. The reference of Luther to the Pope as "the very Antichrist" in the Smalcald Articles was looked upon by Iowa and its predecessors in Germany as more or less an incidental remark, not intended to be a confessional expression. The Missourians, on the other hand, pointing to II Thessalonians 2:2 ff., insisted that Luther's reference must not be so interpreted. In regard to the fulfillment of the "thousand years" in Revelation 20, the Iowa theologians were inclined to allow the right of different interpretation of this passage, while to the Missourians the teaching of chiliasm in any form was incompatible with the language of Article XVII of the Augsburg Confession.

(c) The Iowa theologians held to the view that *unity in the essentials* of faith is sufficient to establish church fellowship, but that doctrinal issues which do not affect the essentials of faith must not interfere with church fellowship. Walther and the other Missourians rejected such a distinction, insisting on complete agreement concerning every Scriptural doctrine.

(d) As to *the question of Sunday observance,* the Augsburg Confession says that those greatly err (*longe errant*) who believe that the observance of Sunday rests on a divine institution (Art. XXVIII). In the seventeenth century the dogmatician Gerhard had taught that, nevertheless, the Church is under divine obligation to set apart one day in seven. Both the Missourians and Iowans were firmly established on the Article XXVIII of the Augsburg Confession. The former, however, wanted to exclude the followers of Gerhard from church fellowship, while the theologians of Iowa considered such a view tolerable.

Previous to the controversy between Walther and the Iowa Synod, the question of Sunday observance had caused some division among the Norwegians with C. L. Clausen, whom we have mentioned above, upholding the view that the Third Commandment has a divine command back of it. Clausen later retracted.[20]

(e) The most important controversy revolved about the question of *eternal predestination.* In this long-protracted and caustic controversy, the Missourians were guided by their desire to safeguard the free efficiency of divine grace to the exclusion

---

[19] For an English translation of these three writings compare Th. Engelder, editor, *Walther and the Church* 1938.

[20] Cf. Rohne, *op. cit.*, pp. 223 ff.

any resemblance of synergism in the doctrine of salvation. Their opponents, the
ologians of the Norwegians (Schmidt),[21] Ohio (Stellhorn), and Iowa (the Fritschel
others) were guided by the principle to make election an organic part of the whole
der of salvation in order to avoid the pending danger of fatalism and despair. To
e Missourians predestination presented a *theological* problem; in the eyes of their
ponents it was a *psychological* question. The latter established themselves on the
sition of the seventeenth century: election takes place *intuitu fidei*. Walther and his
nool objected to this claiming that such a definition is unwarranted both from the
riptures and in the Confessions. Election is, according to them, not *intuitu fidei* but
fidem. Cur alii prae aliis, the question, Why God has elected some men before others,
ist remain an unfathomable mystery. Salvation depends exclusively on this divine
ction; condemnation, however, will result from man's own willful resistance. Though
e Missourians came at times close to the Calvinistic teaching of a double predesti-
tion, they later expressly rejected this view. Walther also rejected the Reformed
aching of final perseverance that no true believer can totally fall from grace. Over
ainst this teaching, Walther believed that a Christian may indeed fall totally from
ace through mortal sin and that the elect must then repent of his sin. Yet he main
ned the view that an elect will inevitably repent before his death, otherwise he could
t be elect.[22] Of the very extensive literature on the subject we refer to *The Error of
odern Missouri* by Stellhorn, Schmidt, and others (1897). The position of Missouri
s received a very exhaustive treatment in *Conversion and Election* by F. Pieper
913).

Note: The controversy split the Norwegian Synod into two opposing factions. To prevent a
ism, the Synod terminated its membership in the Synodical Conference, 1883. In 1887, however,
hmidt and his followers withdrew from the Synod and formed the Anti-Missourian Brotherhood.
rough the merger of 1890 and later of 1917 the men of the Brotherhood became reunited with
e Synod.

While the Ohio and Iowa Synods, in the so-called Chicago Theses of 1929, made a serious
empt to meet the view of the Missourians, the Norwegians rallied around the view of predesti
tion as expressed in Pontopiddan's *Explanation of Luther's Catechism,*[23] which teaches that "God
s predestined all those unto eternal life, whom He from eternity has foreknown as willing to
cept the proffered grace, believe in Christ, and in this belief remain true to the end."

The solution of the age-old problem under discussion is to be seen, according to our opinion
a right synthesis of the truth to be recognized on both sides. Man is, *theologically* speaking,
rely passive in the act of faith. God saves man not because of what man is or does but because
is His nature to love man.[24] But the action of God is accomplished by claiming the natural
culties of man. From the *psychological* point of view man corresponds in *concentrated activity.*
hough the New Testament stresses the monergism of grace in unequivocal terms, it yet charges
in to repent, to believe, to put on the wedding garment, to fight the good fight of faith, etc.
the entire work of salvation man must be denied all credit; but he dare never be relieved of his
ll responsibility. Compare in this connection J. Oman's conception of "persuasive" grace
p. 249 f.), also A. Koeberle, *Quest for Holiness,* p. 254; and E. Brunner, *Man in Revolt,* pp.
8 ff.

[21] The Norwegian Synod had been in close co-operation with the German Missouri Synod when in 1859 a
orwegian professorship was established in Concordia Seminary, St. Louis, with L. Larsen (1833-1915) as its
st incumbent. In 1872 the Norwegian Synod took part in the foundation of the Synodical Conference. F. A.
hmidt, who was on the Concordia faculty, 1872-76, attacked Walther's teaching of predestination as contained
the reports of the Missouri Synod, 1877 and 1879.

[22] *The Proper Distinction Between Law and Gospel,* English translation by W. H. T. Dau, 1929, p. 323.

[23] E. Pontopiddan was a Danish theologian of the age of Pietism. The *Explanation* called, *Sandhed til
dfrygtighed* (Truth unto Godliness) appeared in 1737. In 1842 it was published in an English translation
E. Eielsen.

[24] Cf. the conception of Agape as set forth by Nygrén, *op. cit.* See above, pp. 186 ff.

12. Related to the problem of predestination was the controversy over the meaning of justification and absolution. The Missourians (J. Th. Brohm) as well as the men of the Norwegian Synod (P. L. Larsen) came close to the view of Rosenius and his followers [25] who aimed to identify justification and reconciliation. According to this view, in absolution the forgiveness of sins is imparted to all to whom it is proclaimed "whether they believe it or not (although it is not accepted by all)." Their opponents both in the Iowa Synod and among the pietistic-minded Norwegians adopted the view that absolution has no forgiving effect in case of the unbeliever.[26]

13. In these controversies *the theology of Walther,* through the official recognition of the Missouri Synod, became a powerful factor in American Lutheranism. Its teaching is, undoubtedly, fundamentally sound and evangelical. His thirty-nine lectures on *Die Rechte Unterscheidung von Gesetz und Evangelium* is a real theological classic. With his strict orthodoxy there was always in evidence a sincere evangelical piety. He was a great Luther scholar. He took an active part in preparing the St. Louis edition of Luther's works which is based on the edition of Walch. In his theology he was firmly established upon the Biblical teaching of the *satisfactio vicaria.* He therefore rejected conscientiously the idealistic tenets in the teachings of nineteenth-century Neo-Lutheranism, such as the high church view of the ministry, the conception of the Lord's Supper as implanting in man the seed of immortality, the doctrine of a future probation after death, and chiliasm. In this respect, Walther excelled most of his opponents in discriminative judgment. On the other hand, the Iowa theology distinguished itself by a truer appreciation of the genetic growth of the Christian dogma. Walther's use of Scripture, in his polemical writings, is at times artificial and inconclusive. Likewise, the nominalistic trend inherent in Protestant thought is very pronounced in his conception of the Church.

Note: The caustic sentiment between the once warring synods has more recently given way to a spirit of appeasement and *rapprochement.* In 1916 there existed not less than six different Norwegian synods. Three of these, the Hauge Synod, the Norwegian Synod, and the United Church merged in 1917 to become the Norwegian Lutheran Church. The next year the General Synod, the General Council, and the United Synod of the South merged into the United Lutheran Church in America. The Synods of Buffalo, Ohio, and Iowa formed in 1930 the American Lutheran Church. This body, in turn, joined with the Norwegian Lutheran Church, the (Norwegian) Lutheran Free Church, the United Danish Church, and the (Swedish) Augustana Synod in the formation of the American Lutheran Conference (1930). This Conference, however, is not a unified church body but a federation of independent synods. During the last few years the American Lutheran Church has entered into discussions both with the Missouri Synod and the United Lutheran Church contemplating further unification.

14. Among the leading theologians of the last and present generation affiliated with the Missouri Synod or the larger body, the Synodical Conference, are G. C. STOECKHARDT (died 1913), A. L. GRAEBNER (died 1904), F. A. O. PIEPER (died 1931), G. BENTE (died 1930), A. F. ERNST (died 1924), A. HOENECKE (died 1908), E. L. F. FUEBRINGER, TH. GRAEBNER, P. E. KRETZMANN, W. ARNDT, W. G. POLACK, JOHN T. MUELLER, TH. ENGELDER, W. A. MAIER, *et al.* Most of these men have been voluminous writers. Pieper's *Christliche Dogmatik* (3 vols. 1917 ff., translated into English by W. Albrecht, 1941) will probably mark for America the last major theological publication in a non-English tongue. His position is thoroughly orthodox

---

[25] Cf. above, pp. 140 f.
[26] For the details of this controversy see Rohne, *op. cit.,* pp. 226 ff.

As to the infallibility of the Bible, he says that the Holy Spirit may have accommodated Himself to popular notions, but never to any wrong conceptions. Biblical statements, therefore, in the field of secular sciences are to be considered scientifically correct. (I, 233 ff.).

Of the American Lutheran Church we mention C. H. L. SCHUETTE (died 1926), R. C. H. LENSKI (died 1936), who wrote among other books *A New Commentary on the New Testament* in eleven large volumes (1931 ff.), P. H. BUEHRUNG, and J. M. REU, who, in close contact with European scholarship, has given us a number of books of lasting value (*Quellen zur Geschichte des kirchlichen Unterrichts im evangelischen Deutschland*, 8 vols., 1904-27; *The Augsburg Confession*, 1930; *Luther's German Bible*, 1934, *et al*).

The United Lutheran Church can claim HENRY E. JACOBS (died 1932), an able historian, editorial supervisor of the *Lutheran Commentary* (1895 ff.), as also of the *Lutheran Cyclopedia* (1899), and author of *The Lutheran Movement in England* (1891), *History of the Lutheran Church in the United States* (1893) and *A Summary of the Christian Faith* (1905). Next we mention TH. E. SCHMAUCK (died 1920), with C. T. BENZE (died 1936), author of *The Confessions and the Confessional Principle of the Lutheran Church* (1911), which was aimed as an answer to Richard's book, as referred to; J. W. HAAS (died 1937), who wrote from a more modern point of view *Trends of Thought and Christian Truth*, 1915; *Unity of Faith and Knowledge*, 1926 *What Ought I to Believe?* 1929; *What is Revelation?* 1937; *et al.*; G. H. GERBERDING (died 1927), J. STUMP, with a book on *Ethics* (1930), and *Dogmatics* (1932), CH. M. JACOBS (died 1938), author of *What Then is Christianity?* (1940); L. F. GRUBER (died 1941), famous for his *Creatio ex Nihilo* (title changed to *Whence Came the Universe?* 1921), H. OFFERMANN with very attractive studies in the field of the New Testament, and P. Z. STRODACH, writer along liturgical lines. All of these men had been affiliated with the former General Council. A younger man is the church historian, TH. G. TAPPERT, co-editor of *The Journals of Henry Melchior Muhlenberg* in an English translation.

Of the former General Synod theologians we mention D. H. BAUSLIN (died 1922), who wrote *The Lutheran Movement in the Sixteenth Century* (1918); J. A. SINGMASTER (died 1926), with a book on *Dogmatics* (1927), L. S. KEYSER (died 1937), writer on the confessional question and author of many books, especially on "Modernism," by which he became widely known beyond the confines of the Lutheran church; A. R. WENTZ, known chiefly for his interesting book *The Lutheran Church in American History* (1923, and one subsequent edition) and H. C. ALLEMAN, editor of a *New Testament Commentary* (1936).

Theologians of these bodies translated and edited a selection of *Luther's Works* in modern English, published by the A. J. Holman Company and the United Lutheran Publication House, Philadelphia (6 vols., 1915 ff.).

In the South we have W. H. GREEVER, author of studies in the social field, including *Human Relationships and the Church, A Study of Present-Day Social Problems* (1939), and A. G. VOIGT (died 1933), in whose book *Biblical Dogmatics* (1917, second edition under the title *Between God and Man*, 1925), influences of the Erlangen School are traceable. A scholar of the younger generation is JOHN SCHMIDT. His book *The*

Riches of His Grace (1940) is a keen analysis of the present religious situation in the light of the Reformation theology.

Most outstanding among the Norwegians was H. G. STUB (1849-1931). As the ologian and church leader he held a unique position in Norwegian-American life with a number of books, especially on predestination, to his credit. Also J. N. LENKER (died 1929), translator of Luther, G. M. BRUCE and J. M. ROHNE, O. M. NORLIE, L. P. QUAL BEN, and R. MALMIN, with studies in church history, are well known beyond the confine of their own group.

The theology of the Augustana Synod is marked by a healthy synthesis of a genuine loyalty to the Confessions and an ecumenic conception of the Church. The towering figure here was C. E. LINDBERG (1852-1930). He was well acquainted with the movements in Scandinavia and Germany. Lindberg desired clarity, order, certainty This he found for himself in the classic Lutheran dogmaticians of the seventeenth century. His book *Encheiridion in Dogmatics* has gone through several editions. O the present generation C. BERGENDOFF, author of *Olavus Petri and the Ecclesiastica Transformation in Sweden, 1521-1552* (1928), S. J. SEBELIUS, A. HULT, and A. I MATTSON are outstanding.

Among the Danish Lutherans the pros and cons relative to Grundtvigian view have been of special interest. Prominent among the pro-Grundtvigian Danish Churc are F. L. GRUNDTVIG, pastor in Clinton, Iowa (1883-1900), son of the great Danis leader; S. D. RODHOLM and C. NIELSEN. The United Danish Church can claim J. MAI SEN, writer on liturgical principles, and C. B. LARSEN, author of *Religion and Revela tion* (1934).

Of the Finns, T. A. KANTONEN, present incumbent in the chair of systemat: theology of Hamma Divinity School, Springfield, Ohio, is gaining interdenomination: recognition. We refer especially to his stimulating book, *The Message of the Church t the World of Today* (1941).

While the writings of most of these theologians are an evidence of an ever growin appreciation of the historical Confessions, a decidedly anti-confessional, pietistic no runs through the books of JOHN O. EVJEN (died January, 1942). He was a scholar o no ordinary ability. Educated in the piety of the Norwegian Free Church, he he' membership for many years in the United Lutheran Church. He spent much time ar effort to interpret Sohm's spiritualistic conception of the Church to American Lutherar His numerous publications in English, Norwegian, Danish, and German disclose a wie range of interest.

15. It will have become evident from the foregoing discussion that *Lutheran th ology has succeeded in establishing for itself a new home in the New World* among membership that was not trained to the principle of voluntary self-support. It b secured for Lutheran thought a permanent place in the English-speaking world. comparison with the Reformed denominations, into which liberalism has made serio inroads, Lutheran theology in America has remained loyal to the supernatural found tions of the Christian faith. It did not let Neo-Kantian skepticism take root in its mid

Concerning the problem of an organic unity of all Lutherans in America, the chi obstacle, at present, lies in the difference as to the nature of Scripture and inspiratic The one group of scholars holds the view of the older orthodox school, i.e., they co ceive of the origin of Scripture in such a supernatural way that a concession to t theories of Biblical criticism is regarded here as a deviation from the faith delivered to the Church. These Lutherans are thoroughgoing Fundamentalists in the garb of a strict confessionalism. Over against these men, another group of theologians is more orientated to the historical concept of the Bible as set forth in the older Erlangen theology. The Bible, according to this view, is history, embodying the Word in a record of real historical events and personalities. Consequently the question of authorship, date, and method of composition, requires the same kind of investigation as any other document of antiquity requires. The problem of the Mosaic authorship of the Pentateuch, for example, ought to be decided not *a priori* by a theological presupposition, but *a posteriori* by a critical investigation. Statements pertaining to astronomy and geography are not a product of divine revelation, they say; they rather reflect the condescendence of the Eternal into the finiteness of time and space. This school of thought, therefore, does not look askance at the findings of Biblical criticism, holding that the supernatural character of the Bible is not thereby impaired. The Bible as the Word remains unchanged. Though these two conflicting schools of thought ought not be identified with any single church body — representatives of either view are very likely found in all the major synods — the official pronouncements of the Synodical Conference reflect strongly the unyielding attitude of the orthodox party while many semi-official or private publications of theologians affiliated with the United Lutheran Church point in the other direction.

Chapter Seven

THE TWENTIETH CENTURY

Literature: A. KELLER, *Dynamis*, 1924; *Karl Barth and Christian Unity*, 1933, pp. 177 ff.; H. W. WERDEMANN, *Das religioese Angesicht Amerikas*, 1926; H. SASSE, *Amerikanisches Kirchentum*, 1927; ALBERT C. KNUDSON, *Present Tendencies in Religious Thought*, 1927; GERALD B. SMITH, *Religious Thought in the Last Quarter Century*, 1927; *Current Christian Thinking*, 1928; W. BURG-GRAFF, *The Rise of Liberal Theology in America*, 1930; V. FERM, editor, *Contemporary American Theology*, 2 vols., 1932 f.; EDWIN E. AUBREY, *Present Theological Tendencies*, 1936; HENRY N. WIEMAN-BERNARD E. MELAND, *American Philosophies of Religion*, 1936; CHARLES S. BRADEN, *Varieties of American Religion*, 1936; E. G. HOMRIGHAUSEN, *Christianity in America*, 1936; CHARLES S. MACFARELAND, *Contemporary Christian Thought*, 1936; *Trends of Christian Thinking*, 1937; *The Christian Faith in a Day of Crisis*, 1939; *Current Religious Thought*, 1941; FRANK H. FOSTER, *The Modern Movement in American Theology*, 1939; JOHN HORSCH, *Modern Religious Liberalism*, 3rd edition, 1938; GEORGE P. CONGER, *The Ideologies of Religion*, 1940; HENRY S. COFFIN, *Religion Yesterday and Today*, 1941. For a selective reading of modern authors we refer to *Contemporary Religious Thought, an Anthology*, compiled by THOMAS S. KEPLER, 1941.

1. With the beginning of the twentieth century *the full force of the philosophical revolution,* i.e., the change from the authoritarian medieval mind to the scientific modern mind, began to exert an ever stronger influence on the theological thinking of the American ministry and educated laity. The modern mind is empirical but anti-authoritarian. The conception of an authoritarian Bible or Church is being discarded. The agnostic and positivistic philosophies are diametrically opposed to the idea of religious absolutes. In order not to surrender God and religion in deference to science, theology thought that it was forced to discover a new plank on which its claim might rest. To accomplish this aim, two different possibilities seemed to offer themselves. Theology might try to overcome the limitations of sense-experience, rest religious authority in a broadened conception of experience, and surrender the intellectual implications of religion as being of little or no importance (Ritschl). Such a positivistic bent, how-ever, leaves man in a dualistic position. The theologian then may be, as Jacobi and Sir William Hamilton, a heathen in his thinking but a Christian in his feeling. Over against this dualism, Troeltsch and other recent thinkers have resorted to a new rational defense of religion. Postulating a religious *a priori,* they claim that religion does not lie be-yond the reach of human reason. In addition to experience and reason a third vital factor in modern thinking is the principle of utility. Consequently, theologians have pointed to the ethical tenets in Christianity in order to secure for it a place in modern society. The individual is being taught that "it pays to be good" and society that it can-not progress without the altruistic teachings embodied in historic Christianity. Experi-ence, reason, and utility — these became the pivotal factors around which modern the-ology revolves, whereas the authority of the Bible is now to be found only in the reli-gious spirit which the Bible breathes. Historic Calvinism seems to have suffered a final breakdown in America excepting with scattered Presbyterians and Reformed. Its collapse was greatly hastened by the neglect of, if not actual antagonism toward, creedal state-ments and by a one-sided emphasis on the subjective element in the act of faith (*fides qua*) in the Neo-Calvinistic churches of America. In contrast to this development in

he Reformed denominations, the Lutheran church in America has been affected little
>y Modernism. In fact, she has, on the whole, experienced a decided trend toward a
>etter appreciation of her historic faith as witnessed by the merger of the Norwegians
n 1917, of the General Synod, General Council, and the United Synod of the South into
he United Lutheran Church in 1918, and the subsequent formation of the American
.utheran Church in 1930, and the present trend toward still more inclusive unification
•f the Lutheran church bodies.

2. At the opening of our century the semi-modernistic *Ritschlian theology* was
welcomed *in America*. Ritschlianism was a connective link between the old and the new
heology. Although it abandoned the metaphysical implications of the Church's teaching
n favor of the prevailing agnosticism of the Neo-Kantian school, it purposed to main-
ain the belief in a unique revelation of God reaching its climax in Christ and recorded
n the Bible. Under Ritschl's influence theology became a historical and practical
ldiscipline. It should be remembered that its rise in America coincided with the incep-
ion of James' pragmatism. The quest for the historical Jesus and the historical beginnings of Christianity, and for the practical implications of religion commanded the
nterest of theologians, exemplified, for instance, by the reception of Harnack's lectures
>n *The Essence of Christianity* and A. Schweitzer's *Quest of the Historical Jesus,* both
n England and America. Among the theologians who turned from a study of dogma
o the Bible we find first of all CHARLES A. BRIGGS, who, being suspended in 1893 by
he Presbyterian General Assembly, was received kindly by the Episcopal church.[1] A
Ritschlian influence is also evident in the *Outline of Christian Theology* (1898) by the
Baptist scholar, W. N. CLARKE, who based religious authority plainly on Christian
experience.[2] For a kind of a platform of Ritschlian thought in American garb we may
look to HENRY CHURCHILL KING'S book entitled *Reconstruction of Theology* (1901).
King, in this book, freely refers to Kant, Lotze, Ritschl, Harnack, Herrmann, and Julius
Kaftan. Like Ritschl he wants to restrict theology to experience and phenomena
(p. 54). In his approach King follows the inductive method, standing squarely
opposed "both to the *a priori* abstract supernaturalism which assumes that a record of
divine revelation must be without touch of human error, and to the *a priori* abstract
anti-supernaturalism which assumes that the supernatural is impossible" (p. 113). The
Bible is to him "strictly a record of revelation, rather than the primitive revelation
itself; and, moreover, it is the record even more of what God did, than of what He said."
The unity of ethical life is love; the fatherhood of God is universal (p. 170 f.), and the
Kingdom of God is social, "not personal *and* social, but social *because* personal"
(p. 238). Likewise, the Atonement, he says, must be "conceived as ethical *throughout*"
(p. 182, italics are in the original). The conviction of Christ's divinity is grounded
"on straightforward historical study of the character of Christ, not on metaphysical
speculation" (p. 190). Statements of Christ's divinity are not "philosophical propositions. They must be the outcome of a man's own personal experience with Christ"
(p. 246). The Ritschlian bent of King's mind is especially noticeable in the emphasis
which he places on the personal and ethical as against the mystical and speculative in
religion (pp. 201 ff.). This emphasis on the personal is still more pronounced in

---

[1] *The Authority of the Holy Scriptures,* 1891; *The Messiah of the Gospels,* 1894; *The Messiah of the
Apostles,* 1895; *The Ethical Teaching of Jesus,* 1904, *et al.* See Edwin H. Rian, *The Presbyterian Conflict,* 1940.
[2] Cf. also his later book *The Use of the Scriptures in Theology.* 1906.

King's subsequent volume *Theology and the Social Consciousness* (1902) the quin-
tescence of which is that theology needs a restatement in terms of personality. As th
unity of the human race, he says, "is pre-eminently moral, rather than physical an
mystical" (p. 136), so theology "cannot forget that, if God is a person, and men ar
persons, the adequate self-revelation of God to men can be made only in a truly person
life; and that men need above all, in their relation to God, some manifestation of Hi
ethical will and this can be shown only in the character of a person. A merely meta
physical conception of the Divinity of Christ in terms of substance or essence, as thes
are commonly taught, must therefore wholly fail to satisfy" (p. 184). Such was th
teaching at Oberlin College about 1900, where only a quarter of a century before Finne
and Mahan had preached the supernatural gospel of "entire consecration."

WILLIAM A. BROWN of Union Theological Seminary may also be classified wit
theologians under Ritschlian influence. His Ritschlianism, however, is modified b
Schleiermacher and Hegelian idealism. Brown wants to combine belief in the Absolut
with the experience of progress. With a keen mind he has faced the issue of scienc
and its effect upon Christianity. The technique of science, he holds, is also applicabl
to the religious problems. The final test of truth or falsehood of any view, he says, i
to be seen in its ability "to unify and interpret our experience as a whole." Both fait
and reason, he holds, have a legitimate place in theology. The historic creeds, accordin
to him, are affirmations concerning a great reality, but they are "couched," he argues
"in a language taken from the thought of a bygone age." To be intelligible to th
modern man they need constant restatement and redefinition in the light of the presen
age. These views he has worked out in *The Essence of Christianity* (1902), *Christian
Theology in Outline* (1906), *Beliefs That Matter* (1928), and *Pathways to Certainty*
(1930). Of the historic churches, the Roman church, he states, is pre-eminently a
religion of authority while Protestantism, as he conceives it, is the religion of individualistic faith. To combine the superior qualities of both forms of Christianity, he ha
suggested a third form which he calls "democratic religion." By "democracy" he mean
"the conviction that since God speaks to every man directly according to his capacit
each personality is to be respected by every other." The volumes in which he has se
forth these ideas are *Imperialistic Religion and the Religion of Democracy* (1923),
which was meant by him as a contribution to a "good neighbor policy" between the
Protestants and Catholics of America, and *A Creed for Free Men* (1941).

Two other scholars should not be passed by in this connection: GEORGE W. KNOX
(1853-1912), at one time professor at the Imperial University of Japan, and the church
historian ARTHUR McGIFFERT (1861-1933). Compare specially the volume of the
latter entitled *Christianity as History and Faith*, posthumously edited in 1935.

3. Next to the Neo-Kantian theology of Ritschl, the influence of *Neo-Hegelianism*
extended over the century mark into our own times. Theologians of this type are not
willing to ground religious authority exclusively in the moral and emotional nature of
man. Mere "value judgment" does not satisfy them. They are striving to set up a new
rational authority for the claims of religion, though apart from any sanction of an
external authority such as the Bible or the Church.

4. The teaching of abstract idealism found, as we have stated in Chapter Two,
a strong competitor in *Bowne's philosophy of personalism*. His personalistic approach

to theology has been ably defended by a disciple of Bowne, ALBERT C. KNUDSON, of Boston University.

KNUDSON is a believer in a theistic metaphysics. The dogmatic grounding of theology on a metaphysical dualism, however, he considers obsolete (p. 22). God is to him an absolute, metaphysical and personal Being who is, at the same time, the immanent and causal ground of the universe (*The Doctrine of God,* 1930). The world as the product of God's creative activity stands in a relation of "otherness to God."[3] In anthropology Knudson rules out the older conception of total depravity and imputation of original sin. His harmatology also is strictly personalistic. Sin he defines as "moral imperfection" (*Op. cit.,* p. 249). Every individual begins his life "on the non-moral plane." Our various appetites, instincts, and impulses are ethically neutral (p. 258). The incarnation of the Logos is interpreted by him in terms of divine immanence and inspiration. The difference between Jesus and other men, Knudson maintains, did not consist in His possession of a divine "nature or substance but in the special mode of operation of the immanent divine will upon which He was dependent" (p. 321). The doctrines of the Virgin Birth and the bodily resurrection of Jesus are no essential part of Christology (p. 325). The essential sinlessness of Jesus, he says, consists in His positive and absolute devotion to the kingdom of God; it does not imply "that He never at any time committed any act or entertained any feeling that was out of harmony with the divine will" (pp. 382 f.). The personalistic approach likewise renders the doctrine of imputation of Christ's righteousness impossible. The only way that anyone can be redeemed, according to him, is "by moral transformation" when "the suffering love of God awakens an answering love in the hearts of men" (p. 378). The Christian social ideal will be gradually achieved "through the steadily increasing co-operation of the human with the divine will." This ameliorated human life is to be identified with the kingdom of God (p. 468). However, the question is left open "as to how fully we may expect God to reveal himself in the social and political world" (p. 469). Immortality may be conditional, for "the soul is possessed of no substance or essence or nature that renders it immortal" (p. 496).[4] The Church's doctrine of resurrection Knudson considers crude and obsolete, "but as a symbol of the reality, and the richness of the life hereafter it is still of significance" (p. 500).

From this brief review of Knudson's thought it stands evident that he is thoroughly "liberal." The ultimate authority is neither the Bible nor the Church, rather the individual finite spirit in whom the Infinite arrives at consciousness of Himself. Reason and experience are the underlying principles of his theology. But his emphasis on the metaphysical significance of personality makes his theology more akin to the Biblical world of thought than the teachings of those theologians who are under the influence of abstract idealism.

Another expounder of theological personalism is EDGAR S. BRIGHTMAN, who occupies the chair of philosophy at Boston University. He, too, claims that all reality is personal. Under the impact of evil, Brightman came to accept the teaching of a finite God who is limited by what he calls "The Given," i.e., eternal, uncreated restraints in

---

[3] *The Doctrine of Redemption,* 1933, p. 27. Quotations by permission of the Abingdon-Cokesbury Press, publishers.

[4] As to the doctrine of the immortality of the soul, the prevailing orthodox position is un-Scriptural. According to the Bible, God "only has immortality" (I Tim. 6:16). Man shall live not by an innate quality. Eternal life is a *charisma,* i.e., a gracious gift of God (Rom. 6:23).

His own nature.[5] Other scholars on whom personalism has exerted a telling effect include Ralph T. Flewelling, John W. Buckham, George A. Wilson, and the Methodist bishop Francis J. McConnell.

5. Another type of idealism is seen in *religious mysticism*. The American mystic *par excellence* is RUFUS M. JONES. He holds that "we have no other adequate origin than from the Spiritual Deeps of a World-Mind, or World-Reason, out of which we have emerged into individual form and struck for being into personal bounds." Jones is recognized as a very prolific writer. Among his books are *A Dynamic Faith* (1900), *The Inner Life* (1916), *Religious Foundations* (1923), *Pathways to the Reality of God* (1921), *The Flowering of Mysticism* (1939). The mystic trend was also very pronounced in the late Charles A. Bennett from whose pen we have *A Philosophical Study of Mysticism* (1923) and *The Dilemma of Religious Knowledge* (1931).

6. The emphasis on the practical implications of the divine immanence issued into the conception of the so-called *"Social Gospel."* Tendencies which had been latent in American thought — the Puritan belief in social discipline and a thoroughly Christian-ized society, the optimistic moralism of the Deists, the humanizing of God in revivalism and the emphasis which the revivalists laid on works as an evidence of salvation — all of these gained a new momentum. Add to this the influence of science (evolution, sociology) and the pragmatic bent in the philosophies of the humanists, and you have the forces which created the Social Gospel. Christian activism came to be looked upon as a typically American form of religion.[6]

The stress on the social meaning of the Gospel we may already discern in the work of HORACE BUSHNELL, J. W. H. STUCKENBERG, and later in that of WASHING-TON GLADDEN,[7] FRANCIS G. PEABODY,[8] WILBUR J. TUCKER,[9] and others. But it was left to WALTER RAUSCHENBUSCH (1861-1918) of the Rochester Theological Seminary to bring its full meaning to bear upon our modern age. Kant and Hegel, Darwin and Karl Marx, Pfleiderer, Ritschl, and Dewey have supplied Rauschenbusch with the neces-sary tools of construction. With the passion of a prophet Rauschenbusch set out to contend against indolence and sluggishness of the Church concerning social reforms and economic readjustment. "It (the Kingdom) is not a matter of saving human atoms, but of saving the social organism. It is not a matter of getting individuals to heaven, but of transforming the life on earth into the harmony of heaven."[10] Pathetically he asks, "Does Calvinism deal adequately with a man who appears before the judgment seat of Christ with $50,000,000 and its human corollaries to his credit, and then pleads a free pardon through faith in the atoning sacrifice?" [11] He is convinced that "if we can trust the Bible, God is against capitalism, its method, spirit, and results" (p. 184), and that "the social gospel is God's predestined agent to continue what the Reformation began" (p. 177). Since "freedom, justice, solidarity are among the aims of the social

---

[5] *Religious Values*, 1925; *The Problem of God*, 1930; *The Finding of God*, 1931 (which, as he says, is at once man's finding of God and God's finding of man); *Is God a Person?* 1932; *Personality and Religion*, 1934, *et al.* For criticism of his "figment of a finite God," see John B. Champion, *Personality and the Trinity*, 1940.

[6] Cf. the important book by W. A. Visser 't Hooft, *The Background of the Social Gospel*, 1928.

[7] *Tools and Man*, 1893; *Ruling Ideas of the Present Age*, 1895; *Applied Christianity*, 1899; *Social Salva-tion*, 1902.

[8] *Jesus Christ and the Social Question*, 1902.

[9] *The Function of the Church in Modern Society*, 1911.

[10] *Christianity and the Social Crisis*, 1911, p. 65. By permission of The Macmillan Company, publishers.

[11] *A Theology for the Social Gospel*, 1918, pp. 19, 177, 184. By permission of The Macmillan Company, publishers.

gospel," we need "a theology which will clearly express these in its conception of God" (p. 87). When Jesus called God "Our Father" He democratized the conception of God, and the idea of God today needs such a further cleansing from the historic accretion of despotism. Sin is selfishness. The sinful mind "is the unsocial and anti-social mind" (p. 50). Like Ritschl, Rauschenbusch was chiefly interested in the solidaristic conception of original sin and its social transmission. He interpreted the Biblical conception of the kingdom of evil along the same lines as the "super-individual, collective forces of evil." The social gospel, he says, cannot confine itself in its teaching of salvation to the soul and its personal interests. "Its chief interest is concentrated on those manifestations of sin and redemption which lie beyond the individual soul" (p. 95). "The Kingdom of God is humanity organized according to the will of God." It implies "a progressive reign of love in human affairs" (p. 142). Jesus "bears the weight of the public sins of organized society," but He "did not in any real sense bear the sin of some ancient Briton who beat up his wife in B.C. 56, or of some mountaineer in Tennessee who got drunk in A.D. 1917" (p. 247). Belief in a future life is not exactly denied but it is, as Rauschenbusch says, "not essential to religious faith" (p. 228). In *Christianity and the Social Crisis* he was less skeptical. There he said that a "perfect religious hope" must include both, life eternal for the individual and the "Kingdom of God for humanity" (see pp. 106 f.). In addition to the books discussed Rauschenbusch has set forth the same principles in other works of his, *Prayers of the Social Awakening* (1910), *Christianizing the Social Order* (1912), and *The Social Principles of Jesus* (1916). For a sympathetic interpretation of his life see D. R. Sharpe, *Walter Rauschenbusch* (1941).

In this connection we should not pass by STANLEY JONES' great book, *Christ's Alternative to Communism* (1935). It contains a challenging message. Communism, so runs his argument, seeks to establish a new equalitarian society by force and violence. What have we, Christians, to offer as an alternative to its ruthless methods? We must, he argues, persuade all Christians to live sincerely by the law of the Cross. The Christian alternative to revolution and Communism is "The Lord's Year of Jubilee." Will men heed the call to Christ? "Yes, I think," he writes. "The mind of man is becoming more and more latently Christian." And he adds, "Let men see the Kingdom of God as a really possible way, and the latent Christianity will burst into flame. The Lord's Year of Jubilee may be nearer than we suppose" (pp. 169 f.).[12] It must be established on earth by the efforts of a spiritually united Church which is moved and inspired by the Spirit of God. The Kingdom is by its very nature, he says, a "Co-operative Society" in which competition and acquisitiveness will be outlawed.

Under the impact of these social teachings the so-called *Social Creed of the Churches* was drawn up by Frank Mason North and published by the Federal Council of the Churches of Christ in America in 1908. It was revised in 1912 and again in 1932. (On Shailer Mathews compare below.)

What must be *our criticism of the Social Gospel?* First, as regards its alleged Biblical foundation without doubt its theologians have read back into the teachings of Jesus ideas which were altogether foreign to Him and to His age. These theologians furnish a classical example of what Henry C. Cadbury calls "the peril of modernizing Jesus," in his volume with this title (1937). Next, though we do not want in the

[12] P. 169 f. By permission of the Abingdon-Cokesbury Press, publishers.

least to minimize either the social implications of the Gospel or the sincere passion of Rauschenbusch for social justice, the Social Gospel is, unquestionably, a debasement of the Biblical Gospel inasmuch as it makes the truth of religion subject to an external test. The objective validity of Christianity is, according to the Social Gospel, dependent on its social utility. God is treated as if His sovereignty were limited by popular franchise in a democratic state. The "otherness of God" is lost. Man is held to be essentially good. His shortcomings are due to influences from an unwholesome environment. Consequently, the Social Gospel is not only anti-individual but also anti-ascetic and anti-eschatological. Having lost sight of the meaning of revelation, religion was secularized in the hands of Rauschenbusch. Inasmuch as he inclined to identify reason and revelation, he lost the ability to keep separate the natural and spiritual orders. The Kingdom is not a supernatural reign of God in which God will destroy sin, death, and devil and change the whole cosmic order; in his eyes, the Kingdom is the spiritual reign of reason, liberty, and justice. It is immanent; it will be established by the process of historical evolution. Rauschenbusch's conception of eschatology is that of the left wing of the Hegelians (Strauss and Feuerbach). True, Rauschenbusch was not a genuine Marxist. He had a contrite heart which none of the Marxists ever had. He did not consider his conception of the future state to be a substitute for Biblical eschatology; he rather wrote under the delusion that his portrait of the future state is, in view of the modern, changed *Weltanschauung*, a legitimate recoinage of Biblical ideas. But with Marxism many "social gospelers" have shared the naive and sentimental optimism that "an adequate mechanism of social justice" will automatically create individuals who will be so disciplined as "to give according to their ability and take according to their need."[13]

7. *The social gospel* of a utilitarian, though not necessarily hedonistic, ethics and of a modernistic theology based on reason and experience has gained a wide recognition among the American clergy and educated laity. With most of them its underlying philosophy is a type of naturalism in its many varieties and combinations. They have been drawing heavily upon natural sciences and have vigorously applied themselves to the task of social reconstruction. Their interest centered in a rational defense of universal religion, while the distinctive Christian doctrines, such as the Trinity, the Two Natures, or the sacraments, mean little, if anything, to them. As to their God-concept the naturalistic theologians may conveniently be classified either as *Evolutionary Theists* or as *Empirical Theists*. To the former God is the "Something," a "Cosmic Spirit," or "Purpose," which underlies the phenomena of nature. Here we may mention WILLIAM K. WRIGHT and ROBERT L. CALHOUN.[14] Yet the type of naturalism most commonly held by theologians is that of empirical theism. This latter is "less metaphysical than philosophical theism, yet more inclusive of cosmic interests than religious humanism." [15] Prominent representatives of empirical theism in America are EDWARD S. AMES, Dean of the Disciples' Divinity House at Chicago, HENRY N. WIEMAN, and the late SHAILER MATHEWS. AMES, like Dewey, conceives of God, symbolically, in the term of life's

---

[13] For a further discriminating criticism we refer to A. C. Knudson, pp. 251 ff. See also the keen remarks of Reinhold Niebuhr scattered through his writings such as, for instance, *Moral Man and Immoral Society*, 1932; *Reflections on the End of an Era*, 1934; *An Interpretation of Christian Ethics*, 1935; *Beyond Tragedy*, 1938. For a history of the earlier literature see Shailer Mathews "The Development of Social Christianity in America during the Past Twenty-five Years," *Journal of Religion*, VII (1927), 376 ff., and Charles H. Hopkins, *The Rise of the Social Gospel in America*, 1940.

[14] See the latter's *God and the Common Life*, 1940.

[15] Wieman-Meland, *op. cit.*, p. 272. By permission of Willett, Clark & Company, publishers

function in the world. The word "God" signifies certain proportions of life in its ideal aspect. God is, as he wrote in *The Christian Century* (March 22, 1939) "Reality idealized and personified," or more simply expressed, "God is life as you love it." "God is life, actual and potential, a process, ever becoming, changing and permanent, novel and familiar." "God is the power which makes for righteousness." Among his writings are *Psychology of Religious Experience* (1910) and *Religion* (1929).

WIEMAN holds to a slightly more realistic conception of God. To him God is actually an object of religious experience. However, his God is an impersonal being. God is not personality, he says, He is more than personality. God is "a kind of inter-action between things which generates and magnifies personality and all its highest values" (Ferm, I, 351). Yet, says Wieman, it is his chief concern to promote a theo-centric religion. We must make "the actuality of God Himself, and not our ideas about God, the object of our love and devotion (I, 346). His books include *Religious Experience and Scientific Method* (1926), *The Wrestle of Religion with Truth* (1927), *The Issues of Life* (1931). With Van Dusen he is co-author of *Ventures in Belief* (1930), and with others he edited *Is There a God?* (1932), and *Normative Psychology of Religion* (1935).

A towering figure among the Modernists for many years was SHAILER MATHEWS (1863-1941) of the Divinity School of the University of Chicago. Under his leadership the University of Chicago became a center of religious pragmatism and "applied Christianity." Like Rauschenbusch he conceived of Christianity as a "religious social movement." Yet in contrast to Rauschenbusch, who wrote with the passion of a religious revolutionary, Mathews is a representative of the reformatory type in the Social Gospel movement. Theology likewise was to him a "group belief." It is, he says, a "product of social minds." It therefore is "relative rather than final, functional rather than scientifically correct," and its truthfulness, he adds, is to be determined "by other methods than appeal to authority." [16] Christianity is "creative," he says, "when it acts to transform social conditions into better ones, to lift standards of conduct, to lessen misery and increase welfare." [17] Of late he has re-emphasized the duty of the Church to promote the case of "social morality" in *The Church and the Christian* (1938). As to his influence on the American churches compare the witty remark of Henry C. Cadbury in the volume referred to (p. 203): "A generation ago a favorite *bon mot* among American scholars was to the effect that socialist Germany had substituted for the Gospel of Mark the gospel of Marx; perhaps one could reply that modernist America has substituted for the Gospel of Matthew the gospel of Mathews." [18]

Modernism, he says, is not a new religion,[19] "it is the use of the methods of modern science to find, state, and use the permanent and central values of inherited orthodoxy in meeting the needs of a modern world." [20] It is more an "attitude" than a doctrine (p. 171). Belief in divine immanence and evolution is to Mathews a truer and more satisfying view of God's activity than the old view of miraculous interference

---

[16] Cf. the autobiographical sketch in Ferm, *op. cit.*, II, 163 ff.; also *New Faith for an Old, an Autobiography,* 1936, especially pp. 119 ff.

[17] Cf. *Creative Christianity*, 1935, and his earlier writings *The Church and the Changing Order*, 1907; *The Social Gospel*, 1909; *The Gospel and the Modern Man*, 1910; *Jesus on Social Institutions*, 1928, and other studies.

[18] *The Peril of Modernizing Jesus*, p. 203. By permission of The Macmillan Company, publishers.

[19] See also M. H. Krumbine, editor, *The Progress of Religion*, 1933, which was published in honor of Mathews' seventieth birthday.

[20] *The Faith of Modernism*, 1924, p. 23. Quotations by permission of The Macmillan Company, publishers.

(p. 113). "Human nature is not corrupt, but atavistic" (p. 98). Jesus is the "unique expression of God in an individual" (p. 124). His death and resurrection help us to "interpret that long evolutionary struggle from which human life has emerged and which it carries on" (p. 161). The Modernist's eschatology is hope for a new social order in this world and complete and joyous individuality through death to those possessed of Christlike attitudes (p. 167). We are Christians, in his opinion, not when we hold to a certain body of doctrines, but when our common effort for social life is controlled by the attitudes and convictions which have been the possession of a continuous Christian community (pp. 171 ff.).

How group belief in the past has shaped the conception of the Atonement and God, Mathews has tried to show in two later works, *The Atonement and the Social Process* (1930) and *The Growth of the Idea of God* (1931). There exists between God and man a relationship of dynamic mutuality. He looks upon religion as an outgrowth of the struggle of man to get help from the mysterious forces of nature and environment. Religion developed in the same way as civilization progressed. As the modern mind is dominated by the concept of science, so we must think of God as an activity "that is both creative and environing." Its pattern must include, he argues, "the conception of progress." [21] The object of religion is not a metaphysical being. "It is not the thing-in-itself with which religion deals, but that experience of organism and environment which makes a relationship with objective activities possible." Thus he arrives at defining his view as "conceptual theism" by virtue of which, he says, man is brought into personal relation "with personality-creating, personally responsive, personally conceived activities of the cosmos" (p. 229). Compare also his brief volume *Is God Emeritus?* (1940) in which he reiterates his belief in an evolutionary-pantheistic conception of God and the world. Mathews also was pre-eminently identified with the ecumenical movement of recent times; for liberal theology has an inevitable tendency to discard denominational lines and to advocate tolerance, practical co-operation, and Christian unity.

8. When we come to DOUGLAS C. MACINTOSH of Yale we meet a thinker who combines in his system *the best of the Kantian and Hegelian tradition*. He was nurtured in the revivalistic practice of the nineteenth century with its emphasis on the experimental basis of the religious faith. In keeping with his past he holds that theology is an empirical science. While proceeding from the Ritschlian pragmatism as a starting point he, nevertheless, insists that theology cannot dispense with the task of metaphysics. He has discussed these aspects of theology in two of his earlier writings, *The Reaction Against Metaphysics in Theology* (1911), and *Theology as an Empirical Science* (1919). He also has been a prominent leader in the circles of the philosophical Neo-Realists. In the controversy of these philosophers over the question "whether if one held to realism he could avoid the dualism of the immediately perceived and the independently real" (Ferm, I, 304), he worked out his own theory of knowledge which he calls "critical monism (critical monistic realism, or critical realistic monism)." He has set forth his views concerning these problems in *The Problem of Knowledge* (1915), *The Reasonableness of Christianity* (1925), in the composite volume entitled *Religious Realism* (1931) and in *The Problem of Religious Knowledge* (1940). He

---

[21] *The Growth of the Idea of God*, 1931, pp. 207, 229. Quotations by permission of The Macmillan Company, publishers.

also edited with H. N. Wieman and M. C. Otto *Is There a God?* (1932). As to the specific Biblical doctrines, the concept of a "primeval divine curse imposed upon a nature because of the fall of man," he holds, "has passed through the stages of being believed, questioned, denied, and ridiculed, and is now almost forgotten." [22] The essence of Christianity is to him a sort of "moral optimism." "God the Father is the God of moral optimism," he says, "and He is not a different God from God the Holy Spirit, the God of the religious experience of moral salvation." It is this One God who "indwelt in such a fullness the life of the historic Jesus and gave Him so divine a value and function in human history and experience that He is rightly regarded as the divine man, the historic revelation of God." This, according to his view, is the "religious kernel or essence of Trinitarian Christianity," and constitutes what he calls "the new Christian orthodoxy." [23] In his recent volume entitled *Social Religion* (1939) he has come out as a staunch defender of the now much attacked social conception of the Gospel.

Another prominent theologian who aims to ground theology in the combined evidence of experience and reason is WALTER M. HORTON of Oberlin College. In his earlier writings his thought revolved about a scientific natural theology with his interest centered in the person of God, the reality of evil, and the ethical implications of religion. For information consult his *Theism and the Modern Mind* (1930), *A Psychological Approach to Religion* (1931), and *Theism and the Scientific Spirit* (1932). His next book *Realistic Theology* (1934) with the assertion that Liberalism as a theological system is "dead," marked a turning point in his development. Since that time he has been drawing closer to a Biblical understanding of Christianity. He has lost faith in science as a guide through the perplexing problems of our time, and, as he wrote in *The Christian Century* (May 17, 1939): "I look for concrete light and guidance, above all, to the Biblical revelation of God in the series of mighty acts leading up to the incarnation of Christ, and all that has resulted from the incarnation in subsequent history." He is the co-author with Macintosh of the volume *Religious Realism* and has more lately edited, in co-operation with H. N. Wieman, *The Growth of Religion* (1938). Horton, it seems, is by nature an eclectic. Compare, for example, the summary of his thought in the autobiographical sketch as published in Ferm's symposium (I, 186 f.). The same trend is evident in his recent book *Can Christianity Save Civilization?* (1940), where he veers strongly toward a religious syncretism, while in *Our Eternal Contemporary* (1942) he says that he is led to classify himself as a "liberal Catholic in the Evangelical Protestant camp" (p. 175).

9. Due to lack of space we shall not enter upon a discussion of *other prominent empirical theists.* On the whole subject the reader will find much information in the composite volume of Wieman and Meland, as referred to, pp. 209 ff. We must, however, not pass by one other writer who probably is more popular than any other discussed here. Our reference is to HARRY E. FOSDICK of New York City, preacher, teacher, lecturer, and author. Among his writings are: *The Meaning of Prayer* (1915), *The Meaning of Faith* (1917), *The Meaning of Service* (1920), *Christianity and Progress* (1922), *The Modern Use of the Bible* (1924), *As I See Religion* (1932), *A Guide to Understanding the Bible* (1938).

FOSDICK is thoroughly modernistic, though he does not hold to the sentimental

---

[22] *The Reasonableness of Christianity*, p. 94. Quotations by permission of Scribner's, publishers.
[23] *Ibid.*, pp. 154 f.

optimism of progress and belief that "we can save mankind by the manipulation of outward circumstances." [24] The essence of religion, as he defines it, is self-surrender in the service of humanity. To the religious, God, or the experience which he has of Him, is a power which must be continually translated into ethical service. The realization of the Christian ethics, in his opinion, is much more important than the ontological justification of Christianity. As to the authority of Scripture and Creeds, he distinguishes between the "abiding experiences" of religion and the "passing categories" of theological terminology. It is the modern preacher's responsibility, he claims, "to decode the abiding meanings of Scripture from outgrown phraseology." [25] Thus Fosdick tries to dispense with Biblical categories by the historical-critical method and then to interpret Biblical thought by means of an idealistic philosophy. The Church's insistence on its historical creeds becomes in our age "the ruination of faith" (p. 262). Divine immanence has rendered the idea of supernatural inspiration and miracle unnecessary. The miracle-idea simply was "our forefathers' way of saying that they believed in the living God, whose ways of working are not bound within the narrow limits of man's little knowledge" (p. 158). Likewise angels are said to represent "our fathers' profound and practical consciousness of the reality, friendliness, and availability of the spiritual world" (p. 125). In the same manner, the doctrine of the divinity of Jesus, when released from literal bondage, is in current terms, the expression "of the central experience of the Christian life — finding God in Christ" (p. 261).

These few quotations will suffice to show that Fosdick is not only restating Biblical verities in modern terms. In reality, these are undergoing, in his hands, a complete transformation. With Fosdick, philosophical idealism takes the place of Biblical realism. His theology is, in spite of his appreciative remarks about the personal and concrete nature of the Bible as compared to Platonism (p. 117), philosophical idealism in Christian terminology.

A similar trend of thought and argument is to be seen in Fosdick's recent book *A Guide to Understanding the Bible*. The book is important not for the originality of investigation but rather for the ease and lucidity of style with which the author presents the findings of critical Biblical scholarship. Fosdick traces the growth of six Biblical concepts: those of God, of man, of right and wrong, of suffering, of fellowship with God, and of immortality. The words about God in the Bible, he holds, are of minor importance. Jesus revealed God "not so much in the words He used about Him as in the life He lived with Him" (p. 42).[26] It is doubtful whether the Biblical writers have reported with precision the words of Jesus. The essential thing is the new relation between God and man as exemplified in Jesus. Inspiration, he holds, fortunately has not been stereotyped and is not mechanical. The unfolding of ideas which the Bible presents is dual, he says; seen from one end, it is a "human achievement; seen from the other, a divine revelation" (p. xiv). "The finalities of Scripture are mainly important because they are germinative. They are misinterpretated and misused when employed to stop further developments rather than encourage them" (p. xv).

Note: At this point we shall take the opportunity to direct the attention of the observing reader to a number of critical and for the most part very liberal American and Anglo-American

---

[24] *Christianity and Progress*, p. 89, and other passages.
[25] *The Modern Use of the Bible*, p. 122 f. Quotations by permission of The Macmillan Company, publishers.
[26] Preface, and elsewhere. Quotations by permission of Harper & Brothers, publishers.

scholars in the field of Biblical research: BENJAMIN W. BACON of Yale (died 1932), who wrote *Jesus and Paul* (1921); SHIRLEY J. CASE of Chicago with his two volumes *The Social Origins of Christianity* (1923), and *Jesus: A New Biography* (1927); also *Jesus Through the Centuries* (1931); FRANK C. PORTER, likewise of Yale, *The Mind of Christ in Paul* (1930); ERNEST F. SCOTT, who wrote *The Validity of the Gospel Record* (1938) and many other volumes; JAMES MOFFATT with his widely read book *Love in the New Testament* (1929), and KIRSOPP LAKE, all of Union Seminary, who wrote, among other books, *Landmarks of Early Christianity* (1920). Lake's *Beginnings of Christianity* (5 vols., 1919 ff.), edited in co-operation with FOAKES JACKSON, is a standard work of first importance. The scholar who did in our country the pioneer work in the field of Form Criticism is the Episcopal theologian BURTON SCOTT EASTON with his book *The Gospel Before the Gospels* (1928).

We have followed the main trends in modern theology: the rejection of metaphysics by the Neo-Kantians, the Hegelian emphasis on divine immanence and reason by the Hegelians, and the experimental approach to religion in the fellowship of Schleiermacher and Ritschl.[27] The consistent Americanization of these tendencies led, first, to the religious pragmatism of James, next, to the humanism of Dewey, and finally, to the religious nihilism of Behaviorism. Even those thinkers who maintain a theistic interpretation of religion are more orientated to experience of God than to His self-disclosure in Christ. Thus we are confronted with a new religion marked by belief in a "finite God" without wrath, in man without sin, in redemption through reform inspired by a Christ without a cross. As to the agnostic position of the Neo-Kantians *versus* the teaching of divine immanence, it is true that the Bible speaks of God as being immanent and transcendent. But it is likewise true that the Bible has built its dykes on both sides. The "fall" is the thing that separates the Christian from all naturalistic idealism. The cosmic spirit is not identical with the Holy Spirit. To speak about divine immanence apart from His special revelation is an illusionary and presumptuous undertaking. To boast of possessing the Holy Spirit without the Mediator's atoning and interceding work is "blaspheming the Holy Ghost." Over against all such irreverent, presumptuous thoughts the Bible takes its decided stand on the side of Kant's *Critique of Pure Reason* (Isaiah 55, 8 f., Romans 11, 34 et al.). However, the Bible does not stop there. In contradistinction to Kantian agnosticism, the Bible proclaims with the same fervor the breaking of God into time and space: the Word was made flesh! This is the way of Luther's *theologia crucis*, "In Christ crucified there is to be found true theology and knowledge of God." [28] American theologians, therefore, are right when they refuse to follow Karl Barth. Barth is only a half-way defender of Biblical faith. He is a "prophet" when he contends against the arrogant teaching of divine immanence, but he misses his prophetic call when he fails to contend with equal zeal for the presence of God in Jesus Christ.[29]

10. However, the rise of Modernism has not succeeded completely in extirpating *conservative Christianity* in our country. The gospel of the New Testament has never

---

[27] We must confess that we consider as untenable the line of demarcation as drawn by Wieman-Meland between one modern tendency rooted in Idealism (Kant, Hegel) and the other rooted in Romanticism (Schleiermacher, Ritschl). True, Ritschl accepted the experimental approach of Schleiermacher. But so did Hofmann and Frank. Yet their relation to Schleiermacher was purely formal. A much better classification, in our opinion, would be to list together Kant, Ritschl and their followers with their critical attitude toward metaphysics, on the one hand, and Schleiermacher, Hegel and those who are agreed with them in their emphasis on poetical intuition or dialectical reasoning, on the other. Even Naturalism, which Wieman-Meland consider to represent another distinct tradition in modern theology, may be conceived of as an offshoot of Hegelian philosophy. It is, in its modern form, a sort of *via media* between nineteenth-century spiritualism and materialism, both of which emanated from Hegel. E. S. Brightman is right when he, in the symposium added to the volume under discussion, says: No Hegel, no Marx, no Royce, no Dewey (p. 319).

[28] 20th thesis of the Heidelberg Disputation of 1518, *WA*, I, 362.

[29] For reaction of American theologians to Karl Barth turn to Paragraph 17. Cf. A. Koeberle, *The Quest for Holiness*, 1936, pp. 101 f.

lacked men who have combined faith in the Gospel with scholarly attainment. Among such theologians we may mention first of all JOHN ALFRED FAULKNER, late professor of the Drew Theological Seminary (died 1931), and J. GRESHAM MACHEN (died 1937), the staunch Presbyterian. Faulkner, who at first had distinguished himself as a church historian,[30] later published a systematic treatment of theology in his book entitled *Modernism and the Christian Faith* (1921). He also wrote *The Miraculous Birth of Our Lord* (1924) and *Burning Questions in Historic Christianity* (1930). His position was a mediating theology of the Seeberg type in Germany. "The reason why we believe the Bible is religious authority," he states, "is because the Spirit there meets the Spirit here, and they recognize each other." [31] That is, as we notice, a Coleridgean idea. But inspiration does not mean, we are informed by Faulkner, that all parts of the Bible "are equally divine, that all parts are not also human, that the human and divine do not vary and interplay, that there are no mixtures and errors in its vast evolution" (*ibid.*). As to the question of miracles, Faulkner agrees with Seeberg that "a miracle is only a special combination of natural powers for the bringing forth of a new effect" (p. 70). Of the Trinity, he holds, like the Erlangen theologian Frank, that it is "a truth of Christian experience" (p. 201). Faulkner unreservedly wants to retain the "metaphysical Christ," for "sonship is not a term of reception of influences, but of being" (p. 190). "The Atonement rests securely and alone on Christ's Person and Work" (p. 159), though the idea that Christ suffered on the cross divine punishment in the proper sense, he wants to be excluded from the doctrine of the Atonement. In Chapter Ten of his book under discussion, Faulkner raises the question, "Ritschl or Wesley?" The author makes it quite plain that he is somewhat in sympathy with Ritschl's protest against the intellectualization of faith, but he is not willing to abandon the historical position of Methodism in favor of a purely ethical Christianity of Ritschl. Theology cannot be satisfied with mere "value-judgments." The Ritschlian Christ was not the Christ of Wesley. "You cannot save men with a Unitarian God" (p. 224).

When we come to Machen we meet a theologian of a still more solid fiber. He not only was not in sympathy with the religious anti-intellectual tendencies of the modern age, he definitely saw in the Neo-Kantian skepticism the greatest danger to Christianity. This fundamental thought that the object of faith cannot be separated from the psychological act of faith without destroying the very nature of the Christian faith, runs through both of his systematic studies, *Christianity versus Liberalism* (1923), and *What is Faith?* (1925). In the former book he undertakes to show that the present issue of the Church is not between two varieties of the same religion, but between two essentially different types of thought and life. Christianity, he argues, is not a life as distinguished from doctrine; nor are the doctrinal conceptions of the Bible merely "passing categories," for, as he says (p. 20), with a tinge of Calvinistic legalism, "The originators of the Christian movement . . . did have an inalienable right to legislate for all generations that should choose to bear the name of 'Christian.' " [32] Christ is a life founded on a doctrine. As to the chief purpose of the other book, he says, that he wants to defend "the primacy of the intellect and in particular to try to break the false and disastrous opposition which has been set up between knowledge and faith" (p. 26).

---

[30] *The Methodists*, 1903; *Cyprian*, 1906; *Erasmus* (1908), *et al.*

[31] *Modernism*, pp. 21, 70, 190, 201, 224. Quotations by permission of the Abingdon-Cokesbury Press, publishers.

[32] Pp. 20, 26. By permission of The Macmillan Company, publishers.

For man as a personal being, he claims, faith involves "a person as its object" (p. 46). The faith of which the Church speaks is not, as the Modernists claim, the faith that Jesus had in God, it is faith in Jesus Himself. In some of the further statements about faith, Machen reaches the very heights and depths of the Reformation theology, for instance, when he says: "Faith means receiving something, not doing something or even being something" (p. 173). "The fact to which we refer is this: that it is not as a quality of the soul that faith saves man, but only as the establishment of contact with a real object of the faith" (p. 174). For assurance of salvation man must not think about his faith, but about the object of his faith, i.e., the Person of Christ (p. 250). The historical foundations of Christianity, therefore, are indispensable to faith (p. 149).[33] Machen, no doubt, was one of the finest exponents of Biblical Christianity among the Reformed theologians. He was not satisfied with being a Fundamentalist, he wanted to be a loyal Presbyterian. It therefore is the more significant that in the whole book there is not a single reference to the great historic doctrine of Calvinism: the doctrine of twofold Predestination! [34]

Another man who deserves special mention is A. T. ROBERTSON (died 1934), the late professor of the Interpretation of the New Testament in the Southern Baptist Theological Seminary. He was an able and prolific writer. A number of his books went through several editions. He was also a great linguist. His monumental work, *A Grammar of the New Testament Greek in the Light of Historical Research* (4th edition, 1923) is a rare achievement in the field of American theological scholarship. Robertson never lost sight of the supernatural Christ and His saving grace.

11. Next to these scholarly theologians we have a more popular reaction of conservative forces against Modernism in the so-called *Fundamentalist Movement.* Inasmuch as the modernistic theologians increased in numerical strength in their respective church bodies they naturally succeeded in bringing under their control the responsible and influential positions of their denominations. They seemed to aim at nothing less than a gradual metamorphosis of the theology of their churches. It was this situation that awakened the warning cries of the Fundamentalists. The inception of this movement dates back to the year 1909, when a group of devout believers united in a common effort to preserve the gospel of their fathers in America. In twelve volumes entitled *The Fundamentals,* they set forth the supernatural character of Christianity as they conceived it. The publication of these volumes was largely made possible through the generosity of two wealthy laymen, Lyman and Molton Stewart, who founded in Los Angeles a Bible Institute and established the Stewart Evangelistic Fund for promoting orthodox faith. The paganizing influences of the first World War and the militant spirit which it instilled into the American public gave new and fresh impetus to the movement. In 1918 The World's Christian Fundamentals Association was founded. The Baptist weekly, *The Watchman Examiner,* in an editorial of July 1, 1920, marshalled all men "who mean to do battle royal for the fundamentals." Thus the conservatives became the Fundamentalists. The Fundamentalists pursued two objectives, (1) to restore the primacy of the Biblical gospel in the American churches, (2) to check all anti-Christian tendencies in the secular life and culture of our nation. To obtain its first

---

[33] *Op. cit.,* pp. 46, 149, 173 f., 250.

[34] *Cf.* also his radio addresses *The Christian Faith in a Modern World,* 1936, and *The Christian View of Man,* 1937.

objective they engaged in positive constructive endeavors, such as evangelistic work both by preaching and printed literature in order to win the unchurched (Christian Fund Association). Next, they tried to gather the "saved" into Bible conferences and spiritual retreats. In 1926 the American branch of the English Keswick Conference was founded. And finally they aimed at training a spiritual leadership in Bible schools and orthodox colleges (Moody Bible Institute, Wheaton College, Dallas Theological Seminary). Side by side with these constructive measures the Fundamentalists engaged in a very lively crusade against all kind of modernism in the Church. These polemical attacks upon theological liberalism created a serious friction in all the major churches of the Reformed camp. It became especially bitter in such churches as the Baptist and the Disciples which had hitherto objected to any creedal statement binding upon all members, or in the Methodist church, which had always put a vital experience of Christ above subscription to its *Twenty-five Articles.* The spirited rift created in the church became evident in the duplication of church parties (the Methodist League for Faith and Life; the National Church League, the Churchmen's Alliance, and the Modern Churchmen's Union representing respectively the Protestant, Catholic, and Latitudinarian tradition in the Episcopal church), of church papers (*The Essentialist* perpetuating *The Call to the Colors* of the Methodist fundamentalists; *The Christian Standard* to check the liberalizing influence of *The Christian Century* and of *The Christian Evangelist* among the Disciples), and of theological seminaries (the Northern Baptist Theological Seminary to counteract the influence of the Divinity School in Chicago, the Eastern Baptist Seminary to offset the teachings of Crozier Theological Seminary, and the Westminster Theological Seminary founded as a protest against Princeton). As to the threatening schisms in the various denominations, the Fundamentalists resorted to such an extreme measure only in two cases: the Baptist Fundamentalists organized in 1923, under the leadership of J. Frank Norris, William B. Riley, and T. T. Shields, the Baptist Bible Union of North America, which continued to function till 1930. This group remained, as its name indicates, loyal to the historical tenets of the Baptist church. In the second instance a minority of the Fundamentalists established an independent new denomination on a principle that cuts across all sectarian lines by founding, at the behest of M. S. Kirkland, The American Conference of Undenominational Churches.

For obtaining its second objective, i.e., to put a check on the paganizing tendencies in our public life, the Fundamentalists mainly attempted to interfere with the teaching of evolution in tax-supported schools. The popular reaction against science is especially connected with the name and life of WILLIAM JENNINGS BRYAN (1860-1925). It reached its climax in the famous Scopes trial at Dayton, Tennessee. (Among Bryan's religious writings are: *The Prince of Peace,* 1909; *In His Image,* 1922.) In more recent years the Fundamentalists are engaged in a warfare combatting the alleged communistic forces in our country, which, as they claim, are strengthened by the policy of the Federal Council of the Churches of Christ in America and the Protestant-Catholic-Jewish alliance for "a good neighbor policy." Its leader is Gerald Winrod, editor of *The Defender.* He was defeated in the Kansas primaries of 1938 when he sought nomination for the United States Senate on the Republican ticket.

The conflict between the Modernists and the Fundamentalists chiefly revolves about those doctrines that are especially open to rational attacks such as the literal infallibility of the Bible, special creation, possibility of the miracles, the Virgin Birth and complete deity of Jesus, His atoning death for the sins of the world, His bodily resurrection and return in bodily form to the earth. Concerning all these problems the Fundamentalists have been desirous to defend the strict orthodox view. Their endeavors have the sympathy of conservative theologians although they are not in agreement with them on all points. But the cause of the Fundamentalists is doomed to failure because of the method which they pursue. The mind of the Fundamentalists is pre-scientific. On the grounds of a pre-scientific theology they want to defend and to prove the Biblical truth with rational means. Therefore they cannot win, for historical facts and scientific data cannot be discredited by an appeal to a belief in the super-rationality of the Christian dogma. The apparent inability to distinguish properly between supernatural revelation and its historical setting in the Scriptures is the chief mistake in the theology of Fundamentalism. The object of the Christian faith is the Christ, the Son of God. The man Jesus of Nazareth is certainly not immaterial to faith for "in Him dwelleth all the fulness of the Godhead bodily." But He also was, like the prophets before Him and the Apostles after Him, a representative of an ancient civilization of Western Asia. The Church is not obligated to continue this ancient civilization, it is commanded to preach the saving revelation of God. Since Calvinism, which is more Biblio-centric than Christo-centric, is the common background of the Fundamentalists, the Fundamentalists resented the more bitterly all findings of Biblical criticism for they seemed to be aimed against the very foundation of their faith. But Christianity is not a set of rational doctrines concerning Scriptural infallibility, the Trinity, Virgin Birth, the Two Natures of Christ, etc., important as such concepts may be; the Gospel is a *dynamis* (Rom. 1:16) to save a sinful world through faith in the Crucified and Risen Christ. The Fundamentalist controversy has run its course. The interest in its cause is abating.[35]

12. A special tenet in Fundamentalism is the doctrine of *"Dispensationalism."* According to a definition of the *Scofield Reference Bible* (in a note to Genesis 1:27), "a dispensation is a period of time during which man is tested in respect to some *specific* revelation of the will of God." Scofield distinguishes seven dispensations: (1) the dispensation of Innocence in the Garden of Eden; (2) the dispensation of Conscience which began with the expulsion of Adam and Eve from Eden; (3) the dispensation of Human Government embracing the period extending from the Flood to the call of Abraham when man was put under civil authority; (4) the dispensation of Promise covering the lives of the Patriarchs; (5) the dispensation of the Law extending from the Exodus to the crucifixion of Jesus; (6) the dispensation of Grace, the time of the Church, and (7) the dispensation of the Kingdom.

A similar outline of history is given by W. E. Blackstone in his widely read book *Jesus Is Coming* (first edition, 1908). On the basis of Ephesians 3:11 he presents the following "plan of the aeons" (p. 225): Eden, the aeon (i.e., age) of innocence; (2) the Antediluvian, the aeon of Freedom when conscience was the only restraint; (3) the Postdiluvian, the aeon of Government when man was put under civil authority, terminating with the destruction of Sodom; (4) the Patriarchial, the Pilgrim aeon; (5) the Israelitish aeon terminating with the destruction of Jerusalem in A.D. 70; (6) the aeon of Mystery, the time of the Church; and (7) the Millennium, the aeon of Manifestation (Rom. 8:19). Siding with the pre-Millennial view, i.e., that the Second Coming will

---

[35] For information on the conflict see especially Stewart G. Cole, *The History of Fundamentalism*, 1931, which is replete with references to other literature.

occur at the beginning of the Millennium, the eschatological drama, according to Black-stone, includes the following principal facts: The "first resurrection," the rapture of the saints to meet Christ in the air. Thus the Church escapes the tribulation which will be a period of seven years. At the commencement of this period the Jews who have returned to Palestine in unbelief "enter into a seven-year covenant with the Anti-christ." At the expiration of three and a half years the Antichrist is revealed as the Man of Sin. Under the power of the Devil and his angels he then will bring an unparalleled persecution upon all who have not received his mark. "A third part of the Jews in the land are brought through this time of trouble and are gathered by the Lord in Jeru-salem to be purged of their dross." Upon an attack by the "nations" Jerusalem is taken and half of its people are carried into captivity. But the Lord will go forth for the destruction of His enemies and the deliverance of His people, and establish the Millennial kingdom. At the close of the thousand years Satan is loosed for a "little season" to marshal the "nations" for a final battle against the Lord. But fire from God will destroy them. Then will follow the "resurrection of damnation" and the last judgment.

It is evident that in contrast to liberal theology in general and to the theology of the social gospel in particular, the Fundamentalists have maintained the divine agency in the establishment of the Kingdom. Consequently, the eschatological hope is based in their system not on philosophical speculation but on the promises of the Bible. Yet their interpretation of Scripture is thoroughly literalistic and atomistic, and the mate-rialistic conception of the reign of Christ bears all the earmarks of Judaism. The same is true as regards the development of history as a succession of fixed dispensations.[36] On the other hand, we admit that the purely "spiritual" interpretation of the Old Testa-ment passages in question has often been unsatisfactory. To arrive at a sound view of eschatology, Evangelical theology must be guided here, as always, by the soteriological meaning of the Cross. Jesus came not only "to confirm the promises made unto the fathers," but also to sift and purify the religion of the Old Testament (compare, for example, the Sermon on the Mount). The fulfillment of the Old Testament by Him implies also a criticism of the secular-national hope of Judaism. His cross is the strongest evidence against Israel's claim to world domination. The crucified Messiah is the end of Israel's Messianic expectation. All prophecies concerning Israel's future national glory are not only "spiritually fulfilled" in His Lordship over the world, they are likewise judged and purified by Him. There is no place for a future Messianic reign of Israel or triumphant church upon earth in the plan of God's salvation. It is significant that Lutheran theology, with the exception of the older Erlangen school under the influence of the Reformed theologian Coccejus, has been consistent in rejecting chiliasm as a "Judaistic opinion" (Augsburg Confession, Article 17).[37]

13. In recent years another movement has aroused much interest and has caused considerable discussion. We refer to the *Oxford Group Movement.* Though this movement now bears the name of a venerable English university, it really is a product of American soil. Its originator is the Lutheran clergyman F. N. D. Buchman. Buchman was born June 4, 1878, at Pennsburg, Pa. He is of German-Swiss parentage. Receiving his educa-

---

[36] See the excursus on "The Signs and Calculations of the Days of the Messiah" in Strack-Billerbek's *Kommentar zum Neuen Testament aus Talmud and Midrasch,* Vol. IV, Part II, 1928, pp. 977-1015.

[37] Cf. P. Althaus, *Die letzten Dinge,* 4th edition, 1933, pp. 60 ff., 296 ff.; also Neve, *Churches and Sects of Christendom,* pp. 222 ff., 614 ff., and *Popular Symbolics,* pp. 366 ff. The literature on Pre-Chiliasm and Dispen-sationalism is very large. For a recent study we refer to A. I. Brown, *Into the Clouds,* 1938; for a critical view see W. P. King, *Adventism,* 1941, and Th. Graebner, *War in the Light of Prophecy,* 1941.

tion at Muhlenberg College in Allentown, Pa., and Philadelphia Theological Seminary, he entered the service of the Lutheran church in 1902. While in England in 1907, Buchman became acquainted with the Keswick Movement. It was then that he experienced his "conversion." The movement proper started in 1921 and was originally called "The First Century Christian Fellowship." Since then its growth has been remarkable, having obtained interdenominational as well as some international recognition. Its tremendous success may be ascribed both to the personality of its leader and to the technique in its procedure. This technique consists of Buchman's five "C's": confidence, confession, conviction, conversion, and continuance. The Group does not work with mass meetings but through small house parties. At the climax of such a party one of the leaders will relate the story of how he was saved from a life in bondage of sin. If one of the invited guests wants to have his life changed, he must agree, according to the method adopted by the Group, to give an honest account of his sins, vices, and faults, however petty. Confession must be made to some individual in confidence, not necessarily to the whole party. This is the first step in the process of life-changing. Such a "sharing," as it is called, wipes out, according to the Group, the sense of sin. The second step, the convert finds, is "restitution." "However unnecessary it may seem to him, and however uncomfortable, he must do penance by reparation or apology to persons whom he has injured, however long ago the injury may have been inflicted." The insistence on this principle is justified by stressing the fact that personal humiliation, thus imposed on oneself, puts man in a proper attitude "to welcome the privilege of becoming a willing instrument in God's hand." Those who have surrendered to the will of God must continue under His "guidance." Henceforth a convert will rise half an hour or one hour earlier than required by his worldly duties. With a pencil in hand and a pack of note paper at his side he will wait for "luminous thoughts" from God. In other words, he will "listen in to God."

The Group Movement has often been critized as an "Upper Class Salvation Army," working, as it did, at first especially, if not exclusively, with men of wealth and position. More lately, however, it has extended its service to labor and even to the unemployed. Buchman's theology is a Christianity modified by an overdose of mysticism. The Lutheran background is seen in the fact that, at least theoretically, the divine revelation through the Bible is considered superior to the immediate guidance of the Holy Spirit. Sin is taken seriously; but Buchman's definition of repentance, "That's when a fellow is sorry enough to quit," shows that it lacks the depth of the penitential Psalms and of St. Paul. The Pauline categories such as guilt, forgiveness, repentance, faith, and grace, have no real place in his system. His Christianity is not the religion of the forgiveness of sin as it was with the Reformers, it is the religion of the mystics: complete surrender to God without the mediating work of the Saviour. In its extreme defenders the reference to "Christian" fellowship is even modified since, in their opinion, the restoration of communion with God should, in principle, admit followers of non-Christian religions as well as Christians.

For source material of the Movement we wish to refer to Harold Begbie, *Twice-Born Men* (1932), *Life Changers* (1927), A. J. Russell, *For Sinners Only* (1932), *One Thing I Know* (1934), *Their Religion* (1935), H. J. Rose, *The Quiet Time*, Stephen Foot, *Life Began Yesterday* (1935, Samuel M. Shoemaker, *Religion That Works* (1928), *Realizing Religion* (1931), *The Conversion of the Church* (1933), *The Church Can Save the World* (1938), *God's Control* (1939) et al., Ph. Leon, *The Philosophy of Courage, or The Oxford Group Way* (1939).

For critical studies the reader may be referred to Marjorie Harrison, *Saints Run Mad* (1934), G. C. Gast, *The Oxford Group Movement* (undated). K. von Baalen, *Chaos of Cults* (1938), Chapter Ten; N. G. Schwehn, *What is Buchmanism?* (1940), J. L. Neve, *Churches and Sects of Christendom* (1940), pp. 617 ff.

14. During the last decade there has developed in America a new school of thought, which, conscientiously, aims to bridge the gulf between the religion of redemption and the scientific way of life. This *Neo-Supernaturalism* is an offshoot of the same movement in Continental Theology. It has received its impetus mainly from Karl Barth and from Paul Tillich. The influence of the latter is clearly evident in the writings of the NIEBUHR BROTHERS. REINHOLD, for example, who is greatly interested in problems of social and international reconstruction and who in that respect bears a close resemblance to Rauschenbusch, proceeds from an altogether different principle. He does not share the naive optimism of the Marxian philosophy that the destruction of capital will mean the destruction of evil. Like Tillich, he takes his stand against the hideous evil of demoniac religion and of demoniac living as, especially, exemplified in capitalism and nationalism. But communism, he holds, is equally guilty, for it sets up some goal of social life and worships it as though it were the final objective of humanity, whereas the goal, he holds, must never be less than the unknowable fullness in the perfection of God Who "truly transcends every value and achievement of history." [38] His aim to distinguish properly between the religious intentions and the undeveloped scientific attitude of the Biblical writers becomes apparent when he says that Liberal Christianity "purified Christian theology of some of its grievous errors." It caused theologians to realize that a religious explanation of natural events is not yet a scientific explanation. It taught us to apply, he says, the scientific historical method to the records of our faith and thereby "saved Christianity from the corruption of the profound principle *credo ut intelligam,* into a tyranny of theological authority over human reason." [39] It is in keeping with this view when he, after the manner of Barth and Althaus, accepts the Biblical story of creation as a "description of the quality of existence," but denies that it is "an actual history of origins." Likewise, the Fall is to him not an "account of the origin of evil," but a "description of its nature." [40]

Another representative of Neo-Supernaturalism is the Methodist scholar EDWIN LEWIS, who caused no small sensation when he published in 1934 the volume entitled *A Christian Manifesto.* We shall have occasion to refer to both Reinhold Niebuhr and Lewis again in Paragraph 15.

The most consistent Neo-Supernaturalist is GEORGE W. RICHARDS of the Evangelical and Reformed Church with his book *Beyond Fundamentalism and Modernism* (1934). The Gospel is to him not a *Weltanschauung,* not metaphysics, but a "call to action." It is a serious mistake, he writes, "to assume that the Gospel of God is to supersede, or is in conflict with, the work of the biologist, the psychologist, the social scientist, the moral reformer, humanitarian activities. . . . Again, it is an equally serious error, with woeful consequences, to assume that the scientist, the artist, the statesman, the social servant, are sufficient unto themselves and have no need for the Gospel" (p. 9). Religious assurance cannot come to man by "investigation of science or by

---

[38] *An Interpretation of Christian Ethics,* p. 9. By permission of Harper & Brothers, publishers. Cf. also his other writings as quoted above.

[39] *The Christian Century,* April 26, 1939.

[40] *Christian Ethics,* p. 89.

process of reason" (p. 3). Faith he defines as obedience to God. "Faith comes from God through His word and Spirit each moment, and when it comes, one can say nothing else, astonished and perplexed, but "Lord, I believe, help Thou my unbelief" (p. 4).[41]

15. *In concluding our review of theological thought in America* we cannot pass by the startling series of articles "How My Mind Has Changed," published in *The Christian Century,* beginning with January 18, 1939. Altogether twenty-nine theologians participated in this enterprise, all of them being Americans with the exception of Karl Barth. In an analysis and summary of these articles the editor of *The Christian Century,* Charles C. Morrison, rightly stated that during the last decade "a whole new theological outlook had emerged. The liberalism which had been for nearly a half-century the common presupposition of Christian scholarship had been for the first time effectively challenged in this period. . . . The New Testament presented itself in a new aspect, calling for a radical revision of the prevailing liberal conception of Christianity." To this he adds that in this period the optimistic belief in evolution "was challenged as superficial and unwarranted. A halt had been called to the progressive capitulation of theology to the categories and presuppositions of science" (October 4). The testimonies of the different contributors offer, indeed, a very interesting insight into the development of the American mind during the last decade. Though none of the writers is blind to the trends of the time, liberalism may be "bandaged," ROBERT L. CALHOUN writes, yet it is to him "unbowed" (May 31). "A Changed Liberal — But Still a Liberal," says JOHN C. BENNETT (February 8) though to him, as he says, whose mind is "naturally Pelagian," the strain of Christian thought represented by Paul and Augustine has "come alive." He has abandoned his earlier "utopianism."[42] He has reached the point where man distrusts "the cocksure oversimplifications" of the socialists as to the highly complicated problems of national and international life. Most definite in his reaffirmation of liberalism is EDWARD S. AMES. He is set against Barthianism and what he calls "the resurgence of the old sixteenth-century theology in this twentieth century" (March 22). EDGAR S. BRIGHTMAN is in substantial agreement with him as regards their common aversion against Barthianism. "I view with regret," says he, "the rising tide of neo-supernaturalism and Barthianism" (March 1). As to himself, he describes the change that has taken place in his thinking a change from Rationalism to Empiricism in religion. When he "made it a business of reading Hegel," he discovered, as he says, "to his great surprise that Hegel is not an archrationalist, but rather "the empiricist of consciousness." Likewise, John C. Bennett states that he is more repelled than helped by Barth, and HALFORD E. LUCCOCK writes (August 9), "a wholly other God is no God for me."

With the passing of shallow optimism the naive belief that we have in the social gospel a short cut to universal happiness, *alias* the "Kingdom of God," is shattered. But the social note still is strong in some of the writers with Marxism and pacifism holding sway over the mind of theologians (for example, John C. Bennett, as referred to, Russell H. Stafford, Albert D. Beaven, Walter R. Bowie, A. J. Muste, and, *mutatis mutandis,* Reinhold Niebuhr).

Over against the "unbowed" liberals there is another group which has come much closer to a new understanding and positive appreciation of the supernaturalness of

---

[41] Pp. 3, 41. Quotations by permission of Scribner's, publishers. Cf. *Creative Controversies in Christianity,* 1938; also in Wieman-Meland, *op. cit.,* pp. 77 ff.

[42] See his book *Social Salvation,* 1935, in which he treads in the footsteps of Rauschenbusch.

Christianity. Here we must mention EDWIN LEWIS of the Drew Theological Seminary. While working on *The Abingdon Commentary,* he says, he "discovered the Bible" (June 14). "I saw with a devastating clarity that speculative philosophy, whether it got as far as supernaturalism or whether it stopped with naturalism, could never accommodate itself to Christianity. Instead, it required Christianity to do the accommodating. . . . I found myself faced with the Word of God, given, it is true, by slow process through the words of men, but at last, in Christ, 'made flesh.' The Creator appeared as the Redeemer." And this "can be true," he emphasizes, "only as something revealed, not as something discovered." These views he has set forth more in detail in his stimulating books *A Philosophy of the Christian Revelation* (1940), and *A New Heaven and a New Earth* (1941).

The same change of attitude is recognizable in the article by REINHOLD NIEBUHR (April 26). "I underwent a fairly complete conversion of thought which involved rejection of almost all the liberal theological ideals and ideas with which I ventured forth in 1915." Now liberalism as a creed is gone for him with its faith in man; "faith in his capacity to subdue nature, and faith that the subjection of nature achieves life's final good; faith in man's essential goodness, . . . ; faith in human history which is conceived as a movement upward by a force immanent within it." This liberalism with belief in education as the means to salvation is shallow to him, for it fails to grasp the ultimate religious problem of evil in man. In repudiating "the classic Christology of the God-man," liberalism did not recognize "that this absurd doctrine of the God-man Christ contains the whole essence of the Christian faith, its belief that God transcends history and yet makes Himself known in history." As to the future of society, Niebuhr reaffirms what he wrote some years ago that in his opinion "an adequate spiritual guidance can come only through a more radical political orientation and more conservative religious conviction" (*Reflections on the End of an Era,* 1934, p. ix). His Gifford Lectures of 1939 on *The Nature and Destiny of Man* (Vol. I, 1941), and his contribution, "Religion and Action," to the composite volume *Religion and the Modern World* (1941) are another evidence of the remarkable change that has taken place in his world of thought.

A similar change of mind is seen in HENRY N. WIEMAN, who writes on "Some Blind Spots Removed" (January 25). He has moved away from the prevailing moralistic conception of Christianity and has arrived at a deeper insight into the significance of history. While he at first espoused the cause of theological empiricism, his view is now enriched by the conception that "certain strands of history are powerfully creative of value." In Jesus Christ we see "God incarnate in the historical situation."

The significant change that has come over E. STANLEY JONES is, as he says, "in the content of Christ" (May 3). While formerly the Kingdom was to him "always too large and too impersonal," he now sees that it is personalized and centered in Him.[43] This has helped him to move away from religious individualism and to realize the social and universal claims of the Kingdom. "It is a totalitarian order, more totalitarian than communism and fascism." It embraces time as well as eternity and is both "in God's hands and ours." He explicitly rejects H. Kraemer's purely transcendental Barthian view as expressed in *The Christian Message in a Non-Christian World.*[44]

---

[43] See his recent book *Is the Kingdom of God Realism?* (1940).

[44] This volume was written as stated in the preface, "at the request of the International Missionary Council in order to serve as material for the World Missionary Conference in 1938."

In the same manner, "old phrases like 'the wrath of God,' 'original sin,' 'perdition and judgment,' have come to live again" to WALTER M. HORTON (May 17). However, he declines to say that he has "fallen in" with Augustinianism, he only has "drawn closer" to it. His Barthian friends, he fears, "will continue to look upon him as a spectator and outsider, woefully lacking in 'existential commitment.'"

The Baptist theologian, HAROLD C. PHILLIPS, finds himself preaching more and more on the great themes of historical Christianity. He shows a decided leaning toward the dialectical theology as it is held not by Barth but by Brunner (August 2).

CH. C. MORRISON declines to admit for himself "a shift from one position to another," he rather prefers to speak of a flowing together of two streams of loyalty which, for many years, had been flowing in separate channels," i.e., the heritage which he had received, and his commitment "to the empirical way of thinking" (November 8). The writings of Professor Wieman, he says, have helped him much to arrive at an harmonious synthesis of these two principles in religion. At last, he states, he has discovered that God has revealed Himself, as "righteous, gracious, and loving," not in the "inner life," nor in the "cosmos," but in "history." Christianity is, as he now sees it, "the Incarnation of the living God in Christ, the Christ of history, and the incarnation of the ever living Christ in the Christian community, the living church of history." [45]

Unreserved in his commitment to the new theology is E. G. HOMRIGHAUSEN of Princeton (April 12). He has studied Brunner, Heim, Kutter, Thurneysen. "Yet I must confess," he writes, "it was not these men and events merely, but all of them led me to the two men I now regard as the greatest Christians of all times — Paul and Luther." "Struck" in his liberalism by the dialectic theology, a "gradual detachment from the dialectical movement has set in," and he now has learned "walking on his own theological legs." He has found a home, he says, in the evangelical-Reformed tradition.

16. *Attention also should be called* to the discussion on *"The Meaning of Oxford and Edinburgh"* in *Christendom* (Autumn, 1937) by seventeen American and British theologians. At both conferences it was heavily felt that the historical divisions of Christendom and the tension between the Church and the world can be overcome only by a faithful allegiance to the living Lord. Church unity does not exist, as stated in the resolutions adopted at Edinburgh, August 18, 1937, "in the agreement of our minds or the consent of our wills. It is founded in Jesus Christ Himself, who lived, died, and rose again to bring us to the Father, and who through the Holy Spirit dwells in His Church." In the same soundly Biblical way, the problem of social and economic order should be approached, according to the report of Oxford, "from the standpoint of her (the Church's) faith in the revelation of God in Christ." "The Kingdom of God, as proclaimed in the Gospel, is the reign of God which both has come and is coming." It must not be identified with "a particular social structure or economic mechanism." The penitent and believing attitude as revealed at these two conferences is indeed a promising sign for the future, for only a penitent man is fit for the Kingdom of God.

In summary we state that Liberalism as a creed has lost its sway over the mind of a goodly number of American theologians, especially over those of the younger generation. Is liberalism then doomed to pass out of the picture? As a scientific method of inquiry, many conservatives tell us that the Church cannot dispense with it. Ignorance

---

[45] Cf. his Lyman Beecher Lectures of 1939. *What is Christianity?* published in 1940.

and prejudice as to scientific and historical facts are not an asset to the Church; they constitute a positive danger. Fundamentalism, therefore, cannot win the future. In the past both Orthodoxism and Liberalism have committed the fundamental mistake of confusing theology with philosophy. Both have been Hellenistic in spirit for both have been busy with the search for a comprehensive *Weltanschauung*. Over against this attempt the Reformation stands out not only as a single act of the past, but as "a law of constant critical recurrence to the Word of God." [46] Twentieth-century theology is not asked to canonize all the findings of the Reformers, but Protestant theology is under the serious obligation to learn from them the nature of its own self. As to the modern emphasis on reason and experience, God is known not by reason, but by revelation, and He is apprehended not by experience, but by faith. True, there is an intellectual element in revelation. Theology cannot disregard the question of truth; but faith is not a system of rational definitions. Likewise, there is an experimental element involved in the act of faith; but this psychological aspect is of subordinate importance. Faith in the New Testament is, as with Luther, never a rational apprehension of a divine object, it is trust in the person of God who is operating in majestic love.

And finally a word about the Social Gospel. It has become evident from our discussion that the earlier optimism of its exponents has received a serious setback. Yet, in all likelihood, the Social Gospel will stay.[47] We have no intention to deride the moral earnestness and sacrificial attitude of many of its supporters. Nevertheless, truth compels us to repeat that the theology underlying its convictions is Biblically unsound. There is no political, economic, or social order which can be identified with the Kingdom of God. The Kingdom is not humanity refined, it is the "wholly other." It is human arrogance to undertake to "crown Him Lord of all" through social reform. "It is not for you to know the times or the seasons which the Father hath put in His own power." When during the dark days of the first World War the religious socialists of Switzerland had to stand by helpless at the collapse of a bourgeois as well as a social Christianity in Europe, they turned to the Bible to read it more penitently. "We read it," says Thurneysen, "with the eyes of shipwrecked men, for whom everything has gone overboard. And we did so, as it has turned out, not wholly in vain. The Bible gained a new meaning for us. Beyond all interpretations, its real word again began to speak: The word of forgiveness of sins, the proclamation of the, not humanly, but divinely coming kingdom." (See page 173.) Will American theologians have the same courage to read the Bible *penitently,* thereby to overcome the confusion of thought in which they are trapped? The times are evil. The last quarter century has been a lesson to us that the Kingdom is not at hand when we think it to be. The Kingdom is not of this world; it is not to be identified with any political or social theory; it is supra-mundane. Its consummation lies beyond the possibilities of our present existence. Theologians should be lights directing others to the True Light. That we may become this, "to this may our blessed Father in heaven help us."

[46] George S. Hendry, *God the Creator,* 1937, p. 133.

[47] Cf., for instance, the recent books by Stanley Jones and Douglas C. Macintosh, as referred to; also by F. Ernest Johnson, *The Social Gospel Re-examined,* 1940.

INDEX